Apollos Old Testament
COMMENTARY

15

PROVERBS

TITLES IN THIS SERIES:

EXODUS, T. Desmond Alexander
LEVITICUS, Nobuyoshi Kiuchi
DEUTERONOMY, J. G. McConville
JOSHUA, Pekka M. A. Pitkänen
RUTH, L. Daniel Hawk
1 & 2 SAMUEL, David G. Firth
1 & 2 KINGS, Lissa Wray Beal
PROVERBS, Paul Overland
ECCLESIASTES & THE SONG OF SONGS,
Daniel C. Fredericks & Daniel J. Estes
DANIEL, Ernest C. Lucas
HOSEA, Joshua N. Moon
HAGGAI, ZECHARIAH & MALACHI,
Anthony R. Petterson

APOLLOS OLD TESTAMENT
COMMENTARY

15

PROVERBS

Series Editors
David W. Baker and Gordon J. Wenham

PAUL OVERLAND

Apollos
London, England

APOLLOS (an imprint of Inter-Varsity Press)
36, Causton Street, London SW1P 4ST, England
Email: ivp@ivpbooks.com
Website: www.ivpbooks.com

Inter-Varsity Press, England, publishes Christian books that are true to the Bible and that communicate the gospel, develop discipleship and strengthen the church for its mission in the world.

IVP originated within the Inter-Varsity Fellowship, now the Universities and Colleges Christian Fellowship, a student movement connecting Christian Unions in universities and colleges throughout Great Britain, and a member movement of the International Fellowship of Evangelical Students. That historic association is maintained, and all senior IVP staff and committee members subscribe to the UCCF Basis of Faith. Website: www.uccf.org.uk.

First published 2022

British Library Cataloguing-in-Publication Data
A catalogue record for this book is available from the British Library.

ISBN: 978–1–78359–754–3 (print)
ISBN: 978–1–78359–755–0 (digital)

Set in Sabon 10/12pt
Typeset in Great Britain by CRB Associates, Potterhanworth, Lincolnshire
Printed and bound in Great Britain by TJ Books Limited, Padstow

Printed on paper from sustainable sources.

To Lorie, with deep gratitude:
'You have risen above them all' (Prov. 31:29b)

CONTENTS

EDITORS' PREFACE

The Apollos Old Testament Commentary takes its name from the Alexandrian Jewish Christian who was able to impart his great learning fervently and powerfully through his teaching (Acts 18:24–25). He ably applied his understanding of past events to his contemporary society. This series seeks to do the same, keeping one foot firmly planted in the universe of the original text and the other in that of the target audience, which is preachers, teachers and students of the Bible. The series editors have selected scholars who are adept in both areas, exhibiting scholarly excellence along with practical insight for application.

Translators need to be at home with the linguistic practices and semantic nuances of both the original and target languages in order to be able to transfer the full impact of the one into the other. Commentators, however, serve as interpreters of the text rather than simply its translators. They also need to adopt a dual stance, though theirs needs to be even more solid and diversely anchored than that of translators. While they also must have the linguistic competence to produce their own excellent translations, they must moreover be fully conversant with the literary conventions, sociological and cultural practices, historical background and understanding, and theological perspectives of those who produced the text as well as those whom it concerned. On the other side, they must also understand their own times and culture, able to see where relevance for the original audience is transferable to that of current readers. For this to be accomplished, it is not only necessary to interpret the text; one must also interpret the audience.

Traditionally, commentators have been content to highlight and expound the ancient text. More recently, the need for an anchor in the present day has also become more evident, and this series self-consciously adopts this approach, combining both. Each author analyses the original text through a new translation, textual notes, a discussion of the literary form, structure and background of the passage, as well as commenting on elements of its exegesis. A study of the passage's interpretational development in Scripture and the church concludes each section, serving to bring the passage home to the modern reader. What we intend, therefore, is to provide not only tools of excellence for the academy, but also tools of function for the pulpit.

David W. Baker
Gordon J. Wenham

AUTHOR'S PREFACE

To unlock the riches of Proverbs, a commentary must illumine the biblical text at three levels. First, it must illumine *individual sayings*. In particular, we must resist the temptation to repair expressions that at first glance appear illogical or ungrammatical, lest the sage's subtle and surprising insights go unseen (see §5.7 in the 'Introduction', 'The sage's style: jarring sayings' ['sage' refers to wise persons who wrote Proverbs]). *This commentary seeks to put the reader in touch with the poet's careful composition.*

Second, to help unlock Proverbs a commentary must illumine *clusters of sayings*. What once were regarded as disconnected sayings, recent scholarship – especially in Prov. 10 – 29 – has shown to comprise cohesive poems. Crafted with great care, frequently these poems announce their beginning by introducing from one to three themes – themes that the poet proceeds to expound in the balance of that poem (or lecture). After several subpoints, poems often signal their conclusion with a dynamic climax. Consequently the sense and significance of an individual saying may increase exponentially, due to the way nearby sayings illumine it. By means of poem titles (see Table of contents), poem outlines (located alongside translations) and careful tracing of each poem's progression of thought (under 'Comment'), *this commentary seeks to clarify how each saying belongs to (and so derives meaning from) its surrounding context.*

Third, to unlock Proverbs fully a commentary must illumine how clusters of poems may contribute to *a bookwide instructional scheme*, advancing from first chapter to last. Based on the topics addressed in Prov. 10 – 24, for example, it becomes clear that the author envisions there a different audience than for chs. 1–9. Since the audience of chs. 10–24 no longer ponders whether to pursue wisdom, the sage is free to teach concerning wealth, personal satisfaction and human flourishing. The implicit audience for chs. 25–29 differs yet again – evidently having progressed from apprentice training to employment as wise persons. So the lectures adjust to advise concerning achieving magnificence in one's place of service. Poems in the closing two chapters (chs. 30–31) at once return to basics relevant to all (reverence and contentment-not-greed), while also giving the nation's chief sage (the monarch) pointed instruction for effective management and optimal marriage. Awareness of how a poem fits within the bookwide scheme enables the modern reader to grasp better to whom that poem will speak most incisively, today. *This commentary seeks to illumine the bookwide teaching of Proverbs, explaining how wisdom learners may advance from novice to apprentice, eventually becoming journeymen sages* (see 'Introduction', §3).

My debt of gratitude begins with Brandeis University professors Dr Dwight Young (who taught us to doubt our doubts regarding reliability of the Masoretic Text) and Dr Michael Fishbane (who taught me never to underestimate the Hebr. sages' skill in composition, as intricate as extensive). I am deeply appreciative to the editors of the Apollos Old Testament Commentary series, David Baker and Gordon Wenham, to Philip Duce, Senior Commissioning Editor at Inter-Varsity Press, and to Rima Devereaux, Senior Project Editor, for entrusting to me the privilege of contributing this volume and for their unflagging patience awaiting its completion. This work has benefited immensely from the careful scrutiny of both Eldo Barkhuizen as copy editor and Suzanne Mitchell as proof-reader, for which I am thankful. To the administration of Ashland Theological Seminary I am grateful for generous provision of research leaves, including periods of study at Tyndale House, Cambridge, led by wardens Bruce Winter and Peter Williams, and study of Amenemope artefacts in the Museum of Egyptian Antiquities (Cairo) and in the British Museum. Professor Bruce Waltke generously shared print resources gathered during his research. Dear friends Dale Stoffer and Dave James, together with seminary students and the Carpenters Grace Group, provided valuable inspiration and comment along the way. Beyond all these, my deepest gratitude belongs to my wife, Lorie, who through the decades of this project has given tireless encouragement, all the while excelling both as mother of our now-grown children, Bryan and Kristi, and in her medical profession as well.

Paul Overland

ABBREVIATIONS

TEXTUAL

Arab.	Arabic
Aram.	Aramaic
HB	Hebrew Bible
Hebr.	Hebrew
LXX	Septuagint
MT	Masoretic Text
Syr.	Syriac
Ugar.	Ugaritic

HEBREW GRAMMAR

abs.	absolute
act.	active
adj.	adjective, adjectival
caus.	causative
cohort(s).	cohortative(s)
com.	common (a grammatical form not differentiating masculine from feminine)
conj(s).	conjunction(s)
const.	construct
cop.	copulative
dat.	dative
f.	feminine
fut.	future
hiph.	hiphil
hith.	hithpael
hithpol.	hithpolel
hoph.	hophal
ind.	indicative
infin.	infinitive
juss.	jussive
K	Kethibh (the written Hebrew text)
m.	masculine
mid.	middle
niph.	niphal
pass.	passive

pf.	perfect
pi.	piel
pl.	plural
plpf.	pluperfect
poss.	possessive
prep.	preposition, prepositional
ptc(s).	participle(s)
pu.	pual
Q	Qere (the Hebrew text to be read out)
qat.	qatal
sg.	singular
suff.	suffix
voc.	vocative
wayyiq.	wayyiqtol
weqat.	weqatal
weyiq.	weyiqtol
yiq.	yiqtol

MISCELLANEOUS

ANE	ancient Near East(ern)
AV	Authorized (King James) Version
c.	circa
cm	centimetres
ESV	English Standard Version
ET	English translation
GNT	Good News Translation
in.	inch(es)
lit.	literally
m	metre(s)
NASB	New American Standard Bible
NET	New English Translation
NETS	*New English Translation of the Septuagint*, Oxford: Oxford University Press, 2007; available at <http://ccat.sas.upenn.edu/nets/edition/30-sirach-nets.pdf>, accessed 2 November 2011
NIV	New International Version
NJPS	*Tanakh: The Holy Scriptures: The New Jewish Publication Society Translation according to the Traditional Hebrew Text*
NRSV	New Revised Standard Version
s.v.	under the specified word (*sub verbo*)
TNIV	Today's New International Version
tr.	translated by

JOURNALS, REFERENCE WORKS, SERIES

AB	Anchor Bible
AIL	Ancient Israel and Its Literature
ANET	*Ancient Near Eastern Texts Relating to the Old Testament*, 3rd edn, Princeton: Princeton University Press, 1969
BBRSup	Bulletin for Biblical Research, Supplements
BDB	F. Brown, S. R. Driver and C. A. Briggs, *A Hebrew and English Lexicon of the Old Testament*, Oxford: Clarendon, 1907; repr. Peabody: Hendrickson, 2005
BETL	Bibliotheca ephemeridum theologicarum lovaniensium
BHS	K. Elliger and W. Rudoph (eds.), *Biblia Hebraica Stuttgartensia*, Stuttgart: Deutsche Bibelgesellschaft, 1967–77; notes on *Proverbia* prepared by J. Fichtner
BKAT	Biblischer Kommentar, Altes Testament
BLS	Bible and Literature Series
CBQ	*Catholic Biblical Quarterly*
DCH	D. J. A. Clines (ed.), *The Dictionary of Classical Hebrew*, Sheffield: Sheffield Academic Press, 1993–2014
GKC	E. Kautzsch (ed.), A. E. Cowley (tr.), *Gesenius' Hebrew Grammar*, 2nd edn, Oxford: Clarendon, 1910
HALOT	L. Köhler and W. Baumgartner, *A Hebrew and Aramaic Lexicon of the Old Testament*, Leiden: E. J. Brill, 1994–2000
HSS	Harvard Semitic Studies
IBHS	B. K. Waltke and M. O'Connor, *An Introduction to Biblical Hebrew Syntax*, Winona Lake: Eisenbrauns, 1990
ICC	International Critical Commentary
JBL	*Journal of Biblical Literature*
JETS	*Journal of the Evangelical Theological Society*
Joüon	P. Joüon and T. Muraoka, *A Grammar of Biblical Hebrew*, Rome: Pontificio Istituto Biblico, 2006
JSOTSup	Journal for the Study of the Old Testament, Supplement Series
LCL	Loeb Classical Library
NAC	New American Commentary
NCBC	New Century Bible Commentary
NIBCOT	New International Biblical Commentary on the Old Testament
NICOT	New International Commentary on the Old Testament
OTL	Old Testament Library
PHSC	Perspectives on Hebrew Scriptures and Its Contexts
RB	*Revue Biblique*

REg	*Revue d'Égyptologie*
SBLDS	Society of Biblical Literature Dissertation Series
SOTSMS	Society for Old Testament Studies Monograph Series
VT	*Vetus Testamentum*
VTSup	Supplements to Vetus Testamentum
WAW	Writings from the Ancient World
WBC	Word Biblical Commentary
ZAW	*Zeitschrift für die alttestamentliche Wissenschaft*
ZBK	Zürcher Bibelkommentare
ZTK	*Zeitschrift für Theologie und Kirche*

GLOSSARY

apodosis 'then' portion of a conditional statement (see 'protasis')
apophthegm a concise wisdom statement (used synonymously with 'saying')
assonance words having similar sounds
block the second subdivision level of a poem or lecture
chiasm inversion of components (A, B, B, A), generally within a *single saying*
closure a concentration appearing towards the close of a composition, of words or topics that appeared earlier in that composition
colon (pl. cola) a phrase, two or more of which form a verse (if two, a 'bicolon'; if three, a 'tricolon')
content-based a literary feature that arises from meaning of words employed (e.g. character summary, progression of thought, reversal, thematic continuity; see discussion of macrostructural features for Prov. 1:1–9)
division one of four groups of poems in Proverbs
epigram a pithy wisdom saying (used synonymously with 'saying')
form-based a literary feature that operates without regard to meaning of words employed (e.g. assonance, repetition, closure and inclusio [when identical terms reappear]; see discussion of macrostructural features for Prov. 1:1–9)
inclusio recurrence at or near the close of a composition, of a term or concept that appeared at or near the start of that composition
instruction a verse of wisdom teaching containing an imperative
lecture a cohesive composition within Proverbs, consisting of several sections (interchangeable with 'poem')
macrostructural a feature involving more than one section
maxim a wisdom saying presenting a principle (used synonymously with 'saying')
microstructural a feature confined to one section
palistrophe inversion of terms or concepts involving *more than one verse*
poem a cohesive composition within Proverbs, consisting of several sections (interchangeable with 'lecture')
protasis 'if' portion of a conditional statement (see 'apodosis')
proverb a wise saying or instruction
quatrain two adjacent and thematically related verses, each consisting of a bicolon
saying a verse of wisdom teaching (lacking an imperative, if contrasting an instruction)

section the first subdivision level of a poem or lecture
segment the fourth subdivision level of a poem or lecture
stich colon (see above)
unit the third subdivision level of a poem or lecture

For an exploration of Hebr. terms shaping the sage's moral and philosophical categories, please see §5.6 in the 'Introduction'.

INTRODUCTION

'Read it slowly.'
(W. G. Lambert, when asked how to study Proverbs)

Israelite sages understood wisdom as the observation of order in the natural, social and divine realms, so as to discern by rational choice the path most effectively leading to an optimally flourishing life (Koch 1955; Overland 2018: 499). In contrast to Job's wrestling with divine fairness, and unlike the clever contradictions within Ecclesiastes that probe life's worth and meaning, Proverbs trains the novice pupil to become a mature journeyman sage.

Seven sections comprise the introduction. The first considers the richness of Proverbs for today. The second offers steps for reading Proverbs cohesively. The third suggests a bookwide progression. The fourth explains the translation, headings and terminology found in this commentary. The fifth addresses various aspects of the sages of Proverbs, such as their theology, their understanding of wisdom, adaptation of extra-biblical material, and style of writing. The sixth and seventh deal with authorship and date of composition, respectively. All English translations, unless stated otherwise, are my own.

1. THE RICHNESS OF PROVERBS FOR TODAY

The richness of Proverbs resides in its timeless relevance. Modern headlines decry monetary greed, sexual scandal and self-centred abuse of others. Addressing all these (and more), the inspired sages offer incisive and often passionate advice.

To access the richness within Proverbs requires reading on three levels. First, we must closely translate isolated sayings (see 1.1. 'Closely translate isolated sayings', below).

Second, we must read Proverbs cohesively, noticing clusters of sayings and whole poems. For only as we appreciate the wider sapiential 'forest' (an entire poem) do we begin richly to grasp the worth and impact of an isolated 'tree' (the single saying thoughtfully positioned within its poem; see 1.2. 'Read cohesively, noticing whole poems' and 2. 'Steps towards reading Proverbs cohesively', below). Poem outlines, together with remarks titled 'Comment', seek to illuminate the sage's carefully composed progression of thought. These enable each poem's message to communicate with greater intended impact (see under 'Explanation' for each poem).

Third, we must consider how instruction progresses from one poem to the next and from one group of poems (a division) to the next. Thereby we may discover a bookwide instructional scheme designed to draw the learner forwards through a virtual curriculum within this masterful composition (see 3. 'Progression across Proverbs', below).

1.1. Closely translate isolated sayings

Perhaps no biblical genre suffers loss through translation as does the compact wisdom poetry of Proverbs. Richness returns as we read isolated sayings in close correlation with the original language, even when that yields jarring translations. Those arresting expressions oblige the reader to slow down and consider thoughtfully what the sage intended. To illustrate, consider several samples drawn from this commentary's translation:

- 'A scoffer amounts to wine' (20:1a; contrast NRSV: 'Wine is a [scoffer]'). Verbless Hebr. syntax stipulates 'scoffer' as subject – a topic already introduced in the same poem.
- 'Culpability will scoff at foolish folk' (14:9a; contrast NASB: 'Fools mock at sin'). Grammar indicates 'culpability/sin' as subject.
- 'The core longing of a mortal consists of his faithful love' (19:22a; contrast NRSV: 'What is desirable in a person is loyalty'). Syntax locates faithful love as a self-desire, a longing for one's own character development, rather than a metric for assessing others.
- '[O]ne who works himself into a rage sins against his own appetite' (20:2b; contrast NRSV: 'anyone who provokes him to anger forfeits life itself'). The verb is reflexive (enraging or provoking self), not act. (provoking another).
- 'Many a mortal may proclaim, "A person consists of his faithful love"' (20:6a; contrast NRSV: 'Many proclaim themselves

loyal'). 'To proclaim' is not reflexive. When followed by a Masoretic cantillation pause (as here), it fittingly introduces an epigram.

- 'When an inheritance is despised early on, then its ensuing development cannot be blessed' (20:21; contrast NRSV: 'An estate quickly acquired in the beginning / will not be blessed in the end'). The term 'despised' links to arrogance in the preceding verse. Instead to render 'despised' as 'quickly' requires emendation of the Hebr. and misses the link with arrogance.
- 'They had fled since no one was pursuing the guilty person, but moral folk are like a young lion capable of confidence' (28:1; contrast NRSV: 'The wicked flee when no one pursues, / but the righteous are as bold as a lion'). Grammar and syntax indicate 'guilty/wicked' person as object (of non-pursuit), not subject (who flees). The impunity introduced in this, the opening verse of its poem, foreshadows the importance of a strong and just monarch – which robust role constitutes this poem's central message.

1.2. Read cohesively, noticing whole poems

After closely translating isolated sayings, richness emerges from Proverbs when read cohesively as a series of poems. The conspicuously connected compositions in chs. 1–9 teach us how the sage builds poems. By noticing those same literary building blocks (structures) in subsequent chapters, connected poems materialize – complete with introductions, dynamic development of subpoints and climactic conclusions.

For illustration, notice structures within the lecture spanning Prov. 20:5 – 21:4 (for fuller discussion of structures labelled below in bold, see §2). As to theme, here the sage considers the weighty question 'What is the loftiest expression of human flourishing?'

A **wisdom commendation** signals this poem's start, calling attention to the desirability of wisdom (synonym 'counsel'), without delineating specific behaviour:

> 'Deep water' is counsel in a person's mind,
> but a person with perception may draw it out.
> (20:5)

Of greater prominence than a wisdom commendation is the **wisdom content** that it introduces. This poem's initial wisdom content posits one of the most profound analyses of human character to appear in all of Proverbs:

> Many a mortal may proclaim, 'A person consists of his faithful love'.
> But a person characterized by faithfulness, who can find?
> (20:6)

In other words, one's capacity for exhibiting faithful love and faithfulness marks the extent of that individual's flourishing.

The bulk of this lecture goes on to detail 'faithful love' and 'faithfulness', in three distinct sections. The poem's early lines anticipate those three with a **triple-theme introduction**:

20:7	One who, of his own accord, consistently behaves with personal integrity – he is moral; how fortunate are his children who come after him!	a. Quest to cultivate integrity within
20:8	A king who sits on a throne of justice scatters with his eyes all that is wrong.	b. Quest to vanquish evil without
20:9	Who can say, 'I have cleansed my motives; I have become purified from my sin'?	c. Quest to pursue purity within

'Cultivating integrity within' (20:7) subsequently will be explained in 20:10–23. 'Vanquishing evil without' (20:8) will be expanded in 20:24–28. And 'Pursuing purity within' (20:9) the sage will develop in 20:29 – 21:2.

Dynamic development along these three sectors emerges from specific vocabulary within their respective expansion portions. Each 'quest' corresponds to a successive life-season: youth, life's prime and later years, respectively. In the commentary, **progression of thought** appears initially in outline form alongside the translation of each poem. Under Comment for each poem, a fuller explanation of progression will be found.

Periodically the poet will spotlight a particular saying, showcasing it at the core of a concentric pattern (**palistrophe**). Two palistrophes occur in this lecture. Read in context, the core of the first stresses that the ability to detect integrity-failure originates with the divine:

> A listening ear and a seeing eye,
> the Lord made both of them together.
> (20:12, centred within vv. 10–14)

The core of the second palistrophe similarly stresses that God specializes in detection of duplicity:

> The lamp of the Lord is a mortal's breath;
> it examines all chambers deep within.
> (20:27, centred within vv. 26–28)

Finally, recognition of **climactic conclusions** can clarify a poem's major points. At its close, the sage often will reduce an entire lecture to brief binary alternatives, employing a **character summary**. The lecture spanning 20:5 – 21:4 closes by crystallizing character with a pair of sayings: one positive, one negative.

21:3	Executing morality and justice is more preferable to the LORD than sacrifice.	Positive character
21:4	With its lofty eyes and expansive mind, the lamp of guilty folk is sin.	Negative character

Now the pupil must choose which path he or she will travel.

In addition to recovering dynamic development and climactic conclusions, reading poems cohesively illumines the core theme that binds together a given poem, as suggested by poem titles sampled below (for complete list, see the table of contents).

- 'What counsel does wisdom offer for healthy relationships?' (Prov. 3:1–35)
- 'I seem to have lost my way. What must I do?' (4:10–19)
- 'What does it matter, what I do with my body?' (4:20–27)
- 'Sex between consenting adults . . . What's the harm?' (6:20–35)
- 'When it feels so right, how could it be so wrong?' (7:1–27)
- 'How can I become rich?' (10:1–22)
- 'How can I secure my future?' (10:23–30)
- 'What is the harm in fraudulent riches?' (10:31 – 11:31)
- 'How can I recognize noble character and thus behave as a true friend?' (12:1–28)
- 'How may I achieve true satisfaction?' (13:1–25)
- 'How should I build my house?' (14:1 – 15:6)
- 'What is the loftiest expression of human flourishing?' (20:5 – 21:4)
- 'What strategies will lead to wealth that is worthy and power that is proper?' (21:5 – 22:16)
- 'As I now venture out, what objective must I pursue, above all?' (22:17 – 24:34)
- 'How may a monarchy attain magnificence?' (25:1–12)
- 'In order to become wise, what must one come to know above all else?' (30:1–33)

As suggested by these titles, it is not difficult to bring Proverb's cogent and content-rich biblical counsel to bear on issues relevant to today's public and private life. In view of the contemporary 'epidemic of anxiety' and increased suicide ideation among youth in contemporary Western culture, more than ever we need wisdom that dependably addresses the sorts of questions listed above (Kinnaman and Matlock 2019: 70–88).

Thus close translation and cohesive reading open the way to rich insights in Proverbs. Since cohesive reading marks a recent development in the study of Proverbs, a brief explanation may be helpful.

2. STEPS TOWARDS READING PROVERBS COHESIVELY

To read Proverbs cohesively requires (a) listening patiently, (b) solving riddles and (c) recognizing poems. First, Moshe Greenberg explains how one must listen patiently:

> There is only one way that gives any hope of eliciting the innate conventions and literary formations of a piece of ancient literature, and that is by listening to it patiently and humbly. The critic must curb all temptations to impose his antecedent judgments on the text; he must immerse himself in it again and again, with all his sensors alert to catch every possible stimulus – mental-ideational, aural, aesthetic, linguistic, visual – until its features begin to stand out and their native shape and patterning emerge. (1983: 21)

Second, solve the proverb as a riddle. A saying often compares two items (a basic meaning of *māšāl* 'proverb' involves comparing). The riddle lies in why the sage aligned item A alongside item B – what do they have in common (Kugel 2017: 23)? What facet of A gains clarity when illumined by item B?

These comparisons 'are projected stroboscopically: they are seen quickly side by side, then they are shut off' (Williams 1980: 41). Since 'the impact of the juxtaposition is lost when words are inserted to make the meaning explicit', Murphy opted to translate laconically (1998: xxiii; e.g. 'Hope deferred, sickness of heart; but a tree of life, desire fulfilled' [13:12; 1998: 93]).

Such 'compression cries out for elaboration and elucidation' (Millar 2020: 45). While one must guard against overreading (West 1992: 428), constraints imposed by the elements under comparison will helpfully curb a rich reading (Millar 2020: 70–71).

Third, recognize poems. Our focus must detect 'the movement from line to poem'. Alter explains:

> Poetry is quintessentially the mode of expression in which the surface is the depth, so that through careful scrutiny of the configurations of the surface – the articulation of the line, the

> movement from line to poem, the imagery, the arabesques of syntax and grammar, the design of the poem as a whole – we come to apprehend more fully the depth of the poem's meaning. (1985: 205)

A sage summarized these same steps (listening, riddle-solving and poem-recognition) in a wisdom psalm (where 'harp' indicates song, and thus poem):

> I will listen to a proverb intently;
> I will open up my riddle
> with a harp.
> (Ps. 49:4 [v. 5 MT])

The last – poem-recognition – consists of six sub-steps, from discerning beginnings to detecting progression across multiple poems. Before describing those steps, a brief introduction to Hebr. poetry may be useful.

Individual verses of Hebr. poetry consist typically of two parts or cola, forming a bicolon: 'Roll your work onto the LORD [first colon], so that your plans may be established' [second colon] (16:3). Occasionally the poet employs a tricolon strategically, as with the palistrophic climax in 1:27: 'When your terror comes like a storm [first colon], and your disaster invades like a whirlwind [second colon], when anxiety and affliction come upon you' [third colon]. In any given verse, cola cooperate variously, including cause-and-effect (as with 16:3a and b, above), or synonymous linkage progressing dynamically (as with 1:27).

Unlike classical Greek poetry, Hebr. poetry seldom follows rhythmic conventions (except for the *qinah* lament rhythm, as found in Lamentations). Unlike English poetry, Hebr. is not concerned with end-rhyme. But assonance can play a role, binding together one or more sayings (e.g. *yešārîm*, 'the honest', and *rĕšāʿîm*, 'the guilty', in 2:21–22; *qāṣîn*, 'leader', *qayiṣ*, 'summer', and *qāṣîr*, 'harvest', in 6:7–8).

Beyond the composition of individual verses, six features help cohesive poems come into view. These features enable one more objectively to assess (particularly in chs. 10–29) whether the sayings and instructions of Proverbs comprise a random collection (Longman 2006: 36–42) or were thoughtfully arranged (cf. §2.3. 'Coherence', below).

2.1. Beginnings

Fundamentally, one poem differentiates itself from the next by a shift in theme. Sometimes a conundrum signals that shift, whether by rhetorical question (e.g. 8:1; 31:10), or statement (e.g. 25:13; 28:1).

Most often a wisdom commendation begins a poem, leading to wisdom content. 'Wisdom commendation' refers to one or more verses conveying the desirability of wisdom without situation-specific advice. It may pointedly summon the pupil to esteem wisdom, indicated in this example by 'reproof' and 'insight' (cf. §5.6 in the 'Introduction'):

> Listen, my sons, to a father's reproof,
> and pay attention so that you may learn insight.
> (4:1, leading to wisdom content in vv. 3–9; cf. 3:1–2; 27:11)

Or it may register wisdom's worth without any imperative:

> Whoever loves reproof loves knowledge,
> while one who hates reprimand is dense.
> (12:1, leading to wisdom content in vv. 2–4; cf. 10:1; 15:7; 23:15–16)

Meinhold and Waltke confirm that wisdom commendations introduce wisdom content (1991: 256 and 2004: 21–22, 609, 610, 618, 631, respectively; termed 'rearing' or 'educational' sayings by Waltke). Whybray underscores the structural importance of wisdom commendations, attributing some scholars' misguided groupings of sayings to their failure to take commendations into account (1994c: 90).

2.2. Endings

Together with a change of theme, a poem's ending typically is marked by closure, inclusio, recap, or character summary. Closure results when terms or topics introduced earlier in a composition reappear in concentrated fashion towards the end of a poem (cf. 1:19, closing vv. 10–19). In *Poetic Closure: A Study of How Poems End*, Smith observes, 'The conditions for maximal closure will arise when the structural principles in a poem predetermine its conclusion most rigorously, and when the greatest number or concentration of certain features appear in its terminal lines' (1968: 197).

Inclusio results when closural elements appear at or very near the first and last proverbs of a given poem (e.g. 'surely winds up in need' in 21:5 and 22:16, and 'take note' in 22:17; 24:32). A recap refers to themes encountered earlier in a poem, which reappear towards its end (cf. 13:24–25; 20:2–4).

Finally, sages often close with a binary character summary. Though superficially simplistic, a character summary implicitly challenges the audience: 'Whom will you emulate?'

> Consider this: the moral person on earth will be repaid.
> How much more the guilty sinner!
> (11:31, closing a poem that began in 10:31)

> The house of a moral person is a great treasure,
> but in the revenue of a guilty person there is calamity.
> (15:6, closing a poem that began in 14:1)

For other poem-closing character summaries, see 1:32–33; 3:34–35; 21:3–4. Occasionally character summaries may appear before a poem's close (e.g. 11:8; 14:11, 19, 34).

2.3. Coherence

Scholars are increasingly aware of coherence in Proverbs (e.g. Fox [2000, 2009], Heim [2001], Meinhold [1991], Van Leeuwen [1988] and especially Whybray [1994a] and Waltke [2004, 2005]). Structures such as the six outlined below foster coherence among adjacent proverbs, rendering poems more discernable.

First, repetition fosters coherence. Five sayings within 14:1 – 15:6 refer to both 'wise' and 'foolish'. The root *ʾḥr* (associated with 'future') repeats five times in 23:15 – 24:22.

Second, multiple synonyms (also antonyms) may indicate a cohesive theme. Within 21:5 – 22:16, wealth synonyms occur fifteen times, while power synonyms appear sixteen times. Expressions indicating success-despite-weakness appear seven times across 30:1–33.

Third, an imperative often is followed by an incentive (or explanation; e.g. imperative in 4:20–21, incentive in v. 22). Several such pairs may cluster together in a single poem (e.g. 3:1–2, 5–6, 9–10, 11–12).

Fourth, coherence results when two themes appear preliminarily, with subsequent sequential elaboration (called 'dual-theme introduction'). Examples appear in 1:10a–b (elaborated in vv. 11–14, 15–18) and 11:28a–b (elaborated in vv. 29, 30; cf. 1:2; 21:6–7; 23:13–14, 17–18; 15:7 [triple-theme introduction]). Less commonly, multiple-themes appear in a recap (e.g. dual-theme in 24:19–20; triple-theme in 6:5).

Fifth, coherence pervades a palistrophe (extended chiasm; e.g. 1:11–18, 22–33; 8:5–21; 20:10–14; 21:11–21, 22–29; 22:6–14; 26:1–12). Quantity of concentric steps may vary, yet length of matched steps should correspond (Step B should approximate Step B' in length). Rhetorical focus falls primarily on the centre or pivot, and secondarily on the close.

Sixth, when solution resolves problem, coherence emerges. Problems range from financial entanglement (6:1–2) to the difficulty of finding faithful persons (20:6) or a resourceful wife (31:10). Solutions ensue in 6:3–8, 20:7 – 21:4 and 31:11–31, respectively. More extensively, a problem in one lecture may lead to a solution in the next (e.g. the problem of riches' ephemerality in 10:31 – 11:31 leads to a solution – the lasting wealth of noble character in 12:1–28; liabilities of pursuing wealth and power in 19:10 – 20:4 lead to assets of cultivating faithful love in 20:5 – 21:4).

2.4. Apparent versus actual discontinuity

A poem's coherence would break down at a point of discontinuity. Yet the sage's penchant for riddles (pairing seemingly disparate elements) cautions against premature presumption of discontinuity, especially in Prov. 10 – 29. Whybray warns against

> assum[ing] that the material in these sections of *Proverbs* has been put together in an entirely haphazard way: that the authors or redactors were either indifferent to its arrangement or incapable of imposing any sustained logical structure on their ideas. This assumption is surely unjustified. If modern study of the problem has failed so far to discover the principles on which the material was arranged, this is more likely to be due to the interpreters' inability to find the key than to incompetence on the part of author or redactor. (1979: 154)

First, discontinuity may arise from contradictory counsel within a consistent theme. 'The book of Proverbs hardly shrinks from contradictions; in fact, at times it seems to revel in them' (Kugel 2017: 49).

> Do not reply to a stupid fellow in a manner corresponding
> to his folly,
> lest you become like him – even you!
> Reply to a stupid fellow in a manner corresponding to his folly,
> lest he become wise in his own estimation.
> (Prov. 26:4–5)

Though superficially contradictory, when treated as part of a coherent whole, these counsels teach that 'one size' does not 'fit all'. Wisdom must discern the best response for individual fools.

Second, discontinuity may arise from a seemingly intrusive saying. When explaining Job's suffering as retribution, Bildad pivots from theology to botany: 'Does papyrus grow up without a swamp?' (Job 8:11a). By this proverb, Bildad buttresses his claim that without a prior context of misdeeds (swamp), suffering (papyrus) cannot sprout. Bildad strategically deployed a proverb to reinforce persuasion – a technique Camp calls 'proverb performance'.

So vital is this deployment, that proverbial sayings 'by definition, *require* a performance context to be fully meaningful' (Camp 1985: 166; emphasis original). Once deployed, their new context – with its apparent discontinuity – vitally informs the proverb's meaning. Thus the context of a lesson against thuggery (Prov. 1:10–19) gives meaning to the deployed fowler saying in v. 17 ('a preexisting, self-contained adage', Fox 2000: 88; see also 1:7, 20:6 in respective Comment portions).

Since sages trafficked in deployed sayings, apparent discontinuities must be reconsidered. Else we miss a proverb's meaning by failing to reckon with the fact that a sapiential lecture itself supplies interpretive context. Although 'a proverb in a collection is dead' (Wolfgang Mieder, in Fox 2009: 484), the poems of Proverbs constitute context. Its sayings should no longer be relegated to the status of a mere collection.

2.5. Primary concepts

A poem's coherence grows clearer as constituent concepts come into view. To clarify concepts, outlines appear in this commentary alongside each poem's text.

2.6. Progression of thought

Awareness of a poem's primary concepts positions one to recognize progression of thought through the course of that poem. Since the sage frequently composed lectures to reach a persuasive conclusion, attention to thought progression yields considerable benefit (e.g. 1:10–19; 1:20–33; 2:1–22; 6:1–11; concerning intentional sequencing of sayings beyond Prov. 9, see Waltke 2004: 50).

Insights regarding progression of thought appear under 'Comment', for each poem. These insights arise out of structures indicating (a) a poem's borders, and structures of (b) macrodimensions and (c) microdimensions (discussed for each poem under 'Form and structure').

Just as sequence of concepts indicates progression of thought for an individual poem, progression emerges at a higher level as one considers the sequence of poems – what Whybray calls the 'overall message':

> One who assembled them [i.e. chs. 10–29] in their present order intended them to be seen as a whole. If indeed the purpose of the editors was more than simply one of general convenience but was to imprint some kind of message on the mind of the reader, that overall message must be just as important as the many different 'meanings' of the individual proverbs which make up these collections. (1992: 104–105)

The next portion summarizes progression of thought across multiple poems making up Proverbs. Announcements of named authors suggest a fourfold division of Proverbs: Division I (Prov. 1 – 9, Solomon), Division II (chs. 10–24, Solomon), Division III (chs. 25–29, Solomon and Hezekiah's staff), and Division IV (chs. 30–31, Massaite authorship).

3. PROGRESSION ACROSS PROVERBS

After appreciating progression within individual poems, it is instructive to observe progression from one poem to the next (poem-to-poem progression), and finally, from one division to the next (division-to-division progression; for division borders, see preceding paragraph). Based on content particular to a division, one may infer what audience the sage envisioned at that point.

3.1. Progression of thought in Division I (Prov. 1 – 9): an appeal to the prospective wisdom pupil

Two subunits comprise Prov. 1 – 9. The father-sage speaks to his son in Prov. 1 – 3. That father-sage then retransmits counsel received from his own father (the grandfather-sage) in chs. 4–9.

Poem-to-poem progression. Within the father-sage's five lectures spanning Prov. 1 – 3, wisdom commendation dominates chs. 1–2, beginning with a book-topic introduction (1:1–9). Second, third, and fourth poems seek to persuade the youth to enrol as wisdom's disciple. Negatively, the youth must reject the malicious gang's recruitment overtures (second lecture, 1:10–19). Positively, he must embrace Lady Wisdom's recruitment (third lecture, 1:20–33), and must become profoundly devoted to her (fourth lecture, 2:1–22). Wisdom commendation gives way to wisdom content in ch. 3, issuing counsel concerning wholesome relationships, both divine and human.

Eleven lectures comprise the grandfather-sage's teaching, tracing a cycle of three recurring themes (Prov. 4 – 9). The youth (a) must be receptive to reproof, so he may (b) learn to conduct his physical body in a manner consistent with exemplary inner character. Thus he may (c) interact honourably and safely with influential women, literal and metaphoric.

The grandfather's concern escalates through the last three influential women poems (6:20–35; 7:1–27; 8:1–36), culminating in a showdown-styled conclusion as Lady Wisdom and Dame Folly battle to recruit the youth (9:1–18). Recruitment-competition early (1:10–33) and late (9:1–18) forms a division-level inclusio.

Division-to-division progression. Division I displays simplicity in form and content. Concerning form, poems display clear borders, often with storylines. Content is foundational, instructing concerning relationships, character development, and sexual conduct.

Audience intended for Proverbs 1 – 9. Division I intends a youthful audience of wisdom instruction candidates – persons requiring persuasion before consenting to enlist as pupils. Concerning content, these need training in wisdom values and wisdom behaviour (character traits and healthy relationships).

Concerning form, if they would absorb wisdom teachings in Division II, novice pupils must learn from straightforward poems of Division I to recognize lecture-beginnings, endings, and how the sage groups concepts.

3.2. Progression of thought in Division II (Prov. 10 – 24): advice for the apprentice sage

Poem-to-poem progression. Division II begins by addressing a topic with wide appeal: 'How can I become rich?' (10:1–22). While answering that implicit question, the sage cautions: material wealth cannot satisfy one's deepest need for security. This leads to the next implicit question: 'How, then, can I secure my future?' (10:23–30). Security, the sage explains, arises from careful planning and moral conduct.

The next implicit question fuses moral conduct with wealth (the two preceding lectures): 'What is the harm in fraudulent riches?' (10:31 – 11:31). Immoral pursuit of wealth harms an entire community – a greed resolvable by generosity.

Rather than succumbing to greedy motives that inflict community damage, one should ask, 'How can I recognize noble character and thus behave as a true friend?' (12:1–28). And better than amassing superficial wealth, one should ask: 'How may I achieve true satisfaction?' (13:1–25). The sage explains that joy results from rescuing others (vv. 8–9), practised together with moral behaviour, industry, and receptivity to reproof.

Concern for personal wealth and satisfaction in Prov. 10 – 13 broaden to a concern for corporate success and security in chs. 14 – 24, evident from the next implicit question: 'How should I build my house?' (14:1 – 15:6). Compassion and restraint of power offer the solution, yielding durability both domestic and dynastic.

To lead well a group (domestic or dynastic) requires a well-cultivated mind – nourished by sound counsel, and evidencing psychological resilience attested by joy (15:7 – 17:3; esp. 15:13, 15, 30). Beyond consuming wisdom, effective leaders also will transmit wisdom to others (15:21–24) – a focus appearing with increasing frequency to the close of Division II.

Such a lofty invitation to a well-cultivated mind (15:7 – 17:3) may foster a smug fixation with wisdom, misleading the pupil to suppose that life's struggle will be won, if only one manages to overcome folly. However, beyond the fool lurks a still more-malevolent menace: the evildoer (17:4 – 19:9). The evildoer harms whole communities, hijacking systems of justice for selfish aims.

Benefits associated with wealth (18:2–9) and power (19:4) within the evildoer lecture may tempt the pupil to prioritize pursuit of those assets (earlier cautioned against in 10:1–22 and 10:31 – 11:31 [wealth] and in 14:1 – 15:6 [power]). So the next lecture underscores the priority of generosity in relationships, as the sage answers the implicit question: 'Will not wealth and power reliably bring beauty and benefit, regardless of where they may occur?' (19:10 – 20:4).

After unmasking the base pursuit of wealth and power (19:10 – 20:4), the sage follows with a loftier alternative (20:5 – 21:4). This negative/positive sequence resembles how, after debunking the allure of fraudulent riches (10:31 – 11:31), the sage took up the positive question, 'How can I recognize noble character and thus behave as a true friend?' (12:1–28). But while the two-lecture sequence may be similar, the philosophical and ethical heights now attained in 20:5 – 21:4 range breathtakingly loftier than the teaching about character and friendship in ch. 12. For here the sage explores nothing less than the comprehensive goal of human flourishing (20:5 – 21:4), achieved as one demonstrates faithful love across the three seasons of one's life. A trio of traits marks the three seasons: cultivating integrity within, vanquishing evil without, and pursuing purity within (20:5 – 21:4). These three will return in the next poem (21:5 – 22:16), in the same sequence.

Themes of wealth and power also resurface in that next poem (21:5 – 22:16), though without an attempt to displace the previous trio of goals. As if observing maturation in his pupil, the sage evidently concedes that his pupil must, at some future point, traffic in wealth and power. So he now discloses that pivotal factor spelling success or failure when navigating inevitable rapids of wealth and power – the factor of strategy. A strategy of self-control (bowing before the divine) will lead to authentic power. And a strategy channelling riches to the helpless will yield authentic wealth (21:30 – 22:5).

With a retrospective glance reaching as far back as Prov. 10 (see discussion of 22:20), the sage delivers the last and longest lecture of Division II. Thoughtfully he addresses the youth's implicit query: 'As I now venture out, what objective must I pursue, above all?' (22:17 – 24:34). For, scenarios of upscale social events (23:1–3, 6–8), of power and privilege (22:22–25; 23:4–5) – these envision a youth on the brink of a sapiential career, where he may serve in arenas both judicial (22:21; 24:23–26) and royal (22:29).

Because newfound prestige and power risk seducing the youth, eroding time-tested moral boundaries, therefore the sage twice reinforces, 'Do not move an ancient boundary' (22:28a; 23:10a). Only then will the well-tempered pupil defy deterrence, remaining undeceived by perquisites promised by immoral wealth or power. Only then will he achieve the supreme objective: 'So that in the LORD your confidence may lie' (22:19a).

Strategically concluding the final poem of Division II is a story – reminiscent of stories within Prov. 1 – 9. It is a story that teaches on two levels (24:30–34). For the wisdom trainee it advocates industry, without which the teachings delivered to this point will have been wasted. For the wisdom trainer, this story discloses the sage's secret: how to go about crafting an apophthegm.

Before considering division-to-division progression, a final topic merits attention. Just as the grandfather-sage concluded Lady Wisdom's counsel with advice for wisdom trainers (9:7–9), so also advice for wisdom trainers appears with increasing frequency as Division II progresses. The well-trained mind attains joy as it offers wise counsel to others (15:21–24). The sage supplies script so his pupils may train (a) youth lacking anger-restraint (19:20–24, 27–29) and (b) youth tempted by economic shortcuts (20:15–23). He challenges pupils to train others in proper use of wealth and power (22:6–16). Finally, the longest lecture of Division II presents the longest training for trainers (23:12 – 24:22), including a script stretching forty-three verses, to facilitate training of others on the crucial topic of longings (23:15 – 24:22).

Division-to-division progression. Division I (Prov. 1 – 9) lays a foundation of simpler form and basic content. Regarding form, Waltke observes that Division I (his 'prologue') with its more transparently cohesive poems prepares the reader to detect less-obvious poems comprised of sentence-sayings in Division II. 'The prologue', he observes, 'forges the book's hermeneutical key' (2004: 58). Poems are not so plainly-bounded in Division II, as in Division I (exceptions include poems about alcohol addiction [23:29–35] and proverb-crafting [24:30–34]).

Regarding content, since the youth of Division II requires less expenditure of recruitment energies (fewer wisdom commendations), the sage diversifies wisdom content, ranging from practical (e.g. 'How can I become rich?' [10:1–22]), to philosophical (e.g. 'What is the mind's principal role?' [15:7 – 17:3]). As Division II concludes, the poet readies fledgling sages for their imminent careers by reinforcing core values (22:17 – 24:34).

Audience intended for Proverbs 10 – 24. The audience envisioned for Division II already has embraced Lady Wisdom's invitation (Prov. 9, end of Division I). Consequently they will be receptive to an array of topics, in anticipation of future employment in influential posts. Together with personal advice, they will need skill in administering reproof to their own trainees (e.g. 23:12 – 24:22; see close of Division II 'Poem-to-poem progression', above).

3.3. Progression of thought in Division III (Prov. 25 – 29): advice for the journeyman sage, serving the royal court

Poem-to-poem progression. The four poems spanning Prov. 25 – 29 comprise a master lecture with this objective: to lead a monarchy – both king and courtier – from mediocrity to magnificence. The first lecture identifies both this objective and the twin audiences intended (king and courtier, 25:1–12).

Counsel for the second audience (courtiers) occupies the second lecture (25:13 – 27:22). Before turning to counsel kings in the fourth lecture

(28:1 – 29:27), the third lecture bridges both groups with a brief parable concerning a wise farmer (27:23–27).

Division III closes on a realistic note. The final saying of the fourth lecture portrays forces of morality locked in an interminable struggle with forces of dishonesty (29:27). Thus the sage fortifies courtier and king never to cede the struggle for right.

Division-to-division progression. As Division III begins, pupils readied for bureaucratic employ at the close of Division II now find themselves serving in an atmosphere of power and opulence. They have generated an appetite for counsel to lift their monarchy from mediocrity to magnificence. This focus renders Prov. 25 – 29 the longest thematically cohesive portion in the book (though containing more sayings, Division II is thematically more diverse, embracing the broader objective of personal character formation).

Audience intended for Proverbs 25 – 29. The audience envisioned for Division III has begun to shoulder leadership responsibilities within the community. Yet they are not so near their career's end that they would focus on final wishes (as will Agur in Division IV; cf. 30:7b).

3.4. Progression of thought in Division IV (Prov. 30 – 31): concluding advice for both commoner and king

Poem-to-poem progression. Contentment anchored in knowledge of God (also greed, contentment's nemesis) comprises the first lecture of Division IV (30:1–33, by Agur). Where greed erupts, the king rides forth as appointed agent of just retribution (vv. 24–31). Any who inflict abuse are advised to reform while they yet may (vv. 32–33).

The royal's duty to administer retribution continues in the next lecture (31:1–9, the first by King Lemuel's mother). The crown prince must not default, but must marshal resources to aid the marginalized (vv. 8–9).

Progression emerges from first to second of the queen mother's speeches. First, she cautions Lemuel regarding his relationship with women, lest he destroy himself through wasteful extravagance (31:3). Second, she counsels him to become the sort of husband who can find a supremely resourceful wife (31:10–31).

Division-to-division progression. Division IV registers progression across eight elements of content, and one of form. Concerning content, first consider that, reminiscent of the aged grandfather-sage of Division I, Agur speaks wisdom even nearer his life's end (30:7). Second, reverence, advocated as a principle in Division I (e.g. 1:7), now is embodied in a person (Agur's testimony in 30:2–6). Third, marriage counsel scattered across Divisions I and II (5:1–23; 6:20–35; 7:1–27; 19:13; 21:9, 19) now concentrates in a mother's advice to her son (31:10–31). Fourth, encouragement in Division I to pursue Lady Wisdom as teacher (1:20–33), sister

(7:4), counsellor (ch. 8), and host (9:1–12), now in Division IV transitions to recommend her as lifelong companion (metaphoric wife, 30:10–31). Fifth, in Division I wisdom issues most often from a father (or grandfather; e.g. 4:1–4), while in Division IV it issues from a mother (ch. 31), creating a bookwide inclusio-styled parental merism. Sixth, greed (and conversely contentment) features prominently in the gang's appeal in Division I (1:10–19), in the king's campaign against greed in Division III (29:3–14), and again in Agur's elevation of contentment in Division IV (ch. 30). Seventh, the monarch's responsibility to execute justice appears in Division III (28:1–28; 29:3–14) and again through the queen mother's insistent charge in Division IV (31:8–9). Eighth, the challenge to oppose evil perpetually (29:27, closing Division III) may explain Agur's expression of weariness (30:1, beginning Division IV).

Concerning form, poems with readily-recognizable outer borders characterized Division I. In Division IV self-evident poems return in the numerical sayings comprising the lecture that spans ch. 30, the mother's advice of 31:1–9, and the alphabetic acrostic of 31:10–31.

Audience intended for Proverbs 30 – 31. To this point, the audiences corresponding to successive divisions have grown successively more specialized or mature, ranging from candidates for wisdom recruitment (Division I), then apprentice sages (Division II), leading to journeyman sages (kings and courtiers, Division III). In Division IV the sage resets the audience through the lecture spanning ch. 30. Here he envisions initially a universal group in need of foundational principles (i.e. one must regard the divine with reverence, and fellow humans without greed). Towards the close of that lecture the monarchy resurfaces as the human agent of retribution (30:29–31). The monarchy comprises the focal audience to the balance of Division IV (ch. 31). By beginning with a general audience, then narrowing to a monarchial audience, Division IV recaps the entire book's range of audience.

By including non-Israelites among its authors, Division IV implicitly extends the audience envisioned. If Israel's wisdom has room for foreign authors respectful of Israel's God, non-Israelites in search of wisdom may likewise sense a welcome in the words of this scroll.

4. A GUIDE TO THIS COMMENTARY

4.1. Aim of this translation

To maximize insights arising from Proverb's carefully-composed poetry, this commentary presents a study-translation, preserving much of the Hebr. sense. For example, 1:17 renders 'master-of-flight' (lit. 'master-of-wing') instead of 'bird', registering reversal and closure when 'masters' reappears two verses later: 'Such are the ways of every ruthless profiteer:

the life of its masters shall it take' (1:19). Artful distinction in verb forms also is retained (e.g. *qōtēl* and wayyiq. forms, explained in 'Notes' for 8:35).

Consonantal text (K, 'what is written') is preferred over smoother variants proposed by the Masoretes (Q, 'what should be read aloud'). For K/Q examples, see 'Notes' for 'his path', *ʾŏrḥātô* (22:25) and 'and the weariness of the heavens', *wĕʿāyēp haššāmāyim* (23:5).

4.2. The Septuagint: an early translation

The Greek version known as the Septuagint (LXX) is the earliest translation of the HB, dating to approximately the second century BC. LXX of Proverbs differs from the Masoretic Text (MT) in three regards. The first two described below are drawn from Fox's excellent overview (2000: 361–364).

First, the LXX of Proverbs contains roughly 130 cola and another 30 partial sentences not found in the Hebr. of the MT. Conversely, some lines in the MT do not appear in the LXX.

Second, the sequence of verses within the LXX periodically does not match the Hebr. Notice, for example, how some sayings from ch. 16 were drawn back into ch. 15. Here is the LXX sequence of adjacent sayings: 15:27; 16:6; 15:28; 16:7; 15:29; 16:8, 9; 15:30 (15:31 is lacking in the LXX), 32, 33.

A more substantial displacement appears towards the end of Proverbs. After 30:1–14 there appears 24:23–34, followed by this sequence: 30:15–33, 31:1–9, 25:1 – 29:27, ending with 31:10–31 (with 31:26 before 31:25).

Most salient is the third difference. Where LXX and MT differ, LXX often reads more smoothly. Since smoother readings often are not original (what textual critics term *lectio difficilior potior*, 'the more difficult reading is the stronger'), and since the Hebr. sage regularly used uncommon expressions to arrest attention, one seldom should prefer the LXX over the Hebr. of the MT (for examples, see below under §5.7).

4.3. Recurring commentary headings

The following headings will recur in this commentary.

Title. The title given each poem infers a question that the poem proceeds to answer. No inference is needed for the final lecture's question-title: 'A resourceful wife, who can find . . . ?' (31:10).

Overview. A concise summary ('Overview') begins the discussion of each lecture.

Preceding and ensuing context. Adjacent poems are summarized under 'Preceding and ensuing context'.

What to watch for. To study a poem inductively, notice hints under 'What to watch for'.

Translation and outline. Alongside each translation appears an outline focusing primarily on content, with some indications of form (e.g. wisdom commendations, dual-theme introductions, palistrophes, and character summaries). These outlines, with explanatory progression of thought (located under 'Comment'), comprise this commentary's principal contributions. Horizontal lines suggest verse groupings, to encourage cohesive reading of adjacent sayings contributing to a particular thought.

Notes on the text (or **Notes**). Language-related explanations concerning translational choices, syntax and assonance appear here.

Form and structure: borders. Literary devices marking the outer perimeter of a poem appear under 'Borders'.

Form and structure: macrostructural features. Structural devices of form or content bridging two or more of a poem's largest portions (called 'sections') are summarized under 'Macrostructural features'.

Form and structure: microstructural features. Structural devices of form or content operating within a single section appear under 'Microstructural features'.

Comment. Step-by-step progression of thought coursing through each poem appears under 'Comment', enabling one to distinguish primary from secondary points, and to detect dynamic persuasive momentum that builds to a poem's conclusion. Verse-specific insights unrelated to text notes, structure, or progression of thought appear in smaller font, also under 'Comment'.

Explanation. Biblical insights informing personal transformation appear under 'Explanation'.

4.4. Terms used to describe biblical text

Among terms describing biblical text, a 'poem' (generally interchangeable with 'lecture') refers to a cohesive composition with a demonstrable beginning and ending. The subdivisions within a poem are, in diminishing order: section, block, unit, and segment. 'Division' designates any of the four groups of poems that comprise the entire book (Prov. 1 – 9; 10 – 24; 25 – 29; 30 – 31).

- Division
  - poem (or lecture)
    - section
      - block
        - unit
          - segment

Most verses of Hebr. poetry consist of two lines. Each line is called a 'colon' or 'stich'. A bicolon verse contains two lines (two cola), while a tricolon contains three (see Glossary for additional terms).

5. INSIGHTS CONCERNING THE ISRAELITE SAGE

5.1. The sage's concept of God

The theology of the sage anchors firmly in Israel's God as encountered at Sinai (87 references to Lord [Yahweh] and 5 to God [Elohim]). From God as creator derives nature's orderliness (e.g. 8:22–31; 20:12; 22:2; 29:13; cf. Perdue 1994: 77–122). Ethical order answers to God as ultimate evaluator (e.g. 2:7–8; 3:9–10; 12:22; 16:11; 17:15; 20:10).

A reasonable response to such a deity consists of reverence (1:7; 2:5; 8:13; 9:10; 10:27; 14:27; 15:33; 19:23; 22:4; 31:30) and trust (3:5; 16:3), as one remains satisfied with what he supplies (30:8–9). The loftiest human knowledge consists of acquaintance with the divine (3:6; 30:3, 4d). Divine blessing comprises supreme wealth (10:22).

Though the sage knows of religious ceremonies (7:14), and cautions against spiritual hypocrisy (15:8; 21:3, 27), he employs practical consequences, not divine decrees, to incentivize behaviour (e.g. 1:19; with divine backing in 23:10–11).

The proposal that Yahweh sayings were added late in the editing of Proverbs is difficult to support, due to their strategic placement within the structure of certain poems (*pace* Whybray 1994a: 31–32, 59). From their earliest compositions, the sages responsible for Proverbs subscribed to a world view grounded in Israel's God as encountered at Sinai (cf. palistrophic positioning of 1:29; 19:21, 23; 20:10).

5.2. The sage's definition of wisdom

As observed earlier, wisdom for the Israelite sage may be defined as the observation of order in the natural, social, and divine realms, so as to discern by rational choice the path most effectively leading to an optimally flourishing life (Overland 2018: 499; Koch 1955). The sage chronicles the observation-discernment process (24:30–34) and notes how it should inform decision-making: 'the shrewd fellow noticed [impending] misery and so took cover, but naive fellows kept on going and will be fined' (22:3). Counsel consists of another's discernment that aids one's own decision-making (1:10–19, 20–33; 6:10–11; for an instance of counsel rejected, see 5:7–14).

Since order derives from divine creation, wisdom operates in tandem with ethical conduct (reverent justice).

> In the way of wisdom I had instructed you.
> I had made you travel in honest tracks.
> (4:11)

> Along the path of guilty folk do not venture,
> and do not stride along the way of evil folk.
> (4:14)

Wicked behaviour is patently foolish.

5.3. The sage's concept of humankind

From the sage's teachings emerge six characteristics of humankind. First, with God as Maker, humans possess dignity (cf. 14:31; 17:5; 22:2). Respect towards others is not contingent upon their wealth or status (22:22–23; 30:10).

Second, morals supply navigation, whereas appetites supply motivation. Instead to entrust appetites with navigation invites disaster (16:25 – 17:3).

Third, human greatness issues from the practice of faithful love (20:5 – 21:4), irrespective of wealth or power. Conversely, greed forms the chief of social ills (28:15–16; 30:15–16).

Fourth, the deepest of human longings finds satisfaction, not by receiving love, but by becoming an agent of faithful love (19:22). Greatest personal fulfilment follows love of neighbour.

Fifth, no wealth can exceed the riches accruing to one who rescues others, who treats the helpless with generosity (13:8; 14:25; 21:30 – 22:5). Herein lies joy (13:9).

Sixth, mental health consists not of a towering intellect, but of psychological resilience signified by joy (15:13, 15, 30). A mind marked by joy can guide others to wholeness (17:22).

5.4. The sage's references to women

Proverbs presents women in a variety of roles. As mother, she deserves honour from child (10:1; 15:20; 19:26; 20:20; 23:25; 28:24; 29:15; 30:11, 17) and from husband (31:28–29). As wife, she constitutes a divine gift (18:22a; 19:14), an immense benefit to a wise husband (11:16; 12:4a), who will be faithfully devoted to her (5:18–20). While a wife may contribute to marital strife, context implicates the husband for first failure (12:4b; 19:13; 21:9, 19; 25:24; 27:15). As authoress, two poems composed by a sage-mother conclude the book (31:1–9, 10–31).

The astute youth will guard against harm from evil men (1:10–19; 2:12–15), as from misleading women, whether literal (2:16–19; 6:24–35; 7:1–27; 30:20) or metaphoric (9:13–18). He will beware the Strange Woman, who belongs neither to his trusted kinship network nor to his faith (2:17). He will follow Lady Wisdom closely (1:20–33; ch. 8; 9:1–12; see below, §5.8). He will seek as wife the Resourceful Woman (31:10–31) who, like earlier mothers, instructs wisdom (31:26; cf. 1:8; 6:20; 23:22).

5.5. The sage as caring mentor

Profound parental caring fuelled the sage's determination to mentor youth, evident in exclamations, 'My son':

So why, my son, should you stagger on account of a strange woman
or embrace a foreign woman's bosom?
(5:20)

What, my son!
And what, son of my womb!
And what, son of my vows!
Do not give to women your resources,
nor your behaviour to what is responsible for destroying kings.
(31:2–3)

To this, add parental pride:

For it is the one he loves that the LORD reprimands,
just as would a father, a son of whom he is particularly proud.
(3:12)

For, to their success the sage tethers his own:

My son, if your mind is wise,
my own mind will rejoice as well.
And my inner being will celebrate
when your lips speak what is honest.
(23:15–16)

5.6. Key terms in the sage's vocabulary

Several terms in the sage's vocabulary merit special attention, beginning with synonyms referring to the unwise. (For a brief explanation of poetic terms, please refer to Glossary.)

Synonyms for the unwise. First of four terms describing the unwise is naive (*petî*). These are impressionable, lacking training. So the sage races to recruit the naive, before evil influences may entice them (1:22; 7:7). The root *petî* occurs in fifteen verses in Proverbs.

Unlike the naive, the 'fool', *ʾĕwîl*, knows better but behaves unwisely all the same, in a rather aimless, inattentive manner (10:21). He disregards much-needed reproof (1:7b), supposing he is doing just fine (12:15), even as his words get him into trouble (14:3). The term *ʾĕwîl* occurs in nineteen verses in Proverbs.

Worse than fool is the 'stupid person', *kĕsîl*. He hates wisdom (1:22; cf. 18:2; 23:9) and ridicules forethought (10:23; 21:20). Despite possessing full mental capabilities (he is not mentally deficient), he rejects counsel. 'Stupid' is Proverbs's preferred label for the unwise (forty-nine references). The root *ksl* occurs in fifty-one verses in Proverbs.

Since he influences others, most hazardous is the 'scoffer', *lēṣ*. He foments sedition by mocking wisdom openly (22:10). To reprove him is perilous (9:7–8; 13:1; 15:12). *Lēṣ* occurs in fourteen verses in Proverbs.

Synonyms for correction. The sage elevates 'reproof' (root *ysr*; e.g. 4:13) and 'reprimand' (root *ykḥ*; e.g. 5:12) above all other wisdom, since these offer greatest potential for redirection and consequent benefit. To render either term as 'discipline' risks masking the confrontation they connote. In Proverbs, *ysr* occurs in thirty-five verses, with *ykḥ* in twenty-five verses.

Synonyms for ethical conduct. By *ṣdq*, the first of four terms describing ethical conduct, the sage envisions one who is 'loyal to the claims of all personal relationships' (LaSor et al. 1996: 49), who evidences a 'holistic moral character' (Millar 2020: 103). Thus *ṣdq* is rendered 'moral' in this commentary (e.g. 3:33; as noun, 'equity' in 21:21, or 'morality' in 8:20). Instead to render *ṣdq* as 'righteous(ness)' infers a theology better suited to biblical texts outside of Proverbs. Nevertheless, occasionally the sage associates *ṣdq* with distinctly divine favour, beyond basic morality (3:33; 10:3). The root *ṣdq* occurs in twenty-seven verses in Proverbs.

Yšr, a second term for ethical behaviour, connotes straightness, rectitude (sometimes rendered 'upright'). It will generally be rendered 'honest(y)' in this commentary (e.g. 2:7, 13, 21). This root occurs twenty-five times as an adj., five times as a noun, and five times as a verb.

Mišpāṭ, a third term in this group, carries a judicial connotation, occurring twenty times in Proverbs. To embrace connotations both of vindication and condemnation, this commentary often renders *mišpāṭ* as 'justice' (e.g. 2:8; 8:20), also 'fair decision' (2:9) or 'fairness' (e.g. 12:5).

Tōm (or *tāmîm*), a fourth root expressing ethical behaviour, conveys completeness (sometimes rendered 'perfect'). Occurring thirteen times in Proverbs, this commentary renders *tōm* or *tāmîm* as 'blameless' (e.g. Prov. 2:7, 21) or 'integrity' (e.g. 10:9, 29).

Synonyms for unethical conduct. Four principal terms describe unethical conduct. *Rʿ* refers to what is generally inferior, but as an ethical term is rendered in this commentary as 'evil' (e.g. 1:16; 3:7) or 'harm(ful)' (2:12, 14). Within Proverbs it appears in forty-five verses as adj., in twenty as a noun (e.g. 3:30), and in seven as a verb (e.g. 'inflict hurt', 4:16).

Customarily rendered 'wicked', by *ršʿ* the sage describes one who engages wrong behaviour knowingly, primarily against another in the community (e.g. 10:11; 12:6, 10). So indisputable is his misconduct, that frequently he teeters on the brink of retributive demise (e.g. 10:27, 28, 30; 11:5, 10). This commentary renders *ršʿ* as 'guilty'. Instead to render *ršʿ* as 'wicked' would convey an offence more deeply theological than concerned the sage. Nevertheless, at times the sage associates the guilty with negative divine evaluation (cf. 3:33). Within Proverbs *ršʿ* appears in eighty-four verses.

A third root describing unethical conduct is *ḥṭʾ*, meaning to 'miss the mark' or to 'sin'. Occurring in sixteen verses in Proverbs, the root is rendered 'to sin' or 'sinner' (e.g. 1:10; 13:22) or 'to wrong someone' (8:36). This root occurs in sixteen verses.

A fourth root, *hpk*, is rendered 'devious' (2:12, 14) or 'perversion' (e.g. 6:14 and 16:28, where it connotes a tearing of social fabric). It occurs in twelve verses in Proverbs.

A fifth root, *tʿb*, describes what is 'abhorrent' (e.g. 3:32; 8:7), rendered 'loathsome' (13:19) or 'revolting' (6:16). Within Proverbs, the noun *tôʿēbâ* appears in twenty verses.

Mind. Since the sage traffics in matters of intellect, *lēb* generally should be rendered not as 'heart', but 'mind' (15:14) or 'sense' (11:12). Appearing in ninety-five verses in Proverbs, *lēb* associates with *ydʿ*, 'to know' (3:5; 24:12; 27:23), and with *byn*, 'to perceive' (8:5; 14:33; 15:14; 16:21; 18:15).

Appetite. Fundamental to wisdom is the training of desires. 'Wisdom means not only knowing but also *desiring* to do what is right' (Fox 2000: 133; emphasis original). Since 'in the Old Testament *nepeš* refers to the passionate drives and appetites of *all* breathing creatures, including their hunger for food and sex' (Waltke 2004: 90; emphasis original), in Proverbs *nepeš* often should be rendered 'appetite' (not 'soul', 'person', or 'life'). As an example, see discussion of Prov. 16:17, 26. *Nepeš* occurs in fifty-four verses within Proverbs.

Life. In the sage's vocabulary, 'life', *ḥayyîm*, does not imply mere existence or survival, but robust human flourishing. Any saying where it occurs (there are thirty-eight in Proverbs) should be savoured. Towards the close of her masterfully persuasive speech, Lady Wisdom clinches her argument by extending these benefits: 'Indeed, one who finds me finds *life*, and thus obtained approval from the LORD' (8:35; emphasis added). Later, with this declaration the sage caps off an eleven-verse palistrophe exposing selfishness: 'One who pursues equity and faithful love, he will find *life*, equity, and honour' (21:21; emphasis added).

Synonyms for foreigner. Terms used by biblical writers to designate persons from a different land include 'sojourner', *gēr*, 'stranger', *zār*, and 'foreigner', *nŏkrî*. A sojourner, although alien, would seek not to abuse the hospitality of his hosts. Ruth's father-in-law, Elimelek, for example, is described as a sojourner, not a stranger or foreigner. The LORD repeatedly charged his people to treat with generosity the displaced who sojourned in Israel (Lev. 19:33–34). Frequently sojourners participated as virtual proselytes in Israelite customs. Some who made Israel their home gained heroic reputations (e.g. Rahab and Ruth). In contrast, the Hebr. terms rendered 'stranger' and 'foreigner' signified a difference that boded animosity and suspicion, not a relationship of mutual cooperation. In Proverbs when the sage cautions against hazardous women or men from other cultures, he chooses the term 'stranger', *zār* or *zārâ*, fourteen times, or 'foreigner', *nŏkrî* or *nŏkriyyâ*, nine times. 'Sojourner', *gēr*, does not appear in Proverbs.

5.7. The sage's style: jarring sayings

As intimated earlier, certain of the sage's sayings are jarring. By opacity of terms or obscurity of grammar, they slow the reader, lest she pass too swiftly from that saying to the next.

Hebr. grammar may specify a subject that produces a seemingly awkward message: 'Culpability will scoff at foolish folk' (not 'Foolish folk will scoff at culpability' [cf. NASB], in 14:9a). Or word choice may seem odd. With Q and LXX we expect, 'the *mouth* of stupid folk keeps grazing on folly' (cf. NRSV), rather than the earlier K text: 'the *face* of stupid folk keeps grazing', 15:14b; emphases added). Again, a word may seem superfluous (note second mention of 'truth': 'To make known to you verity, words of truth, so you may return words – *truth* to those who send you?' [22:21; emphasis added]). Additional examples appear in 18:19; 19:1, 7; 23:26 (see under 'Notes' for those texts).

We must restrain the impulse to smooth the text by appealing to exceptional grammar or emending the text too quickly. Routinely the reader who takes the time required to make sense of a jarring saying (adhering to grammar and attending to context) will recover a message both meaningful and unexpectedly insightful.

5.8. Lady Wisdom: creation of the sage

Lady Wisdom stands as an exceptional witness to the sage's literary skill. Artfully he clothes abstract with concrete, transforms principle to person, casting her as lead character in his central story. Winsomely she invites youth to join her group (1:20–33), to marvel at her privileged tutelage (8:1–36), to dine at her lavish feast (not at Dame Folly's, 9:1–18). In a culture traditionally regarding women as inferior, Lady Wisdom's stature commands respect. She casts her long shadow across the Resourceful Wife as well (31:10–31). The settled Israelite theology attested in Proverbs precludes regarding her as a vestigial goddess, a remnant from pre-Israelite worship (see §5.1).

5.9. The sage's initial audience

Based on Proverbs's content, youthful Israelite men comprised the sage's initial audience. Twenty-five times the author calls out, 'My son' (e.g. 1:8, 10, 15; 19:27; 31:2). While *bēn*, 'son', at times refers to children generally (esp. when pl.; e.g. Gen. 3:16; 21:7; Exod. 21:5), the sage's teachings advocating fidelity to one's wife indicate a male audience (e.g. Prov. 5:1–6, 18–20; 6:23–35).

Sayings advising envisioning a monarchial court suggest that some pupils belonged to aristocracy (22:11, 29; 25:6–7). Other sayings instruct a distinctly royal audience (16:10, 12; 20:8, 26, 28; 21:1; 25:5; 31:1–9). For inferences concerning division-specific audiences, please refer to intended-audience observations (§3.1–4, above).

5.10. The sage's mode of transmitting wisdom
The sage transmitted wisdom orally and by writing. Father-sage recalled grandfather-sage's speech: 'He instructed me and said to me, "May your mind lay hold of my words; guard my commands and truly live!"' (4:4). The question, 'Have I not written for you, for some time, concerning counsels and knowledge?' indicates that, like Egyptians and Mesopotamian sages, Israelites transmitted wisdom in written form (22:20). The instruction, 'May [my words] not disappear from your eyes', also may indicate written wisdom (4:21a; Waltke 2004: 297).

5.11. The sage's use of The Instruction of Amenemope
Earliest records from Mesopotamia and Egypt include counsel transmitted to the next generation (Overland 2018: 503–504). Since its publication by Budge in 1923, parallels between the Egyptian wisdom composition, *The Instruction of Amenemope* (hereafter *Amenemope*), and Prov. 22 – 24 have stirred considerable scholarly interest.

With twenty-eight columns of writing, the Budge Papyrus (BM 10474) measures 9.5 inches high (24 cm) by 12 feet 1.5 inches in length (over 3.5 m). It is noteworthy that the Egyptian sage himself divided this massive work into thirty theme-cohesive chapters. Black ink transitions to red for each chapter heading. Such thematic organization dispels any notion that tenth century BC was too early for Israelite scribes to have composed multiple theme-cohesive lectures comprising a substantial book. Roughly two centuries earlier, scribes in Egypt already had produced such a work – a composition with which Israelite sages were acquainted (concerning scribes and wisdom in the ancient world, see Overland 2018).

Amenemope's composition date indicates its priority, relative to Proverbs. My palaeographic examination of the earliest fragment of *Amenemope* (Cairo Ostracon EM 1840-4 = JE 96555) reinforces Posener's provisional dating to the Ramesside Era (Nineteenth–Twentieth Dynasties, spanning 1295–1069 BC; Posener 1975: 195–210), indicating more narrowly the era of Ramesses IV (1153–1147 BC). Laisney similarly dates the Cairo Ostracon to the end of the Twentieth Dynasty (2018: 143). Since by that point *Amenemope* already circulated as a schoolboy text, original composition would date still earlier. Solomon's rule, with its substantial Egyptian exchange, would not begin until roughly 970 BC.

Israelite sages drew from *Amenemope* judiciously. Concerning theology, Thoth (Egyptian god of the scribes) was replaced by the LORD (*Amenemope* col. 4, line 19 [ch. 2.16] and Prov. 22:23). Concerning fauna, geese of Egypt's Nile culture were replaced by the eagle, more fitting for arid Palestine (*Amenemope* col. 10, lines 4–5 [ch. 7.15–16], and Prov. 23:5; Overland 1996: 284, 288).

Of seventeen *Amenemope* parallels appearing in Proverbs, nine evidence significant positioning in the source document, indicating the Israelite sages were attentive to structure in the Egyptian composition with its theme-based chapter divisions (Overland 1996: 290–291). So one should not be surprised to find theme-based lectures in Proverbs, crafted with artful structures.

The evident contact with *Amenemope* raises a question concerning sequencing of *Amenemope* material within Proverbs. Simplest would have been for the order in Proverbs to have mirrored *Amenemope*. Yet such is not the case. Notice how the order of *Amenemope* source chapters oscillates when appearing in Proverbs: Prov. 22:18 ~ *Amenemope* 1.5, 8; Prov. 22:21 ~ *Amenemope*, prologue, line 5; Prov. 22:22 ~ *Amenemope*, prologue, also line 5; Prov. 22:23 ~ *Amenemope* 2.16; Prov. 22:24 ~ *Amenemope* 9.1–2; Prov. 22:25 ~ *Amenemope* 9.35–36; Prov. 22:28 ~ *Amenemope* 6.1–4; Prov. 22:29 ~ *Amenemope* 30.9–10 (final saying before colophon); Prov. 23:1–8 ~ *Amenemope* 23.1–6; Prov. 23:4–5 ~ *Amenemope* 7.1, 9–10, 15–16; Prov. 23:6–8 ~*Amenemope* 11.9–14; and Prov. 23:10–11 ~ *Amenemope* 6.1, 4, 8. Based on the evidence of literary structures, outlines, and progression of thought within the lecture spanning Prov. 22:17 – 24:34, it appears the Hebr. sage resequenced excerpts from *Amenemope* as would best support his own carefully devised rhetorical scheme.

5.12. The question of schools in ancient Israel

Training as a scribe (literacy) formed the foundation of a sage's education in ancient times, whether in Mesopotamia, Syria, or Egypt (Overland 2018: 503–504). In Mesopotamia the home-based *edubba* (tablet house) groomed scribes of ancient Sumer, of Ur III (2111–2003 BC), and of Old Babylon (1894–1595 BC), employing a two-stage curriculum. From the subsequent Kassite period over fifty training tablets were recovered.

In northern Syria multiple instructors staffed the Emar scribal school. Four sons of Nuʻme-Rašap (copyist of the Atra-hasis epic) studied as scribes in Ugarit.

Egypt of the First Intermediate Period (c. 2190–2106 BC) attested schools. The 'house of life' (a temple scriptorium) trained physicians, astronomers, magicians, interpreters of dreams, and priests for the Middle Kingdom (2106–1786 BC). A four-year scribal programme during the New Kingdom (1550–1069 BC) enrolled pupils at age ten, focusing on *sebayit* (moral instructions) and *kemyt* (training that included phrases useful in correspondence).

Recent archaeological evidence renders it highly likely that Mesopotamian school curriculum (training in cuneiform literacy) influenced Canaan at the end of the second millennium BC. This educational tradition may have transitioned to train early alphabetic cultures such as Israel's as well (Schniedewind 2019: 18–20). A scribal apprenticeship system like that of Emar may be indicated by the fact that 'Elihoreph and Ahijah were sons of *Shisha*, scribes', especially if Shisha was not a name, but a corruption of

Egyptian *šs*, referring to a royal scribe (2019: 3; 1 Kgs 4:3; italics in the quote are original).

If, like Syria, schools existed wherever documents have surfaced, then Canaan offered schools as early as the Late Bronze Age (1550–1200 BC; Cohen 2013: 13). As with wisdom compositions and scribal training in Egypt, wisdom literature such as Proverbs may have supplied some of the sequential curriculum (see intended audiences under §3, above, also Crenshaw 1990: 212; Sneed 2011: 71; Shupak 2015: 296).

6. AUTHORSHIP

Among biblical books, Proverbs is unusual for its care in crediting authors. Solomon, third king of Israel (970–930 BC), is credited with composing chs. 1–9 (1:1) and chs. 10–24 (10:1). He constructed Israel's first temple, and gained uncommon fame for prowess in wisdom (1 Kgs 4:29–34; 10:1–13, 24). Under his rule Israel enjoyed remarkable prosperity, expansion of military security, and maritime trade (1 Kgs 4:20–28; 10:14–29). Despite two supernatural encounters with Israel's God, in later years Solomon's affections turned to foreign deities, influenced in part by his decision to marry hundreds of wives (1 Kgs 11:1–13). With Jeroboam's rebellion Israel's monarchy began to fracture during Solomon's reign (1 Kgs 11:26–40).

Solomon's contributions underlie chs. 25–29 as well, although Hezekiah's staff had a hand in the editing process, according to 25:1. Hezekiah began his forty-two-year rule of Southern Israel roughly two centuries after Solomon (728–687 BC, including co-regency with his father, Ahaz). He gained renown by restoring worship of God (2 Kgs 18:1–8; 2 Chr. 29 – 30). During his rule Northern Israel fell to the Assyrians (721 BC, 2 Kgs 18:9–12), and Jerusalem miraculously survived a siege (701 BC, 2 Kgs 18:17 – 19:37).

Although otherwise unknown, Agur (by wordplay with *hammaśśā'*, 'the pronouncement', likely of Massa, a migratory Arabian tribe; Perdue 2000: 251) and the mother of King Lemuel (also of Massa) are credited with chs. 30 and 31, respectively. They respect the God of Israel (note mention of Yahweh in 30:9; 31:30). Another author is the father (unnamed) of the primary author of chs. 1–9, referenced in 4:3–4. Unnamed wise persons are credited in 24:23 as well. As observed above (§5.11.), certain sayings within chs. 22–24 evidently trace to the Egyptian composition, *The Instruction of Amenemope*.

Inclusion of instructions composed by non-Israelite sages illumines the concept of the Bible's inspiration. As observed above, Agur and the mother of King Lemuel each counsel reverence for Israel's God. Analogous to a proselyte, their inclusion among biblical authors may be less surprising than that of the Egyptian sage Amenemope. Incorporation of portions of *Amenemope* demonstrates that individuals outside Israel were regarded as worthy sources of insights for wise living – insights meriting incorporation (after theological modification) into sacred scripture.

Other texts within the Bible from persons who were not followers of the God of the Bible include the prophecies by Balaam of Pethor and, in the New Testament, Greek poets. Though initially reluctant to trespass the terms of his contract with King Balak of Moab, eventually Balaam capitulated, speaking as God directed. So he issued blessings for Israel that included declarations concerning God's character (e.g. Num. 23:19). Centuries later the apostle Paul would cite Greek poets when preaching in Athens (Acts 17:28).

7. DATE

Based on Proverbs's internal attributions of authorship and editing, it is reasonable to conclude that compositional activity corresponds to the periods surrounding the rules of King Solomon (970–930 BC) and King Hezekiah (728–687 BC). *Amenemope* material adapted within Prov. 22–24 would date before Ramesses IV (1153–1147 BC), since by then the composition enjoyed currency as a schoolboy text (see §5.11). Concerning the period of Agur and King Lemuel's mother, we lack information. While one may propose later authorial or editing contributions, paucity of evidence allows little more than speculation (e.g. does Aram. *bar*, 'son' [instead of Hebr. *bēn*], in 31:2 indicate late Israelite composition, or does it preserve evidence that Aram. influenced Massaite culture earlier than it influenced Israelite culture?).

TEXT AND COMMENTARY

DIVISION I (PROV. 1 – 9): AN APPEAL TO THE PROSPECTIVE WISDOM PUPIL

As to form, outer borders and internal cohesion in Division I are indicated by wisdom commendations, character summaries, dual-theme introductions, and palistrophes. As to content, father-sage (chs. 1–3) and grandfather-sage (chs. 4–9) seek to persuade the youth to enrol as a wisdom pupil, reaching a crescendo in the last lecture: 'Whose invitation should I accept: Lady Wisdom's or Dame Folly's?' (9:1–18; see the 'Introduction', §3.1, for inter-poem and inter-division progression).

PROVERBS 1 – 3: INTRODUCTION (A FATHER'S WISDOM)

A book-introduction (1:1–9) begins Prov. 1 – 3, leading rapidly to one of the most impassioned among all of Proverbs's lectures (1:10–19). A youth must be intercepted before joining a deadly gang. The next two poems continue to commend choosing the way of wisdom (1:20–33; 2:1–22). Not until Prov. 3 does the father-sage offer life-specific advice (wisdom content) – foundational lessons for healthy relationships, both divine and human (3:1–35).

PROVERBS 1:1–9
'For whom were these lectures written, and how will they benefit?'

Overview of Proverbs 1:1–9
The poem spanning Prov. 1:1–9 functions as a prologue, setting the course for wisdom training to follow. This lecture answers the implicit question, 'For whom were these lectures written, and how will they benefit?' Here the sage identifies the two groups for whom he has designed this course, and explains how each may benefit from his instruction. In addition, he catalogues various tools (sorts of sayings) used to achieve his objectives.

Before exiting the prologue he will present two teachings – samples of his sapiential instruction. Not random samples, these sayings will epitomize the richest core and deepest foundation within all of his teachings. Thus in his introduction the sage offers an exquisite blend of concision and intricacy, as he readies the reader to enrol in his course of wisdom.

Position of this poem within Proverbs
Ensuing context. Following the prologue, the first lecture will erupt with a desperate appeal from sage to son, as he seeks to divert the youth from the deadly enticement of malevolent companions (1:10–19). The negative tone of that lecture will be balanced by a robustly positive alternative in the second lecture (vv. 20–33). As surely as the youth must steer clear of the band of thugs, he must with equal resolve engage Lady Wisdom as his teacher.

What to watch for
Notice that the verb beginning 1:2b reappears at the start of v. 6. Then consider how v. 2a may introduce vv. 3–5, and how v. 2b may introduce vv. 6–9, all of which focuses attention on the foundational principle in v. 7. Within vv. 3–4, consider the variety of pupils the sage intends to benefit. Consider also the similarity between v. 5 and vv. 8–9.

Translation and outline

Verse	*Translation*	*Outline*
1:1	The proverbs of Solomon, son of David, king of Israel,	I. Description of the book: collected royal wisdom (1:1)
		II. The book's purpose and tools for perception (vv. 2–9)
1:2	For knowing wisdom, even reproof; for perceiving perceptive sayings.	A. Dual-theme introduction: the book's purpose, and tools for perception (v. 2)

		B. The book's purpose: how training in wisdom will benefit two groups, with a bridging exhortation to receptivity (vv. 3–5)
		1. The book's objective: to benefit two groups (vv. 3–4)
1:3	For getting hold of reproof which brings success: equity, fair decision and integrity.	a. Ethical character for the wise (v. 3)
1:4	For giving to naive folk cleverness, to a youth knowledge and schemes.	b. Critical perception for the naive (v. 4)
1:5	May a wise person listen and may he expand training; so will a perceptive person obtain skill in navigation.	2. Dual-theme bridge and exhortation: how receptivity benefits the wise and the perceptive (v. 5)
		C. Tools for perception: catalogue and example of wisdom's materials, with closing exhortation to receptivity (vv. 6–9)
		1. A catalogue and premier example of wisdom materials (vv. 6–7)
1:6	For perceiving a proverb and an allusive expression, words of the wise and their riddles.	a. A catalogue of literary assets (v. 6)
1:7	Reverence for the Lord is the epitome of knowledge; fools despise wisdom and reproof.	b. Reverence: the premier example of a wisdom saying (v. 7)
		2. Closing exhortation to receptivity (vv. 8–9)
1:8	Listen, my son, to your father's reproof, and do not neglect your mother's instruction.	a. Instruction to heed parents (v. 8)
1:9	For a gracious garland are they for your head, and necklaces for your neck.	b. Incentive of adornment (v. 9)

Notes on the text

1:2. 'reproof', *mûsār*: Waltke conveys the confrontational nature of this term by defining 'chastening lesson' (2004: 175).

1:3. 'equity', *ṣedeq*: loyalty, whether in human community or divine community. Association with 'fair decision', *mišpāṭ*, recommends weighting *ṣedeq* in favour of human community; hence 'equity'.

1:4. 'schemes', *mĕzimâ*: alternatively 'discretion'.

1:5. 'May a wise person listen', *yišmaʿ*: juss., due to clause-initial yiq. form, parallel to the weqat. form as indirect juss. found in *wĕyôśēp*, 'may he expand'.

'training', *leqaḥ*: connotes training in rhetoric to enhance persuasive speech (Fox 2000: 62). 'Getting hold of' in v. 3a traces to the same root (*lqḥ*).

1:6. 'and their riddles': i.e. riddles within the 'words of the wise'. Within superficially transparent sayings by the wise lie riddles to be solved. Kugel observes, 'A *māšāl* [proverb] seems to have been deliberately formulated as a kind of riddle whose meaning was not immediately apparent' (2017: 21). For further discussion see the 'Introduction', §2. 'Steps towards reading Proverbs cohesively'.

1:7. 'Reverence', *yirâ*: lit. 'fear', which in this context connotes profound respect rather than dread.

'epitome', *rēʾšît*: implies both the start of something; also its best attestation.

Form and structure

Borders

An authorship attribution begins the book, forming the upper border of the first poem (1:1). Authorship attributions also mark poems' upper borders in 10:1; 25:1; 30:1; 31:1.

Closure and a concluding exhortation mark the lower border. The following elements in the final quatrain (1:8–9) appeared earlier, fostering closure: 'son' (vv. 1, 8), 'reproof' (vv. 2, 3, 7, 8) and 'listen' (vv. 5, 8). 'Epitome' and 'head' link etymologically (vv. 7, 9). Like v. 5, an exhortation to 'listen', with incentive, also marks the lower border (1:8–9). The third lecture of Prov. 1 similarly will close with an emphasis on listening (1:33).

Macrostructural features

Structural features may be based either on form or content. When a feature linking two portions involves grammar or syntax (e.g. an imperative, a negation, a statement of purpose), that link would comprise a 'form-based' feature since it operates apart from the meaning particular to that expression (i.e. apart from what is being specifically commanded, negated or indicated as purpose). Form-based structures may also involve recurring sounds (assonance) or repeated words.

In contrast, a link would be termed 'content-based' when depending on similarity (or dissimilarity) observable only by considering the meaning of an expression. Thus, when occurring in a single lecture, the synonyms 'official', 'ruler' and 'king' would form a content-based feature called thematic continuity, indicating a topic that may be pivotal in that lecture.

In order to grasp the message of each poem, it will be helpful to consider first macrostructures – those features that connect two or more of the highest-level portions that are within that poem. Highest-level portions will be designated 'sections'. Structures joining sections will be termed 'macrostructures'. In contrast, any structure limited to a single section (or some portion of a section) will be termed a 'microstructure'. Portions that make up a 'section' will be labelled, in descending priority, 'blocks', 'units' and 'segments'.

Subject and predicate connection (Sections I and II, form-based). The noun phrase 'The proverbs of' (Section I, 1:1a) serves as subject for a series of five predicates. Thus vv. 1–2a read, 'The proverbs of Solomon . . . [are] for knowing wisdom . . . [v. 2a]; [the proverbs of Solomon . . . are] for perceiving . . . [v. 2b].' Verses 3, 4, 6 similarly supply predicates.

Thematic continuity concerning sayings (Sections I and II, content-based). The commodity of wise sayings appears in Section I ('proverbs', 1:1) and Section II ('perceptive sayings', v. 2b).

Repetition of 'proverb' (Sections I and II, form-based). The term 'proverb(s)' links 1:1, 6.

Microstructural features

Consider next microstructural features – those structural devices that are confined to a single section. Since Section II alone spans more than one verse, all microstructures for the introductory poem operate in that section.

Dual-theme introduction (1:2, 3, 6, form-based). The two cola of 1:2 comprise a dual-theme introduction. Verse 2a will be expanded in vv. 3–4 ('reproof', *mûsār*, appears at the end of v. 2a; then reappears in v. 3a as the first object one gets hold of). Verse 2b will be expanded in vv. 6–9 (the expression 'for perceiving', *lĕhābîn*, opens both v. 2b and v. 6).

Thematic contrast involving benefits and beneficiaries (1:3–4, content-based). The benefit described as 'getting hold' of wisdom (1:3) contrasts 'giving' wisdom (v. 4).

Contrast also joins the beneficiaries of these two actions. Though unnamed here, those who 'get hold of reproof' (1:3) will later prove to be persons already wise. Only they value reproof enough to discount its sting (cf. 12:1; 13:1; 15:32; 17:10; 24:32). In contrast, the 'giving' of wisdom benefits those not-yet wise ('naive' and 'youth', v. 4).

Dual-theme bridge involving wisdom and perception (1:5; also vv. 2, 6, form-based). The first colon of 1:5 bridges back to preceding verses ('wise' in v. 5a, and 'wisdom' of v. 2a, which anticipated vv. 3–4). The second colon of v. 5 bridges to ensuing verses ('perceptive person' in v. 5b links to 'perceiving' in v. 6, and to 'perceiving perceptive sayings' in v. 2b, which anticipated vv. 6–9).

Closure involving the root *lqḥ* (1:5, 3, form-based). The term 'training', *leqaḥ*, in 1:5 traces to the root *lqḥ* found earlier at the start of v. 3 ('for getting hold of', *lāqaḥat*).

Continuity of content-plus-exhortation to 'listen' (1:3–5, 6–9, form-based). The wisdom content spanning 1:3–4 closes with an exhortation to 'listen' in v. 5. The wisdom content spanning vv. 6–7 similarly closes with an exhortation to 'listen' in its final quatrain (in v. 8 of vv. 8–9).

Intensification among related exhortations (1:5, 8–9, form- and content-based). The second closing exhortation intensifies the first formally, escalating from a juss. wish in 1:5 to a pointed imperative in v. 8, and by adding a voc. ('my son'). The appeal to filial honour in v. 8 adds content-based intensification.

Progression among wisdom forms, from general catalogue to specific sample (1:6–7, content-based). A catalogue of wisdom forms appears in 1:6, followed by a specific example of wisdom in v. 7.

Repetition of three adjacent terms (1:2, 7, form-based). A trio of terms in 1:2 reappears in v. 7, and not elsewhere in the HB ('[to] know/knowledge-wisdom-reproof').

Imperative-plus-incentive (1:8–9, form-based). The imperatives of 1:8 are followed by incentives in v. 9.

Comment

Section I (1:1). The first lecture (and entire book) opens with a compact description listing content (proverbs), source (of Solomon, son of David) and author's role (king of Israel, 1:1). To attribute wise sayings to a monarch would enhance their influence, since various biblical leaders were remembered for skill in wisdom (Overland 2005: 985) as well as judicial insight (Liver and Sperling 2007: 167) and military prowess (cf. 1 Sam. 8:20).

Section II (1:2–9). *Block II.A (1:2).* Those proverbs (referred to in 1:1) will accomplish the express purpose of enabling others to gain wisdom thoroughly (note the redundant intensity in 'knowing wisdom', v. 2a). Unwilling to hide the fact that wisdom acquisition at times will entail pain, the sage discloses directly that he will not refrain from administering 'even reproof', when a wisdom lesson may require it.

Tools of the wisdom enterprise consist of perceptive or insightful sayings (1:2b). The sage's role is to help the pupil truly grasp (perceive) lesson content. The saying must not merely glitter as a bauble, but must illumine choices, igniting conduct.

Block II.B (1:3–5). Having introduced the purpose (or end, 1:2a) and tools (or means, v. 2b), the balance of the lecture will unfold those twin dimensions, beginning with its purpose (vv. 3–5). Persons displaying greatest appetite for more wisdom are those already wise. They fairly beg for reproof, that most acerbic form of wisdom, aware that it offers the highest concentration of benefit (v. 3a), shaping even the depths of their very character, chiselling away deficiencies in equity, fairness and integrity (v. 3b).

The character traits begin with 'equity', *ṣedeq* – moral dealing in mutual exchanges. This concept involves your treating me right, and my treating you right. If equity should fail (you treat me right but I treat you wrongly), then the second stage comes into play: obtaining a 'fair decision' to resolve the dispute, *mišpāṭ*. At this stage the aggrieved seeks redress in the form of a just judgement. Should litigation fail (as when those to whom you appeal dismiss or decide against your rightful claims), then the third stage unfolds. Disillusioned and marginalized, you as the aggrieved may then be tempted to resort to retaliation or revenge, executing actions that are less-than-equitable, less-than-fair. How one responds at this stage will prove one's depth of character. One who resists the temptation to take revenge, who resolves instead tenaciously to hold to the high road of 'integrity', *mêšārîm*, despite devolution around him – this one has truly laid hold of success-inducing 'reproof', *mûsār*. Here is one who not only practises equity in mutual exchanges (*ṣedeq*), who issues decisions that are fair (*mišpāṭ*), but who attains a life pervasively characterized by integrity (*mêšārîm*). To inculcate of such a trio of character traits requires tenacious determination, since cross-currents of compounding unfairness mount a formidable tug-of-war, threatening to rip from one's grip those very qualities most necessary to bring about success (note caus. flavour in hiph. stem of 'success', *śkl*, in 1:3a). It is instructive to note that the three qualities here listed as principal indicators of mature wisdom are communal. It would be difficult to cultivate or display them in isolation.

The sage is not content merely to expand wisdom and success of the wise (inferred from 1:3). He aims also to recruit the impressionable 'naive' (v. 4). As yet incapable of 'getting hold' of wisdom for themselves, it must be 'given' them (contrast vv. 3a, 4a).

Moral sensibilities of the naive are yet unformed, rendering him or her a potential pupil for the wise, while also an unwitting prey for the wily. The sage urgently determines to reach them first, as shown in the next poem (1:10–19). Benefits bestowed on the naive and youthful (cleverness, knowledge and schemes) appear tailored to replace indiscriminate naivety, escorting them to join the perceptive.

Whereas a trio of character traits occupied 1:3, the trio of skills found in v. 4 are of a different sort. 'Cleverness', *ʿormâ*, 'knowledge', *daʿat*, and 'schemes', *mĕzimâ*, deal not with ethical behaviour, but with exercising critical perception – the ability to detect authentic worth by unmasking external appearances. So these benefits suitably await the naive and youthful (*pĕtāʾîm* in v. 4a; *naʿar* in v. 4b), persons who merely by their early stage in life (not by moral disinclination) are most at risk of being duped. Fox helpfully observes that 'the ostensive rhetorical setting [for Proverbs] is a man who is speaking to an adolescent son about to enter the adult world' (2000: 62).

Thus the sage has identified the two groups whom he hopes to benefit: the wise (implicit in 1:3) and the naive/youthful (explicit in v. 4). Already some in the audience will have identified with one of those two groups. So he discloses his most sincere longing. He urges each to bring that one trait singularly essential for any who would advance in wisdom – the trait of receptivity (v. 5a). If they will pledge to 'listen', then he may proceed to teach, employing tools of the wisdom trade, helping them truly grasp the wealth concealed in wisdom sayings (v. 5b), as anticipated in the introduction (v. 2b).

Block II.C (1:6–9). The sage's literary tools display rich variety. He itemizes several in 1:6. Frequently he will employ a *māšāl*, 'proverb' – a saying that often illumines by 'comparing' the obscure with the clear, often paradoxically (cf. 12:9). *Māšal* means 'to compare' or 'resemble'.

Incidentally, *māšal* can also mean 'to rule' – a skill inherent to the royal court. Many of the sage's sayings will deal with rule, whether of a realm (cf. 29:4) or of self (cf. 21:23).

In addition to a 'proverb', the sage has at his disposal the *mĕlîṣā*, 'allusive expression', as in this example: 'Better a meal of greens when love is there than [a meal of] fattened cattle with hatred' (15:17). While ostensibly dealing with eating, it alludes more importantly to loving relationships. *Mĕlîṣā* can also describe a mocking poem, as with the keenly polished satire against drunkenness (23:29–35).

Dibrê ḥakāmîm, 'words of the wise', marks a third tool of the sage's trade. As this exact label will head a section known for overlap with international, non-Israelite compositions (22:17 – 24:22), *dibrê ḥakāmîm* here may be the sage's way of acknowledging early on that he lays no exclusive claim to wisdom. He models a humility that allows others to help him perceive aspects of God's truth (without sacrificing convictions concerning Israelite theology – as evident from sayings such as 22:23, on which see below).

Last among his tools the sage lists *ḥîdōtām*, 'their riddles' (i.e. riddles of the wise, 1:6). *Ḥîdâ* attributes a certain sharpness to these sayings, whether due to clever concealment of their meaning (as with paradoxes and riddles), or due to their conscience-pricking quality. An example of a paradoxical riddle emerges from twin instructions concerning how to answer a fool (26:4, 5).

As for a *ḥîdâ* with a conscience-pricking quality, consider this indictment, positioned as the lectures spanning Prov. 10 – 24 draw to a close:

> Rescue those who are being carried off to death, and those who would be tottering towards slaughter, if you were to keep to yourself! Suppose you say, 'Look: we did not know about this!' He who weighs motives, can he not perceive? He who watches over your life, will he not know? Further, will he not repay to a mortal according to his deed? (24:11–12)

Since the catalogue of various sorts of wisdom expressions (1:6) would likely leave his pupils longing for a specific illustration, the sage produces a premier example of wisdom in v. 7.

From among a myriad of sayings, what wisdom should he showcase at this focal point? After considerable reflection, with an aura of solemnity we can picture the sage unfolding to his pupils this foundational principle: 'Reverence for the Lord is the epitome of knowledge; fools despise wisdom and reproof' (v. 7). An attitude misaligned towards the divine betrays that one has neither begun soundly nor finished successfully (v. 7a; 'epitome' renders a word meaning both 'first' and 'ultimate'). And any who bristle at this principle only parade their love of ignorance (v. 7b). Thus the sage discloses in his introduction his finest sapiential conclusion, what Waltke calls 'the quintessential expression of the basic spiritual grammar for understanding the book' (2004: 180). So crucial is this principle that the sage will return to stress reverence in Proverbs another thirteen times.

Just as the sage followed his statement of purpose (to benefit both wise and naive, 1:3–4) with an exhortation to receptivity (v. 5), now again after presenting the varied sorts (v. 6) and a supreme sample of wisdom (v. 7), the sage summons pupils to receptivity (vv. 8–9). He underscores the essential nature of receptivity by marshalling an appeal to filial honour (v. 8). For any who may arrogantly protest that his parents are too out of touch to offer youth any worthwhile advice, the sage warns against 'neglect[ing] your mother's instruction' (v. 8b).

In addition to the exhortation to 'listen', several expressions encountered earlier in the lecture now reappear in 1:8–9, weaving a rich tapestry of closure. These include 'son', 'reproof' and 'head' (a Hebr. root earlier rendered 'epitome').

The sage closes the lecture in 1:9, reinforcing the imperative to 'listen' with a positive incentive. Exquisite honour will adorn those who embrace what the sage is about to disclose to his pupils through the lectures that will follow (v. 9).

1:2. A series of infinitives unfolds the book's aim: knowing, perceiving, getting hold of, giving and again perceiving (vv. 2a, 2b, 3, 4 and 6, respectively). The Egyptian wisdom composition *The Instruction of Amenemope* similarly begins with a series of purpose statements (Fox 2000: 73).

1:6. Skehan speculates that the four wisdom forms in 1:6 may correspond sequentially to subsequent portions of Proverbs (1976: 329–340). Lack of clear delineation of each term's connotation makes this difficult to confirm. Three of the four appear in Hab. 2:6, in the same sequence. Consequently they may have comprised a stock catalogue of wisdom forms ('words of the wise' is lacking in Habakkuk).

1:7. Although 'reverence', *yirâ*, at times may convey terror or fright, that connotation belongs more consistently to other words available to the sage: *paḥad* ('terror' associated with the storm of Prov. 1:26, 27, 33; rendered 'panic' in 3:24,

25) or *ḥărādâ* ('anxiety' in 29:25). Consequently 'reverential awe' better reflects *yirâ* in this setting. It is noteworthy that reverence for the divine here is directed not towards God generally (*ʾĕlōhîm*), but towards the LORD, the God of Israel (*yhwh*), which personal name is indicated in most English versions through small capitals (a convention followed also in this commentary).

Since *rēʾšît* can convey both 'start' and 'best', we should hear both connotations in the foundational axiom concerning wisdom in v. 7. 'Reverence for the LORD is the epitome of wisdom' and 'Wisdom begins with reverence for the LORD' (similarly Ps. 111:10; whereas *tĕḥillat*, 'starting point', occurs in Prov. 9:10). While reverence for the divine was valued in Egyptian and Mesopotamian wisdom literature, it was not accorded the primacy found among Israelite sages (Fox 2000: 71).

Those who disdain the way of wisdom (together with reproof) prove to be 'fools', *ʾĕwîlîm*. By connecting folly with anti-reverence (v. 7a), the sage indicates that, in his vocabulary, a 'fool' identifies not one who is intellectually challenged, but one who by choice behaves with moral deficiency.

1:8–9. 'Father' here carries figurative as well as a literal connotation (for an alternative view cf. Waltke 2004: 62–63). Reference to 'son' was consistent with custom in the ancient world which generally privileged boys, with regard to their education and eventual leadership roles within the community (contrast Deborah [judge and prophetess, Judg. 4 – 5] and Hulda [prophetess, 2 Kgs 22:14]).

Given the patriarchal society of the sapiential author, it is noteworthy that from the outset 'mother' appears together with 'father' as a source of teaching. Female instructors within Proverbs include metaphoric Lady Wisdom (1:20–23), along with King Lemuel's mother (31:1–31) and the Resourceful Wife (31:26).

In Egypt, high judges and viziers wore a necklace bearing a symbol of the goddess Ma'at, since she was associated with truth, justice and order. To Egyptians, this necklace symbolized eternal life (Waltke 2004: 188).

Explanation

Despite dizzying advances in modern technology, wisdom remains in short supply. But, notwithstanding extensive varieties in personal preferences, who among us would purpose to disregard wisdom? Above the landscape of short supply and universal demand, the Israelite sage's offer of wisdom towers with enduring relevance.

The benefits he extends are unparallelled. On the one hand he offers ethical character (1:3). For 'morality is the subject to be taught' (Fox 2000: 75). On the other he promises skill in navigating frequently deceptive pathways of life (v. 4).

Yet not all can gain these benefits. To cultivate ethical character, one must already possess wisdom enough to withstand the inevitable pain of reproof (1:3a). The easily offended need not apply. And to attain skill in life-navigation, one must humbly admit to being naive, accompanied by the indispensable trait of malleability (1:4a).

Put another way, one must present receptivity (1:8), lacking which we should waste neither the sage's time nor ours. Lacking receptivity, his priceless teaching will never bear fruit, but will resemble the seeds in Jesus' early parable that futilely bounced off the surface of a compacted pathway (Mark 4:4; notice that just as an exhortation to receptivity begins Proverbs, so a parable concerning receptivity inaugurated Jesus' teachings). Exquisite insights, unappreciated, will suffer the fate of pearls trampled under the feet of pigs (Matt. 7:6).

To what foundational wisdom principle must the pupil display receptivity? And to what heights should a curriculum in wisdom ultimately aspire? 'Reverence for the LORD is the epitome of knowledge', responds the sage, wrapping in reverence both wisdom's first-step and its ultimate goal (1:7, both conveyed by *rēʾšît*, rendered 'epitome'). In other words, that human who aspires successfully to navigate life will choose to begin by bowing before God – a posture from which he or she will never graduate.

Who is the deity deserving such devotion? Boldly the sage declares that such respect rightly belongs to none other than the LORD, the creator deity manifested to Israel through a history that other parts of the biblical record characterize with words both of tender covenant and pointed chastisement, and by deeds both of miraculous rescue and painful punishment.

Reverence, and receptivity to reproof: these form the foundation of the sage's introductory lecture. As evidence of their importance, these two will return towards the close of the poems spanning Prov. 1 – 9 (cf. 9:7–10).

PROVERBS 1:10–19
'What is the problem with an invitation to pursue wealth?'

Overview of Proverbs 1:10–19

The lecture spanning Prov. 1:10–19 is the first in a collection of three lectures consisting of extensive wisdom commendations (cf. 1:20–33; 2:1–22). Typically, a wisdom commendation is brief, filling one or two verses. Generally, it will appear early within a portion of text, paving the way for more extensive 'wisdom content' that will follow. Thus in the poem of 3:1–12, the first two verses supply a wisdom commendation, with wisdom content filling the balance (vv. 3–12).

In contrast, early in the book the sage felt it necessary to make a grander case for wisdom's worth. So he composed three poems, each an extensive wisdom commendation. The first launches a highly charged warning, cautioning the naive pupil ('son') against the mortally hazardous enticement peddled by a money-hungry gang (1:10–19). This lecture answers the implied question 'What is the problem with an invitation to pursue wealth?'

Position of this poem within Proverbs

Preceding context. The opening lecture of Proverbs consisted of a prologue. There the sage outlined the book's aims, several literary tools one might encounter and two supreme examples of wisdom teaching (1:1–9).

Ensuing context. Following the warning against getting involved with a money-hungry gang (1:10–19), there appear two more wisdom commendations. First will be an opportunity to enrol as Lady Wisdom's disciple, leading to a storm-proof life (1:20–33). Then follows a poem presuming the youth has decided to enrol in wisdom (2:1–22). There the sage clarifies the depth of interest necessary to succeed as a wisdom disciple.

What to watch for

To begin discovering thought groups in this poem, notice when the father's speech quotes the gang, and when his speech addresses the son directly. Next, notice recurring points of logic or argumentation, balancing the gang's comments against the father's direct statements.

Translation and outline

Verse	*Translation*	*Outline*
1:10	My son, if sinners should begin to persuade you, do not go!	I. Dual-theme introduction: enticement and warning (1:10)
		II. Explanation of enticement and warning (vv. 11–18) A. The gang's enticement (vv. 11–14)
1:11	If they say, 'Come with us; let's lie in wait for blood! Let's lurk unprovoked for the innocent.	1. A trap set: inflicting death on others (vv. 11–12)
1:12	'We will swallow them alive like Sheol, and whole – as pit-descenders.	
1:13	'All sorts of precious wealth will we find, and our houses will be filled with booty.	2. Rationale explained: monetary ends (v. 13)
1:14	'Cast your lot with us; there will be a single bag for us all'.	3. Action point: the call to enlist (v. 14)

1:15 My son, do not walk along the lane with them! Withdraw your foot from their footpath. 1:16 For their feet run to evil, and hurry to shed blood. 1:17 Surely it is pointless to spread the net in the sight of any master-of-flight. 1:18 But they – for their own blood do they lie in wait; they lurk for their own lives.	B. The parent's warning (vv. 15–18) 3'. Action point: the call to withdraw (v. 15) 2'. Rationale explained: violent means (v. 16) 1'. Trappers snared: inflicting death on oneself (vv. 17–18)
1:19 Such are the ways of every ruthless profiteer: the life of its masters shall it take.	III. Conclusion: the problem inherent to gain-by-violence (v. 19)

Notes on the text

1:10. 'do not go', *ʾal-tābōʾ*: for the consonants *tbʾ* one must choose either *tābōʾ*, 'go' (indicated by the consonantal text), or *tōbēʾ*, 'consent' (recommended by vowels supplied later by the Masoretes). To vocalize *tābōʾ*, 'go', is fully attested elsewhere in Proverbs (3:25; 4:14; 22:24b), while *tōbēʾ* as 'consent' requires accounting for loss of initial root aleph of *ʾbh*; also an aleph replacing final he (Fox 2000: 85). Thus the vocalization *tābōʾ* is to be preferred, translating 'do not go' rather than 'do not consent' (*pace* NRSV, NIV, NASB, ESV). This injunction against travel ('not go') anticipates the instruction to 'withdraw your foot from their footpath' (1:15) more closely than would 'do not consent'.

'should begin to persuade you': 'begin' inferred from connotation of yiq. conjugation (inception, *IBHS* §31.2.b), and from context since at this point the gang's persuasive efforts have only begun.

1:12. 'as pit-descenders': initially this describes victims. Also it describes unwitting perpetrators.

1:14. 'Cast your lot with us': the sage may have intended both 'lot' as an indication of membership in a pool of participants (e.g. Judg. 20:9; Prov. 16:33; 18:18), and 'lot' referring to one's allotted inheritance or personal fortunes (e.g. Num. 33:54; Ps. 16:5–6).

'bag', *kîs*: both a pouch to contain lot stones, and the robbers' shared purse.

1:17. 'master-of-flight', *baʿal kānāp*: lit. 'master of wing'. Unique in the HB, this highlights birds' particular skill in flying. The sage employs 'master of' in connection with destroyer (18:9), anger (22:24), appetite (23:2), scheming (24:8) and wrath (29:22).

1:19. 'ways', *ʾārḥôt*: with connotation of behaviour, path, process (not 'end', *ʾaḥărît*, *pace BHS* notes).

'ruthless profiteer', *bōṣēʿa bāṣaʿ*: the root *bṣʿ* belongs to the weaving industry, meaning to 'sever the woven part from the threads of the woof', and by extrapolation 'to sever the thread of life'; also 'to make profit', 'to break away from the track' (*HALOT*).

'the life of its masters shall it take': the sage envisions the gang's violent strategies employed as a vicious beast, controlled by the gang. In the end the beast will turn, tearing apart its masters.

Form and structure

Borders

Although many regard the voc. 'my son' and imperatives 'listen' and 'do not neglect' in 1:8 as marking the start of a poem extending through 1:19, the verse pair of vv. 8–9 better contributes to closure for the preceding poem (see Form and structure for 1:1–9; *pace* Murphy 1998: 9 and Fox 2000: 79; Waltke detects modest separation between vv. 8–9 and v. 10 [2004: 185–186]). It is the appearance of voc. and imperative expressions again in v. 10 that recommend recognizing that saying as the upper border of a poem distinct from one ending in v. 9. The balance of this new poem expounds on the caution initiated in v. 10.

Closure in 1:19 marks the lower border. With the exception of summative 'such are' and the verb 'to take', all the terms in v. 19 are prefigured in vv. 10–18. Some are prefigured by reusing the same Hebr. word. Others are prefigured by synonymous expressions (for 'ways' in v. 19, see 'lanes' and 'footpaths' in v. 15; for 'ruthless profiteer', note the policy of violence in vv. 11–12).

Macrostructural features

Two structures operate at the macro level. They involve closure (see under 'Borders', above) and dual-theme introduction.

Dual-theme introduction (1:10, form- and content-based). The dual-theme introduction (Section I, 1:10) links formally with Section II (vv. 11–18) since the conditional structure of protasis (an enticement) in v. 10a, followed by apodosis (a warning) in v. 10b, introduces the structure of vv. 11–14 (protasis of enticement) followed by vv. 15–18 (apodosis of warning). Regarding content, the notion of sinners beginning to persuade (v. 10a) anticipates the theme of enticement in Block II.A (vv. 11–14), while the note of caution ('do not go', v. 10b) anticipates the theme of warning in Block II.B (vv. 15–18).

Microstructural features

Palistrophe (1:11–18, content-based). Three pairs of concepts recur in Section II, arranged so that the two constituent blocks form a palistrophe (extended chiasm). To aid recognition of palistrophes, paired subheadings appear at the same indentation level in outlines alongside translations (cf. II.A.1. 'A trap set' [vv. 11–12], which pairs with II.B.1' 'Trappers snared' [vv. 17–18], in above outline). Thus Block II.A begins by describing the gang's strategy, 'A trap set: inflicting death on others (1:11–12)'. Block II.B closes with reversal by the father's rebuttal, 'Trappers snared: inflicting death on oneself (vv. 17–18)'. The following terms appear both in vv. 11–12 and vv. 17–18: *ʾrb*, 'lie in wait', *ṣpn*, 'lurk', *ḥnm*, 'unprovoked or without cause, pointless or without effect', and *dm*, 'blood' ('blood' also occurs aside from these connected verses, in v. 16).

The middle of Block II.A describes the gang's reasoning with 'Rationale explained: monetary ends (v. 13)', while the middle of Block II.B describes the father's counter-reasoning with 'Rationale explained: violent means (v. 16)'.

Located where we would expect the climax (at the core of any palistrophe), Block II.A ends with the gang issuing an 'Action point: the call to enlist (v. 14)', which the father immediately counters with his own 'Action point: the call to withdraw (v. 15)'. With clever transposition of sounds, the poet contrasts tossing in one's lot in v. 14 (root *grl*) and withdrawing one's foot in v. 15 (root *rgl*).

Another link may be at work here, joining 1:15 and 10. The letters of *tbʾ*, 'go', v. 10b, correspond to the first letters of the fuller prohibition in v. 15, here signified by underscoring: *[ʾl]-t̲lk b̲drk ʾtm*, '[do not] walk along the lane with them' (observed by Michael Fishbane, private conversation).

The recycling structure inherent to a palistrophe ensures that each of the gang's points will be revisited and rebutted. The inverted structure also inherent to the palistrophe turns the gang's argument inside out, producing an instance where 'the literary artistry of the text embodied the text's meaning' (West 1992: 425).

Deployed saying with interpretation (1:17–18, content-based). The fowler apophthegm in 1:17 is a deployed saying, since the surrounding context deals with a different topic (getting rich, not capturing birds). Apophthegms may be positioned late in a speech's sequence to clinch an argument. The next saying (v. 18) interprets the fowler saying (v. 17), showing that even birds are brighter than the gang. For another deployed saying positioned at a poem's close, see 6:10–11.

Comment

Section I (1:10). As the lecture begins, the poet-sage addresses his pupil as father to son. Aware that brigands are on the prowl, looking to enlist recruits, he takes steps to fortify the youth against their seductive rhetoric. In short, the son must learn to refuse their overtures (1:10).

Section II (1:11–18). *Block II.A (1:11–14).* The sage then expands on this concise warning, first by describing – in their own words – how the brigands will lure the youth (1:11–14). They boast like brazen trappers dealing in death (vv. 11–12) for this reason: to get ridiculously rich with minimal effort (v. 13). Having described their enterprise (setting deadly traps) and their reason (to get rich), they issue this directive to the youth: he must join the gang (v. 14a)! Is he hesitant to join? Then this should reassure him: though merely a novice member, he will have equal access to the loot, along with the rest (v. 14b). What is the youth's decision?

Block II.B (1:15–18). As if intercepting the youth at the very point of signing on with the gang, the father issues his counter-command. The youth must withdraw from this group (1:15)! The rationale they offered for getting rich, the father now counters. Their violent means completely undermine any enticing ends they may promise (v. 16). With less than bird brains, they remain wilfully blind to the fact that they will fall – fatally – for the very traps they cleverly set for others (vv. 17–18).

Block II.C (1:19). Now the youth will be able to see what the brigands cannot: the long-term cost of gain-by-violence always outweighs its short-term profit. The menacing monster they presume to control will in the end turn on them and tear them apart (v. 19).

1:17. The fowlers (not the birds; *pace* Crenshaw 1995: 330) are the witless ones, abandoning stealth.

Explanation

No amount of supposed gain outweighs the loss sustained when we loosen our moral moorings. The innocent must be safeguarded, not ambushed. To do less is not merely reprehensible, but suicidal.

As their own violent strategies bring the gang to final demise, the sage discloses a fundamental piece of his world view: retributive justice (cf. Koch 1983: 57–82). To ambush others is to ambush self, as foolish as tripping into one's own deadly trap (1:17–18).

In this lecture it is the lure of loot that deflects the gang's moral compass from true 'north'. Yet riches have no monopoly on moral deflection. Wealth is but a metaphor for seduction of all sorts against which we will wisely beware.

The parent's insightful analysis of the gang's 'ends-justify-means' reasoning, together with a careful point-for-point rebuttal – these model a conversation crucial to engage with youth. Any who carry a concern for the next generation would do well to emulate this model.

PROVERBS 1:20–33
'Who may enrol as Wisdom's disciple, and why is it so critical?'

Overview of Proverbs 1:20–33

In this lecture the sage responds to the implied questions 'Who may enrol as Wisdom's disciple, and why is it so critical that they should do so?' By means of rich personification the poet conveys the lengths to which wisdom (and the sage as its exponent) will go to train youth. Like a teacher enrolling pupils, she promises great benefit to any joining as her disciples. Disaster (not at Wisdom's hand) awaits those who choose to decline.

Position of this poem within Proverbs

Preceding context. The preceding poem operated as an intervention, as parent intercepted son on the verge of joining a murderous gang (1:10–19). The present poem supplies a positive counterpart – an opportunity to enrol as a disciple of Lady Wisdom (1:20–33).

Ensuing context. The poem that follows this composition assumes the youth has become convinced that he should enrol as Lady Wisdom's pupil (2:1–22). At that point the sage will urge the youth to pursue Lady Wisdom energetically, in order to gain full benefit from her instruction.

What to watch for

By noting closely the speaker's references to the audience (directly by second person, or remotely by third person) the poem's subdivisions become clear. Within those divisions, notice recurring elements of persuasive information.

Translation and outline

Verse	*Translation*	*Outline*
		I. Lady Wisdom's circuit (1:20–21)
1:20	In the street Lady Wisdom is giving a ringing cry, in the plaza she is raising her voice.	A. In the street (v. 20a) B. In the market (v. 20b)
1:21	At the onset of roaring she is calling out, at the gateways to the city she is making her speech.	C. At the onset of tumult (v. 21a) D. At the gates (v. 21b)
		II. Lady Wisdom's speech (vv. 22–33) A. Lady Wisdom appeals to potential pupils (vv. 22–27)

Verse	*Translation*	*Outline*
1:22–23a	'How long, naive ones, will you love naivety, and how long will scoffers delight themselves with scoffing, and fools hate knowledge? May you turn to my reprimand!	1. Wisdom's plea: inviting three candidates (vv. 22–23a)
1:23b–c	'Look – would that I might pour my spirit on you; would that I might explain my teachings to you!	2. Wisdom's wish: the prospect of reward (v. 23b–c)
1:24	'Because I called out but you refused, I stretched out my hand but no one paid attention,	3. Wisdom's reason for her response (vv. 24–25)
1:25	'Rather you ignored my every counsel and did not accept my reprimand,	
1:26	'Likewise, for my part I will laugh at your disaster; I will mock when your terror comes,	4. Wisdom's response: ridicule (v. 26)
1:27	'When your terror comes like a storm, and your disaster invades like a whirlwind, when anxiety and affliction come upon you'.	5. Disaster (v. 27)
		B. Lady Wisdom reflects on victims of folly (vv. 28–33)
1:28	'Then they, on their part, will call out to me but I will not answer; they, on their part, will be on the lookout for me, but will not find me.	4'. Wisdom's response: remoteness (v. 28)
1:29	'Since they hated knowledge, and the fear of the LORD they did not choose,	3'. Wisdom's reason for her response (vv. 29–30)
1:30	'They did not accept my counsel; they spurned my every reprimand,	
1:31	'So may they eat of the fruit of their way; then with their plans may they be sated.	2'. Wisdom's wish: the prospect of retribution (v. 31)

1:32	'Surely the waywardness of the naive will slay them, and the fools' complacency will destroy them.	1'. Wisdom's conclusion (with character summary): assessing three candidates (vv. 32–33)
1:33	'But one who listens to me shall dwell securely and will remain undisturbed by dreadful terror'.	

Notes on the text

1:20. 'street', *ḥûṣ*: within a city, *ḥûṣ* designates public space outside one's house.

'Lady Wisdom', *ḥokmôt*: pl., consistent with abstract nouns in Hebr. having sg. meaning (*IBHS* §7.4.2). By this personification the author of 1:20 indicates indebtedness to the grandfather-sage who personified wisdom with the same term in 9:1.

'is giving a ringing cry', *tārōnnâ*: 3 f. sg. of *rnn* (with *-ā* suff. analogous to cohort., GKC §48.c; labelled 'pseudo-cohortative' by Waltke [2004: 197 n., *IBHS* §34.5.3]). Although not nun-energic (the second *n* derives from root *rnn*), yet by using a cohortative-analogous form the sage may indicate that Lady Wisdom announces her message, not coincidentally, but with purposeful determination. By rendering 'sings praise', *hymneitai*, LXX indicates Lady Wisdom uses a publicly audible volume, though musical notion would be metaphoric.

1:21. 'onset', *rōʾš*: may refer to the start of a period of time (Num. 10:10), alternatively referring to head or top of a physical structure.

'roaring', *hōmiyyôt*: associated by assonance with *ḥokmôt*, 'Lady Wisdom', 1:20, *hōmiyyôt* prefigures the howling windstorm of v. 27. Elsewhere it is associated with cities and seas (e.g. Isa. 17:12; 22:2; 51:15). With LXX to emend as 'walls', *ḥōmôt*, is unnecessary, weakening the dynamic progression in nouns of place (see 'Microstructural features').

1:23a. 'May you [pl.] turn': juss., conveying wish or hope.

1:23b–c. 'Would that I might pour . . . would that I might explain': both are first-person cohorts., indicating a strong personal determination to pour and explain.

1:24b. 'I stretched out my hand': parallel to the statement 'Because I called out' in v. 24a, the statement 'I stretched out' further describes Lady Wisdom's overtures. Since it was refused, this gesture signalled generosity, not reprimand (*pace* Jones 2019: 109).

1:27. 'anxiety and affliction', *ṣārâ wĕṣûqâ*: alliteration joins these terms (cf. Isa. 8:22; 30:6).

1:28. 'they, on their part, will call out to me', *yiqrĕʾunnî*: paragogic nun conveys certainty and sets the activity of calling out (with its subject, 'they') in contrast to what preceded (i.e. overtures extended by Lady Wisdom; *IBHS* §31.7.1).

'they, on their part, will be on the lookout', *yĕšaḥărûnnî*: again, a paragogic nun signals contrast.

1:30. 'They did not accept . . . , they spurned': the two cola of 1:30 extend the circumstances begun by the statement 'Since they hated knowledge' in v. 29, with consequences following in v. 31.

1:31. 'So may they eat', *wĕyō'kĕlû*: a weyiq. form (consequential indirect juss.), expressing a hope that this action may come to pass.

'may they be sated': juss., following indirect juss. of *wĕyō'kĕlû*.

Form and structure

Borders

The appearance of Lady Wisdom marks the upper border (1:20–21). She was not present in the preceding poem.

When the parent's voice appears in 2:1, it signals a break following Lady Wisdom's speech that extended through 1:33. A character summary (1:32–33) and a palistrophe's conclusion reinforce v. 33 as the lower border (see under 'Microstructural features', below).

Macrostructural features

Introduction of speaker, followed by speech (Sections I and II, content-based). Sections I and II complement each other since the first introduces Lady Wisdom (1:20–21), while the second presents her speech (vv. 22–33). More than simply introducing Lady Wisdom, by its two progressions Section I fosters an expectation that a public oration soon will appear (see microstructures involving verbs of speech and nouns of place, below).

Microstructural features

Dynamic progression involving verbs of speech (1:20–21, content-based). Four verbs of speech form a progression along twin vectors of (a) decreasing intensity and (b) increasingly complex communication: the ringing cry (highly intense, but not complex, 1:20a), the raising of the voice (increasingly complex, v. 20b), calling out (a more focused address, targeting a particular audience, v. 21a) and saying (very low in intensity, but capable of great complexity, v. 21b).

Dynamic progression involving nouns of place (1:20–21, content-based). Interspersed with the four verbs of speech, four nouns of place trace Lady Wisdom's route, advancing from less to more populated regions (streets in 1:20a, plaza in v. 20b and boisterous public areas in v. 21a, ending with the city gates where speeches would be delivered in v. 21b; concerning boisterous 'onset of roaring', see 'Notes').

Contrast between direct address and oblique reference (1:22–27, 28–33, form-based). Having reached the city gates, Lady Wisdom delivers a two-part speech. In the first (Block II.A, 1:22–27) she addresses prospective pupils directly (e.g. 'I called out but you refused', 1:24). In the second (Block II.B, vv. 28–33), she describes those prospective students obliquely, while talking about them to someone else (e.g. 'Then they, on their part, will call out to me', v. 28).

Thematic continuity involving a trio of potential pupils (1:22–23a, 32–33, content-based). A trio of potential pupils appears in 1:22–23a (naive, scoffers, fools) and in vv. 32–33 (naive, fools, those who listen). Within the latter trio, the new element (listeners) introduces a model for the sage's own audience to emulate. Listeners in v. 33 are those who heeded the plea of v. 23a: 'May you turn to my reprimand!'

Reversal involving the root *šûb* (1:23a, 32, form-based). In 1:23a Lady Wisdom urges the pupils to display receptivity by beneficially 'turning', *tāšûbû* (from root *šûb*) from their resistance to her reprimand. Reversal results when the same root describes fatal 'waywardness', *mĕšûbat*, of the naive (v. 32a).

Grammatical continuity involving wish (1:23b–c, 31, form-based). Lady Wisdom twice expresses what she hopes will come to pass, linking 1:23b–c with v. 31. (While another volitive appears in v. 23a ['May you turn'], it joins with v. 22a–c, not with v. 23b–c, as discussed below under 'Comment'.)

Reversal involving 'spirit' and storm wind (1:23b, 26–27, content-based). Given that 'spirit' may also be rendered 'wind', those invited to Lady Wisdom's training will experience either her benevolent spirit/wind (1:23b), or the wind of a ferocious storm (1:26–27).

Reason followed by response (1:24–25, 26, content-based). The action of pupils in 1:24–25 supplies the reason for Lady Wisdom's response in v. 26.

Triple repetition of 'comes' (1:26, 27, form-based). The expression *bĕbōʾ*, 'when it comes', repeats three times within two verses, like a drum cadence warning of the inevitable approach of disaster (1:26b, 27a, 27c).

Response followed by reason (1:28, 29–30, content-based). Lady Wisdom accounts for her response in 1:28 (refusal to answer) with a rationale in vv. 29–30 ('Since they hated knowledge').

Character summary as conclusion (1:32–33, content-based). A concentrated statement of contrasting characters concludes the poem, forcing the pupil to choose whom he or she wishes to emulate (1:32–33; cf. 2:21–22; 4:18–19). Astute readers will not scan too rapidly such simple-sounding character summaries, but will consider carefully the teachings they review in capsule form.

Palistrophe (1:22–33, content-based). Recurring messages in a concentric pattern reveal a closely fashioned palistrophe spanning vv. 22–33, as reflected in the outline headings opposite the translation, above. The palistrophic links may be seen in these microstructural features, discussed above: thematic continuity involving a trio of potential pupils (vv. 22–23a, 32–33), reversal involving the root *šûb* (vv. 23a, 32), grammatical continuity involving wish (vv. 23b–c, 31), reason followed by response (vv. 24–25, 26) together with response followed by reason (vv. 28, 29–30). Since this palistrophe pivots on a single saying, v. 27 lacks a paired verse. Because a palistrophe customarily focuses greatest attention on its pivotal core, in this poem the core suitably depicts in detail the devastating storm that will befall unreceptive pupils.

The palistrophic structure observed independently by the author shares several features with that presented by Trible (1975: 509–518). Differences involve the following: (a) Trible includes the introduction (Section I, 'Lady Wisdom's circuit', vv. 20–21) as part of the palistrophe rather than treating it as a separate introduction, despite the fact that it is twice the length of the balancing portion (v. 33), (b) Trible does not regard Wisdom's response to rejection in v. 26 as parallel to Wisdom's response to rejection in v. 28, (c) Trible does not treat vv. 29–30 as a 'reason', parallel to the 'reason' that she recognizes in vv. 24–25, and (d) Trible breaks up the three characters in vv. 32–33 into two sections (while keeping the three characters in v. 22 together). Trible's outline is as follows:

A. Introduction: an appeal for listeners (vv. 20–21)
  B. Address to the untutored, scoffers and fools (v. 22)
    C. Declaration of disclosure (v. 23)
      D. Reason for the announcement (vv. 24–25)
        E. Announcement of derisive judgement (vv. 26–27)
      D'. Result of the announcement, with interruption (vv. 28–30)
    C'. Declaration of retribution (v. 31)
  B'. Address about the untutored and fools (v. 32)
A'. Conclusion: an appeal for a hearer (v. 33)

Waltke also detects a palistrophe, limiting it to vv. 22–33 (2004: 201). His omission of v. 26 and (like Trible) the grouping of v. 27 with v. 28 (despite the shift from second to third person) argue against his analysis. The palistrophe proposed by Fox, while appropriately separating v. 27 from v. 28, is still more limited, not accounting for similarities that join vv. 22–23a with vv. 32–33 (2000: 103–104).

Comment

Section I (1:20–21). Like the poem spanning 1:10–19, this composition reads rather like a story. The principal character first appears in obscure regions of the city, perhaps even outside the city (v. 20). She proceeds through increasingly populated regions, calling out with increasing clarity, eventually assembling at the plaza, even at the city gates (the focal point of assembly), those who may wish to hear her speech (v. 21).

1:20. By representing wisdom as a female master-teacher, the sage helps the pupil engage an abstract concept (wisdom) by clothing it in concrete realities (such as a female character). To understand Lady Wisdom as a vestigial goddess would overtax the evidence, simultaneously blunting the impact of this sophisticated literary device (see Fox concerning Lady Wisdom, 2000: 331–345).

Section II (1:22–33). *Block II.A (1:22–27).* She addresses directly three groups who would benefit from her advice: the naive, scoffers and fools. Sadly, they have a history of resisting her overtures (else she would not have lamented, 'How long will you love naivety?', 1:22). Nevertheless, she explains how profoundly she intended to benefit them, withholding not even her innermost self ('my spirit', v. 23).

But these potential pupils' determination to reject her help (1:24–25) leaves Lady Wisdom no alternative. Due to their disinterest, she will turn a similarly deaf ear when their inevitable disaster finally descends (v. 26). It will descend as a devasting storm – reversing the concept of Lady Wisdom's own 'spirit/wind' which she so generously wished to bestow. And how dreadfully will that disaster descend (v. 27)!

Block II.A (1:28–33). By their own choice, those resistant pupils distanced themselves from Lady Wisdom. As her oration continues, she no longer speaks to them, but about them (1:28–33), first reaffirming her deafness to any plea they belatedly may raise (v. 28). She then repeats that her aloofness owes to their rejection of her, not her rejection of them (vv. 29–30).

Lady Wisdom continues to reinforce their culpability for the distress they are about to undergo. In a parade example of retribution, she wishes on them the consequences of their own choices (1:31). Retribution continues into v. 32, since it is their own waywardness that will destroy the naive, as surely as 'fools' complacency will destroy them'.

Happily, an alternative emerges to disrupt this cascading ruin. If one would but listen to Lady Wisdom, the outcome would be vastly different (1:33). Dreadful terror then will be powerless to disturb one who accepts Lady Wisdom's invitation to enrol as pupil.

1:22. The shift from second person ('*you* love') to third person ('*they* delight . . . *they* hate') conveys that scoffers and fools stand more remote from Wisdom than the naive (Plöger 1984: 18). Fox describes the scoffer as 'chronically arrogant and cynical', while the fool is 'smug and thickheaded' (2000: 98).

The palistrophically balanced trio of characters in vv. 32–33 argues against deleting one or more characters from the trio in v. 22 (*pace BHS* notes). Murphy similarly retains all characters in v. 22, although not for palistrophic considerations (1986: 459).

The opening query 'How long . . . ?' implies that Lady Wisdom has challenged these characters over some period of time, reminiscent of a prophet who long indicts a wayward people (cf. Jer. 4:14).

1:23b–c. Lady Wisdom's offer of her spirit conveys a profound, even reckless, determination to bankrupt herself for the benefit of interested students. Her gift will consist of words (cf. John 6:63).

1:22–23a, 23b–c. The customary versification of 1:22–23 assigns three cola to each verse. Four reasons recommend a four-plus-two distribution (not three-plus-three). The four-cola saying would span v. 22 (a, b, c) plus v. 23a. A two-cola saying would comprise the remainder (v. 23b, c).

First, corresponding portions of the poem that present three pupil types are now of equal length. Four cola appear in 1:22–23a, as in vv. 32–33.

Second, the particle 'look!', *hinneh*, now opens a new saying (the bicolon consisting of 1:23b–c), rather than appearing in a later colon. To lead a saying with a particle resembles other line-initial particles in this same poem (e.g. *yaʿan*, 'because', v. 24; *gam-ʾănî*, 'I also', v. 26; *ʾāz*, 'then', v. 28; *taḥat-kî*, 'because', v. 29; and *kî*, 'so', v. 32; for a discussion of the use of particles to lend structure in wisdom admonitions, see Zimmerli 1976: 181–182).

Third, to group the solution 'May you turn . . . !' (1:23a) with the problem 'How long . . . ?' (1:22a–c) creates a more compact problem–solution structure. For other passages combining 'How long . . . ?' with a directive (such as 'return'), see Exod. 10:3, 7; 1 Sam. 1:14; 16:1; 1 Kgs 18:21; Pss 6:3–4; 80:4, 7; 82:2–3; 90:13 (for further discussion, see Overland 1988: 223, n. 188).

Fourth, the new grouping allows the unit containing the expression 'return' (*tāšûbû*, 1:23a) to correspond palistrophically with the unit containing the lexically and structurally related term 'waywardness', *měšûbat* (v. 32; cf. Watson 1984: 152). For observations concerning the structural significance of *šûb* in conjunction with *měšûbat* in Jer. 3:1 – 4:4, see Muilenburg 1953: 105.

1:27. Much is lost when, based on metrical assumptions, one deletes this verse's third phrase (as in Toy 1902: 25, and *BHS* notes). Waltke retains the richness of the tricolon: 'In the chaotic style of a destructive gale [Lady Wisdom] breaks the structure of her otherwise consistently symmetric parallelism with a third and jarring verset' (2004: 208). Fox similarly detects purposeful composition, so that the cumulative effect of repeated consonants 'suggests a relentless snowballing of disasters' (2000: 101).

1:28. Zechariah delivers a remarkably similar warning (Zech. 7:13).

Explanation

This story-poem combines winsome invitation with stern warning to counterbalance carefully the evacuation alarm sounded in 1:10–19. Just as the youth must flee the gang's tantalizing offer of wealth-by-murder, so, conversely, he must embrace Lady Wisdom's rich offer of instruction, even 'pour[ing] her spirit' on him (1:23b–c).

Merely to refrain from wrong never will suffice. Unlike the thugs, the failed candidates within this poem (naive, scoffers, fools) suffered demise, not because of heinous atrocities, but due to disinterest: 'no one paid attention' when Lady Wisdom called (vv. 24–25; cf. the non-responsive audience in Matt. 11:17, and the demise of the cleansed but unoccupied man in Matt. 12:43–45).

The successful candidate, in contrast, displays this trait: he or she listens (1:33). We must not be deceived by the simplicity of that trait, for (as the next poem will disclose), the wise pupil's listening describes intentional and aggressive receptivity, even to reproof (implied by the converse of vv. 25, 30).

What renders receptivity to wisdom so critical is this: for each individual, a storm looms on the horizon. Like the storm in Jesus' parable of the houses built on sand or rock, it is not a question of whether disaster will strike, only when (Matt. 7:24–27). Only that one who has cultivated a habit of heeding wisdom will emerge storm-proof (Prov. 1:33).

The impending disaster arrives not as a revengeful retaliation delivered by Lady Wisdom. It is simply the periodic – and ultimate – misfortune of life in a rebel creation. But because of their disinterest, the naive, scoffers and fools will possess no stores of wisdom to draw upon for rescue. Those who dally, postponing a decision for wisdom, must beware. For persistent refusal wisely to prepare eventually will dawn on a day when time tragically will have run out (cf. the story of five foolish wedding attendants, Matt. 25:1–13).

But until that time, Lady Wisdom models the lengths we should travel to reach those we compassionately care about. Like her, we must go out to them, not waiting for them to come to us. With her, we must speak winsomely, with warning. We must extend a selfless 'spirit' and outstretched 'hands', so that as many as may listen 'will dwell securely and will remain undisturbed by dreadful terror' (1:23–24, 33).

PROVERBS 2:1–22
'What benefits will I gain, if I pursue wisdom with determination?'

Overview of Proverbs 2

In Prov. 2 the sage assumes that the youth has wisely rejected the gang's appeal (1:10–19), choosing instead Lady Wisdom's invitation (vv. 20–33). Now he seeks to convince the youth that, if he would gain full value from what Lady Wisdom has to offer, he must ratchet up his receptivity from mere acquiescence, advancing to aggressive pursuit.

The whole of Prov. 2 promotes the overall worth of wisdom, rather than transmitting specific counsel for living. Thus this poem belongs to the lengthy and layered wisdom commendation that began in Prov. 1.

Prov. 2 unfolds as a proposition – if the pupil will pursue wisdom diligently, then substantial benefits will result (Sections I and II). A character summary completes the lecture (Section III). Although relatively long (22 verses), transparent reasoning governs the logic of this poem, with bright lines rendered unmistakable by verbal markers to signal transitions from one portion to the next.

Position of this poem within Proverbs

Preceding context. The lecture spanning Prov. 2 directly follows a pair of competing appeals that sought to enlist the youth into one of two diametrically opposed groups. Either the appeal of wealth would convince the youth to join the gang – that group of hoodlums whose murderous means disqualify their enriching-but-suicidal ends (1:10–19). Or the youth would be persuaded to accept Lady Wisdom's counter-offer to bestow her very spirit, thereby achieving storm-proof security (vv. 20–33).

Ensuing context. Following the three-part wisdom commendation spanning Prov. 1:10 – 2:22, at last in Prov. 3 the sage will begin to deliver specific wisdom content. This initial lecture with wisdom content will focus on relationships in two axes: divine–human relationships and human–human relationships (3:1–35).

What to watch for

Notice the concentration of 'if' statements appearing in early verses. Next, observe the corresponding 'then' statements. These give way to a concluding statement of purpose and a character summary at the close.

Translation and outline

Verse	*Translation*	*Outline*
		I. If you pursue wisdom undeterred . . . (2:1–4)
2:1	My son, if you get hold of my sayings, if it is my instructions that you treasure within you –	A. If you grasp wisdom tightly (v. 1)
2:2	If – in order for your ears to listen attentively to wisdom – you stretch your mind towards perception,	B. If you listen closely for wisdom (v. 2)
2:3	Especially, if it is insight that you call out to, if it is for perception that you raise your voice –	C. If you call aloud after wisdom (v. 3)

Translation	Outline
2:4 If you seek her as silver, and search for her as for hidden riches,	D. If you undertake an exhaustive search for wisdom (v. 4)
	II. . . . Then you will gain valuable benefits, both rewards and protections (vv. 5–19) A. Two rewards (vv. 5–11) 1. The first-magnitude reward: reverent acquaintance with the divine (vv. 5–8)
2:5 Then you will perceive the fear of the LORD, and knowledge of God will you find.	a. The principle of reverence (v. 5)
2:6 For it is the LORD who can grant wisdom, from his mouth he can grant knowledge and perception,	b. Explanation: the connection between wisdom and reverence (v. 6)
2:7 So he will store up success for honest people, a shield for those who walk blamelessly, 2:8 In order to preserve the paths of justice; and the way of the one devoted to him will he guard.	c. Consequences of reverence: success and protection (vv. 7–8)
	2. The second-magnitude reward: moral character in the community (vv. 9–11)
2:9 Then you will perceive equity, fair decision and integrity – every good track.	a. The principle of moral character (v. 9)
2:10 For wisdom will enter your motives, and knowledge will be delightful to your appetites.	b. Explanation: the connection between wisdom and moral character (v. 10)
2:11 Forethought will guard you; perception will preserve you.	c. Consequences of moral character: protection by preparedness (v. 11)
	B. Two corresponding protections (vv. 12–19) 1. The second-magnitude protection: rescue from a man lacking moral character (vv. 12–15)
2:12 In order to rescue you from a harmful way, from a man who utters devious things,	a. Who he is; how he talks (v. 12)

Verse	*Translation*	*Outline*
2:13	[From] those who abandon paths of honesty in order to walk in ways of darkness,	b. Where he went wrong (v. 13)
2:14	[From] those who enjoy doing harm; they rejoice in devious harm,	c. Harm inflicted on others (v. 14)
2:15	Whose paths are twisted, and who get lost along their tracks.	d. Misguided harm inflicted on themselves (v. 15)
		2. The first-magnitude protection: rescue from a woman misaligned with the divine (vv. 16–19)
2:16	In order to rescue you from the strange woman, from the foreign woman – her words she has lubricated,	a. Who she is; how she talks (v. 16)
2:17	[From one] who abandons the companion of her youth, and has forgotten the covenant with her god.	b. Where she went wrong (v. 17)
2:18	Surely her house has suffered deadly collapse, and her tracks are sinking into the shades.	c. Harm inflicted on herself (v. 18)
2:19	None who approach her will ever return, nor will they ever attain the paths of life.	d. Mortal harm inflicted on others (v. 19)
		III. Conclusion (vv. 20–22)
2:20	For this purpose: so you would walk in the way of good folk, and so you would guard the paths of equitable folk.	A. Purpose of the wisdom quest: to foster equitable community (v. 20)
		B. Character summary: a choice between two alternatives (vv. 21–22)
2:21	Mark this: it is the honest who will settle in the land, and blameless ones are those who will be left standing there.	1. Security of the honest (v. 21)
2:22	But it is the guilty who will be cut off from the land, as the violent are those who keep tearing away from it.	2. Demise of and by the guilty (v. 22)

Notes on the text

2:1. 'you get hold of': the same manner of acquiring wisdom seen in 1:3.

'if it is my instructions', *miṣwotay*: 'if' extends by ellipsis from 2:1a. 'My instructions' is emphasized by fronting.

2:2. 'If': extends by ellipsis from v. 1a. 'If' will reappear explicitly in 2:3a and 4a.

2:3. 'Especially, if', *kî ʾim*: *kî* before 'if' may sharpen the ensuing statement; hence 'especially' (cf. Eccl. 11:8).

2:4. 'seek her': wisdom is personified (cf. 1:20–33).

2:6. 'For it is the LORD who can grant': 'the LORD' is fronted. Capability ('can') is based on the yiq. conjugation. 'He can grant' in 2:6b derives by ellipsis from v. 6a.

2:7. 'So he will store up', reading *wĕṣāpan* with K, not *yiṣpōn*, 'he will store up', with the Q, due to apodosis continuing from 2:5.

'success', *tûšîyyâ*: wholesome initiative rewarded by hoped-for outcomes.

'honest', *yĕšārîm*: connotes uprightness, straightness (see §5.6. in the 'Introduction').

2:8. 'justice', *mišpāṭ*: rendered 'fair decision' in 2:9 (see §5.6. in the 'Introduction').

'the one devoted to him', *ḥăsîdāw*: the sg. in the K is to be preferred to pl. 'the ones devoted to him' of Q. The divine concern for community in 2:7 now focuses on the individual (v. 8b).

2:9. 'equity', *ṣedeq*: this term refers to communal loyalty, whether in human or divine community (see §5.6. in the 'Introduction').

'fair decision', *mišpāṭ*: rendered 'justice' in 2:8 (see §5.6. in the 'Introduction').

2:10. 'motives', *lēb*: 'appetites' in 2:10b recommends 'motives' for *lēb* (see §5.6. in the 'Introduction').

2:12. 'harmful way', *derek rāʿ*: represents the sage's concern better rather than *evil way*. For consistency, *rāʿ* is rendered 'harm(ful)' in v. 14 as well (see §5.6. in the 'Introduction').

'devious things', *taḥpukôt*: a change or perversion from what was originally intended. Fox helpfully renders, 'distortions' (2000: 106; see §5.6. in the 'Introduction').

2:16. 'strange woman', *zārâ*: this term may describe a woman who, although she belongs to one's own people, yet 'does not properly belong to or in a situation' (Fox 2000: 139; e.g. an Israelite woman who is not the subject's wife, therefore does not properly belong in intimate relations with him). This contrasts *nokriyyâ*, 'foreign woman', which typically refers to one who belongs to a region and religion alien to the sage's.

'her words she has lubricated', *ʾămāreyhâ heḥĕlîqâ* (hiph. stem): not 'her words are slippery' (requiring qal stem).

2:17. 'the covenant with her god', *bĕrît ʾĕlōheyhā*: grammatically, 'her' may associate not with 'god', but with 'covenant' ('her covenant involving a god').

Fox (2000: 121) and Waltke (2004: 215) infer a marriage covenant (*pace* Meinhold 1991: 69), perhaps solemnized in the presence of the God of Israel. However, since the sage has identified this woman not merely as 'strange', but ultimately as 'foreign' (2:16b), he thereby establishes that she emerges from outside Israel (Plöger 1984: 26–27). Hence 'her god' is not the God of Israel.

2:18. 'collapse', *šāḥâ*: this derives from *šḥh*, 'it [her house] stooped down' (3 m. sg. ind.), rather than the root *šwḥ*, 'to sink down'.

'her house', *bêtāh*: emending to read 'her path' or 'her byway', *nĕtîbātāh*, is unnecessary and would dilute the vivid portrayal of a shelter reversing to become a hazard (*pace* Fox 2000: 121–122 and Waltke 2004: 215–216, n. 24).

'shades', *rĕpāʾîm*: spirits of the deceased, likely related to *rph*, 'sink downward'.

2:19. 'will ever return', *lōʾ yĕšûbûn*: 'ever' conveys certitude of paragogic nun (*IBHS* §31.7.1).

2:20. 'equitable folk', *ṣaddîqîm*: cf. 2:9; elsewhere rendered 'moral' (see 'moral', §5.6. in the 'Introduction').

'So you . . . would guard the paths of equitable folk': treating yiq. form *tišmōr*, 'guard', as prescriptive, rather than ind. (not 'so that you . . . will guard').

2:21. 'Will be standing', *yiwwātĕrû*: lit. 'will be left', with connotation of surviving or outlasting the others.

2:21–22. The Hebr. emphasizes subjects in 2:21a, 21b, 22a and 22b, rendered as cleft sentences (*It is X who will do Y*).

Ethical reversal produced by contrasting the first positive character (the honest, 2:21a) and the first negative character (the guilty, v. 22a) is cleverly reinforced by reversal of nearly identical sounds in Hebr., *yĕšārîm*, 'the honest', and *rĕšāʿîm*, 'the guilty'.

2:22. 'those who keep tearing away from it', *yissĕḥû mimmennâ*: durative ('keep tearing away') inferred from yiq. conjugation.

The qal pass. vocalization attested in the Cambridge (Cairo) Geniza would read smoothly (echoing the sentiment of 2:22a): 'those who will be torn away from it', *yussĕḥû mimmennâ* (similarly LXX and Targum). However, given the sage's elsewhere-attested intentional use of arresting expression, the plain meaning of the MT is to be preferred (see above, §5.7. in the 'Introduction'). Thus the second colon explains the first. The guilty 'will be cut off from the land' in consequence of their record of 'tear[ing] away from' the land. As they have degraded the land's habitability, so they will be denied habitation within it.

Form and structure

Borders

Whereas Lady Wisdom spoke in 1:22–33, the parent issues a voc., 'My son', in 2:1. This marks the upper border.

Closure and character summary indicate the lower border. As with 1:19 concluding 1:10–19, all but the first word of 2:20 recalls terms already encountered in this chapter. Only a marker of conclusion is unique: *lěmaʿan*, 'for this purpose'. Closure continues in 2:20, 21 by recycling pairs of character traits: 'good' and 'equity' (or 'equitable') in vv. 9, 20, 'honest' and 'blameless(ly)' in vv. 7, 21.

The poem concludes with a character summary. The pupil must choose to align either with the honest-blameless or with the guilty-violent, each of which stands prominently at the front of its saying (2:21–22). Assonance groups the opposing characters. Will the youth side with *yešārîm*, 'the honest', or with *rěšāʿîm*, 'the guilty'?

Macrostructural features

Conditional statements (Sections I and II, form-based). 'If' in the Hebr. of 2:1, 3, 4 signals an extended, compound protasis in Section I (vv. 1–4). Ellipsis supplies 'if' in the English of v. 2.

An extended, compound apodosis in Section II (2:5–19) is signalled by the particle 'then' at the opening of each unit comprising Block II.A (vv. 5, 9). This notion of benefits persists in Block II.B (vv. 12–19), indicated by the expression 'in order to', which similarly appears at the start of each unit in that block (vv. 12, 16).

Intensification (Sections II and III, content-based). In Section II the wisdom follower passively enjoys protection (cf. 2:7–8, 11, 12–19). In Section III passivity intensifies to activity as the youth extends protection to others (v. 20b).

Microstructural features

Dynamic progression (2:1–4, content-based). The sequence of verbs describing wisdom acquisition intensifies across 2:1–4: 'get hold of', 'listen', 'stretch towards', 'call out to', 'raise your voice', 'seek' and 'search'. The progression moves from minimal effort ('get hold of' suggests wisdom is conveniently nearby) to determined exertion ('call out to' and 'search' suggest wisdom no longer is easily accessible, but must be mined like precious metals).

Positive–negative contrast of four benefits (2:5–11, 12–19, content-based). The first pair of benefits that follow pursuit of wisdom are positive: cultivation of reverence (2:5–8) and moral character (vv. 9–11). The second pair of benefits are negative (privative): preventing harm by a dangerous man (vv. 12–15) and woman (vv. 16–19).

Chiasm between four benefits (2:5–19, content-based). A chiasm emerges from the observation that, among the four benefits, the outer two mention the divine (2:5, 6, 17), while the inner two concentrate on human relationships (vv. 9–11, 12–15).

Parallel elements in the first and second rewards (2:5–8, 9–11, form- and content-based). Three sequential elements occur in Unit II.A.1 and again in Unit II.A.2: (a) in each initial verse the expression 'Then you will perceive' is followed by a principle comprising a reward (achieving reverence in 2:5a, and achieving moral community relationships in v. 9a), (b) each second verse contains an explanation accounting for respective rewards (reverence follows wisdom pursuit since tracing wisdom to its source leads one to the LORD in v. 6, and moral community relationships follow wisdom pursuit since thereby wisdom permeates to the level of motives and innate appetites in v. 10), and (c) each third verse presents beneficial consequences accruing to one who embraces the initial principles (reverence brings 'success' and 'shielding' supplied by the LORD in v. 7, and moral rectitude brings protection in v. 11).

The consequence begun in 2:7 flows into v. 8, implying that the benefits afforded by reverence are abundant. In fact, the 'consequence' statement found in the third verse of Unit II.A.2 (v. 11) links more closely to v. 8 than to v. 7, since both vv. 8 and 11 convey the benefits 'preserve' and 'guard' – albeit inverted.

Parallel elements in the first and second protections (2:12–15, 16–19, form- and content-based). Three sequential elements occur in Unit II.B.1 concerning a hazardous man, and in Unit II.B.2 concerning a hazardous woman: (a) each initial verse begins with 'In order to rescue you from', followed by a description of speech issuing from the respective malevolent person (2:12, 16), (b) in each second verse that man or woman has 'abandoned' something valuable (vv. 13, 17) and (c) the final two verses of each describe how they inflict harm on themselves (vv. 15, 18) and on others (vv. 14, 19; note chiastic inversion ending in mortal hazard for others in v. 19).

Summation (2:19, form-based). With a summation the final saying of Section II declares that none of the woman's guests may escape death (2:19).

Comment

Section I (2:1–4). By this point the pupil has declined the gang's offer (1:10–19), determining instead to enrol with Lady Wisdom (vv. 20–33). At issue is the extent of determination the pupil will display in pursuit of her instruction. Over the four verses of Section I the sage maps a progression of escalating determination. If wisdom teachings are conveniently within reach, the youth must grasp hold of them (2:1). If they are slightly beyond reach but still audible, he must silence distractions in order to hear wisdom clearly (v. 2). If wisdom grows so remote that it can be neither conveniently grasped nor easily heard, then the pupil must be insistent enough to raise his voice as if urgently calling for help (v. 3). Finally, if wisdom will not come to you, then you must leave your surroundings and diligently seek her out, just as you would mine for precious minerals (v. 4).

2:1. With twenty-two letters, the sequence of the Hebr. alphabet shares two adjacent 'midpoints', the eleventh (kaf) and twelfth (lamed). Some have viewed the whole of Prov. 2 as a quasi-alphabetic acrostic since (a) it is composed of twenty-two verses, (b) stanzas in the poem's first half begin with the first letter (aleph; cf. vv. 1 [after voc. 'My son'], 5, 9), and (c) the twelfth verse begins with the twelfth letter (*l*, as do stanza-opening verses in the chapter's second half; i.e. vv. 16, 20; cf. Murphy 1998: 14–15 and Waltke 2004: 216–217). The case for an alphabetic acrostic would be stronger if all line-initial occurrences of these letters fitted the pattern (aleph in vv. 4, 15 does not) and if more letters of the alphabet were so sequenced in the poem.

2:2. Of the six Hebr. words comprising this verse, the four outermost words begin with the letter lamed. The third and fourth begin with aleph and taw, respectively: *l . . . l . . . ʾ . . . t . . . l . . . l . . .* Perhaps the poet selected words beginning with aleph and taw because they bound the Hebr. alphabet sequence (as A and Z in English), while *l* represents a midpoint (see above comment on alphabetic acrostic).

2:4. The amount of text devoted to stir youth to pursue wisdom (focused in 2:4, but spanning all of Prov. 1 – 2) demonstrates how deeply Israelite sages cared about youth entrusted to their care. This sentiment was not unique to Israel, as seen in an exhortation by Isocrates (Greek sage, fifth century BC):

> Do not hesitate to travel a long road to those who profess to offer some useful instruction; for it were a shame, when merchants cross vast seas in order to increase their store of wealth, that the young should not endure even journeys by land to improve their understanding. (*To Demonicus*, 1.15, section 19) (Norlin 1966–8)

Section II (2:5–19). *Block II.A (2:5–11).* If the youth pursues wisdom with determination, he or she will attain two sorts of benefits (Section II, 2:5–19). On the one hand he or she will gain outright rewards (Block II.A, vv. 5–11), while at the same time enjoying protection from two hazards (Block II.B, vv. 12–19). The first and greater-magnitude of the two rewards escorts the youth into nothing less than an acquaintance with the divine ('knowledge of God will you find', v. 5b; cf. 3:6a), which issues from reverence ('Then you will perceive the fear of the LORD', v. 5a). In case the youth may be surprised that pursuit of wisdom should channel him or her into a relationship with the divine, the sage explains in v. 6. The divine holds exclusive rights to wisdom of all types. Wisdom is his to give. It follows, then, that pursuit of wisdom would lead to a divine encounter.

That one who thus reverently encounters the divine will enjoy rewards in addition to wisdom. To his devoted ones the divine will grant success and protection as well (2:7–8).

Perception concerning moral rectitude comprises a second, lesser reward, accruing to one who pursues wisdom (2:9). Such perception will extend beyond the intellect, permeating to the level of motives. Even his longings now will align with genuine insight, rather than appetites colouring insight (v. 10). Just as reverence (v. 5) generated protection (vv. 7–8), so will moral alignment yield safety (v. 11).

Block II.B (2:12–19). The second pair of benefits extends the notion of protection (Block II.B, 2:12–19). By pursuing wisdom the youth will enjoy rescue from a trickster – a man who lost his way when he loosened his grip on honesty (vv. 12–15). The harm he inflicts brings him a sick sort of delight (v. 14). Yet there is another, higher-magnitude hazard that threatens the youth.

By pursuing wisdom the youth will receive protection also from the harmful woman (2:16–19). Whereas the devious man abandoned honesty, the hazardous woman has abandoned faithfulness, long since. In a reversal of rich connection with the divine (that first reward of pursuing wisdom, v. 5), it is her relationship with her deity that this woman conveniently has misplaced (v. 17). As she is morally thus unmoored, the pupil should not be surprised to learn that her hazard is fatal. From the hospitality she extends none escape alive (vv. 18–19).

2:5. 'Knowledge of God' as relational (not informational) is conveyed by other parts of the Old and New Testaments (cf. Deut. 29:25; 32:17; Jer. 22:16; 29:13; Hos. 4:1; 6:6; 8:2; John 17:3; Phil. 3:8–11). Waltke identifies this 'knowledge of God' as 'personal intimacy' (2004: 223). Fox understands it rather as a rich, pervasive awareness of God (2000: 112).

In contrast to scholars who have proposed that this lecture's theological messages were absent from the earliest stages of its composition, Fox appropriately observes, 'it is improbable that the tightly knit structure of [this chapter] would have resulted from multiple intrusions' (2000: 128).

2:6. Cf. Job 28:20–28, where the quest for wisdom's source leads to God, with reverence as wisdom's epitome.

2:18. Reference to a netherworld pathway leading to an ominous house appears also in 'The Descent of Ishtar into the Nether World', an Akkadian composition concerning the detention of Ishtar, goddess of fertility:

> Yea, the daughter of Sin {moon deity} set [her] mind
> To the dark house, the abode of Irkal[la] {Queen of the Nether World},
> To the house which none leave who have entered it,
> To the road from which there is no way back.
> (Tr. E. A. Speiser, *ANET*, 107, lines 3–6)

2:19. Sexual overtones underlie the euphemism 'none who approach her' (lit. 'none who enter her'), suggesting that the woman forms a dangerously alluring contrast to the knowledge of God promised in 2:5 (cf. Waltke 2004: 233).

Section III (2:20–22). With a three-verse conclusion the sage sums up the benefits of pursuing wisdom (Section III, 2:20–22). The phrase 'For this purpose' signals his recap (v. 20a). Instead of falling in with (and falling prey to) hazardous men and women, by pursuing wisdom the youth will join the company of 'good folk'. Beyond gaining from the moral strength in their numbers, the youth himself will begin to give back, helping to reinforce moral conduct for the benefit of others (v. 20b).

A binary contrast of character in the closing quatrain crystallizes the benefits of wisdom still more clearly (2:21–22). In the final analysis, one must choose between honest and guilty conduct. The first group will endure, dwelling as a remnant in the land (v. 21). The second not only will find their lease terminated prematurely, but will by their misdeeds contribute to dismantling the land as they are evicted from it (v. 22).

Explanation

How seriously do I desire wisdom? It will not suffice only marginally to prefer Lady Wisdom's invitation (1:20–33) over the gang's deadly overtures (vv. 10–19). Lackadaisical assent amounts to an insult against wisdom. For, to genuinely access Wisdom's assets, our pursuit of Wisdom must advance to an all-consuming passion. When wisdom comes easily, we must 'treasure [it] within' (2:1). When, in contrast, wisdom defies discovery, that must not deter us, but instead drive us to dig after it more deeply (vv. 3–4).

For the magnitude of wisdom's rewards make any effort expended pale by comparison. Greatest of all, pursuit of true wisdom will deepen our awe of God, while at the same time drawing us to his close acquaintance (2:5). Why? Because wisdom pursuit puts us on a vector towards the divine – he is wisdom's source (v. 6). And with him come the derivative benefits of success and safety (vv. 7–8).

Something else will unfold at the same time. There will grow a capacity to discern fairness (2:9). The drives that spur you to action will gain a new compass bearing, as will your subconscious longings (v. 10). You will become farsighted, able to behave shrewdly today because of your insight concerning tomorrow (v. 11).

As if these gleaming benefits were not enough, pursuit of wisdom also brings protection from sinister forces that plot your ruin. You will be able to escape the clutches of people who conceal dishonesty through deceptive speech (2:12–13). While they lose their way, you will advance straight ahead (vv. 14–15).

Sinister also is the one whose solemn commitments to friends and to God produce no lasting constraint (2:16–17). So unencumbered and free she seems! But it is all a mirage, a glittering but deceptive and deadly house of mirrors, whose 'guests' never will find their way back to genuine freedom (vv. 18–19).

In sum, it is absolutely critical to undertake a determined pursuit of moral character achieved through wisdom. The pursuit of wisdom, the embrace of reverence – these make it possible to move forwards in the company of 'good folk' (2:20a). Beyond personal security, the pupil himself or herself will become a preserver of the path, helping those who come after not to lose their way (v. 20b). No other life strategy can assure durable security (2:21). Instead to cut a deal with immoral conduct buys a ticket to rootless existence that only burns others as it crashes (v. 22).

The next lecture expands on two topics introduced here – right relations with God and right relations in human community. In Prov. 3 these will become pointed injunctions – Proverbs's earliest specific instructions for a flourishing life (aside from exhortations to pursue wisdom generally).

PROVERBS 3:1–35
'What counsel does wisdom offer for healthy relationships?'

Overview of Proverbs 3

Five sections comprise the lecture spanning Prov. 3. Section I opens with a wisdom commendation quatrain (3:1–2), then presents focal imperatives requisite for healthy relationships (vv. 3–4). These relationships operate on two axes: divine–human (v. 4bα) and human–human (v. 4bβ).

Section II concentrates on the divine–human dimension (3:5–12). A wisdom commendation in Section III (vv. 13–26) prepares the way for content dealing with human–human relationships in Section IV (vv. 27–33). Section V concludes by returning to wisdom categories with a concluding character summary.

Position of this poem within Proverbs

Preceding context. Across Prov. 1 – 2 the sage developed a case for wisdom. Following a prologue that set forth the book's aim, literary tools and paradigmatic samples (1:1–9), he introduced two parties competing for the youth's devotion. Will he align with the violent gang, lured by its promise of wealth (1:10–19), or will he choose a storm-proof life by adhering to Lady Wisdom's counsel (1:20–33)? Evidently the youth favoured wisdom, for in Prov. 2 the sage maps out the depth of determination such a choice entails for one who truly desires the protection Lady Wisdom has to offer.

Those initial two chapters presented remarkably few life instructions – limited to commands that endorse wisdom generally, without prescribing situation-specific conduct (cf. Fox 2000: 125). Thus Prov. 1 – 2 comprises an extensive wisdom commendation calculated to cultivate the reader's anticipation for instructions that eventually will arise. And arise they do, for no fewer than fifteen command forms crowd into the first twelve verses of Prov. 3, where – at last – the sage's lessons commence. Topping his list of topics is 'Wisdom regarding relationships'.

Ensuing context. A new block of teaching begins in Prov. 4, extending to Prov. 9. This portion features the voice of the sage's father, urging his son to value wisdom. By following a carefully organized scheme, these lectures culminate in a confrontation forcing the youth to decide whom he will follow (Prov. 9). In view of the unified nature of Prov. 4 – 9, Prov. 3 stands out all the more clearly as a conclusion completing Prov. 1 – 2. The sophistication of its composition reveals that it brings to a rich climax these opening three chapters.

What to watch for

Distinguish between verses that tell of wisdom's value (wisdom commendations) and those issuing situation-specific teaching (wisdom content). Among wisdom-content portions, notice instructions advising how to relate to God, in contrast to instructions that involve human–human relationships. Notice how character summaries serve to recap the entire lecture.

Translation and outline

Verse	*Translation*	*Outline*
		I. Introduction: wisdom commendation and universal instructions for relationships (3:1–4)
		A. Wisdom commendation (vv. 1–2)
3:1	My son, my instruction you must not forget, and may your mind preserve my commandments.	1. Imperative: remain receptive to instruction (v. 1)
3:2	For longevity, years of life and peace will they add to you.	2. Incentives: longevity and well-being (v. 2)
		B. Wisdom content: universal instructions for relationships (vv. 3–4)
3:3	Faithful love and faithfulness must not abandon you: tie them about your neck; write them on the tablet of your mind.	1. Primary imperatives for relationships: practise loyal love and faithfulness (v. 3)
3:4	Further, find favour and understanding concerning what is genuinely good, in the esteem of God and mortals.	2. Secondary imperatives for relationships: prioritize favour and discernment (dual-theme, for relationships divine and human, v. 4)

Verse	*Translation*	*Outline*
		II. First tier of relationships: association with the divine (vv. 5–12) A. Three features of a healthy relationship with the divine (vv. 5–10) 1. The importance of reliance (vv. 5–6)
3:5–6a	Incline your confidence towards the Lord with your entire mind, and do not habitually depend on your own insight; in all your ways know him,	a. Imperative: reliance on the Lord (vv. 5–6a)
3:6b	and he personally will straighten your paths.	b. Corresponding incentive: divine straightening of path (v. 6b)
		2. The importance of reverence (vv. 7–8)
3:7	Do not be wise in your own eyes. Revere the Lord and veer away from evil.	a. Imperative: humble reverence towards the Lord, and avoidance of evil (v. 7)
3:8	May healing come to the core of your being, and drink to your bones.	b. Corresponding hope: satisfaction of core longings (v. 8)
		3. The importance of tangible honour (vv. 9–10)
3:9	Honour the Lord out of your substance, even from the earliest of all your revenue.	a. Imperative: honouring the Lord through tangible gifts (v. 9)
3:10	So that your storehouses may be filled with plenty and new wine may burst your vats.	b. Corresponding hope: tangible reward (v. 10)
		B. Conclusion: responding to divine reproof (vv. 11–12)
3:11	It is the reproof of the Lord, my son, that you must not refuse; and do not respond to his reprimand with disgust.	1. Imperative: receptivity to reproof (v. 11)
3:12	For it is the one he loves that the Lord reprimands, just as would a father, a son of whom he is particularly proud.	2. Explanation: reproof proves parental love (v. 12)

<table>
<tr><td>

3:13</td><td>

How fortunate a mortal who has found wisdom, and a mortal who keeps on obtaining perception!</td><td>III. An extended wisdom commendation (vv. 13–26)
A. Descriptions of wisdom's worth, assured in the present and rooted in the past (vv. 13–20)
1. Description of wisdom's worth: an inventory of value assured in the present (vv. 13–18)
a. Dual-theme introduction: an exclamation of wisdom's present worth (v. 13)</td></tr>
<tr><td>3:14

3:15</td><td>For her market value exceeds the market value of silver, and her revenue exceeds gold filigree.
More precious is she than corals, and none of your delights can compare with her.</td><td>b. Wisdom's worth exceeds all tangible assets (vv. 14–15)</td></tr>
<tr><td>3:16

3:17</td><td>Longevity is in her right hand; in her left are wealth and glory.
Her ways are pleasant ways, and all her footpaths are peace.</td><td>b'. Wisdom's worth encompasses all intangible assets (vv. 16–17)</td></tr>
<tr><td>3:18</td><td>A tree of life is she to those who grasp hold of her, and those who attain her are each declared fortunate!</td><td>a'. Wisdom's legendary worth renders one fortunate (v. 18)</td></tr>
<tr><td>

3:19

3:20</td><td>

The Lord himself by wisdom founded the earth, establishing the skies through perception.
By his knowledge the depths were split apart, and clouds may yet overflow with rain.</td><td>2. Description of wisdom's worth: a rehearsal of value rooted in the past (vv. 19–20)
a. Divine use of wisdom at creation to stabilize (v. 19)

b. Dual-theme transition: divine wisdom for controlled destabilization in remote past, with implications for future (v. 20)</td></tr>
</table>

Verse	*Translation*	*Outline*
		B. Prescriptions based on wisdom's worth, looking to the future (vv. 21–26) 1. Prohibition against losing wisdom, with incentives (vv. 21–22)
3:21	My son, they must not disappear from your field of vision; preserve success and forethought,	a. Imperative: do not lose wisdom (v. 21)
3:22	So that they may become life for your inner being and favour about your neck.	b. Incentives: vitality and favour (v. 22)
		2. Detailed assurance when instability threatens (vv. 23–24)
3:23	Then you will travel with confidence along your way and your foot will not trip.	a. Care during activity (v. 23)
3:24	Whenever you lie down you will not feel panic. So you will lie down and delicious will be your sleep.	b. Care during repose (v. 24)
		1'. Prohibition against baseless terror, with explanation (vv. 25–26)
3:25	Do not fear either sudden panic, or the destruction of the guilty – surely it will come.	a. Imperative: do not fear destabilization (v. 25)
3:26	For the LORD will be at your side, and so will guard your foot from capture.	b. Explanation: promise of divine protection (v. 26)
		IV. Second tier of relationships: association with neighbours (vv. 27–33) A. Three features of healthy neighbour relations (vv. 27–31) 1. Imperatives encouraging generosity, while discouraging passive–aggressive behaviour (vv. 27–28)
3:27	Do not refuse good from those deserving it, when it is in your power to do so.	

3:28	Do not say to your neighbours, 'Be gone and come back – tomorrow I will give', although you have it with you.	
3:29 3:30	Do not scheme evil against your neighbour, although he dwells with you in confidence. Do not level baseless charges against a mortal, if he has not worked evil against you.	2. Imperatives against covert aggression (vv. 29–30)
3:31	Do not envy a person characterized by violence, nor choose any of his ways.	3. Imperatives against overt aggression (v. 31)
3:32 3:33	For a crook is abhorrent to the LORD, but he confides in honest folk. The LORD's curse is on a guilty person's household, but even the settlement of moral folk he will bless!	B. The incentive for healthy human relationships: divine consequences of ethical and non-ethical conduct (vv. 32–33)
 3:34 3:35	 As surely as he personally scoffs at the scoffers, so to humble folk he will give favour. Glory is what wise folk will inherit, while stupid folk go on boasting about ignominy.	V. Concluding character summaries: the divine consequences of unwise and wise conduct (vv. 34–35) A. Experience of divine favour depends on respect for the divine (v. 34) B. Experience of glory depends on extent of wisdom (v. 35)

Notes on the text

3:1. 'mind', *lēb*: in wisdom literature this term often refers to intellect or cognitive activity (see §5.6 in the 'Introduction').

3:2. 'longevity', *ʾōrek yāmîm*: lit. 'length of days'.

3:3. 'Faithful love', *ḥesed*: depicts devotion and affection durable enough to weather disappointments.

'faithfulness', *ʾĕmet*: truth as trustworthiness in relationships; LXX renders, *pisteis*, 'trustworthiness'.

'write them on the tablet of your mind': though some would delete this phrase (as in LXX, followed by Toy [1902: 56, 58] and McKane [1970: 291]), all extant Hebr. manuscripts include it (see 'Form and structure' below).

3:4. 'Further, find', *ûmĕṣāʾ*: an imperative, continuing sequence of commands begun in 3:3 (so also LXX; not a consequence of v. 3 as supposed by NRSV, NIV, ESV and NASB).

'understanding concerning what is genuinely good', *śēkel-ṭôb*: lit. 'understanding of [the] good', recognizing *śēkel*, 'understanding', as in const. state (just as *śēkel ʾādām*, 'a mortal's understanding', Prov. 19:11), with *ṭôb*, 'good', functioning as a noun (substantival use of adj.) referring to 'that which is good' (as also in 3:27). Thus a comparable expression in Ps. 111:10 would be rendered, 'The epitome of wisdom is reverence for the LORD; all who practise them [i.e. his commands] possess understanding concerning what is genuinely good' (*śēkel-ṭôb lĕkol-ʿōśêhem*). In Prov. 13:15a *śēkel-ṭôb* and *ḥēn*, 'favour', appear together (as here in Prov. 3:4): *śēkel-ṭôb yiten-ḥēn*, rendered 'an understanding concerning what is genuinely good may grant favour' (cf. 2 Chr. 30:22a).

'mortals', *ʾādām*: lit. 'mortal'. Unlike synonym *ʾîš*, 'man', *ʾādām* often distinguishes the human from the divine.

3:5. 'Incline your confidence towards the LORD', *bĕṭaḥ ʾel yhwh*: by employing the expression *bĕṭaḥ ʾel*, 'trust to, towards', rather than the customary *bĕṭaḥ bĕ*, 'trust in', the sage indicates a habitual inclination.

'and do not habitually depend on your own insight', *wĕʾel bînātĕkā ʾal-tiššāʿēn*: by construing 'depend' with the prep. *ʾel*, 'towards' (not the customary *ʿal*, 'upon'), the sage leaves room for valuing one's intellect, with this proviso: in the event that the counsel of one's intellect were to contradict counsel deriving from the LORD, one habitually must accede to the LORD's counsel.

3:6a. 'know him', *dāʿēhû*: connotes direct acquaintance, so should not be rendered obliquely by terms such as 'acknowledge' (AV, NRSV), 'remember' (GNT) or 'submit to' (TNIV). Closer is 'listen for GOD's voice' (*The Message*).

3:6b. 'personally': reflects the redundant subject pronoun 'he', *hûʾ*, in *wĕhûʾ yĕyaššēr*.

'and he personally will straighten your paths', *wĕhûʾ yĕyaššēr ʾōrḥōtekā*: by introducing an independent personal pronoun (*hûʾ*, rendered 'he personally') at this point in the actions of 3:5–6, the sage stresses the LORD as subject. 'Paths' see less traffic than 'way', *derek*.

3:7. 'Revere', *yĕrāʾ*: when connotations of terror or panic are intended, the poet uses *pḥd*, sometimes combining with *yrʾ* (cf. vv. 24, 25).

3:8. 'May healing come', *ripʾût tĕhî*: lit. 'may healing be' (juss.). By using the juss. with its connotation of a strong wish or hope (and not the ind. *tihyeh*, 'it will happen', attested in 12:24; 14:35; 24:20), the sage tacitly acknowledges that, despite moral character, one may yet succumb to serious or even terminal illness. Elsewhere the sage acknowledges that even wise and moral folk may suffer reversals (e.g. Prov. 15:16; 16:8).

'core of your being', *šārrekā*: lit. 'your navel'.

3:9. 'even from the earliest', *ûmērē'šît*: since one's contribution constitutes a portion of the *rē'šît*, and not all of it, rendering *rē'šît* as 'what is earliest' is preferable to 'the first fruit offering'. For if 'first fruit offering', all should be contributed.

3:10. 'So that . . . may be filled': like the juss., 'May healing come' in 3:8, again the poet expresses a hoped-for outcome (not an assured consequence), this time through a purpose or final clause with an indirect juss. (GKC §165a; Joüon §116d). The LXX correspondingly renders, *hina*, 'so that', plus the subjunctive *pimplētai*, 'it may be filled', expressing potentiality rather than assured results.

'and . . . may burst': this yiq. form also should be taken as juss., expressing another potential consequence, parallel to the expression 'So that [they] may be filled' (3:10a).

3:11. 'reproof', *mûsar*: 'reprimand', *tôkaḥâ*, at the verse's close reinforces the corrective nature of *mûsar*.

3:12. 'a son of whom he is particularly proud', *'et bēn yirṣeh*: use of *'et* with an indefinite noun ('son') is rare, implying definiteness by context (cf. GKC §117d). 'Particularly' is supplied to convey this focus on 'son'.

3:13. 'fortunate', *'ašrê*: an exclamation acknowledging a highly desirable circumstance. Often rendered 'blessed', *'ašrê* does not convey divine benefaction. Nor does it fall to chance (as may be inferred from 'fortune' in 'fortunate' – another common rendition).

'mortal': see v. 4, above.

'who has found . . . who keeps on obtaining', *māṭā' . . . yāpîq*: the first verb is a qat. form (rendered past), while the second is yiq. (rendered durative with future orientation).

3:14. 'her market value', *saḥrāh*: personification of wisdom (grammatically f. in Hebr.) extends through 3:18; hence 'her' (not 'its').

'gold filigree', *ḥārûṣ*: since *ḥrṣ* involves cutting or incising, when applied to gold this term of uncertain meaning may correspond to filigree.

3:15. 'corals': the unusual term *pěniyîm* evidently is a copyist's error for *pěnînîm* (cf. 8:11; 20:15; 31:10). While the meaning of this decorative substance is uncertain, its red hue (based on Lam. 4:7) fits coral better than pearls. Rubies may not have been known to jewellers of the Mediterranean region until the fourth century BC, when first appearing in Greek literature (Waltke 2004: 251, n.).

'can compare', *yišwû*: capability inferred from the yiq. conjugation.

3:18. 'those who attain her', *tōmkêhā*: the present context favours 'attain' (achieving an objective) rather than 'seize' (acquiring an object).

'each declared fortunate', *mě'uššār*: both 'those who grasp hold' and 'those who attain' are pl., while *mě'uššār*, 'are each declared fortunate', is sg. (reflected by supplying 'each').

3:19. 'The Lord himself': 'himself' supplied to reflect fronting of the subject.

3:20. 'may yet overflow with rain', *yir'ăpû ṭāl*: *yir'ăpû* refers to movement of liquid ('drip', 'trickle' or 'run' in *HALOT*). Compare Job 36:28, 'which skies pour down, which flow *yir'ăpû* on mortals abundantly' (*rheō*, 'to gush, stream or flow' in LXX).

'depths were split apart . . . and clouds may yet overflow', *tĕhômôt nibqā'û . . . ûšĕḥāqîm yir'ăpû*: lit. 'depths were split apart . . . and clouds will overflow'. The differentiation between past ('were split apart', alluding to Noahic deluge) and future potential ('may yet overflow') derives from the poet's use of a qat. conjugation for the first (the conjugation associated with certitude), and a yiq. conjugation for the second (the conjugation associated with potentiality). A similar qatal-to-yiq. shift occurred in v. 13 (concerning certitude associated with qat. forms, and potentiality associated with yiq. forms, see Overland 2016, 1: 352–358, and 432–435, respectively).

Through this careful shift in conjugations, the poet indicates that periods of seismic destabilization (over which God ruled in wisdom) were not limited to the Noahic past. Persons still risk undergoing floodlike destabilization. The sage derives confidence as he realizes that such conditions do not prove the divine has lost control, since even they transpire 'by his knowledge'. This lesson (assurance concerning divine oversight in present-day distresses) is foundational to what the sage is about to expound on in 3:21–26.

'rain', *ṭāl*: not 'dew', since associated here with clouds (see further under 'Comment').

3:21. 'your field of vision', *'êneykā*: lit. 'your eyes'.

'success', *tûšiyyâ*: that which leads to lasting prosperity.

'forethought', *mĕzimmâ*: careful planning, as would precede success.

3:22. 'So that they may become', *wĕyihyû*: a weyiq. as indirect juss. yielding a purpose clause after the imperative 'preserve' in the preceding verse.

'life . . . favour', *ḥayyîm . . . ḥēn*: note alliteration in parallel objects.

3:24. 'Whenever . . . So', *'im . . . wĕ*: lit. 'If . . . Then'.

'and delicious', *wĕ'orĕbâ*: lit. 'sweet', an expression assonantally reminiscent of *'ereb*, 'evening', as the typical time of repose.

3:26. 'the Lord will be', *yhwh yihyeh*: while pronunciation of the divine name is uncertain, these words may have been joined by assonance.

3:29. 'evil . . . neighbour', *rē'ăkā rā'â*: these terms are adjacent in Hebr., joined by assonance.

'in confidence', *lābeṭaḥ*: lit. 'trustingly'.

3:34. 'As surely as he personally scoffs at the scoffers', *'im lallēṣîm hû-yālîṣ*: lit. 'If he himself scoffs at the scoffers'. *BHS* notes would convert the conditional particle *'im*, 'If', to a prep. phrase 'With', *'im lēṣîm*. Aside from lack of manuscript support, this proposal should be declined since it detracts from the escalation conveyed by this saying (reasoning from less to greater likelihood).

3:35. 'will inherit . . . go on boasting', *yinḥālû* . . . *mērîm*: a yiq. form ('will inherit'), followed by a ptc. ('go on boasting') suggests that, while the wise will attain (yiq. as fut.) a beneficial tomorrow, stupid folk simply persist in their current and sad delusion (ptc. associated with present time), foolishly supposing ignominy earns esteem.

Form and structure

Borders

Following a character summary that concludes the previous poem (2:21–22), a wisdom commendation with commands marks the upper border of the present lecture (3:1–2). It opens with the voc. 'My son'.

Closure and a character summary mark this poem's lower border. In the final quatrain, closure results from acquiring 'favour' (3:34; also vv. 4, 22), from obtaining 'glory', *kbd*, in 3:35 (which recalls the principle 'Honour [*kbd*] the Lord out of your substance' in v. 9, and recalls receiving 'wealth and glory' from wisdom in v. 16).

Scoffers contrast humble folk in the final quatrain, as wise folk contrast the stupid (3:34–35), producing a character summary. In the final analysis, the ethical behaviour outlined in 3:27–33 is effective because it constitutes wise behaviour.

Macrostructural features

Dual-theme introduction (Section I, connecting Sections II, III and IV, content-based). In the final colon of Section I the sage refers to two levels of relationships: (a) with the divine (3:4bα), and (b) with other mortals (v. 4bβ). Section II expands on the first of these dual-themes through a series of nine commands concerning the divine–human relationship (vv. 5–12).

The term 'mortal', introduced in 3:4bβ, occurs twice in the opening saying of Section III (v. 13), intimating a shift to instruction concerning the second relational dimension (human–human). Despite this intimation, Section III presents not wisdom content, but a wisdom commendation. At last in Section IV the sage presents wisdom content concerning human relationships (vv. 27–33, with mention of 'mortal' in v. 30).

Echoes (Section III, recalling Sections I and II, form- and content-based). Six elements of Section III (especially Block III.B, 3:21–26) echo elements first appearing in Sections I or II. First, the voc., 'My son', opens both Section I and Block III.B (vv. 1, 21), and does not appear elsewhere in this poem. Second is the exhortation to 'preserve' instruction in 3:1, 21 (not elsewhere in this poem). Third, within this poem only 3:3, 22 mention 'neck' as a place to suspend something of value. Fourth, the word-pair 'life' and 'favour' that first were encountered in Section I (3:2 and 4, respectively), now reappear in Block III.B within a single verse, and in the same sequence (v. 22). Each will reappear in this poem only once (vv. 18 and 34, respectively). Fifth, 'confidence' and 'revere/fear' appear in Section II (3:5 and 7, respectively), and again in Section III (vv. 23 and 25, respectively). 'Confidence' occurs only once more (v. 29, Section IV). Sixth, the teaching in Section III that anchors wisdom and security in the LORD (3:19–20, 25–26) is reminiscent of counsel in Section II to cultivate the divine–human relationship.

Based on connections linking Section III with Sections I and II, 'they' in 'they must not disappear' (3:21) refers to wisdom teachings in general (recalling vv. 1–2), and to the universal instructions about relationships in particular (vv. 3–4). That same prohibition ('they must not disappear') further recalls two parallel prohibitions of Section I: 'you must not forget' in v. 1, and '[they] must not abandon you' in v. 3.

Chiastic links (Sections II and IV, form- and content-based). Block II.A consists of three imperatival units (3:5–6, 7–8, 9–10). Block IV.A similarly consists of three imperatival units (vv. 27–28, 29–30, 31). Similarities between respective units result in a chiastic pattern across the two sections. First in Block IV.A is a warning against withholding something of tangible worth (3:27–28), which recalls the exhortation to remit commodities of tangible worth in Block II.A (vv. 9–10). Second in Block IV.A is mention of 'evil' (3:29, 30), which recalls this poem's only other mention of this common term, in Block II.A (v. 7). Third in Block IV.A is the phrase 'any of his ways' (3:31), which parallels the expression 'all [of] your ways' in Block II.A (v. 6a), and does not occur elsewhere in this poem.

Microstructural features

Imperative-plus-incentive (3:1–2, content-based). Block I.A opens with an imperative in 3:1, supported by an incentive in v. 2.

Wisdom commendation followed by wisdom content (3:1–4, content-based). Although imperatives appear both in Block I.A (3:1–2) and in Block I.B (vv. 3–4), they differ. The first unit urges receptivity to wisdom in general (wisdom commendation), which leads to the second – an exhortation to specific behaviour (wisdom content).

Four cycles of imperative-plus-motive (3:5–12, content-based). The instructions in Section II concerning relationship with the divine consist of a fourfold cycle of imperative-plus-motive (3:5–12). The motives encompass incentives (v. 6b), hoped-for consequences (vv. 8, 10) and an explanation of benefit (v. 12). The fourth cycle (3:11–12) concludes the first three, assuring the youth that, though the sage's advice may sting, it demonstrates love.

Dual-theme sayings, introductory and transitional (3:13, 20, form- and content-based). Section III arranges its topic (an extended wisdom commendation) along a vector of time. The descriptive portion (Block III.A,

3:13–20) anchors in both time-present (Unit III.A.1, vv. 13–18) and past (Unit III.A.2, vv. 19–20), while the prescriptive portion focuses on the future (Block III.B, vv. 21–26).

Two verses present dual-theme sayings, referring both to present-or-past and to future. These occur at the start and finish of Block III.A (present in 3:13a and fut. in v. 13b, with past in v. 20a and fut. in v. 20b).

The transition to wisdom's future worth is not incidental, but undergirds the main point of Section III. Just as in the past the LORD maintained wise and sovereign control even when the world was breaking up (Noahic deluge, Block III.A), so also the LORD may be depended on to maintain sovereign control when future disasters may erupt perilously near. For he, too, remains very near (see 3:23–26).

Thematic contrast, wisdom's worth in present and past (3:13–18, 19–20, content-based). Although wisdom's worth dominates all of Block III.A (3:13–20), the first unit focuses on its present value (vv. 13–18), while the second recalls benefits that wisdom brought in the remote past (vv. 19–20).

Inclusio (3:13–18, form-based). The first and last words of Unit III.A.1 involve 'being fortunate', *ʾšr* (3:13a, 18b), creating an inclusio.

Palistrophe (3:13–18, form- and content-based). The quatrain in 3:14–15 resembles vv. 16–17 in content (praising the worth of wisdom) and form (note summation at the close of each quatrain). When combined with the inclusio joining vv. 13 and 18 (see above), a palistrophe emerges.

Merism encompassing both stabilization and destabilization (3:19–20, content-based). By recalling divine sovereignty over stabilization (founding earth, establishing skies in 3:19) and over destabilization (deluge of v. 20; see 'Notes'), the sage proclaims the LORD's comprehensive and trustworthy rule. Therefore the youth need not fear during future disaster (vv. 25–26).

Voc. coinciding with change in theme (3:21, form- and content-based). The voc. 'My son' opening 3:21 creates a rhetorical pause. This formal feature endorses the shift occurring at v. 21, involving both content (description gives way to prescription) and time frame (present-or-past shifts to fut.).

Envelope structure with prohibition quatrains (3:21–22, 25–26, form-based). Prohibition quatrains envelop Block III.B, opening it in 3:21–22, and closing in vv. 25–26.

Merism (3:23–24, content-based). Contrasting scenarios of venturing forth and of retiring for repose comprise a quatrain encompassing all of life (3:23–24).

Palistrophe (3:21–26). The quatrains of prohibition in 3:21–22, 25–26) flank the venturing-and-retiring quatrain in vv. 23–24, producing a six-verse palistrophe in Block III.B.

Grammatical and thematic continuity (3:27–31, form- and content-based). Imperatives appear in each verse spanning 3:27–31, unifying this block. They counsel wholesome relationships, generating thematic continuity.

Dynamic progression among imperative pairs (3:27–31, content-based). Block IV.A segments into three pairs of imperatives concerning neighbourly conduct. The first pair discourages passive–aggressive behaviour (tardy discharge of debt, 3:27–28). The second of this pair ('Do not say') renders specific the first ('Do not refuse').

The second pair discourages aggression of a covert sort (abuse of the legal system, 3:29–30). The second in this pair ('Do not level baseless charges') again sharpens the first ('Do not scheme evil').

A single verse contains the third pair of imperatives, discouraging overt, active violence (*ḥāmās*, 3:31). A summation categorically denouncing the violent person escalates the block's last colon to a universal level: 'nor choose *any* of his ways' (3:31b; emphasis added). The cohesiveness of this block teaches that even passive–aggressive and covert–aggressive misconduct introduce violence into the human community.

Thematic continuity involving incentive (3:32–33, content-based). The quatrain of Block IV.B (3:32–33) coheres as a group of incentives supporting the imperatives of Block IV.A (vv. 27–31).

Thematic continuity involving character (3:34–35, content-based). Each saying in the poem's final verse-pair presents two contrasting characters: scoffers and humble folk, wise and stupid folk (3:34–35). These populate a character summary quatrain.

Comment

Section I (3:1–4). The four-verse introduction comprising Section I opens with a wisdom commendation quatrain (3:1–2). Speaking as a parent, the sage urges his son/pupil to pay close attention to what he is about to say, since his teachings will contribute both quantity and quality to the years of his life.

In the wisdom content which follows, the sage distills grand, overarching imperatives that should characterize all of one's relationships (3:3–4). Above all, loyal love and faithfulness should mark one's relationships indelibly (v. 3, reminiscent of the fundamental character of the LORD disclosed in Exod. 34:6). One should focus not on achieving personal advancement, but on finding favour and understanding (Prov. 3:4a).

As the first section comes to a close, the sage anticipates the balance of the lecture by indicating two tiers of relationships. First, one should attend to divine favour – pursuing what God esteems as truly good (3:4bα). Second, the pupil should behave so that his or her fellow mortals will also be grateful for association with the pupil (v. 4bβ). These two dimensions – with the divine and with fellow mortals – the sage will expand in Sections II and IV, respectively.

3:3. 'Faithful love and faithfulness', *ḥesed wĕʾĕmet*, characterize the LORD (e.g. Exod. 34:6 = Pss 86:15; 25:10; 117:2). 'Faithfulness', *ʾĕmet*, often rendered 'truth', depicts personal reliability over the long haul – truth not only in speech but in consistent character as well (as with the English expression 'a true friend'). 'Faithful love and faithfulness' benefit a monarchy (Prov. 20:28) and interpersonal relationships ('It is through faithful love and faithfulness that iniquity will be atoned, and it is through reverence for the LORD that turning from evil comes about', 16:6).

Also in 3:3, consider the assonantal imperatives 'tie them' and 'write them', *qošrēm, kotbēm*. In the Shema Israel is instructed, 'Tie them as signs on your hand' (Deut. 6:8). Prov. 3:1–12 may serve as a commentary on the Shema (Overland 2000: 424–440). If so, then the sage's locus for attaching (about the neck, contrasting with hand or forehead in Deuteronomy) signals a shift from the more utilitarian (in Deuteronomy) to the more decorative (in Proverbs; cf. 1:9). The sage wants the youth to recognize this teaching as a badge of beauty, not a bond of duty.

Similarly the locus of writing shifts from external (doorposts and gates in Deuteronomy) to internal (on the mind in Proverbs) – a spiritualizing development. Concerning the tendency to spiritualize as 'a characteristic development in the course of tradition history', see Veijola 1992: 537.

By introducing the term 'tablet', *lûaḥ*, together with expressions reminiscent of Deuteronomy ('bind' and 'write'), the sage may have associated with his teaching a degree of prominence derived from the only 'tablets', *lûḥôt*, mentioned in Deuteronomy: those inscribed with the Ten Commandments. While further potential parallels with the Shema will be observed below, these opening correlations invest the call to loyal love and faithfulness with considerable moment, approaching the stature of a sapiential Sinai disclosure.

If Proverbs served in a school setting, pupils would be accustomed to using tablets (stone or wooden). In contrast to the pupil's customary regimen of practice-writing, the lesson about loyal love and faithfulness merited deep inscription on the pupil's mind.

3:4. The Masoretes inserted a *pĕtuḥâ* (a blank space extending to the left margin) before 3:1 and after v. 4, isolating vv. 1–4 as a single segment.

Section II (3:5–12). If the sage ranks reverence as key in relation to the divine (1:7), then in Section II of the present lecture he further explains what reverence entails (3:5–12). A healthy attitude towards the divine begins with high regard for the LORD's capability. This will lead one to rely on him, trusting his counsel primarily (trusting one's own instincts and insights only secondarily, v. 5). This high regard combined with trust should draw the pupil into personal acquaintance, even intimacy, with the divine (v. 6a). In consequence, the serpentine twistedness of one's route through life the LORD will untangle (v. 6b).

The humanistic tendency to rely on one's own powers of assessment and decision-making (to 'be wise in your own eyes') opposes reliance on the divine. Else the sage would not have devoted the second instruction of Section II (3:7–8) to that caution, already embedded in v. 6a ('do not habitually depend on your own insight'). To counteract pride the sage prescribes reverence (v. 7bα). Evidently wilful participation in evil undermines reverence and fosters an inflated sense of personal prowess, for he finds it necessary to add, 'and veer away from evil' (v. 7bβ). Such humility-with-reverence leads to restoration at the deepest level of one's psyche (v. 8).

Although attitudes of profound respect and intimate acquaintance mark the starting point of a right relationship with the divine, it must not stop there. Deep esteem for the divine will express itself through tangible gifts as well. These should not come as an afterthought, but eagerly should lead the way (3:9). Such surrender of tangible resources paradoxically results in their supply (v. 10).

Such candid instruction about relationship with the divine may incite a measure of resistance. So the sage explains how pupils should respond to reproof. Though painful, one must learn to value reproof highly. For reproof proves pedigree, evidencing God's paternal love (3:11–12).

3:5. Chapter 3 contains no fewer than nine of the nineteen references to 'the LORD' found in Prov. 1 – 9. These demonstrate the sage's conviction that genuine wisdom must shape how one relates to the divine. Further, the sage renders transparent his conviction that the divine is none other than the LORD, Israel's God as encountered at Sinai.

One must bear in mind who is advocating reliance on the divine (above reliance on one's own intellect). It is none other than the sage, that premier agent of intellectual prowess.

To resume the idea of connection with the Shema (see comments on 3:3, above), in v. 5 the sage may be clarifying how he seeks to express devotion to the LORD with all his *lēb*, the first sector listed in the Shema ('you shall love the LORD your God with all your heart [*lēb*]', Deut. 6:5). The sage counsels devotion to the divine thus: one must rely upon the LORD even more than one would trust his or her own exceptional powers of reasoning and problem-solving.

3:6. Mention of 'your ways' refers to the conduct of one's life generally, including choices made necessary due to a fork in the road. So it is within the dynamic context of each life-choice that the sage counsels the youth to 'know [the LORD]'. Not only the broader, more routine 'ways', but even the more circuitous, and often meandering, 'paths' of life will grow more direct and purposeful ('straight', *yšr*) on account of the LORD's influence.

The expression *dā ʿēhû*, 'know him', connotes acquaintance with another person, in contrast to gaining information about another person (where 'know' would be followed by *kî*, 'that', as in Ps. 100:3a: *dāʿû kî yhwh hûʾ ʾĕlōhîm*, 'Know that the LORD, he is God'). The expression in Prov. 3:6 closely resembles counsel that Solomon received from his father David when commissioned to build the temple: 'And you, Solomon, my son, know the God of your father' (*daʿ ʾĕlōhê-ʾābîkā*, 1 Chr. 28:9a). Waltke identifies this 'knowledge of God' as 'personal intimacy' (2004: 223; cf. p. 244).

3:8. 'Dry bones' sounds a death knell in Hebr. thinking. Thus the prospect in 3:8 of a 'drink to your bones' signals resilience and vitality (cf. Ezek. 37).

3:9–10. 'Honour' rules out duty-driven worship. With 'the LORD' as object, ostentatious generosity is prohibited (contrast Isa. 43:23, where Israelites failed to 'honour' the LORD with sacrifices).

Intensification escalates from storehouses 'filled' (Prov. 3:10a) to vats 'bursting' (v. 10b) – a picture of irrepressible surplus. 'Storehouse', *ʾāsām*, occurs elsewhere only in the Mount Gerizim blessing passage, a section rich with assurance of material reward for those who obey the LORD's commands (Deut. 28:8). Mention here of prosperous 'storehouses' may have recalled the Deuteronomic promise.

3:11–12. The analogy between divine and parental reproof also appears in Deut. 8:5, so that Prov. 3:11–12 may continue a sapiential commentary on the Shema inferred for earlier verses. The writer of Hebrews later enlarges on these lines from Prov. 3 to urge faithfulness to God as a loving parent, especially during periods of divine reproof (Heb. 12:5–8).

Section III (3:13–26). Following instructions for a healthy human–divine relationship (Section II), and before embarking on the human–human relationship (Section IV), the sage pauses to admire the stunning worth of wisdom, both describing it and prescribing close adherence to it (Section III). It holds value both for the present (3:13a, 14–20a) and for the future (vv. 13b, 20b, 21–26).

In the present, tangible wealth can boast a degree of worth. But it cannot compare to the worth of wisdom (3:14–15). For wisdom offers her followers longevity, pleasant transit along life's journey (vv. 16–17), and even life itself (v. 18). Looking to the past, our trust increases as one recalls the honoured role of wisdom in fashioning the earth, governing both stability and instability (vv. 19–20a).

Since the future may yet hold hazards analogous to a flood, wisdom's ability to survive storms (3:20b) naturally leads the sage to prescribe careful attention to her (Block III.B, 3:21–26; esp. v. 21). Beyond essential rescue ('life'), wisdom brings adornment as well – an asset for healthy relationships (v. 22).

Seasons of instability or supply shortage need cause neither anxiety nor loss of sleep, so long as the pupil consistently esteems wisdom (3:23–24). Periods of bold initiative and periods of repose alike will wisdom oversee with security.

Such freedom from fear (paradoxically benefiting one who fears the LORD) issues from more than simply a willingness to pursue and accept good advice. In a very real sense, security emerges because the LORD whom one trusts (3:5) personally stands guard, ensuring freedom from capture (v. 26).

3:13–20. Now the youth can see for himself that wisdom can also produce benefit as good as – or better than – the financial boon promised by the gang in chapter 1. Allusion to the gang's offer is the more likely since across Prov. 1 – 3 the root *yqr*, 'precious', appears only in these two sections (Prov. 1:13; 3:15), and is rare enough to appear only once more in the whole of Prov. 1 – 9 (6:26).

3:18. By describing wisdom as 'a tree of life' the sage places sapience on a par with that legendary source of vitality and longevity once offered to humankind in the primeval ideal (Plöger 1984: 38). Access to the life-tree, once shut up in Eden's garden, now metaphorically opens again. Such an attribution of primeval dignity paves the way for wisdom's ensuing association with the Creator at the dawn of time (3:19–20).

3:19. The verbs 'to found', *ysd*, and 'to establish', *knn*, refer not so much to the initial act of creation (bringing something into being), but refer rather to that period during which creation congealed, stood firm, took on a sense of order and predictability. This phase when creation grew congealed, solid, reliable is of great importance to the sage. Lacking such reliability, the sage would be powerless to engage in three processes that lie at the core of his profession: (a) he would be powerless to observe cause–effect relationships in the world around him, (b) he would be at a loss to deduce principles and (c) he would have no grounds for advising choices based on predictable outcomes. Thus the contribution of wisdom in bringing creation from a formless void to a grounded universe plays an enormously vital role in how the sage understands life and how he operates within it. In Prov. 8 the sage will present a fuller description of wisdom's role during creation. Yet already in Prov. 3 with laconic strokes he discloses that the stability he so values owes to wisdom an immense debt, a wisdom employed by the Creator at the dawn of time.

3:19–20. Allusion to 'creation-and-flood' appears in Ps. 104:5–9 as well. As observed by Duvdevani, when associated with clouds or skies *ṭāl* refers to substantial precipitation, not gentle dew as has sometimes been supposed (1970: 339–341; I am indebted to Philip Cohen for assistance in reading this article). Scott recognizes in v. 20a a reference to the deluge (1965: 48), while Toy understands all of v. 20 as diluvian (1902: 71–72; *pace* McKane, who interprets the two references to moisture as 'two fertilizing agencies' despite the degree of violence conveyed by the phrase 'depths split apart' in v. 20a [1970: 297]).

The 'splitting of the depths' echoes two terms found towards the onset of flooding in the Noah account: 'In the six hundredth year of Noah's life . . . all the springs of the great deep [*tĕhômôt*] were split open [*nibqāʿû*]' (Gen. 7:11). In only one other case do 'splitting' and 'depths' appear in a single verse. The poet in Ps. 78:15 recalls God's splitting rocks in the wilderness to release pent-up waters in order to give drink to his people. In that instance, 'the depths' serve as a gauge for the immense volume of water issuing from the split rocks, perhaps implying profound subterranean reservoirs or even seas beneath the earth (as envisioned in the earliest cosmologies) that beneficially flooded forth in the wilderness.

If in Prov. 3:19 the sage credits wisdom with developing stability at the dawn of creation, then v. 20 associates wisdom with divinely superintended instability.

By declaring that the LORD employed knowledge to bring about the breaking up of the depths, the sage invokes the Noahic deluge with its 'destruction of the guilty' (note this expression in v. 25) as evidence that God is able to shield his followers during calamity that wreaks retributive havoc against the wicked.

3:20. Lest the youth conclude that wisdom operates with independent initiative (perhaps as a goddess, the consequence of reading as literal the imagery intended as personification), the sage specifies that it was by the LORD's own knowledge that 'the depths were split apart'.

3:25. A demise consisting of 'panic' and 'destruction' mirrors the calamity befalling those who reject Lady Wisdom's overtures in 1:27 (with the sequence reversed). There, the 'hearer' would be able to 'dwell securely', *bṭḥ* (1:33). Similarly the youth who in Prov. 3 embraces wisdom may be assured of 'confident transit', *bṭḥ* (3:23). By recycling from Prov. 1 terms both for hazard and for security, the sage assures the reader of wisdom's comprehensive protection, adequate even for the previously mentioned disaster.

Section IV (3:27–33). After introducing the topic of relationships (Section I), after instructing concerning a healthy relationship with the divine (Section II) and after expanding on the exceptional value of wisdom (Section III), the sage takes up the second dual-theme: human–human relationships (Section IV). A far-reaching notion of generosity leads the list: 'Do not refuse good from those deserving it, when it is in your power to do so' (3:27). Such unsolicited kindness includes but is not limited to care for neighbours in need. Kindness must not suffer indefinite postponement (v. 28).

Contrasting positive generosity, human relationships must be free from baseless, premeditated harm. Especially one must refrain from twisting the legal system to one's advantage (3:29–30).

Building on a foundation of aggressive goodness (3:27–28), with no room for evil scheming (vv. 29–30), a prohibition against even the slightest appeal ('envy') surrounding physical brutality comes as no surprise (v. 31). Ruthless violence has no place in strong neighbourly relationships.

The one who motivates healthy human relationships is the divine. Crooked conduct earns his censure and curse, while the moral gain blessing and intimacy with him (3:32–33).

3:27. The injunction not to delay payment owed is reminiscent of Lev. 19:13.

3:32. 'Abhorrent' registers the most pungent degree of disdain. If the first colon repels with surprising vigour, the second attracts in equal measure ('but he confides in honest folk').

Section V (3:34–35). To close this lecture the sage compactly showcases contrasting characters, presenting clear alternatives between which the pupil must choose (Section V, 3:34–35). Does the youth desire divine favour? Then the choice is simple: abandon scoffing and embrace humility (v. 34). Does he similarly aspire to glory? Then the youth should focus not on glory, but on wisdom (v. 35a). Alternatively any who instead boast about supposedly glorious achievements expose only how ignorant they are (v. 35b).

Explanation

In view of marked deterioration that characterizes relationships across contemporary Western culture, the carefully crafted lecture spanning Prov. 3 speaks with uncommon relevance. Five principles map the way to relational health.

First, notice how high is the priority the sage places on the hard work of cultivating healthy relationships. After investing two chapters commending wisdom's worth (Prov. 1 – 2), he chooses relational health as the premier focus of his wisdom content, rounding out the wisdom commendation-plus-content menu of Prov. 1 – 3. What priority do we devote to healthy relationships, in life and instruction?

Second, consider the two traits isolated by the sage as non-negotiables, if any relationship would thrive: loyal love and faithfulness (3:3). Devoid of devotion that is both selfless and durable, a relationship will wither and die. Where do loyal love and faithfulness rank in our priorities?

Third, notice that relationships both human and divine require cultivation. Significantly, the sage prioritizes divine over human relationships (3:5–12). Three qualities characterize a robust relationship with the divine: supreme reliance (vv. 5–6), reverence (vv. 7–8) and tangible honour (vv. 9–10). Hardest of all may be the task of suppressing our naturally defensive response when the Lord points out deficiencies (vv. 11–12; cf. Gen. 4:6–8). When measured by markers of reliance, reverence, tangible honour and receptivity to reproof, how does our relationship with the divine measure up?

Fourth, when ominous clouds may threaten our future (and inevitably they will), the sage reminds us that it was the Lord who established the cosmos at the dawn of time (3:19). Not only so, he also managed the deluge's destabilization with sovereign wisdom (v. 20). Consequently those who walk wisely may remain confident of the Lord's strong care, even as storm clouds gather.

Fifth, towards our neighbours we must resist the temptation to behave selfishly, in three respects. Are we inclined passively to conserve resources, restraining generosity (3:27–28)? Do we wrong an innocent neighbour, all the while operating within the legal system (vv. 29–30)? Or do we resort to outright violence? From all of these we must desist (v. 31), lest we incur divine censure (vv. 32–33). How healthy are our relationships, when assessed by these metrics?

After establishing in Prov. 3 the importance of relationships, in the next lecture the sage will appeal to wisdom's historic legacy as inherited from his own father. Thus he demonstrates both his own commitment to healthy relationships, and his wise pattern of listening to those who taught him.

PROVERBS 4 – 9: OF PRIMARY IMPORTANCE (A GRANDFATHER'S WISDOM)

The grandfather-sage's counsel occupies Prov. 4 – 9. He accents three principal themes, with trace elements of a fourth: (a) reprimand, (b) body behaviour, (c) influential women and (d) life (conversely death). The first three cycle through Prov. 4 – 9 in an escalating fashion.

To grasp the grandfather's teaching, it is helpful to consider (1) its borders, (2) principal themes and (3) progression across his poems. First, consider borders.

1. Borders of Proverbs 4 – 9

Early in Prov. 4 the father-sage introduces a new wisdom source – his own father (designated here 'grandfather-sage'): 'When I was son to my father . . . He instructed me and said to me, "May your mind lay hold of my words"' (4:3a, 4a). The grandfather's teaching extends until the next author announcement (10:1).

The grandfather addressed an audience of one – his son (the father-sage, in his minority). The father-sage recalls: 'I was . . . a[n] . . . only child' (4:3). The grandfather addresses him in the sg. as 'my son' (5:1, 20; 6:1, 3, 20; 7:1), just as the father-sage referred to his own son in the sg. in Prov. 1 – 3 (1:8, 10, 15; 2:1; 3:1, 11, 21). When, in the course of the grandfather's retransmitted teachings, the pl. 'my sons' appears, this is the interruptive voice of the father-sage, calling out to a wider audience of pupils who now hear him reminisce concerning what he learned at his own father's knee ('Listen, my sons', 4:1; also 5:7; 7:24). It is instructive to observe that, after the initial launch (4:1), both plural-audience interruptions occur at a point of transition from description to prescription – a pivotal point when the father-sage must be certain that his plural audience of 'sons' is paying close attention. ('Sons' in 8:32–33 differs as it quotes Lady Wisdom's voice, not that of a sage-author.)

Differentiation between the father's teachings in chs. 2–3 and the grandfather's in chs. 4–9 suggests that similarities in form (wisdom commendations, character summaries, personification of wisdom and folly) or content (life as a journey, close alliance between wisdom, ethics and reverence) do not constitute incidental repetition by a single author. Rather, their appearance in chs. 1–3 suggests that the father-sage learned these wisdom features as a child, later incorporating them in his own compositions.

2. Principal themes in Proverbs 4 – 9

Three principal themes recur across Prov. 4 – 9: reprimand, body behaviour and influential women. Where themes overlap in a single poem, classification goes to the dominant theme (e.g. 'influential women', not 'body behaviour' in Poem 9 [Prov. 7]).

2.A. Reprimand. Two poems specifically indict wrong behaviour in the youth, evoking a reprimand: Poem 2 (4:10–19; esp. vv. 14–15) and Poem 5 (6:1–11; esp. v. 1). These poems open Cycle I and Cycle II, respectively (see outline, below).

2.B. Body behaviour. Three poems focus on body behaviour: Poem 3 (4:20–27; esp. vv. 24–25), Poem 6 (6:12–15) and Poem 7 (6:16–19). Such language prevented pupils from dissociating advice from concrete conduct.

2.C. Influential women. Most extensive is the theme of influential women: Poem 4 (titled, 'The Strange Woman – what are her dangers and what are my defences?', 5:1–23), Poem 8 ('Sex between consenting adults . . . What's the harm?', 6:20–35), Poem 9 ('When it feels so right, how could it be so wrong?', 7:1–27), and Poem 10 ('What alternative have I, if not the seductress?', 8:1–36). These escalate with increasing vividness. With its artful blend of female characters, reprimand and body behaviour, Poem 11 (Prov. 9) generates a triple-theme conclusion for the grandfather's teachings ('Whose invitation should I accept: Lady Wisdom's or Dame Folly's?', 9:1–18).

By tracing where themes appear, a pattern of expansion emerges (see the table opposite). Cycle I (Poems 2–4) produces one of each theme. Cycle II (Poems 5–10) adds one poem to each successive theme.

Recognition of two cycles with expanding theme-representation solves a puzzle observed by Whybray. He detected a theme joining Poems 4 (5:1–23), 8 (6:20–35) and 9 (7:1–27), but could not account for the pattern (1994a: 34–35).

3. Progression in Proverbs 4 – 9

Poem 1 (4:1–9). Introduction (all themes): 'From the outset, what objective must I pursue, above all?' The grandfather's first lecture lays a foundation with three principal themes, and 'life' (a trace fourth theme). 'Reproof' signals reprimand (first theme, 4:1a). 'May your mind lay hold of my words' commands body behaviour (second theme, v. 4a). Wisdom as (f.) object of love and embrace indicates an influential woman (third theme, vv. 6–9). And the charge to 'guard my commands and truly live!' (v. 4b) involves life, the fourth theme.

Poem 2 (4:10–19). Theme A (reprimand): 'I seem to have lost my way. What must I do?' After the multiple-themed introduction urging acquisition of wisdom (Poem 1), in Poem 2 the grandfather-sage hastens to reprove. The youth is heading the wrong way, evident from the injunction, 'Get off [the wrong route] and move along!' (4:15b).

Pattern of Proverbs 4 – 9		
	Theme	**Title**
Introduction		
Poem 1 (4:1–9)	Introduction (all themes)	'From the outset, what objective must I pursue, above all?'
Cycle I (Poems 2–4)		
Poem 2 (4:10–19)	Theme A (reprimand)	'I seem to have lost my way. What must I do?'
Poem 3 (4:20–27)	Theme B (body behaviour, positive)	'What does it matter, what I do with my body?'
Poem 4 (5:1–23)	Theme C (women, negative and positive)	'The Strange Woman – what are her dangers and what are my defences?'
Cycle II (Poems 5–10)		
Poem 5 (6:1–11)	Theme A (reprimand)	'I have become ensnared! What must I do?'
Poem 6 (6:12–15)	Theme B1 (body behaviour, negative)	'How can I recognize a worthless person?'
Poem 7 (6:16–19)	Theme B2 (body behaviour, negative)	'What about the loathsome person – how can I recognize him?'
Poem 8 (6:20–35)	Theme C1 (women, positive and negative)	'Sex between consenting adults . . . What's the harm?'
Poem 9 (7:1–27)	Theme C2 (women, primarily negative)	'When it feels so right, how could it be so wrong?'
Poem 10 (8:1–36)	Theme C3 (women, positive)	'What alternative have I, if not the seductress?'
Conclusion		
Poem 11 (9:1–18)	Conclusion (all themes)	'Whose invitation should I accept: Lady Wisdom's or Dame Folly's?'

Poem 3 (4:20–27). Theme B (body behaviour): 'What does it matter, what I do with my body?' Reproof (Poem 2) had become necessary, evidently because of harmful body behaviours catalogued here in Poem 3.

Poem 4 (5:1–23). Theme C (women): 'The Strange Woman – what are her dangers and what are my defences?' Disregard for body behaviour cautions (Poem 3) may devolve into greater hazard – falling prey to a negatively influential woman who would bait the youth by means of her own body (Poem 4, 5:1–23). Instead the pupil should counter the peril of illicit sexual pleasure by cultivating a rich and intimate relationship with that one who has been his 'wife since your youth' (vv. 18–19).

Poem 5 (6:1–11). Theme A (reprimand): 'I have become ensnared! What must I do?' Cycle II begins as Poem 5 (6:1–11) launches a reprimand even more incisive than found in Poem 2 (first reprimand poem, 4:10–19). Swiftly the youth must escape his financial entanglement. Caution concerning outsiders continues from Poem 4 (5:3; 6:1), as does voc. urgency (5:20; 6:1).

Poem 6 (6:12–15). Theme B1 (body behaviour): 'How can I recognize a worthless person?' Extent of misfortune swells from ensnarement (Poem 5) to final demise (Poem 6). Note the irremediability of one who, after rejecting reprimand (Poem 5), progresses to harmful body behaviour (Poem 6): 'Instantly he will be broken with none to heal' (6:15b).

By following indictment of indolence (Poem 5) with a portrait of shame (the worthless fellow, Poem 6), the sage implies that the lazy youth has descended to that despicable level. Where reprimand failed to arrest descent (Poem 5), perhaps shame will succeed (Poem 6).

Poem 7 (6:16–19). Theme B2 (body behaviour): 'What about the loathsome person – how can I recognize him?' Poem 7 (like 3 and 6) concentrates on body behaviour. Whereas Poem 3 was positive, Poem 6 turned negative (behaviours of the worthless). Poem 7 grows more negative still, sinking from worthless to loathsome. By implication, if reprimand will not reform the lazy youth of Poem 5 (6:1–11), he may initially digress into worthlessness (Poem 6), then eventually may embrace reprehensible conduct, underscored by divine rejection (Poem 7; esp. 6:16).

Like the worthless (Poem 6), the loathsome person unravels the fabric of resilient community, sowing strife even 'between brothers' (6:19b; cf. 14:c). Wrongdoing is a contagion.

Poem 8 (6:20–35). Theme C1 (women): 'Sex between consenting adults . . . What's the harm?' Just as in Cycle I reprimand (evidently rejected by the youth in Poem 2) followed by failure to guard against bodily misdeeds (Poem 3) led to sexual ensnarement by the Strange Woman (Poem 4), now in Cycle II reprimand (evidently rejected in Poem 5) followed by bodily misdeeds (Poems 6, 7) lead in Poem 8 to sexual victimization by a predatory adulteress (6:26) whose husband will wreak ferocious revenge (vv. 33–35).

The intensified warning in Poem 8 is matched by intensified tenderness. Mother, unmentioned since 4:3, rejoins father in the initial exhortation (6:20). Also, the portrayal of Lady Wisdom, though unnamed, grows more winsome than before (vv. 22–24)

Poem 9 (7:1–27). Theme C2 (women): 'When it feels so right, how could it be so wrong?' Multiple intensifications of content mark Poem 9. Senseless conduct (6:32, Poem 8) now crescendoes to become suicidal (7:23, Poem 9). Internalization of wisdom must exceed merely external adherence (bound upon one's mind, tied about neck, 6:21 in Poem 8). Now the youth must 'guard [wisdom] like the pupil of your eye . . . write [wisdom] on your mind' (7:2b, 3b, Poem 9). The benefactress, unnamed in Poem 8, now is named 'Lady Wisdom' with a relationship (sister), paving the way for her grand parade of accomplishments in Poem 10 (Prov. 8).

Intensification of form also marks Poem 9. A mesmerizing eyewitness report escorts the audience from first misstep to fatal misfortune as, too late, the long-resisted 'reproof' penetrates like a deadly 'arrow' (7:23).

Poem 10 (8:1–36). Theme C3 (women): 'What alternative have I, if not the seductress?' Upon witnessing the foolish youth's grisly death (Poem 9) the pupil may despair: Can no woman be trusted, admired? The grandfather challenges in response: 'Has not Lady Wisdom herself kept on calling? Has not Lady Perception kept on raising her voice?' (8:1, Poem 10). By its close, Poem 10 will have dismantled every excuse against enrolling as a disciple of Lady Wisdom. Unless, of course, the youth entertains a death wish (v. 36).

Poem 11 (9:1–18). Conclusion (all themes): 'Whose invitation should I accept: Lady Wisdom's or Dame Folly's?' As in the grandfather's first lecture (4:1–9), so in his last, he visits the three principal themes, and 'life' (a trace fourth theme). Concerning reprimand, Lady Wisdom imparts the skill of giving reproof (9:7–9). Concerning body behaviour, twice she references *lēb*, 'mind' (in 'lacking sense', 9:4, 16; Poem 1 similarly referred only to *lēb* among body parts). Concerning influential women, in Poem 11 Lady Wisdom competes with Dame Folly to attract guests (or victims). Concerning life (and death), in the end Dame Folly's naive guest descends to Sheol (9:18). Thus in Poem 11 all themes artfully coalesce in a showdown-styled challenge confronting the youth, as the grandfather draws to a climax the compounded rhetorical stratagems that escalated across his previous ten lectures (Prov. 4 – 8).

A topic unique to Poem 11, suitable in closing, unfolds as the sage guides wisdom trainees to become wisdom trainers. Lady Wisdom explains how profitably to issue reproof, that finest form of wisdom (9:7–9).

PROVERBS 4:1–9
'From the outset, what objective must I pursue, above all?' (Poem 1 in Prov. 4 – 9, introduction)

Overview of Proverbs 4:1–9

The poem that opens Prov. 4 – 9 effectively introduces the entire collection, since it touches on each of three recurring themes lending cohesion across those six chapters. Those themes involve reprimand, body behaviour, and influential women (see 'Principal themes in Proverbs 4 – 9', above).

Yet the primary contribution of this poem arises not from three themes, but rather from the way it underscores the immense importance of acquiring wisdom. The father-sage establishes this priority in his own wisdom commendation (4:1–2), paving the way for the grandfather's teaching with its incentive of reciprocal rewards (4:3–9). This poem, inaugurating the cycle extending through Prov. 9, answers the pupil's implicit question: 'From the outset, what objective must I pursue, above all?'

Position of this poem within Proverbs

Preceding context. The father-sage has just concluded his gateway lectures spanning Prov. 1–3. There he constructed a multilayered case for the worth of wisdom across two chapters of wisdom commendations (Prov. 1 – 2), followed by his foundational teaching concerning relationships, both divine and human (Prov. 3). Now he commends to youths a presentation of legacy wisdom – teachings that he as 'only child' inherited from his father. These he now will transmit to his audience of 'sons'. (Concerning the difference between 'son' and 'sons' across Prov. 4 – 9, please refer to 'Borders of Proverbs 4 – 9', above.)

Just as the gateway lectures began with substantial wisdom commendations (Prov. 1 – 2), so also the lessons spanning Prov. 4 – 9 open with more than a cursory wisdom commendation. In this case it comprises the entire first poem (4:1–9). Here we learn how deeply the grandfather-sage prized wisdom.

Ensuing context. Once the wisdom commendation is in place (Poem 1, 4:1–9), the grandfather-sage will initiate the first of two theme-determined cycles (Cycle I, Poems 2–4, 4:10 – 5:23). There he will address in turn: (a) reprimand, (b) body behaviour and (c) influential women. These same topics will recur – in the same sequence – in Cycle II (Poems 5–10, Prov. 6 – 8).

What to watch for

Notice exhortations exhibiting similarity. Often a verse or phrase may be bracketed by two mirroring elements. Consider whether the frame may emphasize the idea located at its core.

Translation and outline

Verse	*Translation*	*Outline*
		I. Father's wisdom commendation (4:1–2)
4:1	Listen, my sons, to a father's reproof, and pay attention so that you may learn insight.	A. Summons to sage's teaching (v. 1)
4:2a	Since I have given you a valuable teaching,	B. Rationale (v. 2a)
4:2b	do not abandon my instruction.	A'. Summons to sage's teaching (again, v. 2b)

		II. Grandfather's inaugural wisdom content concerning life's primary task (vv. 3–9)
4:3	When I was son to my father, a tender, only child in my mother's presence,	A. The setting: a memory that modelled receptivity (v. 3)
		B. Grandfather's principal teaching (first segment, vv. 4–5)
4:4	He instructed me and said to me, 'May your mind lay hold of my words; guard my commands and truly live!	1. Summons to sage's teaching (v. 4)
4:5a	'Acquire wisdom! Acquire insight!	2. Principal teaching: seize life's primary acquisition (v. 5a)
4:5b	'Don't forget! And don't turn from the words of my mouth!	1'. Summons to sage's teaching (again, v. 5b)
		C. Grandfather's principal teaching (second segment, vv. 6–9)
4:6	'Do not abandon her, so she may guard you! Love her so she may protect you.	1. Summons to wisdom, with benefits (v. 6)
4:7	'The principal thing about wisdom is: acquire wisdom! And in all your acquisitions acquire insight!	2'. Principal teaching (again): seize life's primary acquisition (v. 7)
4:8	'Cherish her so she may exalt you; she will honour you if you embrace her.	1'. Summons to wisdom, with benefits (again, vv. 8–9)
4:9	'She will place a gracious garland on your head; a splendid crown will she bestow on you'.	

Notes on the text

4:1. 'reproof', *mûsar*: like *tôkaḥat*, 'reprimand', 5:12, *mûsar* connotes a candid, negative assessment of a given opinion or practice (more confrontational than 'instruction').

'learn', *lāda'at*: often rendered 'to know'.

4:2. 'valuable': lit. 'good'.

4:3. 'When I was son to my father': since it would be needless for any male offspring to point out that he was his father's son, it is the inferiority of role (son-to-father) that the sage emphasizes here. During his minority, the son in an Israelite family stood in a subordinate, learner relationship before his father – a connotation the LXX renders explicit by modifying 'son' with *hypēkoos* 'obedient' (Waltke 2004: 277–278). The sage implicitly urges his youthful audience to follow his example.

4:4. 'and truly live!': lit. 'and live'. It is crucial to recognize that with this simple imperative to 'live' the grandfather is calling his son not merely to exist or survive, but to attain a supremely rich vitality. This connotation – 'to *truly* live', rather than merely existing – should be inferred routinely when encountering the verb 'to live' within Proverbs.

4:5. 'acquire', *qĕnēh*: generally used relative to tangible goods and property, in some instances rendered 'buy' (Gen. 49:30). Occasionally this verb describes formalizing a levirate inheritance involving a wife and property (Ruth 4:10).

'Don't forget! And don't turn from the words of my mouth!': these comprise interjections, urgent appeals for the youth not to ignore the principal teaching in 4:5a to 'acquire wisdom'. This imperative continues in v. 6: 'Do not abandon her.' Like the grandfather, the father himself will also use interjections (cf. 5:7; 7:24).

4:6. 'so she may guard you . . . so she may protect you', *wĕtišmĕrekā* . . . *wĕtiṣṣĕrekā*: a contrastive or emphatic meaning would fit well with the energic nun of these forms, although grammarians disagree whether the energic nun conveys such emphasis, as found in the paragogic nun (cf. GKC §58i; contra Joüon §61f).

4:8. 'Cherish her', *salsĕlehā*: meanings associated with the root *sls* include 'pile high', 'exalt', 'esteem highly'. A notion of unabashed public acclaim (no secret admiration) fits this term (cf. 31:29–31).

4:8–9. 'so she may exalt you', 'you embrace her' and 'she will bestow on you': each expression employs an energic form (see 'Notes' for v. 6, above).

4:9. 'crown', *ʿăṭeret*: while a monarch may wear an *ʿăṭeret*, it may adorn other prominent persons as well. In contrast, *nēzer* more particularly serves as a royal and priestly crown (Waltke 2004: 282).

Form and structure

Borders

After character summaries closed the previous poem (3:34–35), a wisdom commendation with imperatives begins the present lecture (4:1). It opens with the voc. 'Listen, my sons'.

The lower border emerges as double envelope patterns (4:4–5, 6–9) give way to another voc. wisdom commendation marking the start of the next poem in 4:10. The envelope patterns are described under 'Microstructural features', below.

Macrostructural features

Wisdom commendation followed by wisdom content (Sections I and II, content-based). The father's wisdom commendation secures the audience's attention in Section I (4:1–2). The grandfather's wisdom content follows in Section II (vv. 3–9).

Microstructural features
Envelope structure (4:1–2, content-based). An imbalanced envelope structure operates in Section I (4:1–2). A longer summons opens v. 1, while a shorter summons closes v. 2b, encasing a rationale (v. 2a).

Double envelope patterns (4:4–5, 6–9, content-based). The imbalanced envelope structure returns in 4:4–5, 6–9. Summons in vv. 4, 5b surround principal teaching in v. 5a, while summons in vv. 6, 8–9 surround principal teaching in v. 7. Each principal teaching advocates wisdom acquisition.

Repetition of 'words' unites the first envelope (4:4, 5b), while synonyms 'love her' and 'cherish her' unite the second (vv. 6, 8–9). Repetition of both 'acquire wisdom' and 'acquire insight' join the two principal teachings (vv. 5a, 7).

Escalation among related elements (4:4–9, content-based). Considerable escalation operates beneath the seemingly routine repetition of Blocks II.B and C (4:4–9). The summonses of II.C (4:6, 8–9) intensify those of II.B (vv. 4, 5b) by personifying wisdom and by adding reciprocal benefits. The principal teaching of II.C (4:7) intensifies that of II.B (v. 5a) by specifying 'the principal thing' and adding the summation 'in all your acquisitions'.

Escalation among related elements (4:6–9, content-based). Among expressions of wisdom receptivity, 'Do not abandon' (4:6a) becomes 'love' (v. 6b), while 'cherish' (v. 8a) escalates to 'embrace' (v. 8b), forming a vector of increasing intimacy. The blend of summons-plus-benefits found in 4:6 and 8 gives way to benefits-only in v. 9, yielding an incentive-rich conclusion.

Comment

Section I (4:1–2). The grandfather's inaugural lecture displays progression of thought initially as it moves from wisdom commendation (4:1–2) to delivery of wisdom content (vv. 3–9). Within the wisdom commendation, imperatives escalate from 'pay attention' to the more intense charge 'do not abandon my instruction' (vv. 1b, 2b).

4:1. The wisdom commendation with which the father introduces Prov. 4 – 9 resembles his first wisdom commendation of Prov. 1 – 3. Compare 'Listen, my son, to your father's reproof' (1:8a) to 'Listen, my sons, to a father's reproof' (4:1a). The shift from '*your* father's' in ch. 1 to '*a* father's' in ch. 4 may be the father's way of indicating that he now envisions the audience expanding beyond his own family.

'Reproof' leads four wisdom terms in this commendation (4:1–2), signalling how crucial is receptivity to reprimand.

4:2. With receipt of teaching (4:2a) comes responsibility to act accordingly (v. 2b). In the next poem the grandfather will make the same hear-and-act connection: 'I had instructed you . . . I had made you travel' (4:11).

Section II (4:3–9). Within the wisdom content, the father-sage introduces the grandfather's teachings with a fond childhood recollection: 'When I was a son to my father, a tender, only child in my mother's presence' (4:3). The pace accelerates as the tone grows sharper: 'Acquire wisdom! Acquire insight! Don't forget!' (v. 5).

As he draws his lecture to a close, the grandfather suitably shifts, now supplying incentives calculated to motivate a receptive response. Subtly personified, Wisdom is desirable since she will guard, protect, exalt and honour the youth (4:8). She will even adorn him with a gracious garland and a splendid crown (v. 9)! Who would not wish to acquire such a rich, powerful and generous benefactress?

4:3. The designation 'only child of my mother' may fit someone like Solomon, since there is no mention in the historical books of any other surviving son born to Bathsheba and King David. His older full-brother had died in infancy (2 Sam. 12:15–18).

4:5a, 7. Even the LORD, at the outset of his creative activity, modelled the priority of 'acquiring wisdom' (8:22).

The connotations of material property associated with the verb 'acquire' would fit well a court audience comprised of nobles. Here is a class of society more likely to possess disposable income and who thus would enjoy the ability to 'acquire' material goods.

To associate 'acquire' or 'acquisitions' with getting wisdom is reminiscent of the story of Ruth. Boaz 'acquired', *qnh*, Ruth as bride, together with property involved in the levirate transfer (Ruth 4:10; cf. Waltke 2004: 279–280 [esp. n. 25]; Meinhold 1991: 91; contra Fox, who is reluctant to associate marriage with *qnh* until post-biblical Hebr. [2000: 173–174]). Thus in this early reference to acquiring wisdom the poet might have foreshadowed the long-term relationship he hoped his pupils would pursue with wisdom, a relationship resembling marriage fidelity.

Additional links with Ruth include these: (a) the sage will construe wisdom as a wise woman, and (b) Ruth will earn the accolade 'resourceful woman', uniquely resembling the heroine in the latter half of Prov. 31 (cf. Ruth 3:11; Prov. 31:10). In view of later cautions against 'the foreign woman', these potential allusions to Ruth the Moabitess would signal that, from the sage's perspective, foreignness was a matter of ethics, not ethnics. It was possible for a foreigner who left past associations behind to join the Israelite community as an exemplary member.

4:6, 8–9. In wisdom's reciprocal benefits we see an early instance of retribution. By the point of 4:9 the emphasis on benefits is so complete that there is no more mention of what the youth must contribute.

4:9. To portray its great value, the father-sage similarly described wisdom as a 'gracious garland' for the head (1:9a).

Explanation

This poem mentions briefly the three themes developed in later poems: reprimand, body behaviour and influential women. Since it introduces 4:10 – 9:18, it is best read in the light of those subsequent lectures (see 'Progression in Proverbs 4 – 9', above). That context highlights five messages emerging from the introductory poem.

First, the acquisition of wisdom merits priority among anyone's life goals. With insistent urgency the grandfather stresses acquisition of wisdom. Rather than acquiring material wealth, he fairly shouts, 'Ensure that wisdom is your first acquisition – prior to and together with anything else you may attain! Failing that, no other acquisition will be worth owning.' With urgency he would proclaim the same counsel today, addressing acquisition-oriented cultures of our modern world.

Second, the sage highlights reprimand as the sort of wisdom one should learn to prize (4:1a, developed in 5:12). Due to its exceptional value, and in view of the recoil it reflexively produces, the sage's commendation of reprimand deserves careful attention today.

Third, wisdom should be cherished (4:8). Beyond a cost–benefit calculus, wisdom merits affectionate devotion.

Fourth, filial respect models wisdom. The father-sage demonstrates this by the respect he shows for legacy wisdom gained from his own father (4:3–4).

Fifth, authentic wisdom is time-tested. Alarm bells should sound when someone announces a brazenly novel, self-validated insight. Such untried assertions do not mark the wisdom way.

PROVERBS 4:10–19
'I seem to have lost my way. What must I do?' (Poem 2 in Prov. 4 – 9, beginning Cycle I, reprimand theme)

Overview of Proverbs 4:10–19

The second lecture by the grandfather-sage sounds a solemn warning (Prov. 4:10–19). Aware that the youth has chosen an ethically hazardous path, the sage launches a disciplinary intervention, calculated to dislodge the youth from his current trajectory (4:13a). This poem responds to the youth's implicit admission and question 'I seem to have lost my way. What must I do?' (For an overview of the three themes and two cycles, please refer to 'Principal themes in Proverbs 4 – 9' in the introduction to Prov. 4 – 9, above.)

Position of this poem within Proverbs

Preceding context. As the father-sage set the stage for legacy wisdom received from his own father, he reminisced concerning the unparalleled value and priority of embracing wisdom (4:1–9). That poem unfolded a cascading wisdom commendation. Wisdom content now follows in the grandfather-sage's second poem – a rescue-oriented reprimand (vv. 10–19).

Ensuing context. Following the reprimand of 4:10–19 (Poem 2) with its warning of travel along the wrong way, the sage will describe with concrete terms in Poem 3 what it means to travel the route of wisdom (4:20–27). Using imagery of wise behaviour associated with various body parts, this poem represents the body behaviour theme. Thereafter, Poem 4 will deal with the influential women theme (Prov. 5). Poems 2, 3 and 4 (4:10 – 5:23) join to complete Cycle I.

What to watch for

Compare the wisdom commendations appearing in 4:10 and 13. Notice instructions cast as if issued in the past, in contrast to those issued more recently. Consider how a history of disregarding past instructions may influence the tone of new instructions. Observe how concisely the closing quatrain contrasts moral character, positive and negative (vv. 18–19).

Translation and outline

Verse	*Translation*	*Outline*
4:10	Listen, my son, and take my words so may they multiply for you years of life.	I. Wisdom commendation (4:10)
		II. Responsibility for past instruction (vv. 11–12)
4:11	In the way of wisdom I had instructed you. I had made you travel in honest tracks.	A. Record of past instruction (v. 11)
4:12	As you walked, your step would not have been hampered, and if you were to have run, you would not have been tripped.	B. Rationale for past instruction (v. 12)
		III. Introduction of fresh reproof (vv. 13–17)
4:13	Take hold of reproof – don't let go! Protect her, for she is your life.	A. Wisdom commendation concerning reproof, specifically (v. 13)
4:14	Along the path of guilty folk do not venture, and do not stride along the way of evil folk.	B. The imperative: disassociate from the guilty (vv. 14–15)
4:15	Let it go, go no further along it. Get off it and move on along!	

4:16 For they cannot sleep unless they have inflicted hurt – their slumber is stripped away unless they trip. 4:17 For they have feasted on food of guilt, and wine of violence they will go on drinking.	C. The rationale for disassociating: addicted to harm (vv. 16–17)
4:18 Yet the path of moral folk is as the dawning of a bright light, shining more and more brightly until daylight has become well established. 4:19 The way of the guilty is like the darkness: they don't know what they may trip over.	IV. Character summary (vv. 18–19) A. The moral will enjoy an increasingly bright future (v. 18) B. The guilty will suffer a dark, hazardous future (v. 19)

Notes on the text

4:10. 'so may they multiply', *wĕyirbû*: using a weyiq. form as indirect juss. after imperatives *šĕmaʿ*, 'listen', and *wĕqaḥ*, 'and take', the sage indicates what impact he wishes to result from his teachings (Joüon §116d).

4:11. 'I had instructed you. I had made you travel', *hōrētîkā hidraktîkā*: the sage reminds the youth of past efforts to safeguard him. Qat. serves as plpf. in both verbs to fix the instruction of 4:11 prior to the reprimand about to be delivered in 4:14–15.

4:12. 'your step would not have been hampered, and if you were to have run, you would not have been tripped', *lōʾ-yēṣar ṣaʿădekā wĕʾim-tārûṣ lōʾ tikāšēl*: the verse-pair of 4:11–12 consists of instruction (v. 11) supported by rationale (v. 12), both having occurred in the past. The fact that the youth now requires reprimand (vv. 14–15) indicates he did not heed the instruction of v. 11. Consequently the benefits of v. 12 did not materialize.

The qat.–yiq. sequence of Prov. 4:11–12 parallels a similarly unrealized circumstance in Job 19:4. In Job, the past situation is hypothetical: 'If I had indeed erred' (Job 19:4a). In Proverbs, the past situation is actual: 'In the way of wisdom I had instructed you. I had made you travel in honest tracks' (Prov. 4:11).

A consequence follows in Job, expressed with yiq.: 'with me my error would have remained' (Job 19:4b). That consequence (being in error) did not materialize for Job because he did not meet the condition (erring). In Proverbs the consequence phrases similarly employ yiq.: 'your step would not have been hampered' and 'you would not have been tripped' (Prov. 4:12). These consequences did not materialize because the youth failed to follow the sage's instruction of v. 11. Both Job and Proverbs emerge from the unrealized scenarios by issuing directives that draw forward their respective speeches into the next persuasive point: 'Therefore know that God has wronged me' (Job 19:6a), and 'Take hold of reproof!' (Prov. 4:13a).

'To hamper' occurs with 'to trip' also in Job 18:7.

4:13. 'Take hold of reproof – don't let go!': having disregarded earlier wisdom instruction (4:11), the youth now must be receptive to reprimand.

'Protect her, for she is your life': 'her' refers to 'wisdom' in 4:11a, the nearest f. antecedent.

4:14–15. 'do not venture . . . do not stride along . . . Let it go, go no further . . . Get off it and move on along!', *ʿal-tābōʾ . . . ʿal-tĕʾaššēr . . . pĕrāʿēhû ʿal-taʿăbār . . . śĕṭēh . . . waʿăbōr*: this sequence begins with the earliest inclination to take a wrong path, and escalates to mandate that the youth must remove himself from that path. These five commands indicate that the youth is proceeding along a harmful path.

4:15. 'go no further along it . . . and move on along', *ʾal-taʿăbār-bô . . . waʿăbōr*: both verbal expressions ('go further' and 'move on along') employ the verb *ʿbr*.

4:16. 'unless they trip', *ʾim lōʾ yikšôlû*: reflects consonantal text of MT (pausal reading tradition was in place when waw was supplied as *mater lectionis*, before K–Q was added). Subsequent Hebrew scribes revised this to read, 'unless they cause stumbling' [to someone else], *ʾim lōʾ yakšîlû*. While the revision may be smoother (paralleling 'inflict hurt' in the first colon), the earlier reading is to be preferred, since it clarifies that evil folk harm themselves (cf. 1:18).

4:17. 'feasted on food', *lāḥămû leḥem*: lit. 'ate food'; note assonance in Hebr.

4:18. 'shining more and more brightly', *hōlēk wāʾôr*: lit. 'going onwards and shining', an idiom for expansion (cf. *hōlēk wĕsōʿēr* in Jon. 1:11, 13).

Form and structure

Borders

A wisdom commendation marks the upper border of this poem (4:10). Voc. 'my son' and imperatives 'listen' and 'take' sharpen the arresting tone of this opening.

Closure and character summary mark the lower border. As to closure, the terms 'guilty (folk)' and 'way' in 4:19 also appeared in vv. 14, 17 (guilty), vv. 11, 14 (way). 'Trip' is line-terminal in all uses (vv. 12, 16, 19), adding syntax to the closural effect.

The sayings of Section IV cohere in a character summary (4:18–19). A shared theme of illumination reinforces coherence: 'dawning', 'bright light', 'shining more and more brightly', 'daylight' and the antonym 'darkness', together with its consequence of unwittingly 'tripping' over obstacles.

Macrostructural features

Wisdom commendations, recurring in separate sections (Sections I and III, content-based). This lecture begins with a wisdom commendation (Section I, 4:10). By injecting an uncharacteristic second wisdom commendation at the point of Section III (4:13) the grandfather indicates that past admonitions (Section II, vv. 11–12) have fallen on deaf ears. So now he reinitiates a commendation to preface renewed teaching.

Intensification of wisdom commendations (Sections I and III, content-based). The commendation of Section III intensifies that of Section I. The charge to 'take' the sage's 'words' (4:10) escalates to 'take hold' of 'reproof' (v. 13). By specifying 'reproof' the sage signals that the youth has ignored earlier counsel and now requires sterner intervention.

Contrast of time frame (Sections II and III, content-based). Instruction and rationale within Section II recall the past (4:11–12), whereas imperative and rationale within Section III anchor in the present (esp. vv. 14–17).

Thematic continuity involving travel (Sections II, III and IV, content-based). Sections II, III and IV speak of travel: 'way' (4:11, 14, 19), 'to travel' (v. 11), 'tracks' (v. 11), 'to walk' (v. 12, also in idiomatic expression 'progressively' of v. 18), 'step' (v. 12), 'to run' (v. 12), 'to trip' (vv. 12, 16, 19), 'path' (vv. 14, 18), 'to stride' (v. 14), and 'to go further' and 'get on [your] way' (both in v. 15).

Microstructural features

Continuity of past time frame (4:11, 12, content-based). Verbs in both 4:11, 12 establish a past time frame for Section II.

Instruction buttressed by rationale (4:11–12, content-based). Past instruction in 4:11 linked with rationale (v. 12).

Continuity of present time frame through commands (4:13–15, form-based). Nine imperatives establish a present time frame for Section III (esp. 4:13–15).

Imperative buttressed by rationale (4:14–17, content-based). Admonition (4:14–15) is supported by rationale (vv. 16–17).

Comment

Sections I and II (4:10–12). Following the initial wisdom commendation (Section I, 4:10), Poem 2 (4:10–19) traces a progression of thought that begins by recalling, with a sense of disappointment, past instruction the youth has refused to follow (Section II, vv. 11–12). The sage had incentivized instruction (v. 11) with rationale (v. 12), but to no avail.

Section III (4:13–17). Rather than abandon the youth to his past poor choices, with renewed intensity the sage challenges the youth once again (Section III, 4:13–17). Pointedly, he commends this intervention as 'reproof', capable of delivering the youth into life (v. 13). The charge he delivers to the youth amounts to self-extrication from guilty company (v. 14). And he must waste no time about it (v. 15)! To prove the validity of his charge, the sage follows with a quatrain providing rationale (vv. 16–17). As far as the guilty are concerned, inflicting violence on the undeserving fuels their entire enterprise.

4:13. In the explanation 'for she is your life', the youth should have detected a degree of desperation in the sage's voice. If the youth fails to follow this second stage of admonition (Section II was the first stage), he ultimately will forfeit life itself.

4:14–17. The caution against travelling in bad company is reminiscent of the sage's earliest caution (1:10–19; esp. vv. 16–19).

4:17. 'Wickedness has become their necessary nutrient' (Waltke 2004: 291).

Section IV (4:18–19). The ultimate destinations achieved by moral and immoral characters the sage reveals in closing. Simply put, an ever-brighter light will enable safe transit for the moral, while deepening darkness will deprive the guilty of safe progress (Section IV, 4:18–19). In the wake of this lecture's disclosure, failure to choose the right route would evidence folly of an exceptional and intentional magnitude.

4:19. The unflattering observation that 'they don't know what they may trip over' suggests that, along with moral bankruptcy, the guilty manifest folly on the level of an intoxicated bumbler.

Explanation

In Poem 1 (4:1–9) the grandfather urged the youth to pursue wisdom above all other acquisitions. Failing that, no gain can offer lasting worth. Sadly, Poem 2 (4:10–19) reveals that the youth chose as travelling companions folk who are fed and fuelled by evildoing. Foolishly they fail to see that their schemes against others will damage themselves (vv. 16b, 19). Instead of abandoning the youth to suffer the consequences of his damaging decision, the grandfather intercepts his downward drift with a reprimand.

The grandfather employs three additional strategies to intercept the youth. First, instead of shaming or laying blame, he issues crisp, clear directions detailing what the youth now must do. He must proceed no further on this route, but 'get off it, and move on along!' (4:15). Else the damage awaiting the guilty will fall on him as well.

Second, the grandfather associates folly with moral failure (4:14). Conversely moral conduct – not simply 'wisdom' – marks the desired path

(v. 18). Wisdom leads to success because it is moral. Deprived of morality, only failure awaits.

Third, the grandfather incentivizes change by portraying outcomes, as with the closing character summary (4:18–19). For the moral, life will grow steadily brighter until it reaches a zenith. For the guilty, futile darkness will fall until they stumble without knowing why.

It may be helpful to observe elements of the sage's teaching in Prov. 1 – 3 that resemble the grandfather's teaching. Three features in Poem 2 illumine elements appearing earlier – similarities that may help us better grasp how they functioned in previous poems. First, the grandfather's competing journeys in Poem 2 may illumine why the father chose to open his teaching with the two competing invitations, the Appeal of Wealth and the Appeal of Wisdom (1:10–19 and 20–33, respectively). Second, the specific prohibition 'do not go' (in the path of guilty folk, 4:14) resembles closely the father's warning in an earlier poem 'Do not go along the way with them' (1:15). Finally, to close with a character summary is a device that occurs four times in Prov. 1 – 3, of which the last three contrast both positive and negative characters, as appears here in 4:18–19 (cf. 1:19; 1:32–33; 2:21–22; 3:35).

PROVERBS 4:20–27
'What does it matter, what I do with my body?' (Poem 3 in Prov. 4 – 9, body behaviour theme)

Overview of Proverbs 4:20–27

The lecture spanning Prov. 4:20–27 takes up the pupil's implicit question 'What does it matter, what I do with my body?' Here the grandfather-sage leaves no doubt but that to travel the wisdom way will require disciplines of body and mind. This route will yield benefits of resounding well-being that are not exclusively ethereal, but bring health 'for one's entire flesh' (4:22b).

This poem introduces the 'body behaviour' theme, the second of three themes that cycle twice through the grandfather-sage's lectures of Prov. 4 – 9. (For an overview of the three themes and two cycles, please refer to 'Principal themes in Proverbs 4 – 9', in the introduction to Prov. 4 – 9, above.)

Position of this poem within Proverbs

Preceding context. By this point in the lessons spanning Prov. 4 – 9, the father-sage has introduced his own father as an honoured source of legacy wisdom. In response to the implicit question, 'From the outset, what objective must I pursue, above all?', the grandfather exhorted, 'Above all else acquire wisdom!' (Poem 1, 4:1–9). Following that introduction he initiated a three-lecture cycle with a reprimand, as if responding to the implicit question, 'I seem to have lost my way. What must I do?' In reply he urged the youth to cling to the route of reproof by exiting the route of the guilty (Poem 2, 4:10–19). Poem 3 now will continue the journey motif by showing the crucial role particular body parts have to play, if one is serious about travelling in the way of wisdom as commended in Poem 2.

Ensuing context. After fortifying the demands of wisdom's way here in Poem 3, the grandfather will then unveil in Poem 4 (Prov. 5:1–23) a temptation lurking in the shadows. To withstand this temptation will require activation of those disciplines of body and of mind presented in Poem 3. In a lengthy lecture (twenty-three verses) the sage will sound an urgent caution, warning how devastatingly seductive the 'foreign woman' can be, especially in the eyes of a susceptible young man. Nor is this temptress strictly metaphoric, for faithful honour and enjoyment of the youth's own wife poses as the supreme defence (Poem 4, 'The Strange Woman – what are her dangers and what are my defences?', 5:1–23).

What to watch for

Begin by distinguishing the wisdom commendation from the body of the teaching. Observe how imperatives are followed by a supportive rationale or incentive. Notice how many features in 4:27 already appeared in 4:20–26. Consider the practical impact of teaching that is rooted in the conduct or function of various body parts.

Translation and outline

Verse	*Translation*	*Outline*
		I. Wisdom commendation (4:20–22)
4:20	My son, pay attention to my words, to what I say turn your ear.	A. Imperative: engage body to grasp teachings (vv. 20–21)
4:21	May they not disappear from your eyes – guard them within your mind.	
4:22	For they are life itself to those who find them, and for one's entire flesh – healing!	B. Incentive: bodily health (v. 22)
		II. Wisdom content: directives about body behaviour (vv. 23–27)
		A. Avoid these behaviours (vv. 23–24)
4:23	Against every imprisonment protect your mind, for from there life springs forth.	1. Captivity of the mind, with rationale (v. 23)

4:24 Rid yourself of a twisted mouth and put crooked lips far from you.	2. Contortion of the mouth (v. 24)
	B. Engage these behaviours (vv. 25–26)
4:25 May your eyes focus directly ahead, and may even your glances aim straight opposite you.	1. Direction of the eyes (v. 25)
4:26 Pave the track for your feet and all your ways will be made solid.	2. Steadiness of the feet, with incentive (v. 26)
4:27 Don't turn either right or left. Rid your feet of wrong.	C. Conclusion: avoid diversion – except from wrong (v. 27)

Notes on the text

4:21b. 'within your mind', *bĕtôk lĕbābekā*: unlike *bĕ*, 'in', *bĕtôk*, 'within', designates deeper interiority.

4:23a. 'imprisonment', *mišmār*: can refer either to a place of incarceration ('prison'), to the circumstance of restraint ('imprisonment') or to a cohort of soldiers who restrain others ('a division of guards'). To protect one's mind against such imprisonment is necessary since, if confined, the mind is powerless to issue initiatives necessary for true vitality (4:23b). The need to protect from entrapment will continue in 5:9–11.

'Against every imprisonment protect your mind', *mikkol-mišmār nĕṣōr libbekā*: when construed with the verb *nṣr*, 'to protect', the prep. *min* denotes 'separation from' (here rendered 'against'). Thus *nṣr min* means 'to protect [something of value] from or against [a hazard]'. For additional examples of *nṣr min*, cf. Ps. 12:8 (ET v. 7); 32:7; twice in 34:14 (ET v. 13); 64:2 (ET v. 1); 140:2, 5 (ET vv. 1, 4). *Min* with the connotation of separation continues into the next verse: 'Rid yourself *of* [lit. 'from'] a twisted mouth', and 'put crooked lips *far from* you' (Prov. 4:24; emphases added).

Instead with NRSV to render *mikkol-mišmār* as 'with all vigilance' (rather than 'against every imprisonment') follows the LXX (note dat. in *pasēi phylakēi*). Yet this would treat the prep. 'from' as designating the source or the material out of which something is formed (BDB, s.v. '*min*', §§2.b, c). According to this understanding, the sage here would advise the youth to resort to a metaphoric store of 'complete guarding', out of which he must draw a maximum level of fortitude to 'protect' his mind. While possible, this interpretation overlooks *nṣr* construed with *min*, meaning 'to protect against'.

Alternatively, some prefer 'above all else guard your heart', or 'more important than every watch that you must guard [you must guard your heart]' rather than 'against every imprisonment protect your mind' (cf. Fox 2000: 185 and Waltke 2004: 293, respectively). These alternatives treat the prep. *min* as a comparative combined with 'all', as though the sage were directing the youth to guard his mind with a measure of protection that would exceed the extent of vigilance he might exercise towards any other prized possession.

Treating *min* as a comparative is problematic since it overlooks *nṣr min* as 'protect against', and since it strains the rules of Hebr. grammar in two ways. First, the two objects being compared should both be governed by a single verb or condition. For example, when Israel loved Joseph *more than* he loved *all* his sons, both 'Joseph' and 'all his sons' are objects governed by a single verb (both 'Joseph' and 'all his sons' are loved, only in varying degrees, Gen. 37:3). In the case of Prov. 4:23, the two objects corresponding to 'Joseph' and 'all his sons' would be 'your mind' and 'all vigilance'. Yet those two entities are not both governed by the verb 'to protect'. 'All vigilance' is not a normal object of protection (as is 'your mind'). A more suitable object of protection, parallel to mind, would be something of value – such as *kol-ḥăpāṣîm*, 'all precious things' (Prov. 8:11).

Second, the comparatively superior item ('mind', in this case) must belong to the larger set modified by 'all' (BDB, s.v. '*min*', §6). Returning to the example of Israel's loving Joseph more than he loved all his sons, 'Joseph' belongs within the larger set circumscribed by 'all his sons'. According to this principle, the sage's preferred commodity (mind) should belong to the larger set, identified as 'all vigilance'. If the sage intended *mikkol* (lit. 'from all') to convey a comparative ('more than all'), he could have done so with a term such as *kol-bāśār*, 'all flesh' – a term that would circumscribe a larger set that would subsume the subcomponent 'mind'. Such an expression would have communicated that the youth should protect his mind more than he would protect other parts of his body or person. This alternative expression would have been feasible since the expression *kol-bāśār* appears in the immediately preceding colon (Prov. 4:22b). In sum, while the translations offered by NRSV, Fox and Waltke are conceivable, they serve better as wordplay alternatives enriching (but not replacing) the preferred meaning of *mikkol-mišmār nĕṣōr* as 'to protect against every imprisonment', a translation that better fits both the Hebr. idiom as well as the context surrounding Prov. 4:23a.

4:23b. 'for from there life springs forth': lit. 'for out of it [come] the springs of life'. Since the sage conceives of the 'mind' as the grand locus from which 'life springs forth', it seems inadequate to equate it with 'speech' (*pace* Fox 2000: 185). Rather, in this poem dealing with the theme of body parts, 'mind' stands as the premier body part since from within it derives an individual's comprehensive vitality. The mind is 'the agent governing the body's actions' (Waltke 2004: 296). A wholesome and unencumbered mind yields a robust life, whereas a mind-held-hostage would result in a withered, sickly self.

Through assonance, 'spring', *yṣ'*, associated with 'life', *ḥayyîm*, may have reminded hearers of *yṣ'* associated with 'water', *mayim* (cf. Exod. 17:6; Num. 20:8, 10, 11; Deut. 8:7, 15; Judg. 15:19; Neh. 9:15; Ezek. 47:1, 12; Zech. 14:8 ['living waters will spring forth']).

4:26b. 'and all your ways will be made solid': lit. 'and all your ways will be made steadfast' or 'permanent'. Just as commands in 4:20–21 are followed with an incentive in v. 22, v. 26b supplies an incentive (not an imperative; *pace* LXX) supporting the directives of vv. 25–26a.

4:27a. 'turn', *tēṭ*: connotes to stretch or spread out (not simply to shift direction of travel), as if expending energies in futile squandering, the opposite of focused attention in 4:25.

4:27b. 'Rid your feet of wrong', *hāsēr raglĕkā mērā'*: alternatively, 'turn your feet from wrong'. Same verb as 'rid yourself' in 4:24, but not the same as 'Don't turn', v. 27a. 'Rid . . . wrong' roughly approximates assonance in *ḥāsēr raglĕkā mērā'*.

Form and structure

Borders

A character summary closed the last poem (4:18–19). A wisdom commendation combining imperative, voc. and incentive opens the present one (4:20–22), marking the upper border.

The lower border is marked by inclusio and closure. Instruction to 'turn' (positive in 4:20; negative in v. 27) envelops this poem as an inclusio (Waltke 2004: 294). Four recurring features generate closure in 4:27 (Block II.C): 'turn' (v. 20), the negation *'al* ('may they not' in v. 21a; 'don't' in v. 27), 'rid yourself' (v. 24a) and 'feet' (v. 26).

Macrostructural features

Wisdom commendation followed by wisdom content (Sections I and II, content-based). The lecture consists of two sections: a wisdom commendation (Section I, 4:20–22) followed by wisdom content regarding conduct of one's own body (Section II, vv. 23–27).

Thematic continuity involving body parts (Sections I and II, content-based). The theme of body parts begins in the wisdom commendation ('ear', 'eyes', 'mind' and 'one's entire flesh' in Section I, 4:20–22), and expands in the wisdom content of Section II ('mind' in v. 23, 'mouth' and 'lips' in v. 24, 'eyes' in v. 25 and 'feet' in vv. 26, 27).

Repetition of 'life' as motive (Sections I and II, form-based). Twice 'life' motivates desired behaviour. It incentivizes wisdom receptivity in Section I (4:22a). In Section II, one's mind must be kept free, since 'life' issues thence (v. 23).

Repetition of a universal adverb in adjacent sayings (Sections I and II, form-based). By repeating the universal adverb *kōl*, 'entire' or 'every', at the close of Section I (4:22) and again at the start of Section II (v. 23), the intensity achieved through summation at the close of Section I energizes the directives that launch Section II. This adverb occurs also in v. 26 ('all').

Microstructural features

Imperative-plus-incentive (4:20–22, content-based). The wisdom commendation comprising Section I coheres as imperatives (4:20–21) motivated by incentives (v. 22).

Summation ending Section I (4:22, form-based). Section I ends climactically as the summation 'entire' modifies the last in a series of body references: ear (4:20b), eyes (v. 21a), mind (v. 21b) and 'one's entire flesh' (v. 22b).

Negative and positive contrasting commands (4:23–24, 25–26, form-based). Negative commands colour Block II.A (4:23–24), contrasting positive commands of II.B (vv. 25–26). Together these comprise the focal teaching of this poem.

Inclusio involving rationale or incentive (4:23–26, content-based). Within the imperative-rich adjacent quatrains comprising this poem's focal teaching (4:23–24, 25–26), only the outer sayings support imperatives with reasoning (whether rationale in v. 23b or incentive in v. 26b), forming a compact inclusio.

Comment

Section I (4:20–22). Poem 3 (4:20–27) opens with a wisdom commendation – a summons calling the son to pay close attention to what the sage is about to advise (Section I, vv. 20–22). Even within the commendation, the theme of body behaviour begins to emerge. The youth must activate ears, eyes and mind as he eagerly receives counsel (vv. 20–21). If receptive, he will reap superlative benefits that similarly pertain to the body: 'life itself', and 'for one's entire flesh – healing!' (v. 22).

4:21. Since the sage instructs the youth not to let his instructions 'disappear from your eyes', Waltke infers they were circulated in written form (2004: 297).

4:22b. In its closing phrase, the wisdom commendation section (vv. 20–22) leaves the reader with the prospect of physical health – intensified by a summation – with the expression 'and for one's entire flesh – healing!' The central teaching section of the poem proceeds to expand the motif of optimal functioning of one's physical body (vv. 23–27). The picture of physical health in this poem will reverse as 'flesh' in the next poem designates the very arena of the youth's demise after succumbing to the Strange Woman (5:11).

Section II (4:23–27). As the sage shifts from wisdom commendation (Section I) to wisdom content (Section II), directives concerning the body only increase. Certain body behaviours must be avoided, such as letting the mind fall prey to captivity of any sort (4:23), or indulging in untruthfulness ('twisted mouth', 'crooked lips', v. 24). Alternative body behaviours must be embraced, whether training the gaze of one's eyes or directing the path that one's feet travel (vv. 25–26).

In the previous poem the sage worked to dislodge the youth from his habit of travelling along the wrong path (Poem 2; esp. 4:15). Now that the youth has begun again to traverse the correct and moral path, the sage closes Poem 3 by charging him to keep to that route, allowing nothing to divert his progress (v. 27).

4:23a. In a rare use of 'every' to open a list (rather than as a summation at a list's close), the main section of the poem begins with unusual force, as if to extend the crescendo of summation that closed the wisdom commendation in the previous colon (v. 22b): 'for one's *entire* flesh – healing! [So:] Against *every* imprisonment protect'. Nearby lectures specify what sorts of external 'imprisonments' threaten the youth (cf. 4:12, 19, 27; 5:3–14, 22; 6:2; 7:23).

4:25. Fox observes that among the various physiological directives only the instruction to focus the eyes straight ahead could be fulfilled literally. 'The body-posture imagery seeks rather to encourage . . . a certain self-image, an inner carriage, a sense of being straightforward and unequivocal' (2000: 189).

4:26–27. The journey motif so prominent in the previous poem (cf. 4:11, 12, 14, 15, 16, 18, 19) returns through references to 'feet' (twice), 'track', 'way' and staying on course.

Explanation

As indicated in the grandfather's second lecture (4:10–19), the youth made the mistake of choosing friends poorly, which set him on a path littered with hazards (vv. 12, 19). He required a dose of reproof to jolt him back to the right path (vv. 15, 18).

In this third lecture (4:20–27), the grandfather discloses the secret to maintaining a solid, secure path (vv. 26–27). It begins by guarding one's mind (v. 23). This will spread to behaviours of the body (vv. 24–27).

To preserve our mind's true freedom we must begin by repeatedly recalling the sage's teachings (4:20–21). Instead to neglect the written counsel God has provided amounts to forfeiting life and wellness (v. 22; cf. Josh. 1:8; John 6:68). Instead to 'let them disappear', elbowed from our attention, whether by mere lassitude or by preoccupation with urgent-but-lesser concerns – such distraction quietly forges chains and erects bars of mental captivity (4:23a). In the end, genuine personal vitality lies suffocated, straightjacketed by the antinomian promise of liberty from any superior's dictates (v. 23b).

The disciplines that spring from a mind kept truly free will affect how we speak. Gone are posturing and spin-control (4:24).

A mind kept truly free will affect the focus of our attention. Gone are indulgent envies that would divert our focus from the authentically good and noble (4:25). Even momentary distractions will grow increasingly powerless to disrupt our advancement towards godly goals.

A mind kept free will be able to focus on what needs to be done next, smoothing the way of forward progress (4:26). It will be able to unmask and discard the diversionary tactics that attempt to interrupt progress through permissible but irrelevant distractions (v. 27a).

Finally, a mind kept free will recognize when a morally wrong opportunity clamours for recruits (4:27b). That mind will know to respond, 'Not now, not ever.'

PROVERBS 5:1–23
'The Strange Woman – what are her dangers, and what are my defences?' (Poem 4 in Prov. 4 – 9, influential women theme)

Overview of Proverbs 5:1–23

The last lecture stressed the importance of attentively managing one's own body. In the present lecture the sage explores the related implicit question 'The Strange Woman – what are her dangers, for I can see no hazard on the horizon?' In reply the grandfather warns that the youth will find appealing the sort of woman who will spell disaster. That caution leads the sage to answer a corollary implicit question: 'What are my defences against her?' Now the poet helps the pupil to appreciate the vital nature of his bond with his wife. Equipped with this insight, the youth will be able to choose wisely and so may avoid fatal entrapment.

Position of this poem within Proverbs

Preceding context. After opening his legacy wisdom with an urgent call to 'Above all else acquire wisdom' (4:1–9, Poem 1), the grandfather issued his first wisdom-content lesson by jolting the youth with a reprimand calculated to dislodge him from his present hazardous route (4:10–19, Poem 2, Theme of reprimand). With his son thus extricated from the wrong route, the sage proceeded to show that travel along the correct, wisdom way would call for specific body behaviour involving mind, eyes, ears and feet (4:20–27, Poem 3, Theme of body behaviour). The importance of traversing the wisdom way will grow transparently clear through the present poem, as one grasps what pain would result if one were to succumb to the enslaving Strange Woman's allurements (5:1–23, Poem 4, Theme of influential women). As noted in Poem 3, a trio of travel-related terms towards that lecture's close now recur in Poem 4, indicating continuity between these two lectures ('pave', 'track' and 'ways' from 4:26 reappear in 5:21). (For an overview of the three themes and two cycles, please refer to 'Principal themes in Proverbs 4 – 9' in the introduction to Prov. 4 – 9, above.)

Ensuing context. Poem 4 (5:1–23) completes the trio of poems comprising Cycle I, consisting of three themes (reprimand, body behaviour and influential women). Poem 5 (6:1–11) will revisit the first theme (reprimand). There the sage will challenge the youth to escape an economic snare, contrasting with the amorous snare of Poem 4 (whether literal or metaphoric, 5:1–23).

What to watch for
Notice the contrasting yet complementary defences that answer the danger posed by the Strange Woman's seduction. Observe how a character summary brings this poem to a close.

Translation and outline

Verse	*Translation*	*Outline*
		I. Wisdom commendation: an imperative (5:1–2)
5:1	My son, pay attention to my wisdom; to perception turn your ear,	A. Commands (v. 1)
5:2	In order to guard forethought, and so that your lips may protect knowledge.	B. Rationales (v. 2)
		II. Opening incentive (start of wisdom content): the danger posed by the Strange Woman's allure and eventual destination (vv. 3–6)
		A. Her allure and its exposure (vv. 3–4)
5:3	For a dripping honeycomb is a strange woman's lips and her mouth is more slippery than oil.	1. Initial allure (v. 3)
5:4	Her final outcome is bitter as wormwood, sharp as a double-edged sword.	2. Exposure of allure (v. 4)
		B. Ultimate destination (vv. 5–6)
5:5	Her feet are death-descenders; it is Sheol that her steps will take hold of.	1. Death (v. 5)
5:6	Lest she might pave a path to life, her tracks roamed about, she remains unknowing.	2. No life, no knowledge (v. 6)

Verse	*Translation*	*Outline*
		III. Defences against danger (vv. 7–20)
5:7	So now, sons, listen to me: do not turn away from my words.	A. Wisdom commendation interjected by father (v. 7)
		B. Negative defence: keep far from the Strange Woman (vv. 8–14)
5:8	Keep your way a good distance from her, and do not approach the door of her house.	1. Imperative: stay far from the Strange Woman (v. 8)
		2. Incentives (vv. 9–14)
		a. Prospective losses and gains (vv. 9–10)
5:9	Lest you give over to outsiders your splendour, and your years to the cruel.	i. Your losses (v. 9)
5:10	Lest strangers eat their fill of your exertion and of your hard toil, in a foreigner's house.	ii. Strangers' gains (v. 10)
		b. Retrospective confession (vv. 11–14)
5:11	So that you would groan in your last days as your flesh and body waste away.	i. Setting: deterioration of health (v. 11)
5:12	Then you would say, 'How deeply I hated reproof, and my mind spurned reprimand!	ii. Confession: resistant to reprimand (vv. 12–14)
5:13	'And I would not obey my teachers, and towards my instructors I would not turn my ears.	
5:14	'In no time at all I was totally ruined, amid the congregation and the assembly.'	
		C. Positive defence: imperative for marital faithfulness, with hopes for benefits both communal and conjugal (vv. 15–20)
5:15	Drink water from your cistern, and rivulets from your well.	1. Decisive imperative: the case for marital faithfulness (v. 15)
		2. Hopes for benefits both communal and conjugal (vv. 16–19)
		a. Hopes for communal benefit (vv. 16–17)

5:16 May your springs overflow outside, in the plazas – channels of water. 5:17 May they belong to you alone, and not to strangers near you.	i. Benefit to community (v. 16) ii. Benefit of personal sovereignty (v. 17)
5:18 May your fountain be blessed, and rejoice because of the wife from your youth. 5:19 An affectionate fawn and a gentle doe are her breasts; may they quench your thirst at all times; on account of her love you should continually stagger.	b. Hopes for conjugal benefits (vv. 18–19) i. General benefits of joy (v. 18) ii. Particular benefits of enjoyment (v. 19)
5:20 So why, my son, should you stagger on account of a strange woman or embrace a foreign woman's bosom?	1'. Rhetorical question: Is there any case at all, against marital faithfulness? (v. 20)
5:21 If a person's ways are straight before the Lord's eyes, he paves all his tracks. 5:22 His misdeeds will trap the guilty, and in the snares of his sin he will be held fast. 5:23 He will die for lack of reproof, and due to his widespread foolishness he will stagger.	IV. Closing incentive, with character summary (vv. 21–23) A. Travellers who honour the Lord enjoy his care (v. 21) B. But the guilty fall fatally captive, for lack of reprimand (vv. 22–23)

Notes on the text

5:2. 'and so that your lips may protect knowledge': 'lips' provide m. subject of 'to protect' (cf. 10:21, 32).

5:3. 'slippery', *ḥālāq*: connotes both 'smooth' and 'deceptive'.

'mouth', *ḥikkāh*: lit. 'palate', organ of taste and speech.

5:6. 'roamed . . . she remains unknowing', *nāʿû . . . lōʾ tēdāʿ*: the durative ('remains') reflects the sequence of qat. ('roamed') followed by yiq. ('unknowing').

5:11. 'in your last days', *bĕʾaḥărîtekā*: rendered 'final outcome' in 5:4. In Proverbs this is a solemn expression, urging assessment of the present with an eye to the future.

5:12. 'How deeply I hated reproof . . . !': lit. 'How I hated reproof . . . !' 'reproof . . . reprimand', *mûsar . . . tôkaḥat*: see 'Notes' for 4:1.

5:14. 'In no time at all I was totally ruined', *kimĕʿaṭ hāyîtî bĕkol-rāʿ*: not, 'Now I am at the point of utter ruin' (NRSV). For an example of *kimĕʿaṭ* meaning 'in no time at all' rather than 'on the point of', see Song 3:4. For 'I was ruined' rather than 'I am . . . ruin[ed]', note that the past tense setting has been established by 'I hated . . . spurned . . . would not obey . . . would not turn my ears' in Prov. 5:12–13. Thus the next verb having the same form (qat.) also should be rendered as past (barring controverting factors). This plain sense (that there remains no hope of escape) adds to the victim's admission a wrenching tone of hopeless desperation.

'amid the congregation and the assembly': these two terms convey the solemnity of a judicial inquest (Waltke 2004: 316).

5:15. 'cistern', *bôr*; 'well', *bĕʾēr*: assonance intensifies parallelism.

5:16. 'May your springs overflow outside, in the plazas – channels of water', *yāpûṣû maʿyĕnōtēkā ḥûṣâ bārĕḥōbôt palgê-māyim*: instead of reading *yāpûṣû* as an ind. incentive ('[they] will overflow') supporting the imperative 'drink' of v. 15a, it is best to recognize *yāpûṣû* as a long-form juss. meaning 'may [they] overflow' (we would expect short juss. *yāpuṣû*, as in Num. 10:35).

While the sage will at times employ the shorter spelling for hollow-root jussives (e.g. *yāluzû*, 'they must [not] disappear', in place of ind. *yālûzû*, 'they will [not] abandon', Prov. 3:21), to read *yāpûṣû* as a long-form juss. meaning 'may [they] overflow' is endorsed by the nearby long juss. form *tāsûrû* (not *tāsurû*) in 5:7, and by the nearby line-initial juss. in 5:18a, *yĕhî*, 'may [it] be', and line-initial *yihyû lĕ*, 'may they belong' in 5:17a (which is likely a juss. as well).

This verse envisions irrigated verdancy despite an arid Middle Eastern climate. Isaiah uses this imagery of 'channels of water' to describe political leaders who bring benefit to their countries: 'Each will be like a windbreak . . . like channels of water in a dry region, like the shadow of a great rock in a weary land' (Isa. 32:2; cf. John 7:38). It is essential to distinguish the confined waters of 'cistern' and 'well' (metaphors for the youth's wife in Prov. 5:15) from the running waters that overflow outside, into the plaza (v. 16). These two waters are very different (contra NRSV and NIV; see below under Form and structure). Thus a negation is not needed (as supplied by LXX: 'Let not your waters'). Similarly a rhetorical question is not needed (as inferred by NRSV, 'Should your springs be scattered abroad . . . ?'). The secondary waters that bring benefit to the community may refer to the offspring resulting from the pupil's marriage, children who grow up to become upstanding citizens who enrich and fortify the community.

5:17. 'May they belong to you alone', *yihyû-lĕkā lĕbadekā*: reading *yihyû* as juss. The expression 'they belong to' indicates ownership and hence the prerogative to employ them at will (in contrast to the scenario of bondage in 5:9–10, where a slave owner determined how the slave's resources would be spent). To render 'they belong to' is preferable to rendering, 'May they be *for* you alone,' suggesting personal consumption.

5:19. 'fawn . . . gentle doe', *ʾayyelet . . . yaʿălat-ḥēn*: lit. 'female deer [without reference to age] . . . gracious female goat'. The two animals correspond metaphorically to 'her breasts', as evident from Masoretic cantillation separating the verb 'may they refresh you' from the nominal expression 'her breasts' by placing a *dĕḥi* disjunctive (separating) accent following the latter (contra NRSV, which associates the animals with 'wife' of 5:18, and contra NASB and NIV, both of which make the animals a unit to themselves). The terms *ʾayyelet*, 'female deer', and *yaʿălat*, 'female goat', are highly assonantal, achieving a poetic beauty English is powerless to match.

'quench your thirst', *yĕrawwukā*: lit. 'give a drink until saturated', a metaphor for consuming love (cf. 7:18), artfully associated with breasts, and leading to figurative 'staggering' due to intoxication with love, not wine (cf. 20:1; Isa. 28:7).

'on account of her love': by fronting this prep. phrase the sage stresses that the source of one's love-intoxication must come from within the marriage, not outside it (emphasized also in 5:20).

'you should . . . stagger': yiq. of obligation ('should stagger'), not ind. ('will stagger'), since persistence in marital devotion is not inevitable, but must rather be cultivated.

5:20. 'foreign woman', *nokriyyâ*: a m. form of the same term closes 5:10.

5:21. 'If', *kî*: the same particle begins 5:3, rendered 'for'. Although this particle occurs frequently in adjacent chapters (eight times in Prov. 4, seven times in ch. 6), it appears only twice within ch. 5.

'straight before', *nōkaḥ*: the Hebr. prep. connotes 'favourable to' and 'in plain view of' (cf. Judg. 18:6; rendered 'directly ahead' in Prov. 4:25a).

'he paves', *mĕpallēs*: i.e. 'the LORD paves'.

5:22. 'His misdeeds': i.e. 'the misdeeds of the guilty'.

'snares', *ḥablê*: often rendered 'cords'.

5:23. 'He will die', *hû yāmût*: although the redundant pronoun 'he' may be emphatic ('He himself will die', Waltke 2004: 305, n.), more likely the pronoun was supplied to ensure reading *yāmût* as ind. ('He will die'), not juss. ('May he die'). Ind. 'he will die' is endorsed (though not guaranteed) by long-form spelling (not *yāmut*).

'and due to his widespread foolishness he will stagger', *ûbĕrōb ʾiwwaltô yišgeh*: may also be rendered, 'in his widespread foolishness he will err'. Voluminous folly supplies both cause and context of his straying.

Form and structure

Borders

After closure with inclusio drew to a close the preceding poem (4:20–27), a wisdom commendation with imperatives, voc. and rationales marks the upper border of this lecture (5:1–2).

Closure and character summary indicate the lower border. Three expressions resurface in Section IV, resulting in closure: 'to be held fast' (root *tmk* in 5:22, earlier rendered 'to take hold of' in v. 5), 'to pave' (vv. 6, 21) and 'to stagger' (vv. 19, 20, 23). Binary character alternatives summarize the poem, whether ethical (v. 21) or unethical and consequently foolish (vv. 22–23).

Macrostructural features

Wisdom commendation followed by wisdom content (**Sections I and II–IV, form-based**). The lecture opens with a wisdom commendation addressing a summons to the son (Section I, 5:1–2). The balance of the lecture presents wisdom content – the dangers and defences concerning 'the Strange Woman' (Sections II–IV, vv. 3–23).

Reversal involving 'lips' (**Sections I and II, form-based**). In Section I, by his 'lips' the youth must behave defensively (5:2, ending Section I). With reversal, in the next saying it is the Strange Woman's 'lips' that lead the list of allurements by which she would entrap the youth (v. 3).

Thematic continuity involving need for discernment (**Sections I and II, content-based**). The term 'forethought', *mĕzimmôt*, involves both strategizing and skill in discerning when one is falling prey to others' scheming (5:2 in Section I). In Section II the youth admits his need for such discernment (vv. 11–14).

Microstructural features

Thematic coherence regarding disclosing danger (**5:3–6, content-based**). All four verses of Section II disclose the danger posed by the Strange Woman, whether her allurements (5:3–4) or her deadly destinations (vv. 5–6).

Reversal (**5:3–4, content-based**). Desirable sweetness and slippery smoothness (5:3) reverse, becoming undesirable bitterness and the sharp razor's smooth slicing (v. 4).

Wisdom commendation followed by wisdom content (**5:7, 8–20**). A wisdom commendation opens Section III (5:7), introducing wisdom content regarding defences against 'the Strange Woman' (vv. 8–20).

Repetition of root *ʾḥr* (**5:9, 11, form-based**). Two of three occurrences of the root *ʾḥr* (conveying remoteness) help to mark the start of segments: in the first colon of both 5:9–10, 11–14 (Segments III.B.2.a and b, respectively). 'Outsiders', *ʾăḥērîm* (v. 9a), would take advantage of the incautious youth. 'In your last days', *bĕʾaḥărîtekā* (v. 11a), describes the incautious youth's dismal end (a third use, 'her final outcome', lacks structural significance in v. 4).

Thematic contrast concerning zones of benefit (5:16–19, content-based). While all of Unit III.C.2 describes benefits of marital faithfulness (5:16–19), the first segment deals with the benefit marriage brings to the community ('channels of water' in vv. 16–17; see 'Notes' for 5:16 concerning Isa. 32:2, where a benevolent leader is compared to 'channels of water' without any sexual connotation). In contrast, the second segment deals with conjugal benefits (vv. 18–19).

Double summation closing a unit (5:19, form-based). By means of two temporal summations ('at all times' and 'continually') the poet in 5:19 brings to a zenith the benefit of marital faithfulness in Unit III.C.2 (vv. 16–19), a counterargument against promiscuity's lure.

Framing structure concerning marital faithfulness (5:15–20, content-based). Framing Unit III.C.2 (communal and conjugal benefits of marriage in 5:16–19, on which see above) are two sayings that (a) pointedly charge marital fidelity (v. 15, Unit III.C.1) and conversely (b) challenge infidelity (a poignantly rhetorical question, v. 20, Unit III.C.1').

Reversal involving 'stagger' (5:19, 20, form-based). Licit marital delight described as 'to stagger' (5:19) soon reverses, referring to both illicit amorous delight and loss of self-control (v. 20).

Comment

Section I (5:1–2). Emerging from the body-behaviour emphasis in Poem 3 (4:20–27), the pupil would notice mention of 'ears' (the better to hear wisdom) and 'lips' (for protecting knowledge) – both appearing within the wisdom commendation spanning Section I (5:1–2). If lips seem a strange tool for guarding knowledge (they seem irrelevant for fostering wisdom receptivity), the explanation will arrive directly, in the first verse of Section II. For in the company of an alluring woman, a young man's lips serve more than speech.

Section II (5:3–6). The lips of the youth (5:2) segue to the lips of the Strange Woman in 5:3 – at once sweetly attractive and seductively slippery. Now the youth's need for protection (v. 2b) grows clearer. The balance of Section II expands his need of protection, thus supplying an incentive reinforcing the imperative of Section I: 'pay attention to my wisdom' (v. 1).

The opening word of Section II signals incentive with the term 'for', *kî* (5:3a). Although a common particle, within all of Prov. 5 *kî* occurs only at the start of Section II and again at the start of Section IV (rendered 'if') – another portion providing incentive (vv. 21–23). Even the choice in v. 21 to express 'if' by *kî* rather than the more customary *'im* speaks to *kî* as an indicator of structure within this poem.

As the sage exposes the strategies of the Strange Woman, he begins by describing her external allure (sweet and slippery, 5:3), then revealing her harm (bitter and cutting, v. 4). From the Strange Woman's allure, the sage transitions to her ultimate destination (vv. 5–6). With redundant insistence, he emphasizes that she is bound towards death, rejecting any opportunity for life.

5:3. Since the counterpart of the Strange Woman in 5:3 is the youth's wife (vv. 15–19), the foreign woman is a literal figure, not limited to a literary device.

Since the issue of foreignness features in this poem and will surface in Poems 5 (6:1–11), 6 (6:12–15) and 7 (6:16–19) as well, it may be helpful to consider (a) what conditions in ancient times might have prompted one to leave one's homeland, (b) what terms the biblical writers used to designate persons from a different land and (c) why foreigners were treated with caution. First, consider what conditions in ancient times might have led one to leave one's homeland. Unlike today, few would have possessed the means to travel for business or to satisfy curiosity. Due to hazardous zones of lawlessness extending between zones of civilization, any who ventured would require sufficient wealth to afford protection (cf. Ezra 8:21–22, 31).

Personal distress more typically would have prompted migration, whether due to famine (e.g. the family of Elimelek, Ruth 1), enslavement and forced removal from homeland as a prisoner of war or debt (e.g. Naaman's captive Israelite servant girl, 2 Kgs 5:2), or flight from one's own people due to political intrigue (David fleeing to Gath to escape from Saul, 1 Sam. 27:4).

Second, notice how the sage routinely describes someone from a different land. Instead of 'sojourner', *gēr*, he consistently and carefully refers to them as 'stranger', *zār*. For discussion of the difference, refer to §5.6 in the 'Introduction'.

Third, what were the reasons for treating outsiders with a general sense of caution? There were three. First, the stranger would tend to advance his own kinship group at the expense of others. Thus the youth risks suffering harm not only at the hands of one woman, but also at the hands of the entire foreign community, spending the balance of his brief life in servitude to them (5:10).

Second, the tendency to prefer one's own group might have caused other groups to be treated with deception. Thus the Midianites and Gibeonites used deception (Num. 25:18 and Josh. 9, respectively). Herodotus describes deceit perpetrated by Colophonites who, after being expelled by a rival faction, found welcome in Smyrna, then seized that city by treachery during one of its festivals (Herodotus 1.150, 1954: 74). While based in Gath, David lied to the king of Gath concerning which cities he destroyed during periodic raids (1 Sam. 27:10). Due to David's foreignness, Philistine leaders confederate with Gath were hesitant to accept the foreigner David into a joint-forces manoeuvre against the Israelite city of Jezreel, fearing he might revert to Israelite allegiances, causing defeat of Philistia (1 Sam. 29:4).

Third, religious beliefs and practices of strangers might undermine fidelity to one's native faith (cf. the foreign, adulterous woman's peaceable sacrifices and slaughter in 7:14, 22). In this regard men of Israel transgressed and suffered substantially when they succumbed to the lure of women of Moab (Num. 25).

Several elements regarding the hazard of the Strange Woman in Prov. 5:1–23 are reminiscent of the Samson stories (Judg. 14 – 16). To begin with, Samson was repeatedly attracted to foreign women – against whom the sage clearly cautions (here in Poem 4, also in Poems 8 and 9; cf. 6:24; 7:5). He suffered bodily harm as his eyes were gouged out (cf. 5:11). At the end, Samson spent his legendary strength for others as he ground Philistine grain while a captive in their community (cf. 5:9–10). That became the setting of his death, amid a crowd of people (5:14).

5:4. If consumed, the bitter substance known as 'wormwood' could cause illness.

Section III (**5:7–20**). With the Strange Woman hazard so clearly in mind, in Section III the lecture proceeds logically to describe defences one may employ against her wiles (5:7–20).

The father-sage pauses his retelling of the grandfather's lesson, breaking in with a secondary wisdom commendation. A formal marker confirms this shift in content – the line-initial adverbial disjunction 'So now' (5:7; for a helpful discussion of the structural marker *ʿattâ*, 'so now', also *kî*, see Waltke 2004: 306).

Following the interjection by the father-sage in 5:7, the balance of Section III divides between negative defences (Block III.B, 5:8–14) and positive defences (Block III.C, 5:15–20). The negative may be summed up in the exhortation 'Keep your way a good distance from [the Strange Woman]' (5:8a). This imperative verse is followed directly by incentives (vv. 9–14).

The incentives within Block III.B consist of (a) the prospect of bankruptcy suffered by the youth (5:9–10), followed by (b) a prediction that the youth will reflect with remorse, realizing that his refusal of correction brought him to the brink of irreparable ruin (vv. 11–14). In this rare and hypothetical testimonial, the pupils hear how the youth would describe his error. After having fallen victim to his own choices, the youth at last will gain the insight that the sage was trying to supply from the outset: the ability to foresee disastrous outcomes.

The self-indicting incredulity remains rhetorically unassailable, as it represents personal testimony ('How deeply I hated reproof, and my mind spurned reprimand!' 5:12). The wayward youth's pain is all the greater because of public spectacle (v. 14b). As if premature death were not penalty enough, his suffering escalates still further as he anticipates that this soon-approaching death will befall him among foreign oppressors, amid excruciating isolation.

The positive defences against the Strange Woman (Block III.C, 5:15–20) crystallize in the counsel to 'rejoice because of the wife from your youth'

(v. 18b). This clarifies the initial imperative concerning where the youth should go to satisfy his longings: 'Drink water from your cistern, and rivulets from your well' (v. 15, opening Block III.C).

Several hopes in 5:16–19 serve as incentives, supporting the imperative of v. 15. These fall into two groups. First are hopes for communal benefit (vv. 16–17), as the youth with a healthy marriage is, due to his retaining independence (not enslaved), able to supply refreshment to those in the wider community ('in the plazas').

A fine progression involving water volume joins 5:15, 16. The 'channels of water' (v. 16) describe a volume greater than what is drunk from the cistern, greater even than rivulets from one's well (v. 15). In this way the sage indicates that a small but healthy conjugal unit (v. 15) may bring exponential benefit to the greater community (v. 16). While generously benefiting others in the community, these by-products of marriage remain under the youth's domain (v. 17), not seized by strangers (v. 10).

The second group of incentives consists of hopes for conjugal benefits (5:18–19). Joy and rightly intoxicating sexual delight without shame are all part of God's gift to those who wisely shun promiscuity, sidestepping the Strange Woman's strategies.

After thus rehearsing the profound goodness of marital union between a man and a woman, the sage compares with amazement the Strange Woman's competitive offer. He challenges the youth to conjure up any reason that would prefer the Strange Woman's deceptive and deadly proposal in place of the pure and joyous benefits for home and community that issue from life with one's own wife (5:20).

5:7. The pl. expression 'So now, sons, listen' marks a wisdom commendation that the father-sage interjects within the grandfather's lesson (cf. 4:1–2). As in 7:24, the interjection helps ensure that the father's pupils will be paying attention when he resumes the grandfather's teaching – transmitting the forceful imperatives the grandfather delivered to him years before (verbs and pronouns of 5:8 revert to singular).

5:12–14. In terms of content (rhetorical logos) the youth's confession exposes the persistent harm of adolescent disdain for reprimand. In terms of voice (ethos) it speaks as the testimony of a peer, virtually unassailable in terms of persuasive power. In terms of desperation (pathos) the ruin of physical health established in 5:11 and underscored in v. 14a suggests these are the words of a dying man, hoping that his too-late realization of folly may at least serve to safeguard someone else. The rhetorical artistry of this composition is exceeded only by the importance of its message: if only the youth will go against the tide and cultivate receptivity to reprimand, he will sidestep many needless obstacles and thus live a life of rich fulfilment.

By admitting that his 'mind spurned reprimand', the youth validates the grandfather's earlier counsel. One must protect the mind, before any other body part (4:23).

5:14. Concerning the convening of a judicial inquest, youthful promiscuity 'is a social, not just a personal, offense, and it still ruins political careers' (Waltke 2004: 316).

5:16–19. All four benefits within 5:16–19 are not guaranteed outcomes, but benefits the sage hopes will accrue to the youth – rather like wedding wishes (employing juss. mood, not ind.).

5:18. That she is the 'wife of his youth' would recall the delightful memories of early love, and the accumulated strength of a marriage tested through the years.

5:19–20. The tricolon of 5:19 with candour and purity commends to the youth the delight he as husband should find through intimate physical fulfilment with his wife. Similar to the Song of Songs, the poet praises the beauty of the wife's breasts by likening them to a pair of female animals (cf. young fallow deer, female gazelle in Song 4:5 and 7:4 [ET 7:3]). The sage's description of escalating and twice-unending enjoyment paints a picture of supremely exquisite and satisfying marital joy. So lofty a portrayal of worth virtually dares the youth, 'I challenge you to imagine anything better than this!' So it comes as no surprise when, with the next verse, the sage expresses utter amazement that the youth would even consider exchanging for a counterfeit trinket of promiscuity this marriage of such genuine and inestimable value (v. 20).

Section IV (5:21–23). To this point the sage has not appealed to divine directives. He has rested his entire case for marital fidelity, and against promiscuity, on the grounds of observable benefits. Now, at the close, he observes that humans experience all these ethical outcomes because the LORD made it so (Section IV, 5:21–23). He ensures that retribution will reward alike the moral and the guilty. Smooth transit he gives to those he approves (v. 21), while the sin in which the guilty delight will ensnare them (v. 22), ending eventually in death (v. 23; note the reversal of 'stagger', earlier representing wholesome conjugal joy in v. 19). Sadly, all this disaster might have been avoided, had they only been receptive to reproof (v. 23; cf. v. 12).

5:21. Earlier the sage established the value of a track that was 'paved' (4:26). For the LORD now to 'pave one's track' adds still more benefit.

5:22–23. No divine intervention is required for the guilty to encounter their demise. Their own misdeeds and sin retributively will ensnare them.

Explanation

In this fourth lecture (5:1–23) the grandfather discloses why he went to such lengths instructing about proper body behaviour in the previous lecture (Poem 3, 4:20–27). For it is with his body that the youth will either succumb to the seductions of the Strange Woman, suffering in his body consequent deterioration and death, or in his body he will honour the exclusivity of marriage and so will enjoy the exquisite delight and physical refreshing it can bring.

Four primary lessons weave through this poem. First, sexual promiscuity produces hazards both swift and serious (5:3–6, 7–14). Perhaps the tortured experience of Samson with his pursuit of foreign women gave rise to these cautions.

Second, the exclusive bonds of heterosexual marriage comprise a source of exceptional and lasting personal delight. In addition, healthy marriages generate resources that will refresh many in the community.

Third, receptivity to reprimand comprises that character trait ensuring the youth will make the right choice. A testimonial from one who suffered for rebelling against guidance demonstrates the importance of receptivity.

Fourth, one might wonder, 'Where is the LORD within these counsels? Why does the sage not appeal to divinely authorized censures such as "You must never commit adultery"?' In fact, the LORD does feature in this poem, towards its close (5:21). All-seeing, he brings benefit to those whose 'ways are straight' before him. But the punishment of wrongdoers is not attributed to God. Instead the misdeeds themselves work demise (vv. 22–23).

Arising from each of these lessons the sage offers crucial wisdom for societies of today. First, he would caution societies that place a supreme value on sexual euphoria, above the value of marital fidelity between a man and a woman. He warns that those who pursue promiscuity only accelerate towards a deadly destination. So-called 'free love' is not at all free, coming at the cost of emotionally scarred children, aimless, narcissistic adults and hollowed-out communities, a gaunt existence devoid of resilience.

Second, the sage would confront those who dismiss marital fidelity as too constricting, disposable and unfulfilling. The sage teaches instead that it is only within the disciplines of marriage that the most profound fulfilment can be realized – benefiting both the marriage itself and the community composed of such marriages. So rewarding is such a marriage that the sage dares any to propose an illicit relationship capable of generating such deep and lasting benefits.

Third, if some demur at the suggestion of sexual purity and the honour of an exclusive marriage between a woman and a man, the sage would enquire how they would respond to reprimand of other sorts. Perhaps a testimonial of failure would capture their attention. Else such a one 'will die for lack of reproof' (5:23).

Fourth, to those who resort solely to divine censures when issuing counsel, the sage would urge a different approach. Explain that God sees when one chooses the right and will reward it. That God therefore also can see when one does wrong will be patently clear. And point out that misdeeds and sins themselves will be the undoing of the wayward.

A warning about a deadly 'trap' closes this poem (5:22–23). In the next, the 'trap' has been sprung, snaring the son (6:2).

PROVERBS 6:1–11
'I have become ensnared! What must I do?' (Poem 5 in Prov. 4 – 9, reprimand theme)

Overview of Proverbs 6:1–11

After responding with nonchalance in Poem 3 ('What does it matter, what I do with my body?') and with ignorance in Poem 4 ('The Strange Woman – what are her dangers?'), now in Poem 5 (Prov. 6:1–11) the youth exclaims with alarm, 'I have become ensnared! What must I do?' The sage fairly shouts his response, with ten imperatives urging him to extract himself from the hazardous snare he has fallen into.

How did he become ensnared? Due to native laziness, he allowed himself to be conned into a get-rich-quick scheme, masked with an appeal to neighbourly compassion.

Position of this poem within Proverbs

Preceding context. This poem belongs to the legacy wisdom presented by the grandfather-sage spanning Prov. 4 – 9. (For an overview of the three themes and two cycles, please refer to 'Principal themes in Proverbs 4 – 9' in the introduction to Prov. 4 – 9, above.) This lecture follows a lesson concerning influential women (Poem 4, Prov. 5), which formed the final of three themes introduced across Cycle I (Prov. 4:10 – 5:23). In Poem 4 the sage cautioned the youth concerning the enslaving Strange Woman, and urged him to delight in his wife and there to find fruitfulness. Now in Poem 5 (6:1–11) the sage returns to the theme of reprimand – the same theme that initiated Cycle I in Poem 2 (4:10–19).

Ensuing context. After urging the youth to extricate himself from a crisis (reprimand theme in 6:1–11, Poem 5), the sage will advance two brief lectures on the theme of body behaviour in 6:12–15 (Poem 6) and vv. 16–19 (Poem 7). These depict, respectively, worthless and loathsome fellows – how they behave in their bodies.

What to watch for

Observe the tone of reprimand that colours this lecture. Notice the points at which the grandfather gets his son's attention by calling out to him (vocatives). These can mark transition points in this poem's plot. Also observe the shift from problem-identification to solution.

Translation and outline

<table>
<tr><th>Verse</th><th>Translation</th><th>Outline</th></tr>
<tr><td>6:1

6:2</td><td>My son, if you have co-signed a promissory note for your neighbour, if you have clasped your hands with the stranger:
You have been trapped by the sayings of your mouth, you have been caught by the sayings of your mouth.</td><td>I. Introduction to the problem (6:1–2)
A. Seeming prosperity: a lucrative business deal (v. 1)
B. Underlying peril: a sinister snare (v. 2)</td></tr>
<tr><td>6:3a
6:3b

6:3c
6:4

6:5</td><td>Do this, then, my son, and extricate yourself,
for you have come into your neighbour's grip!
Go! Prostrate yourself and badger your neighbour!
Do not keep on granting sleep to your eyes, and slumber to your eyelids!
Extricate yourself like a gazelle from the grasp, and like a bird from the grasp of a trapper!</td><td>II. Solutions for the problem (vv. 3–8)
A. Short-range solutions (vv. 3–5)
1. Concise short-range solution: escape (v. 3a)!
2. Reminder of present peril (v. 3b)
3. Expanded short-range solution (vv. 3c–4)
a. Escape from contract (v. 3c)
b. Escape from complacency (v. 4)
4. Threefold conclusion: concise solution and reminder of present peril (v. 5)</td></tr>
<tr><td>6:6

6:7

6:8</td><td>Go to the ant, lazy fellow, watch its ways and become wise!
Although it has no leader, officer or ruler,
It will prepare its food in the summer; it will have gathered its nourishment at the harvest.</td><td>B. Long-range solution (vv. 6–8)
1. Summons to observe (v. 6)
2. Lesson: escape complacency through self-motivation (vv. 7–8)
a. Despite lack of external leadership . . . (v. 7)
b. . . . There is no lack of internal initiative (v. 8)</td></tr>
<tr><td></td><td></td><td>III. Closing challenge (vv. 9–11)
A. Reprimand by rhetorical question, with reply (vv. 9–10)</td></tr>
</table>

6:9 How long, lazy fellow, are you going to lie there? When are you going to get up from your sleep?	1. Implicit reprimand: exasperated question concerning endless complacency (v. 9)
6:10 'A little sleep, a little slumber, a little folding of hands to lie down'.	2. Deflection of reprimand: patronizing reply (v. 10)
6:11 Then, your poverty will come as a vagabond, and your insolvency like an armed man.	B. Consequent looming peril (v. 11)

Notes on the text

6:1. 'if you have co-signed a promissory note', *ʾim-ʿārabtā*: lit. 'if you have taken on a pledge'. Use of the qat. conjugation with all verbs in 6:1–2 emphasizes that the protasis ('if' portion of the condition) has materialized in the past. The youth has already become snared.

'if you have clasped your hands with the stranger', *tāqaʿtā lazzār kappêkā*: lit. 'you have clasped your palms with the stranger' ('if' is inferred from first colon). Clasping hands indicates an amicable gesture, here ratifying the financial agreement (Jones 2019: 74–75). 'Palms' will be rendered in 6:3b as the neighbour's 'grip'.

'with the stranger', *lazzār*: although the term 'stranger' has appeared in previous poems (2:16; 5:3, 10, 17, 20), to specify with the definite article is new.

6:2. 'sayings of your mouth . . . sayings of your mouth': with uncharacteristic simplicity the sage employs non-differentiation from one parallel colon to the next. For the poet to dispense with literary refinement in this way displays anxiety at least, or even agitation befitting a state of emergency. To emend with Syriac by substituting 'sayings of your lips . . . sayings of your mouth' would mute this vital clue to the sage's anguish over the youth's ensnarement.

6:3. 'then', *ʾēpôʾ*: a particle of pause, escalating urgency and leading to another interjected voc., 'my son' (cf. 5:20a).

'you have come into your neighbour's grip': lit. 'you have come into your neighbour's palm', deftly reversing the amicable, deal-sealing grasp of the pupil's palm (6:1b). Through a seemingly innocent, initial clasp the stranger-borrower gained a dangerous 'grip', *kap*, on the youth-guarantor.

'Go! Prostrate yourself': when 'go' begins a sequence of two imperatives it may signify distinct, coordinated commands (e.g. Gen. 27:13). Alternatively, the first imperative ('go') may simply introduce the second (e.g. Gen. 31:44). Given the youth's need to stir himself to action, 'Go!' should be recognized as a distinct command (cf. Prov. 6:6, 9).

'badger', *rĕhab*: also 'importune', 'storm', 'assault'.

6:4. 'Do not keep on granting sleep': not 'Give no sleep'. Based on the question 'How long . . . are you going to lie there?' (6:9), at issue is whether the youth will ever rouse from sleep, initiating efforts to escape entrapment.

'slumber', *tĕnûmâ*: 'slumber' is a shallower repose than 'sleep' in the first colon, and so intensifies the caution: 'even a bit of snoozing or drowsing can do this to you' (Fox 2000: 213–214).

6:5. 'trapper', *yāqûš*: lit. a fowler, from the same root as 'trapped' in 6:2.

6:6, 9. 'lazy fellow', *ʿāṣēl*: the same person as 'my son', addressed in 6:1–5. Although he regards 6:1–5 and 6:6–11 as referring to distinct inferior persons (loan-guarantor in contrast to sluggard), Waltke notes that the two portions are closely linked by double vocatives (son twice, lazy fellow twice), by the catchwords 'go', 'sleep' and 'slumber', by shared motifs of sleeping when one should be taking action, and by lessons drawn from trapped animals and from insects that take initiative (2004: 328–329). Rather, these links recommend continuity between identity of 'son' and 'lazy fellow'.

6:7. 'Although', *ʾăšer*: lit. 'because' (adversative tone inferred from contrast in 6:8).

6:8. 'It will prepare . . . it will have gathered', *tākîn* . . . *ʾāgĕrâ*: fut. pf. inferred for qat. form *ʾāgĕrâ*, 'gathered', due to fut. sense of yiq. verb *tākîn*, 'It will prepare'.

6:7–8. 'leader . . . summer . . . harvest', *qāṣîn* . . . *qayiṣ* . . . *qāṣîr*: note assonance.

6:9. 'lie there': lit. 'lie down'.

6:9–10. 'How long . . . ? When . . . ? A little . . . a little . . . a little . . . ', *ʿad-mātay* . . . *mātay* . . . *mĕʿaṭ* . . . *mĕʿaṭ* . . . *mĕʿaṭ* . . . : in response to the grandfather's twice-repeated question 'When?', the youth counters assonantally with threefold 'A little'.

6:10–11. This verse-pair comprises a deployed saying. The sage will chronicle in 24:30–34 how he came to compose it. Quotes set off 6:10 to signify that they paraphrase the youth's resistant response to reprimand.

Form and structure

Borders

A character summary combined with an incentive to conclude the preceding lecture (5:21–23), which dealt with marital integrity. The present lecture's upper border is marked by a shift to the topic of economic entrapment, introduced with a voc. in 6:1–2.

A topic shift identifies the lower border. After a challenge to avoid economic entrapment (6:9–11), a new topic (and new lecture) unfolds, delineating the character of a worthless person (6:12–15). Within the present lecture's closing challenge appears a deployed saying, much as the deployed saying of 1:17 appears towards the close of its lecture (1:10–19).

Macrostructural features

Reversal involving 'hands' and 'grip' (Sections I and II, form-based). Although a single term underlies 'hands' (6:1) and 'grip' (v. 3), the connotation shifts from free agency to captivity.

Extended conditional statement (Sections I and II, form-based). Section I consists of an extended protasis (the problem, 6:1–2). Various commands comprise an extended apodosis in Section II (the solution, vv. 3–8; so also Fox 2000: 213).

Repetition of root *yqš*, 'to trap' (Sections I and II, form-based). The root *yqš*, 'trap', appears in the last verse of Section I (6:2) and the last verse of Block II.A (v. 5), contributing to closure for that latter block.

Frequent voc. forms, opening major portions (Sections I, II and III, form-based). Four of this poem's eleven verses employ a voc., each coinciding with the start of a major portion. The expression 'my son' opens the entire poem, then appears in the first colon of Section II (6:1, 3). 'Lazy fellow' occurs in the first colon of Block II.B (v. 6a), and again in the first colon of Section III (v. 9). Frequent and strategic vocatives foster an atmosphere of deep concern.

Statements that have ensnared the pupil (Sections I and III, content-based). Twice the youth is snared by his own statements. A statement of a contractual nature is alluded to in 6:2, while one of complacency is quoted in v. 10.

Microstructural features

Conditional structure (6:1–2, form-based). The two sayings of Section I cohere as an extended protasis (6:1–2; so also Fox 2000: 213). While the youth was aware of making a contract (v. 1), he was unaware that he thereby imperilled himself (v. 2). The clear expression of apodosis beginning in v. 3 discourages treating v. 2 as an apodosis (*pace* Waltke 2004: 331).

Phrase repetition, producing acceleration (6:2, form-based). Twice the phrase 'by the sayings of your mouth' appears in 6:2. So uncharacteristically mundane a repetition suggests the following: (a) the parent-poet is frantic, dispensing with literary refinement in order to sound the alarm swiftly, and (b) the reader should be alert, listening for such a saying (as materializes in v. 10).

Repetition of the imperative 'go' (6:3, 6, form-based). The two blocks of Section II share the imperative 'go'. In 6:3c the sage urges the youth to appeal hastily for release from the loan-guarantee contract, while in v. 6 he urges him to overcome somnolence.

Thematic contrast of imperative (6:3c, 4, content-based). Whereas the imperatives of 6:3c seek to cure contract-entrapment, the imperative of

v. 4 addresses underlying complacency. The poet will focus on this underlying issue in Section III (vv. 9–11).

Block-level closure (6:5, form- and content-based). Several elements in 6:5 foster a sense of closure in Block II.A (vv. 3–5): 'extricate yourself' (vv. 3, 5), synonyms 'grip' and 'grasp' (vv. 3, 5), the terms 'trapped' and 'trapper' (vv. 2, 5), and the notion of captivity (whether in sleep [v. 4] or in a trap [v. 5]).

Thematic contrast involving animals, captive or free (6:5, 6–8, content-based). The two blocks of Section II each present images of animals. Trapped gazelles and birds have lost their liberty (6:5), while mere insects exercise agency, stockpiling food (vv. 6–8).

Comment

Section I (6:1–2). Evidently an outsider has appeared, seeking assistance to secure his loan. Lacking sufficient collateral and character-based credit, he turns to the youth for help. Whether the youth is motivated by compassion or consideration of profit, we do not know. Ben Sirach indicates that gain could be made by securing another's loan:

> A sinner will fall into surety [guaranteeing another's loan],
> and as he pursues profit-taking, he will fall into lawsuits.
> (Sirach 29.19, NETS; cf. Fox 2000: 215)

Regardless of motive, pledges were exchanged, hands were clasped and the deal was sealed. Yet this seeming prosperity produced entrapment – an underlying circumstance not foreseen by the youth.

News of this agreement troubles the grandfather deeply. His speech betrays agitation (Section I, 6:1–2). He hastens to issue a reprimand in hope of rescuing the youth from ruin. (For further exploration of the hazard accompanying economic partnership with a 'stranger', see 'Comment' for Prov. 20:15–23.)

6:1. The parallel terms 'neighbour' and 'stranger' in 6:1 likely refer to the same person, since 'neighbour' alone recurs in v. 3 (cf. Waltke 2004: 331; Fox disagrees [2000: 211]). Initially the audience learns that this individual is a 'neighbour' (v. 1a). His character sharpens in the second colon as the sage discloses that the borrower is a 'stranger'. Similarly when describing the hazardous woman of Poem 8, the sage will delay until the second colon the observation that her language ('tongue') is 'foreign' (6:24).

6:1–2. Elsewhere the sage will urge generosity towards the poor (14:21), showing that in 6:1 the sage is not advocating miserliness. Rather, he cautions here against unsound business dealings (cf. 11:15; 22:26–27). The intensity of concern evident both in the grandfather's introduction (6:1–2) and in the short-range solutions (vv. 3–5) makes sense only if disaster is imminent.

Ben Sirach indicates the extent of risk one may incur by guaranteeing a loan: 'A guarantor's kindness do not forget, for he gave his soul on your behalf' (Sirach 29.15). A Sumerian saying warns, 'Don't act as a guarantor; that man will have a hold on you; and you, don't accept a pledge (that man will be discredited)' (Alster 2005: 65).

Herodotus reports how Persians regarded outsiders in the fifth century BC:

> After their own nation they hold their nearest neighbours most in honour, then the nearest but one – and so on, their respect decreasing as the distance grows, and the most remote being the most despised. Themselves they consider in every way superior to everyone else in the world, and allow other nations a share of good qualities decreasing according to distance, the furthest off being in their view the worst. (Herodotus 1:134, 1954: 69–70)

Section II (6:3–8). The perils he observes are not one, but two, intertwined. Short-range peril stems from a contract trap. Long-range peril stems from a complacency trap. The sage will address both. First he concentrates on the pressing, short-range crisis: 'you have been trapped by the sayings of your mouth' (6:2a). The hope of release from contract suggests it was only recently entered. This crisis dominates the counsel of vv. 3–5 (Block II.A).

Yet this counsel will avail nothing unless the youth acts on the sage's advice, stirring himself to plead with the stranger to cancel his contract. Evidently the youth has a track record of inaction.

That would explain why, early on, the grandfather infuses advice regarding the contract-trap with complacency-trap advice (6:4). He proceeds to guide the youth into a vital discovery by direct observation (the classic avenue to sapiential insight, 6:6–8, Block II.B). The youth should observe that even insignificant insects behave wisely through methodical forethought and routine self-motivation. Thus the grandfather goes beyond rescue from the immediate financial contract crisis. He imparts the greater gift of lasting character reformation – provided, of course, the youth takes it to heart.

6:3–5. Regarding Persians' aversion to financial debt, Herodotus writes, 'They consider telling lies more disgraceful than anything else, and next to that, owing money. There are many reasons for their horror of debt, but the chief is their conviction that a man who owes money is bound also to tell lies' (Herodotus 1:138, 1954: 70). In Prov. 6 the sage is concerned not with debt proper, but with ill-advised liability for the debt of another, who may default on his loan.

Modern students of corporate culture identify the discipline of stirring oneself to action as a requisite skill for executives (e.g. Bossidy and Charan 2002).

Section III (6:9–11). And therein lies the lesson's ending – a sadly tragic conclusion (Section III, 6:9–11). For the youth's response in v. 10 rebuffs his father's reprimand of v. 9, insisting that he has everything 'under control'. 'Under control, indeed!' responds the grandfather. For, sooner than he can possibly realize, the indolent youth and all his fine resources will be spirited away by someone who is on the move – an apt reversal, since the youth refuses to do exactly that: he refuses to move himself into fruitful action.

We may mistakenly infer that the thief who takes advantage of the youth is a stranger – that con man of 6:1, 3. No, replies the grandfather. Were that the case, we could at least confer some blame on another. Instead it is his own laziness that will waylay the youth. In the final analysis, he will have no one to blame but his own, arrogant self. Just as the youth snared himself in v. 2, so in v. 11 the 'vagabond' and 'armed man' who robs him emerges from the youth's own indolence (for self-inflicted disaster, see 1:17–19). To commence life naive is typical. But adamantly to persist in naivety – that is profoundly tragic (cf. 9:6a).

6:10–11. Concerning the origin of this verse-pair, see 'Notes'.

Explanation

Three principles emerge from the grandfather's fifth lecture (6:1–11). The first underscores the importance of cultivating perception. In the absence of perception, we will be unable to avoid the devastating hazards hidden within alluring 'opportunities', financial or otherwise. For the 'neighbour' may prove to be a 'stranger' with devious objectives (v. 1). The contract may constitute a trap (v. 2). And relaxed inattention on our part may spell the sleep of death (vv. 4–5).

The second principle deals with how to help someone unwittingly veering towards disaster. By his example the grandfather models both compassion and candour. Both his love for the youth and the extent of imminent hazard require nothing less than concise and repeated confrontation. To do less would render him uncaring and complicit. Fear of rejection must not deter intervention.

The third principle concerns not content, but concluding persuasive technique. So concerned is the sage to achieve a convincing outcome that he closes with an unmistakable challenge. He fashions it as a rhetorical question: 'How long, lazy fellow, are you going to lie there? When are you going to get up from your sleep?' (6:9). What the youth must do is clear: he must bring his indolence to a full stop.

In case the youth may resist, the sage clinches his argument by portraying negative consequences. If he persists in indolence, the youth will wind up robbing himself (6:10–11). A clear challenge combined with a warning of negative consequences – these components model a persuasive technique worthy of emulation whenever compassion may require us to intervene with candour, intercepting those on the verge of making perilous choices without perception.

PROVERBS 6:12–15
'How can I recognize a worthless person?' (Poem 6 in Prov. 4 – 9, body behaviour theme)

Overview of Proverbs 6:12–15

In Poem 6 (6:12–15) the grandfather-sage responds to the youth's implicit question 'How can I recognize a worthless person?' By considering five body parts (and their sinister misappropriation) he enables the youth to cultivate diagnostic shrewdness. Unlike the internally focused body behaviour lecture of Poem 3 (4:20–27), this lesson ostensibly aids recognition of someone who through unprincipled conduct poses a hazard to the community. Later on, it may implicate the youth him or herself (see under Explanation, for both Poems 6 and 7, below). (For an overview of the three themes and two cycles, please refer to 'Principal themes in Proverbs 4 – 9' in the introduction to Prov. 4 – 9, above.)

The staccato expressions of this poem join with its brevity to reward fairly close scrutiny. For that reason the outline below subdivides even individual verses.

Position of this poem within Proverbs

Preceding context. In Poem 5 (6:1–11) the youth proved incorrigibly complacent – the antithesis of industry and self-motivation. While a positive response to that poem's reprimand would position the youth back on the right track, he yet would emerge vulnerable to new, negative influencers.

Poem 6 (6:12–15) addresses that deficiency, continuing from Poem 5 the shrill sense of alarm (Poems 5–7 bypass any prefatory wisdom commendation in their haste to deliver instruction). If he can help the youth recognize and avoid such a negative influencer as the worthless person, the sage will have advanced far along his quest to help youth finish well.

Ensuing context. The sinister tone of this poem will down-spiral still further in the next lecture – a brief lecture that (like Poem 6) will dispense with any prefatory wisdom commendation. There in Poem 7 (6:16–19) the subject will decline from one who is merely worthless (if that were not bad enough) to one who, in the LORD's opinion, is repugnant.

What to watch for

Distinguish between the behaviour of the worthless fellow and the consequence it brings. Notice cascading references to various body parts and their capacities. Consider whether they may form a progression. Notice contrasts with initial body-behaviour teachings in Poem 3 (4:20–27).

Translation and outline

Verse	*Translation*	*Outline*
		I. Identity and practices of a worthless person (6:12–14)
6:12a	A worthless mortal amounts to a disastrous person;	A. Fundamental identity of a worthless person: a complete liability (v. 12a)
		B. Contributing practices (vv. 12b–14b)
		1. External practices (vv. 12b–13c)
6:12b	he goes about as a twisted mouth,	a. A recruiting mouth (v. 12b)
6:13a	squinting with his eyes,	b. A collusive eye (13a)
6:13b	grinding with his foot,	c. A crushing foot (13b)
6:13c	pointing with his fingers;	d. An accusing finger (13c)
6:14a–b	perversion occupies his mind, scheming evil at every turn,	2. Internal practices: a seditious mind (v. 14a–b)
6:14c	he keeps on unleashing controversies.	A'. Fundamental activity of a worthless person: spreading strife (v. 14c)
		II. Destiny of a worthless person (v. 15)
6:15a	That is why suddenly his calamity will come,	A. Speed of demise: rapid ruin (v. 15a)
6:15b	instantly he will be broken with none to heal.	B. Permanence of demise: rapid and irreversible ruin (v. 15b)

Outline headings such as 'recruiting' mouth and 'collusive' eye seek to reflect the connotations implicit in this otherwise laconic poem. For explanation, see below under 'Comment', also under 'Form and structure'.

Notes on the text

6:12. 'A worthless mortal amounts to a disastrous person': lit. 'A worthless mortal [is] a disastrous person'.

'he goes about as a twisted mouth', *hôlēk ʿiqqešût peh*: unlike the three phrases of 6:13, this expression has no prep. Similar to *hôlēk rākîl*, 'he goes about [as] a slanderer' (11:13; 20:19), the 'twisted mouth' cryptically portrays identity rather than activity.

6:13. 'squinting with his eyes': a derisive or malicious facial expression, perhaps indicating the furrowed brow of one engaged in vicious scheming.

'grinding with his foot': lit. 'scraping or rubbing with his foot'. 'Grinding' reflects the malevolent context.

'pointing with his fingers': a gesture of ridicule in Egyptian and Sumerian wisdom literature (Jones 2019: 32).

6:14. 'perversion occupies his mind': lit. 'perversion [is] in his mind'. Devious tearing of social fabric is the connotation of 'perversion' in this context. Like 6:13–14, the sage will again associate 'perversity' with harm to friends involving non-verbal gestures with eyes and lips in 16:27–30.

'[his mind is] scheming evil at every turn': lit. 'scheming evil at all time[s]'. 'His mind' in 6:14a offers the nearest referent for 'scheming'. Thus the worthless person's mind, not his person in general, is scheming.

'he keeps on unleashing', *yĕšallēaḥ*: as the only finite verb in 6:12–14, 'to unleash' provides a delayed completion of the statement begun in v. 12a: 'A worthless mortal . . . keeps on unleashing'. Thus 'worthless mortal' serves as the subject. The durative connotation ('he keeps on') of the yiq. form *yĕšallēaḥ* is suggested by the expression *bekōl ʿēt*, 'at every turn' (v. 14b).

'controversies', *midyānîm*: K of MT preserves an Aram. spelling *mĕdanîm* (lacking the yod), while the Q supplies a more standard Hebr. spelling (shown here), with no apparent difference in meaning.

Form and structure

Borders

The upper border consists of a theme transition. The previous lecture closes by confronting indolence (6:9–11). A sketch of 'the worthless mortal' begins in v. 12.

In 6:16 begins a new theme (a catalogue of 'things the LORD loathes'), setting v. 15 as lower border for the poem beginning in 6:12. Also, summation (using 'none') escalates the intensity of deterrence in the final phrase of the 'worthless mortal' poem: the worthless person 'will be broken with none to heal' (6:15b). This starkly contrasts a positive summation of benefit, found in the first body behaviour poem (healing for one's 'entire flesh' in 4:22b, closing Section I of Poem 3).

Macrostructural features

Thematic continuity concerning the worthless individual (Sections I and II, content-based). The first verse of this poem introduces 'a worthless mortal' (6:12a), while subsequent verses describe his behaviour (vv. 12b–14, Section I) and destiny (v. 15, Section II). A distinct character – the loathsome person – will occupy the next poem (vv. 16–19).

Microstructural features

Summation (6:14b, form-based). A summation concludes the string of practices engaged by the worthless person (Block I.B, 12b–14b), 'scheming evil at every turn'. With this his malevolent practices reach their zenith.

Continuity through participles (6:12b–14b, form-based). After initially identifying the worthless fellow through a verbless clause (6:12a), there follows a series of five ptcs. describing his behaviour: 'going about', 'squinting', 'grinding', 'pointing' and 'scheming' (6:12b–14b, Block I.B), lending coherence to that block.

Framing through non-participial expressions (6:12a, 14c, form-based). Clauses before and after the five ptcs. of Block I.B (6:12b–14b) are not participial. The statement in v. 12a in Hebr. is verbless ('A worthless mortal [amounts to] a disastrous person'), while a finite verb operates in v. 14c ('he keeps on unleashing controversies'). Since they frame vv. 12b–14b (and so are designated Blocks I.A and I.A'), they evidently present the worthless person's fundamental identity (v. 12a) and fundamental activity (v. 14c).

Contrast of external and internal practices (6:12b–14b, content-based). The worthless fellow's practices distinguish external behaviours (mouth, eyes, foot, finger, in 6:12b–13c, Unit I.B.1) from those that are internal ('perversion occupies his mind, scheming evil at every turn', v. 14a–b).

Contrastive and climactic use of a finite verb, following participles (6:14c, form-based). Participles that dominate 6:12b–14b give way to a single finite verb at the close of Section I: 'he keeps on unleashing' (v. 14c; cf. Waltke 2004: 342). By reserving the finite form until the close, the grandfather conveys that the various untoward behaviours do not float about randomly. Rather, they coalesce to foment divisiveness – that most sinister rending of social fabric.

Thematic continuity and assonance in adverbs (6:15a, b, form- and content-based). The synonymous and assonantal adverbs *pitʾōm*, 'suddenly' (6:15a) and *petaʿ*, 'instantly' (v. 15b) combine to emphasize that the worthless person's destiny will arrive with inescapable rapidity, thus joining the two cola comprising Section II.

Comment

Section I (6:12–14). From the outset, the grandfather summarily assesses the worthless person as 'disastrous' (Block I.A, 6:12a). Particulars follow, in support of that assessment (Block I.B, vv. 12b–14).

A series of five body parts occupies 6:12b–14, beginning with speech ('twisted mouth') and ending with strategy ('scheming mind'). Each of the capacities associated with these parts harms the community, since together they 'unleash controversies' (v. 14c). The list outlines a progression of damage inflicted on one's neighbour.

The first body part expression reads, 'he goes about as a twisted mouth' (6:12b). Such a character mingles in the community, spreading messages that malign others, evidently hoping to recruit supporters persuaded by his slanderous words.

The second expression, 'squinting with his eyes' (6:13a), carries a malicious connotation. Elsewhere, 'squinting eyes' operate in tandem with deceitful speech calculated to harm 'peaceable residents' (Ps. 35:19–20; cf. Prov. 10:10). Just as twisted speech (Prov. 6:12b) assumes an audience, a non-verbal message transmitted by the eyes (v. 13a) similarly envisions one person signalling another. This worthless fellow thus engages in non-verbal collusion, corralling other rogues by means of a knowing signal of the eye.

The third expression, 'grinding with his foot' (6:13b), grows more obvious than subtly squinting the eyes. Feet can connote damaging force, as in crushing an egg (Job 39:15). This foot gesture foreshadows demise of the worthless fellow (Prov. 6:15), which he intended for his victim.

A passage in Isaiah illumines the fourth expression, 'pointing with his fingers' (Prov. 6:13c). 'Pointing with fingers' in Isa. 58:9 belongs to a trio of damaging practices Israel must discontinue, to gain divine aid: applying the 'yoke' (for restraint, Lev. 26:13), 'sending forth of a finger' and 'declaring disaster'. This threefold series maps a sequence of judicial travesty, beginning with an unwarranted arraignment (oppression) and leading to a false indictment (where a malicious person would implicate an innocent person by pointing with a finger; cf. Fox 2000: 221). Then follows in Isaiah a wrongful sentence (a 'declaration of disaster').

Thus 'pointing with his fingers' in the sage's teaching describes the worthless fellow when he singles out his victim before an onlooking crowd. Therefore, the progression from mouth, to eyes, to foot and to fingers traces a path that begins with secretive spreading of rumour while gathering confederates (by calculated speech), escalating to clandestine strategizing (by a winking eye), with quiet glee anticipating their evil victory (by a grinding foot), finally blossoming into boldfaced indictment of the innocent (accusatory fingers).

Fifth, the series of body expressions concludes with the 'mind', a component earning a longer description. The mind is both perverse and evil-scheming (6:14a–b). By delaying until last this mention of 'mind', the sage invites the inference that all reprehensible outward behaviours listed for the worthless person in vv. 12–13 trace to a predictable source – a mind that churns out divisive schemes, perpetually poisoning the community (ceaselessly 'unleashing controversies', v. 14c). In sum, such degeneration coursing through the body parts of 6:12b–14 explains how the individual in Poem 6 earns the designation 'a disastrous person' (v. 12a).

6:12. 'Mortal' often designates humankind as inferior to the supernatural. The next poem will turn to the supernatural, indicating the LORD's evaluation of character (6:16).

Concerning 'a twisted mouth', Fox writes, 'it describes a physical contortion . . . thought to reveal an underlying moral distortion' (2000: 220).

6:13. Concerning malicious gestures of the eye, Ben Sirach states, 'He who make hints . . . with the eye devises evil, and those who know him will avoid him' (Sirach 27.22, quoted by Fox [2000: 220], similarly Jones 2019: 50).

Section II (6:15). The worthless person's identity and practices (Section I) render his sudden and calamitous destiny wholly unsurprising (Section II, 6:15). If its abrupt arrival were not disconcerting enough (v. 15a), its irremediable thoroughness will render that consequence overwhelmingly ominous (v. 15b). Two summations towards the lecture's close escalate to extreme heights both the extent of malevolence ('at every turn', v. 14b) and the depths of consequent demise ('with none to heal', v. 15b).

To locate 'mind' last in this series contrasts the earlier body-behaviour lesson (Poem 3). There the sage presented the same sequence of body capacities as found in Poem 6 (capacities of speech, sight and ambulation in 4:24–27). But in that earlier poem 'mind' appeared before those three capacities, not at their close. Unlike Poem 6, that earlier poem offered constructive guidance, coaching the youth how to nurture his own mind: 'Against every imprisonment protect your mind, for from there life springs forth' (4:23). In contrast, this later poem describes the demise of an individual who fails to guard his own mind, which therefore devolves into an agent of communal destruction.

Explanation

If the youth had heeded the sage's alarm sounding in Poem 5 (6:1–11), he would have escaped the snare of lassitude ('How long, lazy fellow, will you lie there? When will you get up from your sleep?', 6:9). But such leaning towards laziness is not a youth's sole susceptibility. He or she may fall under the spell of other, external influences – individuals whose keen eye and sharp tongue seem heroic by their efforts to uncover fault and expose childish trust.

Today such analysis goes by the label 'deconstruction'. At its best, by encouraging thoughtful and balanced assessment of one's inherited assumptions concerning the nature of the supernatural, the worth of humans, the character of 'good', the meaning of life – 'deconstruction' of this sort forms a vital stage of any youth's maturation into responsible adulthood. It is reminiscent of Socrates' dictum 'The unexamined life is not worth living'.

Yet certain guides along the pathway of deconstruction do not talk so straightly (Prov. 6:12b), skewing argument with unsubstantiated opinion. Prejudice filters and prejudges what they see (v. 13a). So they scheme to trample down others unjustly, sometimes in the name of justice (v. 13b). As their followership swells, a mere pointing with their accusatory finger may bring giants to their knees (v. 13c). What began as a necessary exposure of wrong may, ungoverned, feed on its own success, snowballing into a community-collapsing movement that razes with no thought of rebuilding (v. 14). According to the sage, such an influencer is, in reality, a 'worthless person'.

Despite their seeming success, the end of worthless ones is predictable. The tearing-down they so love they will attain. Only they themselves will become the target suffering 'calamity', and that – 'suddenly' (6:15a).

According to the sage, the levelling agent of retribution is impersonal, nameless. This fact authorizes no vigilante group to 'settle scores' with the worthless.

Similarly absent are any who might soothe their self-inflicted brokenness (6:15b; cf. 28:17b). The worthless suffer a bleak and bitter end.

Wise is the youth – of any age – who by this poem learns to penetrate the arrogant counterpoints of devious deconstruction. Especially wise is he or she who detects and dismantles worthlessness within.

PROVERBS 6:16–19
'What about the loathsome person – how can I recognize him?' (Poem 7 in Prov. 4 – 9, body behaviour theme)

Overview of Proverbs 6:16–19

Like Poem 6 (6:12–15), the sage may have composed Poem 7 (6:16–19) in response to a question concerning character recognition: 'What about the loathsome person – how can I recognize him?' Here the sage will catalogue 'six – even seven' body behaviours distinguishing the loathsome person. As with Poem 6, the climactic liability perpetrated by such a one sows strife, thereby unravelling an entire community (cf. Fox 2000: 223).

Position of this poem within Proverbs

Preceding context. This lesson lies within eleven poems spanning Prov. 4 – 9, focusing on themes of reprimand, body behaviour and women. Like the preceding lesson (Poem 6, 6:12–15), Poem 7 (6:16–19) treats the theme of body behaviour from a negative viewpoint. A shift from the worthless person (Poem 6) to the loathsome (Poem 7) marks a moral descent. (For an overview of the three themes and two cycles, please refer to 'Principal themes in Proverbs 4 – 9' in the introduction to Prov. 4 – 9, above.)

Ensuing context. Following the teachings on body behaviour in Poems 6–7 (6:12 – 6:19), the sage will shift to the theme of women in Poems 8–10 (6:20 – 8:36). Poem 8 (6:20–35) will take up the question 'Sex between consenting adults . . . What's the harm?'

What to watch for

Notice when a given activity or attitude recurs. Observe where 'mind' appears, in relation to other elements that repeat.

Translation and outline

Verse	*Translation*	*Outline*
6:16	There are six things that the Lord loathes, even seven are personally revolting:	I. Announcement of seven sources of divine displeasure (6:16)
		II. List of seven sources of divine displeasure (vv. 17–19)
6:17a	Condescending eyes,	A. A narrow, sneering start (v. 17a)
6:17b	a deceitful tongue,	B. Speech that harms (v. 17b)
6:17c	and hands spilling innocent blood.	C. Limbs that harm (v. 17c)
6:18a	A mind scheming plans of disaster,	D. Control-centre of harm (v. 18a)
6:18b	feet that rush, racing to wrong.	C'. Limbs that harm (v. 18b)
6:19a	A testifier of lies – a deceitful witness,	B'. Speech that harms (v. 19a)
6:19b	one who unleashes controversy between brothers.	A'. An expansive, schismatic end (v. 19b)

Notes on the text

6:16. 'There are six things that the Lord loathes', *šeš-hēnnâ śānē᾿ y[a]hw[e]h*: assonance smooths the sounds surrounding the first three Hebr. words (four, if *y[a]hw[e]h* is the correct vocalization).

'are personally revolting', *tô῾ăbôt napšô*: lit. 'are the revulsions of his soul'.

6:17. 'Condescending eyes': lit. 'exalted, lofty eyes', indicating arrogance (similarly 21:4; 30:13; Jones 2019: 66–71).

6:18. 'feet that rush, racing to wrong', *raglayim měmahărôt lārûṣ lārā῾â*: lit. 'feet which hurry to run to the wrong'. 'Rush', 'racing' and 'to wrong' link assonantally in Hebr.

6:19. 'A testifier of lies – a deceitful witness', *yāpîaḥ kĕzābîm*: the term *yāpîaḥ* can represent both a finite verb (he keeps breathing out) and a noun ('a testifier'; also attested in Ugar.). The noun suits the current context better than the verb, since all other phrases in the list of seven consist of nouns or substantival forms (e.g. eyes, tongue, hands, mind, feet, one who unleashes). Within Proverbs *yāpîaḥ* occurs also in 12:17; 14:5; 14:25; 19:5; 19:9.

Form and structure

Borders

Transition from the 'worthless mortal' theme (ending 6:15) to an enumerated catalogue of 'things the Lord loathes' (beginning v. 16) marks the upper border. The last of seven anticipated traits marks the lower border (v. 19b). Also a palistrophe reaches completion in v. 19b.

Macrostructural features

Numerical anticipation (Sections I and II, form-based). The title verse (6:16, Section I) leads the reader to anticipate a catalogue of seven items. Ensuing verses supply that list (Section II, vv. 17–19).

Microstructural features

A palistrophe (6:17–19, content-based). In Section II the seven features the Lord loathes form a seven-part palistrophe rising to an intensity of divisive conduct at its pivot in 6:18a (step D; observed also by Waltke [2004: 346]). Steps C and C' are linked by aggressive wrongdoing ('hands spilling innocent blood', v. 17c; 'feet that rush, racing to wrong', v. 18b). Steps B and B' each mention 'deceitful' (vv. 17b, 19a). Steps A and A' supply the developmental start and finish of the loathsome person's malevolence, beginning with seemingly innocuous arrogance, but ending with strife that pits brother against brother (vv. 17a, 19b). It is instructive to note that, as in v. 19b, the preceding poem similarly presented 'unleashing controversy' last in its list (v. 14c).

At the palistrophe's focal point is the mind (6:18a). The mind enjoyed prominence as first in the list of Poem 3 (4:21) and last in Poem 6 (6:14).

Stairstep scheme in Poem 7							
	A	B	C	D (Pivot)	C'	B'	A'
Level D: pinnacle of instigation				a mind scheming plans of disaster (6:18a)			
Level C: active imple-mentation			and hands spilling innocent blood (6:17c)		feet that rush, racing to wrong (6:18b)		
Level B: deceptive speech		a deceitful tongue (6:17b)				a testifier of lies – a deceitful witness (6:19a)	
Level A: first step (6:17a) and final outcome (v. 19b)	conde-scending eyes (6:17a)						one who unleashes controversy between brothers (6:19b)

Comment

Section I (6:16). The poem spanning 6:16–19 begins by announcing that there are seven things the Lord loathes (v. 16). The next three verses list those seven features.

6:16. Known as a numerical poem, the 'x-plus-1' pattern conveys plentitude. While the quantity 'x' ('six', in this case) would supply sufficient evidence, there are so many (of whatever commodity is under consideration) that the poet can easily supply one more.

The fact that the Lord is the explicit source of this array escalates dynamism, raising Cycle I to a new level of solemnity at Poem 7. The Lord last appeared in a clinching comment towards the close of Poem 4 (5:21). Here he dominates the poem from the first phrase.

Section II (6:17–19). The sequential arrangement of the seven loathsome features begins interiorly. First is an attitude that regards self superior to others ('condescending eyes', 6:17a).

Before converting attitude (6:17a) to murderous action (v. 17c), the actor spreads a smokescreen of deceitful speech (v. 17b). This lying speech may serve either to lure the unwitting victim into danger, or to fool onlookers into thinking that the actor could not possibly be capable of the wrong-doing about to unfold.

Fuelled by an attitude of superiority, and buttressed by his own speech (liberated from the inconvenience of honesty), the actor then executes his murderous scheme (6:17c). The mind – that strategizing control centre – serves to coordinate those elements of attitude and action (v. 18a). To alter the course of body behaviour, one must reprogramme the mind.

The rate of evil execution reported by the sage ('feet that rush, racing to wrong', 6:18b) next indicates that the actor suffers from no constraint of conscience. As if with seared moral sensibilities, he has no need to think twice. Without hesitation he performs his evil deeds.

If then he may be arraigned in court, challenged to admit his wrongdoing, not even that solemn circumstance can coerce truth from him (6:19a). So dead set is he on self-aggrandizement.

His initial attitude of arrogance (6:17a) ultimately sows dissension even among those whose alliance of mutual aid should be unbreakable (v. 19b). Ancient societies typically placed an extremely high priority on maintaining harmony among family members. For the actor to introduce divisiveness between brothers would mark a climactic disregard for communal values. Thus unrestrained by moral commitments, what began as innocuous personal preferences (an attitude of arrogance) has metastasized, unravelling the very fabric of community.

6:17a. When focusing on the body parts (rather than the attitudes and actions illustrated by those parts) some have observed a top-to-bottom arrangement, starting with the eyes in 6:17a (Meinhold 1991: 115; Fox 2000: 223). However, given that in themselves the body parts are value-neutral, progression of thought surrounding attitudes and actions associated with body parts (rather than the parts themselves) appears more consistent with the sage's ultimate goals.

6:17c. No longer are hands represented merely by fingers that point or indict (cf. 6:13c). Now the hands commit murder.

6:18a. A mind scheming 'disaster', *ʾāben*, recalls the 'disastrous person', *ʾîš ʾāben*, of Poem 6 (6:12a).

6:18b. No longer do the feet symbolically grind the ground – indicating how they intend to crush the neck of an opponent (6:13b). Now they openly and swiftly travel to commit crime.

6:19a. Now talk escalates from conspiracy (6:12b) to boldfaced lies in court proceedings, resulting in undeserved conviction and unfair punishment. The colon 'A testifier of lies – a deceitful witness' is unusual since it layers two titles for the sixth trait (cf. next-to-last element in Poem 6, 6:14a).

6:19b. Although dissolution of community may seem anticlimactic after the vivid violence of 'hands spilling innocent blood' (6:17c) or 'feet that rush, racing to wrong' (v. 18b), by reserving the breakdown of society for last, the sage portrays collective harm exceeding the damage consisting of individual travesties of justice. As isolated travesties accumulate they will snowball, loosening an avalanche a normally resilient community will prove powerless to resist. Swept away, it will doom a host of innocents. It is no wonder that the LORD would assess such a sequence as loathsome.

Explanation

How should the grandfather's teaching concerning the loathsome person in Poem 7 (6:16–19) affect his audience, both then and now? By way of review, the sage had most recently confronted the pupil with a stiff reprimand aimed at breaking him free from snares triggered by chasing easy money (guaranteeing loans) and by coasting into complacency (Poem 5, 6:1–11). When that lecture proved insufficient, the youth must have felt stung by the implication that his complacency was consigning him to a place with the worthless, known for collusion and conspiracy – individuals who destroy community through divisiveness (Poem 6, 6:12–15).

Against this double backdrop (reprimand in Poem 5 and warning of worthlessness in Poem 6), through Poem 7 (6:16–19) the grandfather supplies two strategies to advance caring confrontation one step further. They involve specificity and divine assessment.

Unlike the merely suggestive body behaviours of Poem 6 (twisted mouth, squinting eyes, grinding foot, pointing fingers), those in Poem 7 portray with specificity the sorts of conduct from which one must abstain. Unambiguously the sage indicts 'condescending eyes', 'a deceitful tongue', 'hands spilling innocent blood', 'a mind scheming plans of disaster', 'feet that rush, racing to wrong', 'a testifier of lies, a deceitful witness' and 'one who unleashes controversy between brothers' (6:17–19). After first examining ourselves under this halogen lamp, we must not shrink from warning with specificity those wandering ones for whom we deeply care.

The grandfather's second strategy in Poem 7 consists of connecting the youth directly to divine assessment. Here, at the zenith of his lectures on body behaviours, he ignores any personal authority he might claim for his teaching. For, in the final analysis, it is God with whom the youth – and we, ourselves – must reckon.

Over the next three poems the grandfather will resume the topic of women (6:20 – 8:36). The youth will learn how best to respond to literal and metaphoric women, whether positive or negative.

PROVERBS 6:20–35
'Sex between consenting adults . . . What's the harm?' (Poem 8 in Prov. 4 – 9, influential women theme)

Overview of Proverbs 6:20–35

How should the youth respond to two women? This forms the subject of Poem 8 (Prov. 6:20–35). Although nameless, the first woman corresponds to Lady Wisdom (note 'commandment' and 'instruction' in v. 23). She offers legitimate protection and mental companionship ('she will talk with you', v. 22b).

The second woman appears variously as 'prostitute' (6:26) and 'neighbour's wife' (v. 29). Towards her the youth will sense erotic attraction (vv. 25, 27, 29, 32). Since this lecture principally warns against the folly of satisfying sexual drives illicitly, it is as if the pupil had quizzed his mentor, 'Sex between consenting adults . . . What's the harm?'

Position of this poem within Proverbs

Preceding context. Poem 8 (6:20–35) expands on the theme of influential women that first appeared in the final poem of Cycle I (Poem 4, 5:1–23). Both negative and positive women appear in each of Poems 4 and 8.

The poems in Cycle II leading up to Poem 8 (i.e. Poems 5–7, Prov. 6:1–19) deal with the themes of reprimand and body behaviour, as did the poems of Cycle I that preceded Poem 4 (i.e. Poems 2–3). While Fox notes the thematic continuity joining Poems 4 (5:1–23) and 8 (6:20–35), he does not observe the similarities linking what precedes Poem 4 (Poems 2–3, Prov. 4:10–27) with what precedes Poem 8 (Poems 5–7, Prov. 6:1–19; Fox 2000: 237). For an overview of the three themes and two cycles, please refer to 'Principal themes in Proverbs 4 – 9' in the introduction to Prov. 4 – 9, above.

Ensuing context. Like Poem 8 (6:20–35), Poem 9 (7:1–27) begins with a five-verse exhortation to prize wisdom, personified as Lady Wisdom

(7:1–5). Then follows an extensive chronicle of seduction, a virtual novella depicting a youth who willingly succumbs to the sly appeal of the seductress.

What to watch for

Notice the broad sections that describe distinct women – one who brings benefit and another who brings harm, with a Janus-styled segue linking the two. Observe how the sage buttresses imperatives both by incentives and by illustrations. Consider where in the poem the husband appears, with consequent persuasive impact.

Translation and outline

Verse	*Translation*	*Outline*
		I. Wisdom commendation: prize wisdom, the protectress (6:20–24) A. Imperatives to prize wisdom (vv. 20–21)
6:20	Safeguard, my son, your father's commandment, and do not neglect your mother's instruction.	1. Value parental instruction . . . (v. 20)
6:21	Bind them upon your mind always; tie them about your neck.	2. . . . As precious jewellery (v. 21)
6:22	As you travel about she will escort you; as you lie down she will guard you, and then you will awaken – it is she who will talk with you.	B. Threefold value of wisdom: guidance, protection, companionship (v. 22)
		C. Explanation of wisdom's effectiveness (vv. 23–24)
6:23	For a lamp – that's what a commandment is; instruction is illumination; and a life-giving way – that's what disciplinary reprimands are,	1. Illumination and safe transit . . . (v. 23)
6:24	In order to guard you from Dame Evil, from the slipperiness of a foreign tongue.	2. . . . That provide protection from a sly woman (v. 24)

Verse	Translation	Outline
		II. Caution against succumbing to superficial charm of the huntress (start of wisdom content, vv. 25–31) A. Imperative and incentive against adultery (vv. 25–26)
6:25	Don't let your mind fantasize about her beauty, and don't let her captivate you with her eyelashes.	1. Imperative: restrain your susceptibility to beauty's appeal (v. 25)
6:26	For a prostitute's fee may range as much as a loaf of bread. But in the case of a married woman – it is for a precious life that she will prowl.	2. Incentive: for beauty may bait a deadly trap (v. 26)
		B. Two illustrations that argue against adultery (vv. 27–31) 1. First illustration: fire and the certainty of pain (vv. 27–29) a. The certainty of pain for one playing with fire (vv. 27–28)
6:27	Can a fellow rake fire into his lap without his clothes getting burned?	i. Lap on fire (v. 27)
6:28	If a fellow walks about on the embers, will his feet not become scorched?	ii. Feet on fire (v. 28)
6:29	So is one who cohabits with his neighbour's wife: none who 'touch' her will be exonerated.	b. Certain pain for adultery (v. 29)
6:30	They would not despise the thief, if he would steal to fill his appetite, when he may be hungry.	2. Second illustration: theft and the certainty of punishment (vv. 30–31)
6:31	Yet when he is discovered he must repay sevenfold – he must forfeit his entire household property.	
		III. Recap: certainty and explanation of punishment (vv. 32–35) A. Certainty of punishment for adultery (vv. 32–33)

6:32 One who commits adultery with a woman is senseless. He is self-destructive – he himself keeps on doing it.	1. The self-destructive folly of adultery (v. 32)
6:33 Blows and ignominy will he find, and his shame will not be wiped away.	2. Indelible harm following adultery (v. 33)
6:34 For a strong man's wrath amounts to jealousy, and he will not be lenient on the day of vengeance.	B. Explanation of punishment for adultery: the enraged husband (vv. 34–35)
6:35 No ransom could win his approval; nor will he yield, though you may multiply a bribe.	

Notes on the text

6:22. 'she will escort you', *tanḥeh ʾōtāk*: after referencing parental 'commandment' and 'instruction' (both f. nouns in 6:20) twice with 'them' (m. pl. pronoun in v. 21), the poet personifies that parental teaching in v. 22 (just as 4:6, 8–9). Now the teaching will 'escort', 'guard', 'awaken' and 'talk with you'. Fittingly, the poet assigns the personal pronoun 'she' – corresponding to Lady Wisdom. She embodies the sole guardian capable of defending against the menace of Dame Evil, who will appear in v. 24 and dominate vv. 25–31. To follow versions that render *tanḥeh* of v. 22 with 3 pl. pronoun, 'they', substantially dilutes the poet's pungent imagination (so NRSV, NASB, NIV; NJPS 'it').

6:23. 'For a lamp – that's what a commandment is', *kî nēr miṣwâ*: lit. 'for a lamp [is] a commandment'. By fronting the new information in a verbless expression, the poet emphasizes 'lamp'. Similar is the expression 'and a life-giving way – that's what disciplinary reprimands are', *wĕderek ḥayyîm tôkĕḥôt mûsār*: lit. 'a way of life [are] reprimands of reproof'. The psalmist associates *nēr*, 'lamp', and *ʾôr*, 'illumination' (in that sequence), with divine communication ('your word', *dĕbārekā*, Ps. 119:105).

6:24. 'from Dame Evil', *mēʾēšet rāʿ*: lit. 'a woman [or wife] of evil' (NIV 'a wayward woman'; ESV 'the adulteress'). Since the poem will soon specify involvement with a married woman (6:26, 29, 32), the poet may have chosen *mēʾēšet rāʿ* to suggest she is not unmarried (rather than the adj. *ʾiššâ rāʿâ*, 'an evil woman', analogous to 'evil man' in 29:6). The LXX specifies that she is married (*gynaikos hypandrou*). NRSV follows LXX (which does not mention 'evil'), rendering 'the wife of another' (cf. 'neighbour's wife', 6:29). The close assonance linking *ʾēšet rāʿ*, 'Dame Evil', v. 24, and *ʾēšet rēʿēhû*, 'his neighbour's wife', evidences the sage's literary skill.

'a foreign tongue', *lāšôn nŏkriyyâ*: for this to read 'tongue of a foreign woman', 'tongue' would need to be vocalized *lĕšôn* (const. form; cf. 'tongue of the adulteress' [NASB and NRSV]). Since it is not, this must be a rare instance of 'tongue' with f. gender, modified by the f. adj. *nŏkriyyâ*, 'foreign'.

6:26. 'For a prostitute's fee . . . But in the case of a married woman', *kî bĕʿad-ʾiššâ zônâ . . . wĕʾēšet ʾîš*: lit. 'a prostitute's fee . . . ; but a man's wife'. The grandfather is building a case for greater vigilance due to the greater hazard attending adulterous promiscuity, when compared with the hazard of prostitution. As a noun, *baʿad*, 'price', occurs only here in the HB (*HALOT*). More common is the prep. of the same spelling, meaning 'on behalf of'.

6:27. 'fellow . . . fire', *ʾîš ēš*: the terms 'fellow' and 'fire' are adjacent and assonantal in Hebr. The inverted assonance linking *ʾîš ēš*, 'fellow . . . fire', 6:27, and *ʾēšet ʾîš*, 'married woman', v. 26, transmits a haunting warning: involvement with a married woman brings fire to a fellow.

'lap': rendered 'bosom' in 5:20.

6:28. 'If a fellow walks about . . . will his feet not . . . ?': although no interrogative particle recurs in 6:28, the tone of a rhetorical question extends from v. 27.

In Hebr., 'feet' at times may serve as a euphemism for sexual organs (Waltke 2004: 356). Given the caution against sexual promiscuity central to this poem, mention of 'scorched feet' may imply painful urination, a symptom of sexually transmitted diseases (so also 'fire in his lap' in 6:27).

6:29. 'who "touch"', *hanōgēaʿ*: while the literal meaning is 'touch', quotation marks signal that this expression in 6:29b serves as a euphemism for cohabitation, specifically referred to in v. 29a (Waltke 2004: 357). Fox understands 'touch' literally, making 'the admonition all the more uncompromising: Don't even go *near* her' (2000: 233; emphasis original). In a clever retributive reversal, the grandfather will use the root underlying 'touch' to indicate 'blows' that will befall the promiscuous man (v. 33).

6:30. 'if he would steal', *kî yignôb*: rendering *kî* as 'if' due to hunger introduced as a mitigating circumstance in the balance of the verse.

6:32. 'self-destructive', *mašḥît napšô hûʾ*: lit. 'life-destroying' or 'self-destroying'. The term here rendered 'self' was rendered 'appetite' in v. 30. The thief's justifiable stealing saves his self/appetite, while the adulterer's stealing destroys his self/appetite – evidence of the folly of such actions.

'keeps on doing it', *yaʿăśennâ*: the choice of yiq. here after ptcs. ('commits adultery' and 'self-destructive') suggests a durative connotation.

6:33. 'Blows', *negaʿ*: same root as 'touch' in 6:29, but now with the connotation of injury.

6:34. 'strong man', *gāber*: a single word in Hebr., *geber*, refers to a male community member, including those capable of defending others ('the human male in his strength and competency', Waltke 2004: 360).

6:35. 'No ransom could win his approval', *lōʾ yiśśāʾ pĕnê kol-kōper*: lit. 'he will not lift the face of any ransom'. For a superior person to 'lift the face' of those who approach is to grant them favourable audience. Until accorded such favour, a suppliant would respectfully maintain a downward gaze. Capability (negated) should be inferred from the yiq. conjugation of 'to lift face', based on the context of futility ('nor will he yield').

Form and structure

Borders
A theme of marital fidelity beginning in 6:20 forms the upper border, displacing the preceding poem's theme 'things the Lord loathes'.

Use of recap (6:32–35), inclusio and summation indicate the lower border in v. 35. For inclusio and summation, see under 'Macrostructural features', below.

Macrostructural features
Wisdom commendation followed by wisdom content (Sections I and II–III, content-based). The lecture opens with a section commending the protective properties of wisdom (Section I, 6:20–24). The notion of safeguarding the youth expands in the wisdom content comprising the remainder of this lecture (Sections II–III, vv. 25–35).

Thematic continuity involving influential women (Sections I–III, content-based). Teachings involving influential women characterize Sections I, II and III, whether by f. pronoun (Lady Wisdom is implied in pronouns of 6:22), or by name ('Dame Evil', 6:24). The adulteress dominates Section II (vv. 25–31), while in Section III she is implied through references to her involvement in adultery and by mention of her offended husband (vv. 32–35).

Inclusio by resuming second person (Sections I and III, form-based). Waltke observes that an inclusio joins the imperatives (second person) of Section I with the second person appearing in Section III: 'though you may multiply a bribe' (6:35b; 2004: 350, 361).

Summations at conclusions (Sections II and III, form-based). Three phrases employ a summation, each rendering the term *kōl*. The statement 'none who touch her will be exonerated' concludes Unit II.B.1 (6:29). The statement 'he must forfeit his entire household property' concludes Section II (v. 31), just as the statement 'No ransom could win his approval' closes the entire poem (v. 35, Section III).

Reversal involving 'touch' and 'blows' (Sections II and III, form- and content-based). A reversal involving pain and pleasure involves the root *ngʿ*. 'Touch' in 6:29 euphemistically describes the transgressor's illicit sexual liaison (*nōgēaʿ*). 'Blows' in v. 33 describes corporal punishment inflicted on the adulterer (*negaʿ*).

Reversal by repetition of *nepeš* (Sections II and III, form- and content-based). The terms 'appetite' (6:30) and 'self' (v. 32) render the Hebr. *nepeš*. A reversal is at work, since the first benefits (stealing food to preserve the thief's life), while the second harms (destroying one's own life through adultery).

Microstructural features

Imperatives forming a quatrain (6:20–21, form-based). The quatrain spanning 6:20–21 coheres by imperatives found in each colon: safeguard, do not neglect, bind and tie.

Description of asset, followed by purpose (6:23–24, content-based). Several phrases describing wisdom's teaching (6:22) are linked to a statement explaining its purpose (v. 23). Wisdom protects from Dame Evil.

Envelope structure involving repetition of 'commandment' and 'instruction' (6:20, 23, form-based). The nouns 'commandment' and 'instruction' appear in the initial verses of Block I.A and I.C (6:20, 23). Consequently these blocks frame and elevate the lengthy v. 22 (a tricolon comprising Block I.B).

Wisdom commendation consisting of imperatives with benefits, followed by explanation (6:20–24, content-based). The three blocks of Section I cohere as a series of imperatives (Block I.A, 6:20–21) leading to three benefits (Block I.B, v. 22), supported by a quatrain explaining why those benefits result (Block I.C, vv. 23–24). Fox similarly regards vv. 23–24 as 'parenthetical' (2000: 229). All these commend pursuit of wisdom.

Inclusio involving protection (6:20, 24, content-based). Waltke observes that the synonyms 'safeguard', *nṣr*, opening 6:20, and 'guard', *šmr*, opening v. 24, surround Section I as an inclusio (2004: 350). These operate reciprocally, so that as the pupil safeguards wisdom teaching, that teaching will guard the pupil.

Punishment and its explanation (6:32–35, content-based). Section III begins by recapping the certainty of punishment following adultery (6:32–33). Then the sage explains the source of that punishment: the offended husband's rage, introduced by 'for', *kî* (vv. 34–35).

Comment

Section I (6:20–24). With language paralleling the start of Prov. 3, Section I begins by charging the youth to value highly the instruction his parents delivered to him (Block I.A, 6:20–21). This imperatival portion the sage balances with an incentive portion, introduced with explanatory 'for', *kî* (Block I.C, vv. 23–24). Lodged between imperatives of Block I.A and the explanations of Block I.C (see envelope structure, under 'Microstructural features', above), the sage showcases in Block I.B a threefold benefit of

(a) guidance when the youth is moving about, (b) protection when he rests and (c) companionship when he wakes (v. 22).

Portrayal of wisdom as a lamp (6:23) suggests that even when waking during predawn darkness, wisdom will protect from treachery fostered by Dame Evil (v. 24). In the next lecture her slippery deception will again reappear as darkness falls (7:5, 9). For the sage, wisdom's worth rests in her ability to dispel various shades of darkness, not least of which lies in promiscuity's nocturnal appeal.

6:20. Only here among the grandfather-sage's lectures (Prov. 4 – 9) are both parents connected with wisdom training. The father-sage's lectures (Prov. 1 – 3) credit both parents in 1:8.

6:21. 'Bind . . . , always tie them on your neck' envisions wisdom as an ornament (cf. 7:3). When, later on, the sage-son would write his own counsel, he would model much of 3:1–26 on 6:20–24. The instructions to bind and write are reminiscent of the Shema (Deut. 6:8–9).

6:22. As a tricolon, the length of 6:22 underscores the importance of wisdom's manifold care. Beyond guidance (v. 22a) and protection (v. 22b), wisdom's greatest benefit is this: she can converse and reason, weigh and debate, until – following those dawn conversations – the youth will be ready to engage the day, better prepared for whatever challenges may arise.

6:23. The terms 'reproof' and 'discipline' are not only adjacent (as in 5:12) but also operate in const., yielding the intensified expression 'disciplinary reprimands'. These the grandfather evaluates on a par with 'the life-giving way'. In so doing he offers one of the loftiest endorsements for reprimand as a premier form of wisdom.

6:24. The protection from foreign Dame Evil with her slippery speech is closely paralleled in 7:5, suggesting that Poem 9 (7:1–27) expands and reinforces Poem 8 (6:20–35).

Section II (6:25–31). Without delay, Section II issues a prohibition against the earliest imaginings of adultery (fantasizing, 6:25). The incentive supporting this imperative is as extreme as the prohibition of v. 25 is incisive: whom she lures, the adulteress escorts to death (v. 26). This quatrain (vv. 25–26) comprises the first block of Section II.

For emphasis, the sage follows the imperative and incentive of 6:25–26 with a pair of illustrations portraying inevitable pain (burning, Unit II.B.1, vv. 27–29) and punishment (Unit II.B.2, vv. 30–31) the youth will suffer, if he allows himself to be swayed by the adulteress's slippery words and disarming beauty. The pain of burning escalates from scorching the outer clothing (v. 27) to blistering the soles of one's feet (v. 28; Waltke 2004: 356).

6:25. Women's use of cosmetics from ancient times to enhance the appeal of their eyes is well attested, both by text (2 Kgs 9:30) and by mixing palettes and small spoons recovered by archaeologists (Waltke 2004: 354).

6:26. To the prostitute the youth will forfeit some of the contents of his wallet so she may buy a loaf, while to the married woman he will forfeit his very life as a hunting trophy.

6:31. Israelite law required full restitution. 'Sevenfold' implies generally a repayment that would far exceed the original theft (Fox 2000: 234).

Section III (6:32–35). After describing in detail the sort and certainty of harm awaiting any who succumb to the wiles of Dame Evil (Section II, 6:25–31), the entire poem ends by recapping the certainty of punishment (vv. 32–33, Block III.A; note the addition of shame as a deterrent) and by explaining the source of that punishment, namely the aggrieved husband (vv. 34–35, Block III.B). Bribes cannot be amassed in magnitude sufficient to buy-off the offended and enraged husband.

6:34–35. Unlike the seductress of Poem 4 (5:1–23), the huntress in Poem 8 is married. Her husband's rage will render the youth's promiscuous involvement with his wife supremely regrettable.

Explanation

While the positive woman portrayed in Poem 8 (6:20–35) is figurative (she is Lady Wisdom, yet unnamed), the negative woman is not. By adding to the cast of characters the negative woman's husband, the sage warns that both she and the penalties her offended husband will inflict must be avoided at all cost.

After distinguishing between figurative and literal, one may observe four lessons the grandfather has woven into the tapestry of this lecture. First, any truly interested in wisdom must devote themselves to it, with more than a passing acquaintance (6:21).

Second, those who pursue wisdom must not balk at receiving reproof. Reprimand offers the richest deposits of wisdom, and constitutes the very path of life (6:23).

Third, wisdom's benefits surpass the superficial allure offered by any adulteress, adding neither pain nor shame. Wisdom's care is continual, dispelling darkness and posting guard (6:22–23). Beyond direction and protection, wisdom promises dialogue that fosters instruction (v. 22b).

Fourth, the cost of adultery far exceeds any supposed benefit. Superficial allure only hides a hunt in which the youth is himself the prey (6:25–26). The offended husband can be counted on to ensure that penalties of pain and shame are both costly and non-negotiable (vv. 34–35).

The theme of the married seductress will continue in the next poem (Poem 9, 7:1–27). Instead of lecture, there the grandfather will employ story, unfolding as an eyewitness account.

PROVERBS 7:1–27
'When it feels so right, how could it be so wrong?' (Poem 9 in Prov. 4 – 9, influential women theme)

Overview of Proverbs 7:1–27

The poem spanning Prov. 7 deepens the caution against illicit sex established in the preceding lecture (6:20–35). The sage chronicles how in the case of one hapless youth a sensory assault awakened lusty feelings that overpowered and disarmed his reasoned resistance. In the end, his grisly demise will unfold as graphically as did his sweet seduction. In this manner the sage answers his son's implicit question 'When it feels so right, how could it be so wrong?'

By this eyewitness account the sage takes up the high-stakes 'challenge of making his son feel [the woman's] seduction . . . in such a way that she becomes utterly repugnant to him' (Waltke 2004: 367). The youth's only hope lies in a tenacious attachment to Lady Wisdom and Miss Insight (7:1–5).

Position of this poem within Proverbs

Preceding context. Poem 9 (7:1–27) is the second of three poems within Cycle II devoted to the theme of influential women. Poem 8 (6:20–35) set the scene by describing both the protection Lady Wisdom can provide, together with the considerable harm the youth will inflict on himself if he succumbs to the flirtatious adulteress, Dame Evil (6:20–35). Now in Poem 9 (7:1–27) the sage will chronicle in greater detail both the adulteress's wiles and the youth's deadly demise. (For an overview of the three themes and two cycles, please refer to 'Principal themes in Proverbs 4 – 9' in the introduction to Prov. 4 – 9, above.)

Ensuing context. In Poem 10 (8:1–36) the grandfather will deliver the third poem concerning influential women within Cycle II – an inventory of Lady Wisdom's overwhelming assets. Thus the caution in Prov. 7 (to avoid the seductress at all costs) negatively contrasts the positive recommendation of Lady Wisdom in Prov. 8.

What to watch for

Notice how the shift from warning against promiscuity (Poem 8, 6:20–35) to the present use of a story on the same topic (Poem 9, 7:1–27) intensifies the impact of principles already presented, including stratagems employed by the seductress, and deadly consequences of succumbing to her allures. Observe the effect produced by restricting to the outer two sections the use of imperatives and the voc. 'son(s)'. Consider the role of various references to 'house', as well as elements of architecture and furnishings. Appreciate the cumulative effect of abundant detail.

Translation and outline

Verse	Translation	Outline
		I. Wisdom commendation: compounded exhortations to prize wisdom, as a close relative (7:1–5) A. Imperatives to prize wisdom (vv. 1–4)
7:1	My son, guard my words, and my commands are what you should shelter within you.	1. Guard parental sayings (v. 1)!
7:2	Guard my commands and live! And guard my teaching, as the pupil of your eye.	2. Yes, guard directives deeply (v. 2)!
7:3	Bind them about your fingers, write them on the slate of your mind.	3. Even internalize wisdom indelibly (v. 3)!
7:4	Say to Lady Wisdom, 'My sister are you!', and 'Kin!' may you call to Miss Insight.	4. With relational bonds, cherish wisdom (v. 4)!
7:5	In order to guard you from the strange woman, from the foreign woman – her words she has made slippery.	B. Incentive for prizing wisdom: reciprocal care (v. 5)
		II. A tragic story of one who did not prize wisdom (wisdom content, vv. 6–23) A. From my window I saw a senseless youth (vv. 6–9)
7:6	Indeed, at the window of my house, from my window-lattice I peered down,	1. I noticed . . . (v. 6)
7:7	And then I spied among the naive – I determined to perceive among the sons – a senseless young man.	2. . . . A naive youth (v. 7)
7:8	He was passing through the lane near her corner, he kept striding along the way to her house,	3. . . . Whose steps led in her direction (v. 8)
7:9	At twilight, as day was setting, on into the core of night and deep darkness.	4. . . . As all was growing profoundly dark (v. 9)

	B. . . . And I saw a seductive woman (vv. 10–23)
	1. I noticed how she appears (vv. 10–13)
7:10 At once a woman was there to meet him – seductive of dress and sly of heart.	a. Now an interceptor, clothed and cloaked . . . (v. 10)
7:11 A raucous woman is she and stubborn, her feet never remain long in her house.	b. . . . She prowls a circuit (vv. 11–12)
7:12 Now in the lane, now in the plazas, along every corner she keeps on lurking.	
7:13 In the midst of this she took hold of him and kissed him; she steeled her gaze and then said to him,	c. . . . And attacks with lips (v. 13)
	2. I heard how softly she assaults him with words (vv. 14–20)
7:14 'I had needed to offer some fellowship sacrifices – today I fulfilled my vows!	a. First, she dismantles spiritual defences (v. 14)
7:15 That is why I came out to meet you, to be on the lookout especially for you! And then I found you!	b. Then she woos with affirmation of his worth (v. 15)
7:16 With covers I have spread my couch – embroidered Egyptian linen.	c. Next she paints a picture of her lair – a sensory escapade (vv. 16–17)
7:17 I have perfumed my bed with myrrh, aloes and cinnamon.	
7:18 Come! Let us drink our fill of erotic sensations until morning. Let us delight ourselves in love!	d. Now for the sensuous invitation . . . (v. 18)
7:19 For the husband is not in his house; he has been journeying for quite some time.	e. . . . With assurances of safety (vv. 19–20)
7:20 A moneybag he took with him; at the full moon he will come to his house'.	
	3. I saw that the assault succeeded (vv. 21–23)

Verse	*Translation*	*Outline*
7:21	She steered him aside with her persuasive barrage; with her slippery lips she kept on seducing him.	a. Smooth lips seduced him (v. 21)
7:22	He is going after her, all of a sudden, – like an ox to slaughter he will enter, – like an ankle bangle to a fool's reproof,	b. So off he goes to his deadly destination (vv. 22–23)
7:23	Until an arrow shall thrust deep into his liver, – like the rushing of a bird into a net, unaware that it will cost him his life.	
		III. A closing exhortation to avoid the seductress's seduction (vv. 24–27)
7:24	So now, sons, listen to me! And pay attention to the words of my mouth.	A. Wisdom commendation: a closing exhortation (v. 24)
		B. Wisdom content: an instruction with incentives (vv. 25–27)
7:25	Don't let your mind deviate towards her ways; don't wander about in her paths.	1. Instruction: maintain mental boundaries . . . (v. 25)
		2. Incentives (vv. 26–27)
7:26	For many are the pierced whom she has felled, and countless are all her slain.	a. . . . Due to her high casualty rate (v. 26)
7:27	Her house amounts to Sheol-bound ways – descending to the dark chambers of death.	b. . . . And her deadly destinations (v. 27)

Notes on the text

7:1. 'my commands are what', *ûmiṣwōtay*: 'my words', *ʾămāray* (7:1a), intensifies to 'my commands', *ûmiṣwōtay* (v. 1b); emphasized by fronting the object before the verb 'you should shelter'. Or else 7:1b would likely have begun with imperative *wiṣpōn*, 'and shelter', analogous to imperative *weḥĕyēh*, 'and live' (v. 2a).

'you should shelter': obligation inferred from yiq., in view of imperative 'guard' (7:1a).

7:4. 'to Lady Wisdom . . . to Miss Insight': lit. 'to wisdom . . . to insight'. Titles 'Lady' and 'Miss' are inferred from 'sister' and 'kin', reinforced by personification that pervades Prov. 7, 8.

'may you call': best understood as yiq. of obligation (cf. 'you should shelter', 7:1b). 'To call' escalates the level of vocal energy beyond 'to say' (v. 4a).

7:5. 'her words she has made slippery': lit. made smooth, a metaphor for flattery (cf. 2:16, 'Notes'). 'Slippery' returns in 7:21.

7:6. 'window', *ḥallôm*: derives from *ḥll*, 'to pierce'; presumably because a window 'pierces' the wall where it is located. The root *ḥll* will describe the youth's fatal end (7:26).

7:7. 'I determined to perceive among the sons – a senseless young man', *ʾabînâ babānîm naʿar ḥăsar lēb*: assonance joins this phrase together, while 'perceive' and 'senseless' (lit. 'lacking mind') vividly differentiate the sage and youth. 'Determined' derives from cohort. of *byn*, 'to perceive'.

7:8. 'He was passing through the lane', *ʿōbēr*: after the qat. form 'I peered' (7:6b) followed by wayyiq. 'And then I spied' (v. 7a), the ptc. *ʿōbēr* in v. 8 then reports what the observer espied: '[the youth] was passing'.

'kept striding', *yiṣʿād*: durative 'to keep on', inferred from shift to yiq. For metered, determined progress that defies disruption, see *ṣʿd* in Hab. 3:12.

7:10. 'seductive of dress', *šît zônâ*: lit. 'a garment of a prostitute'.

'and sly of heart', *ûnĕṣurat lēb*: lit. 'covert of mind' or 'of motive'.

7:11. 'stubborn', *sōrāret*: this term always describes 'a person incorrigibly defiant to proper authority' (Fox 2000: 244).

'never remain long', *lōʾ yiškĕnû*: 'never' is inferred from durative connotation of yiq. conjugation. 'Not-at-her-home' describes her consistent pattern: she may be found at someone else's home, perhaps, but cares not for her own.

7:12. 'Now . . . now', *paʿam . . . paʿam*: lit. 'sometimes . . . sometimes'. Since *paʿam* may also be rendered 'foot', a wordplay here may convey that this woman traipses about as her restless feet take her hither and thither (Fox 2000: 245).

'she keeps on lurking', *teʾĕrōb*: durative inferred from yiq. conjugation.

7:13. 'In the midst of this she took hold of him and kissed him', *wĕheḥĕzîkâ wĕnāšĕqâ-llô*: after a dearth of finite verbs across 7:8–12 (only 'he kept striding', 'her feet never remain long' and 'she keeps lurking'), the sage disrupts the dense descriptive atmosphere by launching two finite verbs in rapid succession, as if a stealthily stalking lioness has suddenly pounced upon her prey: 'she took hold of him and kissed him' (v. 13a). The weqat. forms suit well these simultaneous (not sequential) manoeuvres. The phrase 'in the midst of this' is inferred to reflect the abrupt transition from description to action.

'she steeled her gaze', *hʿēzâ pānêhā*: lit. 'she made her face firm' (cf. 21:29).

7:14. 'I had needed to', *ʿālāy*: lit. 'upon me'; plpf. tense inferred since the obligation was prior to act of sacrificing, which was complete before encountering the youth.

'fellowship sacrifices', *šĕlāmîm*: sometimes rendered 'peace sacrifices' or 'sacrifices of well-being', these comprised a typical response when a petition had been divinely granted. 'Fellowship' involves the same root as 'to fulfil', occurring later in the verse. The woman's report of a recent sacrifice conveys she consequently has enough meat (a dietary luxury) left over to share with friends (Fox 2000: 246; Waltke 2004: 377; cf. Lev. 7:15). If her sacrifice involved a Canaanite fertility cult, she would have needed a sex partner such as the gullible youth to finish her pagan ritual (Waltke 2004: 377).

7:15. 'to be on the lookout especially for you': lit. 'to be on the lookout for your face'.

'And then I found you', *wāʾemṣāʾeka*: emphasis connoted by energic form (cf. GKC §58.i).

7:16. 'covers . . . I have spread', *marbadîm . . . rābadtî*: sharing a single root, these terms generate assonance.

'my couch', *ʿaršî*: a divan or couch. This term's capacity to refer to a bed becomes more transparent with the mention of *miškābî*, 'my bed', in 7:17.

'linen', *ʾēṭûn*: a loanword from Egyptian *idmy*, referring to linen dyed red (*HALOT*, s.v. '*ʾēṭûn*'). Egyptians' skill in producing high-quality linen was legendary in ancient commerce. The fact that 'covers' and 'linen' appear only here in the HB suggests that the luxurious furnishings add to the woman's appeal (Fox 2000: 247).

7:18. 'erotic sensations', *dōdîm*: lust is indicated by the context of sexual seduction (*HALOT*).

7:19. 'the husband', *hāʾîš*: lit. 'the man', presumably her husband. Notice the relational formality, even chill, implied by omission of the poss. pronoun in 'my husband', *ʾîšî* (cf. Fox 2000: 248).

'he has been journeying for quite some time', *hālak bĕderek merāḥôq*: cf. Isa. 22:11 and 25:1 regarding *rḥq* as temporal; if *rḥq* is understood spatially, then 'he has gone on a distant trip'. The husband's travels may connect to his family's foreign heritage (Prov. 7:5).

7:21. 'her persuasive barrage', *rōb liqḥāh*: lit. 'the mass of her instruction'.

The root for 'slippery', *ḥlq*, in 7:21b employs the same consonants as 'persuasive' in 7:21a (*lqḥ*), but transposed.

'she kept on seducing him', *tadîḥennû*: the shift from the qat. conjugation in 'she steered him aside' to the yiq. conveys a durative tone. The seductress keeps applying her ploys to ensure that her prey, now captured, will not escape.

7:22. 'all of a sudden', *pitʾom*: lit. 'suddenly'. LXX renders, 'feather-brained', *kepphōtheis*, evidently reading *pĕtāʾyim*, 'naive ones', for *pitʾom*, 'suddenly'.

'slaughter', *ṭābaḥ*: Hebr. listeners would have detected the assonance linking *ṭbḥ*, 'slaughter' (7:22) and *zbḥ*, 'sacrifice' (v. 14), with sinister transformation.

'he will enter', *yābôʾ*: in 7:22b *yābôʾ* applies primarily to the youth (he is the one who will enter), but secondarily applies also to the ox ('the ox will enter *or* go to slaughter'), and similarly by ellipsis supplies a verb for the ankle bangle.

'like an ankle bangle to a fool's reproof', *kĕʿekes ʾel mûsar ʾĕwîl*: an intentionally illogical picture (dressing up for punishment), resembling the youth's illogical delight before his deadly end. Arab. words related to *ʿekes* mean 'to hobble an animal' or 'to hold back the head of a camel, or of some other animal when it is being broken in or slaughtered' (*HALOT*, s.v. '*ʿekes*'). The sense is unnecessarily weakened if emended with the LXX to read, 'like a dog', *hōsper kyōn* (as if Hebr. read *kĕkeleb* in place of *kĕʿekes*).

'reproof', *mûsar*: before Masoretes supplied the consonantal text with vowels, this Hebr. word could have recalled *môsēr*, 'chain', 'fetter', suggesting that the decorative anklet would transform into a means of hobbling the feet (a meaning, incidentally, accompanying the root *ʿks* in Arab.).

7:23. 'shall thrust deep into', *yĕpallaḥ*: lit. 'shall pierce deeply *or* split' (distinct from 'pierce', *ḥll*, in 7:26). Given the explicit context of male sexual activity, this imagery suggests a stark degree of deadly reversal.

'unaware that it will cost him his life': lit. 'and he does not know that it is for his life'. Ironically, 'life' also denotes 'appetite' – the bait that drew the youth to this deadly trap ('let us drink our fill of erotic sensations', 7:18).

7:25. 'Don't . . . deviate', *ʾal-yēśṭ*: four of the six instances of this verb connote deviation from a marriage bond, turning instead towards adultery (Num. 5:12, 19, 20, 29), a connotation corresponding to the youth 'deviating' towards the adulteress's house.

7:26. 'pierced', *ḥll*: depending on the context, this Hebr. root may describe either one who has been wounded in battle (its principal meaning here), or at times it may refer to a woman who has been violated (often translated as 'profaned', Lev. 21:7, 14). The choice of this word (rather than a synonym such as 'the deceased' or 'killed-ones') may signal a fatal reversal, given the promiscuity of those who visit the adulteress's house and are then slain (pierced).

'felled': elsewhere this describes felling trees (2 Kgs 3:19, 25; 6:5). Interestingly, the next noun ('countless', *ʿăṣumîm*) begins with two consonants that spell 'tree', *ʿēṣ*.

Form and structure

Borders

While preceding and present lectures alike deal with marital fidelity, the style shifts at 7:1 from reasoned argumentation to eyewitness anecdote, marking the present poem's upper border. A wisdom commendation with voc. and imperatives reinforces that border (vv. 1–5).

Completion of that story (with closing exhortation) sets the lower boundary at 7:27. Closure in v. 27 and three inclusios in vv. 24–27 reinforce the lower border (see under 'Macrostructural features', below).

Macrostructural features

Wisdom commendation followed by wisdom content (Sections I and II–III, content-based). The lecture opens with a substantial wisdom commendation, urging the pupil to keep close company with Lady Wisdom (Section I, 7:1–5). Wisdom content ensues in Sections II–III, consisting of a narrative description of a youth who favoured Lady Wisdom's competitor, followed by a closing exhortation (vv. 6–23 and 24–27, respectively).

Repetition of *ʾîšôn* as 'pupil' or 'core' (Sections I and II, form-based). Both Sections I and II employ the rare term *ʾîšôn*, rendered 'pupil' (of the eye, 7:2) and 'core' (of night, v. 9). It appears only three more times in the HB. The poet implies that since the youth refuses to retain the father's instruction at the forefront of his vision (v. 2), he thereby consigns himself to stumble about in inky darkness (v. 9).

Closure by repetition of 'house' (Sections II and III, form-based). Most references to 'house' within this poem represent the forbidden territory of the seductress's home (7:8, 11, 19, 20, in Section II). When 'house' reappears in the poem's final line (v. 27), it recalls all the seductive, promiscuous and ultimately fatal entanglements of her lair, effecting closure. A solitary safe house appeared earlier, inhabited by the sage (7:6). There the youth should have remained.

Inclusio involving imperatives (Sections I and III, form-based). Imperative forms appear only in the first and last sections, creating a sense of inclusio (observed also by Waltke 2004: 384). In Section I the sage exhorts his son to 'guard', 'bind', 'write' and 'say' – all calculated to attach the youth closely to Lady Wisdom (7:1, 3, 4). In Section III a group of 'sons' similarly are urged to 'listen', 'pay attention', 'do not let deviate' and 'do not wander' (vv. 24, 25).

Inclusio involving voc. 'son(s)' (Sections I and III, form-based). To buttress the impact of imperatives in Sections I and III, both sections capture their audiences' attention with the voc. 'son' (7:1) or 'sons' (v. 24), fostering an inclusio. Concerning the difference between sg. and pl., refer to 'Borders of Proverbs 4 – 9' in the introduction to Prov. 4.

Inclusio of antonyms involving life or death (Sections I and III, content-based). The opposing concepts of survival and death form an inclusio at the outer edges of this lecture. Initially the grandfather urges his son to 'live!' by cherishing his counsel (7:2). Otherwise the youth will 'fall', 'slain', a permanent resident in the seductress's 'dark chambers of death' (vv. 26–27).

Microstructural features

Imperatives and incentives comprising a wisdom commendation (7:1–5, content-based). A series of imperatives unite 7:1–4 (Block I.A), supported by an incentive in v. 5 (Block I.B).

Inclusio involving 'to guard' (7:1, 2, 5, form-based). A reciprocal inclusio links the outer edges of Section I. The youth must guard wisdom (7:1a, 2a). As he does so, wisdom reciprocally will guard the youth (v. 5a).

Inclusio with reversal involving 'words' (7:1, 5, form-based). The first and last cola of Section I refer to 'words', forming an inclusio. First are the sage's beneficial words (7:1a), followed by the slippery words of the seductress (v. 5b). For his part (and using the same root), the youth must 'say' to Lady Wisdom, 'My sister' (v. 4a).

Repetition of 'house' (7:6, 8, 11, form-based). Two 'houses' appear in Section II. One belongs to the sage (7:6), while the other belongs to the seductress (v. 8) – a house she seldom inhabits (v. 11). Whose house the youth visits will determine his fate.

Repetition of *lēb* as 'mind' or 'heart' (7:7, 10, form- and content-based). A contest of wisdom and wits emerges when the sage recycles the term *lēb* by characterizing the youth as 'lacking sense', *ḥasar-lēb* (7:7), while describing the seductress as 'sly of heart', *nĕṣudat-lēb* (v. 10).

Reversal of slaying in Section II (7:14, 22, content-based). Pious ritual involving ceremonial killing of animals (*zebaḥ*, 7:14) reverses when slaying of a food animal provides a simile for homicide ('like an ox to slaughter [*ṭebaḥ*]', v. 22).

Inclusio involving wisdom terms (7:7, 22–23, content-based). Wisdom terms form an inclusio for Section II, appearing primarily at its start and finish (7:6–23). Towards the start, the eyewitness-sage is perceptive (7:7), while the youth is 'naive' and 'senseless' (also v. 7). Towards the close of Section II, the youth will suffer 'a fool's reproof' (v. 22), unaware (v. 23). 'Sly of heart' presents the only other wisdom term in Section II (v. 10).

Succession of similes (7:22–23, form-based). This poem employs four similes. Three appear in close succession, uniting the final two verses of Section II: 'like an ox to the slaughter', 'like an ankle bangle to a fool's reproof' and 'like the rushing of a bird into a net' (vv. 22, 23, which both happen to be tricola). The first and third (ox and bird) illumine the youth's demise, comparing him with animals destined for slaughter. The second (ankle bangle) evokes a picture of pointless finery worn by one oblivious to imminent punishment. These similes converge for a macabre depiction of the youth's inevitable yet needless death. (The fourth simile appeared in v. 2 of Section I: 'as the pupil of your eye'.)

Wisdom commendation followed by wisdom content (7:24, 25–27, content-based). Section III begins with a wisdom commendation (7:24), followed by wisdom content – a closing exhortation concluding the lecture (vv. 25–27).

Comment

Section I (**7:1–5**). A wisdom commendation opens this poem, urgently exhorting the youth to choose Lady Wisdom as the sole sure protection against her sinister rival (Section I, 7:1–5). Along a vector of escalating particularity and energy, the youth first must preserve general sayings (v. 1), then specific commands (v. 2). He must hold them tightly, then inscribe them indelibly, internally (v. 3). These mandates the youth must cherish, not merely endure (v. 4). Incentive follows imperatives – wisdom's reward of personal protection (7:5).

More than a mere introduction, the imperatives of this commendation comprise the lecture's core instruction. Reminiscent of the grandfather's first lecture (4:1–9), the youth must focus solely on seizing wisdom.

7:2. Since this poem chronicles the death of the hapless youth, the exhortation to 'live!' takes on renewed urgency in this poem (7:2). The grandfather issued a similar exhortation in his first lecture ('Guard my commands and truly live', 4:4), and will repeat it in his last ('Abandon naivety and live!', 9:6a).

7:4. 'Sister' and 'kin' (7:4) may indicate a figurative marriage between the youth and wisdom (Waltke 2004: 369–370). Then wisdom's protection will become effective (v. 5).

Section II (**7:6–23**). *Block II.A (7:6–9).* The elements of Section II (7:6–23) proceed chronologically as an eyewitness report. First, the eyewitness reports his location. He is at home, watching out of his window as a youth strolls along (vv. 6–7).

Next comes information concerning the youth's vulnerable character (naive and senseless, 7:7) and direction of travel ('striding along' in the direction of the foreign woman's house, v. 8). We learn the time of day: daylight has given way to 'deep darkness', *ʾăpēlâ* (a rare term connoting calamitous gloom), foreshadowing the occulted demise awaiting the youth (v. 9).

Block II.B (7:10–23). Attention shifts to the seductress's appearance, words and activities in Block II.B (7:10–23). She has costumed herself to capture attention as she prowls about (v. 11b). Upon seeing the youth, she launches into action: seizing, kissing him, then locking him in her gaze (v. 13).

Then begins her disarming speech (Unit II.B.2, 7:14–20). Deftly she dismantles her mark's moral-spiritual defences, as she attests a sustained and current piety (v. 14). According to her story, some past personal crisis pressed her to petition God with solemn promises – vows whose discharge would be contingent on the divine granting her request. She found favour in God's eyes, so now she faithfully has returned to render the pledged offering. Just now she has emerged from the temple (or so she says). How could one impugn such a pious and faithful person?

With the declaration 'That is why' (7:15) she attributes to vow-performance this evening excursion, which led in turn to seeking out the youth. Exactly why the pious errand should lead her to seek the youth remains unclear. Perhaps it is the sage's way of implying that her story does not quite tally. Without allowing a pause for questioning, she hastens to flatter: 'And then I found you!'

Having penetrated any defences of spiritual misgivings, after dismissing any sense of personal insignificance, she unfolds her preparations of bedding rare and aromas exotic – a spring-loaded snare cunningly camouflaged as a lair (7:16–17). So deliciously she accosts his unguarded appetites! Sensory appeal escalates from visual (v. 16) to aromatic (v. 17), summiting with an invitation – even an imperative – to assuage their lust without restraint (v. 18).

Finally, the seductress dismantles any lingering fear of discovery, assuring that they will have sufficient time for adultery (though she would not name it so), free from detection (7:19–20). The husband is absent and will remain so for some time. To clinch this reassurance, she discloses his itinerary. He is not due back before the start of the next month.

The success of her persuasive barrage becomes clear in the next portion (Unit II.B.3, 7:21–23). Nor will she relent at first success, for she 'kept on seducing' (v. 21b).

At this point the eyewitness shifts to present tense, as if the events are now unfolding: 'He is going after her' (7:22a). In the next colon the report shifts to fut. tense, suggesting that the eyewitness can no longer see them (perhaps they have retreated inside, away from view), so he relates what he knows will unfold for the unfortunate youth from this point onwards: 'he will enter . . . until an arrow shall thrust deep into his liver . . . , [he is] unaware that it will cost him his life' (vv. 22b–23c).

What sort of 'entry' may here be implied? Given the explicitly sexual nature of this poem, it seems reasonable that the sage expected the reader would recognize a sexual connotation in this expression. A sexual euphemism is well attested for the Hebr. verb 'to go after [her]', 'to enter', *bôʾ*, when a man is the subject and a woman's tent or room or general presence is the object (e.g. Gen. 6:4; 16:2; 30:3; Prov. 6:29).

Initial, euphemistic use of 'enter' renders all the more poignant those later, related scenes, due to the reversal that each exposes. Amorous movement of the youth towards the woman is, in reality, like an ox going (entering in) to slaughter (7:22b). Next, the youth's transit also resembles an ankle bangle going (entering in) to a fool's reproof (v. 22c, perhaps evoking an illogical cacophony of jingling, joyous decoration as jewellery collides with painful punishment). Only a glib fool would gaudily dress up for so painful a dressing-down. More transparently, the youth's movement compares to a bird hurriedly going (entering in) to a fowler's net (v. 23b). The decline from an ox to a bird marks the terrible terminus of 'mindless gullibility' (Fox 2000: 250).

As the witless youth learns too late, the seductress's house proves to be a slaughterhouse (Unit II.B.3, 7:21–23). The reader is left with the suspicion that the ritual slaying of 'fellowship sacrifices' earlier boasted by the seductress, in reality consisted of routine slaughter suffered by her most recent human victim (v. 14).

7:6–7. The sage 'peers out', 'spies' and is 'determined to perceive' – underscoring observation as fundamental to the sage's method (7:6–7).

Four expressions in 7:6 are reminiscent of the general Sisera's mother, as from her window she watched in vain for the return of her warrior son ('window', 'peer down', 'from [*bĕʿad*]' and 'window-lattice', Judg. 5:28). The youth, now viewed from the sage's window, would fare no better than Sisera who, as a fugitive from battle, was slain in the tent of a woman named Jael.

Concerning 'lattice', Fox explains that 'windows were enclosed with trelliswork, through which one could peer without being seen' (2000: 242). Since the author 'looked down', his vantage was from an upper-storey room.

7:9. Multiple expressions for night emphasize the nocturnal setting for this rendezvous (7:9). By the story's close, light's recession symbolizes more than literal darkness.

7:14. 'People may be punctilious in ritual and taboo while shabby in ethics' (Fox 2000: 246).

7:20. Since the current night is profoundly dark (not moonlit, 7:9), the husband's return will not be for roughly two weeks, when the moon will again be full (Fox 2000: 248).

7:23. Three aspects of the warning in Prov. 7 are reminiscent of the sin of Israelite men in the Baal of Peor incident (Num. 25). First, the sin involved promiscuity. Second, the men were enticed by foreign women (Moabites). Third, the consequence was fatal. In one especially flagrant case, an Israelite man (and his Moabite consort) was fatally pierced (*dāqar*, 'pierce', in Num. 25:8; cf. Prov. 7:23, where the verb for 'pierce' is *pālaḥ*).

Section III (7:24–27). The closing exhortation (Section III, 7:24–27) begins with an interjection addressing a plural audience (v. 24), reminiscent of the plural exhortation interjected at 5:7. As there, this shift similarly indicates that the father-sage is interrupting his recounting of the grandfather-sage's teaching long enough to seize afresh his own audience's attention (see introduction to Prov. 4 – 9). Then the grandfather's voice resumes as he issues an imperative (addressing a singular audience, 7:25), supported by two incentive lines in closing (vv. 26–27).

This imperative offers no point-for-point rebuttal of the adulteress's slippery lines. Instead the grandfather focuses on the earliest tendencies to drift in her direction. Seduction will remain powerless, so long as the youth refuses his first error – wandering in the direction of 'her' street (7:25; contrast v. 8).

The accompanying incentives hammer home the deadly peril of the adulteress's influence. Her guests fall wounded (7:26a), and then slain (v. 26b). Her hospitality escorts her guests steadily Sheolward (v. 27a), along a pathway that does not slack its methodical descent until gaining the innermost chambers of death (v. 27b).

7:25. If only the victim-youth had taken seriously the caution of Poem 3: 'Against every imprisonment protect your mind' (4:23a)! So the grandfather again cautions his son, 'Don't let your mind deviate towards her ways' (7:25).

Explanation

Similar to the literal warning against promiscuity in Poem 8 (6:20–35), a largely literal interpretation fits Poem 9 (7:1–27) as well. Countering allegorical interpretations, Fox observes, 'The menace of sexual trespass is sufficiently grave to warrant the intensity of the warning it receives' in this poem (2000: 262; for a comprehensive and well-reasoned review of various interpretive options, rabbinic to modern, literal to philosophical and feminist, see Fox 2000: 252–262).

Six practical implications emerge from Poem 9 (7:1–27). First, when trying to convince another of truth, story must accompany principle. Teaching that overlooks illustration risks confrontation without persuasion.

Second, boundaries maintain morals. At night the sage remained safely within the boundaries of his own house. The youth ventured out into the darkness, rendering himself vulnerable.

Third, in certain scenarios stalwart struggle may prove futile, advising 'flight' over 'fight' (7:25). Contending for sexual purity constitutes one such scenario (cf. 1 Cor. 6:18).

Fourth, beware of defence-dismantling strategies (7:14–20). Claims of spirituality form one such strategy, followed by illicit appeals to sensory appetites, and the discounting of harmful consequences (claiming the absent husband would pose no threat). The seductress herself proved the greater hazard.

Fifth, all chambers in a slaughterhouse lead to death. The adulteress's invitation can lead to nothing but a deadly trap. 'Stupid animals see no connection between traps and death, and morally stupid people see no connection between their sin and death' (Waltke 2004: 384).

Sixth, the sure defence consists of overtly and deeply embracing what is good (not simply resisting what is wrong while dismissing what is right). Take initiative to inscribe wisdom deep within. Grant her such a place of prominence that she will be able to extend protection. The grandfather's next (and longest) poem will demonstrate how fully she deserves such honour (Prov. 8).

PROVERBS 8:1–36
'What alternative have I, if not the seductress?'
(Poem 10 in Prov. 4 – 9, influential women theme)

Overview of Proverbs 8:1–36

The sage's resounding renunciation of the seductress's deadly overtures (Prov. 7) would leave the pupil wondering, 'What alternative have I, if not the seductress?' To this implied question the grandfather responds with a question of his own – a double rhetorical inquiry conveying the intensity of an accusation: 'Has not Lady Wisdom herself kept on calling? Has not Lady Perception kept on raising her voice?' (8:1). The seductress's deadly ambush in Prov. 7 easily may be circumvented, if only one would accept the exceptional honour of Lady Wisdom's generous overture. Following that initial challenge (8:1), through this extensive poem the sage constructs a robust case for prizing and pursuing Lady Wisdom.

Already in Cycle II the grandfather has presented two 'influential women' poems. In this, the zenith of 'influential women' compositions, the poet grants Lady Wisdom the most extensive voice of any influential woman. (For an overview of the three themes and two cycles, please refer to 'Principal themes in Proverbs 4 – 9' in the introduction to Prov. 4 – 9, above.)

Position of this poem within Proverbs

Preceding context. This lecture follows a poem chronicling a youth's mortal mistake (Prov. 7). There a youth followed the seductress as an ox lumbering to slaughter, as a witless bird stupidly hurrying into a deadly snare. Now in Prov. 8 the sage demonstrates Lady Wisdom's unparalleled ability to outpace and outclass the slippery-tongued seductress of Prov. 7.

Ensuing context. In Prov. 9 (Poem 11) the grandfather will draw to a close his teaching that began in Prov. 4. There the competing invitations of two influential women will so confront the youth that to postpone his decision will become impossible. He must choose one over the other – a choice that will determine his destiny.

What to watch for

Notice how the grandfather sets the scene in 8:1–3, then follows with Lady Wisdom's speech. Observe how she shifts her persuasive strategy as the lecture unfolds. First she appeals to reason (describing how wisdom will benefit a person in vv. 4–21). Then she urges the youth to trust her on account of her genuine interest in humankind's well-being (based on her long history in vv. 22–31). Finally, she draws the audience to a pivotal decision (vv. 32–36).

Within her appeal to reason, notice the recurring themes of wisdom's morality, accessibility and worth. Note also where (in relation to those recurring themes) she most transparently discloses her identity.

As Lady Wisdom recounts her personal history, observe how often she mentions 'earth'. Consider how successive references to earth depict a region that grows increasingly suitable for human habitation.

When she ultimately draws the audience to a decision, notice how imperative-plus-incentive creates a dual-theme structure. Watch also for the character summary that operates to close the poem.

Translation and outline

Translation with outline

Prov. 8 is remarkable both for length and complexity. For those reasons a more compressed outline without translation appears following the outline with translation immediately below.

Verse	*Translation*	*Outline*
		I. Introduction of Lady Wisdom: the adulteress was not the only person who sought out the youth (8:1–3)
8:1	Has not Lady Wisdom herself kept on calling? Has not Lady Perception kept on raising her voice?	A. Did not someone other than the seductress extend an invitation? (v. 1)
		B. Indeed, Lady Wisdom traversed the city (vv. 2–3)
8:2	Atop promontories alongside the way, at crossroads she has taken her post.	1. She first visited prominent places about town (v. 2)
8:3	Alongside gatehouses at the mouth of the town, at the access to entryways she will give a ringing cry.	2. Then she reached the town square (v. 3)
		II. Appeal by Lady Wisdom: get wisdom (vv. 4–36)!
		A. Get wisdom, due to reason and character (vv. 4–31)!
		1. Get wisdom, due to these reasons (vv. 4–21)!
8:4	It is to you, O men, that I keep on calling; my voice keeps on calling to the sons of mortals.	a. Yes, you are the ones I address (v. 4)

Verse	Translation	Outline
		b. Get wisdom, for these reasons (vv. 5–21)! i. Introduction: get wisdom – from me (vv. 5–6)
8:5	O naive ones – perceive cleverness! And stupid folk – perceive sense!	α. Get wisdom . . . (v. 5)
8:6	Listen! For I will speak of leadership, and the opening of my lips will speak of honesty.	β. . . . By listening closely for valuable training (v. 6)
		ii. First reason: because wisdom is moral, accessible and valuable (first cycle, vv. 7–11)
8:7	For trustworthiness shall my palate savour, but wickedness will be abhorrent to my lips.	α. Wisdom is moral (vv. 7–8)
8:8	Consistent with what is moral are all the words of my mouth; in them is nothing tangling or twisted.	
8:9	They all are forthright to the insightful person, and honest to those who find knowledge.	β. Wisdom is moral and accessible (v. 9)
8:10	Get hold of my reproof, not silver; and knowledge, which is preferable to high-grade gold.	γ. Wisdom is valuable (vv. 10–11)
8:11	For wisdom is better than corals, and nothing delightful can compare with her.	
		iii. Second reason: because of my identity and essence (vv. 12–14)
8:12	I am Lady Wisdom; I inhabit cleverness; and I can find strategic knowledge.	α. My identity (part 1, v. 12)
8:13	To revere the LORD is to hate evil. Pride, presumption, evil ways, and a perverse mouth do I hate.	β. The essence of wisdom: reverence (v. 13)
8:14	Mine are counsel and success; I am insight, mine is might.	α'. My identity (part 2, v. 14)

8:15 By me kings can reign and dignitaries can decree what is moral. 8:16 By me commanders can command, as well as nobles and all who judge by standards that are moral. 8:17 I myself will love those who love it, and those who are on the lookout for me will find me. 8:18 Riches and reputation are with me, time-honoured wealth and morality. 8:19 My fruit is better than high-grade gold and pure gold, and my revenue is preferable to silver.	ii'. First reason, again: because wisdom is moral, highly accessible and supremely valuable (vv. 15–19) α. Wisdom is moral, facilitating rule (vv. 15–16) β. Wisdom is highly accessible (v. 17) γ. Wisdom is supremely valuable (vv. 18–19)
8:20 In the route of morality I routinely walk about, among footpaths of justice. 8:21 So that I may bequeath property to those who love me, and their storerooms I may fill.	i'. Conclusion: where and why to get wisdom (vv. 20–21) α. Moral paths are where you may find me (v. 20) β. My accessibility and value are why you should find me (v. 21)
8:22 The LORD himself acquired me at the outset of his way, the earliest of his acts of old. 8:23 From the dawn of time I was carefully fashioned, since the onset of earth's earliest era.	2. [Get wisdom,] due to my character (vv. 22–31) a. My character is apparent from my employer's confidence (vv. 22–23)
	b. My character is apparent from the focus of my interest (vv. 24–31)

Verse	*Translation*	*Outline*
8:24 8:25 8:26	When as yet there were no primeval depths I was birthed, when as yet there were no springs laden with water. Before the mountains were founded, prior to the hills I was birthed. Until the point when he had not yet made either earth or remote regions, nor earliest dust of habitable land.	i. I was interested in earth, before human habitation was possible (vv. 24–26)
8:27 8:28 8:29	When he set up skies, there was I – when he drew a circle on the surface of the primeval deep. When he congealed clouds overhead, during the defiance of springs in the primeval deep, When he fixed for the sea its limit, so that waters could not trespass his declaration, when he drew the foundations of earth.	ii. I grew even more interested in earth, as human habitation first became conceivable (vv. 27–29)
8:30 8:31	So I came to be by his side as a craftsman, and so I became an intense delight day after day, laughing before him continually. Laughing about the habitable land of his earth, but my delight focused upon the sons of mortals.	iii. I experienced unceasing delight, when at last humans inhabited the earth (vv. 30–31)
		B. Here, then, is what you must do (vv. 32–36) 1. Listen to me, in order to gain good fortune (vv. 32–34)
8:32 8:33	So now, sons, listen to me! And how fortunate are my ways – they go on protecting! Listen to reproof and so become wise, and do not let yourself run wild.	a. Dual theme: a causal connection links (a) listening and (b) good fortune (v. 32) b. Listening requires receptivity even to reproof (v. 33)

8:34 How fortunate is the mortal who listens for me, so he may be alert at my doors day after day, so he may post watch at the doorposts of my entryways.	c. Good fortune requires determined pursuit of wisdom (v. 34)
	2. Character summary: receptivity to wisdom determines well-being (vv. 35–36)
8:35 Indeed, one who finds me finds life, and thus obtained approval from the LORD,	a. The one who finds wisdom ends exceptionally well (v. 35)
8:36 But one who wrongs me assaults his very self; all who hate me have loved death.	b. The one who hates wisdom ends in disaster (v. 36)

Abbreviated outline

To simplify the task of grasping the arrangement of this extensive poem, it may be helpful to view the outline more compactly (without translation), with particular focus on the palistrophic organization of II.A.1.b (8:5–21).

I. Introduction of Lady Wisdom (vv. 1–3)
II. Appeal by Lady Wisdom (vv. 4–36)
  A. Get wisdom, due to reason and character (vv. 4–31)
    1. Get wisdom, due to these reasons (vv. 4–21)
      a. Yes, you are the ones I address (v. 4)
      b. Get wisdom, for these reasons (vv. 5–21)
        i. Introduction: get wisdom – from me (vv. 5–6)
          α. Get wisdom . . . (v. 5)
          β. . . . By listening closely for valuable training (v. 6)
        ii. First reason: because wisdom is moral, accessible, and valuable (first cycle, vv. 7–11)
          α. Wisdom is moral (v. 7–8)
          β. Wisdom is moral and accessible (v. 9)
          γ. Wisdom is valuable (vv. 10–11)
        iii. Second reason: because of my identity and essence (vv. 12–14)
          α. My identity (part 1, v. 12)
          β. The essence of wisdom: reverence (v. 13)
          α'. My identity (part 2, v. 14)
        ii'. First reason, again: because wisdom is moral, highly accessible, and supremely valuable (vv. 15–19)

- α. Wisdom is moral, facilitating rule (vv. 15–16)
- β. Wisdom is highly accessible (v. 17)
- γ. Wisdom is supremely valuable (vv. 18–19)

i′. Conclusion: where and why to get wisdom (vv. 20–21)

- α. Moral paths are where you may find me (v. 20)
- β. My accessibility and value are why you should find me (v. 21)

2. [Get wisdom,] due to my character (vv. 22–31)
   a. My character is apparent from my employer's confidence (vv. 22–23)
   b. My character is apparent from the focus of my interest (vv. 24–31)
      i. I was interested in earth, before human habitation was possible (vv. 24–26)
      ii. I grew even more interested in earth, as human habitation first became conceivable (vv. 27–29)
      iii. I experienced unceasing delight, when at last humans inhabited the earth (vv. 30–31)

B. Here, then, is what you must do (vv. 32–36)

1. Listen to me, in order to gain good fortune (vv. 32–34)
   a. Dual theme: a causal connection links (a) listening and (b) good fortune (v. 32)
   b. Listening requires receptivity even to reproof (v. 33)
   c. Good fortune requires determined pursuit of wisdom (v. 34)
2. Character summary: receptivity to wisdom determines well-being (vv. 35–36)
   a. The one who finds wisdom ends exceptionally well (v. 35)
   b. The one who hates wisdom ends in disaster (v. 36)

Fox recognizes an introduction in 8:1–3 and a conclusion in vv. 32–36, but separates the conclusion from vv. 4–31, despite continuity of Lady Wisdom's voice. Fox recognizes that vv. 22–31 cohere. However, by matching them with vv. 12–21 for an envelope structure, he overlooks evidence of a palistrophe within vv. 5–21 (see under 'Microstructural features', below; Fox 2000: 291–292).

Notes on the text

8:1. 'Has not Lady Wisdom herself kept on calling?', *hălōʾ-ḥokmâ tiqrāʾ*: the poet emphasizes 'Lady Wisdom' by placing the subject before the verb (Fox 2000: 265). The second colon's parallel structure suggests that 'Lady

Perception' would be emphatic. Durative 'kept on calling' and 'kept on raising' is inferred from the yiq. conjugation. Past tense reflects that Lady Wisdom's calling occurred parallel to and competing with the overtures of the adulteress in Prov. 7.

'Lady Wisdom', *ḥŏkmâ*: elsewhere simply 'wisdom', but here rendered with a title due to personification (pl. *ḥŏkmôt* is also rendered 'Lady Wisdom' in 1:20; 9:1). The title 'Lady Perception' is inferred from personification in 8:1b.

8:2. 'at crossroads', *bêt nĕtîbôt*: lit. 'between footpaths'. *Bêt* is a variant of *bên*, 'between'.

8:3. 'she will give a ringing cry', *tārōnnâ*: a 3 f. sg. form with paragogic he (cf. *taʿgĕbâ* in Ezek. 23:20), whereas *tārōnâ* in 1:20 should be read as 3 f. pl., corresponding to a pl. subject (Lady Wisdom is an abstract pl.).

8:4. 'It is to you, O men': by leading with the prep. phrase 'to you', Lady Wisdom stresses her audience above her activity (Fox 2000: 267).

'I keep on calling; my voice keeps on calling to the sons of mortals': lit. 'I keep on calling, my voice [keeps on calling] to sons of mortals'.

8:5. 'perceive . . . perceive', *hābînû . . . hābînû*: while variation would be achieved by the reading *hākînû*, 'establish' (following LXX *enthesthe*), in place of the second *hābînû*, 'perceive', such an emendation would weaken the emphasis of the original and fully comprehensible MT. These naive, foolish candidates for wisdom's tutelage urgently need to 'perceive'.

'naive', *pĕtāʾîm*: assonance may join *pĕtāʾîm* with *pĕtāḥîm*, 'entryways' (8:3).

'sense', *lēb*: lit. 'mind'.

8:6. 'leadership', *nĕgîdîm*: lit. 'princes'. Parallel to the abstract noun 'honesty', *mēšārîm*, *nĕgîdîm* should be understood as referring to topics and skills of concern to nobility and court officials who bear the responsibility to lead others in the community. The sage will further develop the connection between wisdom and leadership in 8:15–16. Thus it is unnecessary to render as 'candid things' (Fox 2000: 263) or as 'what is right' (Waltke 2004: 387). LXX renders *nĕgîdîm* as *semna*, designating things that are august, sacred, lofty or serious.

'will speak of honesty', *mēšārîm*: lit. 'honesty'. The verb 'to speak' is implied from 8:6a by ellipsis.

8:7. 'trustworthiness', *ʾĕmĕt*: often translated as 'truth'.

8:9. 'forthright . . . and honest', *nĕkōḥîm . . . wîšārîm*: both terms have a connotation of straightness.

'insightful person', *mēbîn*: from the root *byn*, rendered 'perceive' in 8:5.

8:11. 'wisdom', *ḥŏkmâ*: rendered 'Lady Wisdom' in 8:1, 12.

'corals', *pĕnînîm*: see 'Notes' for 3:15.

8:12. 'I am Lady Wisdom': lit. 'I [am] wisdom'. Inferring the verb 'to be' (rather than rendering with NRSV, 'I, wisdom') associates this expression with self-identification statements such as 'I am the LORD' (Exod. 6:2) and with extra-biblical royal inscriptions (e.g. 'I am Kilamuwa son of Hayya' or 'I am Azitawadda, blessed by Baal'; Fox 2000: 271).

'strategic knowledge': lit. 'knowledge of schemes' or 'of plans'.

8:13. 'Pride, presumption', *gē'â wĕgā'ôn*: lit. 'pride and presumption', assonantally linked.

8:14. 'success', *tûšiyyâ*: wisdom leading to skill, resulting in successful action.

8:15. 'can reign', *yimlōkû*: yiq. of capability.

8:16. 'nobles', *nĕdîbîm*: related to 'principles of leadership', *nĕgîdîm* (v. 6a), in sound and sense.

'all who judge by standards that are moral', *kol-šōpṭê ṣedeq*: lit. 'all judges of what is moral'. LXX *kratousi*, 'they are judging' (and similarly *BHS* notes), is weaker, losing the summation by omitting 'all'.

8:17. 'I myself will love those who love it', *'ănî 'ōhăbeyhâ 'ēhāb*: following K. The pronoun 'I' is emphatic (Waltke 2004: 404). The 3 f. sg. pronoun 'it' (or 'her') draws the reader back to the f. sg. noun 'wisdom' in 8:12a (rendered 'Lady Wisdom' due to personification) and to her attributes (v. 14), which in Hebr. also happen to be f. sg. nouns (might, insight, success and counsel). If, instead of 'those who love it', the verse were to read, 'those who love me' (as recommended by Q and LXX – an expression occurring in v. 21), it would focus the disciple–mentor bond upon personified Lady Wisdom, rather than upon the actual, non-personified abstract entity of 'wisdom'. When in v. 21 the poet reverts to personification through the expression 'those who love me', he has already established that the relationship joins the disciple with the abstract entity of wisdom, not to be confused with some quasi-deity.

8:18a. 'Riches and reputation': lit. 'riches and honour'. These may form a hendiadys meaning 'honourable wealth' (Fox 2000: 277; cf. Prov. 3:16). The sage realizes that not all riches are honourable (e.g. 'revenue of a guilty person tends towards sin', 10:16b).

'time-honoured wealth': lit. 'old wealth'.

'morality', *šĕdāqâ*: alternatively 'equity' or 'righteousness' (see §5.6 in the 'Introduction').

8:20. 'I routinely walk about', *'ăhallēk*: 'to walk about' reflects pi. stem; 'routinely' reflects yiq. conjugation.

8:21. 'property', *yēš*: lit. 'substance' (not limited to real estate).

8:22. 'The LORD himself acquired me': lit. 'It was the LORD who acquired me' ('himself' added to reflect frontal extrapositioning of subject).

'acquired', *qānānî*: Ugar. attests the root *qnh* meaning both 'to acquire' and 'to create'. However, in Hebr. 'acquire' (not 'create' or 'beget') is the predominant meaning of *qnh*, with derivatives meaning 'wealth', 'property', 'possessions'. For interpreting Prov. 8:22, most significant is the sage's use of *qnh* elsewhere in this book. Of the thirteen remaining instances of *qnh* within Proverbs (across ten sayings), *qnh* always connotes 'to acquire' or 'to purchase' (e.g. 4:5, 7; 16:16; 17:16 [with funds for purchasing]; 23:23; cf. Jenni and Westermann 1997, s.v. '*qnh*'). In all Proverbs instances of *qnh* except 20:14, the object acquired is wisdom or a wisdom synonym. These data discourage following LXX in rendering *qānānî* as '[the Lord] created me' (*ektisen me*; for further discussion, see Waltke 2004: 408–409). Thus the Lord models acquisition of wisdom, an acquisition the sage urges on his pupils.

8:23. 'From the dawn of time', *mēʿôlām*: lit. 'From the earliest period of time'.

'carefully fashioned', *nissaktî*: includes connotations of 'woven' and 'appointed'. This expression together with 'I was birthed' (8:24) may have influenced LXX to render *qānānî* in v. 22 as *ektisen me*, '[the Lord] created me'.

8:24. 'primeval depths', *tĕhōmôt*: refers to the watery deep at the dawn of time (Gen. 1:2). By presenting first the negative scene ('When as yet there were no primeval depths . . . no springs'), Lady Wisdom's description corresponds to the manner of ANE cosmogonies (Waltke 2004: 411).

'I was birthed', *ḥôlālĕtî*: lit. 'I was brought forth through the writhing of birthing pains', distinct from the more common verb *yld*, 'to be born'.

'laden': lit. 'made heavy' (niph. stem).

8:26. 'remote regions', *ḥûṣôt*: lit. '[the] outsides', contrasting 'habitable land' in 8:26b.

'habitable land', *tēbēl*: a synonym for 'earth', sometimes rendered 'world', this term often refers to regions capable of cultivation and human habitation. Particularly since *tēbēl* combines here with 'dust', *ʿāpĕrôt* (from which humankind was formed, Gen. 2:7), and since *tēbēl* in 8:31a refers to the appearance of humankind, mention of *tēbēl* in v. 26 foreshadows the introduction of humankind.

8:28. 'during the defiance', *baʿăzôz*: the fact that the watery depths would require restraint (8:29) is intimated in v. 28 by mention of their 'defiance' (cf. Job 38:10–11). To render 'when he strengthened' (emending by adding a pronominal suff. so that this phrase is parallel to v. 28a, 'when he congealed') would weaken the plain sense of this verse with its semantic link to v. 29 (*pace* Fox 2000: 264, n., and Waltke 2004: 391, n.).

8:29. 'could not trespass': yiq. of (in)capability.

8:30. 'So I came to be', *wāʾĕhĕyĕh*: the sequence of verb forms across 8:24–31 is instructive. In consequence of Lady Wisdom's interest in earth before it was habitable (vv. 24–26, using qat. verb forms to indicate remote past), and in consequence of her interest as it approached habitability (vv. 27–29, using the single verbless clause *šām ʾānî*, 'there [was] I', and six infinitives const., describing nearer-past time frame), she was able to emerge as a joyous craftsman assisting the divine when at last earth became habitable (v. 30a–b, twice using the wayyiq. form *wāʾĕhĕyĕh*, 'so I came to be/became', describing the most recent among several past events).

The double use consisting of *ʾĕhĕyĕh . . . ʾĕhĕyĕh*, 'so I came to be/became', within a single verse (whether yiq. or wayyiq.) occurs twice elsewhere in the HB, one of which unveils the divine name, 'I am who I am' (Exod. 3:14; cf. Zech. 2:9). If the sage intended an allusion to the divine name here at the close of the creation-recollection (vv. 22–31), perhaps he did so to discourage the reader from regarding wisdom as an independent entity, indicating instead that wisdom resides fully within God's own person and divine repertoire.

'craftsman', *ʾāmôn*: as summarized by Fox (2000: 285–287) and Waltke (2004: 417–420), the search for a conclusive translation of *ʾāmôn* has revolved around three primary proposals: (a) artisan, (b) constant(ly) and (c) nurturing. Given that the LXX renders the term as *harmozoysa*, 'one who fits [things] together', and in view of the possibility that *ʾāmôn* may be an alternative (albeit unique) representation of *ʾommān*, 'artisan', it seems best to render as 'craftsman', rather than 'constantly' or 'nurturing'.

'laughing', *mĕśaḥeqet*: a pleasant exuberance, not mocking.

8:31b. 'but my delight', *wĕšaʿăšuʿay*: after presenting cola 8:30c and 31a in rapid succession without any conj., the appearance of a conj. at v. 31b suggests that Wisdom's interest in 'sons of mortals' may stand in elevated contrast to prior joyous information of vv. 30c and 31a, recommending the adversative conj. 'but'.

8:32. 'how fortunate are my ways – they go on protecting!', *wĕʾašrê dĕrākay yišmōrû*: Wisdom's ways prove 'fortunate' because of the ongoing protection they provide. Hebr. manuscript evidence does not support rendering the finite form *yišmōrû*, 'they go on protecting', as if it were the ptc. *šōmrîm*, 'those who keep' or 'protect' (as in 'those who keep my ways'; cf. LXX, NRSV, NASB, NIV). Of twenty-nine instances of *ʾašrê* in the HB, only in Ps. 65:5 (ET v. 4) does a finite form appear to operate as a ptc. designating the entity, which is 'fortunate'. In all other instances it is a nominal entity (noun, pronoun or relative clause) that is 'fortunate'. Although to read with LXX (and others) would be smoother, the more difficult reading is grammatically more sound, rendering 'my ways' as the 'fortunate' entity in 8:32. This paves the way for mortals who are receptive to Lady Wisdom similarly to earn the designation 'fortunate' (v. 34a).

'fortunate', *ʾăšrê*: unlike words derived from *brk*, *ʾăšrê* connotes 'enviable', lacking the connotation of issuing a benediction (a connotation often inferred from the English term 'blessed'). For examples of *brk*, 'bless', in Proverbs, see 3:33; 27:14; 30:11.

8:35. 'Indeed', *kî*: not 'since' or 'for', because the character summary comprising 8:35–36 operates as a concluding declaration, not an explanation.

'one who finds me finds life', *mōṣĕʾî mōṣĕʾî ḥayyîm*: in the first *mōṣĕʾî*, the *î* represents 'me' (1 com. sg. suff.). In the second *mōṣĕʾî*, the *î* is best understood as an archaic ending (*hireq compaginis*, GKC §90.l, Joüon §93.n and esp. with ptcs. in Joüon §93.o; also *IBHS* §8.2.e). The *hireq compaginis* connects the ptc. 'one who finds' with the object 'life'. Thus it is not necessary with the Q to omit the yod (reading *māṣāʾ*, 'he found', instead of *mōṣĕʾî*, 'finds'). The alternative offered in *BHS* notes, while retaining the yod, vocalizes both ptcs. as pl. (cf. LXX), which does not conform to the sg. verb in 8:35b ('obtained').

'and thus obtained', *wayyāpeq*: wayyiq. summarizing what has preceded (*IBHS* §33.2.1d).

8:36. 'have loved death', *ʾāhăbû māwet*: like 8:35, ptcs. in the first colon give way to a finite form in the second (summarizing wayyiq. in v. 35b, qat. in v. 36b). The effect of qat. '[they] have loved death' as a simple ind. both accounts for and consigns to ultimate demise those who 'wrong' wisdom.

Form and structure

Borders

The upper border consists of a theme transition. The story of the adulteress and her youthful victim concludes in 7:27. A poem concerning Lady Wisdom begins in 8:1.

The lower border is marked by the continuity of Lady Wisdom's accolades that conclude in 8:36, by character summary and by closure. Two contrasting characters close the lecture. One deserves emulation, having discovered Lady Wisdom and thereby divine approval (v. 35), while the other harms himself mortally by attacking her (v. 36).

Eight elements appearing earlier foster closure in the concluding block (8:32–36). They include 'sons' (vv. 31, 32), 'listen' (vv. 6, 32, 33), 'way' (vv. 13, 32), 'reproof' (vv. 10, 33), 'mortal' (vv. 4, 31, 34), 'LORD' (vv. 13, 22, 35), 'hate' (vv. 13, 36) and 'love' (vv. 17, 36).

Macrostructural features

Owing to the brevity of Section I (three verses, compared with thirty-three verses in Section II), macrostructural links are few. Conversely, the length of Section II means that devices operating at the block-, unit-, and even segment-levels tend to involve a larger span of verses than would customarily be the case.

Repetition of 'to keep on calling' and 'voice' (Sections I and II, form-based). By repeating 'to keep on calling' and 'voice' in 8:1a and b of Section I, and again in 8:4a and b, the poet establishes that this poem consists of Lady Wisdom's communication, anticipated and then delivered. Notice that v. 4 opens the first block of Section II.

Repetition of root and word (Sections I and II, form-based). The root *rʾš*, 'head' or 'outset', and the word 'way' appear in 8:2a and in v. 22a. Notice that v. 22 opens the second unit of Block II.A. Thus v. 1 anchors a repetition that will open the first unit of Block II.A (see 'calling' and 'voice' repetition, above), while v. 2 anchors a repetition that will open the second.

Speech following itinerary of speaker (Sections I and II, content-based). Before reporting Lady Wisdom's speech (Section II, 8:4–36), the grandfather-sage describes her recruitment itinerary (Section I, vv. 1–3). He similarly described the adulteress's recruitment itinerary (7:10–13) before reporting her persuasive message (7:14–20).

Wordplay involving 'mouth' (Sections I and II, content-based). Section II consists of a speech delivered by Lady Wisdom, referring to her 'mouth' in 8:8, 13. When in Section I she calls out 'at the mouth of the town' (v. 3a), 'mouth' indicates a locale and, by wordplay, alludes to her addressing the city.

Microstructural features

Third-person perspective (8:1–3, form-based). Description of Lady Wisdom in the third person characterizes 8:1–3. A first-person voice characterizes the balance of the poem.

Section-level closure (8:3, content-based). Two themes dominate 8:1–3: speech (v. 1) and urban locales (v. 2). When both appear in v. 3 closure results.

Block-level inclusio involving 'sons of mortals' (8:4, 31, form-based). The expression 'sons of mortals' appears in Prov. 8 only at vv. 4, 31 (line-terminal in each case), bracketing Block II.A precisely. Following v. 31 Lady Wisdom transitions to deliver a closing exhortation (vv. 32–36). Although Waltke recognizes the recurrence of 'the sons of mortals' as a 'striking and meaningful frame', he divides the poem so that v. 4 is lodged amid vv. 1–5, not at the outset of vv. 4–31 (2004: 392, 422).

***Kî* ('for') as incentive marker (8:5–6, 10–11, form-based).** The quatrain of 8:5–6 initiates a pattern of imperative buttressed by incentive, with incentive introduced by explanatory *kî*, 'for'. When vv. 7–9 open with *kî*, they extend the explanatory thrust initiated in v. 6b. When vv. 10–11 present another imperative buttressed by incentive with *kî*, the pattern repeats yet again, not to recur in this poem. (When *kî* in v. 35 opens the final quatrain, it should be rendered as a reflective exclamation, 'indeed', rather than an incentive, 'for'.)

Thematic coherence regarding morality (8:7–8, content-based). The theme of morality appears in each colon of 8:7–8, unifying this verse-pair.

Summation (8:8, form-based). Positive and negative summations in 8:8 ('moral are all the words of my mouth' and 'in them is nothing tangling or twisted') intensify the theme of morality that began in v. 7.

Summation (8:11, form-based). A summation similarly closes and contributes a climax to the quatrain spanning 8:10–11: 'nothing delightful can compare with her'. This fosters a sense of climax for the portion spanning vv. 7–11 as well.

Dual-theme expressions (8:13, form-based). Tight structure governs the three parts of 8:13 (a tricolon). The Hebr. of the first portion (v. 13a) concludes with 'hate evil'. 'Evil' then recurs as the last word in the Hebr. of v. 13b, while 'hate' recurs as the last word of v. 13c (also noted as chiastic in Waltke 2004: 388, n.). In this manner the final two words of v. 13a serve as a compact dual-theme phrase, anticipating the close of vv. 13b and 13c. As Waltke observes, this structure argues against the hypothesis that v. 13a is a later addition (Waltke 2004: 388, n.; *pace* Fox 2000: 263, n., 272).

Inclusio (8:12, 14, form- and content-based). The outer verses of 8:12–14 join formally by repeating 'I', *ʾănî*, otherwise appearing in this chapter only in vv. 17, 27. Concerning content, they differ from v. 13 since they list Lady Wisdom's sapiential assets (whereas v. 13 posits a reverential principle). This inclusio contributes to the larger palistrophe operating in vv. 5–21, showcasing its pivot in v. 13 (see concerning palistrophe, below).

Repetition of 'by me' (8:15–16, form-based). By repeating 'By me' at the start of 8:15, 16, Lady Wisdom reviews what influential clients have sought her leadership counsel.

Summation (8:16, form-based). Summation accentuates the last in a list of four leaders populating the quatrain of 8:15–16: 'all who judge' (v. 16b).

Unit-level closure (Unit II.A.1, 8:20–21, content-based). The three themes of wisdom's moral character, accessibility and wealth appeared first in 8:7–11, and again in vv. 15–19. They generate closure when they recur in vv. 20–21. Lady Wisdom travels 'the route of morality . . . among footpaths of justice' (v. 20). In v. 21 she promises both accessibility (for 'those who love me', cf. v. 17) and wealth (property and full storerooms).

Palistrophic structure (8:5–21, content-based, with formal elements). A pattern of themes and terms recur across 8:5–21 to create a palistrophe. Consider, first, how three components within vv. 7–11 reappear within vv. 15–19, in the same sequence. These involve the morality of wisdom (vv. 7–8, 15–16), wisdom's accessibility (vv. 9, 17) and wisdom's wealth (vv. 10–11, 18–19). The link between the quatrain of vv. 10–11 and the quatrain of vv. 18–19, together with expressions linking vv. 10, 19, endorse the compositional integrity of v. 19 (*pace* Fox 2000: 264, n.).

Consider next how 8:5–6 balances vv. 20–21 as an introduction balances a conclusion. As observed above, the quatrain of vv. 5–6 initiates a form (imperative-plus-incentive) surrounding a theme (wisdom acquisition) that largely characterizes vv. 7–19. Closure points to the role of vv. 20–21 as a conclusion (see above).

Consider, finally, the palistrophic core in 8:12–14. As observed above, the independent personal pronoun 'I', *ʾănî*, appears in vv. 12a, 14b (inclusio) to express Lady Wisdom's identity, while synonyms for wisdom dominate the content of those two verses. At the core of this trio of verses, and of the entire palistrophe, Lady Wisdom discloses that reverence comprises the essence of her identity (v. 13).

Thus the saying in 8:13 does not so much 'break the continuity' that joins vv. 12, 14 (*pace* Waltke 2004: 388, n.), but rather draws to a focal climax the palistrophe spanning vv. 5–21 by establishing as divinely moral the foundation supporting the wisdom that vv. 12, 14 describe.

Terminal placement of 'earth', with synonyms (8:23, 26, 29, 31, form- and content-based). Terminal placement of 'earth' (along with synonyms 'remote regions', 'dust' and 'habitable land') repeatedly indicates structure across 8:22–31. 'Earth' appears in the last colon of vv. 22–23, a quatrain that coheres by anchoring a general introduction to Lady Wisdom's service during creation. 'Earth' (together with synonyms 'remote regions', 'dust' and 'habitable land) appears in the last saying of vv. 24–26, a portion portraying the uninhabitable era.

'Earth' appears in the last colon of 8:27–29, even line-terminal (as in v. 23). Those three sayings describe increasing human habitability.

'Earth' (also 'habitable land') appears in the latter saying of 8:30–31. Those lines cohere in Lady Wisdom's delight over the appearance of humankind.

By observing the deployment of 'earth' and synonyms, one may recognize both the outer boundaries encompassing all of Unit II.A.2 (operating initially in 8:22–23 and finally in the terminal line of vv. 30–31), as well as its inner portions (ending vv. 24–26 and vv. 27–29). As to its meaning, across the landscape of creation Lady Wisdom's attention focuses on 'earth' since humankind – those frail 'sons of mortals' – comprise her object of greatest delight (v. 31b).

Chiasm involving 'delight' and 'laugh' (8:30–31, form-based). 'Laughing' follows 'delight' in 8:30, chiastically reversing in v. 31 (Waltke 2004: 417).

Transitional closing pivot (8:30–31, 32–36, content-based). The quatrain unified by 'delight' and 'laugh' (8:30–31) closes this poem's longest block (Block II.A, vv. 4–31). There Lady Wisdom pivots from delighting in various geologic, atmospheric and oceanic developments (vv. 24–31a). Instead her delight now focuses on humankind itself (v. 31b). This pivot transitions to the next block – a concluding charge to her human recruits (vv. 32–36). The realization that her delight rests most keenly on them will incline them to believe that her directives have their best interests at heart.

Dual-theme introduction of 'listen' and 'fortunate' (8:32, form- and content-based). 'Listen', line-initial in 8:33, recalls 'listen' in v. 32a. 'Fortunate', line-initial in v. 34, recalls 'fortunate', colon-initial in v. 32b. Furthermore, 'listen . . . fortunate' in each case link as incentive-and-imperative, a content-based similarity. Thus v. 32a and b comprise a dual-theme introduction, expanded in vv. 33, 34. Whybray's proposal to excise v. 32a as an interpolation and to omit v. 33 as 'metrically deficient' overlooks the artistry of vv. 32–34 (1966: 494). Without noting the dual-theme structure, Fox counters that 'the MT in this section is meaningful and well designed as it stands' (2000: 289).

Assonance linking 'listen' and 'protecting' (8:32, form-based). The terms 'listen', *šimʿû*, and 'protecting', *yišmōrû*, overlap assonantally in 8:32. This formal link reinforces the content-based link of imperative-plus-incentive that also operates in these terms.

Positioning of 'Lord' across Section II (8:4–36, form-based). Within each portion where it occurs, the term 'Lord' is strategically positioned. During the appeal to reason (8:4–21), 'Lord' occurs at a palistrophic pivot

(v. 13 within vv. 5–21). During the appeal to character (vv. 22–31), 'LORD' occurs line-initial in the opening verse. During the conclusion (vv. 32–36), 'LORD' appears in the closing quatrain (vv. 35–36).

Comment

Section I (8:1–3). As observed above, the stern tone of rhetorical questions in 8:1 maintains the momentum of crisis surrounding the youth's demise at the close of Prov. 7. No wisdom commendation retards the launch of Prov. 8. The audience must wake up to the fact that the seductress was not the only one seeking to gain the hapless youth's attention. Lady Wisdom and Lady Perception also have been summoning him (8:1). As if anticipating the youth's plea of ignorance, the grandfather reviews Lady Wisdom's typical itinerary as she would circuit through town – proof of her accessibility (vv. 2–3). She begins her circuit in rather obscure communities, ending at the plaza customarily located before the city's gate-guarded entryway. Here one would expect to hear a reasoned and passionate discourse, such as follows directly in vv. 4–36 (analogous to the city-gates discourse of 1:22–33 that followed a circuit through the town in 1:20–21).

8:1. Wisdom and perception form a fixed pair (cf. 2:6; 3:13, 19; 21:30; 23:23). Within the grandfather's lectures they appear only in 5:1 (start of the first influential women poem, Cycle I), and in 8:1 (start of final influential women poem, Cycle II).

8:2–3. Compare Wisdom's similar circuit and verbs of speech in 1:20–21, reaching a destination of gates, with the objective of delivering a speech.

Section II (8:4–36). *Block II.A (8:4–31).* Within the longer, first block of Section II (Block II.A, 8:4–31), Lady Wisdom urges pursuit of wisdom based on an appeal to reason (logos of classical rhetoric), and based on her sterling character (ethos). The shorter, final block calls the audience to act on the evidence she has produced (Block II.B, vv. 32–36).

Unit II.A.1 (8:4–21). The appeal to reason begins with a pointed address ('It is to you, O men, that I keep on calling', 8:4a), and a prescription for expected behaviour: 'O naive ones – perceive cleverness! And stupid folk – perceive sense! Listen!' (vv. 5–6aα).

Incentives support these imperatives. As a preliminary incentive, she explains that wisdom will facilitate leadership, resting on a foundation of morality (8:6). Her ensuing comments present two grand arguments further incentivizing pursuit of wisdom.

Then Lady Wisdom gives three reasons for pursuing wisdom: she is moral, accessible and valuable. These appear first in 8:7–11, and again in vv. 15–19 (with greater intimacy).

After establishing wisdom's moral character, accessibility and worth in 8:7–11, Lady Wisdom focuses the youths' attention on herself as she discloses her identity: 'I am Lady Wisdom' (8:12aα). Then follows an axiom defining piety in ethical terms: 'To revere the LORD is to hate evil' (8:13a). Lest one may question whether Lady Wisdom subscribes personally to this value, she affirms, 'Pride, presumption, evil ways and a perverse mouth do I hate' (v. 13b–c).

The uncommon structural prominence enjoyed by the axiom in 8:13 emerges as Lady Wisdom turns to disclose her identity once again in v. 14: 'I am insight; mine is might'. Here begins the retracing of the palistrophe that the poet commenced in v. 5. The piety axiom of v. 13 stands at the palistrophe's pinnacle-pivot.

The morality of wisdom, first stressed in 8:7–8, returns in vv. 15–16, with 'moral' in each verse. Leadership now expands the discussion of morality.

Accessibility of wisdom, first suggested in 8:9, returns with greater clarity in v. 17. Anyone receptive to her will find Lady Wisdom.

The worth of wisdom, first declared in 8:10–11, returns in vv. 18–19. Three expressions of value in the earlier quatrain (silver, high-grade gold and corals) expand to five in the latter (riches, wealth, high-grade gold, pure gold and silver).

The double series of three incentives dominating Unit II.A.1 (8:4–21) draws to a close as Lady Wisdom reviews those three reasons in the unit's concluding quatrain. First, Wisdom confines herself to moral lanes (v. 20a, b). Second, she is accessible, rewarding any who love her (v. 21a). Third, her reward amounts to substantial worth ('property' and 'storerooms' made full in v. 21).

Unit II.A.2 (8:22–31). After the appeal to reason (8:4–21), in Unit II.A.2 (vv. 22–31) Lady Wisdom pursues an autobiographical approach, calculated to persuade by virtue of her character (ethos, in classical rhetoric).

A review of past employers and a rehearsal of service in venerable antiquity form the backbone of the first portion of her autobiography (8:22–23). As to past employers, no less than the LORD himself enlisted her aid. As to antiquity, her work history reaches back to earth's earliest era. (Concerning the structural importance of 'earth' and related synonyms appearing in terminal lines, refer to 'Microstructural features', above.)

Thereafter Lady Wisdom recalls where her interests were focused – fostering conditions of increasing human habitability (briefly noted by Waltke [2004: 411, 415], in contrast to the universal present/remote past organization proposed by Fox [2000: 281]). When she first arrived, human habitation remained unthinkable. As yet there was no dry land (8:24–26). Then waters supernaturally abated, creating habitable space (vv. 27–29). Consequently her joy knew no bounds (vv. 30–31). T. T. Perowne appropriately observes, 'Wisdom, who found glad exercise in every part and state of creation as it advanced, had her consummated joy in the adaptation of the complete whole to be the dwelling-place of man' (*Proverbs* [Cambridge: Cambridge University Press, 1916], p. 82, quoted in Waltke 2004: 422).

Such character-based persuasion should dismantle any lingering hesitation the youths may harbour towards Lady Wisdom. Surely she has their best interests at heart.

Block II.B (8:32–36). After producing reasons that recommend her offer of training (8:4–21), and after dispelling uncertainty concerning her true motives (vv. 22–31), Lady Wisdom advances to clinch her appeal. It remains only to help the youths crystallize the choice they now must make. With two strategies she addresses this task (vv. 32–36).

The first strategy presents four imperatives, plainly recapping what the youths must do (8:32–34). Her directive to 'listen', twice in vv. 32–33, may have reminded them of the imperative to 'perceive' that appeared twice in v. 5 (also 'listen' in v. 6). (For the dual-theme dimension of vv. 32–34, see under 'Microstructural features', above.)

These imperatives Lady Wisdom supports with incentives beckoning to great good fortune ('how fortunate are my ways' in 8:32b, and 'how fortunate is the mortal' in v. 34a). More than painting scenes of good fortune, Lady Wisdom is concerned to help youths visualize what authentic receptivity entails. Thus she explains that one who 'listens' should 'be alert at my doors day after day' (v. 34b). He should go so far as to 'post watch at the doorposts of my entryways' (v. 34c). These characterize the depth of receptivity within 'a mortal who listens to me'.

As a second strategy to consolidate the youths' choice, Lady Wisdom portrays two characters (8:35–36). Such concise word pictures would linger as reminders of the dramatically contrasting destinies awaiting either receptivity or refusal of wisdom. On the one hand, to discover Lady Wisdom will yield the staggering, twofold reward of life itself, together with divine favour (v. 35). Conversely, one would be hard-pressed to imagine any consequence more undesirable than what will befall those who 'wrong me' (lit. 'who sin against me', v. 36). They suffer self-harm, a veritably suicidal death-wish, determining to 'love death' (contrast vv. 17, 21). Now the youths must choose.

8:5. 'Cleverness' would uniquely aid the 'naive', characterized by gullibility.

8:8. 'The physical imagery of ethics throughout Prov 1 – 9 is consistent: Honesty is bright, straight, directly to the front. Dishonesty is dark, crooked, and off to the side – a departure from the right and bright path' (Fox 2000: 269–270). 'Tangled' and 'twisted' also appear in Deut. 32:5 and Ps. 18:26 [MT v. 27], suggesting that they function as a hendiadys (Waltke 2004: 398).

8:9. 'But in the eyes of the fool they will seem contrary and contradictory to one another' (medieval Jewish commentator Riyqam, quoted in Fox 2000: 270).

8:10. 'Get hold of my reproof' resembles a primary purpose of Proverbs (1:3).

8:10–11. The precious materials, their sequence and the expression 'nothing delightful can compare' closely parallels 3:14–15. The proposal to omit 8:11 because it might have been added later (adapted from 3:15), and because alone in 8:11 is wisdom referred to in the third person overlooks the following features (*pace* Waltke 2004: 388, n.). First, while 8:11 holds much in common with 3:15, they are not identical. Second, the expression 'those who love her' in 8:17 similarly refers to wisdom in the third person. Third, the structure whereby the three topics of 8:7–8, 9 and 10–11 respectively recycle in the three topics of 8:15–16, 17 and 18–19 indicates that v. 11 is not a later addition, but rather is integral to a larger scheme linking vv. 10–11 with vv. 18–19. Fourth, as suggested in the introduction to Prov. 4, similarities between Prov. 1 – 3 and 4 – 9 more likely result from influence of the latter six chapters upon later composition of the first three.

8:12. The sequence 'cleverness . . . strategic knowledge [lit. 'knowledge of strategies', *mĕzimmôt*]' resembles 'cleverness . . . knowledge and schemes [*mĕzimmâ*]' in 1:4.

8:13. 'For Proverbs, love and hate are not two emotions among many. They are the polar mind-sets that define the basic shape of a person's character. The wise are typified by love of wisdom and hate of deceit, fools by their perverse loves and hatreds' (Fox 2000: 275).

8:22. While superficially appealing, to identify Lady Wisdom with the second person of the Christian Trinity (as if identical with the Logos of John 1) lacks exegetical basis within Proverbs. The sage's depiction of God's employing Lady Wisdom at creation was his way of artfully announcing, 'God determined that wisdom would course through all of creation.'

8:27. Lady Wisdom carefully avoids claiming responsibility for creation. She was in attendance, a subordinate offering advice and skill. It was the LORD who brought about the various aspects of creation.

8:30–31. Fourfold mention of delight and laughter portrays the creation occasion as, above all, a period of intense joy, exuberance and celebration. As with the account in Gen. 1, here also the appearance of humankind marks a high point of creative effort.

8:32. To this point when the declaration 'So now, sons, listen to me' appears within the grandfather's lectures, it comes from the father-sage as he interrupts his rehearsal of the grandfather's poems, in order to capture afresh the wandering attention of his audience of 'sons' (5:7; 7:24). Although the expression in 8:32 is identical, here Lady Wisdom still speaks, evident by continuity of a plural audience reaching back to vv. 5–6 and continuing with the plural verbs 'listen', 'become wise' and 'run wild' in v. 33.

8:33. Repeatedly the grandfather has elevated reproof as that facet of wisdom most to be prized – from the start (4:1), at strategic junctures (5:12; 6:23; 7:22; 8:10) and at the close of Cycles I and II (5:23 and 8:33, respectively). Nothing is so calculated and capable of leading the youth out of naivety into wisdom as reproof (8:33a). And nothing is so likely to stir resentment and defiant autonomy (v. 33b).

8:35. 'One who has found a wife has found a good thing, and so has obtained approval from the LORD' (18:22).

Explanation

After exposing in Prov. 7 the fatal consequences awaiting those who succumb to seduction of illicit pleasures, now in Prov. 8 the grandfather-sage expends time and considerable skill to showcase the alternative. 'Everything in the chapter serves the rhetorical goal of influencing the reader to desire wisdom' (Fox 2000: 293).

The counsel within Prov. 8 clusters around two primary themes. The nature of authentic wisdom marks the first, while the second involves qualities of an effective wisdom teacher.

The nature of authentic wisdom

The sage traces the nature of wisdom to a pair of underlying axioms. First, wisdom is rooted unalterably in soil that is moral (8:5–9, 13, 15–16, 18, 20). Second, reverence supplies the substratum for that soil (v. 13).

The twin axioms of reverence and morality translate into a caution. One must beware of any advice masquerading as 'wisdom', when that advice (a) springs from an attitude lacking reverence, or (b) leads to activities lacking morality. For example, although the sage would argue that wisdom is eminently 'pragmatic', that pragmatism (a) must not be dismissive of the divine and (b) must not advance self at the expense of others.

These two axioms lead to three corollaries. First, piety without morality is a logical impossibility (8:13a). Second, rule requires morality. Without morality, responsible rule dissolves into cruel tyranny (vv. 15–16). Third, unwise wealth – the sort gained or spent without morality – can only impoverish (vv. 10–11, 18–19, 21).

Wisdom of this reverent and moral sort will lead to doubly desirable consequences. It will result in a life marked by profound vitality and divine approval (8:35). Those who dismiss wisdom's invitation self-destruct (v. 36).

The voice of wisdom is readily audible. '*Something* is calling, some voice is heard. But whose? It is, the author declares, surely Wisdom whose voice we hear everywhere, loud and clear – unless we perversely choose to stopple [plug] our ears' (Fox 2000: 265; emphasis original).

A response of eager receptivity must follow detection of wisdom's voice. That receptivity will embrace even reproof (8:10a, 33). Only then will maximal benefit follow (vv. 32–34). If reprimand instead provokes either indiscipline or defiant autonomy, we must beware.

Qualities of a teacher of wisdom

Alongside the nature of authentic wisdom, this lecture also portrays three aspects of an effective wisdom teacher. They involve the teacher's inner character, how he or she relates to pupils and how the teacher approaches the craft of communication.

The teacher's inner character

Reverence towards the God of Israel will permeate the wisdom teacher, as through life (8:22–23), so through lecture (v. 13). Some may deign to teach without reverence. But it will not be wisdom they instruct.

Consistent with reverence, a sage's teaching will be characterized by what is ethical and reliable. It will avoid moral compromise and misleading messages (8:7–8).

The teacher's relationship with pupils

The well-being of pupils will matter deeply to the effective wisdom teacher (8:30–31). 'However lofty her origins and status, Wisdom cares about people, even the less worthy, and seeks them out' (Fox 2000: 267). Such a teacher will respond with loving generosity towards those affectionately devoted to wisdom (vv. 17, 34).

The perceptive sage will not prematurely exclude seemingly unlikely learners. Even for the naive and stupid he or she will map a way forward, leading them to success (8:5). For wisdom remains available to any who display interest (v. 4).

The teacher's craft of communication

Propelled by a deep caring for her or his students, the wisdom teacher refuses to sit idly, waiting for potential pupils to take initiative. 'Far from being esoteric or academic, Wisdom plunges into the midst of this hustle and bustle to reach people where *they* are' (Fox 2000: 267; emphasis original; 8:2–3). When reason will be most effective, his communication will resound with logic (vv. 4–21). When reason requires balance through character-illustration, logic will give way to story (vv. 22–31).

Through Poem 9 (7:1–27) and Poem 10 (8:1–36) the grandfather-sage portrayed competing characters. First emerged the sly adulteress, with her sweet-smelling but deadly bed. Then appeared Lady Wisdom, combining reason and story with reverence and morality, ultimately leading to robust vitality and divine approval. With the scene thus set, Poem 11 (9:1–18) will match these same figures in a final contest. Whom will the youth follow?

PROVERBS 9:1–18
'Whose invitation should I accept: Lady Wisdom's or Dame Folly's?' (Poem 11 in Prov. 4 – 9, conclusion)

Overview of Proverbs 9:1–18

With Prov. 9 (Poem 11) the grandfather-sage concludes his lectures much as he commenced them (Poem 1, 4:1–9), weaving together themes of reprimand, body behaviour and influential women. For an overview of themes, refer to 'Principal themes in Proverbs 4 – 9' in the introduction to Prov. 4 – 9, above.

The drama unfolding in Prov. 9 presents two figurative women who compete for a single prize. Through their respective banquet invitations, coupled with meal preparation (or lack thereof), they hope to persuade the 'naive' and 'senseless' to attend their respective feasts.

Several mysteries naturally follow. Whose invitation will the guests accept? And where will those invitations ultimately lead? Since both invitations sound so similar, how can candidates wisely discern the better? Each of these puzzles the grandfather-sage concisely, carefully resolves in this, his climactic lecture.

Position of this poem within Proverbs

Preceding context. The rival women of Prov. 9 are not new to the sage's lessons. The actress who played the adulteress of Prov. 7 now returns, more clearly costumed (i.e. labelled) as 'Dame Folly' – Lady Wisdom's unmistakable rival (9:13–18).

Unlike the sly adulteress, Lady Wisdom is by nature a candid character. Consequently her 'costume' (her character label) in 9:1–12 remains virtually unchanged from her prior performance in Prov. 8. She remains 'Lady Wisdom' as before, only more so. In 8:1 the sg. 'wisdom', *ḥokmâ*, identified her, whereas now she bears the title 'wisdoms', *ḥokmôt* (9:1, as in 1:20; Hebr. often employs a pl. to designate an abstract concept).

In addition to previewing characters that play in Prov. 9, preceding context also foreshadows those destinies to which each woman will conduct her guests. The one reliably leads to ever-expanding life, while the other leads inexorably to death (contrast 8:35 and 9:11 with 7:27 and 9:18).

Ensuing context. The second major division of the book will begin following Prov. 9 – a division introduced by the heading beginning Prov. 10: 'The proverbs of Solomon'. Aside from a subheading at 24:23a ('These, too, pertain to the wise'), the lectures commencing in Prov. 10 will extend until the material edited by Hezekiah's staff, signalled by yet another major heading: 'These, too, are Solomonic proverbs, which the men of Hezekiah, king of Judah, arranged' (25:1).

Regarding topics, in Prov. 10 – 24 the sage will expend less energy arguing the worth of wisdom. Instead he will concentrate on situation-specific counsels. For example, in his first lecture he anticipates that his youthful audience may desire wealth, and so offers advice for that specific situation (10:1–22). In the second he advises concerning how to weather adverse life experiences (10:23–30).

What to watch for

A shift of characters marks the large-scale structure of Prov. 9, beginning with Lady Wisdom in the first twelve verses, and transitioning to Dame Folly in the remaining six. While their respective invitations differ little, pronounced contrasts mark the extent of preparation, the 'food' provided for guests, and ultimate consequences enjoyed (or suffered) by guests.

It is instructive to listen for a second layer within Lady Wisdom's counsel. This deeper layer would benefit not the novice wisdom adherents, but those guests who had matured to the point of becoming the next wisdom hosts, sages who would perpetuate the tradition by discipling the next generation of naive youth.

Translation and outline

Verse	*Translation*	*Outline*
		I. Industrious Lady Wisdom invites guests; then offers beneficial counsel (9:1–12)
		A. Introduction of industrious Lady Wisdom (vv. 1–3)
9:1	Lady Wisdom has built her house, she has quarried her seven pillars.	1. She has built her house (v. 1)
9:2	She has butchered her meat, she has mixed her wine; she has even spread her table!	2. She has spread her banquet (v. 2)
9:3	Having sent out her maidens, she began to call out, atop the city's lofty sites.	3. She has dispatched her messengers (v. 3)
		B. Invitation to Lady Wisdom's banquet (vv. 4–6)
9:4	'Whoever is naive, may he turn aside here! O senseless one!' she said to him.	1. The focus of invitation: the naive and senseless (v. 4)
9:5	'Come! Feast on my food and drink of my mixed wine!	2. The appeal of legitimate food (v. 5)
9:6	'Part company with naive folk, and live! Straight on, now, in the way of insight!'	3. A redirection into life (v. 6)
		C. Her banquet's two courses, with rationales (vv. 7–12)
		1. Two courses of counsel (vv. 7–10)
9:7	'One who reproves a scoffer grasps for himself disgrace, and one who reprimands a guilty person, his injury.	a. First course: a wisdom commendation concerning issuing reproof to wise and to scoffer (vv. 7–9)
9:8	'Do not reprimand a scoffer lest he hate you; reprimand a wise person so he may love you.	

Verse	Translation	Outline
9:9	'Give it to a wise person so he may grow wiser still; educate a moral person so he may expand training.	
9:10	'The starting point of wisdom is reverence for the Lord; and knowledge of the Holy One is insight.	b. Second course: wisdom content concerning reverence for Israel's God (v. 10)
		2. Rationales for embracing Lady Wisdom's invitation (vv. 11–12)
9:11	'For it is by me that your days will multiply, so that they may increase for you years of vitality.	a. Wisdom's reward of longevity (v. 11)
9:12	'If you have been wise, you have been wise for yourself; but if you have been scoffing, you alone must bear the consequences'.	b. Character summary and dual-theme conclusion: retributive consequences for wise and scoffer (v. 12)
		II. Indolent Dame Folly invites guests; then inflicts deadly consequences (vv. 13–18) A. Introduction of indolent Dame Folly (vv. 13–15)
9:13	Dame Folly makes a lot of racket – naivety! And she knows utterly nothing.	1. She builds only commotion (v. 13)
9:14	So also she sits at the doorway of her house, upon a chair among the city's lofty sites,	2. She presumes a position of honour (v. 14)
9:15	In order to call out to wayfarers, to those who are making their paths straight.	3. She only waylays persons already on a mission (v. 15)
		B. Invitation from Dame Folly (vv. 16–17)
9:16	'Whoever is naive, may he turn aside here – the senseless one too!' so also she said to him.	1. The focus of invitation: the naive and senseless (v. 16)
9:17	'Stolen waters can be sweet, and secret food can be delightful.'	2. The appeal of illicit food (v. 17)
9:18	But he does not know that the shades are there; in the depths of Sheol are her guests.	C. Rationale for rejecting Dame Folly's invitation: a deadly destiny (v. 18)

Notes on the text

9:1. 'Lady Wisdom', *ḥokmôt*: lit. 'wisdoms' (as in 1:20). Although pl., the verbs *ḥokmôt* governs in 9:1–3 are sg. ('built', 'quarried', 'prepared', 'mixed', 'spread' and 'sent out'; see 'Notes' for 1:20). The shift from sg. *ḥokmâ*, 'Lady Wisdom, in Prov. 8:1 to pl. *ḥokmôt*, 'Lady Wisdom', in 9:1 may signify an escalation or consolidation of dignity.

'[she] has built her house, she has quarried her seven pillars', *bānĕtâ bêtāh ḥāṣĕbâ ʿammûdeyhā šibĕʿâ*: assonance joins 'built', *bānĕtâ*, with 'her house', *bêtāh*. 'To quarry' and 'pillars' may refer to the fashioning of great wooden posts (cf. 1 Kgs 7:2; Isa. 10:15).

9:2. 'she has butchered her meat', *ṭābḥâ ṭibḥāh*: the shared root *ṭbḥ* results in assonance.

'she has mixed her wine': 'mixed wine' has been reconstituted, often enhanced with spice or honey (also 9:5).

9:2b–3a. 'her table! Having sent out her maidens', *šālĕḥâ naʿărōteyhā*: assonance again joins adjacent words, here linking the end of 9:2 with the beginning of v. 3.

9:3a. 'Having sent out her maidens, she began to call out': inceptive 'began to' inferred based on the syntax of preparatory activity, 'sending out' (qat. conjugation) contrasting present activity, 'calling out', to invite guests (yiq. conjugation; cf. Fox 2000: 295–296).

9:3b. 'atop the city's lofty sites': lit. 'upon an elevation of lofty parts of a city' – a remarkably public setting within the city (Fox 2000: 298).

9:5. 'Come! Feast on my food', *lĕkû laḥămû bĕlaḥămî*: linked by assonance surrounding the root *lḥm*, 'food', 'bread'. The verbs of vv. 5–6 are pl., envisioning a group. In 9:7–12 verbs focus on a single learner.

'of my mixed wine': lit. 'of wine [that] I have mixed'.

9:6. 'naive folk', *pĕtāʾyîm*: not 'naivety' (which will appear in 9:13; Waltke 2004: 427, n.; *pace* Fox 2000: 295, who renders, 'callowness').

9:7b. 'and one who reprimands a guilty person, his injury', *ûmôkîaḥ lĕrāšāʿ mûmô*: the expression 'grasps for himself' is implied by ellipsis from the first colon ('and one who reprimands a guilty person [grasps for himself] his injury').

9:8. 'so he may love you', *wĕyeʾĕhābekā*: a weyiq. verb (such as 'to love') following a command (such as 'Do not reprimand') expresses an indirect juss. with a sense of consequence (Joüon §116d).

9:9. 'Give it to a wise person': lit. 'give to a wise person'. Fox correctly infers that, based on 9:7–8, the gift one should 'give' to a wise person would consist of reprimand (2000: 296). Unlike the scoffer of vv. 6–7, a wise person will prize such a gift.

'so he may grow wiser still', *wĕyeḥkam ʿôd*: another indirect juss. conveying consequence (9:8, above); similarly 'so he may expand' (v. 9b) and 'so that they may increase' (v. 11b).

9:10. 'The starting point', *tĕḥillat*: by employing *tĕḥillat* instead of *rē'šît* (as appears in Prov. 1:7), Lady Wisdom establishes reverence for the LORD as the onset of wisdom rather than its zenith.

'and knowledge of the Holy One': this designates not information about, but personal acquaintance with, the divine, corresponding to the sage's injunction to 'know him' (see 'Notes' for 3:6 and Fox 2000: 309). Near the book's close Agur affirms 'knowledge of the Holy One' (30:3).

'the Holy One': an honorific pl. conveying majesty or sovereignty, thus rendered sg. ('Holy One', not 'holy ones'; cf. GKC §124h and Prov. 30:3; also Hos. 11:12 [MT 12:1]).

9:11. 'For it is by me that your days will multiply', *kî-bî yirbû yāmeykā*: the agency of Lady Wisdom (above the service she provides) is emphasized by locating 'by me' ahead of the verb 'to multiply'.

To emend *bî*, 'by me', to read *bāh*, 'by it' (i.e. by wisdom), as suggested by LXX, Syriac and Targum (also Waltke 2004: 428, n., 442) is inadvisable for several reasons. First, such an emendation would diminish the sense of closure achieved, as *bî*, 'by me', resumes in the rationale-portion (9:11–12) the first-person address Lady Wisdom began in v. 4. Second, the change would blunt the rhetorical impact of Lady Wisdom's parting remarks in vv. 11–12. Instead of forcefully and personally confronting the prospective guest by declaring, in effect, 'Son, when you look at me you are looking at your ticket to longevity – take it or leave it!', the emendation 'by it' would cancel the personification, weakly replacing it with a reference to abstract wisdom. Third, the emendation makes it harder to recognize vv. 7–10 as a unit of wisdom teaching intentionally encased within the larger invitation extended by personified wisdom. This unit comprises a premier sample of Lady Wisdom's teaching – the sort of metaphoric 'meal' she is so eager to offer her guest-pupils. To convert 'by me' to 'by it' superficially smooths the text by solving a seeming irregularity – a jarring expression calculated by the poet to seize the reader's attention, so he or she will not miss the forceful conclusion the sage delivers at that point.

'so that they may increase for you years of vitality', *wĕyôsîpû lĕkā šĕnôt ḥayyîm*: the expression 'your days' (9:11a) supplies the subject-antecedent of 'they': 'so that [your days] may increase for you years of vitality'. Unnecessary is the LXX rendition 'so that years of vitality may be added for you' (requiring emendation of hiph. *wĕyôsîpû* with niph. *wĕyiwwāsĕpû* for a pass. meaning).

It is similarly unnecessary to treat 'they' in 'they may increase' as an indefinite subject without antecedent (*pace* Waltke, who renders, 'and years of life will be added to you' [2004: 428]). Although Fox affirms the original hiph., he overlooks 'your days' as the antecedent subject, resulting in an expression similar to LXX and Waltke: 'and years be added to your life' (Fox 2000: 299–300). It should be noted that the noun 'years' (f.) in 9:11b cannot stand as the subject of the verb *yôsîpû*, 'increase' (m.), without appealing to exceptional Hebr. grammar.

9:12. 'If you have been wise . . . ; but if you have been scoffing', *ʾim-ḥākamtā . . . wĕlaṣtā*: 'if' in 'but if you have been scoffing' is inferred from the first colon by ellipsis. The protasis verbs ('you have been wise' and 'you have been scoffing') are either qat. or cop. weqat. forms, indicating a condition already fulfilled (GKC §159.1). As a result the apodoses ('you have been wise' and 'you alone must bear the consequences') describe not potential but assured outcomes, whether realized already ('you have been wise for yourself'), or still pending ('you alone must bear the consequences').

'you have been wise for yourself': alternatively this may mean 'you have gained wisdom concerning yourself'.

'you alone must bear the consequences': lit. 'you alone will lift up', here implying 'to bear a load'; especially a load of consequential suffering (cf. Prov. 30:21, which, like 9:12, lacks an object). The mandate 'must' is inferred also from the yiq., in the context of ominous outcomes. The object 'consequences' is inferred for the verb 'lift up' (cf. Prov. 30:21 and *HALOT*, s.v. '*nśʾ*').

9:13. 'Dame Folly', *ʾēšet kĕsîlût*: lit. 'wife/woman of folly' or 'foolish wife/woman'. The designation *ʾēšet*, 'wife', helps cement the connection between Dame Folly of Prov. 9 and the adulteress of Prov. 7 (Waltke 2004: 443). A similar expression appeared in 6:24: *ʾēšet rāʿ*, 'Dame Evil'.

'naivety!', *pĕtayyût*: unaccompanied, the abstract concept 'naivety' stands as an exclamation. To this the sage appends with a sense of exasperation: 'And [what is more,] she knows utterly nothing!' Assonance joins *pĕtayyût*, 'naivety' (9:13b), with *kĕsîlût*, 'folly' (v. 13a).

'racket': this term describes the adulteress's boisterous conduct (rendered 'raucous' in 7:11; Waltke 2004: 443).

9:14. 'upon a chair among the city's lofty sites': Dame Folly displays presumption by positioning herself on a chair with a regal connotation ('throne'), since chairs were generally reserved for persons of honour – especially monarchs (Waltke 2004: 429, 444).

9:17. 'secret food', *leḥem setārîm*: secrecy associated with Dame Folly's meal may refer both to its source (obtained by theft) and its effect (inflicting death; cf. 9:18). 'The wise recognize her words as an unintended warning to be wary of sweet pleasures, for the sweetness is just a coating for their poison' (Fox 2000: 302).

Form and structure

Borders

The upper border is marked by thematic transition from the extensive poem describing Lady Wisdom (ending 8:36), shifting to the competing invitations from Lady Wisdom and Dame Folly (beginning 9:1).

As Dame Folly's invitation ends (with the sage's analysis), so also does the poem (9:18). An inclusio reinforces the lower border. 'Not knowing' encircles all of Dame Folly's section, appearing in vv. 13, 18 (so also Waltke 2004: 430).

Macrostructural features

Rival characters (Sections I and II, content-based). The entire poem revolves around two characters, Lady Wisdom (9:1–12) and Dame Folly (vv. 13–18). They compete for guests, coaxed to their banquets.

Reversals involving food and ultimate destinations (Sections I and II, content-based). Where Lady Wisdom offers legitimate wine (9:5), Dame Folly substitutes stolen water (v. 17). Where Lady Wisdom promises robust vitality (v. 6), Dame Folly escorts her guests to the deadly netherworld (v. 18).

Microstructural features

Thematic continuity concerning Lady Wisdom's estate (9:1–3, form-based). Various aspects of Lady Wisdom's estate dominate her introduction. House, pillars, meat, wine, table and maidens – all belong to 'her' (9:1–3).

Inclusio regarding 'naive' (9:4, 6, form-based). Mention of 'naive' encircles Lady Wisdom's three lines of invitation, appearing in the first colon of both 9:4 and 9:6 (so also Waltke 2004: 436).

Wisdom commendation followed by wisdom content (9:7–9, 10, content-based). The emphasis on receptivity to reproof in 9:7–9 marks these verses as a wisdom commendation. They lead to wisdom content concerning the foundational nature of reverence in the next saying (v. 10).

Counsels followed by rationale (9:7–12, content-based). Lady Wisdom follows her counsels (receptivity to reproof in 9:7–9, and reverence in v. 10) with rationales introduced by explanatory *kî*, 'for' (vv. 11–12). Rationales consist of longevity and retribution.

Dual-theme conclusion with character summary (9:12, form-based). Of the various characters referred to in 9:7–9, two are mentioned twice. The scoffer appears first (vv. 7a, 8a), followed by the wise person (vv. 8b, 9a). Words deriving from the roots for 'scoffer' and 'wise person' recur in v. 12, using verbal forms rather than nouns ('to be wise' rather than 'wise person', 'to engage in scoffing' rather than 'scoffer'). Since v. 12 comprises the final line of Lady Wisdom's instruction-speech, mention of wise and scoffing in that verse forms a dual-theme conclusion to Lady Wisdom's speech. In typical dual-theme fashion, each term occupies its own colon (albeit in reverse order, ending with scoffing). Since the two themes consist of contrasting characters and appear at the close of a speech, they operate also as a character summary.

Repetition of root for 'naivety' (9:13, 16, form-based). The term *pĕtayyût*, 'naivety', appears in 9:13, the opening verse of Dame Folly's introduction (vv. 13–15). *Petî*, 'naive', a term sharing the same root, appears in v. 16, the opening verse of her invitation (vv. 16–17). Since she embodies 'naivety', Dame Folly is as much in need of wise guidance as are her naive guests.

Comment

To suggest that Prov. 1 – 8 would conclude more persuasively if Prov. 9 were omitted underestimates the zenith of confrontation achieved by placing in tandem fashion, within a single lecture, the competing appeals of Wisdom and Folly (*pace* Fox 2000: 307). The youth cannot escape making a choice, either for or against Wisdom (cf. Waltke 2004: 429).

Overview of progression of thought. *Section I (9:1–12).* The story or parable of invitations by Lady Wisdom and by Dame Folly unfolds in two parallel scenes, producing what may be the simplest structure of the entire book. Lady Wisdom begins by making preparations (9:1–3). Then she issues guest invitations (vv. 4–6). Since the meal is metaphoric, her fare consists of valuable counsel (vv. 7–12). These three (preparation, invitation and counsel) comprise Section I (vv. 1–12).

9:1. While the indication of 'seven' pillars in 9:1 has inclined some to seek a sevenfold division of Prov. 1 – 9 (Skehan 1947), it seems better to regard 'seven pillars' as a device portraying the magnificence of Lady Wisdom's metaphoric mansion, boasting nearly twice the grandeur of a typical four-pillared house.

9:8. In an Egyptian wisdom collection bearing his name, Anchsheshonq advises along the lines of 9:8, 'Do not instruct a fool, lest he hate you. Do not instruct him who will not listen to you' (7.4–5, M. Lichtheim, *Late Egyptian Wisdom Literature in the International Context: A Study of Demotic Instructions* [1983: 72], in Fox 2000: 311).

9:10. Concerning reverence as the source point of wisdom (9:10), Waltke observes, 'The wise, who deserve to sit at Wisdom's table, begin their educability with their submission to the highest Authority, the Lord' (2004: 441).

Section II (9:13–18). Then follows Dame Folly's competing appeal, featuring the same three components in the same order (Section II, 9:13–18). Yet something has gone awry. Her preparation rings hollow (vv. 13–15), her invitation is suspect (vv. 16–17), and the wisdom counsel located here comes not from Dame Folly, but from the sage, as he warns the pupil to avoid her at all costs (v. 18).

9:13. As shown by Fox, it is not necessary to look beyond a figurative contrast to Lady Wisdom when inquiring about the origins of Dame Folly (2000: 303–305). Speculations that Dame Folly might have been modelled on fertility goddesses fail to convince, owing both to insufficient evidence and the diminution of her (im)moral influence that would follow such foreign modelling.

9:15. The 'wayfarers . . . who are making their paths straight' (9:15) may correspond to the messengers of Lady Wisdom. If so, Dame Folly does not hesitate to divert even Lady Wisdom's choice emissaries, strategically undercutting her opponent's overtures.

9:17. Concerning the sweetness of stolen waters (9:17), Fox comments:

> Stolen, clandestine pleasures have a special tang because they give a feeling of surplus of possession, of having more than is one's due. There is a special sense of power to be had from defying authority and transgressing boundaries, and in that way furtively imposing one's will on a corner of the moral economy. (2000: 302)

Arab. culture offers a parallel saying: 'Everything forbidden is sweet' (J. L. Burckhardt, *Arabic Proverbs*, in Thomas 1965: 272).

9:18. A text from Ugarit in ancient Syria describes the high god El hosting 'shades' for a banquet, spread at his palace (Fox 2000: 302–303). In contrast, although a meal invitation tantalized in Prov. 9:13, all sense of festivity disappears by the time Dame Folly's guests reach their final destination in the netherworld (v. 18).

Contrast in progression of parallel components. Comparison of corresponding elements in the parallel appeals yields several observations. Consider first how progression within Lady Wisdom's introduction differs from progression of Dame Folly's introduction.

Host preparations (9:1–3, 13–15). The sage introduces Lady Wisdom with an aura of industry, elegance and orderliness. With forethought she builds an impressive home (9:1). She proceeds to prepare a sumptuous feast (v. 2). So elegant a mansion and feast would incline passersby to wonder whether they might be so fortunate as to gain admittance. The answer arrives at once, when the hostess dispatches her messengers with guest invitations (v. 3).

In contrast, the introduction of Dame Folly features noisy and ignorant indolence. Despite generating 'a lot of racket' (perhaps imitating the commotion of grand construction emanating from Lady Wisdom's property), Dame Folly has nothing to show for it. Consistent with her name, she 'knows utterly nothing' (9:13). Instead of spreading a table with food, her preparations (if such they can be called) consist of seating herself in a chair of honour, motionless (v. 14). The only noise she makes is brazenly to accost and intercept 'wayfarers' who purposefully stride past, intent on their business (v. 15). Dame Folly's indolence is no surprise, since she embodies naivety (v. 13b).

Invitations extended (9:4–6, 16–17). Like her introduction, Lady Wisdom's invitation moves through three orderly steps (9:4–6). First, she secures the attention of potential guests individually ('"O senseless one!" she said to him', v. 4; Waltke 2004: 437). Next, she indicates what they must do (partaking of her feast, v. 5). That meal transitions from literal to metaphoric as she directs them to part ways with the 'naive' and proceed straight ahead into 'insight' (v. 6).

Dame Folly mimics the opening lines of Lady Wisdom's invitation, cunningly riding the coattails of Lady Wisdom's credibility (cf. vv. 4, 16). Yet Folly's meal results from theft, not honest industry. Lest her illicit fare deter prospective guests, she admits moral bankruptcy, while brazenly portraying it as an exotic opportunity: 'stolen waters can be sweet, and secret food can be delightful' (v. 17).

Specific counsel (9:7–12, 18). A third contrast that distinguishes the approaches of the two women pertains to the counsels that follow their respective invitations in Sections I and II. After Lady Wisdom invites to a metaphoric meal (9:4–6), she serves two 'courses' (*pace* Fox, who regards vv. 7–10 as a later addition, relocating them after v. 18 [2000: 306]). At this point she narrows her focus from the wider audience of vv. 5–6 (2 pl.), now addressing an audience of one in vv. 7–12.

The initial course in her metaphoric meal trains pupils concerning how to issue reproof (9:7–9). Three features are noteworthy. First, persons who issue reproof would not be novices, but wisdom teachers-in-training. Here, at the close of his teachings, the grandfather franchises wisdom instruction, ensuring its transmission long after he is gone.

Second, by specifying reproof rather than other wisdom forms, the grandfather elevates adversative counsel (9:7–9). Here is wisdom of the highest grade.

Third, it is noteworthy that, although a distinct skill is advocated here (in 9:7–9 one must learn to distinguish who will be receptive to reproof), because this skill is intrinsic to a wisdom teacher's career, this teaching belongs to the category of a wisdom commendation.

After training concerning issuing reproof, Lady Wisdom features reverence as second course in her metaphoric meal. Here is the wisdom content she presents. It is an eminently suitable selection, since reverence constitutes 'the starting point' (9:10a). Yet authentic reverence will not remain the end point, a dread and distant awareness of the divine. For it will lead to close acquaintance, reverently anchored in his transcendence as the Holy One (v. 10b; concerning 'knowledge' as acquaintance, see on 3:6).

As an aside, consider how the topics of reproof and reverence in Lady Wisdom's teaching (9:7–10) parallel the sage-son's inaugural lecture (1:1–9). Only 'reproof' appears twice among a trio of wisdom synonyms in 1:2–3. And when that poet selected two principles to feature in that first lecture, his choice fell on reverence and receptivity-to-reproof (1:7 and 8–9, respectively). Thus the sage-son created a broad inclusio by commencing his own lectures (Prov. 1 – 3) with a pair of principles that featured most prominently in the last of the grandfather-sage's lectures (Prov. 4 – 9).

Lady Wisdom concludes her teaching with a pair of sayings that buttress her exhortations with rationales (9:11–12). The first rationale declares that it is through her one may achieve robust longevity (v. 11a) of a sort far superior to mere existence (v. 11b) – a stark contrast to the deadly outcome suffered by Dame Folly's guests (v. 18).

Her second rationale explains that the pupil's every choice, whether for wisdom or scoffing, will recoil upon the pupil, bringing its own consequences (9:12). The principle of retribution – that bedrock of the sage's world view – ensures that each choice privileging wisdom will be in the pupil's own best interests.

In Lady Wisdom's rationales, the return of multiple themes generates a strong sense of closure (9:11–12). The return of first-person language ('by me' in v. 11a) is reminiscent of v. 5 ('my food'). 'Vitality' (lit. 'life', v. 11) recalls 'live' from v. 6a. As Fox observes, v. 11 'directly reinforces v. 6' (2000: 299). Mention of both wise and scoffer in v. 12 recalls these concepts from vv. 7–9 (also noted in Waltke 2004: 439; *pace* Fox, who considers v. 12 a later addition [2000: 317]).

Since Lady Wisdom follows up her invitation (9:4–6) by presenting her counsel and rationale (vv. 7–12), the parallel structure of this poem leads one to expect that counsel and rationale would follow Dame Folly's invitation in vv. 16–17. However, only rationale follows in v. 18, without counsel. The silence of Dame Folly precisely on the point of counsel exposes her wisdom bankruptcy.

Even the rationale that appears in 9:18 is unconventional. For instead of Dame Folly's voice (which we would expect), the grandfather's voice breaks in. And in place of rationale arguing *for* the preceding invitation, this rationale argues vigorously *against* it. Disaster will befall any who ignorantly accept her invitation. For, contrary to popular thought, what you don't know *will* hurt you: 'But he does not know that the shades are there, in the depths of Sheol are her guests' (9:18; cf. 7:23, where the youth 'does not know' how fatal his foolish choice will prove). What a striking contrast to Lady Wisdom's incentive of 'multiplied days' and 'increased vitality' (v. 11)!

Explanation

So compact and carefully framed is the grandfather's closing poem, that scarcely a line lacks a lesson for life. Consider first how Lady Wisdom as host epitomizes the master-teacher of wisdom.

Lady Wisdom as master-teacher does not pontificate. Instead she spends herself for others, with generosity and industry inviting, then training the next generation of learners (9:1–3). Her generosity is not unqualified, however. Those who would qualify as guests must demonstrate genuine hunger (v. 5) combined with a willingness to replace old and harmful associations with a new direction in life (v. 6).

The wise master-teacher prepares her learners to become the next generation of teachers, helping them identify potential disciples based on two features. First, their future pupils must display receptivity even when confronted with reproof, that most precious of all forms of wisdom (9:7–9). Lacking receptivity, no counsels can possibly take root in the resistant soil of the student's heart. According to Mark, Jesus similarly inaugurated his teachings with a parable requiring receptivity (Mark 4:1–20). Within it he queried his disciples, 'You don't understand this parable? Then how are you going to understand any [other] parables?' (Mark 4:13).

Reverence for the LORD comprises the first principle to which a wisdom aspirant must respond with receptivity (9:10a). The pupil dismissive of reverence will proceed hopelessly at cross-purposes to the design of the universe as configured by the divine.

Beyond initial and persistent reverence (9:10a) one must progress to personal acquaintance with the divine in his inestimable holiness (v. 10b). 'Such knowledge is not erudition, but an untutored awareness of divinity – God's presence, will, and works' (Fox 2000: 309).

Only wisdom will yield vibrant longevity (9:11). This outcome is dependable, since the retributive nature of wisdom and folly is woven into the fabric of creation (v. 12).

Folly, Wisdom's rival, launches a competitive but hollow appeal, with nothing to back it up (9:13–14). Her enterprise is parasitic. Whatever temporary prize her followers may obtain issues from theft, advertised by the allure of the illicit. When Folly's guests pause to savour her fare, they must do so furtively, fugitives on the run (v. 17).

Whereas Wisdom offers life (9:6), Folly can promise nothing but death. Her past customers now lodge in the bleak netherworld (v. 18). By launching these two starkly opposing invitations side by side within this final lecture of Prov. 1 – 9, the sage disallows further delay of decision. Will the youth follow Lady Wisdom into life? Or will he be led to death by Dame Folly?

DIVISION II (PROV. 10 – 24): ADVICE FOR THE APPRENTICE SAGE

Like Division I (Prov. 1 – 9), Division II (chs. 10–24) is attributed to Solomon. This portion displays greater subtlety of form than Division I. Poem borders are less distinct, leading the medieval Jewish scholar Sa'adia Gaon (AD 882–942) to conclude that what follows Prov. 9 'consists of proverbs and words of instruction in disconnected utterances' (quoted in Fox 2000: 318). Nevertheless, structures that foster beginnings, endings, separations, cohesion and progression in Division I persist in Division II (cf. §2 in 'Introduction'). As if to stress continuity of structures, the first lecture (10:1–22) presents no fewer than six wisdom commendations (vv. 1, 8, 13, 14, 17, 21).

Regarding content, Division II expends less energy convincing the youth to enrol as wisdom's pupil. Evidently, he has already crossed that bridge. So the poet undertakes a wider range of questions, such as 'How can I become rich?' (10:1–22) and 'How may I achieve true satisfaction?' (13:1–25).

Along with teaching wisdom learners, in Division II the sage cultivates wisdom trainers. Of the final six lectures (15:7 – 24:34), five include advice – even scripts – equipping pupils to counsel others. For a fuller discussion of inter-poem progression, inter-division progression and the audience intended for Division II, see §3.2 in the 'Introduction'.

PROVERBS 10 – 13: PERSONAL WEALTH AND SATISFACTION

Unlike the corporate outlook that often will characterize Prov. 14 – 24, teachings about wealth and satisfaction of a personal sort dominate Prov. 10 – 13.

PROVERBS 10:1–22
'How can I become rich?'

Overview of Proverbs 10:1–22
The initial lecture of Prov. 10 – 24 addresses the implicit question 'How can I become rich?' (10:1–22). Yet this lecture will not confine itself to tangible wealth. After advising timely diligence (10:4–5), the sage will move beyond tangible wealth to address intangible assets (vv. 6–22).

Two axioms dominate this lecture: tangible riches are limited, while intangible wealth exceeds the value of tangible riches. Both principles emerge early (within Section I, 10:1–7). They resurface periodically before reaching a profound climax in the concluding verse (v. 22).

Position of this poem within Proverbs
Preceding context. The grandfather-sage's teaching closed in Prov. 9 by confronting the pupil with a life-and-death choice: Whom would he follow? Would he enrol with generous Lady Wisdom to enjoy her sumptuous 'meal', focusing on receptivity-to-reproof and reverence? Or would he succumb to the allure of the illicit, furtively feeding on a fugitive's meagre fare – the best Dame Folly can offer? Against this backdrop, pursuit of tangible riches in Prov. 10 comprises one of the lures Dame Folly would dangle before a prospective guest-pupil she seeks to entice. It is instructive to observe that, aside from an introductory poem (1:1–9), a lecture

cautioning against pursuit of illicit riches comprises the book's first lecture (1:10–19; so also Waltke 2004: 452).

Ensuing context. After explaining that assets such as security exceed the worth of tangible riches (10:1–22), the sage will offer counsel for those times when security is threatened (10:23–30). There reverence and moral conduct will emerge as anchors of security.

What to watch for

Note wisdom commendations, since they mark multiple section boundaries. Within each section, observe how the sage approaches the topic of riches, exposing what they can and cannot provide. Also notice what assets lie outside the category of 'tangible riches'. Watch for patterns that result when entire phrases (not merely isolated words) repeat wholesale, such as 'the person who is foolish-of-lips will be put down', or 'while the mouth of guilty folk keeps on covering violence'. Finally, notice how many concepts in 10:22 appeared earlier in the lecture.

Translation and outline

Verse	*Translation*	*Outline*
		I. Authentic wealth (10:1–7)
10:1	The Proverbs of Solomon. A wise son will bring a father joy, while a stupid son is his mother's grief.	A. Authorial note and wisdom commendation: wisdom consists of filial honour (v. 1)
		B. Wisdom content: tangible and intangible riches (vv. 2–7) 1. Learning to distinguish between tangible and intangible riches (vv. 2–3)
10:2	Treasures of a guilty person cannot bring profit, but moral conduct can rescue from death.	a. Morality brings security – worth more than tangible riches (v. 2)
10:3	The LORD will not bring hunger upon the appetite of a moral person, but what guilty folk desire he will put beyond reach.	b. Divine favour satisfies (v. 3)
		2. Advice for achieving riches, tangible and intangible (vv. 4–7)
10:4	A poor person produces a lazy grip, while the hand of diligent folk will enrich.	a. Advice for achieving tangible riches: timely diligence (vv. 4–5)

10:5 One who gathers during the summer is a skilful son; one who nods off during the harvest is a disgraceful son.	
10:6 Blessings are upon the moral person's head, while the mouth of guilty folk keeps on covering violence. 10:7 The reputation of a moral person results in a blessing, while the name of guilty folk will rot.	b. Advice for achieving intangible riches: ethical conduct leading to communal favour (vv. 6–7)
	II. Two assets that exceed tangible riches: security and vitality (vv. 8–13)
10:8 The person who is mentally wise will take up orders, while the person who is foolish-of-lips will be put down.	A. Wisdom commendation: the sensible person takes direction (v. 8)
	B. Wisdom content: the surpassing worth of security and vitality (vv. 9–12)
10:9 One who proceeds with integrity can proceed securely, but one who twists his ways will be exposed. 10:10 One who squints his eyes will give pain, while the person who is foolish-of-lips will be put down.	1. The worth of personal security, deriving from individual ethical behaviour (vv. 9–10)
10:11 A fountain of life is a moral person's mouth, while the mouth of guilty folk keeps on covering violence. 10:12 Hatred will awaken strife, but over all transgressions love will form a covering.	2. The worth of vitality, pouring from the mouth of the merciful (vv. 11–12)
10:13 In a perceptive person's lips wisdom can be found, while a rod is destined for the back of one lacking sense.	A'. Wisdom commendation: the senseless person receives a beating (v. 13)

Verse	*Translation*	*Outline*
		III. Do not be fooled: security derives from morality (vv. 14–16)
10:14	Wise folk keep on storing up knowledge, while a fool's mouth amounts to imminent ruin.	A. Wisdom commendation: secure reserves result from wisdom (v. 14)
		B. Wisdom content: riches offer only superficial security, while moral conduct yields supreme security (vv. 15–16)
10:15	A rich person's wealth is his strong city; the ruin of poor folk is their poverty.	1. While riches offer superficial security (v. 15) . . .
10:16	A moral person's wage tends towards life; revenue of a guilty person tends towards sin.	2. . . . It is morality that yields supreme vitality (v. 16)
		IV. Value-laden speech can extend security to many (vv. 17–22)
10:17	A path tending towards life is one who guards reproof, but one who forsakes reprimand causes others to stray.	A. Wisdom commendation: reproof-receptivity can multiply supreme security (v. 17)
		B. Wisdom content: the worth of speech in community (vv. 18–20)
10:18	Lying lips cover hatred, and one who brings forth defamation – that one is stupid.	1. Worthy speech will not arise from hatred (v. 18)
10:19	Through lots of talk transgression cannot cease, but one who restrains his lips is successful.	2. Worthy speech will be sparse (v. 19)
10:20	Choice silver is a moral person's tongue; the mind of guilty folk amounts to little.	3. Worthy speech arises from morality (v. 20)
10:21	A moral person's lips can nourish many, but fools for lack of sense may die.	A'. Wisdom commendation as character summary: the communal effect of moral and foolish speech (v. 21)
10:22	The blessing of the LORD – that is what will enrich a person, and he will not add pain to it.	C. Conclusion: supremely authentic wealth consists of words conveying divine favour (v. 22)

Notes on the text

10:1. 'will bring . . . joy': yiq. conjugation conveys dynamic potential rather than a static trait (contrast ptcs. 'produces', 'gathers' and 'nods off' in 10:4a, 5).

'a father . . . his mother': the familial bond intensifies in the second colon by adding 'mother' and 'grief'.

10:2. 'moral conduct', *ṣĕdāqâ*: often rendered 'righteousness' (see 'moral' under §5.6 in the 'Introduction').

'cannot bring profit' and 'can rescue': (in)capability inferred from yiq. conjugation.

10:3. 'appetite', *nepeš*: often rendered 'soul' (see 'appetite' under §5.6 in the 'Introduction').

'he will put beyond reach': lit. 'he will push away'.

10:4. 'A poor person produces', *rā ʾš ʿōśeh*: *rā ʾš*, 'a poor person', is a m. sg. ptc. of the root *rwš*, 'to be poor', so supplies the m. subject required by *ʿōśeh*, 'produces', resulting in the phrase 'a poor person produces'. The noun *kap*, 'grip' or 'palm', is f., so cannot serve as the subject (*pace* Vulgate). Consequently we may not render, 'A lazy grip produces a poor person' (*pace* NRSV: 'A slack hand causes poverty'). LXX follows the MT, treating *rā ʾš* as the subject (although rendering it with the abstract noun 'poverty' [as if vocalized *rē ʾš*] rather than the ptc. 'a poor person' [*rā ʾš*]).

'grip', *kap*: lit. 'palm', refers to one's hand when describing a hand clasp to conclude an agreement (cf. 6:1; for the more common synonym 'hand', *yād*, cf. 10:4b).

'produces a lazy grip', *ʿōśeh kap rĕmîyâ*: not 'works *with* a lazy grip' (which would employ the prep. *bĕ*, 'by means of' [cf. Neh. 4:17]). The lazy grip designates not the means by which work is (or is not) performed, but is itself the product fashioned by the poor person.

10:5. 'one who nods off', *nirdām*: the root *rdm* describes sleep or insensibility when one ought to be alert (not *yšn*, the normal sleep of nocturnal rest; Fox 2009: 513).

10:6. 'blessings are upon the moral person's head', *bĕrākôt lĕrō ʾš ṣaddîq*: the expressions of 10:6–7 depict the community petitioning the divine that well-being may reward the moral person (cf. Gen. 49:26; Prov. 11:26; contrast *ʾašrê*, 'How fortunate . . . !', Ps. 1:1; Prov. 3:13).

'while the mouth of guilty folk keeps on covering violence': durative connotation ('keeps on') inferred from yiq. Instead to render as 'but violence overwhelms the mouth of the wicked' weakens the reversal between 'blessings' in 10:6a and words that conceal violence in v. 6b (*pace* Waltke 2004: 448).

10:7. 'reputation': lit. 'remembrance'.

10:8. 'will be put down', *yillābēṭ*: contrasts 'can proceed securely' in 10:9. In the HB the root *lbṭ* is attested only here, in v. 10, and in Hos. 4:14.

10:9. 'will be exposed': lit. 'will become known'.

10:10. 'will give': contrast 'take' in 10:8a.

'will be put down', *yillābēṭ*: see 10:8, above.

10:11. 'life', *ḥayyîm*: the sage employs this term to convey robust vitality (see under §5.6 in the 'Introduction').

'keeps on covering': durative connotation inferred from yiq.

10:13. 'In . . . lips . . . while a rod', *běśiptê . . . wěšēbeṭ*: linked by assonance. In Hebr. these terms begin their respective cola.

'can be found': capability inferred from yiq.

'a rod is destined for the back of one lacking sense', *wěšēbeṭ lěgēw ḥăsar-lēb*: lit. 'a rod is for'. Note extent of assonance, particularly if *w* and the fricative form of *b* were both pronounced as *v*: *věšēveṭ lěgēv ḥăsar-lēv*.

10:14. 'keep on storing up': lit. 'will hide'. Iterative is inferred from yiq. conjugation.

10:15. 'a rich person', *ʿāšîr*: from *ʿšr*, the same root as 'enrich' (10:4b, 22b).

'his strong city': lit. 'the city of his strength'.

10:16. 'tends towards life . . . tends towards sin', *lěḥayyîm . . . lěḥaṭṭāʾt*: lit. 'to life . . . to sin'. The 'wage' or 'revenue' obtained by respective characters does not conclude their conduct. As if reinvested, those proceeds figuratively fund still greater expansion in the direction of either robust vitality ('life' for self and others; cf. 10:11a), or of misguided offence towards the divine and harm towards self and others ('sin'). Assonance links the parallel, antithetical phrases of *lěḥayyîm . . . lěḥaṭṭāʾt*, which may further explain why the second expression does not read *lěmāwet*, 'towards death', as might have been expected. *Lěḥayyîm* recurs in v. 17.

'sin', *ḥaṭṭāʾt*: with a connotation of missing the mark, 'sin' corresponds to 'straying', *matʿeh*, in 10:17b.

10:17. 'one who guards reproof': this one both treasures and abides by reproof received.

10:19. 'cannot cease': (in)capability inferred from yiq.

'successful', *maśkîl*: possessing understanding that causes one to prosper.

10:21. 'can nourish . . . may die': capability/possibility inferred from yiq. In context, what nourishes are the caring, sparse, moral and 'choice silver' words of reproof (10:17–20).

'sense', *lēb*: rendered 'mind' in 10:20. In context, the sense lacked by the foolish is the reproof (10:17–20), for which nourishment they have no appetite.

10:22. 'blessing of the LORD', *birkat yhwh*: see 'Notes' for 10:6 for 'blessings'.

Form and structure

Borders

The upper border is marked by authorship attribution and a wisdom commendation in 10:1. Also at that point content shifts from competing invitations issued by Lady Wisdom and Dame Folly (Prov. 9), transitioning to a lecture focusing on wealth acquisition (10:1–22).

Features indicating a lower border in 10:22 include an alphabetic acrostic (see under 'Macrostructural features', below), inclusio and closure. Inclusio consists of five elements in 10:2–3 that reappear in vv. 21–22, spanning the entire lecture (excepting the authorial heading and wisdom commendation in v. 1). First, the moral person appears in both portions (vv. 2, 3, 21). Second, both refer to abundance (treasures in v. 2, sufficiency to nourish others in v. 21, and enrichment in v. 22). Third, both refer to deficiency, whether unsatisfied desires (v. 3) or a deficit of sense (v. 21). Fourth, the influence of the LORD will not produce disadvantage, whether 'hunger' (v. 3) or 'pain' (v. 22). The term 'LORD' does not appear in this poem aside from those two verses. Fifth, some will enjoy rescue from death (v. 2), while others may suffer death (v. 21). Mention of death enjoys greatest precision, appearing exclusively one saying removed from the poem's outer edges.

The lecture's last verse fosters closure through four terms and three topics. Two overlap with the inclusio described above. Heim similarly notes several of these elements and concludes that 10:22 'indeed rounds off the unit', although he stops short of proposing 10:1–22 as a cohesive lecture (2001: 126).

Of the four repeated terms, three appeared first in Section I: 'the LORD' (10:3), 'enrich' (v. 4) and 'bless(ing)' (vv. 6, 7), and not again until v. 22: 'The blessing of the LORD – that is what will enrich a person' (v. 22a). A fourth term, 'pain', appeared first in v. 10, and not again until the final verse: 'and he will not add pain to it' (v. 22b).

Three topics similarly link 10:22 with earlier portions: authentic wealth, absence of harm, and speech. Authentic wealth featured prominently in Section III ('rich', 'wealth', 'poor', 'poverty' in v. 15, and 'wage' and 'revenue' in v. 16). It resurfaced in Section IV through the expression 'choice silver' (v. 20) and conversely through 'little' in v. 20. Authentic wealth returned in v. 22 with the terms 'blessing', 'enrich' and 'add'.

Absence of harm (the second closural topic) appears in 10:2 in the phrase 'rescue from death'. In v. 22 that topic is conveyed by the phrase 'he will not add pain to it'. Related to this is the fact that 'the LORD will not bring hunger' (v. 3), which resembles '[the LORD] will not add pain' (v. 22).

The third closural topic, speech, is connoted by expressions such as 'reproof' and 'reprimand' (v. 17), 'lying lips' and 'defamation' (v. 18), 'lots of talk' and 'restraining one's lips' (v. 19), 'tongue' (v. 20) and 'lips' (v. 21). The sage shifts the topic of speech from human to divine through his mention of 'blessing' in v. 22.

The impact of each closural component intensifies when appearing in the poem's final verse, escalating persuasive effectiveness. 'Blessing' in

10:22 specifies divine favour, not human (contrast vv. 6–7). 'The Lord' in v. 3 refrains from harming, while in v. 22 he positively enriches. Enrichment followed diligent exertion in v. 4, but signals the Lord's munificence in v. 22. Pain follows deception in v. 10, while in v. 22 the Lord shields from pain.

Macrostructural features

Concept-rich introduction (Sections I–IV, content-based). The introductory quatrain in Section I (10:2–3) initiates four concepts that will be revisited in subsequent sections. These include (a) the topic of riches and poverty (v. 2a; cf. vv. 4, 14, 15, 16), (b) the supposed worth of tangible riches, in contrast to the superior worth of security (v. 2; cf. vv. 7, 11, 16, 20), (c) the divine as source of ultimate satisfaction (v. 3; cf. v. 22) and (d) the principle that satisfaction is not possible without moral conduct (both vv. 2 and 3; cf. vv. 6, 7, 9, 11, 16, 21).

Wisdom commendations marking section boundaries (Sections I, II, III and IV, content-based). Aside from the authorial note in 10:1a, each section begins with a wisdom commendation (10:1b–c, 8, 14, 17). Wisdom commendations also appear at the close of Section II (v. 13, with *ḥăsar-lēb*, 'lacking sense') and as the poem's penultimate saying (v. 21, Section IV, again with *ḥăsar-lēb*, 'lacking sense'). So high a concentration of wisdom commendations in the first lecture of Division II (Prov. 10 – 24) encourages the pupil to cultivate alertness to structural markers this device may signal.

Alphabetic poem with acrostic (Sections I, II, III and IV, form-based). The sayings of this poem number twenty-two – the number of letters (consonants) comprising the Hebr. alphabet. Four sayings begin with the letter matching their alphabet sequence (allowing for the inversion of 'ayin and pe found in some presentations of the Hebr. alphabet, although admittedly not in the fully alphabetic acrostic poem of Prov. 31:10–31). The four letters are zayin (*zēker*, 'reputation', v. 7), ḥeth (*ḥăkam*, 'wise', v. 8), pe (*pĕʿullat*, 'wage', v. 16), and sin/shin (*śiptê*, 'lips', v. 21). These sayings appear either at a section's start (10:8), at a section's close (vv. 7, 16) or very near the poem's close (v. 21). Similarly, yet with only one alphabet-corresponding line-initial letter, some regard the twenty-two verses of Prov. 2 as alphabetic (*lĕhaṣîlĕka*, 'to rescue you', in the twelfth verse corresponds to lamed, the twelfth letter; Murphy 1998: 14).

Taken in sequence, the acrostic letters may spell '*z*[*ĕh*] *ḥpś*', suggesting 'this is a cleverly devised thing'. As a verb the *ḥpś* root appears in Prov. 2:4, where the sage stirred the youth to 'seek', *bqš*, wisdom and to 'track it down', *ḥpś*, as if wisdom were a precious commodity. As a noun, *ḥēpeś* refers to a cleverly devised scheme only the careful enquirer will uncover (attested only in Ps. 64:6 [MT v. 7]). With the acrostic of Prov. 10:1–22 the sage may have challenged the pupil, 'This (wisdom poem) merits careful searching-out.' Alternatively he may have implied, 'This (wisdom poem) will itself search out and reveal what sort of wealth you, the pupil, actually hold dear.'

Repetition of 'wise' or 'wisdom' in wisdom commendations (**Sections I, II and III, form-based**). Of six wisdom commendations in this poem, each of the first four employs the root *ḥkm*, 'wise' (in 10:1, 8, 14; 'wisdom' in v. 13), a root not appearing elsewhere in this lecture. Repeated association of *ḥkm* with wisdom commendations so early in Division II may have been the sage's way to help pupils recognize wisdom commendations more readily. Not every fut. use of *ḥkm* signals a wisdom commendation (e.g. 11:2 in a later lecture).

Repetition of phrases creating a palistrophe (**Sections I and II, form-based**). Although wisdom commendations serve to mark this poem's principal boundaries (see above), two pairs of identical phrases defy this scheme, crossing over the seam separating Sections I and II. The first pair involves the phrase 'while the mouth of guilty folk keeps on covering violence', appearing in 10:6b, 11b. The second pair involves the phrase 'while the person who is foolish-of-lips will be put down', vv. 8, 10. Antonyms 'take up' and 'give' further join v. 8 with v. 10.

'Blessing' joins 10:6–7, and 'covering' joins vv. 11–12. Consequently the inner repeated phrase ('while the person who is foolish-of-lips will be put down') nests just inside those quatrains (vv. 6–7 and 11–12).

The high level of literary craftsmanship that characterizes so much of this book argues against dismissing such lengthy repetitions as compositional carelessness. Instead we must conclude that, in addition to thought divisions marked by wisdom commendations, the sage wished to focus attention on the causal relationship between security and integrity featured in the palistrophic pivot of 10:9 (so also Heim 2001: 114). By means of this palistrophe the sage underscores the principle that tangible wealth fades before the intangible asset of integrity, due to the security it yields.

Achieving community favour – introduction and specification (**Sections I and II, content-based**). Section I ends by extolling the value of community favour, without specifying how favour may be earned ('blessings' in 10:6–7; see 'Notes'). The last wisdom-content colon of Section II describes one who ameliorates the transgressions of others by covering with love (v. 12b). Since this merciful 'covering' contrasts the stealthy 'covering' over of violence in v. 6 (also v. 11), covering transgressions with love in v. 12b specifies how the moral person of vv. 6–7 achieves community favour introduced in Section I.

Mention of 'moral' and 'guilty' to close a section (**Sections I and III, form-based**). Double use of the antonym-pair 'moral', *ṣdq*, and 'guilty', *ršʿ*, in the introductory verse-pair establishes ethics as a foundational concept for the entire lecture (10:2, 3). Double use of this antonym-pair also closes Section I (vv. 6–7), while single use closes Section III (v. 16). Remaining instances of the word-pair further establish the theme, without offering structural significance (vv. 11, 20).

Microstructural features

Repeated terms and syntax, with reversed topic (10:2–3, form- and content-based). As already noted in a macrostructure, the terms 'guilty' and 'morality' (or 'moral') appear in both 10:2 and, chiastically reversed, in v. 3 (so also Waltke 2004: 452). Syntax is parallel, since each verse opens with the negation *lō*ʾ, followed by a hiph. verb in yiq. conjugation, and a subject. The verses reverse topics, with insufficiency in v. 2, and non-deficiency in v. 3. Taken together, this quatrain teaches that although illegitimate means (guilty conduct) may yield ostensible benefit (v. 2a), what a person ultimately requires (rescue from death, v. 2b) follows moral conduct that is reflective of alliance with the LORD, who alone satisfies wholly one's deepest longings (vv. 3a–3b).

Thematic continuity involving diligence (10:4–5, content-based). The quatrain spanning 10:4–5 coheres in the theme of diligence ('diligent' in v. 4b, 'gathers' in v. 5a, with the antonym 'nods off' in v. 5b).

Thematic continuity involving wealth and poverty (10:2–5, content-based). Through the expressions 'poor' (10:4a), 'enrich' (v. 4b) and 'harvest' (v. 5), the quatrain spanning vv. 4–5 links with the theme of wealth and poverty introduced in vv. 2–3 ('profit', 'not . . . hunger' and 'desire' that is 'beyond reach').

Repeated terms ('guilty', 'moral' and 'blessing') and the topic of honour and shame (10:6–7, form- and content-based). The terms 'guilty', 'moral' and 'blessing' join 10:6, 7, appearing in each verse. Together they address honour for the moral (vv. 6a and 7a) and shame for the guilty (v. 7b).

Inclusio involving 'death' and 'rot' (10:2, 7, content-based). The term 'death' (line-terminal in 10:2) overlaps semantically with 'rot' (line-terminal in v. 7). These form an inclusio around the wisdom content of Section I (Block I.B, vv. 2–7).

Thematic continuity involving concealment, with reversal (10:9–12, content-based). Concealment or misdirection comprises the most frequently recurring theme in Block II.B (10:9–12). It appears in the term 'twisted' and conversely as loss of concealment ('exposed', both in v. 9b), as eyes that 'squint' (v. 10a) and as veiled violence (v. 11b). While the preceding were malevolent, with reversal even kindness works through concealment – to the extent that benevolence covers comprehensively the transgression of others (v. 12b).

Inclusio involving wisdom commendations (10:8, 13, content-based). Section II (10:8–13) begins and ends with wisdom commendations (vv. 8 and 13, respectively; see 23:15–25 for another portion with opening and closing wisdom commendations).

Thematic continuity involving ethical behaviour (10:9a, 11a, content-based). Between the wisdom content inclusio of 10:8 and 13 (noted earlier) the quatrains of vv. 9–10 and 11–12 each begin with ethical behaviour. Verse 9a features 'integrity', with 'moral' appearing in v. 11a.

Thematic continuity involving intangible benefits (10:9, 11, content-based). Benefits consisting of security (10:9a) and vitality (v. 11a) foster a continuity of intangible benefits in Block II.B (vv. 9–12), contrasting tangible riches of the first wisdom content (cf. vv. 2a, 4).

Ostensible wisdom corrected by genuine wisdom (10:15, 16, content-based). The sayings in 10:15, 16 join as seeming wisdom (v. 15) is corrected by genuine wisdom (v. 16), addressing the lecture's central theme of authentic wealth and security. Initially, tangible wealth appears to supply security, while poverty seems to spell ruin (v. 15). However, attentive pupils would have questioned the veracity of this apophthegm, since it bypasses any moral ingredient (contrast v. 2). Such a thinly veiled fallacy may typify the sort of clandestine speech spoken by the 'mouth of the guilty' (vv. 6b, 11b). Instead it is morality that will generate robust vitality (v. 16a), more valuable even than the rich person's 'strong city'. Deprived of morality, one's revenues ultimately amount only to 'sin' (v. 16b).

Inclusio involving life and death (10:17, 21, content-based). The first colon of Section IV (10:17a) refers to life, forming an inclusio of antonyms with mention of death in the section's penultimate verse (v. 21b).

A leader's influence upon followers (10:17, 18, 21, content-based). At three points the sayings of Section IV extend beyond private experience, describing a leader's influence on others. In 10:17a, the person who guards reproof gains vitality not only for himself. As a life-giving 'path' he benefits others also who may come after. Conversely, one who forsakes reprimand does not simply lose his own way. He 'causes others to stray' (v. 17b).

Reference to speech (lying lips, defamation) in 10:18 should be read in the light of speech-as-reproof in v. 17. Thus the influence on others portrayed in v. 18a depicts needed reproof one refuses to administer to another (thereby lying). Although this may appear kind, such deception amounts to hatred. Leviticus similarly cautions, 'You must not hate your brother in your heart. Firmly reprimand your associate, and do not incur sin in this regard' (Lev. 19:17).

The opposite appears in 10:18b, where a superior administers nothing but negative evaluations (reproof). While not hateful (contrasting v. 18a), such a leader is 'stupid', failing to grasp his or her role.

A leader's capacity to influence others appears also in 10:21a: 'A moral person's lips can nourish many.' This sentiment parallels the benefit to others resulting from a 'path tending towards life' (v. 17a).

Comment

Progression of thought develops through this poem both generally, and through its six wisdom commendations. Consider first how wisdom commendations display progression.

Progression of thought within wisdom commendations. Two concurrent progressions weave through this poem's six wisdom commendations (10:1, 8, 13, 14, 17, 21). One involves varied sorts of wisdom, advancing from generic to confrontational. The second portrays consequences that follow folly, along a vector of decreasing desirability.

Among varied sorts of wisdom, the first is basic, evident in a respectful parent–child relationship ('a wise son', 10:1). The second narrows, portraying the wisdom of willing cooperation (the 'mentally wise will take up orders', v. 8a) in contrast to folly suffering forcible subjugation ('the person who is foolish-of-lips will be put down', v. 8b). The third describes one who has accumulated wisdom enough to transmit it to others ('in a perceptive person's lips wisdom can be found', v. 13). The fourth refines the notion of transmission, implying that with their accumulation of wisdom, the wise also have learned when not to speak (v. 14). The fifth introduces confrontational wisdom (reproof and reprimand) – wisdom's most valuable form – yielding the supreme benefit: robust vitality (v. 17).

The wisdom-commendation progression surrounding sorts of wisdom reaches its apex in a pair of climactic alternatives. Either a person will supply nourishment to many, or that person will perish, depending on one's folly or morality (10:21).

Here a wisdom commendation blends with a character summary. Where one would expect a guilty person to contrast the moral person of 10:21a, a sense-deficient fool appears instead. The character summary invites the pupil not merely to survive individually, but by his words ('lips') to 'nourish many' others as well (recall beneficial 'lips' of v. 13). Else he will perish a senseless fool (v. 21b).

The second wisdom-commendation progression concerns folly's undesirable consequences. At first, maternal grief results from a stupid son (10:1b). The second stage results in personal demotion – a step costlier than disappointing a parent (v. 8b). When physical beating and ruin appear in the third and fourth stages, negative consequences have taken tangible form ('rod' in v. 13 and 'ruin' in v. 14). Fifth, one who discards reproof not only misses the life-path himself or herself, but misleads others as well (v. 17b). Sixth, folly will be fatal ('but fools for lack of sense may die', v. 21b).

Progression of thought through the entire poem. *Section I (10:1–7).* After a heading attributing Solomonic authorship (10:1a), a wisdom commendation anchors wisdom instruction within the parent–child relationship. The pupil does not exist unto himself or herself. Response to instruction inevitably has an impact on parents (10:1b–c).

Wisdom content of Section I follows in two parts. First, a verse-pair (10:2–3) introduces four concepts that appear repeatedly through the poem. These include (a) riches and poverty, (b) illusive versus authentic worth, (c) satisfaction deriving from the divine, and (d) satisfaction deriving from moral behaviour.

In the second wisdom content of Section I, the sage offers specific advice for achieving tangible wealth (vv. 4–5). When applied in a timely fashion, sincere diligence yields a good harvest.

After advice concerning tangible wealth comes counsel for intangible wealth. By opting for moral conduct rather than clandestine destruction ('covering violence', 10:6), one may gain favour as the community issues affirmation, calling down 'blessings' (vv. 6a, 7a). Conversely, guilty conduct will rot one's reputation in the community – the nadir of failure in an honour–shame culture. This quatrain concludes Section I. The wisdom content of Section II (vv. 9–12) similarly addresses community dynamics.

10:1–16. Waltke similarly regards 10:1–16 as a connected whole, treating wealth in vv. 1–5, communication in vv. 6–14 (with 'centerline' in v. 10) and wealth again in vv. 15–16 (2004: 450–465). Yet the theme of wealth may continue in vv. 6–12, transitioning from tangible to intangible wealth encompassing communal favour (vv. 6–7), security (vv. 9–10) and vitality (vv. 11–12). Further, inclusio and other closural indicators involving vv. 17–22 are better accounted for if the poem does not stop at v. 16, but extends to v. 22 (see 'Macrostructural features', above).

10:3. The sage establishes a close connection between moral behaviour and the God of Israel, here in the early lines of Division II (Prov. 10 – 24).

Section II (10:8–13). After a wisdom commendation advocating receptivity towards another's directives (10:8), Section II builds on 'rescue from death' (10:2), teaching that security and vitality exceed the value of tangible riches. Security issues from integrity (v. 9). Instead to scheme evilly brings pain (v. 10). By leaving the pain-victim unspecified, the sage allows the inference that retributive pain will rebound on the perpetrator. His silent scheming will escalate to spoken folly, working his own downfall (v. 10b). By repeating the wisdom commendation of v. 8b within the moral instruction of v. 10 the sage teaches that folly fails for lack of morality.

Beyond supplying security for the individual of integrity (10:9–10), moral conduct brings communal benefits (vv. 11–12). From the moral person others gain vivifying instruction (v. 11a). When transgression threatens to splinter the community, a response of love (evidently by the moral person) soothes and mends, forming a covering (v. 12b) – a masterful reversal of concealed malevolence (v. 11b).

Section II ends (10:13) as it began (v. 8), with a wisdom commendation. The perceptive become a winsome wisdom source (reminiscent of life issuing from a moral person's mouth, v. 11).

In contrast, not only are the senseless unable to distribute wisdom – they refuse even to receive advice for themselves, until that advice bruises their backs through a caning (10:13b). This punishment illustrates the demotion predicted when they refuse to receive orders – unlike the wise who 'take up orders' willingly (v. 8).

Antonyms in the outermost cola link opposing characters of Section II. Those receptive to orders are mentally wise (*ḥăkam-lēb*, 'wise-of-mind', 10:8a), while those who destine themselves for corporal discipline lack sense (*ḥăsar-lēb*, 'deficient-of-mind', v. 13b). For the sage this entails moral resistance, not mental incompetence.

Thus in Section II the sage commends pursuit of intangible, authentic wealth, in the form of personal security and a magnanimous, merciful vitality. Such treasures result from ethical conduct (cf. 'integrity' and 'moral' in 10:9 and 11, respectively), and explain earlier exclamations of blessing the community will call down on the benefactor, rendering him or her richer still (10:6–7).

10:10, 11. Ostensibly schemers (10:10) and the guilty (v. 11) inflict (not receive) pain and violence. However, by not specifying victims, and by including subterfuge ('covering violence'), the sage leaves open the possibility that the harm schemers and the guilty create may retributively rebound on them (cf. 1:18–19).

10:12. 'Even if we do not condone another's offence, we need not rake it up and put it on display' (Fox 2009: 518). The second colon of 10:12 may have influenced the writer of 1 Peter 4:8 ('love covers a multitude of sins'; cf. Prov. 17:9).

Section III (10:14–16). After a wisdom commendation attributing insecurity to folly (10:14), Section III resumes the topic of wealth begun in Section I ('to store up', 'rich', 'wealth', 'poor', 'poverty', 'wage' and 'revenue' in vv. 14–16). Security and insecurity also feature prominently in Section III ('strong city', 'life', 'ruin').

In striking fashion Section III upends the assumption that material riches guarantee security. Informed by earlier cautions (10:2a), the attentive pupil would have grown suspicious upon hearing that 'a rich person's wealth is his strong city; the ruin of poor folk is their poverty' (v. 15). The Jewish scholar Shadal (AD 1800–65) similarly regards v. 15a as delusional, reflecting the erroneous assumptions about wealth entertained by certain affluent persons (noted in Fox 2009: 519). In a later lecture the sage will disclose conditions that rank inferior even to poverty (28:6, 11).

A correction to the delusion of 10:15 follows directly. Security will reward not the rich, but the moral person. Furthermore, such folk will achieve the zenith of security – even robust vitality (v. 16a; recall v. 11).

Section III closes with 'sin' – a distinctly theological term (10:16b). Thus the sage escalates the threat level attending guilty conduct. Insecurity resulting from guilt will persist until its offence against the divine has been resolved.

Section III thus extends the lecture-wide theme of riches by teaching that tangible wealth pales in comparison to vitality, a derivative of morality. Mention of sin reminds the pupil that theology frames the sage's world view (cf. 10:3, 22).

10:15–16. The sage corrects in 10:16 the conventional (but inaccurate) wisdom of v. 15. Similarly the parent in 1:15–19 corrects the violent gang's philosophy of vv. 10–14. In Ecclesiastes also the sage periodically presents, then corrects, a widely held principle (e.g. 'all is supremely pointless' in Eccles. 1:2, contrasted with 'it is good to eat and drink and recognize worth in all one's toil' in Eccles. 5:18 [v. 17 MT]).

Section IV (10:17–22). Section IV (10:17–22) deals with communication, seemingly disconnected from the theme of authentic wealth. However, after establishing superlative wisdom (reproof and reprimand) as the communication under consideration, the sage joins this communication with superlative worth, since it leads to robust vitality, v. 17 (notice the seamless link 'tending towards life' forms with v. 16a). Instead to discard such discipline will cause not only oneself, but others as well, to miss the path leading to life (see 'Notes' linking 'sin' in v. 16b with 'stray' in v. 17b).

Then follow three principles for assessing richness in communication. First, deceptive communication conceals not only truth, but hatred as well (10:18). Given the context of reproof in v. 17, hateful lying lips of v. 18 would refuse to reprove others, thus misleading them by implying all is well. Second, communication's quality varies inversely to its quantity (v. 19). Third, ultimately it is morality that determines communication's worth (v. 20).

Thereupon the sage begins to summarize his lecture advocating pursuit of authentic wealth. Those who make morality their aim gain vitality not only for themselves, but also 'nourish' others by what they say (10:21a, implying speech that includes reproof [cf. v. 17]). Instead to fail morality is to embrace death-by-folly (v. 21b). For morality supplies wisdom's foundation. And the LORD, the ground of morality, is the agent of ultimate wealth. To secure his favour spells riches without painful recoil (v. 22).

10:20–21. By placing 'fools' in 10:21b in contrast to 'a moral person' in v. 21a, and synonymous to 'guilty folk' in v. 20b, the sage indicates that folly – at least of the *ʾĕwîl* sort – involves some degree of moral failure.

10:22. Through a cleft sentence ('It is X [rather than Y] that is [or does] Z') the poet elevates 'the blessing of the LORD' as the ultimate source of enrichment. When it comes to wealth-generation, the youth should disregard every other strategy and instead should concentrate all efforts on securing the blessing of the LORD.

Some may question whether sayings such as 10:22 with its mention of 'the LORD' reflect a later addition. 'The LORD' was already mentioned towards the outset of the poem (v. 3a). If v. 3 were not original, its absence would disrupt the smoothly flowing trio of quatrains in Section I (vv. 2–3, 4–5, 6–7) and the twenty-two-member partial-alphabetic acrostic.

Fox renders 'pain', *ʿeṣeb*, as 'striving' (exerting effort) and treats it as the subject of 10:22b: 'and striving adds nothing more thereto' (2009: 522). While grammatically possible, this would disrupt the twofold closural link with v. 3, since 'he [i.e. the LORD] will not add pain' in v. 22b resembles the statement 'the LORD will not bring hunger' (v. 3b). Elsewhere the sage acknowledges that morality does not always ensure prosperity (cf. 15:16, 17; 16:8 and 19).

Explanation

Money, sex and power often rank among the most high-profile of pitfalls. Money, the first of these, begins to tantalize youth as early as his or her first pay cheque. Since passing years may only intensify the longing for riches, the sage could scarcely have chosen a more timeless topic to open Division II (Prov. 10 – 24).

The sage's lecture on riches may be summarized in ten points – a quantity indicating how thoughtful was his analysis. To sense the cumulative impact of his multipoint message, the following paraphrased summary may help.

1. **The myth of riches.** Profit gained illegitimately cannot satisfy. For satisfaction, pursue God (which presumes moral conduct, 10:2–3).
2. **The need for diligence.** If you want to get rich, get to work. Don't put it off (10:4–5).
3. **The mandate for morality.** In case you overlooked what the sage said in 10:2–3, pay close attention: in the pursuit of wealth, morality is non-negotiable. In contrast, deceptive speech works injury (10:6–7).
4. **The worth of communal favour.** Moral conduct will win favour from your community network – a sort of wealth far superior to mere riches. Else you will wind up with a rotten reputation (also 10:6–7).
5. **The need for supervision.** Don't arrogantly suppose you know it all. Accept supervision (10:8).
6. **The worth of security.** Like favour, security exceeds the worth of mere riches. Also like favour, it derives from ethical behaviour (10:9–10).
7. **The worth of mercy.** At times, you will be presented with an opportunity to express mercy. The dividends issuing from mercy will prove far more desirable than those resulting from foolish words of hatred (10:11–13).
8. **Recap.** Are you getting the picture? The security afforded by riches is only illusory. For robust vitality, try morality (10:15–16).

9. **The supreme wealth within wisdom.** If truly interested in wealth, realize that to receive reprimand is to acquire a rare treasure (10:17). Its confrontation must not arise from hatred (v. 18). It should be measured, rather than overwhelming the recipient of reprimand (v. 19). It will carry supreme worth, when arising from a person marked by moral conduct (v. 20). Paradoxically, the wealth of moral reprimand has the capacity of nourishing many in the community, while those who foolishly refuse it will go fatally hungry (v. 21).
10. **Ultimate enrichment.** Most enriching of all are choice words of favour ('blessing') deriving from the LORD himself – the ground of all caring and morality. His blessing will leave no bitter aftertaste (10:22).

PROVERBS 10:23–30
'How can I secure my future?'

Overview of Proverbs 10:23–30

The lecture spanning Prov. 10:23–30 trains the pupil to sidestep treachery, embracing instead a secure future. The implicit question that undergirds this lecture asks, 'In view of storms looming on the horizon, how can I secure my future?'

Future-oriented expressions include 'planning' (10:23), 'dread' and 'longing' (v. 24), 'expectation' and 'hope' (v. 28). Prospects may be dark: a 'whirlwind' (v. 25), years-grown-short (v. 27), 'ruin' (v. 29) and inability to 'reside in the land' (v. 30). Alternatively prospects may be bright: a 'permanent foundation' (v. 25), 'add[ed] days' (v. 27), a 'refuge' (v. 29) and remaining unmoved (v. 30).

Position of this poem within Proverbs

Preceding context (remote). Themes dominating the first two poems of Prov. 10 – 31 to a remarkable degree resemble themes found in the first two poems of Prov. 1 – 9 (after the book introduction of 1:1–9). The first poem's topic in each case involves the allure of wealth (1:10–19; 10:1–22). The second poem in each group warns that a tempest is brewing (1:20–33; 10:23–30). Two terms identify the tempest in Prov. 1:27: *šôʾâ*, 'storm', and *sûpâ*, 'whirlwind'. *Sûpâ* describes the hazardous weather looming in 10:25 as well. *Sûpâ* does not occur elsewhere in Proverbs.

Preceding context (near). The lecture just concluded moved from tangible wealth to the greater but intangible asset of security (10:1–22). The theme of security the sage will expand in this present lecture. The close connection of these poems is evident from the fact that 'the LORD' in 10:22 serves as the referent of 'he will grant' in v. 24b.

Ensuing context. A wisdom commendation follows in 10:31–32, signalling the upper boundary of the next poem. That lecture will again examine the topic of wealth, addressing particularly those problems created by fraudulent riches. It will span 10:31 – 11:31.

What to watch for

Begin by noting terms pertaining to security or insecurity. Consider how the term 'planning' in the opening verse of the lecture establishes the theme of future security. Notice the positioning of any verses that seem to convey similar messages. Consider how the scenario of dispatching someone on a mission may pertain to a quest for future security (10:26). What does the poet believe concerning the impact of moral conduct on future security? After examining the final verse (v. 30), review what precedes, noting concepts that appeared earlier in the poem.

Translation and outline

Verse	*Translation*	*Outline*
10:23	To engage in planning seems like a joke to a stupid person, but it is wisdom to a perceptive person.	I. Introduction with wisdom commendation: the importance of planning (10:23)
		II. How moral conduct affects plans (start of wisdom content, vv. 24–25)
10:24	What a guilty person dreads – that is what will come to him, but he will grant the longing of moral folk.	A. Plans backfire or thrive, depending on moral conduct (v. 24)
10:25	When the whirlwind blows through, a guilty person is no more, but a moral person is a permanent foundation.	B. Security vanishes or materializes, depending on moral conduct (v. 25)
		III. Two keys concerning future security (vv. 26–27)
10:26	As vinegar to the teeth and as smoke to the eyes, so is a lazy person to those who dispatched him.	A. Indolence: the key to disappointment (v. 26)
10:27	Reverence for the LORD will add days, while the years of guilty folk will grow short.	B. Reverence: the key to longevity (v. 27)

	II'. How moral conduct affects hope (vv. 28–29)
10:28 The expectation of moral persons amounts to joy, while the hope of guilty folk will perish.	A. Hope thrives or perishes, depending on moral conduct (v. 28)
10:29 The way of the LORD is a refuge to a person of integrity, but ruin to those who deal in iniquity.	B. Security materializes or disintegrates, depending on moral conduct (v. 29)
10:30 A moral person for ever shall not be moved, but guilty folk will be unable to reside in the land.	I'. Conclusion with character summary: the importance of morality, for future security (v. 30)

Notes on the text

10:23. 'planning', *zimmâ*: although sometimes designating devious scheming, this lecture's theme of careful preparation for a secure future recommends *zimmâ* as 'planning' (*pace* LXX 'evil', and Fox, who renders, 'vice' [2009: 525]). Fut. is indicated by 'dreads' and 'will come' (10:24), secure permanence (v. 25), life lengthened or shortened (v. 27), 'expectation' and 'hope' (v. 28), 'not be moved' and 'unable to reside' (v. 30).

'but it is wisdom to a perceptive person', *ḥŏkmâ lĕʾîš tĕbûnâ*: lit. 'wisdom to a perceptive person'. 'To engage in planning' in Hebr. closes the first colon. By ellipsis it carries into the second colon, where it corresponds to 'wisdom'; *pace* Fox, who treats 'wisdom' as the subject of the second colon: 'but wisdom (is thus [i.e. like amusement]) to the man of good sense' (2009: 525; cf. Waltke 2004: 467).

'seems like a joke': lit. 'is like a joke'.

10:24. 'will come to him', *tĕbôʾennû*: links assonantally with 'perceptive person', *tĕbûnâ* of 10:23b.

'he will grant', *yittēn*: the simplest antecedent of 'he' is 'the LORD', from the preceding poem's close (10:22a; so also Heim 2001: 128 and Fox 2009: 525). It is unnecessary to render as a verb with pass. connotation and an indefinite subject ('it will be given'; *pace* Waltke 2004: 467, n.).

10:25. 'a permanent foundation', *yĕsôd ʿôlām*: *yĕsôd*, 'foundation', is a noun (so NASB), not a verb, *pace* NRSV ('the righteous are established for ever') and NIV ('but the righteous stand firm for ever').

10:26. 'to the teeth . . . to the eyes', *laššinnayim . . . lāʿênayim*: note assonance in this deployed proverb.

10:30. 'for ever', *ʿôlām*: rendered 'permanent' in 10:25b. Locating 'for ever' before 'shall not be moved' produces emphasis.

'shall not be moved', *bal yimmôṭ*: negation with *bal* can convey emphasis.

'will be unable to reside': (in)capability inferred from yiq.

Form and structure

Borders

Thematically, a transition from wealth acquisition to concern for the future begins at 10:23. (As described under 'Macrostructural features', a palistrophe also begins in that saying, reinforcing the upper border.)

The completion of a palistrophe ('Macrostructural features', below), character summary and closure set the lower border at 10:30. A character summary foresees permanence for moral folk and displacement for the guilty.

Three terms or topics in 10:30 foster closure. These include 'permanent'/'for ever' (both *ʿôlām*, vv. 25b and 30a, respectively), security or longevity (vv. 27, 29, 30), and the word-pair 'moral' and 'guilty' (vv. 24, 25, 28, 30).

Macrostructural features

Wisdom commendation followed by wisdom content (Sections I and II, III, II' and I', content-based). The lecture opens with a wisdom commendation concerning the desirability of planning (Section I, 10:23). The balance of the lecture supplies wisdom content concerning readiness for the future (Sections II, III, II' and I', vv. 24–30).

Palistrophe spanning Sections I, II, III, II' and I' (content-based). Similarities linking Sections II and II' begin to suggest a palistrophic structure. The connection between Sections I and I' supports that hypothesis, so that Section III operates as a palistrophic core. Consider first the links joining Sections II and II'.

Section II (10:24–25) and Section II' (vv. 28–29): how moral conduct affects plans and hope. Both 10:24–25 and vv. 28–29 deal with the impact of moral conduct. Both quatrains present guilty and moral alternatives. In Section II, plans will either backfire, generating the most feared insecurity (vv. 24a, 25a), or succeed, bringing divine supply and storm-proof security (vv. 24b, 25b), depending on one's moral conduct. In Section II', hope will either give way to ruin (10:28b, 29b) or will thrive (v. 28a) with a divine refuge (v. 29a), depending once again on one's moral conduct.

Section I (10:23) and Section I' (v. 30): introduction and conclusion. Section I introduces the activity of planning, an obvious prerequisite for the lecture's theme – securing one's future. Section I' resumes that aim of future security, but stresses the less-obvious prerequisite of moral conduct – a component of security that the intervening sections sought to underscore.

When the closing verse links moral behaviour with the eminently desirable goal of remaining unmoved, even for ever, this in effect marks the zenith of successful planning (10:30a). Conversely, to be consigned to continual wandering ('unable to reside in the land') depicts the darkest doom. To scoff at planning (as do the stupid, v. 23a) will consign one to a future of endless insecurity. Thus Section I joins palistrophically with Section I' as a straightforward introduction joins with a magnificent conclusion.

Pivot in Section III: two keys concerning future security (10:26–27). At the palistrophic core, Section III locates side-by-side sayings concerning (a) the disappointment caused by a lazy emissary and (b) longevity resulting from reverence (10:26 and 27, respectively). Since the notion of an emissary is otherwise foreign to this poem, it functions as a deployed proverb – a saying characterized by (a) internal, axiomatic veracity, and by (b) lack of immediate connection with the poem in which it is located (cf. 1:17, where a deployed saying about a fowler appears in a lecture discouraging illicit wealth). Deployed proverbs win general acceptance since they are axiomatic, supplying persuasive capital that the poet can leverage to rhetorical advantage in the larger poem.

The emissary saying relates to the lecture's theme of future security thus: just as a dignitary may dispatch an advance team to prepare for a future visit to a particular space, so a wise pupil will engage in thoughtful planning to prepare for his future arrival to a particular season of life. The discipline of planning functions like a wise, metaphoric messenger who has been sent on ahead. Instead if one lazily fails to plan, one should expect only bitter 'food' for that future 'trip' ('vinegar to the teeth'), and the 'light' for finding one's way into the future will only diminish vision, not enhance it ('smoke to the eyes').

In place of a lazy emissary, what sort of metaphoric messenger ought one to dispatch to secure one's future? The sage answers in his next saying: 'Reverence for the LORD will add days, while the years of guilty folk will grow short' (10:27). Reverence today readies best for a secure tomorrow. Conversely, immoral conduct cannot but detract.

Situated as they are at this lecture's palistrophic core, the sayings concerning the lazy emissary and reverence enjoy exponential prominence. The condemnation of indolence in planning and the commendation of reverence emerge as monumental guideposts pointing the way to future security.

Reference to 'the LORD' (Sections II, III and II', form-based). 'The LORD' is referenced in 10:27 of Section III and in v. 29 of Section II'. In addition, prominent mention of 'the LORD' at the close of the last lecture (v. 22) offers the best antecedent subject for v. 24b of Section II: 'but he [i.e. the LORD] will grant the longing of moral folk' (see 'Notes', above).

Microstructural features

Repetition of 'guilty' and 'moral' (10:24–25, form-based). 'Guilty' and 'moral' appear in both 10:24 and 25, joining these verses. This word-pair recurs elsewhere in this poem, but not in adjacent verses (cf. vv. 28, 30).

Movement from general to specific (10:24–25, content-based). The general dread afflicting the guilty in 10:24a grows specific in v. 25a, taking the form of a devastating whirlwind. The general longing of moral folk in v. 24b grows specific in v. 25b – a permanent foundation.

Escalation in terms of time (10:27, content-based). The span of 'days' escalates to 'years' within the two cola of 10:27.

Effect, and cause (10:28–29, content-based). In 10:28 the sage describes how the moral and guilty regard the future. These effects result from the causes in v. 29, whether travelling along the Lord's way, or dealing in iniquity.

Comment

Section I (10:23). The lecture opens with a wisdom commendation (10:23). 'Planning' introduces the lecture's theme, epitomizing the shape of wisdom that the sage here commends to the pupil.

10:23. 'Planning' is the middle word of the seven-word Hebr. saying opening this poem.

Section II (10:24–25). In Section II the poet cautions that how one prioritizes moral conduct will determine whether the plans of Section I will backfire or succeed. If they backfire, not only will the pupil fail to gain hoped-for security. Still worse, the insecurity he most dreaded will descend on him (10:24a, 25a).

Successful plans signal divine favour (10:24b; for an explanation of 'he will grant' as implying the divine, see 'Preceding context', in lecture introduction). Such a one by moral character will weather the same storm that will uproot the guilty (v. 25).

10:25. Like the unavoidable windstorm of 10:25, inescapable retribution will surface in 11:21, 31.

Section III (10:26–27). Next the sage portrays moral conduct as an imaginary emissary dispatched to prepare for the pupil's eventual arrival. One must take care that the emissary (i.e. one's own conduct) is not morally indolent, but demonstrates moral industry epitomized by reverence (Section III, 10:26–27).

10:26. Vinegar as an unpalatable beverage contributes to punishment in Ps. 69:21 (v. 22 MT, Waltke 2004: 476).

Contrasting the lazy employee of 10:26, the 'faithful' messenger of 25:13 brings his masters unexpected refreshing.

10:27. It is instructive that the first occurrence of 'reverence for the LORD' to appear outside Prov. 1 – 9 emerges not haphazardly, but in a poem consumed with genuine dread of impending disaster. Here 'fear of the LORD' frees the moral person from intimidation of other sorts – even the great and inevitable windstorm (10:25). The expression 'reverence for the LORD' will not reappear until 14:27.

Reverence serves as bookends for Prov. 1 – 9 (in 1:7; 9:10) and 10 – 31, appearing in the penultimate verse of the book's final poem (31:30).

Section II' (10:28–29). Section II' resembles Section II since both portions develop the connection between moral-or-guilty and success-or-failure (compare 10:24–25 with vv. 28–29). This time, however, the nature of success or failure is much more profound than in Section II. No longer is it the plans that will backfire or succeed. Now it is hope itself that will either thrive or wither away. When hope thrives for the moral person, a robust anticipation unfolds with such irrepressible confidence that it blossoms into joy even before the hoped-for objective (a divine refuge) materializes (vv. 28a, 29a).

In contrast, guilty behaviour resulting in failure now spells not merely the arrival of dreaded consequences (as in 10:24a, 25a) but the very death of hope itself (v. 28b). Here is an accelerating maelstrom of despair that will not end until it reaches total ruin (v. 29b). Paradoxically, 'the way of the LORD' alternatively produces refuge for some, and ruin for others.

Section I' (10:30). By means of a character summary in the last verse, the sage reduces to a few words the lecture's fundamental principle (10:30). Future security will follow moral conduct, both reliably and durably. In contrast, to favour guilty conduct will ensure ceaseless instability. The endless extent of security (v. 30a) combines with the dismal prospect of perpetual wandering (v. 30b) to foster a sense of climax in this closing verse. Waltke similarly marks v. 30 as the close of a portion dealing with 'Security of the Righteous' (2004: 477).

10:30. Inability to 'reside in the land' (due to death, expulsion or captivity) represented a particularly grim prospect for any in ancient times.

Explanation

This poem prepares the youth for life's inevitable storms, a theme found in Prov. 1:20–33 as well. Just as this poem comprises the second poem of Prov. 10 – 31, so also the poem of 1:20–33 is the second in Prov. 1 – 9 (aside from the book introduction in 1:1–9). With this early and recurring theme the sage signals that storm-proofing his pupils ranks high among his priorities.

Section I (10:23)
Wisdom consists of carefully assessing the future, resulting in responsible action today. Lack of forethought amounts to wilful stupidity.

Section II (10:24–25)
Moral behaviour links inextricably to ultimate security. A probing storm dependably will descend upon moral and guilty, with dependably different results. Perhaps Jesus had this passage in mind when at the conclusion of the Sermon on the Mount he told of a single storm with divergent outcomes (cf. Matt. 7:24–27).

Section III (10:26–27)
Everyone dispatches his or her moral conduct of today as an 'emissary' (10:26) into the future, in hope of securing a refuge (see earlier discussion under 'Macrostructural features', especially Section III under Palistrophe spanning 10:23–30). The character of our emissary – whether morally lazy or morally courageous – will determine whether we survive the looming storm. Reverence today comprises the sole 'emissary' leading to a secure tomorrow.

Section II' (10:28–29)
Even before attaining future security, hope and joy will spring up along the way of reverence and moral conduct.

Section I' (10:30)
Hurricanes of various sorts inevitably descend, whether of wealth, health, politics or relationships. After the windstorm has blown through, the reverent will re-emerge, rocklike, appearing where they stood before the storm struck. But those who refused to invest in a godly life will be swept away without a trace.

PROVERBS 10:31 – 11:31
'What is the harm in fraudulent riches?'

Overview of Proverbs 10:31 – 11:31
The topic of riches that occupied the lecture spanning 10:1–22 returns in 10:31 – 11:31. Four perspectives now expand the earlier lecture: (a) the lure of wealth pursued by fraudulent means, (b) the impact on community when one member pursues riches, (c) the paradox of generosity and (d) the certainty of retribution.

This poem draws to a close as multiple threads join in Section IV (11:28–31). Several connotations the reader might allege from Sections I–III grow transparent in that final section, as if the sage withheld interpretive keys until the closing four verses. Consequently after absorbing as much of the poem as possible (especially Sections I–III), it is profitable to reread it in the light of Section IV.

Position of this poem within Proverbs

Preceding context. The first lecture of Prov. 10 – 31 distinguished between tangible and authentic wealth, in answer to the implicit youthful aspiration 'How can I become rich?' (10:1–22). True wealth ultimately results from ethical behaviour that secures divine favour. Then followed a lecture addressing the question 'How can I secure my future?' (10:23–30). Moral living marked by reverence for the LORD offers the only reliable route to security.

Ensuing context. After establishing in this lecture the fact that relationships exceed the value of tangible riches (10:31 – 11:31), in the next the sage will explore the nature of authentic friendship (12:1–28). There the concept of approval or acceptance will loom large.

What to watch for

Notice mention of tangible riches. Then observe relational terms such as 'approval', 'neighbour', 'community', 'nation', 'city', 'husband', 'wife' or 'household'. Watch for paradoxical combination of riches and relationships, as in 11:24. Observe how wisdom commendations can mark the start of a portion, and how character summaries can mark conclusions. Be alert for recurring messages that at times may form a palistrophe, and at other times may mark a dual-theme summary.

Translation and outline

Verse	*Translation*	*Outline*
		I. The poverty of immoral riches (10:31 – 11:8) A. Wisdom commendation: wisdom derives from moral conduct and generates relational favour (10:31–32)
10:31	A moral person's mouth will bear fruit of wisdom, but a perverse tongue will be cut off.	1. Wisdom derives from morality (10:31)
10:32	Lips of a moral person will thoroughly know approval, but the mouth of guilty folk, perversion.	2. Wisdom generates favour (10:32)

Verse	*Translation*	*Outline*
		B. The liability of illicit wealth, the asset of humble integrity (start of wisdom content, 11:1–4)
11:1	Deceptive balances are abhorrent to the LORD, while an accurate weight has his approval.	1. The ultimate liability of illicit wealth (11:1)
11:2	When insolence arrives then arrives disgrace; but with humble folk is wisdom.	2. The asset of humble integrity (11:2–3)
11:3	Integrity of honest folk will guide them, while crookedness is what treacherous folk amount to, even their own devastation.	
11:4	Wealth will not profit on a day of wrath, but moral living will defend against death.	1'. The ultimate futility of illicit wealth (11:4)
11:5	The morality of a person of integrity will straighten his way; while because of his guilt the guilty will fall.	C. The progressive stages of moral and guilty conduct (11:5–7)
11:6	The morality of honest folk will rescue them, while because of their greed, treacherous ones will become trapped.	
11:7	As soon as a guilty mortal dies, hope will perish; but the expectation of the powerful had perished already.	
11:8	A moral person from distress was delivered, and then the guilty entered in his stead.	D. Character summary: retribution by replacement (11:8)
		II. The wealth of moral relationships (11:9–13)
11:9	By mouth the godless can annihilate his neighbour, while by knowledge moral folk can be delivered.	A. Wisdom commendation: moral behaviour begins by benefiting self (11:9)
11:10	Due to the goodness of moral folk a city may rejoice, but due to the ruin of guilty folk there is a shout of joy.	B. Moral behaviour extends to benefit one's city (start of wisdom content, 11:10–11)

Translation	Outline
11:11 Through the blessing of honest folk a city will gain prominence, while by the mouth of guilty persons it will be torn down. 11:12 One who expresses contempt for his neighbour lacks sense, but a perceptive person would keep quiet. 11:13 One who goes about slandering discloses secrets, while one with a trustworthy temperament covers a matter.	C. Moral behaviour benefits even the lone individual who needs mercy (11:12–13)
11:14 For want of navigation a community will collapse, but there is deliverance through much counsel.	III. Interaction between riches and relationships, human and divine (11:14–27) A. Pursuing riches harms human relationships (11:14–18) 1. Wisdom commendation: successful community requires counsel (11:14)
11:15 One will suffer substantial harm because he has guaranteed a loan for a stranger, while one who hates such handshakes trusts. 11:16 A gracious wife will lay hold of glory, while ruthless folk will lay hold of riches. 11:17 One who has weaned his appetite is a husband who loves faithfully, but one who is cruel entangles his next-of-kin. 11:18 A guilty person works a false deal, while one who plants morality – a true wage.	2. Valuing community above riches yields gain (start of wisdom content, 11:15–18) a. The short-sightedness of financial dealings outside the community (11:15) b. Marriage relationship: a wife's graciousness, not greed, achieves glory (11:16) b'. Marriage relationship: a husband who has outgrown self-centredness has learned to love (11:17) a'. The short-sightedness of shady financial dealings (11:18)
11:19 Thus it is that morality tends to life while one who pursues harm tends to his death.	B. The divine as guarantor of moral retribution (11:19–21) 1. The outcomes of moral conduct are staggering (11:19)

Verse	*Translation*	*Outline*
11:20	Abhorrent to the Lord are the twisted-of-mind, while those who journey with integrity receive his approval.	2. It is the Lord who evaluates (11:20)
11:21	Be sure of this: a person who causes harm will not go unpunished, while children of moral folk will have fled to safety.	1'. The outcomes of moral conduct are unavoidable (11:21)
		A'. Pursuing generosity helps human relationships (11:22–27)
11:22	A gold ring in a pig's snout – such is an attractive woman who turns away from discriminating taste.	1. Wisdom commendation (deployed proverb): it is comedic when wealth outstrips discernment (11:22)
		2. Wisdom content: how generosity and greed play out paradoxically in community (11:23–27)
11:23	The core longing of moral folk is strictly good; the hope of guilty folk is an angry outburst.	a. What one desires for others will determine what one can hope to receive (11:23)
11:24	There is one who scatters generously yet gains still more, while one who holds back from straight dealing surely winds up in want.	b. The generous neighbour will not lack, while the miserly will run short (11:24)
11:25	An appetite for blessing others will itself be made fat, just as one who waters thoroughly will himself be watered.	c. Paradoxical ideal: a hunger for generosity will enjoy a feast (11:25)
11:26	A nation will curse one who withholds grain, while a blessing is upon the head of one who offers grain for sale.	b'. The miserly neighbour will gain disgrace, while the generous neighbour will gain favour (11:26)
11:27	One who is on the lookout for good will seek approval, but one in search of harm will get precisely that.	a'. What one seeks for others will determine what one may hope to get (11:27)
		IV. Summary: generosity in relationships, not greed, will reward with rich vitality (11:28–31)
		A. Dual-theme summary regarding greed and generosity (11:28–30)

11:28 Whoever trusts in his riches – that one will fall, while moral persons will sprout out like a leaf.	1. Dual-theme summary: the poverty of trusting tangible riches and the vitality-wealth of morality (11:28)
11:29 One who entangles his household will inherit wind, and a fool is servant to the wise-of-mind.	2. First theme: the poverty of tangible riches secured at the expense of relationships (11:29)
11:30 The fruit of a moral person is a tree of life, and one who gains lives is wise.	3. Second theme: the vitality-wealth that follows the morality of greed kept in check (11:30)
11:31 Consider this: the moral person on the earth will be repaid. How much more the guilty sinner!	B. Character summary conclusion: moral retribution is sure (11:31)

Waltke similarly detects sections ending at 11:8, 27, 31 (2004: 480–481, 504, 509).

Notes on the text

10:31–32. 'perverse' and 'perversion' (*tahpukōt* in both instances): since the root *hpk* involves changing or overturning, *tahpukōt* introduces precisely the devious weight-falsification crime appearing next (11:1).

10:32. 'will thoroughly know approval', *yêdĕʿûn rāṣôn*: 'know' implies 'to know by experience', with 'thoroughly' representing the verb's energic nun. It is not necessary to emend *yêdĕʿûn rāṣôn*, 'thoroughly know approval', to read *yabbîʿûn rāṣôn*, 'express approval', since this would treat 'approval' as an opinion issued, rather than a commendation received – a connotation found in 11:1, 20, 27 (*pace* Fox 2009: 529).

11:1. 'accurate', *šĕlēmâ*: lit. 'complete, whole'. Within this poem the root *šlm* will recur only in the poem's final verse ('will be repaid', *yĕšullām*, 11:31), contributing to closure.

11:3. 'honest folk', *yĕšārîm*: with a basic meaning of 'straight', the root *yšr* appears in 'straight dealing' (11:24), contrasting *selep*, 'crookedness' (v. 3b).

'while crookedness is what treacherous folk amount to, even their own devastation', *wĕselep bôgdîm wĕšŏddām*: i.e. treacherous folk embody crookedness, and they are their own undoing (following K, two verbless clauses revolving around the identity of treacherous folk). To read *wĕšŏddām* not as a noun (devastation), but a verb (yiq. *yĕšŏddēm*, 'will devastate them', so Q), would produce in 11:3b a simpler syntax ('while the crookedness of treacherous folk will devastate them') neatly mirroring v. 3a (cf. Waltke 2004: 480–481, n.). However, the syntax of K – though jarring – remains comprehensible as it stands, and delivers to treacherous folk a sharper indictment, a more ominous prognosis. They amount to crookedness and are themselves the cause for their own collapse under the weight of ethical emptiness.

11:4. 'will not profit': echoing 'treasures of a guilty person cannot bring profit' (10:2).

11:7. 'will perish . . . had perished already', *tōʾbad . . . ʾābādâ*: shift from yiq. to qat. of the same verb ('perish') suggests plpf. 'had . . . already' for the second verb.

'but the expectation of the powerful': rendering with adversative conj. 'but' reflects this saying's indication that, long before the demise of sinister hopes entertained by the guilty person (11:7a), already the nefarious expectations held by the powerful had diminished into empty threats (v. 7b). Parallel to 'guilty' in v. 7a, 'the powerful' carries a malevolent connotation.

11:10. 'Due to the goodness of moral folk': i.e. goodness exhibited by moral folk (cf. 11:23, 27).

'there is a shout of joy': lit. 'a shout of joy' (11:10b is a verbless clause).

11:11. 'the blessing of honest folk': i.e. a blessing generously issued by honest folk (cf. generous actions in 11:24a, 25b, 26b). Actions that similarly have an impact on others (not self) continue in v. 12 ('one who expresses contempt for his neighbour'). In contrast to actions that affect others, 'a blessing is upon the head' refers to receipt of blessing for oneself (v. 26b).

'city', *qāret*: synonymous with *qiryâ*, also rendered 'city' (11:10).

11:12. 'lacks sense', *ḥăsar-lēb*: lit. 'lacking-of-mind', contrasting *ḥăkam-lēb*, 'wise-of-mind' in 11:29b.

11:13. 'a trustworthy temperament': lit. 'faithful of spirit', implying control over one's emotions.

11:14. 'navigation', *taḥbulôt*: assonantally linked to *tahpukôt*, 'perverse' (10:31, 32), a term thematically vital to this poem, appearing twice in its opening quatrain.

11:15. 'trusts': or 'is confident' (also in 11:28). Paradoxically, one who refrains from an outward expression of trust (solemnizing an agreement through a handshake with a stranger) still maintains trusting relationships with others – presumably with persons within a closer circle, who require no confirming handshake (see 6:1, 'Notes').

11:16. 'wife', *ʾēšet*: not simply 'woman', but 'wife', due to these relational terms in the context: 'neighbour' (11:9, 12), 'community' (v. 14), 'next-of-kin' (v. 17), 'children' (v. 21) and 'household' (v. 29).

'ruthless', *ʿārîṣîm*: emending to read *ḥārûṣîm*, 'diligent', misses how that colon contributes to the theme of harmful, headlong pursuit of riches (*pace* Fox 2009: 537; cf. 11:1, 4, 15, 22, 24, 26, 28).

11:17. 'weaned his appetite', *gōmēl napšô*: in 11:17 (as in v. 25) 'appetite' offers the best meaning for *nepeš*. Consequently *gml* should not be rendered 'to reward', but 'to wean' (cf. *gml* as 'to wean', twice with *nepeš* in Ps. 131:2).

'husband', *ʾîš*: not 'man' or 'person', due to proximity to 'wife' in 11:16.

11:20. 'receive his approval': lit. '[are] his approval'.

11:21. 'a person who causes harm': the adj. *rāʿ* here designates a person who brings harm (rendered 'wicked person' in 24:20).

'will have fled', *nimlāṭ*: fut. pf., since the action of 11:21b occurs prior to the punishment of wrongdoer in v. 21a.

11:23. 'The core longing of moral folk is strictly good', *taʾăwat ṣaddîqîm ʾak-ṭôb*: i.e. moral folk yearn only that good may come to others (cf. 19:22).

'an angry outburst', *ʿebrâ*: the concepts of overflow and anger combine in this term, rendered 'wrath' in 11:4.

11:24. 'scatters generously': lit. 'scatters', with generosity implied by context (cf. 11:26).

'straight dealing', *yōšer*: describes one's minimally reasonable response to others in the community (see 'Notes' for 11:3). To 'scatter generously' would exceed this threshold of neighbourly fairness.

11:25. 'appetite': expressions such as 'to be made fat', 'to water' and 'to be watered' recommend rendering *nepeš* as 'appetite' (also 11:17).

'blessing others': lit. 'blessing'; 'others' is inferred (cf. note on 11:11).

11:27. 'One who is on the lookout for good', *šōḥar ṭôb*: one who seeks opportunities to bring goodness to others (not to reap benefit for himself; cf. 11:10, 23).

'will get precisely that', *tĕbôʾennû*: lit. 'it will enter him'.

11:29. 'entangles', *ʿôkēr*: lit. 'causes trouble for'.

'wise-of-mind', *ḥăkam-lēb*: opposite of *ḥăsar-lēb*, 'lacking-of-mind' (11:12).

11:30. 'and one who gains': lit. 'one who takes (or grasps, seizes)'. While 'to gain' resembles accumulating wealth, here it involves securing benefit for others by rescuing them. Alternatively, 'to seize' or 'grasp' can refer to controlling one's own self (Jer. 23:31) – a connotation that may foster wordplay surrounding *nĕpāšôt* (see below).

'lives', *nĕpāšôt*: the spelling *nĕpāśôt* in Codex Leningradensius should be regarded as a scribal error for *nĕpāšôt*, 'lives', since, aside from this verse, Hebr. attests no root spelled *npś* or *nps*. As discussed below ('Macrostructural features'), the phrase *lōqēaḥ nepeš* may present a wordplay, both grasping others' lives in order to rescue them (Waltke 2004: 513) and keeping a restraining grip on one's own appetite – an alternative translation of sg. *nepeš* (cf. 11:17a).

11:31. 'Consider this': lit. 'behold'.

'guilty sinner': lit. 'guilty and sinner' (hendiadys). Mention of 'sinner' underscores divine involvement in retribution (cf. 11:1, 20).

Form and structure

Borders

Thematic transition and a wisdom commendation mark the upper border. Themes transition from future security (preceding poem, ending with a character summary in 10:30) to fraudulent riches (present poem). That theme begins directly after an initial wisdom commendation (10:31–32).

A character summary, intensification and dense closure mark the lower border. Regarding character summary, although various verses in this lecture contrast good and bad behaviour (e.g. 11:6, 9, 11), at the lecture's final verse the antonyms 'moral person' and 'guilty sinner' confront the pupil with stark binary contrast characteristic of a character summary. Regarding intensification, the expressions 'consider this' and 'how much more' intensify a climactic sense of conclusion in the lecture's final verse (11:31; so also Waltke 2004: 513).

Dense closure is achieved by six terms or topics introduced earlier in the lecture that reappear in the final section. The first involves misplaced confidence, trusting in illicit riches (mention of 'moral' in 11:28b implies that the riches of v. 28a are illicit). Flawed reliance on riches also appeared in 11:1, 4, 15.

A second closural element involves valuing relationships. Those who harmfully entangle family relationships will hollow out their inheritance (11:29a). Relationships were featured earlier in 11:9–13, 14–18, 24–27.

Third is the concept of falling, which in 11:28 is suffered by those who value riches above relationships. Earlier, the guilty fall (v. 5), suffering punishment wrongly destined for the innocent (v. 8). Entire communities also may fall (v. 14).

The fourth closural topic involves the robust vitality (beyond mere security or survival) that will follow moral living, metaphorically portrayed as a fruitful tree (11:28, 30). As noted below, the poem's initial colon alluded to a fruitful tree (also pruning): 'A moral person's mouth will bear fruit, but a perverse tongue will be cut off' (10:31a; Fox 2009: 544), creating a lecture-wide inclusio.

The fifth closural topic involves magnanimity. Rather than grasping at tangible riches, a moral person extends 'life' to others, 'grasping' them (for rescue, 11:30; cf. 13:8). Magnanimity appeared earlier in 11:13, 23–27.

Retribution constitutes the sixth and last closural topic, appearing in each verse of Section IV, most forcefully in the poem's last verse: 'Consider this: the moral person on the earth will be repaid. How much more the guilty sinner' (11:31). Retribution features prominently in 11:3–8, 19, 21, 23–27. The root 'to repay', *šlm*, appeared in the first wisdom content saying as 'accurate' weights, *šlm* (11:1).

Macrostructural features

Repetition of 'moral' (Sections I–IV, form-based). Although not displaying significant positioning, the frequency of terms tracing to the root *ṣdq*, 'moral' or 'righteous', involves all four sections of this lecture, appearing in fifteen of its thirty-three verses (10:31, 32; 11:4, 5, 6, 8, 9, 10, 18, 19, 21, 23, 28, 30, 31).

Thematic continuity involving crookedness (Sections I and III) and straightness (Sections I–IV, content-based). The theme of crookedness/straightness similarly crosses all four sections, appearing in sixteen instances spread over one-third of this lecture's sayings (thirteen of thirty-three verses). As with the term 'moral' (see above), the theme of crookedness is anchored in each saying of the initial wisdom commendation quatrain ('perverse' in 10:31 and 'perversion' v. 32). Related negative terms include 'deceptive' (11:1) and 'crookedness' (11:3) in Section I, and 'twisted' (11:20) and 'to hold back from straight [*yšr*] dealing' (11:24) in Section III.

The theme of straightness, the positive counterpart of crookedness, appears in all four sections, evident in the root *šlm* ('accurate' in 11:1; 'repaid' in 11:31), in the root *yšr* ('straighten' in 11:5; 'honest' in 11:3, 6, 11) and in the root *ʾmn* ('trustworthy' in 11:13; 'true' in 11:18). Two terms indicating safe transit through uncertain situations further contribute to the concept of straightness: 'to guide' (11:3) and 'navigation' (*taḥbulôt* in 11:14; assonantally linked to *tahpukōt*, 'perverse', in 10:31, 32).

Thematic continuity involving community relationships (Sections I–IV, content-based). With numerous terms indicating community relationships the sage builds a case for valuing relationships beyond pursuit of riches. Relationship is indicated through (a) expressions of approval/disapproval, (b) specific labels and (c) behaviours presuming relationships.

Expressions of approval/disapproval involve the term 'approval' (10:32; 11:1, 20, 27), 'gracious' (11:16) and 'blessing' (receiving affirmation, 11:11, 25, 26). Disfavour takes the form of 'abhorrence' (11:1, 20) and 'to curse' (11:26).

Specific labels indicating community include 'neighbour' (11:9a, 12), 'city' (vv. 10, 11), 'community' (v. 14), 'wife/woman' (v. 16), 'man/husband' (v. 17), 'next-of-kin' (v. 17), 'children' (lit. 'descendants', v. 21), and 'servant' and 'master' (v. 29). The 'stranger' signifies someone outside the natural boundaries of familiar and trustworthy community (v. 15).

Behaviours indicative of relationships include 'to scatter generously' (11:24), 'to water others' (v. 25) and 'to offer grain for sale (v. 26). Negative behaviours include 'to entangle one's household' (vv. 17, 29), 'to hold back' from treating others fairly (v. 24) and 'to keep back' grain that others wish to buy (v. 26).

Repetition of 'deliver' (Sections I and II, form-based). The last saying of Section I (11:8) and the first of Section II (v. 9) contain this lecture's only mention of 'deliver' (Waltke 2004: 489). This continuity links the two sections at their point of adjacency.

Wisdom commendation, with repetition of 'mouth' (Sections I and II, form- and content-based). 'Mouth' is repeated in each saying of the two-verse wisdom commendation opening Section I (10:31–32), and again in the wisdom commendation opening Section II (11:9). The first leads to wisdom content spanning the balance of Section I (11:1–8). The second introduces wisdom content completing Section II (11:10–13).

Thematic continuity surrounding fruitfulness and growth (Sections I, III and IV, content-based). Several expressions point to a theme of fruitfulness and growth. These include 'to bear fruit' (10:31) 'to plant' (11:18), 'children' (lit. 'seed', 11:21), 'to gain still more' (11:24), 'to be made fat' (11:25), 'to be watered' (11:25), 'fruit' and 'tree of life' (both in 11:30). Contrasting fruitfulness are the expressions 'to be cut off' (10:31) and 'to be in want' (11:24).

Thematic continuity surrounding generosity and the futility of illicit riches (Sections I, III and IV, content-based). Three of the lecture's four sections contrast generosity and the futility of illicit riches. In Section I, dishonest scales speak to the futility of illicit riches, directly after the initial wisdom commendation (11:1). The declaration 'Wealth will not profit on a day of wrath' categorically devalues riches (v. 4).

In Section III, the sage explains how damaging to community and family relationships is the headlong pursuit of riches (11:15, 16b, 17b, with implications for vv. 19–21 as well). In contrast, grace and faithful love mark the ideal woman and man, respectively (vv. 16a, 17a). Instead of pursuing futile riches, one should earn an honest living (v. 18b). Wealth is wasted on one who is oblivious to what is truly valuable (v. 22, a negative wisdom commendation and deployed proverb). One should aim generously to meet the needs of others, rather than destroying others in pursuit of one's own longings (vv. 23–27).

The final section opens with this caution: 'Whoever trusts in his riches – that one will fall' (11:28a in Section IV). Rather than accumulating wealth, one should seek to 'gain' or 'seize' human lives (v. 30b, with a sense of rescue; cf. 14:25). A subsequent lecture recommends depleting riches in order to ransom another's life (13:8). Since the term for 'life', *nepeš*, also means 'appetite' when sg. (11:17, 25), a wordplay may operate here, urging both the protection of others' lives, and restraint of one's own desires.

Closure involving 'good', 'approval' and 'harm' (Section III, form-based). Due to their appearance in earlier sections, three terms that occur in the last verse of Section III foster a sense of closure for that section. The terms 'good', 'approval' and 'harm' all occur in 11:27. 'Good' appeared earlier in Section II (v. 10), also in Section III (v. 23); 'approval' appeared in Sections I (10:32; 11:1) and III (11:20). 'Harm' appeared earlier in Section III, together with other terms also stemming from the root *ra'* (11:15, 19, 21). The closure that these foster at the end of Section III contributes to the effectiveness of Section IV as a summary.

Deployed proverb involving discernment of wealth (11:22 in Section III, and Sections I, II and IV, content-based). A deployed proverb concerning wise discernment of genuine wealth opens Block III.A': 'A gold ring in a pig's snout – such is an attractive woman who turns away from discriminating taste' (11:22). Tangible wealth without an appreciation for what in life is truly valuable will only make of a person a laughable pig, however highly decorated he or she may appear (cf. Waltke 2004: 504). Since the theme of proper esteem for riches, relative to relationships, features prominently in all other sections of the lecture, this deployed proverb functions adroitly within this poem.

Microstructural features

Section I (10:31 – 11:8). *Wisdom commendation (10:31–32, content-based).* Expressions involving 'wisdom' (10:31), 'to thoroughly know' (10:32) and speech (both verses) suggest that this quatrain serves as a section-opening wisdom commendation.

Repetition of 'perverse' and 'moral' connected with speech (10:31–32, form- and content-based). Each verse of the initial wisdom commendation begins with the topic of moral speech: 'A moral person's mouth' and 'Lips of a moral person'. 'Perverse' or 'perversion' also appears in each saying (the noun *tahpukôt* in each case, 10:31b, 32b), a term occurring only twice more in Proverbs (16:28, 30).

Repetition of 'approval' (10:32; 11:1, form-based). 'Approval' in 11:1 recalls use of that term in 10:32 (Waltke 2004: 482), linking wisdom commendation (Block I.A) with wisdom content (Block I.B), and initiating the value of relationships that features prominently in this lecture.

Frame and core (11:1 and 4, 2 and 3, content-based). The sage presents the shortcomings of wealth in 11:1 and 4 (also Garrett 1993: 124–125). Divine evaluation, whether negative or positive, also marks each verse. These sayings frame a core in vv. 2–3 recommending humility and integrity while exposing arrogance and sly dealing. This frame and core comprise Block I.B.

Dynamic progressions (11:5–7, content-based). Repeated expressions link 11:5, 6: 'The morality of [a positive entity enjoying benefit]' in the first cola, contrasted in the second cola by the statement 'while because of [a negative entity suffering demise]'. The successive benefits escalate in desirability (Waltke 2004: 486).

A progression of worsening demise characterizes 11:5–7. Fortunes of the guilty deteriorate from falling (v. 5b), to entrapment (v. 6b), ending in death (v. 7a). This outcome in no way surprises the sage, since 'the expectation of the powerful had perished already' (v. 7b; see 'Notes'). Three terms for death in v. 7 ('perish' twice, and 'dies') seal the three-verse block with a sense of finality (11:5–7, Block I.C).

Character summary (11:8, content-based). The binary alternatives of moral and guilty characters conclude Section I in 11:8, with one refinement. Instead of isolated opposites (as is usually the case with character summaries), these interrelate retributively as the guilty replaces the moral, rightly receiving the disaster that nearly befell the innocent.

Inclusio with reversal (11:8, content-based). Substitution operates in 11:1, 8, creating an inclusio for the wisdom-commendation portion of Section I. In v. 1 the deceptive merchant substituted false weights for true. In v. 8, a guilty person substitutes for a moral person. Reversal operates here, since v. 1 described dishonesty, while v. 8 described retribution.

Section II (11:9–13). *Wisdom commendation (11:9, content-based)*. Mention of speaking and knowledge, without advising a specific course of action – this signals a wisdom commendation at the start of Section II (11:9).

Thematic continuity involving relationships (11:9–13, content-based). Relationships dominate 11:9–13. 'Neighbour' appears in vv. 9, 12, with 'city' in vv. 10, 11 (synonyms deriving from the root *qrb*). Waltke, citing Goldingay, also notes the theme of relationships in these verses (2004: 490). Each colon of the relational message of 11:12 intensifies in v. 13, both for ill (first cola) and for good (second cola).

Dynamic progression involving the recipient of benefit or harm (11:9–13, content-based). A dynamic progression concerning the recipient of benefit or harm emerges in 11:9–13. Initially, the moral individual receives benefit (v. 9b). Next is the city (vv. 10–11; Waltke similarly regards these as a quatrain [2004: 491]). Last among beneficiaries is an individual whose behaviour could reflect negatively on himself, were it to become public knowledge (vv. 12–13).

Assonance (11:11, 12, form-based). Although 11:11 and 12 belong to separate blocks, assonance joining the last word of each verse smooths the transition from one theme to the next. *Tēhārēs̆*, 'it will be torn down', closes v. 11, while *yaḥărîs̆*, 'keeps quiet', closes v. 12.

Section III (11:14–27). *Wisdom commendation (11:14, content-based)*. Mention of 'navigation' and 'counsel' mark 11:14 as a wisdom commendation. It opens Section III.

Double inclusio involving repetition of 'harm' (11:15, 27, 19, 21, form-based). Positioning of four sayings with the Hebr. root *ra*ʿ, 'harm', results in two inclusios. It appears in 11:15 (twice) and 27 – the first wisdom-content verse of Section III and the section's final verse. It also appears in vv. 19, 21, the start and finish of Block III.B. It occurs nowhere else in this lecture.

Palistrophe (11:15–18, form- and content-based). A two-step palistrophe unifies 11:15–18. The outer step warns against damaging deals, whether with strangers (v. 15), or based on unethical practices (v. 18). The inner step contrasts noble marriage partners with those who harm others due to greed (vv. 16–17).

Thematic continuity regarding the concept of harm (11:14, 16, 17, 19, 21, 23, content-based). Together with repetition of *ra*ʿ, 'harm', warning against harm inflicted in relationships is conveyed in Section III by six related expressions. These include 'collapse' (11:14), 'ruthless' (v. 16), 'to entangle' (v. 17), 'death' (vs. 'life', v. 19), 'not-unpunished' (v. 21) and 'an angry outburst' (v. 23).

Through this theme the sage teaches that harm befalls those who contract with someone foreign to their community relationships, in hope of securing monetary gain (11:15). To aim at wealth will cost one's close relationships (vv. 16–17; Waltke also recognizes that these form a quatrain [2004: 499]). This will lead to death (v. 19), an outcome reinforced by the LORD himself (vv. 20–21).

Those who prioritize profit above neighbourly relations (11:26) can expect to be repaid with an 'angry outburst' from their neighbours (v. 23). For, 'One who is on the lookout for good will seek approval [i.e. will cultivate appreciative relationships], but one in search of harm will get precisely that' (v. 27).

Thematic continuity regarding accountability (11:19–21, content-based). Accountability characterizes Block III.B (11:19–21). Expression of consequences ('So it is') concerning life/death ultimacy leads v. 19, while certitude ('Be sure of this') concerning retribution leads v. 21. Between these the sage affirms that it is the LORD's evaluation that matters most of all.

Palistrophe (11:23–27, form- and content-based). A three-step palistrophe unifies 11:23–27. Within this lecture, the adj. 'good' appears only in 11:23, 27, forming an inclusio framing Unit III.A'.2 (the first palistrophic step). 'Goodness' in v. 10 is a noun, contrasting the adj. 'good' in vv. 23, 27. Waltke also observed the repetition of 'good' in vv. 23, 27 (2004: 505; cf. Meinhold 1991, 1: 197–200). As a second palistrophic step, each of 11:24, 26 features neighbours who are either generous or miserly (chiastically reversed). Third, the poet stresses the principle of generosity, showcasing it at the palistrophic core (v. 25).

Section IV (11:28–31). *Dual-theme summary (11:28, content-based).* Section IV opens with a dual-theme verse contrasting (a) the harm of pursuing riches (11:28a) with (b) vitality following moral living (v. 28b). Verse 29 expands the harm of pursuing riches (note that 'entanglement' implies pursuing riches, based on vv. 16–17). Verse 30 expands on the vitality theme, with its mention of fruit and tree of life. Waltke similarly observed that v. 28 prefigures vv. 29, 30 (2004: 512–513).

Closure (11:31, form- and content-based). Both dual-themes anchored in 11:28 return in the final verse (v. 31), effecting closure. The second dual-theme appears first, signalled by 'moral' (v. 31a; cf. vv. 28b, 30). The first dual-theme (the harm of pursuing riches) follows in v. 31b, as the 'guilty sinner' receives repayment (cf. vv. 28a, 29).

Comment

Section I (10:31 – 11:8). Section I cautions against the impoverishment of immoral riches. Even the initial wisdom commendation establishes that moral conduct will yield communal approval (10:31–32, Block I.A).

Next the sage takes up the lecture's principal topic: pursuit of wealth. Unless grounded in morality, pursuit of wealth will incur the supreme catastrophe of divine disfavour (11:1). Conversely, morality in the marketplace results in divine favour (note repetition of 'approval' in 10:32 and 11:1). Disregard for divine supremacy and integrity will bring self-destruction (vv. 2–3). The liability of immorality (and contrasting asset of morality) reaches a climax with the expressions 'day of wrath' and 'defend against death' in v. 4, closing Block I.B.

The next block reviews successive stages of moral and guilty conduct, ending again with death for the guilty (11:5–7, Block I.C). The moral enjoy unimpeded travel (v. 5a) and ultimate rescue (v. 6a). The guilty, by contrast, will trip (v. 5b), will become trapped (v. 6b) and ultimately will perish (v. 7). In a character summary with reversal, the moral enjoy deliverance as the guilty arrive on the scene to suffer fairly the disaster that was on the verge of striking the moral unfairly (v. 8, Block II.D).

11:1. The Pentateuch and *Amenemope* similarly caution against falsifying weights and measures (cf. Lev. 19:36; Deut. 25:15; *Amenemope* col. 17, line 18 – col. 19, line 3 [ch. 16.1 – 17.12]).

11:5. The expression *běriš ʿatô*, 'because of his guilt', may have reminded hearers of the Hebr. expression *běrištô*, 'into his net', hinting at the following statement: 'into his net the guilty will fall' (so Kselman, noted in Fox 2009: 532).

11:8b. The writer of Ecclesiastes would concur: 'to the sinner [God] has appointed a task of gathering and amassing in order to give it to one who is good in God's estimation' (Eccles. 2:26b).

Section II (11:9–13). The sage contrasts the liability of riches immorally obtained (Section I) by presenting the immense intangible worth of relationships (Section II). Beyond benefiting self with rescue (11:9, recapping v. 8 of the preceding section), moral conduct spreads joy and prosperity to one's community as well (vv. 10–11). General community benefit will aid individuals as well, for moral people will refrain from expressing contempt towards individuals with whom they disagree (v. 12). Further, when another's failings come to light, the moral may be trusted to be discreet (v. 13, closing Section II).

11:12–13. Practising kindness by preserving confidentiality recalls 10:11–12, another section-closing quatrain.

Section III (11:14–27). Section III brings together the themes of (a) the cost of illicit riches (Section I) and (b) the worth of relationships undergirded by morality (Section II), showing how riches affect relationships, both human and divine, for good or ill. The theme of relationships begins in the section-opening wisdom commendation ('community', 'much counsel' in 11:14).

The poet proceeds to outline two types of 'community': business relationships and marriage relationships (11:15–18, Unit III.A.2). In each case, selfish pursuit of riches will backfire. In business, pursuit of wealth will incline one to venture outside the trustworthy boundaries of community, resulting in 'substantial harm', whereas truly trustworthy relationships require no 'handshake' (v. 15).

In marriage, one who values tangible wealth above gracious relationships will treat relationships with ruthlessness (11:16). A husband must 'wean' himself from such narcissism, learning instead selflessly to love those in dearest relationship (v. 17). The choice amounts to opting for truth over falsehood. In the end, only moral conduct will reward by paying a true wage (note the implication of wealth in v. 18, a saying that closes the unit spanning vv. 15–18).

One may rely on these grand principles (the futility of illicit wealth, and the reward of integrity), for this reason: they are established and maintained by the divine. He guarantees moral retribution (Block III.B, 11:19–21).

Whereas Block III.A cautioned against greedy pursuit of wealth, Block III.A' commends generosity (11:22–27). The poet opens with a comedic wisdom commendation drawn from the barnyard (v. 22): one who pursues riches with utter abandon (discerning no other value) will become a clownish absurdity.

The paradox of generosity – desiring good for others – contrasts such greed (11:23a). Generosity consistently reaps a greater harvest than parsimony (v. 24). Returning to the language of 'appetite' (cf. v. 17), the sage summarizes the paradox in v. 25: to prosper ('become fat') one must hunger for others' well-being ('blessing'). Such kindness will win the community's favour, enriching one's store of relationships (v. 26). Such is the benefit for seeking 'good' – which, as the pupil would now realize, must mean 'what is good for my neighbour' (v. 27). 'What you seek for others, you will find for yourself' (Waltke 2004: 509).

11:17. Children customarily were weaned about age 3 (Exum 1996: 766). A child who insisted on mother's milk beyond the normal suckling age would be regarded as encumbering its mother by its delayed maturation.

11:22. Still today Bedouin women wear a ring of this sort in the right wall of the nostril (cf. Gen. 24:22; Waltke 2004: 503). Mention of 'a gracious woman' who lays hold of glory (11:16) in the vicinity of a negative depiction of 'an attractive woman' who lacks taste (v. 22) commends the inner beauty of generosity above outward glamour.

To suggest that the ignorant pig represents the beautiful woman's unappreciative husband (rather than describing her own ignorant conduct) would not provide a f. subject required by the verb 'turns away'. It must describe the woman who no longer manifests the ability to distinguish between beauty and barnyard (*pace* Fox 2009: 540; concerning construal of the prep. 'from' with the verb 'to turn away', cf. 2 Chr. 8:15; 20:33).

11:24–25. Paradoxically, generosity is self-serving. 'It is better to give than to receive' (Acts 20:35).

11:26. In hope of greedily driving up the sale price one might constrict supply (Waltke 2004: 508).

Section IV (11:28–31). In point-for-point fashion, Section IV summarizes this lecture's contrast of (a) the poverty of immoral riches and (b) the wealth of moral relationships. Both appear in 11:28: tangible riches offer unreliable support, while moral behaviour assures irrepressible vitality. Greedy riches dominate v. 29: one who sacrifices relationships ('his household') in hope of acquiring riches will gain nothing but wind. In v. 30 the supreme wealth of 'life' itself, issuing through moral relationships, is signified by a fruitful tree that benefits others, and by restraint of one's own appetites.

In closing, the sage assures the reader that retribution will reliably arrive, for moral and guilty alike. Mention of 'sinner' adds a theological layer, implying that God will guarantee moral repayment. So the pupil must choose what sort of repayment he wishes to receive from him (11:31).

11:28. A cleft sentence as found here also closes a lecture in 10:22b: 'The blessing of the LORD – that is what will enrich a person.'

11:30. Mention of 'fruit' in connection with a 'tree of life' raises the possibility of allusion to the two trees account of Gen. 3.

Explanation

To pursue riches at the expense of community amounts to a bad business plan, for returns always will favour the generous. And 'returns' there will be, for the moral as for the guilty.

Section I. The poverty of immoral riches (10:31 – 11:8)

Riches strongly allure. Yet they deliver nothing with enduring worth. Pursuit of riches follows a twisted path, escorting the traveller away from divine favour, leading into tripping, entrapment and the universal death of hope.

Section II. The wealth of moral relationships (11:9–13)

We may realize that riches never deliver as promised. But are we commensurately aware of the returns that follow investing in relationships? In particular, one should invest (a) by cultivating generosity and (b) by choosing not to repeat a matter that would inflict needless harm.

Section III. Interaction between riches and relationships, human and divine (11:14–27)

Instead of subscribing to a scarcity world view that advocates wealth-pursuit and hoarding, communities need families composed of gracious wives and husbands weaned of self-serving greed (11:16–17). Only then will neighbourhoods grow vibrant. Only then will the next generation escape ruin. For surely there will be a reckoning.

After all the sage's cautions against damaging the community, we must face this question: 'How deeply do we prize relationships (11:24–26)?' Are they worth no more to us than jewellery to a pig (11:22)?

Two factors provide the answer to this question. First, to what degree do we value people around us? Are people only a means to an end? Or are relationships, in themselves, the 'end'? As someone has advised, 'Use things to do [i.e. develop] people, not people to do things.'

Second, do we engage others with an 'appetite to bless'? Or do we hoard, fearing that generosity will deplete our limited supply? As the sage declared at the zenith of a palistrophe, an outlook of generosity that attends to the needs of others marks the path leading to richest personal fulfilment (11:25).

Section IV. Summary: generosity in relationships, not greed, will reward with rich vitality (11:28–31)

To rely on riches for security is to lean on a support sure to collapse. Only as the greedy thus falls will he bring gladness to his community (11:28a, 29).

To test whether riches have become our goal, we should assess family relationships. Are we spending down our reserve of relationships in order to secure riches? To bankrupt family relationships in pursuit of riches will prove a poor and enslaving trade (11:29).

Or have we discovered the greater wealth of snatching others from destruction (11:30)? Such a one cultivates an appetite for generosity.

One who consistently chooses the morally high road will achieve a lasting reward of robust vitality both for self and for those nearby. For the reward resulting from moral conduct will be as dependable as that following guilty conduct (11:28b, 30–31).

PROVERBS 12:1–28
'How can I recognize noble character and thus behave as a true friend?'

Overview of Proverbs 12:1–28

The lecture spanning Prov. 12 portrays the character of one meriting the pupil's trust as a true friend (specified in 12:26). For the discerning pupil, this poem will become a self-portrait.

Position of this poem within Proverbs

Preceding context. The last lecture stressed the importance of generously investing in relationships, both human and divine, rather than pursuing tangible riches (10:31 – 11:31). This sets the stage for the present lecture's exploration of genuine friendship. The term 'approval', which signalled healthy relationships in the previous lecture (10:32; 11:1, 20, 27), appears in the first wisdom content colon of this lecture: 'A good person will obtain approval from the LORD' (12:2a).

Ensuing context. Just as a wisdom commendation concentrating on reproof opens the lecture spanning Prov. 12, so another dealing with reproof will open the next (13:1). That lecture will address the implied question 'How may I achieve true satisfaction?' (13:1–25).

What to watch for

Observe how much of this lecture focuses on persons (12:2, 4) or personal traits pivotal for authentic relationships. Notice how advice concerning relational prowess progresses from general (Section I) to specific (Section II), climaxing with mention of life and death in the final verse. Watch for patterns generated by repeated concepts. Consider whether wisdom commendations that feature receptivity, and conclusions that feature retribution, respectively may locate the start and finish of sections.

Translation and outline

Verse	*Translation*	*Outline*
		I. Words and deeds reveal noble character (12:1–14) A. Introduction: recognize two principal relationships (vv. 1–4)
12:1	Whoever loves reproof loves knowledge, while one who hates reprimand is dense.	1. Wisdom commendation about receptivity (v. 1)
		2. Wisdom content: two primary relationships (vv. 2–4)
12:2	A good person will obtain approval from the LORD, while a person known for scheming will he declare as guilty.	a. Relationship with the divine (v. 2)
12:3	A mortal cannot become established through guilty behaviour, while the root of moral folk cannot become dislodged.	b. Security results from moral character (v. 3)
12:4	A resourceful wife is her husband's crown, while rottenness in his bones is a shameful wife.	a'. Relationship with one's spouse (v. 4)

	B. Words that reveal noble character: bringing healing and honour (vv. 5–8)
12:5 The plans of moral folk operate with fairness; navigation of guilty folk is a deception.	1. Wisdom commendation about moral planning (v. 5)
	2. Wisdom content: words should bring healing and honour (vv. 6–8)
12:6 Words of guilty folk are a blood-spattered ambush, but the mouth of honest folk will rescue them.	a. Words will bring harm or healing (v. 6)
12:7 Overturn guilty folk, and they will vanish; but a house of moral folk will stand firm.	b. Security results from moral character (v. 7)
12:8 According to his insightful statement a man will be praised, but one with a bent mind will become despised.	a'. Words will bring honour or shame (v. 8)
	C. Deeds that reveal noble character: industrious and generous (vv. 9–12)
12:9 Better to be regarded as insignificant while employing a worker than to be pompous while lacking food.	1. Deeds should focus on quiet industry (v. 9)
12:10 A moral person is aware of his animal's appetite, but the tenderness of guilty folk amounts to cruelty.	2. Deeds should be generous, not malevolent (v. 10)
12:11 One who works his soil will be satisfied with food, but one who pursues empty aims lacks sense.	1'. Again, deeds should focus on quiet industry (v. 11)
12:12 A guilty person delights in a trap of evil folk, but the root of moral folk keeps on giving.	2'. Again, deeds should be generous, not malevolent (v. 12)
	D. Conclusion: retribution will reward words and deeds (vv. 13–14)
12:13 In transgression of the lips is a defective snare, but a moral person fully emerged from distress.	1. Ensnaring words, or morality's escape (v. 13)
12:14 From the fruit of a person's mouth one may be satisfied with good, and the deed of a mortal's hands will repay him.	2. Retributive words and deeds (v. 14)

Verse	*Translation*	*Outline*
		II. Noble character responds with faithfulness and counsel during a friend's adversity (vv. 15–28)
12:15	A fool's way is straight in his own eyes, but one who listens to counsel is wise.	A. Another wisdom commendation about receptivity (v. 15)
		B. Wisdom content: noble character remains faithful during a friend's adversity (vv. 16–23)
12:16	As for a fool, his vexation at once becomes known, while one who conceals an insult is discreet.	1. Speaking before thinking, or exercising discretion (v. 16)
12:17	A faithful testifier keeps declaring, 'Moral!', while a false witness keeps declaring, 'It's a deception!'	2. Faithful or false: witness-assertions by friend and foe (v. 17)
12:18	There is a gossip who is like sword-thrusts, while the tongue of the wise heals.	3. Misery: inflicted or soothed (v. 18)
12:19	Truthful lips will be established for ever, while a false tongue is fleeting.	4. The future durability (long or short) of the words of a witness (true or false, v. 19)
12:20	Deception is intended by those who devise evil, yet those who counsel wholeness will experience joy.	4'. The future aims and outcomes of their respective behaviours (misery or joy, v. 20)
12:21	From utter disaster a moral person will be exempted, while guilty folk are full of misery.	3'. Misery: avoided or suffered (v. 21)
12:22	False lips are an abhorrence to the Lord, but those who work at faithfulness he approves.	2'. False or faithful: assessment by the Lord (v. 22)
12:23	A mortal who is discreet conceals what he knows, while the mind of stupid folk will blurt out folly.	1'. Exercising discretion, or speaking before thinking (v. 23)
		C. A true friend offers counsel, with diligence and confidentiality (vv. 24–27)
12:24	The diligent hand will come to rule, but laziness will lead to forced labour.	1. Diligence wins over laziness (*rĕmiyyâ*, v. 24)

12:25 As to anxiety in a person's mind – although he may manage to suppress it, a good word can turn it into joy. 12:26 A moral person will conduct a reconnaissance on behalf of his friend, but the way of guilty folk will cause them to wander. 12:27 His [a moral person's] hunt will not set deceit in motion; rather, a mortal's precious wealth is diligence.	2. Changing anxiety into joy through good counsel . . . (v. 25) 2'. . . . such is the diligent work of a moral friend (v. 26) 1'. Deceit (*rĕmiyyâ*) enabled by divulging confidences cannot entice the diligent (v. 27)
12:28 Along the path of morality is life, and may there be no death along the journey of its footpath.	D. Conclusion: moral retribution involves mortal stakes (v. 28)

Notes on the text

12:2. 'approval', *rāṣôn*: favour, acceptance (also 12:22).

12:3. 'cannot become dislodged', *bal-yimmôṭ*: (in)capability inferred from yiq. For another instance of *bal* negating 'dislodged', see 10:30.

12:4. 'resourceful wife', *ʾēšet-ḥayil*: this recurs in 31:10.

'a shameful wife', *mĕbîšâ*: lit. 'a shameful woman'.

12:5. 'operate with fairness', *mišpāṭ*: lit. '[are] fair, just'.

'navigation of guilty folk is a deception': i.e. the ethical compass of guilty folk cannot consistently locate true north.

12:6. 'blood-spattered ambush': lit. 'an ambush of blood'.

12:7. 'Overturn guilty folk, and they will vanish', *hāpôk rĕšāîm wĕʾênām*: lit. '[the] overturning of guilty folk – then they do not exist'. This use of an infin. abs. ('to overturn') is not a genuine imperative, operating rather like a conditional clause: 'If guilty folk were to be overturned, they would vanish.' Fox terms it a 'rhetorical imperative' (2009: 549, n.; cf. Waltke 2004: 515, n.). For additional examples, see *hālôk*, 'walk', 13:20, and *ḥāgô*, 'remove', 25:4, 5.

'house': 'house' also connotes 'household'.

12:9. 'while employing a worker', *wĕʿebed lô*: 'and he has a worker', sometimes rendered 'slave' or 'servant' (lexically linked to *ʿôbēd*, 'one who works', 12:11a).

12:12. 'trap of evil folk', *mĕṣôd rāʿîm*: not 'fortress' (with BDB; *pace HALOT*), since this term is parallel to 'snare' in 12:13. *Rāʿîm* refers to evil people (cf. Prov. 14:19; 15:3), while *rāʿôt* refers to abstract evil (e.g. 15:28).

The expression 'trap of evil folk' may ambiguously be set by evil folk to snare others, or may capture the evil folk who set it up, as in 12:21 (so also Fox 2009: 553).

'keeps on giving', *yittēn*: durative connotation inferred from yiq. conjugation. To emend, reading *ʾêtān*, 'is secure', in place of *yittēn* would diminish the pungent and fundamental contrast between the subtractive strategy of the guilty with their traps, contrasting the generosity of moral folk with their 'giving' (*pace* Waltke 2004: 516; Fox 2009: 553).

12:13. 'a defective snare': lit. 'a bad snare'. Since a good snare will trap prey, a snare that is 'bad' must be defective, harming not only prey, but also predator-trapper.

'but . . . fully emerged', *wayyēṣēʾ*: lit. 'and [he] went out'. The wayyiq. form contributes certitude to the contrast of this saying's second colon.

12:14. 'From the fruit of a person's mouth one may be satisfied with good': potentiality derives from yiq. (cf. 13:2a).

'and the deed . . . will repay him', *ûgĕmûl . . . yāšûb*: the hiph. alternative offered in the Q (*yāšîb*, 'he/it will cause to repay') is not needed. The K conveys that a person's deed will work retributively.

12:15. 'straight': may also be rendered 'honest' or 'right'.

12:16. 'his vexation . . . , while one who conceals', *kaʿĕsô wĕkōseh*: assonance links these adjacent Hebr. expressions.

'at once': lit. 'in the day'.

'an insult': lit. 'a disgrace'. Upon suffering an insult, a person of noble character will not react with impulsive defensiveness, but will demonstrate discretion, downplaying the insult (Waltke 2004: 517).

'discreet', *ʿārûm*: lit. 'clever, shrewd'. A positive connotation accompanies *ʿārûm* here (cf. 12:23).

12:17. 'A faithful testifier': lit. 'one who testifies faithfulness', contrasting one who testifies falsehoods (6:19; 14:5; 19:5, 9).

'keeps declaring', *yāggîd*: in a juridical context (as implied by 'testifier' and 'witness'), the verb *nagad* can mean 'to give evidence' (cf. Lev. 5:1). The iterative connotation ('[he] keeps declaring') derives from yiq.

'Moral!', *ṣedeq*: lit. 'righteous'. The author uses the adj. form here, opting for neither the abstract noun 'righteousness', nor for 'righteous person' (as he will in 12:10, 21). Since this adj. follows a verb of speech – a verb used to deliver testimony in court – the term *ṣedeq* here reports the statement uttered by the testifier with regard to the defendant in a court case. By so saying, the witness declares that the defendant is in the right. We might expect the verb *lēʾmōr*, 'saying', to introduce the exclamation 'Moral!', after *ngd*, 'to declare'. The omission here of *lēʾmōr* may owe to the compressed nature of sapiential expression (cf. omission of *ʾmr*, 'to say', between *qrʾ*, 'to cry out', and the ensuing quoted speech in Gen. 12:18).

'while a false witness keeps declaring, "It's a deception!"': lit. 'but a false witness – a deception' ('deception' also occurs in 12:5, 20). The phrase 'keeps declaring' is inferred in v. 17b by ellipsis from the previous colon ('[he] keeps declaring'; so also Waltke 2004: 517). If one does not infer 'keeps declaring' by ellipsis, v. 17b would be meaninglessly tautological: 'while a false witness [is] a deception'.

Mirmâ, 'deception', stands parallel to the declaration *ṣedeq*, 'Moral!' Each declaration reports the differing testimony offered by respective witnesses. This verse envisions that the first witness in a case is steeling himself to remain stalwart on the witness stand. His need for inner resolve suggests that the prosecution has intimidated him with threat of harm. Nevertheless, he declares boldly what he knows to be true: 'The defendant behaved morally! He is innocent of all charges against him!' Upon hearing this, the witness for the prosecution – who is a false witness – contests with equal vehemence, 'That testimony you just now heard was rigged! It's a deception! I bear witness that the defendant is guilty!'

12:19. 'truthful': the same root as 'faithful' (12:17a).

'for ever, while . . . fleeting', *lāʿad wĕʿad ʾargîʿâ*: lit. 'until always, and until a moment'. The time references are adjacent in Hebr., intensifying contrast.

12:20. 'Deception is intended by': lit. 'deception is in the mind of'. Deception both describes the clandestine strategy employed by schemers, and diagnoses the disorder by which they are retributively afflicted, severely impairing their judgement.

'wholeness', *šālôm*: when contrasting divisiveness (as in this saying), 'wholeness' renders *šālôm* better than 'peace'.

'will experience joy': lit. 'joy'. Futurity ('will experience') is inferred from the sense of anticipation inherent in 'intended' (12:20a).

12:21. 'will be exempted': lit. utter disaster 'will not be allowed to befall' a moral person.

'are full of misery', *mālĕʾû rāʿ*: the notion of retribution in 12:21a recommends *rāʿ* as 'misery' in v. 21b (rendered 'evil' in v. 20).

12:23. 'discreet', *ʿārûm*: see 'Notes' for 12:16.

'what he knows': lit. 'knowledge'. Beyond humility, this concealed knowledge may refer to information unearthed, which would damage another, were confidences violated (cf. 12:26–27).

12:24. 'diligent hand': lit. 'hand of diligences'; this may be rendered 'hand of diligent ones'.

'laziness', *rĕmiyyâ*: or 'deceit' (as in 12:27).

'will lead to': lit. 'will be'.

12:25. 'As to anxiety in a person's mind – although he may manage to suppress it', *dĕʾāgâ bĕlēb-ʾîš yašḥennâ*: lit. 'anxiety in a person's mind he may suppress it'. Identifying the subject of the verb 'suppress' is the first pivotal issue for understanding this verse. Since this finite verb specifies a 3 m. sg. subject (whether pronoun 'he', 'it', or specific m. noun), the f. noun 'anxiety' will not do (unless one invokes exceptional grammar, as do Waltke 2004: 518 and Fox 2009: 558). The simplest 3 m. sg. subject responsible for 'suppressing' something is the pronoun 'he' – that *ʾîš*, 'person', in whose mind the anxiety resides. The expression 'manage' is supplied to clarify the contrast between energies expended in hope of quelling anxious thoughts (12:25a), and the winsome conversion of anxiety into joy, resulting from another's 'good word' of counsel or encouragement (v. 25b).

The second pivotal issue centres on who or what is being suppressed; i.e. the object of the verbal expression 'he may suppress it'. Since 'it' in this expression is 3 f. sg., and since the fellow is m. (defined by m. *ʾîš*, 'person'), it cannot be that the man is being suppressed or 'weighed down'. Such a translation would require the reverse of the above exceptional grammar: understanding a m. entity as the antecedent indicated by a f. pronoun suff. Those who follow this course simply propose an emendation (so Fox 2009: 558) or, curiously, suggest that the f. suff. overrode the m. to create a smoother flow of sounds (Waltke 2004: 513). A simpler solution is to regard the f. noun 'anxiety' as the pronominal antecedent, resulting in the translation 'he may suppress it [i.e. the anxiety in his mind]'.

In order to reflect the Hebr. emphasis on the object ('anxiety' is fronted), the English must preface that object with 'as to' or 'regarding'. Also added for clarification is the adversative conj. 'although'. This elucidates the problem–solution relationship linking first and second cola. A more wooden translation would position that particle at the start of the second colon to reflect the conj. *wĕ*, 'but'.

'anxiety': 'the extreme emotional distress caused by the situation of fearing to lose something vital to life' (Waltke 2004: 541).

'a good word can turn it into joy', *wĕdābār ṭôb yaśḥennâ*: lit. 'but a good word can turn it into joy'. In this expression the pivotal issue involves identifying the antecedent of the 3 f. sg. pronoun suff. 'it' in *yeśammĕḥennâ*, 'can turn it to joy'. Since 'mind' and 'person' are m., neither of these is eligible (thus disallowing NRSV ['but a good word cheers it up'] and NIV ['but a kind word cheers it up']). 'Anxiety' offers the only available 3 f. sg. antecedent. Thus the sage teaches that, under the influence of a 'good word' (likely a perceptive and supportive word of advice) anxiety may transform into joy. This translation requires neither exceptional grammar nor textual emendation.

12:26. 'will conduct a reconnaissance on behalf of his friend', *yātēr mērēʿēhû*: the root *twr* connotes to spy out, to survey a region ('to send out for intelligence information before a [military] operation', *HALOT*; cf. Num. 13:2, 16, 17, 21, 25, 32; 'searches out' [Waltke 2004: 518]). The prep. *min* can convey 'on account of', 'by reason of' or 'on the side of' (BDB). Here it identifies that person on whose behalf the perceptive exploration is to be conducted (see Jer. 9:3 for similar syntax). To help his distressed friend, the moral person sets out to investigate the circumstances leading up to that person's anxiety. Instead to revocalize *yātēr* as *yuttar* ('is released', a hoph. form of the root *ntr*) unnecessarily alters the portrait of a friend's aid as intended by the sage (*pace* Fox 2009: 559). Similarly unnecessary is the suggestion to emend *mērēʿēhû* to read *mērāʿāh*, 'from misfortune' (559).

12:27. 'His hunt', *ṣêdô*: 'his' in the expression 'his hunt' is sg., referring to the reconnaissance conducted by 'the moral person' in 12:26a. Since 'his' is sg., it cannot refer to the 'guilty folk' of v. 26b, as they are pl. in number.

'Hunt' is the only m. sg. noun eligible as the subject for the verbal expression *lōʾ-yaḥărōk*, '[he or it] will not set in motion'. The noun 'deceit' (sometimes rendered 'laziness') is f. (cf. 12:24b).

Three accommodations are necessary if one is to arrive at a translation for 12:27a such as is found in NRSV: 'The lazy do not roast their game'. First, one must invoke exceptional grammar allowing the f. *rĕmiyyâ* (whether rendered 'laziness' or 'deceit') to serve as subject of the m. verbal expression *lōʾ-yaḥărōk*, '[he or it] will not set in motion'. Second, one must infer that 'setting in motion' refers narrowly to the motion of rotating meat on a spit over a fire. Third, one must infer that 'hunt' represents the end product of a successful hunt (the meat resulting from butchering the captured animal) rather than the broader process of hunting. Although these three accommodations are possible (supported by Fox 2009: 559), they depend on exceptional grammar and excessively narrow definitions. A simpler understanding treats 'hunt' (alluding to the earlier reconnaissance of v. 26) as the m. subject fitting with the m. verb 'will not set in motion'. The object that is not to be set in motion is 'deceit' (where 'deceit' refers to the cunning abuse of damning information unearthed in the process of researching [hunting] the client-friend's future opportunities). These connotations fit with the exploration phase of judicial proceedings implied by vv. 17, 22 (cf. Heim 2001: 155).

'deceit', *rĕmiyyâ*: the meaning 'deceit' is to be preferred over 'laziness' (12:24), despite the tight contrast that would form with 'diligence' in v. 27b, if *rĕmiyyâ* were to be rendered 'laziness' in v. 27a. Deceit is preferable since it better accounts for the caution concerning proper behaviour following the 'hunt'. The hunt refers to the uncovering of information resulting from the studied reconnaissance of a friend in v. 26. In the wrong hands, such information may cause damage, and so must be treated with confidentiality, not deception.

'diligence', *ḥârûṣ*: this word can mean both 'diligent' (with the adj. understood here as substantival, as a noun) and 'gold' (cf. Prov. 3:14; 8:10, 19; 16:16). When the sage likens diligence to wealth, the double meaning of diligence as 'gold' intensifies this saying's impact.

12:28. 'Along the path of morality', *bĕʾōraḥ ṣĕdāqâ*: *bĕ*, 'in', implies that the entire journey is enveloped in vitality (rendered 'along'). Instead to use 'to', *lĕ*, would identify the destination towards which a given road leads, as in 'a path [leading] to life' (*ʾōraḥ lĕḥayîm*, 10:17).

'may there be no death', *ʾal-māwet*: lit. 'may it not – death'. To construe the juss. (wish) negation *ʾal* with a noun ('death') instead of a verb is rare.

It implies a juss. or imperative connotation (Fox 2009: 560, n.). By expressing this truth as a wish (not an established fact), the sage subtly acknowledges that, while he sincerely hopes misfortune will not befall moral people, he is aware that, for a time, they may suffer harm undeservedly. Another example of the juss. negation *ʾal* followed by a noun (without a verb) occurs in the expression *ʾal-domî*, 'take no rest'; lit. 'may it not – cessation' (Isa. 62:6). To revocalize *ʾal*, 'may it not', as *ʾel*, 'to', needlessly complicates matters, since it blunts the subtle sense of the wish, and requires insertion of a noun such as 'wickedness' ('while the way of [wickedness] leads to death'; so Fox 2009: 560).

'its footpath', *nĕtîbâ*: *nātîb*, 'footpath', with a 3 f. sg. suff. pronoun (not the similar f. noun *netîbâ*). 'Its' refers to the f. noun 'morality', found in the first colon.

Form and structure

Borders

Theme transition and a wisdom commendation mark the upper border. Themes transition from fraudulent riches (preceding poem) to noble character as the foundation for lasting relationships (present poem). Two primary relationships unfold following a wisdom commendation in 12:1.

A section-level inclusio and a climactic conclusion indicate the lower border. Concerning inclusio, 'path', 'journey', *derek* and 'footpath' in 12:28 recall 'way', *derek*, from the first verse of Section II (v. 15), where it was line-initial. The terms 'life' and 'death' draw this lecture to a climactic close in v. 28.

Macrostructural features

Thematic continuity concerning receptivity, in section-initial wisdom commendations (Sections I and II, content-based). Wisdom commendations in 12:1, 15 stress the importance of receptivity to counsel – including openness to counsel of a confrontational sort. Waltke similarly recognizes that receptivity-to-instruction links vv. 1 and 15, initiating two equal sections that comprise a lecture spanning Prov. 12 (2004: 518).

Thematic continuity in section conclusions concerning retribution (Sections I and II, content-based). The theme of retribution emerges in the last sayings of Sections I and II (12:14, 28). Waltke observes that the two sections comprising Prov. 12 close with sayings 'promising the righteous life now [v. 14] and forevermore [v. 28]' (2004: 518).

Closure involving navigation (Sections I and II, content-based). In 12:5 the sage warns that 'navigation of guilty folk is a deception'. The concept of navigation returns in v. 26. There a noble individual supplies a friend with life-guidance through 'reconnaissance', while navigation practised by guilty folk results only in wandering.

Alphabetic acrostic (vv. 1–22 in Sections I and II, form-based). An alphabetic acrostic may operate in the first twenty-two verses of this lecture. The first verse begins with the Hebr. alphabet's first letter (aleph for *ʾōhēb*, 'one who loves'), while 12:22 begins with the last (taw for *tôʿăbat*, 'abhorrent'). Two more verses begin with the sequentially corresponding alphabetic letter (teth for *ṭôb*, 'good', in v. 9, and yod for *yôdēaʿ*, 'knows', in v. 10). Taken in alphabetic sequence, these words may convey the following sentiment: 'One who loves what is good knows what is abhorrent.'

Since a palistrophe concludes with 12:23, not v. 22 (see 'Microstructural features', below), at first glance the lower boundary of the acrostic does not appear to coincide with the boundary of a unit of thought. It is instructive to note, however, that the letter beginning v. 23 is aleph (in *ʾādām* 'a mortal'), thereby creating an alphabetic inclusio with v. 1. Verse 23 closes a portion of thought (Block II.B, vv. 16–23).

Microstructural features

Section I (12:1–14). *Thematic continuity concerning vital relationships (12:2–4, content-based).* Block I.A concentrates on two relationships: with the LORD (12:2), and with one's wife (v. 4). With each, one's conduct should be moral (v. 3). Even the wisdom commendation uses verbs often associated with relationships (love and hate, v. 1).

Parallel structures involving wisdom commendations (content-based). Blocks I.A (12:1–4) and I.B (12:5–8) each begin with a wisdom commendation (vv. 1, 5). The remainder of each block follows with three verses wherein outer sayings have a shared theme (the theme of primary relationships in vv. 2, 4, and the impact of words in vv. 6, 8). The inner saying of each trio presents a single principle: security that results from morality (vv. 3, 7).

Thematic continuity regarding speech (12:5, 6, 8, content-based). Block I.B (12:5–8) focuses on speech: 'plans' (v. 5), 'words' and 'mouth' (v. 6), and 'insightful statement' and 'praised' (v. 8). The fact that 'mouth' appears at the start of v. 6b and in the Hebr. for 'according to', *lĕpî*, of v. 8a forms a speech-related inclusio for Unit I.B.2 (vv. 6–8).

Thematic continuity regarding actions (12:9–12, content-based). Whereas Block I.B focuses on speech, Block I.C (12:9–12) deals with action. Waltke observes these two themes, but curiously groups v. 8 with vv. 9–12 as dealing with actions (2004: 519; similarly Heim 2001: 150).

Thematic alternation involving industry and generosity (12:9–12, content-based). Themes of steady industry (12:9, 11) and generosity (vv. 10, 12) alternate in an A-B-A'-B' pattern within Block I.C.

Section-level closure (12:13–14, content-based). The final two verses of Section I revisit two earlier themes, involving words ('lips' in 12:13; 'mouth' in v. 14) and actions ('deed of a mortal's hand' in v. 14). Deeds of generosity performed by the moral person of v. 12 carry forward to characterize the moral person of v. 13b. (The close connection between vv. 12 and 13 consists of 'trap' and 'snare', 'guilty' and 'evil', 'moral folk' and 'moral person'.) Waltke also notices that vv. 13–14 recap the portion beginning at v. 1 (2004: 519).

Two further elements of closure include reference to escaping a snare in 12:13b (cf. 'rescue' in v. 6b) and mention of 'good' in v. 14 (cf. 'good' in v. 2 and 'better' in v. 9 ['better' in Hebr. employs the term 'good']). 'Good' in vv. 2 and 14 'essentially frames the subunit' spanning Section I (12:1–14, Waltke 2004: 519). Within the entire lecture 'good' will occur only once more (v. 25).

Section II (12:15–28). *Wisdom commendation (12:15, content-based).* A wisdom commendation opens Section II at 12:15, with wisdom content following in vv. 16–28 (Blocks II.B–D).

Palistrophe (12:16–23). Concentric links spanning 12:16–23 assemble a palistrophe. While not proposing a palistrophe, Fox senses that 12:16–19 coheres, perhaps even vv. 15–23, unified in the topic of 'speech' (2009: 555).

At the palistrophe's outermost level, a fool blurts out what he is feeling, unlike one exercising discretion (12:16, 23). Waltke also joins v. 16 with v. 23 and v. 17 with v. 22 (2004: 533; Heim proposes an irregular palistrophe, not accounting for v. 18 – joining v. 16 with v. 23, vv. 17 and 19 with v. 22, and v. 20 with v. 21 [2001: 154]).

Within this lecture 'faithful' or 'faithfulness' (the same Hebr. word) appears only in 12:17 and 22, joining these sayings in the second palistrophic level. The root *šqr*, 'falsehood', also occurs in those verses (and again in v. 19).

The notion of misery joins 12:18 with 21. These comprise the third palistrophic level.

The notion of pretence joins 12:19 ('false tongue') and v. 20 ('deception'), as well as a perspective of futurity. In v. 19 futurity measures the durability of a witness's testimony. In v. 20 future intentions drive the behaviour of evil schemers, while those who counsel wholeness will experience joy.

To recap the palistrophic content, the first level commends the silence demonstrating discretion (12:16, 23). However, when a colleague's character languishes under false accusation, one must replace such silence with courageous assertions of truth, favoured by the Lord (second level, vv. 17, 22).

If an adversary escalates a barrage of harmful words, a trustworthy colleague will counter with words to heal his comrade. The colleague will remain safe, while the adversary's harmful attack will rebound with misery (third level, 12:18, 21).

What, ultimately, will become of those lacerating words? Hurtful words will fade, while their spokespersons will deceive their own selves, arriving at the evil destination they intended for others. Exponents of truth suffer no such deterioration, achieving joy instead (fourth level, 12:19, 20).

Thematic coherence involving friendship (12:24–27, content-based). Block II.C revolves around character and conduct associated with authentic friendship. A true friend exhibits concern for a comrade burdened by anxiety (12:25a). He or she seeks to buoy up the other's spirits (v. 25b) by looking ahead, exploring opportunities and forecasting hazards that may loom on the horizon (v. 26a). Moral conduct and diligence mark the friend's character (vv. 24, 26a, 27). He will never harm his friend by betraying confidences (v. 27).

Palistrophe (12:24–27, form- and content-based). The teachings of Block II.C form a four-verse palistrophe (also Waltke 2004: 540; Heim links 12:24 with 27 [2001: 158–159]. In 12:24 and 27 appear both 'diligence' (or 'diligent') and *rĕmiyyâ* (rendered 'laziness' in v. 24, 'deceit' in v. 27). While words related to *rĕmiyyâ* occur also in vv. 5, 17, 20, those associated with the root of 'diligence', *ḥrṣ*, occur only in vv. 24, 27. These sayings extol the ascendancy (v. 24a) and kindness (v. 27) of a diligent friend, while cautioning against abasement (v. 24b) and manipulative harm (v. 27) of a fraud.

The sayings in 12:25 and 26 join to depict a scenario involving three individuals or groups: one afflicted with anxiety (client-friend), one offering counsel (counsellor-friend) and guilty folk. The client-friend attempts to dull his anxiety, suppressing it by force of will (v. 25a). A better strategy would treat anxiety with sound counsel ('a good word', v. 25b), replacing anxiety with joy. The counsellor-friend is able to supply sound counsel in the form of 'reconnaissance' conducted for his client-friend (v. 26a).

'Conducting reconnaissance', *twr* (12:26), requires (a) that one be aware of the client-friend's location, and (b) that one be able to survey optimal routes for the client-friend's future progress (including alerting him or her to potential hazards along that way). Often translated as 'to spy-out', *twr* occurs most frequently in connection with Israel's finding their way through unfamiliar territory in Canaan (see 'Notes' for v. 26).

Ineffective navigation, the converse of reconnaissance, appears in the next colon. Instead of discerning reliable direction for self or others, 'the way of guilty folk will cause them to wander' (12:26b).

Thus 12:25, 26 coheres by producing this lecture's clearest picture of a counsellor-friend's conduct. This quatrain deservedly occupies the palistrophic focal point within vv. 24–27.

Continuity of characters (12:16–17, 25–27, content-based). In 12:16–17 the sage portrays two characters. The first, a fool, harms others by disclosing damaging information (the 'insult' of v. 16b), while attempting to discredit any who would support the wrongly accused (v. 17b).

The second character shows discretion concerning information that would damage another (12:16b). He faithfully defends the wrongly accused (v. 17a).

That second, faithful character resurfaces in 12:26, in the form of one who will 'conduct a reconnaissance on behalf of his friend'. What he uncovers in the course of that investigation he handles with discretion, not manipulating it to his own advantage (v. 27). That faithful person can supply a 'good word' of counsel, transforming his discouraged friend's anxiety into joy (v. 25b).

On this basis, it follows that the first character (who harms others by indiscreet disclosures, 12:16) may be the cause of anxiety plaguing the mind of the anguished person (v. 25a). He is guilty, aimless (v. 26b), the exponent of deceit (v. 27a) he blames on others (v. 17b). These two characters create a continuity between Blocks II.B and C.

Comment

Section I (12:1–14). *Block I.A (12:1–4).* The sage begins by challenging the youth to adopt a receptive attitude towards reproof (wisdom commendation in 12:1, resembling another that opens Section II in v. 15). Evidently, he sensed that the principles he was about to reveal could evoke a resentful reaction in his audience.

Before explaining how words (12:5–8) and deeds (vv. 9–12) disclose inner character, the sage points out two primary relationships that merit careful attention. First is one's relationship with the Lord (12:2). Securing divine approval is keenly important, contingent on moral conduct.

Second is the youth's relationship with his wife (12:4). She can make or break him.

Lodged between these two primary characters lies the sage's fundamental counsel for healthy relationships: morality fosters durability (12:3). Moral character will enjoy relationships capable of weathering life's storms. These four verses comprise Block I.A (vv. 1–4).

Block I.B (12:5–8). The balance of Section I examines words and actions – twin components indicative of noble character (Blocks I.B, C, and D). The wisdom commendation that opens Block I.B recalls the core of Block I.A by stressing again the importance of moral conduct, free from trickery (12:5; cf. v. 3).

Speech (as an indicator of character) dominates the remainder of Block I.B. How one speaks can bring harm or healing (12:6), honour or shame (v. 8). Security derives from morality (v. 7). That morality saying nests between the two related sayings (vv. 6, 8), just as an earlier saying about morality (v. 3) nested between two statements sharing the theme of relationships (vv. 2, 4).

Block I.C (12:9–12). In Block I.C the sage turns from speech, focusing instead on actions as an index of character (12:9–12). In the arena of deeds, what matters is neither prestige nor popularity, but quiet industry. Behind a glittering mask, hunger may hide (v. 9). A person of noble character will add to industry the practice of non-manipulative generosity (v. 10). Lest the youth miss these two principles, the poet restates them.

Most essential are the traits of quiet industry (v. 11) and generosity untainted by sinister motives (v. 12).

Block I.D (12:13–14). The sage follows teachings about words (Block I.B) and deeds (Block I.C) by revisiting both in a two-verse block concluding Section I (Block I.D, 12:13–14). Transgressive words will entrap, while morality escorts to safety (v. 13). Any desiring satisfaction should watch what they say and do. For their words and deeds will either reward or penalize them (v. 14).

12:1. 'Reproof' and 'reprimand' appear together in eight other sayings in Proverbs (3:11; 5:12; 6:23; 10:17; 13:18; 15:5, 10, 32). 'Dense', *bāʿār*, is among the most pejorative of the sage's descriptions for stupidity.

12:3. Like 'root', terms of vegetation appeared towards the close of the last lecture: 'leaf' (11:28), 'fruit' and 'tree' (11:30). Mention of 'fruit' will close this section (12:14).

12:4. A 'resourceful' person (often rendered 'valiant', 'valorous') is one who can take care of himself or herself, with sufficient resources and energy to care for others as well. Bravery, maturity, initiative and a healthy sense of self-confidence combine in this term, a word often describing military might. In a patriarchal society such as ancient Israel, it is instructive to observe that a skilful female poses neither threat nor liability to her husband, but is rather a highly honoured asset. 'Resourceful' adds dimensions of capability to the trait of generosity, a trait characterizing the woman of 11:16. Superficial beauty is conspicuous by its absence from the sage's list of preferred feminine traits.

The terms 'good', 'LORD', 'favour' and 'wife' found in 12:2, 4 also appear in 18:22: 'He found a wife, he found a good thing, and he obtained approval from the LORD'. Thus the divine 'approval' of 12:2 may, in the sage's reasoning, account for a husband finding 'a resourceful wife' in 12:4.

12:11. Most of this saying repeats in 28:19.

Section II (12:15–28). *Block II.A (12:15).* After a wisdom commendation urging receptivity to counsel (12:15; cf. v. 1), Section II examines how a person of noble character will treat friends when they encounter adversity (vv. 16–28).

Block II.B (12:16–23). Next the sage describes how two onlookers respond to negative behaviour they observed (Block II.B, 12:16–23). The first onlooker, a fool, at once gives angry vent to his feeling of offence (v. 16a). The second onlooker, a discreet person, works to control the damage caused by another's initial insult (v. 16b). Perhaps 'transgression of the lips' in v. 13 refers to an insult, unwisely uttered by the discreet person's friend.

Evidently the fool's allegations of offence were sufficient to warrant examination by litigation, for the next line relates how these onlookers, who now serve as witnesses, respond in court (12:17). The discreet person of v. 16b is first to appear in v. 17a. He 'keeps declaring, "Moral!"' – repeatedly affirming for others to hear that his friend, despite having uttered the original insult, merits respect as an upstanding member of the community.

The need repeatedly to affirm his friend's worthy character implies that the litigious currents swirling around him are whispering that the vexatious person was guilty of something more heinous than an insult. So the discreet friend steels himself, courageously declaring aloud that the accused is 'Moral!' By describing the offending friend as 'moral', as opposed to 'blameless, innocent', *nqh*, the wise friend affirms the underlying character of the offender, implying that this recent unspecified offence was out of character for his friend, who has a history of behaving in a fundamentally moral manner. In contrast, the opposing onlooker seeks to undermine the credibility of the first witness by accusing, 'It's a deception!' (12:17b).

As proceedings continue, the foolish opponent seems bent on revenge and humiliation, stooping to smear tactics in order to inflict wounds of hearsay (12:18a). The discreet fellow (here classed with the wise) refuses to respond in kind. Instead he applies a salve consisting of sayings that heal (v. 18b).

The sage then discloses the outcome – the future impact of their respective testimonies. Long-lasting will be the effect of the truthful report, while unfounded falsehoods will soon fade (12:19).

Having looked forward to the lasting impact of testimony, the sage then looks back – or rather looks beneath – to expose the ultimate aims that motivated the two figures. Deceit, of which the fool was so quick to accuse others (12:17b), the sage now reveals as the driving force within the fool himself (v. 20a). Not surprisingly, the wise-discreet person is driven by a longing for wholeness. His inner engine will lead not merely to survival or fairness, but will issue even in joy (v. 20b).

What will the future look like for these two? Exemption from disaster awaits the moral person, while an abundance of misery awaits the fool – now glossed as 'guilty' (12:21).

How certain is this future expectation? Assuring these outcomes is none other than the LORD himself. For he it is who weighed their falsehood and faithfulness (12:22; recall v. 2, and notice the contrast of 'lips' [speech] and 'work' [actions], seen earlier in the contrast between Blocks I.B and I.C).

To sum up Block II.B, discretion holds great worth. This is particularly true for that sort of self-control that guards as confidential any personal knowledge concerning another person (knowledge the indiscreet might manipulate to their own advantage, 12:23a). In contrast, although to divulge such information may secure momentary advantage (at another's expense), in reality such a strategy amounts to stupid thinking (v. 23b).

Block II.C (12:24–27). Building on earlier cautions against deception (12:5, 17, 20), the sage begins Block II.C by advocating diligence as the antidote to deception. For diligence will result in leadership, not enslavement (v. 24).

Then he portrays how such a leader might use his or her elevated role to serve others. In this scenario, anxiety troubles a member of the community. Rather than abandoning the beleaguered fellow to fight his fears in isolation, the diligent leader of 12:24 searches for a way to inject a 'good word' – well-reasoned counsel capable of converting that anxiety into joy (v. 25). This friend's diligence takes the form of exploring what opportunities (or hazards) lie before the troubled person – opportunities to which the afflicted one may be insensitive or blind (v. 26a).

To undertake such an exploration without personal moral grounding will harm, not help. It will generate aimless pseudo-guidance (12:26b). In contrast, noble character will prevent misuse of any confidential information his search may unearth (v. 27a). He realizes that true gain comes through diligence, not by divulging confidences (v. 27b).

Block II.D (12:28). Life or death – so drastic are the alternatives associated with morality (12:28)! With this vivid declaration and desire ('may there be no death') the sage concludes his lecture concerning noble personal character and friendships that are true.

12:22. Notice the contrast between words (first colon) and deeds (second colon), as also between falsehood and faithfulness.

Explanation

In the lecture immediately prior, the sage made a case for investing in relationships, both human and divine, rather than pursuing tangible riches (10:31 – 11:31). The practical counsel concerning friendship appearing in the present lecture would richly benefit members of any group wishing to enrich their relationships in authentic ways.

Section I, Block A. Introduction: recognize two principal relationships (12:1–4)

Since trusting relationships wield considerable influence, recognizing trustworthy friends holds immense importance. If those we advise have already chosen friends poorly, we would do well to prepare them for the chastening counsel they deeply need (12:1).

Relationship with the divine holds primary importance (12:2). To seek approval elsewhere is to relinquish what is truly good. One's relationship with the Lord stands superior only to the relationship with one's spouse (v. 4). To devalue one's spouse is to disregard a source of splendour, preferring inward decay instead.

Section I, Block B. Words that reveal noble character: bringing healing and honour (12:5–8)

Training youth to notice carefully what their peers say will cultivate character assessment. Are conversations crafted to entrap or to rescue? Do they promote self at the expense of others, or serve others at personal expense? Is there a congruence between promises and performance (cf. Ps. 15:4)? Or do their words simply churn out a smokescreen of deception? Impression management through social media offers one arena for applying principles of character assessment.

Section I, Block C. Deeds that reveal noble character: industrious and generous (12:9–12)

No one enjoys being treated as insignificant. As A. W. Tozer observed, 'The heart's fierce effort to protect itself from every slight, to shield its touchy honour from the bad opinion of friend and enemy, will never let the mind have rest' (1982: 112). In 12:9 the sage points the way to discount empty dismissals: simply respond by assessing your well-being, and then recall that flapping mouths (as would voice empty disrespect) make for hungry stomachs.

Not only will a wise person know how to discount slights that disregard his or her worth. He or she will make it a point also to show regard for others, especially for those easily overlooked due to their subordinate station in life, whether human or even animal (12:10). Violence must never rear its head in a domestic setting, except when needed sacrificially to safeguard those entrusted to one's care. Such conduct (attentive care and self-sacrifice) characterizes the storm-proof and drought-proof generosity that lies at the core of a moral person's identity (v. 12).

Section I, Block D. Conclusion: retribution will reward words and deeds (12:13–14)

Perceptive is the person who regards speech and actions as an investment with an exceptionally reliable rate of return. In due time all will be repaid, with interest.

Section II, Block B. Noble character remains faithful during a friend's adversity (12:16–23)

Friendship must consist of far more than common meals, overlapping interests in entertainment, or even shared service projects. The true test of friendship is this: how we respond when one we count as a friend suffers adversity, or when he or she may even be responsible for disappointment inflicted on us. Do we cry, 'Foul!' for all to hear? Do we resort to stiletto wounds of gossip? Or do we remain faithful, asserting truth aimed at wholeness, leading to joy (12:20)?

The business of faithfulness requires exertion. But faithfulness rewards the effort, since it assuredly wins approval from none other than the LORD himself (12:22b).

Section II, Block C. A true friend offers counsel, with diligence and confidentiality (12:24–27)

The first work of a faithful friend looks beyond the hurtful act of his or her comrade, uncovering instead his anxious heart (12:25–26). The second work wisely communicates 'a good word' – counsel whose truth will disarm deceit with its power to enslave. On the heels of this counsel will spring up joy (v. 25; cf. v. 20). The final work of a faithful friend practises diligent discretion – concealing again what has been confidentially revealed, lest that information fall into the wrong hands (vv. 24, 27).

Section II, Block D. Conclusion: moral retribution involves mortal stakes (12:28)
The challenge to recognize persons worthy of trust, together with the invitation to become a moral and therefore trustworthy friend – these rank among the most important lessons one may learn in life. Robust life will reward those who travel this pathway.

PROVERBS 13:1–25
'How may I achieve true satisfaction?'

Overview of Proverbs 13:1–25
In the lecture spanning Prov. 13:1–25 the sage responds to the implied question 'How may I achieve true satisfaction?' This lecture begins by outlining four concomitants of satisfaction: receptivity to reproof, appetite-management, moral orientation and correct assessment of wealth (Section I, 13:1–9). After stressing again the importance of receptivity, the sage proceeds to explain that simply to isolate a worthy aspiration will not suffice. One must invest diligent effort (Section II, vv. 10–15). One's diligent effort should focus especially on this: responding to reproof with receptivity (Section III, 13:16–19). Only then may benefits be realized. Otherwise, reproof is wasted. By the close of Section III the youth should have embraced the uncommon importance of reproof.

Next the sage explains where the youth may find sources of reproof (Section IV, 13:20–23). Incentives that close Section IV lead the youth to lift his gaze, investing in generations yet to come.

A final section fuses together the entire lecture. Here the sage revisits themes of parental reproof and moral conduct, all in service of achieving lasting satisfaction (Section V, 13:24–25).

Position of this poem within Proverbs
Preceding context. Rather crass implicit questions of personal ease ('How can I get rich?' in Prov. 10:1–22) and survival ('How can I secure my future?' in Prov. 10:23–30) began the lectures of Division II. Then the sage returned to the topic of riches, but with a difference – contrasting riches and community relationships ('What is the harm in fraudulent riches?' in Prov. 10:31 – 11:31). In the lecture just concluded, the sage taught the importance of investing in those relationships sacrificially ('How can I recognize noble character and thus behave as a true friend?', Prov. 12:1–28). Upon

this substantial foundation, the present lecture's analysis of wealth, poverty and the value of community relationships rises as a carefully crafted capital, crowning a massive sapiential column (cf. 13:7–8, 10).

Ensuing context. Masoretes detected a transition following Prov. 13 (see v. 25, under 'Comment'). Near the close of Prov. 13 with its largely individualistic focus, the sage broadens the youth's attention to invest in future generations, beginning with his own grandchildren (13:22). The ensuing lecture will expand this idea, explaining how to build one's metaphoric 'house', whether domestic or dynastic (14:1 – 15:6).

What to watch for

Attention to the following topics will illumine this lecture's organization: reproof (including reprimand, rebuke, and speech associated with the wise), satisfaction (including appetite, mouth, lips, belly, food, longing and expectation) and wealth (including riches, poverty, honour and disgrace). After noticing how the three themes of reproof, satisfaction and wealth emerge at various points, notice especially how they populate 13:21–24, and especially the final two verses. Consider, finally, how the final quatrain reflects the opening quatrain (compare vv. 24–25 with vv. 1–2). Recall that 'mouth' may associate with both reproof (by uttering corrective advice) and with the satisfying of one's appetite (consuming food).

Translation and outline

Verse	*Translation*	*Outline*
		I. Four signposts to satisfaction: receptivity to reproof, appetite-management, moral orientation and correct assessment of wealth (13:1–9)
13:1	A wise son embodies a father's reproof; but a scoffer paid no attention to a rebuke.	A. Wisdom commendation: receptivity to reproof is essential (v. 1)
		B. Appetite-management: discernment and diligence regarding appetite will determine satisfaction (start of wisdom content, vv. 2–4)
13:2	From the fruit of a person's mouth one may feed on what is good, but the appetite of treacherous folk will feed on what is violent.	1. Satisfaction rewards those with an appetite for instruction (v. 2)

13:3 One who watches over his mouth safeguards his appetite, but one who opens wide his lips – he has ruin.	2. Become a discerning consumer (v. 3)
13:4 What craves with nothing to show for it? His appetite! Whose? A sluggard's! But the appetite of diligent folk will be made fat.	3. Become a diligent consumer (v. 4)
	C. Moral orientation: satisfaction follows reproof governed by morality (vv. 5–6)
13:5 A moral person will hate a false word, but a guilty person will both have a bad odour and will act shamefully.	1. Misreporting* either will be detected and rejected, or will be embraced unsuspectingly, depending on one's moral compass (v. 5)
13:6 Morality will watch over one whose way is characterized by integrity; but wickedness will relabel sin.	2. Protected progress or a hazard misreported – one's moral orientation determines what one will experience (v. 6)
	D. Pursuit of wealth (a sample appetite): satisfaction depends on correctly discerning the nature of true riches (vv. 7–8)
13:7 There is one who feigns riches, and yet – there is nothing at all; another feigns poverty, and yet – much wealth!	1. Some measures of wealth are misleading (v. 7)
13:8 His riches consist of this: ransoming a person's life. But poor is the person who paid no attention to a rebuke.	2. Authentic wealth consists of rescuing lives, while poverty results from resisting this message of reproof (v. 8)
13:9 Light emanating from moral folk will be joyful, while the lamp of guilty folk will go out.	E. Character summary: personal morality disburses joy – evidence of deep satisfaction (v. 9)
	II. To achieve satisfaction, welcome reproof and invest diligent effort (vv. 10–15)
13:10 By insolence alone can one keep engendering strife, but with those who accept advice is wisdom.	A. Wisdom commendation: welcome reproof* . . . (v. 10)

Verse	*Translation*	*Outline*
		B. Then invest diligent effort . . . (start of wisdom content, vv. 11–12)
13:11	Wealth originating from vapour will diminish, but one who consistently gathers by handfuls can make it multiply.	1. While patient diligence marks the route to lasting satisfaction . . . (v. 11)
13:12	Expectation that must be dragged along renders the mind ill, but a veritable tree of life – such is a longing that comes to pass.	2. . . . Hope too long delayed debilitates (v. 12)
		C. Incentive: . . . and so receive the reward (vv. 13–15)
13:13	Whoever shows contempt for a directive – he will be obliged to fulfil it; but as for one who shows respect for a commandment, he it is who will be repaid.	1. Only receptivity to reproof* will repay with a reward (v. 13)
		2. Receiving life and giving grace are rewards that follow receptivity to reproof* (vv. 14–15)
13:14	A wise person's instruction is a spring of life, in order to veer away from the snares of death.	a. Reward of receiving life, instead of death (v. 14)
13:15	Insight that is good will keep engendering grace, while the way of treacherous folk is interminable.	b. Reward of giving grace, instead of being consigned to journey endlessly (v. 15)
		III. To execute reproof faithfully – that is what will achieve satisfaction (vv. 16–19)
		A. Reproof-counsel must be executed faithfully (vv. 16–17)
13:16	Any sensible person will act on knowledge, but a stupid person will make an open display of folly.	1. Wisdom commendation: a sensible person will execute plans, translating reproof*-counsel into action (v. 16)
13:17	A guilty messenger will fall into misery, but a faithful envoy is a cure.	2. Wisdom content: a reliable messenger exemplifies the reward of execution (v. 17)

	B. Incentive: honour and satisfaction reward execution of reliable reproof (vv. 18–19)
13:18 Poverty and disgrace characterize one who forsakes reproof, but one who safeguards reprimand will be honoured.	1. Acting on reproof results in honour, not disgraceful poverty (v. 18)
13:19 A longing that has come to pass will be pleasing to the appetite, but loathsome to stupid folk is veering away from misery.	2. Acting on reproof* results in satisfaction, with misery as alternative (v. 19)
	IV. Conclusion: to achieve lasting satisfaction, pursue wise agents of reproof (vv. 20–23) A. How to find wise agents of reproof* (vv. 20–21)
13:20 Walk in the company of wise folk and become wise; but a friend of stupid folk will be treated badly.	1. Wisdom commendation: a directive commending wise companionship (v. 20)
13:21 It is sinners that misery will pursue; but in the company of moral folk good will repay.	2. Wisdom content: the benefit of companions who are moral (v. 21)
	B. Incentive: the lasting satisfaction of morality, and the needless demise in poverty (vv. 22–23)
13:22 A good person will leave an inheritance for grandchildren, but a sinner's property is stored up for the person who is moral.	1. The ultimate satisfaction of morality: it will bequeath generational riches, even acquiring sinners' wealth (v. 22)
13:23 An arable field belonging to poor folk represents a lot of food; but someone is being plundered, and that without redress.	2. The ultimate dissatisfaction of poverty: despite rich potential, poor will suffer plundering, unrequited (v. 23)
	V. Recap of themes: parental reproof, morality and achieving satisfaction (vv. 24–25)
13:24 One who refrains from using his rod hates his son, whereas one who loves him watches attentively for an opportunity to reprove him.	A. Parents must not shirk their responsibility to issue reproof (v. 24)

Verse	Translation	Outline
13:25	A moral person eats to the point of his appetite's satisfaction, but the belly of guilty folk will keep on suffering want.	B. Character summary: morality will determine satisfaction or unremitting hunger (v. 25)

*The importance of reproof (evidenced by 'reproof', 'rebuke' and 'reprimand') is anchored early (13:1a, b) and late (v. 24b) in the lecture, then recurs along the middle as well (vv. 8b, 18a, b). Owing to the dominance of this theme, and in order to clarify the broader reach of this theme among related but less explicit synonyms, several outline headings include the word 'reproof' even if the corresponding designation for an influential message at that point in the text is more general than the confrontive sort of instruction specified by 'reproof'. Related terms include a [false] 'word' or report (v. 5), 'advice' (v. 10), a 'commandment' (v. 13) and 'knowledge' (v. 16). Reproof is implicit also in v. 19 (where refusal to turn from misery implies that reproof has been rejected) and in vv. 20–21 (where wise and moral companions in this context would serve as sources of wise counsel, including reproof).

Notes on the text

13:1. 'A wise son embodies a father's reproof': lit. 'A wise son [is] a father's reproof'. Fox terms this verbless syntax 'blunt juxtaposition', rendering, 'A wise son – a father's discipline' (2009: 561). This is to be preferred over borrowing the verb 'to pay attention' from the second colon (*pace* LXX, Targum and Waltke 2004: 545).

'paid no attention': lit. 'did not hear' (also in 13:8b). One who in the past paid no attention to rebuke subsequently devolved to the level of a scoffer.

13:2. 'From the fruit of a person's mouth one may feed on what is good': when read in isolation this colon appears to teach retribution, so that the person who speaks and the person who feeds are one and the same. Such was the case in the nearly verbatim occurrence of this colon in 12:14a. This reflexive message (wherein it is the speaker who reaps the consequences of his or her own speech) would be more clearly expressed if it were to read 'from the fruit of *his* mouth' (as in 13:3a), rather than 'from the fruit of *a person's* mouth'. By specifying 'a person's' mouth, the sage opens the opportunity for it to refer to the mouth of someone other than the person on whom the consequences will fall.

When read in context with 13:1, it is the father's reproving mouth (v. 1a) that speaks reproof and so issues valuable fruit (v. 2aα), upon which the attentive son may feed (v. 2aβ). The second cola of vv. 1, 2 are similarly parallel.

Since 'good' elsewhere associated with 'eat' describes clearly the object that is eaten, it should not here be understood as describing the subject doing the eating ('a good person may eat'), but rather the object (food that is good). For grammatically unambiguous examples of 'good' and 'eat', cf. *ṭôb*, 'good', in Isa. 55:2, *ṭôbâ*, 'good', in Job 21:25, and *ṭûb*, 'goodness', in Isa. 1:19 and Ezra 9:12. As with the parallel in 12:14, potentiality (one may feed) derives from the yiq.

'but the appetite of treacherous folk will feed on what is violent': the verb 'will feed on' is inferred from the first colon by ellipsis. 'Violence' describes the metaphoric food the appetite consumes, as 'good' in the first colon described what was there consumed.

13:3. 'appetite', *nepeš*: not 'life' (contrast 13:8), due to mention of foods, eating, mouth, lips, craving and becoming fat in vv. 2–4.

13:4. 'What craves with nothing to show for it? His appetite! Whose? A sluggard's!', *mitʾawwâ wāʾayin napšô ʿāṣēl*: lit. 'That which craves (fem.) but there is nothing; his appetite (fem.), a sluggard'. The interrogatives 'What?' and 'Whose?' have been supplied to capture the sense of a question-and-answer riddle contained here.

Concerning the declaration 'His appetite!', Fox appropriately observes, 'The delay of the identification of the subject until the end of the clause, after the predicate, gives 13:4a the feel of a riddle. What hungers but has nothing? The appetite of the sluggard' (2009: 562). Not only is the subject 'appetite' delayed, but also the antecedent of 'his' in 'his appetite' is similarly delayed until the climactic and final word 'sluggard'. For this reason the second interrogative, 'Whose?', appears in the translation.

'with nothing to show for it', *wāʾayin*: lit. 'and there is nothing'.

13:5. 'will both have a bad odour and will act shamefully', *yabʾîš wĕyaḥpîr*: the objectionable odour is part and parcel of the objectionable behaviour (indicated by waw-conjunctive *wĕyaḥpîr*).

13:6. 'wickedness . . . sin', *rišʿâ . . . ḥaṭṭāʾt*: lit. 'wickedness [or guilt] . . . sin [or sin-offering]'. Both are abstract nouns (like 'morality', *ṣedāqâ*, in 13:6a), and so should not be rendered as 'the wicked [person]' or 'the sinner' (*pace* NRSV and NASB, respectively). If the sage intended 'sinner' and not 'sin', he would have used the ptc. *ḥôṭēʾ*, 'sinner', as he will later in this lecture (13:22b; *pace* Fox 2009: 563). Like 'morality', 'wickedness' is the subject of its respective verb (*pace* NRSV, which renders v. 6b, 'sin overthrows the wicked').

The condemnation of falsehood immediately prior ('A moral person will hate a false word', 13:5a) reinforces the meaning of v. 6b as cautioning against schemes that attempt to market sin as harmless or even noble.

Waltke infers 'way' from 13:6a, and so renders v. 6b, 'wickedness will overturn the sinful [way]', explaining that 'unreliable lies subvert and ruin sinners' (2004: 556). However, 'way' does not easily pass by ellipsis from

v. 6a into v. 6b. For in the first colon, 'way' is lodged in a phrase that identifies the character of a person ('one whose way is characterized by integrity'). The converse in v. 6b should read, 'one whose way is characterized by sin' – a notion that Hebr. would convey with the ptc. noted above (*ḥôṭēʾ*, 'sinner'), without use of 'way'. The fact that the sage uses instead the term *ḥaṭṭāʾt*, 'sin', leads to the conclusion that he was referring to the relabelling of sin, not the overturning (or undermining) of sinful persons or a sinful way of life.

'will relabel', *tĕsallep*: lit. 'will twist, misrepresent, bring to ruin'.

13:7. 'one who feigns riches . . . another feigns poverty', *mitʿaššēr . . . mitrôšēš*: both ptcs. employ an h-t stem (hith. or hithpol.), a formation occurring elsewhere in this poem only in 'that which craves', *mitʾawwâ*, of 13:4a. In both v. 4a and 7a the form is followed by the negative expression *wĕʾayin* (or *wĕʾên* in const.), rendered 'with nothing to show for it' or 'and yet – there is nothing at all'. These similarities form a connection between vv. 4 and 7, verses that bracket the teaching about morality in vv. 5–6.

Since in Hebr. 'to feign poverty' may also imply 'to impoverish oneself', the sage invites the inference that this person became poor knowingly, exhausting personal resources to help another (BDB; cf. 13:8a and 2 Cor. 8:9).

13:8. 'His riches consist of this: ransoming a person's life', *kōper nepeš-ʾîš ʿošrô*: lit. 'ransoming a person's life [is] his riches'. The pronoun 'his' refers to the second of the pair described in the preceding verse – the person who, despite apparent poverty, is truly rich (13:7b). Now in the first phrase of v. 8a (in the Hebr. syntax) the sage discloses the nature of that person's hidden wealth.

To understand 13:8a as observing that someone with a reserve of material wealth may ransom (buy or bribe) his own way out of misfortune (or misdeed) may fit the text if read in isolation (Waltke 2004: 558; Fox 2009: 563). However, when read in conjunction with 13:7, the sage in v. 8a teaches that the reason the wealth of the seemingly poor person of v. 7b goes unnoticed is this: he or she invests in ransoming others. Consequently he has little (but ransomed lives) to show for it.

'ransoming a person's life', *kōper nepeš-ʾîš*: lit. 'ransom of a person's life'. The word *nepeš* (here rendered 'life') is central to this lecture, since it can also mean 'appetite' (13:2, 4, 19, 25).

'But poor is the person who paid no attention to a rebuke', *wĕrāš lʾō-šāmaʿ gĕʿārâ*: lit. 'But a poor person will not listen to a rebuke'. Since in 13:8a the sage specifies the true nature of riches (ransoming another), the parallel sense in v. 8b will specify what constitutes the true nature of poverty (rather than describing what a person who is poor does or does not do). To identify poverty with a non-receptive response to rebuke corresponds remarkably to the sage's valuation of reproof-receptivity, beginning even in this lecture's opening line (13:1), and reinforced again near its close (v. 24). Between those verses, the sage reinforces reproof-receptivity four more times, either explicitly or implicitly (vv. 10, 14, 16, 18). Regarding 'paying attention', see 'Notes' for 13:1.

It is not his poverty that causes the poor person to disregard a word of reproof (as if his inability to finance a bribe removes all hope of his dodging the reproof's effects – so Waltke 2004: 559). Rather, his poverty flows from his insolent refusal, upon hearing the reproof, to take corrective action.

13:10. 'can one keep engendering': lit. 'can one give'. The subject is indefinite (*IBHS* §4.4.2), indicating that insolence supplies the environment necessary for sustaining strife. Capability and durability ('can it keep engendering') are inferred from the yiq.

13:11. 'originating from vapour . . . by handfuls', *mēhebel . . . ʿal yād*: lit. 'from vapour . . . upon a hand'. These parallel expressions contrast means of generating wealth. The first specifies the source material as insubstantial ('from vapour', which Waltke glosses as 'by unsound means', 2004: 547). Emending 'vapour' to read *mĕbōhāl*, 'in a rush', weakens the plain and picturesque quality of the original expression (*pace* Fox 2009: 565).

The second expression ('by handfuls') presents a unique use of the prep. 'upon' plus the noun 'hand' when in absolute state. Gathering 'upon-a-hand' at least implies 'by personal effort' (Fox 2009: 566), or even may contrast use of a mediating tool, whether harvesting with a scythe or digging into a pile of loose grain with a pitcher or other device for scooping. Instead of gathering by a tool, the worker is gathering directly by hand(fuls).

'one who consistently gathers': lit. 'one who gathers'. Use of a ptc. connotes a persistent trait ('consistently').

13:12. 'Expectation . . . ill', *tôḥelet . . . maḥălâ*: assonance joins these words.

'a veritable tree of life', *ʿēṣ-ḥayyîm*: lit. 'a tree of life'. 'Veritable' is supplied to reflect emphasis of phrase-initial positioning of the expression. *Ḥayyîm* refers to life in the abstract, in contrast to *nepeš*, which refers to the life (or appetite) of an individual.

13:13. 'directive', *dābār*: lit. 'word, message, edict, command'. Since the resistant hearer will be 'obliged to fulfil' this message, and since it is parallel to 'commandment', the sage envisions a behavioural expectation.

'he will be obliged to fulfil it', *yēḥābel lô*: lit. 'he will become pledged to it' (BDB) or 'a pledge is seized from him' (*HALOT*). Instead to render *yēḥābel lô* as 'he will be harmed' loses the specificity of retribution, whereas 'obliged to fulfil it' shows that, though dismissed, the duty returns to haunt the dodger (*pace* Fox 2009: 566; similarly Waltke 2004: 547).

13:15. 'will keep engendering grace': lit. 'will grant grace'. Durative is inferred from the yiq. (cf. 'engendering strife', 13:10). An insightful person will generate grace that benefits others (just as 'strife' would harm others in v. 10a). Thus grace here is relational, not reflexive 'favour' (*pace* Waltke, 'Good judgment wins favor' [2004: 548]).

'the way of treacherous folk is interminable', *wĕderek bōgedîm ʾêtān*: lit. 'the way of treacherous folk [is] continual'. A delay may inflict mental distress (13:12). Thus a transit never reaching its destination ('interminable') amounts to endless agony. Rendering *ʾêtān* as 'interminable' (cf. Job 33:19) is preferable to emending the Hebr. to read *ʾēdām*, 'perishing' (as proposed by *BHS* notes, following LXX).

13:16. 'sensible', *ʿārûm*: outside Proverbs this term often is sinister, rendered 'clever'. Within Proverbs it is uniformly admirable, distinguishing the wise from the naive (e.g. 'discreet' in 12:23).

13:18. 'Poverty and disgrace characterize one who forsakes reproof': a verbless clause, 'characterize' is inferred.

'disgrace', *qālôn*: often rendered 'shame'; a synonym of 'to act shamefully', *ḥpr*, in 13:5.

13:19. 'longing . . . but loathsome', *taʾăwâ . . . wĕtôʿăbat*: assonantally linked but semantically opposed.

13:20. 'Walk', *hālôk*: reading infin. abs. (as rhetorical imperative) with K, not ptc. (*hōlēk*, 'one who walks') with Q (cf. 12:7; 25:4, 5).

'in the company of wise folk': lit. 'with wise folk'.

'and become wise', *waḥăkām*: reading imperative, with K.

'but a friend . . . will be treated badly', *wĕrōʿeh . . . yērôaʿ*: assonantally linked but semantically opposed: 'friend', *rʿh*, and 'treated badly', *rʿʿ* (also Fox 2009: 569).

13:21. 'but in the company of moral folk', *wĕʾet-ṣadîqîm*: lit. 'but with moral folk'. Indefiniteness of 'moral folk' identifies *ʾet* as the prep. 'with' or 'in the company of', as was the case in 13:20a ('Walk in the company of wise folk'). Moral folk in v. 21b join with the wise folk of v. 20a, designating the sort of companions the sage commends to the pupil (*pace* Fox 2009: 569 and Waltke 2004: 549).

'good will repay', *yĕšallēm-ṭôb*: the contrasting qualities of *rāʿā*, 'misery', and *ṭôbâ*, 'goodness', often appear in connection with the verb *šlm*, 'to repay' or 'to be repaid' (Gen. 44:4; 1 Sam. 24:19 [MT v. 20]; Pss 35:12; 38:20 [MT v. 21]; Jer. 18:20). Since 'misery' here operates as a subject ('misery will pursue'), it is likely that 'good' also serves not as the commodity being repaid, but as the subject ('good will repay'), even though the sage employed *ṭôb* (adj.) and not *ṭôbâ* (noun). Waltke similarly renders, 'good things reward' (2004: 549). The poet previously employed the adj. 'good' as a subject in 12:2 and will do so again in 13:22.

13:22. 'property', *ḥêl*: this term overlaps with the semantic field of *hôn*, 'wealth' (13:7, 11).

13:23. 'but someone is being plundered', *wĕyēš nispeh*: lit. 'but there is one who is plundered' (ptc.). Devastation compounds with anonymity of helplessness ('one who is plundered'). The victim was the poor person, according to the preceding colon (13:23a).

'redress', *mišpāṭ*: or 'judgement', a verdict effecting justice in a legal dispute. *Nispeh*, 'a plundered person', and *bĕlōʾ mišpāṭ*, 'without redress', are assonantally linked but semantically opposed.

13:25. 'will keep on suffering want', *teḥsār*: durative inferred from yiq., contrasting a ptc. (*ʾōkēl*, 'eats') in the first colon.

Form and structure

Borders

A theme of noble character as foundation for lasting relationships dominated the preceding poem. This transitions to a quest for true satisfaction (present poem), which theme begins within a wisdom commendation marking the upper border (13:1).

Recap, character summary, closure and inclusio mark the lower border in 13:25. A recap of three themes occupies 13:24–25: parental reproof, morality and achieving satisfaction. A character summary contrasting moral and guilty appears in 13:25.

Themes contributing to closure in the final quatrain (13:24–25) include parental reproof (cf. v. 1 most specifically, and corrective instruction more widely, with special emphasis in vv. 8, 18), morality (cf. vv. 5, 6, 9, 15, 17, 21, 22) and achieving satisfaction (for specific satisfaction, together with a range of desirable outcomes, see vv. 2, 4, 9, 12, 14, 18, 19, 21, 22).

Concerning lecture-wide inclusio, the terms rendered 'son', 'reproof', 'eat' and 'appetite' occur in 13:1–2. They recur in vv. 24–25, creating a lecture-wide form-based inclusio. 'Reproof' and 'appetite' occur elsewhere in this poem, fostering closure when they appear in vv. 24–25 ('reproof' in v. 18; 'appetite' in vv. 3, 4, 8 [where *nepeš* is rendered 'life'], 19). Waltke similarly notes that 'eat' and 'appetite' in v. 2 create an inclusio with v. 25, and later observes the link formed by reproof's appearance in vv. 1, 24 (2004: 550 and 570, respectively).

Reference to satisfaction as a derivative of reproof creates a content-based inclusio. This also begins in 13:1–2, returning in vv. 24–25.

It is instructive to note that by associating 'love' with 'reproof' in 13:24, the sage links the close of this lecture with the opening verse of the preceding lecture: 'Whoever loves reproof loves knowledge' (12:1a, opening the lecture spanning 12:1–28). This joins with the end of Prov. 13 to create a sense of closure grander than simply the conclusion of a single lecture. Here the poet fosters closure at the level of multiple lectures.

Macrostructural features

Thematic continuity regarding satisfaction (Sections I–V, content-based). This lecture centres in the concept of satisfying one's appetite or, in more philosophical terms, achieving fulfilment in life. The concepts of appetite or hunger, satisfaction/dissatisfaction, reward, vitality, fulfilment and failure of yearnings – all of these crop up repeatedly across the poem (cf. 'feed' and 'appetite' in 13:2, 'appetite', 'mouth' and 'lips' in v. 3, 'crave', 'appetite' and 'made fat' in v. 4, expectation-denied, emotional distress, 'tree of life' and longing-fulfilled in v. 12, reward in v. 13, 'spring of life' in v. 14, 'longing' and 'appetite' in v. 19, repayment in v. 21, a quantity of food in v. 23, and 'eat[ing]', 'appetite', 'satisfaction' and 'suffering want' in v. 25). When the concept of satisfaction is extended to include notions of wealth–poverty, and light–darkness, then the following verses contribute to the overarching theme of satisfaction: 'riches' and 'wealth' in v. 7; 'riches' in v. 8; 'light', 'joy' and 'lamp' in v. 9; 'wealth' and expansion in v. 11; 'poverty' in v. 18; and 'inheritance' and 'property' in v. 22.

Syntax-related refrain (Sections I, II, III and V, form-based). Four of this poem's five sections conclude with a particular syntactic expression in the last colon. Each of the following section-closing phrases may be represented as 'X of Y is (or does) Z'. The expressions are 'the lamp [element 'X'] of guilty folk [element 'Y'] will go out [element 'Z']' (13:9b, Section I), 'the way of treacherous folk is interminable' (v. 15b, Section II), 'loathsome to [lit. an abhorrence of] stupid folk is veering away from misery' (v. 19b, Section III) and 'the belly of guilty folk will keep on suffering want' (v. 25b, Section V). This syntax appears also in v. 4b (closing Block I.B) and v. 20b (not structurally significant).

Thematic continuity regarding corrective communication (Sections I, II, III and V, content-based). Corrective communication features prominently in this lecture, indicated by 'reproof', 'rebuke' and 'reprimand' (13:1, 8, 18, 24). Both 'reproof' and 'rebuke' appear in the first verse. Related expressions include 'the fruit of a person's mouth' (v. 2, associated with 'reproof' and 'rebuke' in v. 1), 'a false word' (v. 5, representing unfounded reproof), 'accepting advice' (v. 10), 'a directive' and 'a commandment' (v. 13), 'a wise person's instruction' (v. 14), 'insight that is good' (v. 15), 'acting on knowledge' (v. 16) and being influenced by wise and moral folk (vv. 20–21). These amount to thirteen of this lecture's twenty-five verses.

Inclusio involving 'good' and 'treacherous' (Sections I and II, form-based). The terms 'good' and 'treacherous folk' appear in 13:2 (near the opening of Section I) and in v. 15 (closing Section II), contributing to an inclusio for Sections I and II. These are the sole instances of 'treacherous folk' in this poem. 'Good' appears also in vv. 21, 22.

Thematic continuity regarding kindness (Sections I and II, content-based). The penultimate saying of Section I and the final saying of Section II showcase compassionate conduct, creating a climactic continuity of character within each section (13:8, 15).

Thematic continuity concerning community relationships (Sections I and II, content-based). Strategic placement of sayings fostering community relationships signals a profound connection between healthy relationships and the lecture's principal theme of personal satisfaction. The sage defines wealth in terms of lives one has successfully ransomed (13:8). Such moral persons benefit those around them by emitting light of a joyous (not blinding) sort, a sign that they have achieved an abundance of satisfaction (v. 9). These two relational sayings climactically close Section I.

Community discord radiates uniquely when pride rejects another's counsel (13:10). In contrast, relationships undergirded by patient kindness flourish through the operation of valuable insight (v. 15; see 'Notes'). Wisdom will not enrich self at the expense of community.

Thus Sections I and II cooperate to advance the importance of relationships, if one would achieve satisfaction. While other sayings allude to relationships, they are limited to more customary family ties (vv. 1, 22, 24).

Thematic continuity concerning progeny (Sections I and IV, content-based). A person's lamp may refer to one's offspring (13:9b; Fox 2009: 564). Mention of grandchildren reinforces this concept (13:22a). These appear in the last verse of Section I and in the penultimate verse of Section IV.

Exhortation, plus incentive (Sections II, III and IV, content-based). Incentive portions follow exhortations (whether explicit or implicit) in Sections II, III and IV. These present (a) the importance of diligent effort (13:11–12 followed by incentives in vv. 13–15), (b) the need to act on reproof (vv. 16–17, followed by vv. 18–19) and (c) the importance of finding reliable agents of reproof (vv. 20–21, followed by vv. 22–23).

Microstructural features

Section I (13:1–9). *Wisdom commendation and character summary, for section-level framing (13:1, 9, content-based).* Section I begins with a wisdom commendation (13:1; wisdom content spans the balance of Section I, vv. 2–9). The stark contrast of 'guilty' and 'moral' folk, with a sombre sense of finality ('the lamp of guilty folk will go out') supplies a character summary at this section's close (v. 9). The poet deploys these components often enough in this manner (opening with a wisdom commendation, as in 10:8, 14, 17, 23, 31, and closing with a character summary as in 10:30; 11:8, 31; 13:25), so that when both appear in a single section, they frame the section.

Thematic continuity concerning manner of consumption (13:2–4, form- and content-based). The notion of beneficial eating, begun in 13:2, in vv. 3–4 concentrates on how one eats. One must consume with discernment (v. 3) and diligence (v. 4). Whereas reproof was the object of consumption in vv. 1–2, vv. 3–4 seem to address appetite and ambition more generally. Waltke detects in v. 4 a substantial contribution to the lecture's theme of appetites and aspirations (2004: 552).

Continuity involving morality (13:5–6, form- and content-based). The quatrain of 13:5–6 coheres by repeating 'moral' in the first colon of each saying (so also Waltke 2004: 555). In addition, each second colon refers to 'guilty' or 'wickedness' (both stemming from the root *rš'*). The terms 'false' (v. 5) and 'integrity' (v. 6) expand the theme of morality. Diligent morality enables one to discern as advised in v. 3, distinguishing between valid and baseless words of reproof.

Thematic continuity concerning deception (13:5, 6, content-based). Mention of 'a false word' (13:5) and the practice of 'relabel[ling] sin' (v. 6) involve deception, helping to link these two sayings.

Framing with negation and stem-related verbs (13:4a, 7a, form-based). The verse-pair in 13:5–6 is framed by two features found in vv. 4a and 7a. First, these cola use the negation *wĕʾayin* (in the phrase 'with nothing to show for it' in v. 4a, and in 'and yet – there is nothing at all' in v. 7a). *ʾAyin* does not occur elsewhere in this poem.

Second, preceding the expression *wĕʾayin* appear the ptcs. 'craves' (13:4a) and 'feigns riches' (v. 7a). Although the verbal roots differ, they share an h-t stem (whether hith. or hithpol.). Within this poem, an h-t stem verb occurs only once more ('another feigns poverty' in v. 7b). Waltke likewise notes these similarities linking vv. 4 and 7, but, due to differences in section boundaries, does not observe how they frame vv. 5–6 (2004: 557).

Repetition of root involving 'riches' (13:7–8, form-based). Both the ptc. 'one who feigns riches' in 13:7 and the noun 'riches' in v. 8 trace to the root *ʿšr*, 'riches', a root not appearing elsewhere in this poem.

Near-inclusio involving 'rebuke' (13:1, 8, form-based). The phrase 'paid no attention to a rebuke' (line-terminal in 13:1b) reinforced the theme of reprimand introduced with 'reproof', v. 1a. The same phrase reappears in v. 8b, section-terminal except for a character summary in v. 9. The link between vv. 1 and 8 approximates an inclusio for Section I, indicative of carefully structured composition (also Waltke 2004: 551), not a copyist's error (*pace* Fox 2009: 564).

Section II (13:10–15). *Wisdom commendation followed by wisdom content (13:10, 11–15, content-based).* Section II begins with a wisdom commendation about reproof (13:10), which leads to wisdom content advocating diligent effort (vv. 11–15).

Thematic contrast concerning diligence (13:11–12, content-based). In one verse the sage counsels persistent effort (gathering 'by handfuls') in order to achieve one's goals (13:11). The next saying brings balance by cautioning against excessively prolonging the deferral of gratification, lest mental illness set in (v. 12; so also Van Leeuwen [in Fox 2009: 566]). Thus to read v. 12 in concert with v. 11 is to be preferred over severing the train of thought by treating v. 12 as the start of a new unit (*pace* Waltke, who links vv. 12 and 19 [2004: 562]). References to reproof, not longings-fulfilled, provide a more reliable indicator of the start of new portions in this lecture (see 'Thematic continuity regarding corrective communication', under 'Macrostructural features', above).

Advice supported by incentive (13:11–12, 13–15, content-based). After advising diligent effort in pursuit of goals (13:11–12), the sage supports that advice with rich incentives. These include repayment (v. 13), a spring of life and escape from death (v. 14), and a resilient capacity to bestow grace, rather than suffering the demise of ever travelling while never arriving (v. 15).

Inclusio with contrast concerning 'engendering' (13:10, 15, form-based). The outer sayings of Section II refer to 'engendering', *yittēn*. First, insolence 'will keep engendering strife' (13:10a). In contrast, 'insight' of a good sort (resembling wisely accepting advice in v. 10b) 'will keep engendering grace' (v. 15a). The root yielding 'engender', *ntn*, does not otherwise appear in this lecture (most recently appearing in 12:12, and next in 21:26, in both instances rendered 'keeps on giving'). For grace to offset strife is consistent with the sage's high esteem for the life of another (13:8a).

Closure concerning non-arrival (13:12, 15, content-based). The fate of never arriving at one's intended destination or goal (13:15b) recalls the mental malaise associated with an expectation whose fulfilment delays too long (v. 12a). This contributes to closure.

Section III (13:16–19). *Wisdom commendation followed by wisdom content (13:16, 17, content-based).* Section III begins with a wisdom commendation about decisions based on knowledge (13:16), leading to wisdom content concerning messengers (v. 17).

Principle-plus-illustration (13:16–17, content-based). This principle appears in 13:16: a sensible person will execute knowledge he has received. In context such knowledge entails reproof.

A saying about a faithful envoy follows next, illustrating the principle of execution. The messenger's responsibility has been discharged only once he has delivered the message (13:17). A guilty messenger, in contrast, either alters the message or fails to deliver it. 'Folly' in v. 16b therefore consists of receiving knowledge concerning what one must do (v. 16a), but failing to act on it. Such a one fails to experience a cure (recall the mental malaise of v. 12a).

Advice supported by incentive (13:16–17, 18–19, content-based). A collection of benefits in 13:18–19 supports the importance of execution in vv. 16–17. Those benefits include avoiding poverty and disgrace, receiving honour, obtaining a satisfied appetite and avoiding misery.

Section IV (13:20–23). *Wisdom commendation followed by wisdom content (13:20, 21, content-based).* Section IV begins with a wisdom commendation about wise friends (13:20), which leads to wisdom content advocating companions who are moral (v. 21).

Thematic continuity concerning wise friendships (13:20–21, content-based). After teaching the value of reproof, the sage recommends friendships with wise and moral individuals (13:20, 21). They will constitute sources of reliable reproof. Admirable persons are pl. in this quatrain, adding to coherence (in the next they are sg.).

Imperative supported by incentive (13:20–21, 22–23, content-based). In 13:20–21 the sage commends the practice of securing wise friends. Incentives follow: wealth will be secured for generations (v. 22), while one may avoid suffering poverty and exploitation (v. 23).

Frame and hinge words (13:21–22, form- and content-based). The quatrains dealing with exhortation (13:20–21) and incentive (vv. 22–23) are joined by two formal features at the quatrains' point of contact (between vv. 21 and 22). 'Sinners' is line-initial in v. 21 and line-terminal in v. 22. 'Good' is line-terminal in v. 21 and line-initial in v. 22 (Waltke 2004: 570).

Misery connects 13:21, 22 on a content level. The 'misery' that pursues sinners in v. 21a amounts to this: property they hoard for themselves winds up benefiting a moral person (v. 22b; cf. Eccles. 2:26).

Thematic contrast concerning bequeathable assets (13:22, 23, content-based). Although 13:22, 23 join in presenting incentives that support the exhortation to acquire wise friends (vv. 20–21), they do so through stark contrast. Positive incentive arises from the prospect of being able both to acquire and to bequeath assets to future generations (v. 22a). In contrast, the sinner will be unable to retain what property he may acquire (v. 22b). The contrast extends in v. 23. There the poor (who, within the context of this lecture, refer to those who have rejected reproof [vv. 8b, 18a]) must forfeit their field with its capacity for food and revenue (or must forfeit at least its harvest, v. 23a). To add insult to injury, they entertain no hope for redress (v. 23b).

Section V (13:24–25). *Closure (13:24–25, content-based).* Closure in Section V was described under Borders, above.

Comment

Section I (13:1–9). In Section I (13:1–9) the sage indicates four signposts that point one towards satisfaction. Those signposts begin with receptivity-to-reproof (vv. 1–2). Second, the sage unveils the category he will address with words of reproof: one's appetites and aspirations (vv. 3–4; see 'Microstructural features', above). The third signpost establishes the moral environment that must permeate the process of receiving and issuing messages of reproof (without which one might wrongly conform to misguided reproof, or one might disregard valid messages of reproof, vv. 5–6). The fourth signpost considers one specific ambition – perhaps the most commonly pursued of all life-goals: amassing wealth (vv. 7–8). Here the sage trains the pupil to distinguish between apparent and authentic wealth.

Within all of Proverbs, this portion houses two of the most monumental disclosures of the sage's entire value system. First, true wealth consists of rescuing others (13:8a). Second, poverty traces primarily to treating reproof with indifference (v. 8b; in v. 23 the sage will add that poverty is not ultimately a matter of insufficient resources).

The sage concludes this series of four quatrains (13:1–8) with a single-verse character summary presenting a test to determine whether one has correctly assessed the true nature of wealth (v. 9). Joy and brightness will characterize an individual whose inner morality has correctly defined wealth in terms of rescuing others. Conversely, a life of escalating gloom traces to a mistaken ambition that values tangible wealth above persons.

13:1. The term 'father' has not appeared since 10:1 (where it joined with 'son'), and will not return until 15:5. Across Prov. 10 – 13, 'son' occurs only in the outer lectures (four times in the first lecture [twice in each of 10:1, 5] and four times in the last lecture [13:1, twice in 13:22, and in 13:24]). This suggests that the lecture beginning in 13:1 may bring to a close the poems that began in 10:1. By combining in 13:1 the closeness of a father–son relationship with the mention of both 'reproof' and 'rebuke', the sage may indicate, in effect, 'I now invite you to what is at once the finest and most challenging level of wisdom instruction.'

13:2. The genius of this saying emerges in its reversals. Instead of consuming destructively, the mouth may supply desirable nourishment (13:2a; cf. Mark 7:15). The treacherous inflict their violence overtly on others, yet 'it boomerangs against themselves' (Waltke 2004: 553).

13:5. Any who value truth will easily identify the moral inverse, even with eyes closed.

13:6. The root *slp*, 'relabel', described the greedy merchant's despicable ploy to switch marketplace weights (11:3).

Section II (13:10–15). After mapping out four way-markers leading to satisfaction (Section I), Section II adds the crucial ingredient of diligence and the incentive of profound reward. This section opens by reinforcing the importance of receptivity to reproof – in case the youth had insufficiently embraced this principle at the opening of Section I (13:10; cf. vv. 1–2). Then the sage introduces the critical need for diligence in the pursuit of aspirations (vv. 11–12). Without consistent moral industry (not chasing mirages), even a noble aspiration may transmute into a denizen of despair, simply due to the interminable postponement of its elusive achievement. But the pupil who responds willingly to reproof, who applies diligence in the pursuit of honourable aspirations, that individual will one day achieve the reward – a reward consisting of robust vitality for oneself and, for those around, grace (vv. 13–15). A dismal end describes the alternative: being consigned ever to journey, but never to make port in the hoped-for harbour of satisfaction (note parallel despair in v. 12a).

13:11. Although it is true that 13:7 ends with 'much wealth', and that words associated with those roots appear first and last in v. 11 ('multiply' and 'wealth'), to infer that this brackets a portion spanning vv. 7–11 (so Waltke 2004: 556) accounts neither for the lecture's theme of 'reproof' appearing in v. 10, nor for the inclusio with 'engendering strife' and 'engendering grace' in vv. 10, 15 (see 'Microstructural features').

Section III (13:16–19). Evidently, the sage had observed individuals who possessed the right aspirations, who were oriented by proper morals, who even seemed to welcome helpful reproof, but who yet failed to achieve the desired goals. They failed at the point of execution – stopping at the point of converting into action the reproof they had received. So the poet devotes Section III to underscore the importance of execution (13:16–19). Like an envoy (v. 17) who has been entrusted with a physician's therapeutic message, so a counsel of 'reproof' (v. 18a) or a sterner counsel of 'reprimand' (v. 18b) remains powerless to effect its 'cure' (also v. 17), unless the envoy faithfully completes his task. The pupil's responsibility with respect to regarding reproof does not stop at the point of merely responding with respectful inaction. He must 'act on knowledge' (v. 16a). Only then has the metaphoric messenger of v. 17 finished his mission. Only then can 'cure' begin – a cure that generates honour together with the longed-for satisfaction (vv. 18–19).

Since 13:19b deals with failure to avoid misery (evidently by rejecting reproof), conversely the 'longing that has come to pass' in v. 19a results implicitly from embracing reproof. Hence the outline heading 'Acting on reproof results in satisfaction, with misery as alternative'. Waltke similarly regards this saying as closing a portion: 'In sum, a person's [attaining fulfilment in] life depends on finding his drives and appetites satisfied' (2004: 570).

13:17. Fox infers that a *ṣîr*, 'envoy', travelled on missions more distant than a *malʾāk*, 'messenger' (2009: 568).

Section IV (13:20–23). What more can the sage add to this lofty summit? Only this: to help the pupil locate reliable agents of reproof. That explains his commendation of wise companionship in the first quatrain of Section IV (13:20–21). The remaining quatrain of Section IV (vv. 22–23) conducts a general survey of outcomes, creating a sense of conclusion for this section. For the person who is good, wealth will abound to multiple generations – even acquiring assets initially accumulated by a bad person (v. 22; keeping in mind that the sage established his own definition of 'wealth' in v. 8). In sad contrast, the poor will suffer plundering without redress (v. 23).

At this point an interpretive aside is necessary, exploring the meaning of 13:23. At the outset, it is essential to bear in mind how the sage conceives of poverty. According to vv. 8, 18, within this lecture the poor describes those who resist reproof. By implication, the truly 'rich' refers to those who embrace reproof.

The fact that the poor are those who resist reproof significantly influences the meaning of 13:23b. Initially that colon smacks of gross injustice: they appear as victims of plundering, without redress. Yet, on further reflection, the notion that reproof-resistant persons should fail to gain profit from their field (despite its fertility) comes as no surprise. To resist reproof is folly, and folly generates no profit.

In response to the scenario in 13:23 the reader cannot help but wonder, 'Who has done this despicable deed, this plundering with impunity?' Yet the sage remains silent, leaving the reader to ponder. From the pass. voice (with no agent disclosed), we know only that the poor field owner is 'being plundered'. Some understandably might wrongly conclude that this colon admits faults within an otherwise reliable justice system, exceptions wherein only the wealthy can secure vindication – exceptions permitting them to abuse others with impunity (cf. Waltke 2004: 573; Fox 2009: 570).

But to reach this conclusion loses sight of what the sage established earlier in 13:8, 18. There he explained that, within the context of this lecture, the poor is poor neither for lack of a fertile field, nor for lack of justice, but because he resists reproof (elsewhere the sage teaches that one must advocate for the disadvantaged; cf. 24:10–12). Gradually it would dawn on the pupil that the one plundering the poor person – the one preventing the poor from gaining a profit – is the poor person himself. By implication, at some point he has rejected critical reproof. In context, that reproof would likely have pertained to effective farm- or fiscal-management. Perhaps financial mismanagement forced him to forfeit his field. So he became 'plundered', by his own reproof-resistant hand. Now it becomes clear why he receives no redress. When a crime has been self-inflicted, nothing will be gained by punishing the criminal. The justice system is powerless to recover and repay to the poor man what he has stolen from himself.

Section V (13:24–25). A pair of verses follows the conclusion lodged in Section IV. There the sage reviews and reinforces large themes to which the lecture devoted itself. First, parents must own their responsibility as reliable agents of reproof (13:24; cf. v. 1). Second, beyond any other single feature, it is his own moral conduct that ultimately will determine whether the pupil will achieve satisfaction, or be consigned to gnawing hunger (v. 25). In this manner Section V serves the entire lecture as a recap.

13:24. To shrink from humanely reproving one's children constitutes no lenient love, but a clandestine hatred of one's own offspring. Loving parental interdiction first appeared in 1:15–19.

The corporal nature of this reproof is reminiscent of the physical violence that consumes the appetite of treacherous folk (13:2b), with this difference: that earlier physical harm served selfish ends. Here, physical pain serves only to benefit the youth, to set him back on a road where morality, initiative and self-control will enable him to achieve his goal of satisfaction through self-sacrifice.

13:25. Masoretes located a *pětuḥâ* composition break (a blank space extending to the margin, as found at the end of each paragraph in this book) in the middle of 10:1, directly after the title 'The proverbs of Solomon'. The next *pětuḥâ* break does not appear until the end of 13:25. In this way the Masoretes communicated that, in their opinion, Prov. 10 – 13 enjoys a sense of coherence. That coherence may involve a shift from individual interests (Prov. 10 – 13) to interests that address community health (Prov. 14:1 – 15:6). Waltke detects closure in v. 25 that reaches back to 10:3 (2004: 570). Both sayings describe how the guilty will go hungry.

Whole-lecture theme of achieving personal satisfaction. Regarding progression of thought, one additional observation merits notice. It concerns how the theme of achieving personal satisfaction operates within each of Sections I–V. Consider especially the five section-ending verses. When taken in sequence, these five sayings form a progression of thought. They speak in a uniformly negative fashion, explaining how one may fail to achieve personal satisfaction. Initially, we learn that the meagre lamp-light of the guilty is succumbing to darkness – a failure of satisfaction (13:9b). Next, the treacherous travellers discover that they have yet to reach their destination – another failure of satisfaction (v. 15b). Sadly, in their stupidity they still refuse to turn from misery in order to find a better route – explaining the cause of their eventual dissatisfaction (v. 19b). Impoverished not by lack of opportunity, but by rejecting reproof (according to v. 8b), they suffer added loss without hope of justice – a dismal formula for dis-satisfaction (v. 23). In the end, these unfortunate travellers (once again in v. 25 labelled 'guilty folk', as in v. 9) are consigned to the failed-destination of interminable hunger. Their expedition bound for satisfaction has failed, and miserably so.

Explanation

As the sage draws to a close the lectures spanning Prov. 10 – 13, he takes up a universal human question: How may one achieve lasting satisfaction? His timeless principles fall into five categories.

First and foremost, one must prize reproof. So essential is reproof that the sage introduces it in the lecture's first verse (13:1), then underscores it near the first section's close (v. 8b). It reappears at the opening of both the second and third sections (vv. 10 and 16, respectively). The challenge of discovering reliable sources of reproof dominates the fourth section (cf. vv. 20–21). Among reliable sources, parents rank first (vv. 1, 24).

Second, one must cultivate discernment concerning what appetites one will pursue in the quest for satisfaction. Not all that appears sweet will nourish. One must distinguish what will be useful, and then pursue it with diligence (13:3–4).

Third, by cultivating moral conduct one's powers of discernment will be sharpened. Moral conduct defines the skill necessary to distinguish between appetites that nourish and those that bring harm. For, an inner compass of moral character will offer the best insurance against either (a) being bullied by unfounded reproof or (b) being enticed to pursue misleading ambitions whose immoral means or ends have been cleverly disguised through relabelling (13:5–6).

Fourth, the nature of true wealth merits careful consideration. Much that masquerades as wealth misleads. Conversely, the materially penniless may die as the richest of all (13:7). Of what, then, does genuine wealth consist? Of greatest worth is to ransom the life of another (v. 8a). To disregard this principle will relegate oneself to penury, notwithstanding heaps of accumulated material riches (v. 8b). Jesus underscored this principle in his account of Lazarus and the rich man (Luke 16:19–31), with the story of the short-sighted barn-builder (Luke 12:16–21), and principally with his own life: 'For the Son of Man did not come to receive service, but in order to serve, even giving his life to ransom many' (Mark 10:45).

Ironically, it is not ledger balances, but joy issuing from moral conduct, that reveals authentic wealth (13:9). Lesser ambitions spawn only treachery, strife and interminable violence (vv. 2, 10, 15).

Fifth, wisely selected appetites and heartily welcomed reproof matter little, until catalysed by diligent industry. One must act on the reproof that one has received, carrying it to completion (13:4, 16–17).

The pupil who acts on these principles will circumvent the pitfalls of illusive satisfactions (13:3b) and elusive ambitions (vv. 12a, 15b). He or she will attain authentic wealth (vv. 8, 12b), passing it along even to another generation (v. 22) – a portrait of enduring satisfaction (v. 25). Offsetting this splendid prospect looms the ominous fate 'the belly of guilty folk will keep on suffering want' (v. 25b) – a destiny analogous to the treacherous who were consigned ever to journey, but never to arrive (v. 15b).

PROVERBS 14 – 24: CORPORATE SUCCESS AND SECURITY

Counsel for individual success has characterized much of Prov. 10 – 13. Now the sage shifts to corporate success, indicated by *bayit*, 'house', a term referring either to a material structure (e.g. 'a house of cedar', 2 Sam. 7:2) or to a household (Prov. 14:1). Lectures extending through Prov. 24 (closing Division II) address increasingly lofty themes, as the instructor readies the youth to assume responsibility as a sage in his own right.

PROVERBS 14:1 – 15:6
'How should I build my house?'

Overview of Proverbs 14:1 – 15:6

Both a domestic house and a dynastic house feature in the introduction to the lecture spanning Prov. 14:1 – 15:6 (Section I, 14:1–4). Then follows counsel for securing an honourable domestic house (Section II, 14:5–27). Metaphors of building (14:1) and navigation (14:2) intertwine at strategic points. After the domestic house, in Section III the poet takes up the dynastic house (14:28 – 15:4), followed by a two-verse conclusion joining wisdom commendation with character summary (Section IV, 15:5–6). The pupil emerges with a palace template as stunning as it will be secure.

Position of this poem within Proverbs

Preceding context. Prov. 10 – 13 comprised a group of lectures that began with a self-centred focus, as evident from these titles: 'How can I become rich?' (10:1–22), 'How can I secure my future?' (10:23–30) and 'What is the harm in fraudulent riches?' (10:31 – 11:31). The next lecture concerned relationships: 'How can I recognize noble character and thus behave as a true friend?' (12:1–28). The last lecture in that cycle returned to an inward focus: 'How may I achieve true satisfaction?' (13:1–25). Yet even there the sage embedded a relationally oriented redefinition of wealth: 'riches consist of this: ransoming a person's life' (13:8). As noted above, the present lecture turns from the solitary individual, examining instead the metaphoric 'house' (or household) the youth seeks to build.

Ensuing context. After a character summary closing the present lecture (15:6), a wisdom commendation opens the next: 'The lips of wise folk keep on winnowing information, but the mind of stupid folk is not so' (15:7). Embedded within that saying is the next lecture's objective: to isolate the mind's primary role (*lēb*), and then to sharpen its capacity for critical thinking (15:7 – 17:3).

What to watch for

Distinguish portions envisioning a smaller organization (such as a family) from those dealing with a broader, even national, perspective. Also notice the metaphors of (a) build-and-collapse and (b) navigating, particularly in 14:1–27 and 15:6. Observe the concepts of morality and discretion. The opposite of naivety, discretion will assess before it trusts. Block II.B (14:8–19) especially features discretion and moral conduct. Distinguish between conventional wisdom (e.g. 14:20, 28) and the sage's corrective immediately following. Notice how the word-pair 'wise' and 'foolish' enjoy strategic positioning towards the start of a new portion.

Translation and outline

Verse	*Translation*	*Outline*
		I. Dual-theme introduction: how to build a house, domestic and dynastic (14:1–4) A. How to navigate building a domestic house (14:1–2)

Translation	Outline
14:1 Women who are wise have built their house, but Folly with her hands will demolish it. 14:2 One who reveres the Lord walks according to his straight standards, while one who despises him strays along his ways.	1. Wisdom commendation: wisdom builds a house, while folly destroys it (14:1) 2. Wisdom content: morality will determine navigational soundness (14:2)
14:3 In a fool's mouth is an arrogant rod, while lips of wise folk will safeguard them. 14:4 Where there are no cattle a feeding trough is clean, but great revenues result from the strength of an ox.	B. How to build a dynastic house (14:3–4) 1. Wisdom commendation: a fool's speech abuses power, wise speech protects from the powerful (14:3) 2. Wisdom content: the power of productivity is messy (14:4)
14:5 A trustworthy witness will not lie, while one who testifies falsehoods is a false witness. 14:6 A scoffer was looking for wisdom, but there was none. Yet for a perceptive person, knowledge came easily. 14:7 Depart from before a stupid fellow, since you do not yet distinguish knowledgeable speech.	II. How to navigate building a domestic house (14:5–27) A. Start with reliable sources of information (14:5–7) 1. Reliability of information depends on the character of the source, not the sound of his words (14:5) 2. Obtaining wisdom depends on the character of the seeker, not the adequacy of supply (14:6) 3. The naive should avoid stupid companions (14:7)
	B. Then focus on discretion and morality, generally: the keys to navigating effectively and building securely (14:8–19) 1. Discretion and morality ensure positive outcomes (14:8–13) a. Effective navigation and house-building require discretion and morality (14:8–11)

Verse	*Translation*	*Outline*
14:8	Wisdom characterized by discretion rendered perceptible the way one should travel, while the folly of stupid folk will deceive.	i. Discretion enables navigation (otherwise suffer deception, 14:8)
14:9	Culpability will scoff at foolish folk, but among honest folk is favour.	ii. Morality brings favour (otherwise suffer humiliation, 14:9)
14:10	A mind knows the bitterness of its inner longings, and in its joy a stranger cannot participate.	i'. Discretion evidences wisdom (14:10)
14:11	The house of guilty folk will be destroyed, while the tent of honest folk will blossom.	ii'. Character summary: morality determines the demise or flourishing of one's house (14:11)
		b. In navigation, the discretion that perceives ultimate outcomes is essential (14:12–13)
14:12	There is a way that from a human perspective is straight; but in the final analysis, it consists of ways leading to death.	i. Verify the information-source of morals, or suffer fatal navigation hazards (14:12)
14:13	Despite laughter the heart keeps on aching; and in the final analysis, joy consists of grief.	ii. A veneer of hilarity may conceal underlying heartache (14:13)
		2. To disregard reliable information initiates a downward spiral of dissatisfaction ending in disgrace (14:14–19)
14:14	From its own ways a deviating mind must draw satisfaction, while far from him will a good person be satisfied.	a. Axiom of navigation: morality of route chosen determines ultimate satisfaction (14:14)
14:15	A naive person will believe anything, while a discreet person will exercise perception concerning his step.	b. Naive or discreet: their contrasting assessments of information determine misstep or navigational safety (14:15)

14:16 A wise person regards warning seriously and so turns from wrong, but a stupid fellow gets angry, so self-confident is he.	c. Resentful anger fuelled by self-rightness follows previous misstep (14:16)
14:17 A short fuse will generate folly, but a person known for schemes will be hated.	c'. Resentful anger fuels more folly, which fuels scheming, which earns rejection (14:17)
14:18 Naive folk have bequeathed folly, while discreet folk will bestow knowledge as a diadem.	b'. In consequence of either naivety or discretion, ensuing generations will either fade or flourish in wisdom (14:18)
14:19 Bad folk bowed before good folk, and the guilty – at the gates of a moral person.	a'. Character summary and axiom of building: morality determines ultimate abasement, or honour (14:19)
	C. Proceed to focus on morality, specifically: valuing persons discloses true wealth or poverty (14:20–22)
14:20 A poor person will be hated even by his neighbour, while those who love a wealthy person are many.	1. Conventional wisdom: tangible wealth determines worth (14:20)
14:21 One who despises his neighbour sins, but it is the one who practises compassion towards the oppressed who is truly fortunate!	2. Corrected wisdom: authentic wealth consists of a compassionate response to the oppressed, whose value is not contingent (14:21)
14:22 Will not they wander, who are devising misery? But those who devise good embody faithful love and faithfulness.	3. To devalue one's neighbour breeds wicked designs, which will result in navigational drift (14:22)
	D. Section conclusion: a call to action with four-part review (14:23–27)
14:23 From any sort of toil profit will result, while mere talk amounts only to lack.	1. Introduction: act decisively (14:23)
14:24 The crown of wise folk is their wealth, yet the folly of stupid folk is folly.	2. First: begin with a right understanding of wealth (i.e. compassion, 14:24; cf. 14:20–22)
14:25 A truthful witness rescues lives, but one who testifies falsehood embodies deception.	3. Second: speak reliably to effect life-saving compassion (14:25; cf. 14:5–7)

Verse *Translation*	*Outline*
14:26 In reverence for the LORD lies a mighty confidence, and for his children there will be a place of refuge. 14:27 Reverence for the LORD is a spring of life, in order to turn oneself from the snares of death.	4. Third and fourth: pursue reverence, to attain secure building and successful navigation (14:26–27; cf. 14:2, 8–19) a. Building: a secure dwelling ultimately results from reverence (14:26) b. Navigation: lifegiving navigation ultimately traces to reverence (14:27)
14:28 A great mass of people comprises a king's splendour, but zero population comprises a dignitary's ruin.	III. How to build a dynastic house (14:28 – 15:4) A. Advice for superiors (14:28–34) 1. Conventional metric for leadership greatness (14:28)
14:29 Restraining one's own anger amounts to great insight, but a short temper exalts folly. 14:30 An ambition to bring healing to others results in vitality for one's own body, but rottenness of the bones is envy. 14:31 One who exploits the helpless has reproached the one who made him, but one who shows grace to the poor honours him. 14:32 By his wrongdoing a guilty person will be pushed down, but it is a moral person who takes refuge in his death.	2. Corrected metrics for leadership greatness (14:29–32) a. Begin with patience, not anger (14:29) b. Escalate to healing others, not envy (14:30) c. Proceed to extending grace, not exploitation (14:31) d. Incentive: moral choices result in ultimate consequences (14:32)
14:33 In the mind of a perceptive person wisdom will come to rest, and among stupid folk it can be recognized.	3. Conclusion concerning leadership greatness (14:33–34) a. Wisdom commendation: receptivity indicates perception (14:33)

14:34 Morality is what will lift a nation up, but sin brings a populace reproach.	b. Character summary: morality forms the basis for national honour (14:34)
14:35 A king's favour belongs to a skilful servant, but his fury will become a shameful thing. 15:1 A gentle reply can divert rage, but a hurtful word can escalate anger.	B. Advice for subordinates (14:35 – 15:1) 1. A subordinate's dilemma concerning royal favour and fury (14:35) 2. A subordinate's response to fury (15:1)
15:2 The tongue of wise folk will enhance knowledge, but the mouth of stupid folk will gush folly. 15:3 In every place – there are the eyes of the LORD, examining bad folk and good. 15:4 A healing tongue is a tree of life, but when twisted it brings a shattering of spirit.	C. Section conclusion (15:2–4) 1. Wisdom commendation: source of speech determines its worth (15:2) 2. All are accountable to the supreme sovereign (start of wisdom content, 15:3) 3. Aim to specialize in healing speech, not harshness (15:4)
15:5 A fool will spurn his father's reproof, but one who safeguards reprimand develops discretion. 15:6 The house of a moral person is a great treasure, but in the revenue of a guilty person there is calamity.	IV. Lecture conclusion (15:5–6) A. Wisdom commendation: receptivity to reproof (15:5) B. Character summary: morality builds a palace (15:6)

Notes on the text

14:1. 'Women who are wise have built their house', *ḥakmôt nāšîm bāntâ bētâ*: lit. 'wise ones [f.] of [or among] women, she built her house'. The use of the adj. *ḥakmôt* in place of noun *ḥŏkmôt* (as in Prov. 9:1) prevents inferring Lady Wisdom for this expression (so also Waltke 2004: 576, n.). As recognized by translators of the LXX, the writer has in mind those among women who are wise (*sophai gynaikes*). This is one of several places in the HB where a f. pl. subject (*ḥakmôt*) precedes a f. sg. verb (*bāntâ*, not pl. *bānû*; cf. Gen. 49:22, Isa. 59:12, Jer. 2:15 [where Q proposes a pl. verb], and Jer. 48:41). As Waltke also infers, here is a group of wise women, each one of whom shoulders her own load as she constructs her own house (or household; 2004: 576, n.). The saying in 14:1 envisions the ways in which women can influence their households. From this base the sage will proceed to discuss healthy and unhealthy organizational practices.

'Folly': this noun is gendered f., as are many other abstract nouns (e.g. righteousness, truth, wisdom). Although 14:1a refers to wise females, 'folly' in v. 1b designates a trait irrespective of the gender of one who practises it (as also in 14:18; so Fox 2009: 572; *pace* Waltke 2004: 584). Equipped with metaphoric 'hands', Folly here enjoys a preliminary degree of personification. Yet she does not fill so well-developed a role as Dame Folly in Prov. 9 (for which 14:1 may have supplied inspiration, as suggested by Fox [2009: 572]).

14:2. 'walks according to his straight standards': lit. 'is walking in his straightness' or 'honesty'. In 14:2a 'his straight standards' refer to the LORD's standards, not those of the pious person. In v. 2b the expression 'despises him' refers to despising the LORD, while straying along 'his ways' refers to the pathways travelled by the person who despises the LORD. As he travels along his ways, the one who holds the LORD in low esteem will unwittingly wander. The ultimate destination of these wanderings emerges in 14:12.

14:3. 'will safeguard them', *tišmûrēm*: the f. pl. subject 'lips' serves as the subject of this 3 f. sg. verb (where one would expect 3 f. sg. vocalization *tišmĕrēm*, as in Ps. 12:8). As Fox points out, the 3 f. sg. *plene* spelling with *û* is attested in *taʿăbûrî* of Ruth 2:8 (2009: 572). To follow manuscripts and versions that read a 2 m. pl. form (*tišmĕrûm*) only complicates the issue, as it infers a quasi-imperative ('You [pl.] shall guard lips of wise folk'). A genuine imperative occurs in Prov. 14:7a. To infer such in 14:3b significantly disrupts the surrounding texture, which consists of sayings, not instructions with their imperatives.

14:5. 'one who testifies', *yāpîaḥ*: lit. 'a witness' (a substantive with prefixed *y*-, not a yiq. form).

14:7. 'from before', *minneged lĕ*: followed by *lĕ*, the compound prep. *minneged* portrays new separation from a position that previously was both near and opposite, facing, or otherwise closely engaged (cf. Gen. 21:16; 2 Kgs 2:7; Deut. 28:66; *pace* Fox 2009: 574). Thus the sage points out that the pupil must disengage from the present close association between the pupil and his companion, who is stupid.

'since you do not yet distinguish': lit. 'and you do not know' (Waltke similarly regards 14:7b as the cause for v. 7a [2004: 577, n.]).

14:8. 'rendered perceptible', *hābîn*: the hiph. stem of *byn* can convey 'to make perceptible' or 'to teach'.

'the way one should travel': lit. 'his way', implying the direction along which a person should proceed.

'will deceive', *mirmâ*: lit. '[is] deception'. Ostensibly, these folk deceive others. Yet the poet's expression allows that they may fool even themselves. 'Hence the deceit in question is self-delusion' (Fox 2009: 574).

14:9. 'Culpability will scoff', *yālîṣ ʾāšām*: the 3 m. sg. subject required by *yālîṣ*, 'will scoff', is supplied by *ʾāšām*, 'culpability, guilt'. Discord of number means that 'foolish folk' pl. can serve as the subject only by exceptional grammar (as Fox correctly observes [2009: 576]), thus discouraging translations such as 'Fools mock' (NRSV). Instead 'fools' serves as the object, the target of personified culpability's scoffing. Regarding attributing figurative action to an abstract entity such as guilt, note sins' action in Isa. 59:2. As also maintained by Meinhold, this grammar is clear, requiring no emendation (1991: 232; *pace* Waltke 2004: 578; Fox 2009: 575). The sage has composed an intentionally jarring message that indicts the foolish for the immoral deception in which they have indulged (14:8b).

'honest folk', *yĕšārîm*: the root *yšr* is rendered 'straight' in 14:2a and 12a. It consequently contributes to the theme of navigation, even in vv. 9, 11.

14:10. 'A mind knows', *lēb yôdēaʿ*: both terms belong to wisdom vocabulary. Although the connotation of this saying is unmistakably emotional (favouring *lēb* as 'heart' rather than 'mind'), to detect the wisdom flavour of this phrase it is best translated as 'a mind knows'. The sage thus conveys that the discreet behaviour described in this verse depicts how wise people will conduct themselves. This accounts for the outline heading for this verse: 'Discretion evidences wisdom'.

'inner longings', *napšô*: lit. 'soul', 'appetite', 'self'. This term refers to one's inner self, especially in terms of its capacity to register needs or longings.

14:12. 'but in the final analysis, it consists of': lit. 'and its outcome'. The antecedent of 'its' is the deceptive 'way' of 14:12a.

'ways leading to death': lit. 'ways of death'.

14:13. 'Despite laughter': lit. 'even in laughter'.

'heart', *lēb*: often rendered 'mind', the context of psychological anguish recommends rendering *lēb* as 'heart', with its emotion-laden connotations.

'keeps on aching': durative sense inferred from yiq.

'and in the final analysis, joy consists of grief', *wĕʾaḥărîtāh śimḥâ tûgâ*: lit. 'and its outcome [i.e. the outcome of the self-deluded 'way' in 14:12a]: joy [is] grief'. This verbless colon jarringly juxtaposes three noun expressions. In the long run, the sage explains, the façade of joy displayed with such seeming confidence by the self-deluded will reveal an underbelly of gnawing sorrow.

Consequently the message of 14:12–13 may be paraphrased as follows: 'A pattern of conduct founded on morals that are merely self-referential will, over time, result in deadly consequences [v. 12]. Furthermore, although the noise of lighthearted laughter may surround such an ill-authorized pattern of conduct, that laughter will be powerless to cure the heart's ongoing anguish [v. 13a]. Over time that self-deceiving pattern of conduct will crumble, exposing the veneer of joyous laughter for what it truly is – no more than a mask's painted smile – itself an ironic evidence that beneath it lies a pool of irrepressible tears [v. 13b].' (It is important to distinguish the theme of deception at work in the inward–outward contrast of v. 13 [continued from v. 12], not to be confused with the theme of judicious discretion present in the inward–outward contrast of v. 10.)

14:14. 'a deviating mind', *sûg-lēb*: A similar expression in Ps. 44:19 connotes devotion that has been compromised, rather than intellectual redirection. The nature of the deviation grows clearer from Prov. 14:14b. By implication, the 'deviating mind' turns away from completing duties others may reasonably rely on him or her to perform.

'must draw satisfaction': lit. 'will be satisfied'. Obligation is inferred from yiq.

'while far from him', *ûmēʿālāyw*: lit. 'while away from him'. The sage consistently uses this compound prep. to convey separation (cf. Prov. 4:15; 5:8; 24:18; 27:22). While it is appealing to emend to read *ûmimmaʿălĕālyw*, 'from his deeds' (so Waltke 2004: 579, n.; Fox 2009: 578), the Hebr. as it stands is meaningful, underscoring the distance that separates the futile source of satisfaction for a mind that is off-course, when contrasted with the trajectory of a good person. They stand light years apart. Alternatively, the phrase may be rendered 'and from his obligations' (i.e. actions he would be responsible to perform, so Meinhold 1991: 235; cf. 7:14).

'be satisfied': inferred by ellipsis from the first colon.

14:15. 'anything': lit. 'every word' (Waltke 2004: 579, n.).

14:16. 'regards warning seriously and so turns from wrong': lit. 'fears and turns from evil [or misery]'. Although the fear sensed by the wise person may be limited to an awareness of impending harm, it may also imply reverence (so Waltke 2004: 595), since three times in this poem fear is directed towards the LORD (14:2, 26, 27). For that reason an ethical dimension should be detected in *rāʿ*, 'evil' or 'wrong', not a neutral sense of misery.

'gets angry': this term connotes an abundance of angry emotions that overflow their normal restraints. The course correction embraced by the wise person in 14:16a suggests that a warning-laden reproof has come to light. The wise and stupid respond to it in opposite fashions. Versions that omit the dimension of anger miss the connection with anger in v. 17 (alternatives to 'get angry' include 'throws off restraint' [NRSV] and 'is arrogant' [NASB]).

'so self-confident is he': lit. 'and he is trusting'. The sage presents confidence as a concomitant, bound up in the stupid fellow's angry response. Confidence here does not correspond to the admirable sort of reverent reliance elsewhere endorsed by the sage (cf. 3:5–6). Instead the sage is referring to an unfounded attitude of self-reliance. Since in 14:16a the wise person has detected a hazard requiring an evasive manoeuvre (turning away from wrong), the unfounded confidence exhibited by the stupid fellow would amount to this: the stupid fellow dismisses any warning, while boasting to others that the circumstance poses no threat, and so blunders blindly forwards with even increased speed.

14:17. 'A short fuse', *qĕṣar-ʾappayim*: lit. 'shortness of anger'. This measures rapidity of anger's onset, not its duration, and differs little from 'short temper', *qĕṣar-rûaḥ*, in 14:29b.

14:18. 'have bequeathed': often rendered 'to inherit', 'to bequeath' as an alternative meaning follows better the sentiment of generating folly in 14:17a (rather than receiving folly another has produced). Also the notion of passing folly along to the next generation better fits the overarching theme of building a house (to shelter self and dependants), a theme reappearing in 'gates' of v. 19.

'will bestow knowledge as a diadem': lit. 'will throw out crowns consisting of knowledge' (cf. BDB). Although often rendered as wearing, not making, a diadem, the sense of producing and distributing diadems better fits this context with its connotation of creating something that may be bequeathed to others, whether folly (14:18a) or knowledge (v. 18b). Forethought for future generations becomes even clearer in v. 26b.

14:19. 'the gates of a moral person': given the specification 'of a moral person' (note the sg.), these 'gates' mark the entrance to a substantial compound, an estate belonging to a righteous person, not gates of a city governed by a group of righteous individuals (pl.; *pace* Fox 2009: 580).

14:21. 'who is truly fortunate!': lit. 'O, the good fortune (or blessedness) of him!' Customary syntax would locate this phrase ahead of the expression identifying the person. By placing it after, the sage accents the paradox. It is not the crass and manipulative corporate climbers who have achieved supreme success. Rather, it is the compassionate who truly come out ahead.

14:22. 'Will not . . . ?': As a negated polar question, this expression adds marked intensity, suitable for the last verse of a block (Waltke 2004: 581, n.).

'But those who devise good embody faithful love and faithfulness', *ʿwĕḥesed weʾĕmet ḥōrĕšê ṭôb*: lit. 'but faithful love and faithfulness, those who are devising good'. Unlike the first colon, this expression is verbless. The subject ('those who are devising good') is juxtaposed directly with the predicate ('faithful love and faithfulness'), creating an identity statement (Fox 2009: 581). To infer a more nuanced verbal element dissipates the force of this identity statement (*pace BHS* notes, which infer a prep. [*lĕḥōrĕšê ṭôb*], which in turn would account for a translation such as by Waltke: 'and do not the planners of good meet with reliable kindness?' [2004: 581]).

14:23. 'while mere talk': lit. 'but a word of lips'.

14:24. 'crown . . . folly': a mild degree of assonance joins these parallel terms, each of which opens its colon. While the LXX rendition of 'folly' as 'pastime' ('the pastime of stupid folk is folly') removes the tautology, by so doing it loses the insipidity achieved by that very tautology: 'the folly of stupid folk is [i.e. cannot be passed off as anything other than] folly'.

On its surface 14:24a appears to teach that monetary wealth constitutes the 'crown' of the wise – that aspect concerning which the wearer is most proud. Yet the general tenor of the book teaches that a wise person would not measure wealth in monetary terms. If you were to ask the sage, 'What constitutes your true wealth?', he would reply, 'My wisdom – that is my greatest asset.' More specifically, the sage disclosed in 14:21 that to regard the oppressed with compassion constitutes true fortune. In this light, v. 24a means, 'Wisdom – and especially the practice of compassion, constitutes the wise person's "crown jewel." That is what they regard as their greatest asset (i.e. their wealth).'

14:25. 'rescues': lit. 'one who snatches [to safety]'.

'one who testifies': see on 14:5.

'but one who testifies falsehood embodies deception': lit. 'but one who testifies falsehood, deception'. Like 14:22b, this expression presents a verbless identity statement.

14:29. 'short temper', *qĕṣar-rûaḥ*: lit. 'short of spirit'. See note on 'short fuse' (14:17).

14:30. 'An ambition to bring healing to others results in vitality for one's own body', *ḥayyê bĕśārîm lēb marpēʾ*: lit. 'life for flesh is a mind [or heart] of healing'. Two issues surround this verse: whether to translate *marpēʾ* as 'healing' or as 'calm', and if 'healing', whether the healing focuses on others or on self. As to 'healing' or 'calm', Hebr. allows either but favours the first (*pace* Fox, who renders, 'gentle heart' [2009: 584]). As Hebr. favours 'healing', the translator should endeavour first to make sense of that option.

As to bringing healing to others, versus experiencing healing for oneself, the context is helpful. In 14:28, the king and dignitary are set in relation to their subordinates. In v. 29, the emotions of patience and anger assume relationship with others, as also exploitation and showing grace in v. 31. In v. 30b, 'envy' indicates relationship with others. In this context, a heart or mind characterized by healing would be one that responds to those in the surrounding environs so as to spread healing to them.

As the ambition or mind of the individual in 14:30 aims to benefit others, such an outlook coincidentally returns to the healer the immense benefit of vitality. Conversely, in v. 30b envy directed at others afflicts the envious person with inner decay.

'one's own': inferred from the principle of favourable retribution seen earlier in this lecture (14:20–23).

14:31. 'honours him': i.e. the gracious person honours God.

14:32. 'but it is a moral person who takes refuge in his death', *wĕḥoseh bĕmôtô ṣaddîq*: lit. 'but one who takes refuge in his death is a moral person'. Since it is the harder reading, *bĕmôtô*, 'in his death', is likely the original reading (rather than *bĕtummô*, 'in his innocence', as implied by LXX and preferred by Fox [2009: 585]).

At issue is the identity of the dying person, whether the exploiter of 14:32a or the moral individual of v. 32b. If the exploiter, then his initial demise ('pushed down') climaxes in his death, at which point the person he has been oppressing experiences relief – a circuitous sort of refuge (so B. Vater, cited in Fox 2009: 586, n.).

If, on the other hand, it is through the moral person's own death that he 'takes refuge' (experiences relief from hazard), then this constitutes one of the few passages in the HB that looks to the afterlife for ultimate retribution (Waltke 2004: 582, n., 607–608; cf. Heim's thoughtful discussion [2001: 189–190]). This interpretation is grammatically the more straightforward, and would be consonant with the psalmist's expression of hope:

> With your counsel you will guide me,
> and afterwards, into glory you will take me.
> Who is my advocate in the heavens aside from you?
> And, having you, I desire nothing else on earth.
> My flesh and my heart are come to an end;
> God is my heart's rock and my portion, for ever . . .
> As for me, what is good is the nearness of God;
> I have placed my refuge in God the LORD,
> so as to report all of your deeds.
> (Ps. 73:24–26, 28)

14:33. 'it can be recognized', *tiwwādēaʿ*: lit. 'it will be known'. Presumably in order to resolve the paradox of stupid folk gaining insight, LXX inserts a negation: 'it will not be known'. The solution rather should be found in the yiq. conjugation conveying capability. Earlier the sage indicated that due to their arrogant attitude, scoffers prove incapable of securing wisdom, though they may seek it. In contrast, the perceptive find wisdom easily (14:6). Now he extends this principle, showing how deeply the perceptive welcome wisdom (v. 33a). At the same time he allows that even the less perceptive are capable of noticing wisdom (v. 33b).

14:34. 'reproach', *ḥesed*: a wordplay may be at work, since the meaning 'reproach' applies to this word only here in the entire HB. 'Reproach' is homonymous with 'faithful love'. Perhaps the sage had in mind occasions when a self-serving leader attempted to relabel despicable practices by claiming, 'This policy will benefit all,' knowing full well the opposite was true (cf. 13:6).

14:35. 'but his fury will become a shameful thing', *wĕʾebrātô tihyeh mēbîš*: lit. 'but his fury will become something that produces shame'. The person shamed by a display of royal wrath is the person who generated that wrath – the king himself. The shame may dawn gradually; hence the yiq. verb *tihyeh*, 'will become'. Instead to render with NASB (and similarly NRSV) 'but his anger is toward him who acts shamefully' requires a prep. ('toward') absent from the Hebr. saying.

15:4. 'but when twisted it brings a shattering of spirit': lit. 'but a twisting in it [is] a shattering spirit'. 'It' refers to the tongue, as both are f.

15:5. 'one who safeguards', *šōmēr*: mention of 'great treasure' and 'revenue' in 15:6 suggests that *šōmēr* be rendered 'safeguard', not merely 'heed'.

15:6. 'The house of', *bēt*: by flatly equating 'the house of a moral person' with 'great treasure', the sage links the close of the lecture with its beginning. The metaphoric 'house' (encompassing household, organization, even nation) concerning which the sage has lectured carefully since 14:1 – this securely built house constitutes the treasure. If the poet had intended to say 'in the house of the moral is great treasure', he would have supplied the prep. 'in' (*bĕbēt* in place of *bēt*; *pace* Fox 2009: 590–591, who follows Targum, Syriac and LXX). Waltke properly cautions against this emendation: 'The metaphor of the MT and Vulg[ate] is the harder reading and so preferable' (2004: 616).

Form and structure

Borders

The quest for true satisfaction (preceding poem) gives way to counsel for building one's 'house' (present poem). A wisdom commendation initiates the new theme, marking the upper border (14:1).

The lower border is indicated by a character summary (15:6), by an inclusio involving 'house' (14:1; 15:6) and by three closural features appearing in Section IV (15:5–6). First, by referring to the pupil's father as a reliable source of wisdom (15:5), the sage recalls roles within the domestic household (14:1) as well as the importance of securing reliable sources of information (14:5–7). Second, the terms 'great' and 'revenue' in 15:6 recall the phrase 'great revenue' in 14:4. Third, mention of 'great treasure' in the moral person's house (15:6a) recalls the sage's redefinition of wealth in terms of the worth of a person (14:20–22).

Macrostructural features

Thematic continuity regarding build-and-collapse (Sections I, II, III and IV, content-based). The theme creating greatest cohesion across this lecture involves the positive and negative counterparts, build-and-collapse. Expressions that contribute to the positive portion (build) include terms for architecture (house in 14:1, 11; 15:6; tent in 14:11; gates in 14:19), for shelter (mighty confidence and place of refuge, both in 14:26), together with associated verbs (to build in 14:1, and finding refuge in 14:32).

The following expressions contribute to the negative half of the theme (collapse): 'demolish' (14:1), 'to be destroyed' (14:11), 'ruin' (14:28), 'to be pushed down' (14:32), also 'twisting' (since it also may be rendered 'ruin') and 'to shatter' (both in 15:4). Especially noteworthy is the object within that final entry: 'a shattering of spirit' (15:4). There at last the sage dispenses with the metaphor of a physical structure (a house). All along, the ultimate aim of this lecture centres on how a leader values persons – whether one abusively diminishes or graciously affirms the worth already conferred on them by their Maker (14:21a, 31).

Each section participates in the build-and-collapse theme. As later macrostructures will show, often this theme occurs at structurally significant junctures.

Repetition of word-pair 'wise' and 'foolish' (Sections I, II and III, form-based). Of the fourteen sayings in Proverbs that contain word-pairs tracing to the roots *ḥkm*, 'wise', and *ʾwl*, 'foolish', five appear in this lecture (14:1, 3, 8, 24; 15:2). Each displays strategic positioning, beginning with the opening verse (14:1). There the poet anchors the metaphors of the domestic house and of navigation, introducing concepts Section II will expand. The second instance of the word-pair initiates the second block (Block I.B, 14:3–4), which anticipates Section III and the topic of building a dynastic house. When the word-pair next appears (14:8), it begins this lecture's most extensive block (Block II.B, 14:8–19).

The fourth saying mentioning wise and foolish (14:24) similarly occurs in Section II. That saying is the first of four verses (vv. 24–27), which together review the four themes in Section II (wealth, reliable information, building and navigation). Only an initial call to action in v. 23 precedes the cluster of four review sayings of Block II.D, concluding Section II.

The last instance of the wise–foolish word-pair occurs in 15:2. This saying is structurally significant since it opens the final block of Section III (Block III.C, 15:2–4).

Framing with metaphors of navigation and building (Sections I and II, content-based). The metaphors of building and navigation appear in 14:1 and 2, respectively. Terms associated with these metaphors frame two subsequent portions (navigation ['travel'] in 14:8 and buildings ['house' and 'tent'] in v. 11 frame Segment II.B.1.a; navigation ['ways' and 'deviating'] in 14:14 and building ['gates'] in v. 19 frame Unit II.B.2).

The five sayings of Block II.D close by referring to building ['a place of refuge'] in 14:26 and navigation ['to turn from'] in v. 27. Appearance of these themes at this point contributes to closure for Section II.

Framing with 'wisdom' and 'house' (Sections I and II, form-based). Section I mentions 'wise' and 'house' in the lecture's first colon (14:1a). 'House' next appears in v. 11, closing a four-verse portion that began with 'wisdom' (v. 8), fostering a frame for Segment II.B.1.a (14:8–11). Non-structural instances of 'wise' occur in vv. 3, 6, 24.

Thematic continuity concerning navigation (Sections I and II, content-based). The second saying of Section I introduces the concept of navigation with the expressions 'to walk', 'straight', 'to stray' and 'ways' (14:2). Section II develops this metaphor with nine instances spread over eight of the twenty-three verses found in that section. These include 'depart' (14:7), 'way' (vv. 8, 12, 12, 14), 'step' (v. 15), 'turn' (v. 16) and 'wander' (v. 22), ending with a second mention of 'turn' (v. 27). No further expressions dealing with navigation appear in this poem.

Section-level closure involving theme of building-and-collapse (Sections I and II, content-based). As noted above, in the lecture's first verse the term 'house' initiates the general theme of buildings as a source of security (14:1, Section I). Within Section II, the expressions 'mighty confidence' and 'place of refuge' belong to the semantic field of shelter (both in 14:26). Since they occur within the final block of a section (Block II.D), these expressions contribute to closure for their section. By describing these shelters as exceptionally secure and extensive enough to provide multigenerational safety, the sage expands exponentially the notion of 'house' as a source of security.

Section-level closure involving reverence (Sections I and II, form-based). The sage commends reverence for the LORD early in Section I (14:2). Within this lecture, reverence for the LORD appears twice more – in a quatrain that concludes Section II (14:26, 27), creating closure for that section.

Thematic continuity concerning national leadership (Sections I and III, content-based). Section I presents intimations of a national perspective that Section III develops extensively. Consider first the evidence of a national or monarchial perspective in Section III. From its opening line, Section III envisions an enterprise grander than the domestic house (note 'king', 'crowd of people' and 'dignitary' in 14:28, opening Block III.A). The second block similarly mentions kings and servants in its first line (14:35, Block III.B). The following elements in Section III also comport well with securing a dynastic (rather than domestic) house. A leader may engage in abusive anger, cautioned against in 14:29. One can envision that a ruler wielding power may need counsel against misguided ambition, envy and exploitation of helpless persons (14:30–31). An interest in national well-being appears when the sage observes, 'Morality is what will lift a nation up, but sin brings a populace reproach' (14:34). Just as fury in 14:35 issues explicitly from a monarch, it is likely that rage and anger in the next verse similarly envision a royal source (15:1). When the sage in 15:2 refers to wise persons who 'enhance knowledge', he likely envisions councillors who behave shrewdly when their monarch is enraged (cf. 14:35 – 15:1). Instead of reacting to royal animus with abrasive counter-challenges (thereby 'gushing folly' like stupid folk, 15:2b), the wise advisor will supply the king with additional information. Such councillors will seek to broaden the monarch's perspective, encouraging him to take into consideration critical factors (such as the harmful fallout of explosive wrath) that in his hasty rage he might have overlooked.

Turning to Section I, intimations of a national perspective appear there already. The description of harsh corporal punishment ('an arrogant rod'), while not uniquely designating a monarch, evokes a picture of power manipulated with excessive cruelty (14:3).

In addition, the terms *ʾălāpîm*, 'cattle', and *šôr*, 'ox', in 14:4 lay the groundwork for a perspective grander than domestic 'houses'. Consider first *ʾălāpîm*. While appropriately rendered 'cattle' in 14:4, in other settings that same term is rendered 'thousands' of people, whether large subgroups of the Israelite population (Num. 1:16) or military troops (Num. 31:14). Thus *ʾălāpîm* offers a wordplay hinting at a multitude of people.

Consider next *šôr*, 'ox', also in 14:4. Aside from Prov. 14:4, *šôr* and *ʾălāpîm* appear together only in Deut. 33:17. That Deuteronomic passage appears within Moses' benedictory poem, occurring in the stanza most descriptive of leadership influence (the blessing of Joseph, Deut. 33:13–17). There 'ox' represents a leader noted for strength. In Deut. 33:17, *ʾălāpîm* refers to thousands of people (not cattle). In this way Section I introduces a national perspective, which Section III develops at length.

Similar section conclusions (Sections II and III, form-based). Both Sections II and III close with mention of 'LORD' and 'life' in their final two verses (14:26–27; 15:3–4). They combine to contribute a sense of ultimacy to these section endings.

Section-level closure involving speech and life (Sections II and III, form-based). Closure results from mention of 'tongue' and 'tree of life' in 15:4 (Section III). Speech and parts of the mouth appeared earlier in Sections II (14:23) and III (15:1–2). 'Life' appeared previously in the last saying of Section II (14:27), as well as in 14:30 (Section III).

Microstructural features

Section I (14:1–4). *Wisdom commendation and wisdom content verse-pairs (14:1–2, 3–4, content-based).* A verse of wisdom commendation in 14:1 pairs with one verse of wisdom content in v. 2. When this pairing repeats in vv. 3–4, it delineates two blocks comprising Section I (*pace* Heim, who notes the similarity of vv. 1, 3 and, by overlooking commendation-plus-content pairing that encompasses v. 4, infers an inclusio of vv. 1–3 [2001: 171]).

Thematic continuity regarding rule (14:3–4, content-based). A theme of rule or power unites Block I.B (14:3–4). An arrogant rod (referring to the fool's speech) portrays abuse of power (v. 3a). 'Safeguard' issuing through the speech of the wise similarly implies that some risk victimization due to abusive rule (v. 3b).

'The strength of an ox' also contributes to the theme of power, exercised not for abuse, but for productivity. As observed in a macrostructure above, the terms 'cattle' and 'ox' in 14:4 may connote, respectively, a group of people and a powerful ruler who leads them (see above, under macro-structures involving Section III). Although community life may get messy (v. 4a), strong and wise leadership can bring the reward of revenue.

Section II (14:5–27). *Thematic continuity involving reliable information (14:5–7, content-based).* The expressions 'falsehood' and 'false witness' in 14:5 introduce for Block II.A the theme of differentiating between deceptive and trustworthy sources of information (14:5–7). That theme continues in v. 6 with the quest for wisdom information, extending into v. 7 with the need to 'distinguish knowledgeable speech' (also Waltke notices that speech-source links vv. 5–7 [2004: 584]).

Thematic continuity involving deception (14:5, 8, content-based). By recycling in the opening verse of Block II.B the idea of deception ('the folly of stupid folk will deceive', 14:8b), the sage forms a connection with the misleading witness of v. 5 (Block II.A). In view of v. 8, the deceptive witness is not clever, but stupid. He will lose his way.

Portions opening with 'way' (14:8, 12, 14, form-based). When the term 'way' occurs in Section II, it appears in the first colon of a saying that opens a portion (14:8–11, 12–13, 14–19). Within this lecture, 'way' appears only once more (14:2).

Framing with themes of navigation and building (14:8–11, 14–19, content-based). As noted in connection with macrostructural devices, the themes of navigation and building combine to frame two independent portions within Section II. Both Segment II.B.1.a and Unit II.B.2 open with navigation and end with some component of a building (14:8–11, 14–19). Evidence of the navigation and building themes undermines Garrett's proposal concerning a palistrophe spanning 14:8–15 (1993: 142–143).

Alternating themes of discretion and morality (14:8–11, content-based). The four verses of Segment II.B.1.a (14:8–11) oscillate evenly between the themes of discretion and moral conduct. 'Discretion' appears in 14:8 ('Wisdom characterized by discretion'), while morality emerges in v. 9 ('culpability' and 'honest'). Discretion returns in 14:10 as the sage describes one who excludes a stranger from participating in his or her inmost feelings. Moral conduct reappears in 14:11 as within a character summary guilty folk are contrasted with the honest.

Character summary concluding a segment (14:11, content-based). A character summary in 14:11 closes a four-verse segment spanning vv. 8–11 (Segment II.B.1.a). Whether one suffers demise or flourishes will depend on whether one is numbered among the guilty or the honest.

Repetition of 'in the final analysis' (14:12, 13, form-based). The expression 'in the final analysis' occurs in both 14:12b and 13b, joining these adjacent sayings into a single segment (Segment II.B.1.b).

Palistrophe (14:14–19, content-based). The six verses comprising Unit II.B.2 (14:14–19) form a palistrophe of three steps. The theme of anger joins vv. 16 and 17 to form the core or pivot. The word-pair 'naive' and 'discreet' appears in each saying alongside the core (vv. 15, 18). Although 'discreet' appears elsewhere in this lecture, only in these verses does 'naive' occur. (Waltke similarly links vv. 15 and 18 through this word-pair as a framing inclusio; he does not include additional elements of the palistrophe encompassing vv. 14–19 [2004: 594].)

Each saying in the next palistrophic step features the adj. 'good' (14:14, 19). While this adj. appears also in 14:22 and 15:3, it seems beyond coincidence that its first two occurrences are positioned to enlarge the palistrophe. As noted elsewhere, these outermost orbits of the palistrophic structure also feature the twin themes of navigation (v. 14) and building (v. 19).

One observation arises from this palistrophe. By lodging it at the palistrophic core, the sage stresses the hazard of combustible, defensive anger.

Character summary (14:19, content-based). The stark contrast of 'bad' and 'good folk', of 'guilty' and 'moral' persons constitutes a character summary in 14:19. It helps to mark the close of Block II.B (14:8–19).

Repetition of the word-pair 'bad' and 'good' (14:19, 22, form-based). Twice the antonymous word-pair *rāʿ*, 'bad' or 'misery', and *ṭôb*, 'good', appears in the last saying of a block (14:19 closes vv. 8–19 [Block II.B], while 14:22 closes vv. 20–22 [Block II.C]). Waltke also senses closure in 14:22 through mention of 'good' and 'bad' (2004: 600). The word-pair appears once more in 15:3, near the close of Section III (14:28 – 15:4).

Thematic continuity involving wealth (14:18, 19, 20, 21, content-based). 'Diadem' (14:18) and 'gates' of a residence (v. 19) introduce the theme of wealth at the close of Block II.B. That theme expands in Block II.C with the expressions 'poor' and 'wealthy' (v. 20), and 'fortunate' (v. 21).

Intensification by rhetorical question and progression of thought (14:22, content-based). The persuasive impact of Block II.C (14:20–22) intensifies by posing a rhetorical question in its last verse ('Will they not wander . . . ?'). Also, the attitude that began by 'despising' a neighbour in v. 21 now sharpens to the point of 'devising misery' in v. 22.

Section-level closure by review of topics (14:23–27, content-based). The last four sayings of Section II contribute to closure by reviewing four topics introduced in the previous three blocks of that section. The first defines true wealth in terms of wisdom (14:24), linking to teaching about wealth and the worth of the individual (Block II.C, 14:20–22). The second associates the words of a reliable witness with rescuing lives (14:25), recalling the importance of reliable witnesses as sources of information (Block II.A, 14:5–7). The third asserts that reverence results in 'a mighty confidence' and 'a place of refuge' both for the pupil and for his family (14:26), recalling the theme of a secure building – a theme that marked portion-endings within Block II.B (at 14:11, 19). The fourth saying explains that reverence is required for effective navigation (14:27), recalling the theme of travel that marked the start of three portions in Section II (14:8, 12, 14).

Closure by repetition of terms (14:23–27, form-based). Mention of 'deception' in 14:25 and 'death' in 14:27 contributes to closure for the final block of Section II (Block II.D, 14:23–27). 'Deception' earlier appeared in 14:8, while 'death' appeared in 14:12. In all four instances these terms occur in line-terminal position.

Section III (14:28 – 15:4). *Thematic continuity concerning national leadership (14:28 – 15:4, content-based).* Just as Section II focused on strengthening the domestic 'house' or family, Section III coheres by supplying advice for a strong nation or dynasty (see 'Thematic continuity concerning national leadership' under 'Macrostructural features', above).

Progression leading to mortal climax (14:29–32, content-based). A progression of malevolence begins in 14:29, ending with a climactic (and paradoxical) victory achieved by the moral person (14:32). Malevolence begins in anger badly managed (v. 29). This escalates to scheming envy (v. 30). Next comes exploitation (v. 31) and vivid oppression, where the victim is 'pushed down' (v. 32a). Consequently when in v. 32b even death cannot thwart the moral person from achieving refuge, this marks climactic failure of evil and a correspondingly stunning retributive victory for the moral person (Waltke 2004: 607; cf. 'Notes', above).

Wisdom commendations opening distinct portions (14:33; 15:2, content-based). Wisdom commendations appear in both 14:33 and 15:2. Each saying opens a portion, whether Unit III.A.3 (14:33–34) or Block III.C (15:2–4).

Character summary concluding a unit (14:34, content-based). Unit III.A.3 spans only two verses. As noted above, it begins with a wisdom commendation (14:33). It closes directly with a character summary offering moral counsel on a national scale (14:34).

Thematic continuity involving anger (14:35 – 15:1, content-based). The quatrain spanning 14:35 – 15:1 coheres in the theme of hostile emotion (fury, rage, anger). Due to the royal context of 14:35, the principal exponent of rage envisioned in 15:1 is the monarch. As Fox observes, chapter divisions periodically obscure cohesion joining adjacent sayings (2009: 588).

Continuity and inclusio (15:2–4, form-based). 'Tongue' is mentioned in both 15:2 and v. 4, fostering an inclusio for the block spanning these three verses (Block III.C). The root meaning 'good' forms a continuity linking v. 2 (rendered 'enhance') with v. 3 (so also Waltke, who recognizes a new portion beginning in 15:5 [2004: 614–615]).

Closure (15:2–4, content-based). Since speech featured prominently in Section III, mention of tongue (15:2, 4) and mouth (v. 2) in that section's final block fosters closure. The 'tongue of wise folk' in 15:2 follows fittingly the earlier exhortation to give 'a gentle reply' (15:1). The caution against use of the tongue to shatter the spirit recalls the harm perpetrated by royal rage in 14:35 – 15:1. 'Healing' and 'life' in 15:4 recall the same terms from 14:30 (also in Section III).

Section IV (15:5–6). *Wisdom commendation opening a portion (15:5, content-based).* Three elements combine to render the wisdom commendation that opens Section IV particularly potent (15:5). They involve an attitude of receptivity, the highest-value (and most disagreeable) wisdom commodity of 'reproof' (also 'reprimand') and a parent as the source of that corrective counsel. Such an intense wisdom commendation directs sharp focus on the wisdom content to follow, a lecture-closing character summary (v. 6; the compact combination of wisdom commendation followed directly by character summary also appeared in 14:33–34).

Character summary concluding a section (15:6, content-based). A character summary concludes Section IV – and with it the entire lecture (15:6). The moral person with his or her 'great treasure' (associated with his 'house[hold]') starkly contrasts the calamity harvested by the guilty. For a review of inclusio and closural features operating in Section IV, please refer to 'Borders' (above).

Comment

Section I (14:1–4). Both domestic and dynastic houses are anticipated in Section I (14:1–4), with two verses devoted to each level. Section II expands on the domestic level, while Section III develops the dynastic level.

In the initial verse of Section I, reference to women who are establishing their house signals the domestic level of relationships – the cultivation of one's household or family (14:1). Reverence is paramount for this enterprise (14:2). The sage will doubly underscore reverence in 14:26–27, at the close of Section II – the section that develops the domestic house.

Just as Block I.A introduces the domestic house (14:1–2), so Block I.B introduces the dynastic house (14:3–4). Without yet naming the monarch's role, the power of a rod and the productive potential of an ox suggest a domain exceeding domestic (see explanation of 'ox' under 'Thematic continuity concerning national leadership', within macrostructures, above). Section III (14:28 – 15:4) focuses on counsel for a dynastic house, naming the king in 14:28, 35.

Dynastic well-being requires the leader to curb his or her bent towards abuse of power (14:3). As for the commoner, to enjoy the sort of corporate productivity made possible through strong leadership, one must learn to put up with the messiness such a leader will leave behind (14:4).

14:1. Similarity of expressions in 9:1 and 14:1 leads Waltke to infer a section beginning in 14:1, as in 9:1 (2004: 583).

14:1–2. Waltke's proposal to link vv. 6–7 with vv. 1–2 palistrophically would be more defensible if the imperative of v. 7 mirrored an imperative in vv. 1–2 (2004: 583).

Section II (14:5–27). *Block II.A (14:5–7).* The next section divides into four blocks that present extensive counsel enhancing the operation of a domestic house. The first establishes the importance of obtaining reliable information (Block II.A, 14:5–7). Since this block is not principally concerned with the judicial system, the opening teaching concerning true and false witnesses functions as a deployed proverb distinguishing between true and false information (14:5; cf. the deployed proverb about the fowler in 1:17). Like a trial process, wisdom also cannot operate without discovering reliable information – known as 'trustworthy witnesses'. To this metaphor the sage will return in the review (14:25 within 14:23–27).

Looking still farther ahead, the concept of a reliable wisdom source (corresponding to a faithful witness) will reappear in the conclusion of Section IV. There the sage will elevate the youth's father as a worthy source of reproof (15:5).

Block II.B (14:8–19). After counselling the pupil to concentrate on reliable information sources as a first step towards gaining wisdom (Block II.A, 14:5–7), in Block II.B (vv. 8–19) the sage recommends discretion and moral conduct (Segment II.B.1.a, vv. 8–11). The twin traits of discretion and moral conduct will enable the pupil both to successfully 'navigate' his life-journey (14:8) and to 'build his house' securely (14:11), thus book-ending that segment with metaphors drawn from 14:2 (navigation) and 14:1 (building).

The paired traits of discretion and moral conduct oscillate evenly through 14:8–11. First to appear is discretion – the aptitude necessary for effective navigation (v. 8). Failing discretion, the fool will fool only himself (v. 8b). Moral conduct then appears, signalled by honesty and contrasted by culpability (v. 9). The folly that deceived the stupid in v. 8b the sage now exposes. Fools who made light of wrongdoing will become the butt of ridicule spawned by their own guilt (v. 9a).

The trait of discretion returns in 14:10 as the sage implies that a mind knowledgeable concerning heartache will not divulge to strangers its innermost experiences. The sage here may envision the knowledgeable leader of an organization – one whose access to confidential information requires him or her to shoulder certain of the pains and pleasures of leadership in complete solitude.

Morality reappears in 14:11 through a character summary contrasting guilt with honesty. To show that he has not drifted from the lecture's original focus, the poet employs the metaphor of dismantling a 'house' (line-initial). Although the guilty may boast a grand house, their guilt guarantees its collapse. Others, in contrast, inhabit but a mere tent. Yet their meagre tent will endure and flourish, anchored in honesty (recycling 'honesty' from v. 9).

In the next segment the sage urges scrutiny of the eventual destination of one's chosen path (Segment II.B.1.b, 14:12–13). Such scrutiny presumes discretion. Discretion is not optional, but mission-essential. Lacking discretion, the traveller will mistake his or her way, finally arriving at a deadly destination only thinly concealed by hollow hilarity. When the purported 'straightness' of one's route derives from self-referential ethics rather than divine reverence (recall 'straight' from v. 2a), navigation will fail fatally (v. 12; note link to concept of deception in v. 8b).

The notion of a deceptive façade of purportedly dependable navigation (14:12) colours the meaning of v. 13 as well. Superficial laughter in v. 13a corresponds to hollow navigational reassurances of v. 12a that intone, 'Don't worry about me – I know where I'm heading.' The aching heart of v. 13 corresponds to the hidden fears of the outwardly confident traveller – one who has substituted self-reference for divine reverence (v. 12). Over time, grief will erode the confident façade, as deception ultimately escorts this traveller to a destination devoid of any laughter (note the parallel concept of ultimacy in vv. 12b and 13b). Unlike the healthy partition separating public persona from private in the life of the discreet leader (v. 10), the barrier that in v. 13 separates external cheer from inward anguish anchors in the shifting sands of self-referential morality. It will collapse with passage of time.

After first introducing the dual topics of domestic and dynastic well-being (Section I), to this point in Section II the sage has urged his pupil to begin building his domestic house by obtaining reliable information (Block II.A). After securing solid counsel, he is ready to 'navigate' the 'building' of his 'house' through discretion and moral conduct (Segment II.B.1.a, 14:8–11). Along that route, he must guard against indulging in self-referential ethics, or else in the end he will be dismayed to discover that he has veered into a concealed and catastrophic conclusion (Segment II.B.1.b, 14:12–13).

Such a warning would seem a sufficiently climactic ending for the sage's lessons about navigating and building through discretion and morality. But the sage determined to add two more ingredients: (a) a caution against hurtful anger, and (b) consideration of generational consequences. These the sage unfolds in Unit II.B.2 (14:14–19).

That six-verse unit (incidentally, a palistrophe) begins with a two-verse review (14:14–15). Here the sage points out that, for good or ill, satisfaction will depend entirely on which route one chooses to navigate – whether moral or immoral (v. 14; note the concept of satisfaction, which featured prominently in the preceding lecture). Then follows a caution against indiscriminate trust (v. 15). Reminiscent of the importance of reliable information (vv. 5–7), the sage urges discretion. Only those who begin their journey with reliable counsel (v. 15) will be able to choose their steps safely (v. 14).

After these two review teachings, in his third point the sage takes up the issue of anger (14:16). Whereas a wise person responds to reliable counsel by drawing his foot back from a hazardous step, a stupid fellow responds by overflowing with anger, foolishly confident that his own insight is superior to any cautionary alarm others may sound (reminiscent of 14:12; cf. 3:5b).

The fourth statement continues to focus on anger (14:17, linking palistrophically to anger in v. 16). Folly that refuses warning (v. 16) now bursts forth with anger, which in turn spawns still more folly, yet with one sinister expansion. Now folly sets itself to scheming. At this point the fool has blundered forward and tripped, his ears resolutely plugged so as not to hear the navigational warnings issued by others. Upon getting up again, he angrily maligns those nearby. He determines (schemes) to lay blame and bring harm to whoever may be at fault for his recent demise. For surely, he protests, he cannot possibly be blamed for his own downfall! Is it any wonder that others come to hate him (v. 17b)?

The fifth statement of Unit II.B.2 extends the trajectories of the discreet in contrast to the naive, envisioning how they will influence their future generations (14:18, linking palistrophically to 'naive' and 'discreet' in v. 15). As for the naive, who believe all and stumble, who then respond with anger, who begin to scheme and so make enemies – the only inheritance they have amassed for their descendants consists of a bumper crop of folly. In contrast, those who began by exercising discretion in their search for trustworthy information will ultimately fashion out of knowledge precious diadems, presumably passing these heirlooms along to their offspring.

The sage concludes Unit II.B.2 with a double character summary ('bad folk', 'good folk', 'the guilty' and 'a moral person' in 14:19, with 'good folk' linking palistrophically to 'good person' in v. 14). He depicts how conduct will lead either to humiliation or to exaltation, depending on its moral character. To portray the success of the moral person, the sage envisions the enclosure of a wealthy estate, guarded by a gate (notice the language of a building, balancing language of navigation in palistrophically linked v. 14). To portray the failure of the guilty person, the sage envisions him arriving at that same gate, humbly bowing. His bowed posture indicates social demotion occasioned by his prior moral collapse.

Block II.C (14:20–22). While Block II.B emphasized moral conduct generally, Block II.C focuses on a specific aspect of moral conduct: the valuation of material wealth, relative to the worth of a person (14:20–22). People easily resent a poor neighbour, being attracted instead to a rich person (v. 20). Such a value system stands on its head a system of godly ethics (v. 21a). In contrast, right-side-up ethics recognizes in the genuinely needy a paradoxical opportunity to acquire authentic wealth – the by-product of generosity motivated by compassion (v. 21b).

The sage intensifies the conclusion of Block II.C with a rhetorical question which exposes the fact that by overlooking compassion one may devolve into inflicting misery (14:22a; Waltke 2004: 600). The sage leaves open whether that misery is destined for the ill-used person, or reciprocally for the short-sighted miser. To devise misery ultimately proves counterproductive, since it steers the traveller off-course, thwarting the greater goal of navigation (v. 22a). In contrast, for the compassionate 'faithful love and faithfulness' take on mythic proportions, determining good for the generous (v. 22b). These traits are among the core qualities of the divine (Waltke 2004: 600; cf. Exod. 34:6).

Block II.D (14:23–27). The sage recaps in a section conclusion (Block II.D, 14:23–27) four teachings that recall the first three blocks of Section II

(14:5–22). Before revisiting these four earlier pieces of advice, he impresses on the pupil the importance of execution (14:23). Notwithstanding its enthralling sound, mere talk will benefit nothing. What one requires is decisive action.

The topic of genuine wealth (the most recent principle in Block II.C, 14:20–22) the sage reviews first (14:24). When he states that 'The crown of wise folk is their wealth,' he intends the pupil to recall his earlier definition of genuine wealth. A person will accumulate true wealth in direct proportion to his or her compassionate response to persons in need (14:21). Such is the wealth wise folk are pleased to wear as a crown.

The second point of review (14:25) assumes that the pupil has endorsed the first (valuing persons above material riches). Consequently rescuing lives would matter immensely to such an individual. Rescue, the sage explains, results from reliable information ('a trustworthy witness'). If the connection between informant and rescue seems remote, consider that one who 'bears witness' by informing a neighbour his house is on fire becomes a rescuer by supplying that vital information. The connotation of 'witness' should not be limited to a judicial process, as observed when the term occurred in Block II.A (14:5–7). Thus 14:25 reviews the first teaching of Section II, just as 14:24 reviewed Block II.C, the last teaching prior to the present Block II.D.

The third and fourth elements of review recycle the metaphors of building a secure house (14:26) and navigating a road (v. 27). With these motifs, the sage reaches back – in the same sequence – to the first and second verses of the entire lecture (14:1, 2). He assures that reverence for the LORD will result in unassailable security, not only for the pious person, but for his descendants as well (14:26). As one reveres the LORD, he or she will be able to navigate in a manner that sidesteps deadly snares, securing instead an endless supply of life (14:27).

Line-initial mention of fear of the LORD in both 14:26 and 27 underscores the same point introduced in 14:2. Since reverence is largely synonymous with moral conduct, by mentioning reverence twice in this closing quatrain of Section II, the sage effects a review of moral conduct, a priority repeatedly emphasized in Block II.B (14:8–19).

14:7. A similar call to dissociate appeared in 1:15.

14:8. Whom does their folly deceive? Others, thinking it is wise? Or themselves, thinking it clever?

Waltke proposes a four-step palistrophe spanning 14:8–15, centred on vv. 11, 12 (2004: 588). This accounts for the repetition of 'discretion' in vv. 8, 15, and 'mind' in vv. 10, 13. However, themes of navigation and house building, together with a palistrophe spanning vv. 14–19, suggest a different configuration (see 'Microstructural features' for Section II, above).

14:12. 'The house of the wicked is annihilated [v. 11a] because it is built on the flimsy foundation of human epistemology, the relative truth accessible to human sight' (Waltke 2004: 592). Since this saying reappears at 16:25, the sage must have valued it highly.

14:15. 'The gullible does not give heed to his lifestyle, and the shrewd, who keep [*sic*] a wary eye against one false step, does not rely on human opinion' (Waltke 2004: 593).

14:21. For generosity, see 11:25.

14:23. Waltke detects an intensification at 14:23 (2004: 601) – fitting preparation for the lecture's four-part review that unfolds directly in vv. 24–27.

14:26. This saying contributes to the theme of sheltering architecture, since *mibṭaḥ*, 'confidence', and *maḥseh*, 'a place of refuge', can refer to physical structures (for *mibṭaḥ*, a spider's 'house' [i.e. web] in Job 8:14, a tent in Job 18:14; for *maḥseh*, cliffs that shelter animals, Ps. 104:18).

14:26–27. Reverence for the LORD appears in adjacent verses only here and in Isa. 11:2–3.

14:27. This saying draws on a principal instruction from the preceding poem concerning wealth in relationships (13:14).

Section III (14:28 – 15:4). *Block III.A (14:28–34).* After a four-point review of Section II in its final block (14:23–27), a new section suitably opens with the next saying (v. 28). Here the sage turns from advice concerning a domestic house, treating instead issues related to rulers and the development of a dynastic house (Section III, 14:28 – 15:4). The sage fashions counsel both for superiors (Block III.A, 14:28–34) and subordinates (Block III.B, 14:35 – 15:1). This section ends with a three-verse conclusion (Block III.C, 15:2–4).

The sage opens his teaching about rulers with a commonly accepted metric of greatness: a leader's worth can be measured by the size of the group he leads (14:28). The conventional wisdom of such a statement is calculated to win easy confirmation by the audience. However, in the four sayings that follow, the sage will move in a different direction (14:29–32). These sayings make it clear that the sage discards the metric of 'bigger is better' – regarding it as inadequate at best, and at worst misleading. An escalation from inner attitude (whether anger or patience) to outward action (exploitation or grace) marks these four steps, ending with ultimate consequences (concerning the progression from v. 30 to v. 31 see Waltke 2004: 607).

When 'greatness' that is found in 14:28 returns in the next verse, it is instructive to observe that it refers to greatness of insight, not of population (v. 29). Instead of population-control, the sage advises anger-control. For the sage, the first step in greatness consists of self-control when irritated or wronged.

If the scenario in 14:29 envisions patience when wronged, v. 30 portrays even greater kindness. Now the offended leader goes so far as to restore ('heal') the offender. Refusal to do so, the sage explains, inevitably will infect the offended leader with deep decay.

The fact that the sage mentions grace in the next verse (14:31b) suggests that the anger in v. 29 came in response to an offence. In such a case, the offended superior may opt either for oppression (v. 31a) or for grace (v. 31b). Lest the leader take this choice lightly, the sage observes that the Maker sides with the poor (that person subject to the leader's whims), so that responses of cruelty or kindness shown to the poor have an impact on their Maker as well.

The fourth and final corrective to the notion that 'bigger is better' unfolds as an incentive statement (14:32). There is good reason why one should restrain anger, exhibit gentleness and extend grace. Failure to do so will result in the abusive leader himself suffering demotion (being 'pushed down'). In contrast, one who embraces this moral teaching will attain an ultimate 'refuge' (v. 32b; see 'Notes'). A shelter so secure as this constitutes an impregnable dynastic house, highly desirable to any leader.

After redefining dynastic greatness from a leader's perspective in the first five verses of Section III.A (Units III.A.1–2, 14:28–32), the sage issues a concentrated wisdom commendation (v. 33), signalling he wishes to focus attention on a particular saying that will follow in v. 34. In that next saying, by means of a character summary, he reduces the formula for national benefit-and-harm to a single determining factor. Just as moral misconduct will abase an individual (v. 32), conversely an entire nation will be exalted to the extent that it pursues a course of morality (v. 34a). Sin, in contrast, will bring national (and dynastic) disgrace (v. 34b).

Block III.B (14:35 – 15:1). Having counselled leaders in Block III.A, the sage advises subordinates in Block III.B (14:35 – 15:1). By mentioning 'king' in 14:35 the sage shows that the dynastic perspective persists in these verses. Consequently 'servant' of 14:35 envisions primarily a court official.

Just as leadership training at the dynastic level first addressed the leader's need to restrain his or her anger (14:29), so the topic of anger returns as the sage advises subordinates. They should execute with skill any duties assigned by the king, so as to earn his favour and not his fury (14:35). But if one should happen to encounter a king's rage, the preferred response of gentleness will de-escalate confrontation (15:1). Direct opposition would only fan the flames.

Block III.C (15:2–4). The next three verses conclude Section III. They consist of a wisdom commendation followed by two sayings that reinforce principles already presented in this section (15:2–4). Through the wisdom commendation the sage implicitly urges the pupil to seek out wise people, as they will supply knowledge worth hearing (15:2; cf. Block II.A, 14:5–7).

After the wisdom commendation of 15:2, the first of two sayings reminds the pupil that the LORD is everywhere watching and assessing conduct (v. 3). This divine perspective was last seen when the sage urged leaders to extend grace to the less fortunate, since 'one who exploits the helpless has reproached the one who made him, but one who shows grace to the poor honours him' (14:31).

The second saying employs the term 'healing' (15:4), thus reinforcing earlier use of this term – 'an ambition to bring healing' (14:30). Now in the Section conclusion the sage enjoins control over what one says, since with the tongue lies the power either to heal or to shatter another's spirit (reminiscent of the havoc that began with anger in 14:29).

14:31. Jesus similarly taught that kindness shown to the hungry, the stranger, the unclothed, the ill, or the imprisoned was, in fact, kindness bestowed on his own self – albeit in a distressing disguise, to borrow Mother Teresa's expression (Matt. 25:35–40).

15:2. 'The wise do not merely speak the truth bluntly; they give it elegant form' (Fox 2009: 589). The rhetorical care evident in the composition of extended lectures within Proverbs evidences this sapiential priority.

Section IV (15:5–6). The entire lecture ends with a two-verse conclusion (Section IV, 15:5–6). A wisdom commendation once again indicates that pivotal teaching will follow. By urging receptivity even to reproof the sage conveys a particular intensity at the lecture's close (15:5).

Just as this lecture began with the metaphor of a house (14:1), so also it closes (line-initial, 15:6). Repeatedly the sage has elevated moral conduct, stressing that gracious treatment of one's neighbours defines true wealth (14:20–22) and displays proper regard for God (14:31). So it comes as no surprise to learn that 'the house of a moral person is a great treasure' (15:6a). And although the guilty may amass revenue, their immoral means ensure only that they will suffer destructive ends (v. 6b).

15:6. To contrast a guilty person's calamity with the house of a moral person is reminiscent of folly dismantling her house, while wise women were at work building their house (14:1).

'Though the wealth of the wicked might well be great, it is contaminated by disquiet' (Fox 2009: 590).

Explanation

Since by nature humans are social creatures, much of Proverbs addresses relationships. What is unusual in Prov. 14:1 – 15:6 is the extent of communal advice. It is as if a pupil had appealed for expert guidance in how to lead his or her social group effectively. To that end the sage offers insights concerning groups as small as a family (Section II) and as large as a nation (Section III).

Section I. Dual-theme introduction: how to build a house, domestic and dynastic (14:1–4)

Dynamics differ according to a group's size. A group may be as small as a household (14:1–2), or so large that it requires a strong-as-an-ox leader to achieve collective goals (vv. 3–4).

It is impossible for a group to remain static. Relationships will either atrophy or grow stronger. Each member inevitably contributes to the culture of the group, whether wisely building it up (14:1a) or foolishly dismantling it (v. 1b), most especially the leaders entitled to call it 'my house'.

Reverence comprises the most fundamental tenet for even the smallest of groups. Irreverence conversely ensures that a group will get lost in the weeds (14:2).

Power, whether assigned or assumed, will vary among group members. Wise is the leader who exercises power not to abuse others but to protect – especially when employing the power of speech (14:3). And wise is the group which reckons with the fact that, although communal life comes with inherent messiness, through strong leadership the group may grow highly productive (v. 4).

Section II. How to navigate building a domestic house (14:5–27)

A healthy group will monitor the trustworthiness of information sources (14:5–7). Consider the importance of external information, whether for a family or a company. Without reliable information concerning a family's changing neighbourhood or a company's changing market, the group will form poor decisions concerning the advisability of relocating, or shifting product lines.

Internal information is equally vital. Effective groups practise trustworthy internal communication, pursuing aggressive transparency in order to deter misunderstandings and extinguish gossip.

While specific goals will differ according to the mission of a given group, two principles remain universal: morality and discretion (14:8–13). When confronted with right-or-wrong choices, a commitment to morality will enable the group and its leadership resolutely to choose the 'high road', despite grade and isolation. Above all they must beware of fashioning self-referential ethics (v. 12).

When confronted not by right-or-wrong, but by good/better/best alternatives, discretion will equip the group and its leadership to penetrate misleading hype in order to distinguish the path most effectively leading the group to achieve its goals (14:8, 10). Lacking discretion, the group will perish through misdirection.

An effective group and its leadership will guard against responding with self-justifying resentment when confronted with caution or critique (14:14–19). Such anger will only accelerate a downward spiral that will cause them to be discredited in the community.

Beyond the two universal priorities of morality and discretion, there is one value to which all healthy groups must subscribe. It is the value of persons, in contrast to profits (14:20–22). Wise is the group whose decisions are driven by a determination to value persons – most especially persons who otherwise may seem dispensable. They only are rich who come to the aid of the oppressed (v. 21, echoing the sage's earlier teaching: 'riches consist of this: the ransom of a person's life' [13:8a]).

Within a family, this value would safeguard persons who otherwise might be relegated to the status of 'trophy spouse', merely a decorative accessory to another's star-studded career. This value protects the very young and the very old from sacrifice on the altar of 'the unwanted', whether actively through abortion or euthanasia, or passively through neglect.

A company that values persons will not remain content with a record of merely sterile fairness (as important as fairness is). Beyond antiseptic equity, a wise company will fundamentally believe and consequently will behave so that all within its reach (whether employees, customers, suppliers or auditors) sense that they are seen – noticed as persons, not invisible automatons valued solely for their ability to execute a task.

Discovering the foregoing principles of a healthy group constitutes a necessary first step. But discovery without decisive action yields a net deficit (14:23). We must begin by understanding the principle that authentic wealth consists of aiding the oppressed (v. 24). Next, we must diligently ferret out reliable information and engage in faithful communication, as if the lives of others – and perhaps our own – depended on it (v. 25). And, above all, we must anchor ourselves individually and collectively on the bedrock of reverence – the sole sure refuge for future generations (v. 26). Similarly the only life-giving, death-avoiding navigation issues from the LORD, accessible to those who revere him (v. 27).

Section III. How to build a dynastic house (14:28 – 15:4)

As a group grows, extending even to encompass a nation, certain dynamics merit particular attention (Section III). Of initial concern is how a group defines greatness (14:28). While it may be true that 'a leader with no followers is only taking a walk', the sage's subsequent teachings envision a sort of greatness not tethered to the size of one's following.

Consider, first, the greatness of a leader who, when justifiably angry, curbs that reaction in favour of seeking a healing solution (14:29–30). Since 'it is the one who practises compassion towards the oppressed who is truly fortunate' (v. 21b), truly great is the leader who treats the impoverished person with grace (v. 31). Gracious treatment demonstrates a leader's greatness especially if the recipient of grace was the cause of justifiable anger (vv. 29, 31). A leader who instead crushes subordinates will be demoted, while not even death can threaten the one who treats others with compassion modelled by morality (v. 32). Receptivity to this sort of moral wisdom will ensure a nation's prosperity (vv. 33–34).

Consider, second, the greatness paradoxically found in gentleness expressed by a subordinate. This obtains especially when one's superior fails to curb an angry reaction (14:35 – 15:1).

Thus those who wish to help an organization achieve greatness will evidence wisdom (15:2) as they bear in mind that all – from greatest to least – stand accountable to the LORD's supreme oversight (15:3). By words they speak they will strive to mend and heal, resolutely avoiding the demoralization caused by manipulative messages (15:4).

Section IV. Lecture conclusion (15:5–6)
If aspects of this lecture revealed shortcomings, and if we react by disregarding these caring but painful warnings, our response shows that we have traded discretion for folly (15:5). We must turn instead to prize reproof. Especially we must realize that our grand treasure consists of the morally grounded organization – our 'house'. We must recognize the worth of each member. Although survival requires solvency, an organization's true treasure lies not in its economic success. For the group that sacrifices moral conduct is bound for collapse, regardless of the seeming splendour of its present bottom line (15:6).

PROVERBS 15:7 – 17:3
'What is the mind's principal role, and how may I cultivate it?'

Overview of Proverbs 15:7 – 17:3
Since Prov. 10, the sage has focused on specific dilemmas such as, 'How can I become rich?' (cf. Prov. 10:1–22), 'How can I secure my future?' (10:23–30) or, most recently, 'How should I build my house (whether domestic or dynastic)?' (14:1 – 15:6). The present lecture (15:7 – 17:3) turns from such specific projects, probing instead the operation of the mind itself. 'Mind' (often translated as 'heart', whether *lēb* or its synonym *lēbāb*) appears in this lecture with four times the frequency found in the rest of Proverbs.

Fuelling the sage's entire enterprise was his determination to help pupils achieve intellectual vibrancy. He desired not that they would accumulate towering stores of information, but rather attain mental resilience evidenced, remarkably, by joy. To achieve joy, the mind should concentrate on its principal role – its twofold capacity for discernment and counsel.

Discernment entails thinking critically in order to detect motives. Motives, in turn, forecast the ultimate success or failure of a given plan.

Since blind spots are inherent to personal discernment (16:2, 25), one must also cultivate external sources of morality-based counsel – even and especially when that counsel takes the form of painful reproof. Highest among reproofs is counsel that deepens reverence. Divine counsel then will ensue – counsel that is exclusively moral and that draws on infinite discernment. Divine counsel will lead to strategies assured to materialize, thereby resulting in joy.

By developing the skill of discernment, and by deepening one's ability to receive and give sound counsel, the mind will flourish as intended.

Intellectual vitality, marked by joy, enabled by discernment and moral counsel – these facets comprise the sapiential gem gleaming in this lecture.

Position of this poem within Proverbs

Preceding context. The lecture spanning 14:1 – 15:6 turned from a focus on individual success, advising instead how a group may attain success – whether a domestic group (a well-functioning household) or a national group (a durable dynasty). Themes of discretion, morality, proper use of power, and astute response to one's superiors featured prominently in that lecture.

Closure in the final two verses of 14:1 – 15:6 combines with a wisdom commendation at the start of the present lecture (15:7) to distinguish former lecture from latter. Embedded within the present lecture's commendation are three concepts: (a) discernment, (b) disbursing counsel and (c) a healthy mind (see under 'Macrostructural features', below).

Ensuing context. In the present lecture the sage will explore the inner workings of a robust, joyful mind, achieved by cultivating inner discernment and by pursuing outside counsel, including reproof culminating in reverence. In the next lecture he will turn from reverence to analyse evil – a condition more hazardous even than folly (17:4 – 19:9). He will alert pupils to ways evil may infiltrate their own behaviour and relationships.

What to watch for

Notice references to the mind, especially in connection with joy. Pay particular attention to sayings that speak of (a) a capability (or need) to gather and critically evaluate information (discerning, perceiving), and (b) the nature and contribution of counsel (associated with replies, instruction and reproof), whether received for oneself or administered to others. Observe how reproof connects with reverence.

Translation and outline

Verse	*Translation*	*Outline*
		I. Discernment: the route to a healthy mind (15:7–19) A. Introduction to discernment: the importance of discernment, for mental health (15:7–14)
15:7	The lips of wise folk keep on winnowing information, but the mind of stupid folk is not so.	1. Triple-theme wisdom commendation: discernment (winnowing) and giving counsel (lips of wise) constitute core attributes of a healthy (not-stupid) mind (15:7)

Translation	Outline
15:8 A sacrifice from guilty folk is abhorrent to the LORD, but prayer from honest folk is pleasing to him. 15:9 The way of a guilty person is abhorrent to the LORD, but one who pursues morality he will love. 15:10 Reproof is regarded as evil for one who regularly abandons the path; one who hates reprimand will die.	2. Discernment and counsel: their genesis in the divine (start of wisdom content, 15:8–12) a. Initial evidence of divine discernment, with preliminary warning about counsel-of-reproof (15:8–10) i. Initial information discerned by the divine (15:8–9) ii. Initial warning concerning reproof-resistance (15:10)
15:11 Sheol and the Place of Destruction are plainly visible before the LORD: how much more the motives of mere mortals! 15:12 A scoffer will not love when he is reprimanded; unto wise folk he will not go.	b. Increased evidence of divine discernment, with greater warning about counsel-of-reproof (15:11–12) i. Increased evidence of divine discernment (15:11) ii. Increased warning concerning reproof-resistance (15:12)
15:13 A mind characterized by joy will cheer one's face, but by mental anxiety one's spirit is crushed. 15:14 The mind of a perceptive person keeps on searching for information, but the face of stupid folk keeps grazing on folly.	3. The healthy human mind: its capacity and cultivation (15:13–14) a. The capacity of the mind for pervasive joy or profound discouragement (15:13) b. The cultivation of a discerning mind through seeking information (15:14)

Verse *Translation*	*Outline*
	B. Demonstration of discernment: the role of discernment in discovering plenty despite relative poverty (15:15–19)
15:15 All the days of an oppressed person are miserable, while a person with an optimistic outlook is a continual banquet.	1. Key principle: the mind holds the key to discernment within the dilemma of relative poverty (15:15)
	2. Discernment enables release from relative poverty (15:16–17)
15:16 Better a little bit with reverence towards the LORD than vast treasure with uneasiness mixed in. 15:17 Better a meal of greens where there is love than a fattened ox with hatred mixed in.	a. Discernment directed towards divine: release from poverty through reverence for the divine (15:16) b. Discernment directed towards neighbour: release from poverty through love of neighbour (15:17)
	3. A bleak future awaits those who remain captives of relative poverty (15:18–19)
15:18 A person characterized by rage will stir up strife, while restraint of anger will appease a dispute. 15:19 A sluggard's way is like a hedge of briars, but the path of honest folk is a highway.	a. Rage: a reaction towards others, displayed by one who remains poverty's captive (15:18) b. Indolence: a reaction towards self, displayed by one who remains poverty's captive (15:19)
	II. Moral counsel: the route to joy (15:20 – 16:15) A. Introduction to moral counsel: the importance of receiving and giving moral (reverent) counsel, in order to achieve joy (15:20 – 16:9) 1. Why moral counsel leads to joy (15:20–32) a. The connection between counsellors (wisdom dispensers) and joy (15:20–24)

15:20 A wise son will bring his father joy, but stupid is the mortal who despises his mother. 15:21 Folly passes for joy to one lacking sense, but a person characterized by perception will be able to travel in a straight manner. 15:22 The absence of candid counsel makes plans fall apart, but through many advisors they will hold up. 15:23 Joy comes to a person through the reply of his mouth, and a saying in its proper time – how good! 15:24 A life-giving, ascending path belongs to one who instructs, with this intent – to turn oneself from Sheol below.	i. Wisdom commendation: wise behaviour distributes joy; stupidity scorns counsel-source (15:20) ii. Perception-driven progress results in authentic joy (start of wisdom content, 15:21) iii. Counsel results in plans-fulfilled (15:22) iv. That is why joy rewards perceptive counsellors (15:23) v. Eventual lofty destination for counsellors: life itself (15:24)
15:25 A house of proud folk will the Lord tear down, but a widow's boundary will he set in place. 15:26 Abhorrent to the Lord are evil plans, but pure are beautiful sayings. 15:27 A ruthless profiteer ruins his house, but he who hates gifts will live.	b. The converse: the connection between arrogance (resistance to moral counsel) and self-destruction (15:25–27) i. Arrogance or humility determine divine response (15:25) ii. Morality determines counsel's worth (15:26) iii. And counsel-strategies determine self-destruction or success (15:27)
15:28 The mind of a moral person meditates how to respond, but the mouth of guilty folk gushes evil. 15:29 The Lord is far from guilty folk, but prayer from moral folk he will hear.	c. Morality: the moderator of counsel, human and divine (15:28–29) i. Morality of a counsellor will moderate his response (15:28) ii. Morality of supplicant will determine divine response (15:29)

Verse *Translation*	*Outline*
	d. Recap linking receptivity, joy and increased wisdom (15:30–32)
15:30 The lamp of the eyes brings joy to the mind; good news will fatten the bones.	i. Counsel-receptivity leads to joy (15:30)
15:31 An ear that listens to life-giving reprimand will spend the night in the company of wise folk.	ii. Reproof-receptivity leads to increased wisdom (15:31)
15:32 One who pays no attention to reproof rejects his own life, but one who listens to reprimand acquires a mind.	iii. Reproof-rejection fosters self-hate, forfeiting wisdom's prize (15:32)
	2. Reverence: the zenith of moral counsel, cast as reproof (15:33 – 16:9)
15:33 Reverence for the LORD constitutes wisdom's reproof, and prior to honour is humility.	a. Reverence constitutes the zenith of reproof, the inverse of reproof-rejection (15:33)
16:1 To a mortal belong the strategies of one's mind, but from the LORD is a tongue's reply.	b. Such humility accesses divine insight, beyond human discernment (16:1)
16:2 All a person's ways appear clean in his own eyes, but the one who weighs spirits is the LORD.	c. For to humans all plans may seem moral, yet God can discern motives (16:2)
16:3 Roll your work onto the LORD, so that your plans may be established.	d. So, wisely surrender your plans to God, for him to secure (16:3)!
16:4 Everything is managed by the LORD in keeping with his own purpose, including the guilty person for a day of misery.	c'. For God coordinates all with his overarching objective, including the immoral (16:4)
16:5 Abhorrent to the LORD is every intellectually arrogant attitude; most assuredly he will not be acquitted.	b'. Lack of humility earns divine disfavour and punishment (16:5)

16:6 Through faithful love and truth iniquity will be atoned for, and through reverence for the LORD comes turning from evil. 16:7 When the LORD is pleased with a person's ways, he will make even his enemies to be at peace with him. 16:8 Better is a little with morality than much revenue deprived of fairness in judicial proceedings. 16:9 A mortal's mind should plan his way, but it is the LORD who will establish his step.	a'. But renewed reverence will initiate repentance, leading to atonement (16:6) b''. Then, even opponents sue for peace due to divine favour (16:7) c''. Although morality may seem the poorer choice (16:8) . . . d'. . . . God will secure the progress of those in league with him (16:9)
16:10 An oracular verdict is on a king's lips; in judicial proceedings his mouth should not behave unfaithfully. 16:11 Floor balances and hand-held scales of justice belong to the LORD; all the weights in the bag are his work.	B. Demonstration of moral counsel: the role of moral (reverent) counsel, to facilitate stability and prosperity within the monarchy (16:10–15) 1. What moral counsel the king gives should derive from the celestial king, since morality is his domain (16:10–11) a. As judge, the king receives divine counsel, which he must faithfully transmit (16:10) b. All moral counsel belongs to the divine domain (16:11)
16:12 Doing wrong is abhorrent to kings, for it is through morality that a throne will grow firm. 16:13 Kings' pleasure results from lips that are moral, and it loves one who speaks honesty.	2. Furthermore, moral conduct is in the best interest of kings and their courtiers (16:12–13) a. Kings should embrace morality for dynastic durability (16:12) b. Courtiers should embrace morality when offering counsel (16:13)

Verse	*Translation*	*Outline*
		3. Make no mistake: a monarch's extreme power recommends courtier compliance with moral standards (16:14–15)
16:14	A king's rage amounts to death-messengers, but a person who is wise will be able to appease it.	a. Death looms for councillors who infuriate the king (16:14)
16:15	In the light of a king's face is life, and his pleasure is as a spring rain cloud.	b. A prosperous life awaits councillors who gain royal favour (16:15)
		III. Review: underscoring the importance of moral counsel and discernment (16:16 – 17:3) A. The profound importance of composing moral counsel (16:16–24) 1. The superior worth of wisdom (16:16–20)
16:16	Acquisition of wisdom – how much better than gold, and acquisition of insight – preferred above silver!	a. Wisdom commendation: the incomparable value of wisdom (16:16)
		b. Essential wisdom content: morality and humility (16:17–19)
16:17	Turning from evil is a highway for honest folk; one who guards his appetite protects his way.	i. Navigation by morality that restrains appetites (16:17)
		ii. The asset that is humility (16:18–19)
16:18	Prior to breakage – elevation; and prior to stumbling – loftiness of spirit.	α. Arrogance harms (16:18)
16:19	Better is a lowly spirit with humble folk than dividing spoil with proud folk.	β. Humility helps (16:19)
16:20	One who instructs concerning a saying will discover good, but it is the one who trusts in the Lord who is truly fortunate.	c. The exceptional value of composing counsel, inferior only to reliance on the divine (16:20)

16:21 A person who is wise-of-mind will be called 'perceptive', and sweetness of lips will expand learning. 16:22 Instruction is for one who masters it a spring of life, but reproof of fools is folly. 16:23 A wise person's mind will instruct his mouth, and learning will expand on his lips. 16:24 Beautiful sayings are an abundant supply of honey, sweet to the appetite and healing to the bones.	2. The superior worth of composing counsel, within the wisdom tradition (16:21–24) a. The output of wise counsel: sweetness that develops out of discernment and expands learning (16:21) b. Instruction: the spring of life (16:22) b' Instruction: the sign of a mind that expands learning (16:23) a'. The intake of wise counsel: a healing sweetness (16:24)
16:25 There is a way that from an individual's perspective is straight, but its outcome is death's ways.	B. The profound importance of cultivating discernment (16:25 – 17:3) 1. The problem: the critical need for discernment (16:25)
16:26 The appetite of a labourer labours for him, for his mouth keeps putting pressure on him. 16:27 A person characterized by worthlessness digs up evil, and it is upon his lips as a scorching fire. 16:28 A person characterized by perversity will dispatch strife, and a slanderer alienates a close friend. 16:29 A person characterized by violence will attempt to allure his friend, so he will bring him along a way that is not good.	2. The wrong solution: trusting appetites for navigational discernment (16:26–30) a. Appetites serve well for motivation (16:26) b. Navigation by appetite: four catastrophes (16:27–30) i. Appetite that damages self (16:27) ii. Appetite that isolates from friends (16:28) iii. Appetite that entices others into evil (16:29)

Verse	*Translation*	*Outline*
16:30	One who shuts his eyes for planning perversity, one who purses his lips, has brought evil to completion.	iv. Appetite that ultimately anaesthetizes one's conscience to scheming evil (16:30)
		3. The right solution: trusting morals for navigational discernment (16:31 – 17:3)
16:31	A splendid crown is grey hair, along the way of morality it can be found.	a. Magnificent longevity: evidence of a life navigated by morality (16:31)
		b. Discernment for navigating disappointment (16:32 – 17:2)
		i. Navigating disappointment when someone wrongs you (16:32–33)
16:32	Better is restraint of anger than belligerence; and one who rules over his spirit than one who captures a city.	α. Exercise self-control towards neighbours . . . (16:32)
16:33	Into a lap the lot is thrown, but from the LORD comes its every judicial decision.	β. . . . And maintain trust in divine justice (16:33)
		ii. Navigating disappointment when allotted a smaller portion (17:1–2)
17:1	Better is a dry morsel along with calm than a house filled with contentious feasts.	α. Demonstrate trust in moral conduct . . . (17:1)
17:2	A servant who instructs will rule over a shameful son, and will have a portion of the inheritance among brothers.	β. . . . For a lowly wisdom instructor will acquire supremacy and an equal share (17:2)
17:3	A crucible for silver and a smelting furnace for gold, but the one who sets up tests for motives is the LORD.	c. Ultimate trust in morality: discernment by the divine (17:3)

Notes on the text

15:7. 'keep on winnowing', *yĕzārû*: the verb *zārâ*, 'to winnow', can connote discerning or scrutinizing (cf. Ps. 139:3, where it is synonymous with 'to know in detail'). Alternatively, *zārâ* can connote scattering or dispersing (as with threshed grain heaved into the air so a crosswind will carry away useless hulls). Each meaning (discern and scatter) corresponds to a principal theme of this poem. Durative ('keeps on') derives from yiq.

'information': lit. 'knowledge'.

'mind', *lēb*: lit. 'mind', 'heart' (contrast 15:11 and 17:3, where pl. *libbôt* is rendered 'motives').

'the mind of stupid folk is not so', *wĕlēb kĕsîlîm lō'-kēn*: *kēn*, 'so', links this second colon closely to the first. How wise folk employ their mental assets is not how stupid folk use theirs. In this lecture the sage will return frequently to the matter of properly cultivating one's mental capabilities (e.g. showing how to 'acquire a mind', 15:32b).

Also latent in *lō'-kēn* is the sense of 'not right' or 'not functioning as it should' (cf. Waltke 2004: 620). However, to render *kēn* as 'right' (rather than 'so') conceals the close connection between first and second cola (Fox 2009: 591).

15:8. 'sacrifice from guilty folk': 'sacrifice' encompasses more than ritual slaying of animals for atonement (e.g. peace offerings in Lev. 3:1).

'is pleasing to him': lit. 'is his pleasure', earning his approval.

15:10. 'Reproof is regarded as evil': lit. 'reproof [is] evil'. Treating 'evil' as predicative adj. establishes the first colon as the circumstance (disregard for reproof) leading to the second colon consequence (death of such a one). Of the forty-seven occurrences in Proverbs of the adj. *rāʿ*, 'evil', thirty-six function either in a predicative or substantive manner (as here). Rendered attributively, the first colon would read, 'There is severe discipline for one who forsakes the way' (NRSV).

'for one who regularly abandons the path': 'regularly' implied by use of ptc.

15:11. 'the Place of Destruction', *'ăbaddôn*: an afterlife destination much worse than Sheol, which is a synonym for death (Waltke 2004: 622–623).

'plainly visible before', *neged*: lit. 'opposite'. *Neged* locates an object pointedly in front of a person.

'motives', *libbôt*: see 'Notes' for 'mind' in 15:7.

'mere mortals': lit. 'children of a mortal'. Contrast with divine in 15:11a underscores insignificance of humans.

15:13. 'A mind characterized by joy': lit. 'a joyful mind'.

15:14. 'keeps on searching' and 'keeps grazing': durative inferred from yiq.

'information': see 'Notes' for 15:7.

'face of', *pĕnê*: 'face' here connotes 'attention'. Stupid folk are preoccupied with finding more folly. They refuse the hard work of 'searching for information' that would enable wise decisions, which would lead to joy cheering one's 'face' (15:13).

Discord of subject (pl. 'faces') and verb (sg. 'graze') may owe to *pānîm* being grammatically pl. but sg. in meaning (*plurale tantum*, Joüon §90f). Thus the Q (and LXX) alternative *pî*, 'mouth of' (sg.), is not needed.

15:15. 'while a person with an optimistic outlook is a continual banquet', *wĕṭôb-lēb mišteh tāmîd*: lit. 'and a good-of-mind [is] a continual banquet'. 'Good-of-mind' describes a positive attitude, whether warranted (1 Kgs 8:66; 2 Chr. 7:10), chemically induced (2 Sam. 13:28; Esth. 1:10) or unwarranted (Judg. 16:25; Esth. 5:9). Since in Hebr. this expression involves the term 'mind', it contributes to this lecture's theme of cultivating one's mind, controlling one's outlook by choosing either to bow beneath negative circumstances ('oppressed') or to rise above them ('optimistic'). The sage of Ecclesiastes uses an evidently synonymous expression (*leb-ṭôb*) when encouraging the reader to counsel cheerful enjoyment of basic pleasures, confident of divine approval (Eccles. 9:7). By beginning each of Prov. 15:16 and 17 with *ṭôb*, 'better', the sage explains how a person may cultivate the 'goodness-of-mind' (optimism) described in v. 15.

Some versions describe the optimistic outlook as *having* a continual banquet (e.g. NRSV and NASB). However, Hebr. credits the optimistic outlook with *embodying* such a banquet (so also Waltke 2004: 617). When this person enters a room, he or she brings a 'banquet' to others because of the cheerfulness he radiates.

15:16. 'uneasiness', *mĕhûmâ*: this term can range from disquietude to panic.

15:21. 'lacking sense': lit. 'lacking mind'.

15:22. 'plans . . . will hold up', *maḥăšĕbôt . . . tāqûm*: lack of agreement between the subject (f. pl. 'plans') and verb (f. sg.) reflects the tendency to treat f. pl. nouns of objects or animals as collectives (Joüon §150g).

15:23. 'the reply . . . a saying', *maʿănê . . . dābār*: in the context of 'counsel', 'plans' and 'advisors' (15:22), 'reply' refers to advice offered in response to a problem (Waltke 2004: 633; cf. 'reply' in 16:1, 'saying' in v. 20).

15:24. 'one who instructs', *maśkîl*: more than simply 'being wise' (NRSV, NASB, NIV), the hiph. stem of the root *śkl* means 'to instruct' – aiding another to gain insight or success (cf. 16:20, 23; 17:2).

'with this intent – to turn oneself from Sheol below', *lĕmaʿan sûr miššĕʾôl māṭṭâ*: since 'turn' implies departing from a wrong path, it suggests the instructor transmitted reproof (for 'reproof' and 'abandoning the [right] path', cf. 15:10; for 'Sheol' cf. v. 11).

15:26. 'sayings', *ʾimrê*: from *ʾmr*, a synonym of *dbr* in 15:23.

15:27. 'gifts', *mattānôt*: in the context of greed (15:27a), 'gifts' implies bribes.

15:30. 'The lamp of the eyes', *mĕʾôr-ʿênayim*: by this image the sage paradoxically describes the eye as a perception-enhancing organ of metaphoric illumination (revelatory illumination also associates with the face in the expression *mĕʾôr-pāneykā*, 'the lamp of your countenance', Ps. 90:8). The importance of seeing clearly the sage already established ('winnowing information', Prov. 15:7) and illustrated (being wise enough to see greater value in simpler fare, vv. 16–17). Instead to render *mĕʾôr-ʿênayim* as 'bright eyes' (NASB) or 'light in a messenger's eyes' (NIV) misses the point. It is not happiness ('bright eyes') that 'brings joy' but keen perception (observant eyes).

15:32. 'his own life', *napšô*: this saying offers a choice between 'suicide versus survival' (Waltke 2005: 8). Later in this lecture, *nepeš* will refer to 'appetite', not simply 'life' or 'self' (16:17, 24, 26).

'but one who listens to reprimand acquires a mind', *wĕšômēaʿ tôkaḥat qôneh lēb*: given this lecture's focus on the role and cultivation of the mind, a sense of climax accompanies this declaration.

16:1. 'the strategies of one's mind', *maʿarkê-lēb*: the root *ʿrk* of this hapax legomenon (a word occurring only once) indicates 'to arrange' as the underlying sense of 'strategies'. Given this lecture's repeated mention of 'plan' (15:22, 26; 16:3, 9), the notion of 'arrangements' associated with 'mind' recommends the meaning 'strategies'.

'a tongue's reply', *maʿănēh lāšôn*: see 'Notes' for 15:23a.

16:2. 'but the one who weighs spirits': 'spirits' refers to intentions outwardly undiscernible. A similar saying appears in 21:2: 'Every way of a person is honest in his own eyes, but the one who weighs motives is the LORD.'

16:4. 'Everything is managed by the LORD': lit. 'all the LORD worked' or 'accomplished'. Syntactic emphasis rests on 'everything'. Since the second colon looks to the future, the qat. form 'is managed' conveys certitude not limited to the past. In this saying to render *pāʿal* as 'made' misleads, suggesting divine determinism. Waltke renders 16:4a, 'The LORD works everything to its appropriate end' (2005: 4).

'in keeping with his own purpose', *lammaʿănēhû*: *maʿăneh* can mean either 'purpose' or 'reply'. The perspective of comprehensive divine oversight recommends 'purpose' here, in contrast to 15:23 and 16:1, where *maʿăneh* is rendered 'reply'.

The uncharacteristic use of both definite article and poss. pronoun in a phrase such as *lammaʿănēhû* accounts for the term 'own' in 'his own purpose' (cf. 'my own tent' in Josh. 7:21, and 'your own proportion' in Lev. 27:23). Consequently the 'purpose' in question rests uniquely under the LORD's purview.

'including the guilty person for a day of misery': if he were to observe the guilty profiting by misconduct, one who has 'roll[ed his] work onto the LORD' (16:3) may grow concerned. This saying reassures that the LORD may be relied on to bring to the guilty the retributive consequences their choices have set in motion. This saying does not teach divine determinism.

16:5. 'every intellectually arrogant attitude': lit. 'every loftiness of mind'.

'most assuredly': lit. 'hand to hand' – a solemn assurance, likely envisioning two persons clasping hands in pledge (in HB attested only here and Prov. 11:21, both times followed by 'he will not be acquitted').

'he will not be acquitted': i.e. the 'guilty person' of 16:4, who exhibits an arrogant attitude in v. 5a.

16:9. 'A mortal's mind should plan': lit. 'a mortal's mind will plan' (obligation inferred from yiq.).

16:10. 'An oracular verdict', *qesem*: in the context of *mišpāṭ*, 'judicial proceedings', *qesem* refers to a verdict derived by consulting the divine. The discovery of Achan by lots is analogous, though *qesem* does not appear there (Josh. 7:14–15). In some instances *qesem* refers to a form of divination prohibited in Israel (Deut. 18:10).

'should not behave unfaithfully': lit. 'will not be unfaithful' (obligation inferred from yiq.).

16:11. 'and hand-held scales of justice', *ûmōʾzĕnēy mišpāṭ*: the context of judicial proceedings (16:10) recommends *mišpāṭ* as 'justice', not 'honest' (NRSV) or 'just' (NASB). *Mišpāṭ* is rendered 'fairness in judicial proceedings' in 16:8, 'judicial proceedings' in 16:10 and 'judicial decision' in 16:33.

'weights in the bag': lit. 'stones of a bag'; i.e. a bag containing weights with predetermined dimensions, often of smoothed stone incised with a symbol indicating dimension.

16:12. 'wrong', *rešaʿ*: often rendered 'guilty'.

16:13. 'Kings' pleasure results from lips that are moral': lit. 'pleasure of kings is moral lips'.

'it loves one who speaks honesty': lit. 'one who speaks honesty, it loves'. 'Loves' requires a sg. subject, fitting 'pleasure' but not 'kings'.

16:13, 15. 'pleasure': see 'Notes' for 15:8.

16:14. 'will be able to appease it': capability inferred from yiq.

16:16. 'Acquisition of wisdom', *qĕnōh ḥŏkmâ*: lit. 'to acquire wisdom'. While not presenting the *-ôt* ending expected for an infin. const. of a III-he verb, since the sage elsewhere uses the *-ôt* ending for a III-he infinitive construct (e.g. *ʿăśōh*, 'to make', 21:3), and since outside Proverbs *qĕnōh* regularly serves as infin. const. of the verb 'to acquire', *qĕnōh* here should not be emended (with some Hebr. manuscripts) as an imperative *qĕnê ḥŏkmâ*, 'acquire wisdom' (though that imperative is attested in Prov. 4:5, 7).

16:20. 'a saying', *dābār*: as in 15:23, and as confirmed by description of attractive, thoughtfully crafted speech in 16:21, 23, 24, *dābār* here refers to verbal advice (not merely 'thing' or 'matter').

'One who instructs', *maśkîl*: see 'Notes' for 15:24. This may refer to one who is 'competent in speech', who transitions from consuming wisdom, now to begin sharing counsel with others, which role in v. 21 will unfold as a teacher (Waltke 2005: 28–29).

16:22. 'Instruction', *śēkel*: see 'Notes' for 15:24. The likelihood that *śēkel* here connotes 'instruction' transmitted to another (rather than insight kept to oneself) increases by virtue of the fact that 'reproof' in the second colon indicates training of another person (Fox 2009: 620).

16:23. 'instruct', *yaśkîl*: see 'Notes' for 15:24.

16:25. 'from an individual's perspective': lit. 'in front of a person'.

16:28, 30. 'perversity': lit. 'crookedness'.

16:30. 'shuts': lit. 'shut' (perhaps 'wink'). While this word occurs only here in the HB, non-verbal gestures with eyes and lips are associated with the 'worthless person' and 'perversion' in 6:12–14.

'purses his lips': this verb conveys a devious gesture when referring to a narrowing of the eyes (6:13; 10:10).

16:32. 'than belligerence': lit. 'than a warrior'.

'spirit', *rûaḥ*: 'spirit' indicates the primary locus of one's emotion, since it is here that reactions such as 'anger' and 'belligerence' can be restrained (not in one's 'mind/heart', *lēb*).

16:33. 'lot': a divinely directed means ensuring humanly impartial selection, consisting of one or more small stones shaken from a garment-fold or a container, until one would fall out, thereby indicating a selection or decision (BDB; Waltke 2005: 37).

'its every judicial decision', *kŏl-mišpāṭô*: i.e. a judicial verdict, in this instance determined by casting lots thrown into a lap. The noun *mišpāṭ* is rendered 'fairness in judicial proceedings' in 16:8 and 'justice' in v. 11.

17:1. 'contentious feasts': lit. 'sacrifices of strife'. This expression would have seemed oxymoronic, since such sacrificial meals were 'intended to enhance harmony among the participants and between them and God' (Fox 2009: 624). Note the contrast between 'full' of contention and emptiness of a 'dry morsel'.

17:2. '[one] who instructs', *maśkîl*: see 'Notes' for 15:24.

17:3. 'one who sets up tests', *bōḥēn*: when associated with precious metal, *bḥn*, 'to test', describes use of heat to assay purity. There is evidence that when used in conjunction with *ṣrp*, 'to smelt, refine', *bḥn* may connotate purification (improving a commodity's worth, not simply evaluating it, as in Zech. 13:9). That connotation should not be inferred here, however. Rather, while the LORD mercifully exposes (evaluates) impurities through reproof, that event constitutes an invitation, an opportunity for the subject to display wise and moral character by reverentially turning from evil (16:6), rather than resisting reproof (15:10, 12). Thus, if the LORD here refines (improves quality), and does not merely expose impurities, he does so indirectly (*pace* Fox, who infers that the LORD here purifies through testing [2009: 625]). The root *bḥn* does not appear elsewhere in Proverbs.

'motives', *libbôt*: lit. 'minds', with connotation of thought processes and underlying intentions, as in 15:11.

Form and structure

Borders

The theme of identifying and cultivating the mind's principal role dominates the present poem (contrasting counsel for building one's 'house' in the preceding poem). That theme emerges promptly from the initial wisdom commendation with its introduction of three subthemes, concisely establishing the upper border (15:7).

The lower border consists of macro- and microstructures involving closure, inclusio and climax. Macro-level closure (spanning more than one section) appears in the final saying: 'the one who sets up tests for motives is the LORD' (17:3). Already the sage had referenced the divine's capacity for profound interior examination (15:8–9; 16:2).

Macro-level closure appears again as the sage observes that, while well-suited for motivation, appetites are unqualified for navigation (contrast 16:26–30 with 16:31 – 17:3). Earlier in the lecture stupid folk succumbed to their appetite, routinely 'grazing on folly' (15:14b).

The closing verse displays macro-level inclusio. The divine capacity for separating precious from worthless in 17:3 recalls how the wise person is able to 'winnow' information, separating useful from useless (15:7). As an example of closure, the capacity for discernment associates specifically with the divine in 15:8–9, 11, and then again in 17:3.

Micro-level inclusio (within a single section) marks the lower border when discernment-deficiency leads to a deadly destination (16:25, beginning Block III.B). This reverses as complete discernment even to the level of motives is associated with the divine, as noted above in 17:3 (ending Block III.B and the entire poem).

Micro-level closure operates as themes of humility, wealth and divine trustworthiness appear in Section III, prior to their return in 17:2–3. Humility seen in the servant of 17:2 also appeared in the expressions 'lowly', 'humble folk', not 'proud folk', in 16:19. Wealth indicated in 17:2 by 'having a portion of the inheritance' recalls 'dividing spoil' in 16:19. The LORD's ability to establish 'tests for the motives' indicates that moral folk may entrust their well-being to the divine's capacity for fair assessment (17:3b). This recalls the confidence expressed in 16:20: 'one who trusts in the LORD . . . is truly fortunate'.

Macrostructural features

Wisdom commendations that introduce sections (Sections I–III, content-based). Despite its length (sixty-three sayings), this poem contains only three wisdom commendations, each of which marks the opening of each section. The first opens Section I in 15:7, a second opens Section II at 15:20 and the third opens Section III (16:16).

Triple-theme within a wisdom commendation (15:7, with links to Sections I–III, content-based). The concentration of themes in the lecture's opening verse merits careful notice (15:7). First, given its connotation of 'separating', 'winnowing' anticipates the theme of discernment that dominates Section I (also Block III.B).

Second, an alternative connotation of 'winnowing' as 'scattering' anticipates the theme of disbursing counsel. The theme of counsel dominates Section II (also Block III.A).

Third, mention of 'mind' introduces for this lecture the concept of intellect (15:7b). Properly trained, one's mind will be able to 'winnow', both distinguishing useful from useless and disbursing counsel to receptive persons. Failure of the stupid traces to a 'mind' that is 'not so' – a mind disengaged from the disciplines of intellectual discernment and composing counsel.

Repetition of 'mind' (Sections I–III, form-based). In this lecture the term *lēb* (and its synonym *lēbāb*) occurs frequently, rendered variously as 'mind', 'motives', 'outlook', 'sense' and 'intellectually'. These synonyms occur in this poem with a density higher (by a factor of four) than in the balance of Proverbs (sixteen times across these 63 verses, contrasting eighty-two times across the remaining 852 verses). *Lēb* or *lēbāb* appears in each section: Section I (15:7, 11, 13 [twice], 14; 15:15), Section II (15:21, 28, 30, 32; 16:1, 5, 9), and Section III (16:21, 23; 17:3).

The sage makes substantial claims concerning *lēb* or *lēbāb*. The *lēb* is the organ of planning (16:1, 9). The *lēb* designates that region where arrogance can operate (16:5, contrasting reverence in v. 6). Although humanly inscrutable, the LORD can examine and assess it with ease (15:11; 17:3). It may be moral (15:28; contrast 11:20 and 12:20). Although one may be lacking in *lēb* ('senseless', 15:21), it is possible to acquire *lēb* (15:32).

The frequent references to *lēb* or *lēbāb*, together with the substantial claims made concerning it – these combine to indicate the lecture's principal theme. This lecture trains youths to grasp the mind's principal role, and to learn how they may cultivate a healthy, well-disciplined mind.

Aware of how central is 'mind' within this poem, its mention at the lecture's opening assumes a programmatic function. After elevating the wise with their capacity for 'winnowing information' (15:7a), the sage conversely diagnoses the problem among stupid folk as mental: 'but the mind of stupid folk is not so' (or 'is not right', v. 7b). By cultivating a healthy mind one may join the wise, while escaping those who are not. The remainder of the lecture is devoted to cultivation of the mind.

Thematic continuity involving respectful regard for the LORD (Sections I–III, content-based). This lecture refers to the divine four times more frequently than does the balance of Proverbs (twenty times across 63 verses, in contrast to sixty-seven times over 852 verses). Most involve reverence: in Section I (15:8–9, 16), in Section II (15:25–26, 33; 16:1, 2, 4–7, 11) and in Section III (17:3). Remaining references to the divine focus on benefits flowing from the divine, rather than respect due him (16:3, 9 in Section II; 16:20, 33 in Section III).

Recurrence of 'better' sayings (Sections I–III, form-based). While not unique to this lecture, so-called 'better sayings' appear in each section, teaching that less paradoxically is more. They occur in Section I (15:16, 17), in Section II (16:8) and in Section III (16:19, 32; 17:1). The 'better saying' form suits well the lecture's aim of cultivating discernment (found particularly in Section I and Block III.B). 'Better sayings' display the analytic or discerning side of wisdom, thus revealing the methods of wisdom, rather than simply asserting its conclusions without explanatory comparisons (Perry 1993: 95).

Repetition of 'joy' (Sections I and II, form-based). Of the twenty-eight references to the root *śmḥ*, 'joy', across Proverbs, five appear within this lecture, marking joy as a prominent concept for this poem.

A block of introduction, followed by a block of demonstration (Sections I and II, content-based). Sections I and II concentrate on distinct themes (discernment and counsel, respectively). Yet they follow a parallel development, beginning with theme-introduction in Block A of respective sections, followed by theme-demonstration in Block B. Notice the contrast of 'introduction' and 'demonstration' within each of the next two macrostructures (theme of discernment and theme of counsel).

Thematic continuity involving discernment (Sections I and III, content-based). The themes of discernment and counsel comprise the most comprehensive themes giving cohesion to this lecture. Consider first the theme of discernment. It dominates Section I, through both introduction (Block I.A, 15:7–14) and demonstration (Block I.B, 15:15–19). After a brief appearance in Section II (which concentrates rather on the theme of counsel), discernment returns in Section III, governing its closing block (Block III.B, 16:25 – 17:3).

In Section I the theme of discernment is introduced through a connotation associated with *zārâ*, 'to winnow', in the poem's opening colon (15:7a; see 'Notes'). For the second connotation, see 'Thematic continuity involving counsel', below.

Discernment characterizes the divine. With ease he assesses worshippers' sincerity (15:8), probing even to the nether regions of one's motives (vv. 9, 11).

Discernment characterizes also the ideal human. He or she continually searches out more information (lit. 'knowledge', 15:14), which his 'perceptive' mind then assesses. Such disciplined collection and evaluation of information accounts for his psychological equilibrium, enabling him to surmount negative circumstances, reframing them within an outlook that is more comprehensive and consequently more optimistic (15:13).

In the demonstration portion of Section I (Block I.B), one's powers of discernment determine whether one will enjoy 'a continuous banquet', or will remain captive to perpetual misery (15:15, where 'outlook' renders *lēb*, 'mind'). Discernment's core outlook consists of reverence (15:16). When one surveys relative impoverishment from the divine overlook of reverence, 'a little bit' exceeds a 'vast treasure'. And when coupled with a neighbourly outlook of 'love', 'a meal of greens' offers better succulence than 'a fattened ox' (15:17, recalling the 'continual banquet' of 15:15). Such is the transforming centrality of discernment.

Discernment appears seldom in Section II, receding before the theme of counsel (15:20 – 16:15). First, joy comes to the mind due to 'the lamp of the eyes' – one's ability to illumine and consequently discern information (15:30). Second, the sage teaches that a mortal's capacity for self-discernment is universally compromised (16:2a). The divine, in contrast, suffers no such deficiency, discerning hidden motives as if weighed on a delicate scale (v. 2b).

Section III (16:16 – 17:3) reviews earlier themes. Boldly the theme of discernment returns at the final block's opening saying: 'There is a way that from an individual's perspective is straight, but its outcome is death's ways' (16:25). To avoid that fatal destination, one's appetites must bow to discernment (16:26). Although well suited for motivation, appetites are feckless for navigation.

The sage then illustrates the catastrophe resulting from navigation by appetite. A series of four characters prove this point, each more toxic than the last. Heedless of any moral compass, they make a colossal wreck of things (16:27–30).

A lone noble figure follows these four, distinguished by this trait: he steers by a moral compass. Consequently he achieves enviable longevity and radiant splendour (16:31).

Longevity and splendour come despite disappointments, as the victim responds not with a reflexive appetite for revenge, but through restraint of anger (16:32). Self-discipline is a derivative of discernment.

As with 'better' sayings appearing earlier in this poem (15:16, 17), again one requires discernment to perceive when ostensible 'less' amounts to 'more' (16:32; 17:1). That person who is unaware of divine oversight may conclude – erroneously – that life is but a cruel and capricious role of die (16:33), perversely rewarding diligent industry with but a morsel (17:1a). In contrast, the ability to discern that crusts-plus-calm satisfy better than feasts-with-fighting (17:1b; cf. 15:16) can extricate one from the mental sinkhole which infers that every day is miserable (15:15a), escorting instead to banquets appearing prodigally across all of life (15:15b).

The lecture's closing verse brings to a climax the theme of discernment, declaring both (a) the divine's unparalleled ability to discern, and (b) the superior worth of pure motives, when compared with tangible wealth. 'A crucible for silver and a smelting furnace for gold, but the one who sets up tests for motives is the LORD' (17:3; cf. 15:11). Such a conclusion would move the receptive pupil to value and pursue reverence and moral conduct above inferior riches (cf. 16:6–9).

Thematic continuity involving counsel, both consumed and composed (Sections II and III, content-based). Consider next the theme of counsel, both consumed and composed. The theme of counsel dominates Section II (15:20 – 16:15). This theme returns in the review provided by Section III, governing its first block (Block III.A, 16:16–24). Section II is primarily (though not exclusively) concerned with counsel consumed by the pupil, while the perspective of composing counsel distinguishes Block III.A.

Block II.A introduces the idea of moral counsel (15:20 – 16:9). Block II.B demonstrates how moral counsel may operate in a monarchy (16:10–15).

The introduction portion (Block II.A) begins by connecting moral counsel with joy (Unit II.A.1, 15:20–32; esp. vv. 20–23; cf. 15:13). Indications of counsel in Unit II.A.1 include the following: despising one's mother (foolishly rejecting counsel she may offer, 15:20), 'candid counsel' and 'advisors' (15:22), 'the reply of [one's] mouth . . . a saying in its proper time' (15:23), 'instructs' (15:24), 'beautiful sayings' (15:26), 'meditat[ing] how to respond' (not 'gush[ing] evil', 15:28), 'listen[ing] to life-giving reprimand' (15:31), and either 'pay[ing] no attention to reproof' or listen[ing] to reprimand' (15:32).

After connecting moral counsel and joy (Unit II.A.1), the sage draws attention to reverence as a select sample of counsel (Unit II.A.2, 15:33 – 16:9). Indications of counsel in Unit II.A.2 include 'reverence' as 'wisdom's reproof' (15:33), 'a tongue's reply' (divine counsel here contrasts internal discernment, expressed as 'the strategies of one's mind', 16:1), 'intellectually arrogant' (opposite of reverence, 16:5) and 'reverence', once again (16:6).

The demonstration portion (Block II.B, 16:10–15) focuses on moral counsel operating within a monarchy. Counsel connects to the following: 'oracular verdict' (when presiding over judicial cases, a wise king will seek divine counsel before issuing a verdict, 16:10), 'weights in the bag' (objective standards morality used to critique objects in question, 16:11), 'lips that are moral' and 'one who speaks honesty' (councillors who supply the king with moral advice, 16:13).

In the blend of consuming-counsel and composing-counsel, Section II favoured the former, while Section III will favour the latter. Expressions from Section III that indicate counsel (whether consumed or composed) begin with these: 'acquisition of wisdom', 'acquisition of insight' (both 16:16) and 'one who instructs concerning a saying will discover good' (16:20a; cf. 15:24). The magnitude of attainment ('good') there associated with 'instructing' is surpassed only by the fortune of one's trusting in the divine (16:20b). Thus the sage conveys exceptionally high esteem for any who compose and dispense counsel.

Counsel-related expressions continue in Block III.A. While 'wise-of-mind' may refer to internal discernment (note mention of 'perceptive'), composing counsel for others is indicated by the statement 'sweetness of lips will expand learning' (16:21).

Consider next the statement 'instruction is for one who masters it a spring of life' (16:22a). Since 'instruction' and 'instructor' share the root *śkl*, 16:22 refers to prowess in composing wisdom sayings that will benefit others. Thereby one achieves the pinnacle of robust living. The likelihood that 'instruction' in colon A refers to composing wisdom increases, in view of the message of colon B (16:22b): 'the reproof of fools is folly'. This may be paraphrased, 'A reproof statement composed by fools is but hollow blathering.'

Further counsel-related expressions in Block III.A include these: 'a wise person's mind will instruct his mouth' (i.e. the mind of the wise instructs his mouth to expound wisdom, 16:23a), and 'learning will expand on his lips' (i.e. drawing upon his learning, he then will compose counsel to benefit others, 16:23b; note that *skl*, 'instruct', contributes a form-based macrostructure joining 15:24 in Section II and 16:20, 22, 23 in Section III). The sage concludes this block by observing, 'beautiful sayings are . . . sweet' (i.e. wisely composed counsel will prove delicious when consumed by its beneficiaries, 16:24).

Two sayings outside Section II and Block III.A also pertain to the theme of composing and dispensing counsel. First, in the lecture's opening saying the verb *zārâ*, 'to winnow', offers the initial indication of dispensing counsel (15:7). For, in addition to describing separation of chaff from the kernel of grain (suggesting differentiation or discernment), 'to winnow' also describes the process of dispersing chaff. Counsel similarly must be disbursed.

Second, as the lecture draws to a close, the sage observes, paradoxically, that a servant who can 'instruct' (dispense counsel) will catapult ahead even of those who rank as aristocratic heirs (17:2). An earlier link between 'instruction' and the process of composing and dispensing of wise sayings indicates that the servant's instruction consists of counsel (cf. 15:24; 16:20, 22, 23).

Dual-theme verse (Sections II and III, content-based). The two cola of 16:2 in Section II anticipate with uncanny precision the start and finish of Block III.B. Thus 'All a person's ways appear clean in his own eyes' (16:2a) resembles the start of Block III.B: 'There is a way that from an individual's perspective is straight' (16:25a). Similarly 'the one who weighs spirits is the LORD' (16:2b) resembles the close of Block III.B: 'the one who sets up tests for motives is the LORD' (17:3b). Apart from reinforcement of themes, it is unclear why this dual-theme teaching (16:2) should be at such a distance from its corresponding portion (Block III.B).

Microstructural features

Section I (15:7–19). *Thematic continuity concerning discernment (15:7–19, content-based).* The theme of discernment joins together the two blocks of Section I. In the first the sage introduces the topic of discernment (Block I.A, 15:7–14). In the second he presents a demonstration showing the importance of discernment (Block I.B, 15:15–19). For evidence of this theme in Section I, please refer to 'Thematic continuity involving discernment' within 'Macrostructural features', above.

Wisdom commendation (15:7, content-based). A wisdom commendation opens Section I, honouring speech of the wise while discrediting thoughts of the stupid (15:7).

Thematic continuity involving discernment exercised by the divine (15:8–12, content-based). The capacity of the LORD to discern motives and conditions – even beyond physical death (in Sheol and the Place of Destruction) – binds together 15:8–9, 11. Divine reproof follows each of those in vv. 10, 12. This fosters cohesion for material ending at v. 12 (also noted in Waltke, who begins the portion at 15:5, however [2004: 622–623]; see remark on 15:10 under 'Comment', below).

Closure regarding wise folk (15:12, form-based). Mention of wise folk at the end of Unit 1.A.2 (15:12) recalls the same in the lecture's opening verse (15:7), fostering unit-level closure.

Repetition of 'mind' (15:13–14, form-based). The term 'mind' appears line-initial in both 15:13 and 14, joining these lines together to form Unit I.A.3. Double reference to 'mind' in 15:13 underscores the prominence of this term.

Thematic continuity concerning mental health (15:13–14, content-based). The parallel sayings comprising Unit I.A.3 deal with mental health (15:13–14), whether joyful and well informed, or anxious and poorly informed.

Inclusio involving 'mind', 'information' and 'stupid folk' (15:7, 14, form-based). When the same trio of expressions ('mind', 'information' and 'stupid folk') appears in the first and last sayings of Block I.A, an inclusio results (15:7, 14).

Thematic continuity surrounding poverty versus contentment (15:15–19, content-based). A contrast of poverty and contentment brings thematic continuity to 15:15–19. Suffering oppression contrasts enjoyment of a banquet in 15:15. Poverty and simple fare contrast treasure and feasting in 15:16–17. Rage may reasonably follow resentment upon realization of one's relative poverty (15:18). When poverty and contentment are expressed in a metaphor of travel, they emerge as 'a hedge of [restrictive] briars' in contrast to 'a highway' (15:19). Waltke similarly recognizes a conclusion at 15:19 (although he begins the portion at 15:13; 2004: 624).

Introduction and specification involving the adj. ṭôb *'good' (15:15, 16, 17, form-based).* The adj. *ṭôb* appears in each of 15:15, 16, 17 (rendered 'optimistic' and 'better'), fostering coherence. The first introduces the concept of an optimistic outlook, while the second and third specify how one can maintain that cheerful outlook, despite relative poverty. The root *ṭôb* appears nine more times in this lecture (15:23, 30; 16:8, 16, 19, 20, 29, 32; 17:1).

Waltke similarly observes the structuring effect of *ṭôb* in 15:15–17, but includes the related verb *yṭb*, 'to cheer', in 15:13 as well (2004: 624). However, based on the inclusio that unites 15:7, 14, it is preferable to recognize 15:13 as part of that introduction to discernment (Block I.A, 15:7–14), whose echoes would reasonably reach into the demonstration of discernment in the next block (Block I.B, 15:15–19).

Thematic complement encompassing comprehensive relationships (15:16, 17, content-based). The 'better-sayings' in 15:16, 17 complement each other by encompassing relationships comprehensively. The divine–human relationship occupies v. 16, while v. 17 deals with human–human relations.

Positive and negative patterning (15:16–17 contrasting vv. 18–19, content-based). Positive scenarios occupy the first colon in each of 15:16, 17 (typical for 'better-sayings'), while negative scenarios appear first in 15:18, 19. When joined with thematically related 15:15, this patterning recommends treating 15:15–19 as a connected group (Block I.B).

Thematic continuity of lack of self-control (15:18–19, content-based). Both the enraged person of 15:18a and the indolent person of v. 19a lack self-control (Waltke 2004: 628–629).

Assonantal link (15:18–19, form-based). Assonance involving *ʾerek*, 'restraint', and *ʾōraḥ*, 'path', joins 15:18b with 15:19b. Even *ʾăruḥat*, 'a meal', in 15:17 shares similarities of sound (Waltke 2004: 628).

Section II (15:20 – 16:15). *Thematic continuity concerning giving and receiving counsel (Blocks II.A and II.B, content-based).* The theme of counsel unifies the two blocks of Section II – introduced in Block II.A (15:20 – 16:9), and demonstrated in Block II.B (16:10–15; see 'Thematic continuity involving counsel, consumed and composed' within 'Macro-structural features', above). Although Waltke does not recognize the continuity of counsel, instruction and reproof beginning with 15:20 and extending through 15:32, he does observe considerable continuity joining 15:30 – 16:9 with 16:10–15 (2005: 5–6).

Wisdom commendation (15:20, content-based). As noted earlier, 15:20 operates as a wisdom commendation, opening Section II. Meinhold and Waltke similarly observe that a new portion begins in 15:20 (Meinhold 1991: 256; Waltke 2004: 631). They label this type of saying as 'educational' (Meinhold) or 'child-rearing' (Waltke).

Thematic continuity involving giving counsel (15:22–24, content-based). The theme of giving counsel appears in 15:22 ('candid counsel' and 'many advisors'), in v. 23 ('the reply of his mouth' and 'a saying'), and in v. 24 ('one who instructs').

Inclusio involving travel (15:21, 24, content-based). After the wisdom commendation of 15:20, the first verse of the wisdom content spanning 15:21–24 ends by portraying 'travel in a straight manner' (v. 21a). An inclusio for the wisdom content portion results when the theme of travel recurs at that portion's close (progress along an ascending path, 15:24).

Repetition of 'LORD' (15:25–26, form-based). The LORD is mentioned in both 15:25 and 26. This is the only mention of 'LORD' within the span of 15:20–27.

Double framing using the theme of household and the term 'life' (15:20–24, 25–27, content- and form-based). Each of two adjacent segments is framed by beginning with the theme of household and ending with the term 'life'. Thus a household is connoted in 15:20 by mention of 'son', 'father' and 'mother', while 'life' appears in 15:24, framing Segment IIA.1.a. Again, 'house' appears in 15:25, with the verb 'to live' in 15:27, framing Segment IIA.1.b.

Double inclusio involving 'house' (15:20, 25, 27, form- and content-based). Mention of 'house' in 15:27 creates a form-based inclusio with 'house' in v. 25 (Waltke also observes that 15:25–27 is framed by 'house' [2004: 635]). It also creates a content-based inclusio with the theme of household observed earlier in v. 20.

Repetition of 'moral' and 'guilty' (15:28–29, form-based). 'Moral' and 'guilty' appear in each of 15:28, 29, creating a quatrain (observed also by Waltke, as chiastic [2004: 635]).

Closure involving discernment, counsel and joy (15:30–32, form- and content-based). Closure marks the final segment of Unit II.A.1 by revisiting themes of discernment and counsel, and by repeating the term 'joy' (Segment II.A.1.d, 15:30–32). Perception is signified by observant eyes and attentive ears (15:30, 31), recalling the theme of discernment from Section I. Counsel, signified by 'reproof' and 'reprimand' (15:31, 32), recalls the same terms from 15:10, 12 in Section I, which then expanded into the theme of counsel in Segments II.A.1.a–c, 15:20–29). 'Joy' appeared expressly in 15:13, 20, 21, 23, before returning in 15:30.

Double palistrophe (15:33 – 16:9, form- and content-based). A double palistrophe comprised of repeated expressions (form-based) and related concepts (content-based) spans 15:33 – 16:9 (Unit II.A.2). The first palistrophe encompasses 15:33 through 16:6, pivoting in 16:3. The second overlaps the first, encompassing 16:3 through 16:9 and pivoting in 16:6.

The first palistrophe links balancing verses in the following manner. 'Reverence for the LORD' joins the first (outermost) steps (15:33a; 16:6b).

The second pair of steps describes human initiative (strategies, 16:1a), which may venture to the extent of human arrogance (16:5a). These prove no match for divine counsel (16:1b) and cannot withstand supernaturally determined punishment (16:5b).

In Hebr. the line-initial mention of 'all' links the third pair of steps: whether 'all a person's ways' or 'the LORD has engineered all' (16:2a and 4a, respectively). While 'all' appears in 16:5 as well, it is not line-initial.

A single pivot verse comprises the initial palistrophe's fourth step (16:3). Here the sage issues an imperative urging the pupil no longer to presume ultimate control (nor to assume ultimate responsibility) regarding his work. As the sole imperative in the entire lecture spanning 15:7 – 17:3, this instruction forms a striking palistrophic core, positioning the human planner to benefit maximally from divine counsel.

The second palistrophe (16:3–9) overlaps with the first (15:33 – 16:6). Sayings in the outermost step portray the LORD's 'establishing' a person's plans (16:3) or steps (16:9).

Respective components of the second step connect by the moral antonyms 'guilty' (16:4) and 'morality' (16:8). Though relatively common terms, within the double palistrophe (15:33 – 16:9) these terms occur only in 16:4, 8.

The third palistrophic step similarly involves opposites. The divine responds either with abhorrence (of arrogance, 16:5a) or with approval (bringing peace, 16:7a). Waltke similarly observes antonyms in 16:5, 7 framing v. 6 (2005: 12).

Once again, a single pivot verse forms the fourth step, this time addressing atonement (16:6; cf. pivot in v. 3). To position at a palistrophic pivot a statement concerning atonement underscores its significance in the sage's thinking.

Of the ten verses that occupy balanced steps in this palistrophe (15:33 – 16:9), Heim recognizes seven, whether in pairs or trios: 15:33 with 16:6, 16:2 with 4 and 8, and 16:5 with 7, contributing a measure of confirmation (2001: 207–210).

Closure (16:9, form-based). Five elements in 16:9 appeared earlier, creating closure for Block II.A (15:20 – 16:9): 'mind' (cf. 15:7, 13, 14, 15, 21, 28, 30, 32; 16:1), 'mortal' (cf. 16:1), 'devise', *ḥšb* (cf. 'plans', also from *ḥšb* in *ḥ*, 15:22, 26; 16:3), 'establishing' (16:3) and 'way' (16:2, 7). Heim similarly detects a break after 16:9, concluding a portion that began at 16:1 (2001: 206–210).

Repetition of 'king' (16:10, 12–15). Cohesion results from mention of 'king' in all but one verse of Block II.B (16:10–15). Meinhold similarly groups these verses due to the monarchial theme (1991: 269). Mention of the LORD, alone in the sole verse without mention of the human monarch, implies that the divine ranks as celestial monarch (16:11).

Repetition of 'justice' (16:10–11, form-based). Repetition of *mišpāṭ* in 16:10, 11 forms these sayings into a unit (Unit II.B.1). *Mišpāṭ* is rendered 'judicial proceedings' in 16:10, and 'justice' in v. 11.

Assonance (16:10–11, form-based). Line-initial in both 16:10 and 11 are nouns with a distinctive (and less common) segholate (*e-e*) vowel pattern: *qesem*, 'oracular verdict' (16:10), and *peles*, 'floor balances' (v. 11).

For Waltke also, repetition (of *mišpāṭ*, 'justice') and assonance connect 16:10–11. This verse-pair comprises the first of three quatrains that make up the block spanning vv. 10–15. Waltke labels them, 'The King's Authority' (16:10–11), 'The King's Moral Sensibility' (vv. 12–13) and 'The King's Power' (vv. 14–15; 2005: 16–22). Most if not all of the microstructural devices noted here in connection with vv. 10–15 are also observed by Waltke.

Progression from large to small, with summation (16:11, content-based). Tools for weighing array from large (floor scale) to small (mere weights, 16:11). To modify 'weights' with 'all' adds a summation, raising to a climax this final element of the series.

Repetition of 'moral' root (16:12–13, form-based). The root *ṭdq*, 'moral', joins 16:12 with v. 13. Mention of 'honesty' in v. 13 underscores moral conduct as the theme linking these two verses.

Grouping of pl. 'kings' and sg. 'king' (16:12–13, 14–15). Although 'king' appears in each verse of 16:12–15, it is pl. in vv. 12–13 and sg. in 14–15. This helps to distinguish the adjacent quatrains.

Positive and negative patterns in parallel quatrains, with repetition of 'pleasure' (16:12–13, 14–15, form-based). The two quatrains spanning 16:12–13, 14–15 display a similar positive–negative pattern. The first saying of each quatrain begins the positive and ends the negative (vv. 12, 14), while the second verse of each is wholly positive (vv. 13, 15). Also linking vv. 13 and 15 is the repetition of 'pleasure'.

Contrast of disfavour and favour (16:12–13, content-based). The quatrain of 16:12–13 coheres by contrasting opposing evaluations, both issued by the monarchy. Guilty deeds they loathe (v. 12a), while moral speech they favour and love (v. 13).

Contrast of death and life (16:14–15, content-based). The quatrain of 16:14–15 coheres through the antonyms 'death' (v. 14a) and 'life' (v. 15a).

Section III (16:16 – 17:3). *Wisdom commendation (16:16, form-based).* As observed earlier, Section III opens with a wisdom commendation in 16:16.

Thematic continuity concerning humility and arrogance (16:18, 19, content-based). The benefit of humility (and, conversely, the harm of arrogance) links 16:18, 19. Terms such as 'elevation', 'stumbling', 'loftiness', 'lowly', 'humble folk' and 'proud folk' contribute to this theme.

Framing with root g'h *(16:18–19, form-based).* A single root (*gʾh*) gives rise to 'elevation' and 'proud folk', framing the quatrain of 16:18, 19 in its outermost cola.

Repetition of 'spirit' (16:18, 19, form-based). Repetition of 'spirit' joins 16:18 and 19.

Inclusio concerning 'better' and 'good' (16:16, 20, form-based). The term *ṭôb* appears in 16:16 ('better') and 20 ('good'), creating a unit-level inclusio (Unit III.A.1, 16:16–20). Whereas acquiring wisdom is better than wealth (16:16), one who advances to the point of imparting wisdom to others ultimately attains what is 'good' (v. 20).

Between these two, the sage uses *ṭôb* also to teach that humility is better than great wealth (16:19). That saying joins with the second colon of v. 20 to elevate the worth of humble trust in the Lord.

Thematic continuity of transmitting wisdom (16:21, 23, 24, content-based). The theme of transmitting wisdom appears in 'lips' (16:21, 23), 'mouth' (v. 23) and 'beautiful sayings' (v. 24).

Inclusio involving 'sweet' (16:21, 24, form-based). The term 'sweet(ness)' appears in the outer verses of Unit III.A.2, creating an inclusio (16:21, 24). Mention of honey in v. 24 reinforces this theme. The first verse refers to expounding wisdom (v. 21). The closing verse deals with ingesting nutritious metaphoric honey (v. 24).

Repetition of 'wise' in connection with 'mind' (16:21, 23, form-based). Given the attention paid to 'mind' in this lecture (cf. 15:7, 13, 14, 28, 30, 32;

16:1, 5, 9), the line-initial combination of 'mind' with 'wisdom' to form 'a person who is wise-of-mind', *laḥăkam-lēb*, in 16:21 announces a signal achievement in wisdom maturation. That level earns the designation 'perceptive' – a term that earlier described the discerning person (cf. 15:14).

In 16:23 the two nouns are inverted, again line-initial: *lēb ḥākām*, 'a wise person's mind'. This time the wise person exhibits the skill of a wisdom composer (as also in 16:21b, 22). These foster continuity linking 16:21–23.

Closure by problem and solution concerning appetite (16:24, content-based). When 'appetite' first appears in 16:17b, it marks the locus where restraint must be exercised, lest immoral attractions lure the traveller off-course. When 'appetite' returns in the final verse of Block III.A, it fosters closure (16:24). There the appetite achieves wholesome satisfaction, as newly composed counsel proves 'sweet' to the 'appetite' and brings healing even to profound levels of inner illness.

Repetition of 'a person characterized by' (16:27–29, form-based). Of four negative characters listed in 16:27–30, the first three are closely connected since each verse opens with *ʾîš*, 'a person characterized by'.

Thematic continuity of negative characters (16:27–30, content-based). Following the series of three negative characters in 16:27–29 introduced by the expression 'a person characterized by', there appears one more in v. 30. That character exceeds the others by 'bringing evil to completion'. These four form a unity (16:27–30).

Inclusio involving 'lips' and 'evil' (16:27, 30, form-based). Mention of 'lips' and 'evil' in 16:27 and again in v. 30 creates an inclusio framing the four negative characters spanning 16:27–30. Although a common term, within this lecture the noun *rāʿâ*, 'evil', occurs elsewhere only in 15:28 and 16:4 (rendered 'misery'; 'evil' [*rāʿ*] in v. 6 is an adj.).

Assonance in the two verbs preceding *rāʿâ* further reinforces the use of 'evil' in 16:27, 30. In 16:27 the Hebr. phrase reads *kōreh rāʿâ*, 'digs up evil', while in v. 30 it reads *killâ rāʿâ*, 'brings evil to completion'.

Unit-level closure involving 'perversity' (16:30, form-based). In addition to inclusio involving 'lips' and 'evil', the last of four negative-character verses (16:30) reflects unit-level closure by repeating from 16:28 the term 'perversity'.

Thematic contrast between disastrous and desirable solutions (16:25, 26–30; 16:31 – 17:3, content-based). Block III.B opens with a dilemma: humans' natural deficit of critical faculties renders them unable to discern a desirable route in life (16:25). Two navigational strategies then follow – one disastrous, and one desirable. The disastrous strategy elevates appetites to the status of navigator (16:26), with four character-outcomes, each more despicable than the last (vv. 27–30).

Then follows a desirable character. He navigates by morals, not appetites (16:31). He discerns authentic value amid disappointments in life

(16:32 – 17:2), ultimately drawing confidence from God's sovereign discernment and implicit fairness (17:3). The combination of disastrous and desirable solutions to the dilemma of discernment-deficit creates cohesion for Block III.B (16:25 – 17:3).

Thematic continuity concerning perceived disadvantages (16:32 – 17:2, content-based, with formal component). Each saying within 16:32 – 17:2 describes a perceived disadvantage: inferior physical strength (16:32), inferior opportunity (v. 33), inferior riches (17:1) and inferior pedigree (17:2). Aided by the sage's discernment, the pupil discovers that none need pose an irreversible liability. Each can be either disproven or reversed outright.

Comment

Section I (15:7–19). In order to explain the mind's principal role and how to cultivate it, the sage begins by explaining the importance of discernment (Section I, 15:7–19). Lacking discernment, the youth will remain powerless to probe beneath the superficial in order to recognize what is truly worthwhile in life. To show the value of discernment, the poet introduces mental vitality together with the strategic nature of counsel obtained from others (Block I.A, 15:7–14). Then he will demonstrate how discernment can bring illumination (Block I.B, 15:15–19).

Block I.A (15:7–14). The lecture-opening wisdom commendation in 15:7 initiates (a) the theme of discernment ('winnowing information'), together with the need for (b) counsel ('the lips of wise folk'), both of which function in (c) the realm of the mind (negatively indicated by 'the mind of stupid folk'). The first two of this trio (discernment and counsel) originate in the divine, as the sage explains in two cycles. First, the divine can discern between sincere and pretentious piety (15:8–9). Unfortunately, counsel of reproof that the divine might bestow would be wasted on an evil, pretentious person, since he 'hates reprimand' (v. 10). In the second cycle, divine discernment penetrates even to the netherworld (v. 11)! Like the evil person, the scoffer (that most inveterate of wisdom-resistant persons) refuses to seek counsel (v. 12; cf. 'hates' of v. 10 with 'will not love' of v. 12).

After anchoring discernment and counsel in the divine, the sage explores how the third component of the trio – the mind – operates healthily among humans. Optimally, a mind spreads joy. If hobbled by anxiety instead, the mind will spawn despair (15:13). Fox concurs that v. 13 presents two options between which the pupil may choose, rather than stating irreversible conditions (2009: 594; cf. volitional alternatives in v. 15).

The sage then explains what characterizes a perceptive mind (15:14), implying that whether an individual chose joy or despair (v. 13) depended on whether he or she cultivated a perceptive mind. A mind that is perceptive will display thirst for information (v. 14a). Information comprises that raw material the mind must sift and assess, discerning between authentic and deceptive. Supplied with information properly discerned, the mind will be positioned to formulate wise decisions, to forge strategy, and select a course of action that generates reward and consequent joy. Later in this lecture the sage will identify as 'perceptive' one who achieves the pinnacle, becoming 'wise-of-mind' (16:21). Instead to refuse the route of perception is to let one's mind lazily graze, cattle-like, on anodyne diversions (v. 14b; cf. Waltke 2004: 625).

Block I.B (15:15–19). After proposing that discernment and counsel can foster a vibrant, joyous mind (Block I.A), the sage takes up a case in point. In Block I.B he demonstrates what a difference discernment can make, when applied to a specific predicament – the dilemma of relative poverty (15:15–19).

The sage begins this demonstration with an expansive claim: '*All* the days of an oppressed person are miserable, while a person with an optimistic outlook is a *continual* banquet' (15:15; emphases added; concerning embodiment of a banquet, see 'Notes'). Such far-reaching expressions as 'all' and 'continual' typically appear in a closing summation, not at the start of a portion. Such grand claims would capture hearers' attention, stirring wonder, if not doubt. Is the life of the oppressed universally miserable? Has he no moments of happiness? Conversely, is there never a ripple of sorrow or disappointment for the optimist?

A quandary still more core to the sage's message is this: Why would an 'optimistic outlook' (15:15b) counterbalance the 'oppressed person' (v. 15a)? Should not the 'continual banquet' in v. 15b associate with one freed-from-oppression? No, and precisely therein lies the sage's point. The optimist differs from the oppressed not due to chance attainment of freedom. The sage nowhere implies that the cheerful person has sidestepped all misfortune.

Rather, the difference is fundamentally mental in nature. The person perceiving plenty has cultivated *ṭôb-lēb* – literally, 'goodness of mind' (rendered 'an optimistic outlook'). He or she has developed the skill of perceiving (winnowing) information pertaining to his or her circumstances (cf. 15:7a, 14a). In contrast, the oppressed person is unable (v. 19a implies indolent unwillingness) to look beyond the face value of oppression he or she suffers, as unjust as it may be.

It would be erroneous to infer from this instruction that the sage was unconcerned about unjust suffering, as other sayings make clear (cf. 16:10, 11, 33; 24:10–12). But he has observed some who allow their experience of injustice to define their entire identity. They perceive nothing beyond their own oppression. For them the sage maps a way of escape, a path to recover lost joy, even though justice may yet delay.

Thus, after positing the shocking observation that some experience only misery where others enjoy an endless banquet (15:15), the sage supplies evidence through four sayings. In the first two, the pupil would realize that less may amount to more. For, when mixed with reverence (v. 16a) and served with love (v. 17a), a meagre fare exceeds the worth of great treasure or a sumptuous feast. Conversely, without reverence uneasiness will devalue treasure (v. 16b), just as hatred ruins an otherwise sumptuous feast (v. 17b).

By issuing in 15:16–17 the counsel to remember reverence and incorporate love, the sage illustrates an earlier point – the importance of seeking out pertinent information (v. 14). For the counsel transmitted through this information (urging reverence and love) provides the key to transform one's perception of relative poverty, exchanging mental misery for joy (v. 13).

Next the sage takes up personal discipline and its converse. When mixed with indiscipline, hatred (already brewing in 15:17b) boils into rage – angry eruptions that only repel reconciliation (v. 18a). Better by far is restraint that enables disputing parties to restore relationships (v. 18b).

As Section I draws to a close, the sage focuses on the importance of personal discipline (15:19). While passing for motionlessness, indiscipline is deceptive. For the barricading briar hedge will not suspend its gradual sprouting up, simply because the indolent chooses to remain immobile (15:19a).

In contrast, those characterized by moral progress ('honest folk') will discover their unimproved beginnings ('path') opening into a route engineered for reliable forward progress ('highway', 15:19b). When read against the backdrop of Section I, these 'honest folk' embody that personal discipline characterized by resolutely gathering and winnowing informative counsel (such as the importance of reverence towards God and love towards one's neighbour, 15:16–17). Discernment of this counsel facilitates joy as it reorients perception (transforming into an endless banquet one's outlook concerning oppression, v. 15). They restrain their inclination towards anger bred of resentment (v. 18), and so make steady headway (v. 19b), leaving behind the undisciplined person, imprisoned by his thorny hedge of indolence (v. 19a).

Thus one who with personal discipline cultivates a perceptive mind will become an interminable banquet (15:15b), not an unending tale of misery (v. 15a). For a healthy mental outlook comes not by accident.

15:8. The two actions listed here constituted for the Israelite 'the two essential acts of worship: slaying a costly animal and offering an accompanying prayer for favor' (Waltke 2004: 621).

15:17. Consumption of meat was generally restricted to sacrificial meals associated with a religious feast. Most days the menu consisted of grains and greens (Fox 2009: 596).

15:19. Paradoxically, the narrower 'path' offers greater progress than along the broader 'highway'.

Section II (15:20 – 16:15). After teaching that discernment yields a healthy mind (Section I), in Section II the sage identifies joy – a by-product of moral counsel – as the primary evidence of a healthy mind (15:20 – 16:15). Whereas cultivating discernment (Section I) fortifies one's internal capacity to assess the merits of information received, to obtain moral counsel (Section II) substantially accelerates progress towards joy, since it supplies the individual with practical advice from an external source, exceeding what that person may deduce by internal discernment.

Like Section I, after a wisdom commendation Section II presents an introduction, followed by a demonstration. The introduction explains the importance of receiving and giving moral (reverent) counsel, in order to achieve joy (Block II.A, 15:20 – 16:9). The demonstration focuses on a royal context, showing how moral counsel facilitates stability and prosperity in that arena (Block II.B, 16:10–15).

Block II.A (15:20 – 16:9). The sage introduces moral counsel in Block II.A in two parts. First, he explains why moral counsel results in joy (Unit II.A.1, 15:20–32). Second, he showcases reverence as the zenith of moral counsel (Unit II.A.2, 15:33 – 16:9).

The wisdom commendation opening Section II resumes the theme of joy encountered earlier in 15:13–14: 'A wise son will bring his father joy' (15:20). So universally desirable is joy, that even those who lack sense will attempt to counterfeit it (15:21a), parading a facsimile cobbled together of silly and insubstantial diversions (cf. 15:14b). Genuine joy, however, materializes as a perceptive person marks steady progress towards his or her objectives (v. 21b), a progress aided by 'candid counsel' from 'many advisors' (v. 22).

Joy accrues not only to the recipient of counsel, but also to its composers (15:23). They experience joy by watching pupils capitalize on instruction imparted, thereby attaining new heights of success. Chief among a counsellor's joy is the rescue that results when a pupil welcomes reproof, thereby 'turn[ing him]self from Sheol below' (see 'Notes' for 15:24).

Conversely, how tragic when the proud reject counsel, inviting instead destruction by the LORD's own agency (15:25a)! By simply embracing meekness they might have enjoyed divine deliverance instead of destruction (v. 25b). Although the arrogant followed counsel, it was not moral but 'evil plans' (v. 26a), urging reckless pursuit of economic gain (v. 27a). In contrast, 'beautiful' counsel, shunning graft, wins divine favour (vv. 26b, 27b).

For, morality alone determines the worthiness of a counsel-response (15:28). This obtains since only the moral counsellor enjoys divine intimacy (v. 29).

A recap concludes the first unit of Block II.A, sequentially reviewing discernment, joy, reproof-receptivity, counsellor-friends and ultimately the acquisition of a mature mind (15:30–32). The first colon embraces the entire process: 'The lamp of the eyes brings joy to the mind' (v. 30a). Joy characterizes a healthy mind, nourished by perceiving information (cf. vv. 7, 13, 14, 20–22). When that information constitutes 'good news' (moral counsel), deep inner health will ensue (it 'will fatten the bones', v. 30b).

Gathering of information continues with 'an ear that listens' (15:31a), now specifically welcoming 'reprimand'. Such a one cultivates a steady supply of life-giving counsel (v. 31b; cf. v. 22 and contrast v. 12). Instead to disregard reproof is symptomatic of poor self-esteem (v. 32a; for wordplay on 'life' as 'appetite', see 'Notes'). 'The ill-disciplined, uncontrollable person is on some level unhappy with himself and unconsciously self-destructive' (Fox 2009: 604). In contrast, those who embrace reproof attain the ultimate goal: a mature, morally formed mind (v. 32b).

In the unit just ended, the sage explained that joy results from receptivity to moral counsel, especially when that counsel takes the form of reproof (Unit II.A.1, 15:20–32). Now he will showcase reverence as the zenith of reproof (Unit II.A.2, 15:33 – 16:9).

Reverence is not new to this lecture. In the demonstration portion of Section I (Unit I.B, 15:15–19), reverence comprised the first information one might discern, resulting in joy (15:16).

In form, the present unit (Unit II.A.2) unfolds as a double palistrophe. Elegance of form reinforces importance of content (see under 'Microstructural features'). To trace progression of thought, the current discussion considers how the sage's thoughts unfold sequentially, not palistrophically.

After anchoring reverence as 'wisdom's reproof' (15:33a), the sage describes wisdom's worth. Reverence (implied by 'humility' in v. 33b) holds considerable worth, since it leads to honour (also v. 33b). Further, reverence registers worth since it gives access to superior, divine counsel (16:1b; see 'Notes').

Humans require that objective, divine counsel since too often we drift off-course, crediting ourselves with untainted motives (16:2; cf. 15:8–9, 11). 'What God examines is human sincerity in its depths, even beneath a person's delusive opinions of himself' (Fox 2009: 608). Wise are those who embrace the sage's imperative, entrusting their work to the divine, thus reinforcing human strategy with divine security (16:3; 'roll' is the sole imperative in 15:7 – 17:3). Then he will add confirmation to his counsel, for thereby they 'make [their] plans congruent with God's will' (Fox 2009: 609).

Thus to entrust one's work to the Lord is only reasonable, due to his sovereign oversight (16:4a). For God works reliably, bringing to fruition what he has counselled (cf. the counsel of his inspired 'reply' in 16:1b). Events will unfold reliably even for the guilty person. The day will come when he will suffer retributive misery – just as the sage cautioned (16:4b; cf. 15:8–9, 25–27, 29).

Refusal humbly to fit into God's coordinated plans will earn divine disfavour and punishment (16:5). Nevertheless, due to divine love even such iniquity as arrogance can be resolved, if one would but return to reverence (v. 6). Once restored to divine favour, enemies will become allies (v. 7). What is more, a meagre supply mixed with morality will exceed the value of riches amassed through immorality (16:8), reiterating the discernment registered in Section I (15:16). So seamless a progression of thought counters Fox's assessment of 16:8 as 'extraneous and perhaps added later' (2009: 606).

The unit's final saying sums up the instruction concerning reverence as the zenith of moral counsel, a teaching that began in 15:33. A wise person will engage all his mental faculties to plot an optimal life course (16:9a). Yet his confidence rests not in his brilliance, but in the LORD, whom the sage has taught the pupil to regard with reverence (15:33; cf. 15:9b and 16:3–4). For the divine will reliably secure his steps (16:9b).

Block II.B (16:10–15). After introducing moral counsel as a pathway to mental joy (Block II.A, 15:20–16:9), the sage demonstrates how moral counsel functions in the context of a monarchy (Block II.B, 16:10–15). A first glimpse of the monarch in this portion shows him obtaining divine ('oracular') counsel. This he must not compromise as he delivers a judicial verdict (16:10).

It would be reasonable for an earthly monarch to appeal to the celestial monarch for counsel. For all moral counsel, great or small, belongs to the divine domain (16:11; see 'Notes' concerning wordplay involving 'justice' and 'honest').

Aside from the wisdom of securing divinely moral counsel (16:10), specific conduct of monarchs should be moral, if they would foster a durable dynasty (v. 12). By extension, also those who counsel kings should embrace integrity (v. 13; note pl. 'kings' in vv. 12, 13).

Advice to courtiers begun in 16:13 intensifies in vv. 14–15 ('king' is sg. in both verses). Pupils must beware infuriating a monarch. By moral conduct and counsel courtiers will secure royal favour (vv. 12–13).

Depictions of royal favour ('the light of [his] face is life' in 16:15a, and 'his pleasure is as a spring rain cloud' in v. 15b) recall joy-filled outcomes earlier associated with wise behaviour (15:20–24, 30). Thus in the final quatrain of Section II the sage extends another implicit invitation to joy – achieved as the courtier observes the monarch's moral standards (16:14b, 15). In contrast, the courtier careless of moral conduct and counsel invites a confrontation with deadly rage (16:14a). Nowhere does the sage advise mindless assent to a ruler's immoral demands.

15:27. Mention of one who through greed would 'trouble [*ʿōkēr*] his house' may recall the sad saga of Achan. By greedily determining to secrete some of Jericho's forbidden booty beneath his tent, he brought his household to a violent end. So that valley came to be called the Valley of Achor, or the Valley of Trouble (*ʿākôr*, Josh. 7:26).

15:29–33. Fox proposes that 15:29–33 is connected by mention of hearing and reproof (2009: 603). While these are present, the flow of thought becomes clearer when vv. 28, 29 are linked by repetition of antonyms 'moral'–'guilty', with vv. 30–32 serving as a recap recalling earlier emphasis on joy and reproof (see progression of thought for Block II.A, above). Then 15:33 initiates the double palistrophe about reverence that reaches to 16:9 (see 'Double palistrophe' under 'Microstructural features' for Section II, above). At a later point Fox allows that v. 33 'may serve equally well to introduce 16:1–9' (2009: 605). This position, in my opinion, is better supported by structural evidence.

16:2. 'Weighing' as a metaphor for divine moral assessment of mortals at death appears in Egyptian culture as well. A wall painting in the chapel adjacent to the craftsmen's village of Deir el-Medina (serving the Valley of the Kings) portrays the heart of the deceased, resting on one of two pans suspended from the crossbeam of a balance-scale. On the other pan is a vertical feather, the emblem of Ma'at, goddess of truth, justice and order. Welfare of the deceased in the afterlife was thought to depend on how he or she would 'weigh', relative to the metric of divine truth.

16:10. In view of the prior context that (a) urged the necessity of outside counsel (15:20–32), and (b) ranked divine direction as the most prized of all counsels (15:33 – 16:9), the expression 'oracular verdict' refers to supernatural guidance aiding the monarch when weighing disputants' contradictory claims (cf. 16:33b; similarly, Waltke [2005: 17]; *pace* Fox, who questions whether 16:10 describes the monarch benefiting from supernatural direction in judicial decisions [2009: 615]).

16:14. See 14:35–36 concerning the hazard of a monarch's wrath.

Section III (16:16 – 17:3). After establishing that (a) the skill of discernment is requisite for a healthy mind (Section I), and after teaching that (b) moral counsel yields joy – that metric of a healthy mind (Section II; esp. 15:22–24, 28, 30–32, 33; 16:4, 9) – in this poem's final section the sage reviews those same themes: discernment and counsel. Block III.A revisits the theme of counsel (16:16–24), while Block III.B returns to the theme of discernment (16:25 – 17:3). When viewed alongside Sections I and II, discernment and counsel in Section III reach a higher level of intensity.

Block III.A (16:16–24). The first block of Section III (Block III.A, 16:16–24) underscores the importance of moral counsel as follows. The sage begins by asserting the value of wisdom, using a wisdom commendation that should – by this point – easily win pupils' assent: 'Acquisition of wisdom – how much better than gold, and acquisition of insight – preferred above silver!' (16:16).

Next he specifies two fundamental traits of wisdom. The first is morality, as 'honest folk' reject 'evil' (v. 17). Morality has featured prominently in this lecture (cf. 15:8–9, 26, 28–29, 33; 16:8–9, 10–13). Here in Section III morality entails restraint of appetites, requisite for any wishing to advance along life's 'highway'.

The second trait intrinsic to wisdom is humility (16:18–19). This too is a review, since earlier the sage advocated humility by urging receptivity to reproof (15:10, 12, 13–32), by commending reverence (15:16, 33; 16:6) and by valuing meekness while lamenting arrogance (15:25, 33; 16:5). By according pride (16:18–19) one saying more than morality (16:17), the poet emphasizes the hazard it poses. Double mention of one's 'spirit' (attitude, 16:18, 19) recalls the last mention of 'spirit', within a warning against discounting what is impure in one's own conduct (16:2). The core of self-excuse is arrogance, not ignorance.

It is well, personally, to travel the path of morality and humility. Still better is to counsel others along this way, thereby achieving the supreme 'good' (16:20a). Lest this lofty achievement seduce one into smug self-reliance, the sage concludes this unit, swiftly adding, 'but it is the one who trusts in the LORD who is truly fortunate' (v. 20b). Trust in the divine constitutes humility of the highest order.

The next unit extends the worth of composing counsel (Unit III.A.2, 16:21–24). One who fashions 'sweet' counsel attains high acclaim as a 'perceptive' person (16:21) – a trait with rank already established in this lecture (15:14, 21; also Fox [2009: 619] and Waltke [2005: 29–30] remark that this portion indicates an instructor, not merely a wisdom consumer). The master-instructor achieves not less than a veritable 'spring of life' (16:22), imparting instruction that keeps growing, compounding learning (v. 23).

In its final verse Unit III.A.2 escalates to a singular summit the sage's acclaim for crafting counsel (16:24). Newly composed sayings nourish as would sweet honey, satisfying at last that appetite which earlier required restraint from immoral conduct (16:17). These teachings heal brokenness even at the level of a person's inner core (v. 24). Waltke similarly notices the sense of climax attained in v. 24 (2005: 30).

Block III.B (16:25 – 17:3). After revisiting in Block III.A the value of composing counsel, the poet develops in Block III.B the importance of discernment, especially when choosing a path in life. This block opens, not with a wisdom commendation, but with a dilemma concerning navigation (16:25). Confronted with a fork in the road, the traveller must choose. Left to his own discernment, we are informed that the traveller will err – fatally.

Next the poet outlines two solutions – alternative sources of navigational discernment. The first is one's own appetite (16:26–30). Since hunger effectively motivates (16:26), may it not also reliably navigate?

As if in reply, the sage produces a series of four characters (16:27–30). Mention of 'lips' in connection with the first (v. 27) and last (v. 30) suggests that each exemplifies an appetite gone awry (link 'lips' with 'appetite' and 'mouth' from v. 26). The lips of the first are scorched, as if by greedily devouring roasted food before it had a chance to cool down. What he should have let alone to 'cool down' was news of evil that had been mercifully buried, put out of sight. Instead this 'worthless' fellow exhumes it, evidently hungry to launch a smear campaign. Such an appetite will not end well.

Worse than the 'worthless' fellow of 16:27 is the 'perverse' person (v. 28). He speaks evil even of close friends, harming himself by repelling them.

When the third character replaces slanderous words with tangible violence, even recruiting others to join him, the negative cascade has reached a new low (16:29). To be 'not good' denotes a condition worse than the mere words suggest (Fox 2009: 622).

The list reaches its nadir as the fourth character 'plans perversity' with eyes tightly shut (either to concentrate or to silence the conscience). He then executes premeditated 'evil' (16:30, recalling 'evil' earlier exhumed in v. 27; Waltke also detects a climax in this character [2005: 31]). These four characters demonstrate that appetites entrusted with navigation escort with fatal predictability (cf. v. 25).

Whereas appetites are faulty guides, morality emerges as a time-tested means of navigation (16:31). In a culture of short life expectancy, longevity proves the success of morality ('a splendid crown is grey hair').

The sage proceeds to sketch the contours of this morality. Unlike the licence of appetites unbridled, morality begins with restraint – such as reining-in one's natural tendency to rage and revenge when wronged (16:32a). It is self-control, not boisterous revenge, that signals authentic greatness (v. 32b). Such a one keeps sight of the fact that, although near-term outcomes may bring random misfortune or unfairness ('into a lap the lot is thrown'), God has not surrendered sovereign control. He ensures eventual justice (v. 33).

Such awareness of divine control (16:33) will foster contentment despite meagre fare that follows moral conduct (17:1; recall divine trust, 16:20b). For, although refusing to resort to 'contention' (recall '[self-] restraint of anger' in 16:32) may yield a mere 'dry morsel' instead of overflowing 'feasts', yet such trust in moral conduct surpasses the worth of overflowing 'feasts' poisoned by 'contention' (17:1). Here again, navigation by appetites fails.

The scenario of contentment despite a smaller allotment extends into 17:2. By cultivating sapiential skills, one born to inferior status ('servant') may achieve honours surpassing even those enjoyed by aristocratic heirs. Specifically, those sapiential skills involve 'instructing' – composing and dispensing wisdom.

Is one misguided or naive, when placing in morality such confidence for navigation, such dependance for ultimate fairness? Not at all, assures the sage. For the divine can be depended on to discern and uphold morality, assessing even the hidden recesses of individual motives (17:3). Recalling the picture of winnowing grain from this lecture's opening saying (15:7), divine powers of discernment far exceed the finest metallurgist's skill in determining when a precious metal has reached purity. Appetites, in contrast, can only lead astray. For they remain powerless to render moral direction.

16:25. This saying appeared verbatim in 14:12. Perhaps it was in Jesus' thinking when he cautioned against the spacious road that leads to destruction (Matt. 7:13).

Explanation

In this lecture the sage's advice focuses inward, exploring the mind's principal role and how to cultivate it. He seeks to help pupils cultivate minds characterized by health and vigour, so they may weather inevitable turbulence with resilience, even joy. That joy will result from a mind that has been trained for its focal, twofold role: to exercise discernment and engage counsel (receiving and composing it).

Section I. Discernment: the route to a healthy mind (15:7–19)
Consider first the importance of discernment. To cultivate discernment, one must winnow information (15:7) one has sought out (v. 14).

Discernment originates with God. He weighs the sincerity of every pious act (15:8–12). He cannot be fooled by hypocritical piety, but will show favour, even love, to any who pursue moral living.

When discernment unveils reproof that requires a change of thought or behaviour, we must not bristle (15:10). Else we risk shutting down a source of crucial information (v. 12). Doing so would shut out joy, consigning ourselves instead to a crushing load of mental anxiety (v. 13).

Robust discernment enables us to take two steps that defy bitterness, giving us access to a banquet instead (15:15). The first step regards God with steady reverence (v. 16), while the second regards our neighbour with love (v. 17). We must beware the temptation to react to relative poverty with either rage or indolence. These will only perpetuate dissatisfaction and thwart personal progress (vv. 18–19). For, a mind enslaved to lassitude refuses to pursue information and consequently renders the intellect anaemic, deprived of the very fuel that could enable it to escape an egocentric orbit. Instead it will remain paralysed by negative circumstances.

Section II. Moral counsel: the route to joy (15:20 – 16:15)
After discernment, moral counsel marks the second step towards cultivating a mind that accesses joy. Joy belongs, first, to those who cultivate their ability to instruct others in moral, life-giving counsel (15:20–24). Those who arrogantly resist the offer of moral counsel will suffer ruin (vv. 25–27). For joy belongs, second, to those who are receptive to the illumination provided by moral counsel (vv. 28–31). Resistance to reproof amounts to self-hatred (v. 32).

The premier reproof consists of a call to reverence (15:33). Through the gateway of reverence we may obtain divine counsel (16:1) that dispels the fog of self-delusions (16:2). Divine counsel is worthy of trust (16:3), since the LORD ensures that his intended outcomes will materialize (16:4), including (but not limited to) undesirable outcomes unwittingly chosen by those who reject reverence (16:5–6). Contentment, a correlative of joy, follows those whose lives reflect morality (a derivative of reverence, 16:8), who plan as best they can, all the while relying on God's care over ultimate outcomes (16:9).

Those entrusted with leadership should be among the first to seek counsel – particularly divine counsel (16:10). For the fairness they must model and instil originates with the LORD (v. 11). Both leaders and their subordinates can only benefit by a policy of morality in deed and word (vv. 12–15).

Section III. Review: underscoring the importance of moral counsel and discernment (16:16 – 17:3)

Discernment, and giving-and-receiving counsel – these two signposts mark the path to a vibrant mind. Regarding the second of these, that counsellor who learns to offer instruction anchored in morality (16:17) and in humility (vv. 18–19) – he or she attains what is truly good, surpassed only by one who steadfastly depends on the divine (v. 20). Such an instructor will discover the healing sweetness of life at its best (vv. 21–24).

Regarding the first of these, failure to cultivate discernment will bring lethal consequences (16:25). In particular, a failure to discern the incapacity of appetites to provide reliable moral navigation – this failure will prove catastrophic, injuring self, damaging close friendships, misleading friends and climactically anaesthetizing all ethical sensibilities (vv. 26–30).

For motivation, we may enlist the aid of appetites (16:26). However, in order to identify worthy aims towards which appetite-driven motivation should be unleashed, we must first appeal to morals (v. 31). Otherwise, if innate appetites are permitted to authorize objectives, and if those objectives then trespass otherwise-attested moral boundaries, we may erroneously conclude that, through ostensibly God-given appetites (therefore exempt from moral restraint), 'I am being tempted by God.' James incisively cautions against this faulty logic, for it endorses a suicidal captivity at the hands of one's own desires (Jas 1:13b–16).

When morals, not appetites, are entrusted with navigation, they lead to longevity (16:31). When the inevitable neighbourly offence occurs, those morals respond with resilient self-control and divine reliance, rather than belligerence and faithlessness (16:32–33).

When the inevitable unfair compensation disappoints, those morals map a response informed by discernment of what is truly worthwhile (17:1), combined with a determination to rise above disappointment by excelling in wisdom instruction (17:2). For, the individual governed by morality can rest secure in the confidence that the LORD, who hears and loves the moral (15:8–9), and who discerns motives with ease (15:11), can be counted on to uphold cosmic standards of morality (with associated fairness), distinguishing right from wrong, sincere from deceptive, even to the depth of assessing an individual's motives (17:3).

PROVERBS 17:4 – 19:9
'Can any hazard exceed a fool's?'

Overview of Proverbs 17:4 – 19:9

To the extent that length and compositional refinement signal a topic's importance, the lecture warning against evildoers must in the sage's thinking rank as exceptionally vital (Prov. 17:4 – 19:9). Here the poet reveals that he could not rest content if, at the conclusion of their training, his pupils were to surmise that a simple strategy of folly-avoidance would be sufficient to ensure a flourishing life.

Through this lecture the pupil will learn that, superior to and interweaving twin categories of wisdom and folly, there towers the moral category of good, which suffers cunning and unrelenting attack from evil. As foul as is the fool, there looms another far worse – the malevolent. Wise is the pupil who learns both to evade folly, and also to recognize and reckon with the evildoer.

What characterizes the evildoer? Through falsehood focused in slander he specializes in predatory litigation, hijacking systems of justice to satisfy selfish aims. Alert to those strategies for subverting the judiciary, the sage sounds a klaxon concerning the first inklings of strife that will later metastasize into legal disputes (17:14; 18:1).

The lecture closes with counsel for the rejected-poor (Section IV, 18:23 – 19:9). Initially they seem an appendix, disconnected from the evildoer except, perhaps, as victims. However, sentiments hauntingly reminiscent of the lecture's earlier scenarios intimate that past suffering of rejection may have marginalized the disaffected and so may have given rise to the archetypal evildoer – the malevolent loner.

A reminder concerning reading contextually may be helpful. As the more transparently theme-cohesive poems of Prov. 1 – 9 recede further into the background, increasingly the sage invites us to recognize meaning intended for a given saying by listening closely to its immediate context. Thus, at various points in this poem, adjacent sayings that by structure cluster together are treated as contributing to the theme of that cluster, even though the theme may not appear explicitly in each of the cluster's sayings. As before, observations concerning progression of thought (condensed in outline headings, subsequently explained under 'Comment') seek to illumine the dynamic configuration of such clusters.

Position of this poem within Proverbs

Preceding context. In the lecture just concluded (15:7– 17:3) the sage turned from offering counsel concerning various desirable life-destinations that began in Prov. 10 (achieving wealth, security, a more noble character, a secure 'house'). In contrast, that last poem focused on the mind itself – that part of one's person responsible for escorting the pupil towards those desirable life-destinations. A distinctly climactic verse closed that lecture (17:3), leading to a new subject in 17:4.

Like the last lecture, the present poem refrains from helping the pupil attain a specific life goal. Instead the sage cautions concerning evil – that universal obstacle capable of blocking progress towards any goal.

Ensuing context. The next lecture returns to topics of wealth and power, but with a strategic shift (19:10 – 20:4). Increasingly the sage trains pupils so they, in turn, may train others.

What to watch for

An advanced degree of subtlety marks this lecture. It appears as though the poet assumes the pupil's skill in grasping wisdom poems has steadily advanced. So he supplies fewer way-markers to announce themes, less literary rigging for tracing train-of-thought. As Heim observes, 'there is a greater variety of themes in Proverbs 17 than in previous chapters, and obvious links are missing . . . [T]he method by which clusters are arranged are [*sic*] different' (2001: 225). Nevertheless, method does exist, and themes are present. As outlined directly below, three compositional techniques dominate the sage's method of arrangement, while the lecture's themes concentrate on three pairs of opposing topics.

Three compositional techniques

1. Two-plus-one clusters of sayings. Six times the sage presents a trio of adjacent sayings. Two initial verses present a single theme, while the third contrasts (trio designated in the outline by 'two-plus-one'). The first two trios are contiguous, addressing similar themes. Together these two trios establish the evildoer's ostensible destiny (attaining splendour in 17:4–6; attaining popularity). His destiny follows in vv. 10–11 (suffering a cruel fate).

Four trios remain, unified by wisdom commendations that occupy the first two sayings of each. Then follows wisdom content in each third verse (17:21–23, 24–26; 17:27 – 18:1; 18:20–22). Of these four trios, the first two are contiguous, closing Section II. They treat evil arising from family members (II.C, 17:21–23, 24–26). The two remaining trios frame all of Section III, a section identifying the evildoer as a malevolent loner (17:27 – 18:1; 18:20–22).

In addition to this form-based framing of Section III with trios at start and finish, even the topic of speech within wisdom commendations opening that section (17:27–28) resembles the topic of speech in closing wisdom commendations (18:20–21). Further, the respective wisdom contents connect as a problem (loneliness, 18:1) and a solution (marriage, 18:22; see under 'Microstructural features').

2. Frequent use of wisdom commendations. Fourteen times (using nineteen sayings) the sage uses a wisdom commendation to introduce wisdom content. Ten commendations operate in pairs (quatrains). Not every saying containing wisdom vocabulary qualifies as a wisdom commendation (e.g. 18:12; 19:2, 3, 7, 8).

Thirteen of the nineteen function as expected for wisdom commendations. These describe wisdom's worth, without recommending situationally specific behaviour: 17:10, 12, 16, 21–22, 24–25, 27–28; 18:2, 4, 6–7.

Six remaining sayings qualify as wisdom commendations (despite recommending certain conduct) for three reasons. They (a) employ wisdom vocabulary, (b) lack general continuity with preceding content and (c) lead directly to wisdom content (e.g. 17:18; 18:13, 15, 20–21; 19:1).

It should be acknowledged that two of these six display a measure of continuity with preceding content since they are embedded in larger theme-related portions. Thus 'friend' appears both in 17:16–17 and again in the wisdom commendation of 17:18, since vv. 16–17 introduce the section extending through v. 26 (Section II). That section deals with 'Evil arising from unexpected sources', including sources such as 'friends'. Similarly 18:23–24 deals with poverty, as does the wisdom commendation of 19:1, because 18:23–24 introduces Section IV (18:23 – 19:9), a section dealing with loneliness induced by poverty.

Finally, the fact that wisdom traffics in words results in several wisdom commendations that address speech (cf. 17:27–28; 18:2, 4, 6–7). Their use of wisdom vocabulary and their customary function (serving to introduce wisdom content; cf. 18:1, 3, 5, 8–9) lessen the focus on speech within those wisdom commendations, resulting in greater focus on the ensuing wisdom content.

3. Semantic obscurity. Periodically, the poet composes a saying with syntax so jarring that it defies rapid comprehension. Such is the case in 17:12, 26; 18:19; 19:1, 7. This obscurity is no accident, no scribal error, but rather evidences strategic composition. By this means the sage obliges the reader to decelerate, slowing to a deliberate pace. He or she must consider more deeply the topics caught in that saying. It may require review of other parts of the lecture to consider connections and connotations (see 'Notes', 'Comment' and 'Microstructural features' for these sayings; for further discussion of jarring sayings, see §5.7 in the 'Introduction').

Three opposing topic-pairs

The theme-related pairs involving (a) evil–good, (b) wealth–poverty and (c) isolation–community illumine most of the sage's aims within this lecture. These three are not partitioned, but interweave across the poem. Thus the evildoer (first theme) wields wealth (second theme) in a manipulative manner and splinters the community (third theme). Due to the scope and compositional refinement of this lecture, the following catalogue of topics may prove helpful.

1. Evil versus good. The role of 'evildoer' initiates with *mēra'*, the lecture's opening word ('one who perpetrates evil', 17:4). 'Guilty' and 'evil' serve as synonyms, enlarging the portrait of an evildoer (cf. 17:11, 13, 15, 23; 18:3, 5).

Strategies associated with evildoers include deceit and slander (17:4, 7; 18:8; 19:5, 9). Their deceit may take the form of false gifts or bribery (17:8, 23; 18:16). Or deceit may disguise the sinister reality of relationships masquerading as trustworthy (17:17, 18, 21, 24–25). In the final analysis, deceivers will be unable to dodge the penalty of their behaviour (17:5; 19:5, 9).

Evildoers foster strife and litigation (cf. 17:11a, 14; 18:1, 6, 17, 18, 19). They are drawn to inflict damage, cruelty and destruction (17:13), especially indirectly or under the protection of the law (17:15, 23, 26; 18:5). Such destruction afflicts others initially, but eventually will rebound upon themselves (17:4, 11b, 14, 19, 22, 26; 18:1, 6, 7, 12, 14, 23, 24; 19:5, 9).

Opposite evil is *ṭôb*, 'the good' – a term the poet employs seven times, both positively and negatively ('not good'). Between bookend sayings ('not finding good' in 17:20, and 'finding good' in 19:8), five more involve this theme (17:26; 18:5, 22; 19:1, 2). Also opposing evil are moral persons (root *ṣdq*, the antonym of 'guilty'). Within this lecture they occupy a role that is passive, victimized or illusory, thus underscoring the sage's focus on the evildoer (17:15, 26; 18:5, 10, 17).

2. Wealth versus poverty. Due to their wealth, some gain popularity while others suffer rejection (17:5; 18:23; 19:4, 6, 7). Consequently some erroneously regard wealth as their ultimate security (18:11), leading them to jettison integrity in pursuit of wealth (19:1). Some wield wealth to overturn justice – an especially sinister strategy of the evildoer (17:23; 18:16). What draws them to such misconduct is an unrestrained craving (18:1, 7; 19:2, 8).

3. Isolation versus community. Instead of building community, relationships characterized by evil (first theme) and wealth (second theme) breed only isolation (17:5, 9; 18:1, 19; 19:4, 7). In contrast, the sage commends community characterized by affirmation and mercy, epitomized by marriage and the family (17:6, 9; 18:22).

Translation and outline

Verse	*Translation*	*Outline*
		I. Introduction of evildoers (17:4–15) A. The evildoer's desired destiny: splendour and popularity (17:4–9) 1. The evildoer counterfeits splendour through destruction, with alternative (17:4–6, two-plus-one)

17:4 One who perpetrates evil pays attention to a dialect of disaster; falsehood keeps an ear out for language of destruction. 17:5 One who mocks the poor taunts his Maker; one who experiences joy over calamity will not be acquitted.	a. Two destructive strategies: demise of others and devaluing of others (17:4–5) i. Demise of others counterfeits splendour for self (17:4) ii. Devaluing of others counterfeits an inflated value of self (17:5)
17:6 Grandchildren are a crown for the elderly, and splendour of sons is their fathers.	b. One exemplary alternative: authentic splendour radiates through intergenerational honour (17:6)
17:7 Gushing language is not attractive for a good-for-nothing; how much worse for a prince is a language of falsehood! 17:8 A stone of favour is the bribe, in the opinion of its owner; wherever he turns he has success.	2. The evildoer counterfeits popularity through false generosity, with alternative (17:7–9, two-plus-one) a. Two strategies of counterfeit generosity: flattery and bribes (17:7–8) i. Flattery counterfeits verbal generosity (17:7) ii. Bribes counterfeit material generosity (17:8)
17:9 One who covers transgression seeks love, but one who repeats an issue alienates a close friend.	b. One exemplary alternative: authentic generosity conveys mercy (17:9)
17:10 A rebuke will penetrate an insightful person more thoroughly than a hundred blows will a stupid fellow.	B. The evildoer's destiny, and a warning to dissuade him (17:10–15) 1. Destiny of the evildoer (17:10–11) a. Wisdom commendation: blows of reproof are wasted on the stupid . . . (17:10)

Verse Translation	Outline
17:11 Nothing but contention will an evil person seek. So a cruel messenger will be sent against him.	b. Wisdom content: . . . but they paradoxically are not wasted on the evil person, since contention is his aim and cruelty his destiny (17:11)
17:12 May a bereaved bear encounter a person, rather than a stupid fellow encountering his folly.	2. A warning to dissuade the evildoer (17:12–15) a. Wisdom commendation: although rampant stupidity is worth evading . . . (17:12) b. Wisdom content: . . . still worse is rampant evil – it must be arrested early (17:13–15)
17:13 One who returns evil for good: evil will not depart from his house.	i. Caution: ethics overturned reap persistent evil (17:13)
17:14 Water escaping is the start of strife. So, before a lawsuit breaks out give it up!	ii. Charge to evildoer: to avoid irreversible retribution, desist from evil strife early (17:14)!
17:15 One who justifies the guilty and one who renders the just guilty – abhorrent to the LORD are both.	i'. Caution: ethics overturned reap divine disfavour (17:15)
17:16 How is it possible that in the hand of a stupid fellow there would be tuition to invest in wisdom, since what he is missing is sense?	II. Evil arising from unexpected sources (17:16–26) A. Introduction: unexpected sources of evil (17:16–17) 1. Wisdom commendation: the illogic of the senseless (17:16)
17:17 At all times a friend loves, and a brother for distress will be born.	2. Wisdom content, with dual-theme introduction: by definition, friends and family should be devoid of evil . . . (17:17)
	B. . . . But evil may arise unexpectedly from among so-called 'friends' (17:18–20)

17:18 A mortal lacking sense will shake hands, emphatically guaranteeing a loan before his friend. 17:19 One who loves trespass loves a brawl; one who makes lofty his entryway seeks collapse. 17:20 A twisted mind cannot find good, and one who pivots with his tongue will fall into evil.	1. Wisdom commendation: the illogic of the senseless, who pledge for a supposed 'friend' (17:18) 2. Wisdom content: twisted love and deceptive pledges (17:19–20) a. The focus of a person's love exposes his character (17:19) b. Unreliable pledges plunge one into misery (17:20)
17:21 One fathers a stupid fellow to his grief, and the father of a good-for-nothing cannot rejoice. 17:22 A mind characterized by joy can make a cure appealing, but a crushed spirit will desiccate bones.	C. . . . And evil may arise unexpectedly from among family members (17:21–26) 1. It is evil when wealth overturns justice (17:21–23, two-plus-one) a. Wisdom commendation: parental grief or joy (17:21–22) i. Filial stupidity brings only anguish to one's parent (17:21) ii. Cure offered in response to that stupidity will either sweeten or scorch, depending on counsellor's foundation in joy (17:22)
17:23 A guilty person will take a bribe out of a breast pocket, to divert paths of justice.	b. Wisdom content: evildoers overturn justice by subversive monetary gifts (17:23)
17:24 In the presence of an insightful person, there awaits wisdom; but a stupid fellow's eyes are on the ends of the earth.	2. It is evil when force overturns justice (17:24–26, two-plus-one) a. Wisdom commendation: a son's flitting focus brings parental grief (17:24–25) ii'. Mental focus would foster wisdom, instead of stupid speculations – (17:24)

Verse	*Translation*	*Outline*
17:25	A stupid son is a vexation to his father, and bitterness to her who gave birth to him.	i'. – A stupid sort of speculation that brings only anguish to both parents (17:25)
17:26	Also to impose a fine on the moral person is not good, to strike princes for being honest.	b. Wisdom content: having already overturned justice (cf. 17:23), evildoers proceed to extract monetary fines from the innocent (17:26)
		III. The evildoer's nature and strategy, with safeguards against them (17:27 – 18:22) A. Introduction to the evildoer's outward strategy and inward nature (17:27 – 18:1, two-plus-one) 1. Wisdom commendation: he pursues an illusive strategy of restrained speech (17:27–28)
17:27	One who restrains his words is very knowledgeable, and a cool spirit is a person of perception.	a. He restrains his speech . . . (17:27)
17:28	Even a fool who keeps quiet may be regarded as wise; one who shuts his lips is a perceptive person.	b. . . . And so simulates wisdom (17:28)
18:1	What he craves – that is what a loner will seek; with consummate competence he will break into a lawsuit.	2. Wisdom content: the evildoer is by nature an egocentric loner, by strategy a persuasive litigator (18:1)
		B. Exposure of the evildoer's predatory, litigious strategies (18:2–9) 1. Initially restrained, in time he launches an opening gambit of scorn-filled indictments (18:2–3)
18:2	A stupid fellow cannot take delight in perception, but rather in laying bare his mind.	a. Wisdom commendation: unlike the stupid, the evildoer practises verbal restraint (18:2, contrast 17:27–28)
18:3	When a guilty person enters, contempt enters, too; and with ignominy, reviling.	b. Wisdom content: his first tactic heaps up scorn on the defendant (18:3)

Translation	Outline
18:4 Words of a person's mouth are deep waters; a spring of wisdom is a rushing stream. 18:5 Showing partiality towards a guilty person is not good, thrusting aside the moral person in the courtroom.	2. Those scornful indictments require close scrutiny, for they scheme to overturn justice (18:4–5) a. Wisdom commendation: using subtle and sinister words, so unlike wisdom . . . (18:4) b. Wisdom content: . . . Those scornful indictments would blind the bench to fairness (18:5)
18:6 Lips of a stupid fellow will enter into a lawsuit, and his mouth will call for beatings. 18:7 A stupid fellow's mouth is his destruction, and his lips are a snare for his appetite.	3. After scorn, he resorts to a second tactic: slander (18:6–9) a. Wisdom commendation: again, the evildoer contrasts the stupid, who shows no restraint in court (18:6–7) i. Only a stupid fellow would litigate rashly . . . (18:6) ii. . . . Convicting himself in the process (18:7)
18:8 Words of a slanderer are like delicacies, so they descend deep within a person. 18:9 Also, one who is careless about his work is brother to the master-destroyer.	b. Wisdom content: the evildoer's second tactic escalates to combine . . . (18:8–9) i. . . . Slander of defendant (18:8) ii. . . . With sleepiness on the bench (18:9)
18:10 A strong tower is the LORD's name; into it a moral person will rush, and so will be perched high.	C. Offer of safeguards to protect against his litigious strategy (18:10–19) 1. Impregnable divine protection for the moral (18:10)
18:11 A rich person's wealth is his strong city, and like a high town wall in his imagination.	2. Wealth may supply momentary protection . . . (18:11–12) a. The wealthy presume riches will protect from litigation (18:11)

Verse	*Translation*	*Outline*
18:12	Before breakage a person's mind will become lofty; and before honour, humility.	b. But that very pride foreshadows their downfall (18:12)
		3. . . . But judicial diligence and impartiality supply monumental protection (18:13–19) a. The need for judicial diligence (18:13–14)
18:13	One who issues a verdict before he may even hear: that is folly for him, and an insult.	i. Wisdom commendation: the folly of lazy impatience during discovery phase of a court case (18:13)
18:14	A person's spirit may endure when he is ill, but a crushed spirit, who can bear it?	ii. Wisdom content: the unbearable heaviness of justice denied (18:14)
		b. The need for judicial impartiality (18:15–19)
18:15	The mind of a perceptive person will keep on investing in information, and the ears of wise folk will keep on searching for information.	i. Wisdom commendation: the wisdom of diligence during discovery phase of a court case (18:15)
		ii. Wisdom content: the importance of judicial impartiality (18:16–18)
18:16	A mortal's gift will make room for him, and it can escort him into the presence of great people.	α. Risk of judicial subversion: influence must not be for sale (18:16)
18:17	The first person to appear in his lawsuit is moral; his neighbour will come and cross-examine him.	β. Due process must not be circumvented (18:17)
18:18	The lot can bring strife to a close, and can create space between mighty opponents.	α'. Risk of judicial subversion: a divine decision can resolve the threat of violent conflict (18:18)
18:19	A brother who has suffered transgression by a 'strong city', and by strivings, is like a citadel bar.	iii. Final warning: justice subverted imprisons the innocent (18:19)

	D. Conclusion: the retributive power of words, and a cure for the loner (18:20–22, two-plus-one) 1. Wisdom commendation: the retributive effect of words (18:20–21)
18:20 From the fruit of a person's mouth will his belly be satisfied; with the revenue of his lips will he be satisfied.	a. Speech eventually rewards the speaker . . . (18:20)
18:21 Death and life are in the power of the tongue, and one who loves it will eat of its fruit.	b. . . . With death-or-life consequences (18:21)
18:22 He who has found a wife has found what is good, and has obtained approval from the LORD.	2. Wisdom content: in marriage lies the LORD's solution for the loner (18:22)
	IV. Loneliness: the problem of uninvited isolation, with strategies for success (18:23 – 19:9) A. Introduction: the problem of the isolated-poor, with strategies for success (18:23–24)
18:23 A poor person keeps on uttering pleas for help, but a rich person keeps on replying stridently.	1. Problem: suffering isolation due to poverty (18:23)
18:24 A person known for friends will suffer ruin; but there is one who loves, who clings more loyally than a brother.	2. Solution: overcoming isolation, not by quantity of friends, but by quality (18:24)
	B. A strategy for success despite isolation due to poverty (19:1–9)
19:1 Better a poor person who walks in his integrity, than if he were to operate with twisted lips – and so would prove to be a stupid person.	1. Wisdom commendation: integrity-safeguarded, despite poverty, will ensure personal worth – and wisdom (19:1)
19:2 Furthermore, to be ignorant about appetites is not good, and hasty feet sin.	2. Ignorance concerning one's appetites will thwart success (start of wisdom content, 19:2)

Verse	*Translation*	*Outline*
19:3	A mortal's folly will misdirect his way, yet it is against the LORD that his mind will rage.	3. The disappointment concerning that foolish personal failure will incline one to alienate from the divine (19:3)
19:4	Wealth may multiply friends many times over, but a helpless person will be isolated from his friend.	4. A deceptive truth: so-called friends multiply proportional to one's wealth (19:4)
19:5	A perjurer will not be acquitted, but will breathe out violence; he will not be rescued.	5. Integrity sacrificed will ensure hazardous isolation (19:5)
19:6	Many will flatter a generous person to his face, and everyone is friend to a person known for giving gifts.	4'. A deceptive truth: so-called friends multiply proportional to one's generosity (19:6)
19:7	All the brothers of a poor person hate him; how much more his close friend – they separate themselves from him; he is pursuing words of wisdom; they are not.	3'. Disappointment over alienation due to material poverty need not prevent one from pursuing wisdom (19:7)
19:8	One who acquires sense loves his appetite; he preserves perception – so as to find what is good.	2'. Acquiring wisdom will nurture appetites and will achieve success (19:8)
19:9	A perjurer will not be acquitted, but will breathe out violence; he will perish.	1'. Integrity sacrificed will ensure deadly peril (19:9)

Notes on the text

17:4. 'One who perpetrates evil', *mēra‘*: beyond being evil (substantival use of the adj. *ra‘*), this character inflicts evil on others (hiph. ptc. of the root *r‘‘* appears in Proverbs only here and 24:19). Positioned as the entire lecture's opening word, this robust and rare depiction of evil character effectively introduces the lecture's theme.

'keeps an ear out', *mēzîn*: beyond the typical verb for 'hearing', *šm‘*, this verb suggests focused listening.

17:5. 'his Maker': although 'his' initially recalls 'the poor', upon reflection it implicates the mocker as well.

17:6. 'their fathers': 'fathers' can include both parents and more remote ancestors (Fox 2009: 627).

17:7. 'not attractive for a good-for-nothing', *lōʾ nāʾwâ lĕnābāl*: note assonance, particularly if 'w' and 'b' in *nābāl* were pronounced as a 'v': *lōʾ nāʾvâ lĕnāvāl*.

'Gushing language . . . language of falsehood', *śĕpat yeter . . . śĕpat šāqer*: lit. 'lip of surplus . . . lip of falsehood'. A degree of assonance joins *yeter*, 'gushing', with *šāqer*, 'falsehood'. Flattery is connoted by 'gushing language', since 17:7–8 negatively contrasts the generosity theme of v. 9.

17:8. 'A stone of favour': lit. 'a stone of (or generating) grace'. This stone causes others to be undeservedly well disposed towards its owner (Waltke 2005: 48).

'in the opinion of': lit. 'in the eyes of'.

'he has success', *yaśkîl*: since a bribe ('stone of favour') is the catalyst, the root *śkl* should be rendered 'success', not 'instruct' (as was the case in 15:24).

17:10. 'an insightful person', *mēbîn*: from the root *bin* (as is *nābôn*, 'perceptive', in 17:28b).

17:11. 'So a cruel messenger': LXX specifies that the LORD will send this messenger.

17:12. 'May . . . encounter', *pāgôš*: lit. 'to encounter'. Volition is inferred for the infin. abs. 'to encounter', due to the negative volitional particle *ʾal*, 'may . . . not . . .' in the second colon (Fox 2009: 631). *Pgš*, 'to encounter', is more fateful than a synonym such as *qrʾ*, 'to meet or happen upon' (cf. the encounter with a bear in Hos. 13:8).

'encounter a person', *pāgôš . . . bĕʾîš*: the person is the object encountered by the bear, as indicated by the prep. phrase *bĕʾîš* (lit. 'upon a person'; so also Fox 2009: 630–631; *pace* Waltke who, while allowing this possibility, prefers to regard *bĕʾîš* as the agent of bereavement, 'by a man' [2005: 44, n.]).

'rather than a stupid fellow encountering his folly', *wĕʾal-kĕsîl bĕʾiwwaltô*: lit. 'and not a stupid fellow upon his folly'. 'Encountering' is inferred from the first colon. The prep. phrase *bĕʾiwwaltô* (lit. 'upon his folly') identifies what the stupid fellow encounters (as the phrase 'upon a person' in the first colon identified what the bear came upon). Thus the sage declares that it is disastrous to encounter an unwise person at the point when he is wantonly revelling in unimpeded folly. As a wisdom commendation, this dismaying caution prepares the pupil for the even more horrifying disintegration of social ethics unveiled in the wisdom content that follows (17:13–15).

17:14. 'give it up': lit. 'let [it] alone' (directed towards the strife monger; cf. 17:11).

17:16, 18. 'sense', *lēb*: lit. 'mind' or 'heart'.

17:16. 'How is it possible', *lāmmâ-zzeh*: lit. 'how [is] this'. Incredulity accompanies this rhetorical question, resembling the English idiom 'How in the world . . . ?' (as also Waltke 2005: 44).

'tuition to invest in', *mĕḥîr liqĕnôt*: lit. 'payment for acquiring' or 'buying' (cf. 18:15 and 19:8, where the same root [*qnh*] involves acquiring wisdom).

'since what he is missing is sense': lit. 'and a mind there is not'. By fronting 'sense' the Hebr. syntax emphasizes this component, rather than the fact of lack ('missing').

17:18. 'emphatically guaranteeing a loan before his friend', *ʿōrēb ʿărubbâ lipnē rēʿēhû*: an unwise fellow solemnly guarantees a loan for someone claiming friendship, even as that 'friend' looks on (so also LXX, NIV and NRSV; contra 'in the presence of his neighbour', NASB and ESV). Elsewhere the sage cautions that one seeking a loan guarantee may pass as a friend, but prove to be an untrustworthy 'stranger' (6:1; also with clasping hands). Fox allows that 'friend/neighbour' may designate a 'greedy neighbour' (2009: 633).

Loan guaranteeing is not elsewhere construed with *lipnē*, 'before'. Since that prep. often depicts an inferior before a superior, the sage may imply that the 'friend' is hovering oppressively, pressuring the unwise person to complete the financial pledge.

17:20. 'one who pivots with his tongue': in the context of a deceptive financial scheme (17:18), a 'pivoting tongue' would correspond to an unreliable borrower who, despite pledges, has no intention of repaying his debt.

'cannot find good': (in)capability inferred from yiq.

17:21. 'cannot rejoice': (in)capability inferred from yiq.

17:22. 'can make . . . appealing': lit. 'will make good, beautiful' (capability inferred from yiq.).

17:24. 'In the presence of an insightful person, there awaits wisdom', *ʾet-pĕnê mēbîn ḥŏkmâ*: lit. 'accompanying a countenance of an insightful person is wisdom'. The compound prep. *ʾet-pĕnê* envisions an attendant who waits on his or her superior (Waltke 2005: 62).

17:26. 'Also': this conj. signals that unjust fines and silencing of whistle-blowers (17:26) join the culpability of bribery (v. 23, a link also recognized by Heim [2001: 239]; *pace* Waltke, who treats 'also' as emphatic ['even'] rather than additive [2005: 46]). Structurally, v. 23 parallels v. 26, as each comprises one apophthegm of wisdom content after two apophthegms of wisdom commendation (vv. 21–22 and 24–25, respectively).

17:27. 'is very knowledgeable': lit. 'knows knowledge'.

'and a cool spirit', *wĕqar-rûaḥ*: a clear expression, rendering unnecessary the Q proposal of *yĕqar-rûaḥ*, 'precious of spirit'. LXX renders as 'patient'.

17:28. 'a fool who keeps quiet may be regarded as wise': lit. 'a fool who keeps quiet, wise he will be regarded'. Modal 'may' is inferred from yiq. of 'to regard'.

18:1. 'What he craves – that is what a loner will seek', *lĕtaʾăwâ yĕbaqqēš niprād*: lit. 'For a craving one who is separated will seek'. To render instead as 'The misfit seeks pretexts' (emending *lĕtaʾăwâ* to read *lĕtōʾăbâ*) blunts the plain and incisive sense of the MT (*pace* Fox 2009: 638).

'loner', *niprād*: lit. 'one who is separated', one who declines the benefits and costs of customary community relationships.

'with consummate competence', *bĕkōl tûšš iyyâ*: lit. 'with all competence', construed with *bĕ* of agency (not a prep. identifying the target against which the loner directs his opposition; *pace* Waltke 2005: 65; Fox 2009: 637). Of the three times the verb *galaʿ*, 'to break forth', occurs, only here is it construed with a prep. Thus context is the best indicator of connotation (whether *bĕ* of agency or target). Due to the cleverness of nefarious strategies conceived by evil persons elsewhere in this lecture (especially co-opting the judicial system in 17:23, 26), to render *kōl tûššiyyâ* as 'consummate competence' fits better than 'complete sound judgement'.

'he will break into a lawsuit', *yitgallāʿ*: lit. 'he will break forth', with connotation of 'explicitly initiating' or 'filing suit'. 'Lawsuit' is inferred from 17:14, where the sage connects 'lawsuit' explicitly with the verb 'to break forth': 'So, before a lawsuit breaks out, give it up!' (see 'lawsuit' and 'to break forth' in 20:3 – the only other instance of 'to break forth' in Proverbs). The courtroom context will become explicit in 18:5b.

18:2. 'cannot take delight': (in)capability inferred from yiq.

18:4. 'deep waters': depth indicates a well or cistern, not a lake or river (Fox 2009: 639). Since depth complicates water retrieval (20:5), depth describes distance to the water's surface, not the well's bottom. Thus 'deep waters' convey hazard, whereas 'spring' and 'a rushing stream' (18:4b) convey fresh, safely retrievable water.

18:5. 'in the courtroom': lit. 'in the judgement' or 'through the verdict'.

18:6. 'and his mouth will call for beatings': i.e. the punishment he petitions loudly against his opponent lands on himself instead.

18:7. 'his appetite', *napšô*: or 'his life', with wordplay implying fatal attraction (see 19:2 for the importance of gaining knowledge concerning one's appetite).

18:13. 'One who issues a verdict': lit. 'One who responds with a word' (judicial context inferred from 18:5, 8–9, 16–17).

18:14. 'may endure . . . can bear it': modal meanings inferred from yiq.

18:15. 'will keep on investing in', *yiqneh*: lit. 'will buy' or 'will acquire' (cf. 17:16 and 'acquire' in 19:8). Iterative 'will keep on' is inferred from yiq. (similarly, *tĕbaqqeš*, 'will keep on searching for').

'information': lit. 'knowledge', as in 15:7, 14.

18:17. 'The first person to appear . . . is moral': lit. 'moral [is] the first person'. Closer scrutiny of this first individual may alter the initial positive assessment (18:17b).

'his neighbour', *rēʿēhû*: although this term can designate a genuine 'friend' (17:17), or a sly friend-in-name-only (v. 18), the effect of this individual (rather than his precise relationship to the litigant) merits the greater focus. By his cross-examination, this individual contributes substantially to discovery of facts, reinforcing the quest for diligent judicial process (vv. 13, 15–16). Consequently *rēʿēhû* should be understood not as 'friend', but more generally as 'neighbour' – someone in the community qualified to engage in such scrutiny, perhaps referring to the opposing counsel or *antidikos*, 'defendant' (LXX).

18:18. 'The lot': casting of lots offered a means of referring a question to God for divine counsel or decision.

'can create space between': lit. 'will keep apart from one another' (capability inferred from yiq.).

'mighty opponents', *ʿăṣûmîm*: lit. 'mighty ones'. 'Opponents' is inferred from the courtroom context.

18:19. 'A brother who has suffered transgression by a "strong city"', *ʾāḥ nipšāʿ miqqiryat-ʿōz*: lit. 'one who has been trespassed-against by a city of strength'. This is a jarring saying, owing to initial opacity (for alternative explanations, see Fox 2009: 645). One searches this verse in vain for a comparative adj. to allow a translation such as 'An offended brother is [insert comparative adj.] than a strong city'. MT will not allow the translation 'stronger than a city' (NRSV), since 'city' is in const. with the noun 'strength', yielding 'strong city'.

Alternatively, the obscurity would quickly resolve by replacing the initial kaph with mem, so 'by a strong city', *miqqiryat-ʿōz*, would read '[is] like a strong city', *kĕqqiryat-ʿōz* (so LXX; preferred by Fox [2009: 644] and Waltke [2005: 67], who observes that kaph and mem at times were confused).

Since the prep. *min* does not here contribute to a comparative expression ('than'), it indicates agency ('by means of'; for a niph. verb [such as *nipšāʿ*] with agency signalled by *min*, see Job 24:1; Eccles. 12:11). The agent that here perpetrates the 'transgression' is 'a strong city'. The sage recently observed that the wealthy mistakenly rely on riches to provide security, like a 'strong city' (18:11). Thus to be transgressed by a metaphoric 'strong city' would involve being wronged by someone wielding wealth to bring about injustice (i.e. judicial bribery). ('Strong city' is set off by quotes to signal that it is metaphoric.) As recently as in 18:16 the sage cautioned against gaining unfair judicial advantage by wealth distributed as a bribe. Thus to read v. 19a in the light of (a) 'a strong city' of v. 11 and (b) bribery in v. 16 yields the following paraphrase: 'A close relative who has been deprived of justice by means of bribery.'

Proceeding to the second colon of 18:19, the phrase 'and by strivings' stands parallel to 'by a "strong city"', that metaphoric agency of transgression. If ellipsis of the prep. 'by' were not in play it would read, 'by a strong city and strivings'. Consequently the whole of 18:19 may be paraphrased as follows: 'A close relative, who has been victimized (transgressed against) in court by means of bribery that upends justice and sows strife, can scarcely be restored to a trusting relationship. It would be easier to break through a heavily fortified citadel door than to reconcile with the offended relative.' By specifying that the victim is a close relative, the sage implies that the perpetrator and the victim are near relations. Both vv. 13–14 and 19 lament the high cost of graft, whether to the individual spirit (v. 14) or to the fabric of families (v. 19).

The LXX of 18:19 varies considerably from the MT, suggesting puzzlement on the part of translators, or a different Hebr. exemplar. The LXX reads, 'A brother who is aided by a brother is as a stout and lofty city, mighty as a firmly founded palace.'

18:23. 'keeps on uttering . . . keeps on replying': lit. 'will utter . . . will reply' (durative inferred from yiq.).

'stridently', *ʿazzôt*: lit. 'with strength, ferocity'.

18:24. 'A person known for friends', *ʾîš rēʿîm*: lit. 'a person of friends'. The phrase, 'a person of', indicates that the ensuing expression characterizes that person in a comprehensive manner (cf. *ʾîš mattān*, 'a person known for giving gifts', 19:6).

'will suffer ruin', *lĕhitrōʿēaʿ*: this expression of 'ruin' would have evoked in hearers the notion of 'evil', since the underlying root in each case is spelled *rāʿaʿ*. Consequently the disaster in 18:24a links by homonym to the lecture's theme of the evildoer. Assonance similarly linked 'ruin' (root *rāʿaʿ*) with 'friends' (root *rēaʿ*).

'one who loves': as a m. ptc., this person is not the literal wife of 18:22. The identity of this true friend grows clearer as in the next block the sage exposes that wealth is powerless to acquire authentic friends (Block IV.B, 19:1–9). As that block draws to a close, the poet repeats the term 'love': 'One who acquires sense loves his appetite; he preserves perception – so as to find what is good' (19:8). It is by acquiring sense (not a myriad of so-called friends) that oneself is nourished. So it is wisdom that comprises the dependable, loving companion of 18:24b. Wisdom as companion may be seen in Prov. 2, 8, 9, 31. For an instance where 'acquire' refers to obtaining a wife, cf. Ruth 4:10.

'more loyally than a brother', *dābēq mēʾāḥ*: lit. 'clings, sticks more closely than a brother'. This verb connotes proximity and persistence. It describes a marital bond in Gen. 2:24.

19:1. 'than if he were to operate with twisted lips': lit. 'than twisted of his lips'. This refers to the poor person's lips.

'and so would prove to be a stupid person', *wĕhûʾ kĕsîl*: lit. 'and he [is] a stupid person'. Following Syriac, Fox emends *kĕsîl*, 'a stupid person', to read *ʿāšîr*, 'wealthy': 'Better a poor man who walks in his innocence than a man of crooked lips who is rich' (2009: 647). Although simpler, this alteration sacrifices the pungency of the sage's implication that perfidy lowers oneself to stupidity.

19:2. 'Furthermore, to be ignorant about appetites is not good', *gam bĕlōʾ-daʿat nepeš lōʾ-ṭôb*: lit. 'Also in not knowledge-of-appetite [is] not good'. 'Knowledge' grammatically governs 'appetite', preventing disconnect between 'desire' [i.e. appetite] and 'knowledge' found in NRSV: 'Desire without knowledge is not good.' Specifically, it is the category of 'appetites' wherein knowledge-deficiency is 'not good'. 'Desires ungoverned by good sense propel one to rush in pursuit of their fulfillment' (Fox 2009: 648).

19:4. 'but a helpless person will be isolated from his friend', *wĕdāl mērē ʿhû yippārēd*: since 'wealth' serves as the subject in the first colon, so 'helpless person' (not 'his friend') offers the simplest subject for the second (so also Fox 2009: 649). If *mērē ʿhû*, 'from his friend', had been vocalized *mĕrē ʿhû*, 'his close friend' (as in 19:7, and as in v. 4 in Hebr. manuscripts other than Codex Leningradensius), 19:4b could mean 'but as for the poor person, his close companion separates himself' (so Waltke 2005: 88).

19:5. 'be rescued', *yimmālēṭ*: although rare for the niph. stem of the root *mlṭ*, a pass. meaning fits well the context of 19:4–6. When the deceptive person ('perjurer') suffers disaster, he will not 'be rescued' by others, since his practice of purchasing fans (vv. 4, 6) has discouraged genuine friendships.

19:6. 'friend': lit. 'the friend'. The definite article establishes 'friend' as a special category.

'a person known for giving gifts', *ʾîš mattān*: lit. 'a person of gifts' (cf. 'a person known for friends', in note for 18:24, above).

19:7. 'how much more his close friend': narrowing from pl. 'brothers' to sg. 'close friend' intensifies poignancy of loss. The ensuing pl. ('they separate themselves from him') encompasses 'brothers' and 'close friend'.

'he is pursuing words of wisdom, they are not', *mĕraddēp ʾămārîm lōʿ hēmmâ*: lit. 'he is pursuing words, they are not'. 'Words' worthy of pursuit would consist of wise sayings, as the ensuing colon clarifies by commending the acquisition of 'sense' (19:8a; cf. 'words of knowledge' in 19:27).

'they are not', *lōʾ-hēmmâ*: i.e. they are not pursuing words of wisdom. This trait, more than poverty, distinguishes this discarded person in contrast to wealthy and arrogant family and friends. Understood thus, it is neither necessary nor preferable to dismiss the laconic statement 'they are not' as an 'unintelligible fragment' (*pace* Fox 2009: 650). If the sage meant to convey their demise ('they are no longer alive'), *ʾênām* likely would have appeared instead (e.g. Gen. 37:30; 42:13, 32).

19:8. 'One who acquires sense', *qōneh lēb*: lit. 'one who acquires (or buys) a mind'. Earlier the root *qnh* described an ill-prepared person who presumed to invest in wisdom (17:16). In contrast, the investor of 19:8 is sagacious.

'loves his appetite', *ʾōhēb napšô*: to render *nepeš* as 'soul' instead of 'appetite' would disconnect this saying from the notion of personal desires – a major theme in this lecture. For it is at the expense of others that the loner selfishly pursues his cravings, becoming the archetypal evildoer (18:1). He appears to 'love his appetite', letting its satisfaction dictate his behaviour. But his plans will miscarry because he is 'ignorant about [his] appetites' (19:2, a saying palistrophically linked to 'appetite' and the worth of wisdom in v. 8). Only those wise enough to curb their cravings within ethical boundaries truly 'love their appetites', ultimately 'find[ing] what is good' (v. 8b).

Form and structure

Borders

After addressing the mind's principal role in the previous lecture (with a striking climax in its closing saying, 17:3), in the present lecture the sage cautions concerning evildoers. The opening apophthegm introduces this theme, setting the upper boundary (17:4).

Three classes of structure indicate 19:9 as the lower boundary: closure, inclusio and palistrophe. Closure results when the sage underscores the importance of integrity early in the first section (17:4, 7) and again in the last (19:1, 5, 9).

Inclusio operates through assonance involving 'calamity', *ʾêd* (17:5) and witness', *ʿēd* (19:5, 9). Inclusio also emerges with repetition of *šeqer* ('falsehood' in 17:4 and as a component in 'perjurer' in 19:9). It appears twice more, not far from the first and last sayings ('falsehood' in 17:7 and as an element of 'perjurer' in 19:5). *Nqh*, 'to acquit', generates an inclusio as it appears in the lecture's second saying (17:5) and in its last (19:9; elsewhere in this poem only in 19:5). An inclusio also surfaces since in the first saying the evildoer shows interest in destruction (17:4), while in the last he suffers destruction (19:9).

A palistrophe beginning in 19:1 reinforces 19:9 as the lower border since the palistrophe does not extend beyond that saying. For additional poem-concluding features involving 19:7, 8, see the following under 'Macrostructural features', below: 'Closure with reversal concerning favour', 'Closure involving "poor"', 'Closure through repetition of *ʾămārîm*', 'Closure with correction', 'Closure involving "finding good"', and 'Closure with reversal involving "investing in/acquiring" wisdom or sense'.

Macrostructural features

Thematic continuity related to evildoer (Sections I–IV, content-based). With its first word this poem introduces *mēraʿ*, 'one who perpetrates evil', or simply 'evildoer'. The root for 'evil', *rʿ*, repeats four more times within the first seventeen sayings (17:11, 13, 13, 20). When surveying for evil behaviours (without using that root), a considerable number appear, representing each section of the poem. Section I includes ones who delight in disaster (17:4), mock the poor (v. 5), offer bribes (v. 8), foster contention (v. 11, repeating 'evil'), repay good with evil (v. 13, 'evil' twice), are litigious (v. 14) and who justify the guilty while condemning the innocent (v. 15). Section II refers to one who loves a trespass (17:19), is twisted in mind and duplicitous in speech (v. 20, repeating 'evil'), offers bribes to overturn justice (v. 23) and penalizes the moral leaders (v. 26). Behaviours connoting evil in Section III include one who is litigious (18:1), reviles others (v. 3), overturns justice (v. 5), slanders (v. 8), ignores evidence when issuing verdicts (v. 13) and receives bribes (v. 16). In Section IV the sage twice condemns perjury, suggesting that calculated deception lies at the core of the evildoer's conduct (19:5, 9; see discussion concerning borders, above).

Repetition of 'love' (Sections I and II, form-based). Contrasting the evildoer, Block I.A. closes with a picture of one who overlooks wrongdoing, and so 'seeks love' (17:9). When a 'friend' appears early in Section II, he is characterized by constancy of 'love' (17:17). Conversely, love misdirected exposes one who merely masquerades as a friend. In reality, that one 'loves trespass' and 'loves a brawl' (17:19). Thus the object of love can reveal true character.

Reversal involving 'evil' and 'good' (Sections I and II, form-based). Both 'evil' and 'good' appear in 17:13 and again in v. 20. In the first, malevolent schemes transpose good for evil. In the second, evildoers suffer evil instead of the good they hoped for, effecting a reversal.

Reversal involving family honour (Sections I and II, content-based). Family members honour each other in Section I (17:6). In Section II they bring distress (17:21, 25).

Family serving as solution to a problem (Sections I and III, 17:6 and 18:22, content-based). Family operates as a solution in Sections I and III. In Section I, generously affirming family relationships (17:6) answer the harm caused by the self-seeking evildoer (17:4–5). In Section III marriage (18:22) resolves the core defect of the malevolent loner (18:1).

Assonance with reversal involving 'love' and 'crave'; also repetition of 'seek' (Sections I and III, form- and content-based). Assonance joins a saying that celebrates healing of fractured relationships (17:9) with a saying revealing the evildoer's nature as lacking nurturing relationships (18:1). 'Love', *ʾahăbâ*, in 17:9 assonantally resembles what one 'craves', *taʾăwâ*, in 18:1. Semantically the two are reversed, since love connotes generosity while craving centres on self. 'To seek' appears in each, a form-based link (also in 17:11, 19; 18:15).

Repetition of 'break out/into' (Sections I and III, form-based). Of three instances of 'to break out/into' (root *glʿ*) across Proverbs, two occur within this lecture (17:14; 18:1). The first is significant since it brings Section I to a climax, issuing the poem's only imperative. Since the second reveals the evildoer's core nature, it too bears significance.

Repetition and thematic continuity concerning isolation (Sections I, III and IV, form- and content-based). The concept of isolation is conveyed by the expressions 'to alienate' in 17:9 and 'loner' in 18:1, both derived from *prd*, 'to separate'. Separation also obtains when the poor suffer rejection (18:23; 19:4, 7). Thus isolation (whether voluntary or involuntary) displays escalating prominence across three sections of this lecture.

Thematic continuity concerning initiating conflict (Sections II and III, content-based). The sage describes the character and conduct of the loner in Section III (labelled in 18:1). Instead of honest industry, he concentrates on conflict, especially litigation. Consequently he aligns with the evildoer of Section II, known for fomenting conflict ('loves a brawl', 17:19). By using bribes 'to divert paths of justice' (v. 23) and by imposing unjust fines (v. 26), the evildoer of Section II identifies even more closely with the loner of Section III, known for launching sinister litigation.

Repetition of 'brother' (Sections II, III and IV, form-based. The term 'brother' designates a close sibling four times in this lecture, spread over Sections II–IV (the use in 18:9 is metaphoric). Through these four sayings the sage reveals dimensions of the sibling role that prove central to this lecture. Beginning with the introduction to Section II, the sage presents the ideal brother – one marked by undeterred loyalty (17:17). Within this dual-theme introduction, 'brother' anchors the category of family – a pool whence evildoers may arise unexpectedly (see 17:21–26).

'Brother' appears late within the sage's appeal for an unimpeachable judiciary to combat the evildoer (final saying of 18:13–19). Should that judiciary fail, a 'brother' will fall victim (to brother), fracturing community due to impenetrable barriers of resentment.

'Brother' occurs early (18:24) and late (19:7) in the final section (18:23 – 19:9). Mysteriously, the sage offers that, although to possess a corps of 'friends' may not shield one from 'ruin' (18:24a; cf. 19:4, 6–7a), nevertheless there exists 'a loving person who clings more loyally than a brother' (18:24b). Yet the identity of that loyal person remains enigmatic, implied only in 19:8 (see 'Comment', below).

The sage underscores the need for a person of such integrity by observing quite comprehensively within the final brother-saying that 'all the brothers of a poor person hate him' (19:7a). The poet reveals where these brothers err since, unlike the poor individual who maintains integrity (cf. 19:1), they have left off 'pursuing words of wisdom' (v. 7b). For this lecture teaches that wisdom aligns with integrity ('sense' and 'perception' contrast 'perjury' in 19:8–9).

Repetition of 'crushed spirit' and thematic continuity of graft (Sections II and III, form- and content-based). A 'crushed spirit' appears in 17:22 and 18:14 (again only in 15:13 in the entire HB). A theme of graft appears in 17:23 ('bribe') and 18:16 ('gift').

The two contexts connect as follows. Crushed of spirit is the father (17:22) whose son foolishly schemes to overturn justice by graft (17:23). And the victim of miscarried justice will similarly suffer a crushed spirit (18:14), since graft has truncated due process (18:16; cf. vv. 13, 17).

Thematic continuity of predatory litigation (Sections II, III and IV, form- and content-based). In Section II the sage alerts the pupil concerning those who overturn justice through predatory litigation (bribes in 17:23; illegal fines in v. 26). In Section III predatory litigation, slander and subversion of the judiciary comprise the malevolent loner's preferred strategy (18:5, 8, 13–19).

With the assessment 'not good' the sage twice censures predation, whether through illegal fines (17:26) or through preferential treatment of the guilty (18:5). And twice in Section IV he cautions against deception in legal proceedings: 'A perjurer will not be acquitted' (first in 19:5, then in v. 9 – the lecture's final saying).

Thematic continuity of aloneness (Sections III and IV, content-based). As in Section III the sage probes the evildoer's nature, a picture of intentional aloneness emerges (esp. 18:1). In contrast, unsolicited aloneness features in Section IV as the rich regard the poor with disdain (18:23; 19:4, 7).

Closure. *Closure with reversal concerning favour (Section IV, with Section I, form-based).* In Section I a valuable gem secures favour as a bribe (17:8). In Section IV the poor seek favour by their pleas, but encounter rejection instead (18:23). Both 'favour' in the phrase 'stone of favour' and the verb 'to utter pleas for help' trace to *ḥnn* (favour or grace).

Closure involving 'poor' (Section IV, with Section I, form-based). In the lecture's second verse the sage warns against mocking the 'poor' (17:5, Section I). Similar concern over mistreatment of the poor accompanies this lecture's three remaining uses of that term, all in Section IV (18:23; 19:1, 7).

Closure involving assonance (Section IV, with Section I, form-based). The lecture's first word is *mēraʿ*, 'an evildoer' (17:4). Towards the lecture's close, a similar sound occurs twice: *mērēʿēhû* ('from his friend', 19:4; see 'Notes' for vocalization), and *mĕrēʿēhû* ('his close friend', 19:7). Thus through assonance the poet alludes to the lecture's principal theme: cultivating awareness of evildoers.

Closure involving 'brother' and 'friend' (Section IV, with Section II, form-based). Early in Section II 'friend' and 'brother' appeared as two groups unexpectedly capable of spawning evildoers (17:17). Closure results when those terms reappear in Section IV, dismissing an impoverished family member and friend (19:7).

Closure through repetition of ʾămārîm *('words', Section IV, with Section III, form-based).* Within this lecture, the term *ʾămārîm*, 'words', appears only in 17:27 (opening Section III) and in 19:7 (three verses from the lecture's close). Since *ʾămārîm* occurs fairly frequently in Proverbs (twenty-two times), to appear only twice in a poem suggests structural significance, fostering closure in 19:7. The nearest uses outside this lecture appear in 16:24 and 19:27.

Closure with correction: loving self rightly (Section IV, with Section III, content-based). The sage characterizes the malevolent loner as loving himself ('What he craves – that is what a loner will seek', 18:1a in Section III). That narrow focus on self seems to reappear in the poem's end, as the sage describes one who 'loves his appetite' (19:8a). However, a substantial correction is at work. For it is 'one who acquires sense' who 'loves his appetite'. Thus through closure the sage teaches that pursuit of wisdom (not of cravings) provides the sole avenue to actualize love of self.

Closure involving 'finding good' (Section IV, with Sections II and III, form-based). Three times this lecture refers to 'finding good'. 'A twisted mind cannot find good' (17:20a), whereas to find a wife is to 'find good' – an indication of divine approval (18:22). Closure results when, in the lecture's penultimate saying, one who 'acquires sense' will 'find what is good' (19:8).

Closure with reversal involving 'investing in/acquiring' wisdom or sense (Section IV, with Section II, form- and content-based). *Lēb*, rendered 'sense' or 'mind', occurs nine times in this lecture. In the first, someone lacking sense attempts unsuccessfully to 'invest', *qnh*, in wisdom (17:16). Closure results when, in the last, someone successfully 'acquires', *qnh*, sense, thereby gaining 'what is good' (19:8).

Microstructural features

Section I (17:4–15). *Thematic continuity concerning hazard (17:4–5, content-based).* A theme of hazard joins 'disaster' and 'destruction' in 17:4 with 'calamity' and 'not acquitted' in v. 5.

Two-plus-one verse-trios, with repetition of 'falsehood' (17:4–6, 7–9, form- and content-based). Six times the poet groups a trio of adjacent sayings, wherein a common theme links the first and second sayings, contrasted by a third saying. Mention of 'falsehood' in both initial sayings links the first two trios (17:4–6, 7–9). The second saying of each describes a negative practice, whether mocking the poor (v. 5) or using wealth (bribes) to gain unfair advantage (v. 8). The third presents a positive contrast, whether a nourishing family network (v. 6) or a merciful response to wrongdoing (v. 9).

Summation concerning falsehood (17:8, form-based). The negative sentiments concerning false compliments and false gifts in 17:7–8 culminate in a summation concerning the seeming success of one's issuing a bribe: 'wherever he turns he has success' (v. 8b). This accentuates the contrast mercy applies to wrongdoing in v. 9.

Inclusio involving assonance (17:4, 9, form-based). Assonance links the outer sayings of Block I.A (17:4–9) due to transposition of sounds in *maqšîb*, 'pays attention' (17:4), and *mĕbaqqēš*, 'seeks' (v. 9).

Inclusio with reversal regarding reports about others (17:4, 9, content-based). The outer sayings of Block I.A are further linked by the concept of reports about others. In the first saying, evildoers misuse damaging reports about others ('a dialect of disaster, language of destruction', 17:4). That block's last verse teaches that one should not broadcast, but should bury such damaging information (v. 9), forming an inclusio with reversal for Block I.A.

Wisdom commendations and wisdom content, repeating 'stupid' and 'evil' (17:10–15, form- and content-based). The structure of 17:10–15 divides into two segments (vv. 10–11, 12–15), each consisting of a wisdom commendation (vv. 10, 12) followed by wisdom content (vv. 11, 13–15). Each wisdom commendation mentions 'stupid' (vv. 10, 12), while 'evil' appears in the first colon of each wisdom content (v. 11a, and twice in v. 13a). Waltke similarly recognizes vv. 10–15 as a discrete portion, observing the wisdom tone linking vv. 10, 12, and the recurrence of 'evil' in vv. 11, 13 (2005: 50).

Dynamic progression concerning hazard (17:10–11, 12–15, content-based). A progression from bad to worse transpires when moving from wisdom commendation of 17:10 to wisdom content of v. 11. While the stupid person is bad (v. 10), the evil person focused on contention is worse (v. 11).

Similar is the next wisdom commendation and wisdom content. The stupid fellow given free rein of folly is bad (17:12), yet 'one who returns evil for good' is worse (v. 13).

Escalation also surfaces when comparing the two stupid-to-evil progressions. Folly is more rampant with the second stupid fellow (17:12) than the first (v. 10). Evil similarly swells from contention (v. 11) to more overt malevolence (v. 13), ending in a corrupt judiciary that earns divine disapprobation (v. 15).

Framing an imperative with theme-related sayings (17:13, 15, content-based). The charge 'So, before a lawsuit breaks out, give it up' (17:14) contains this lecture's sole imperative form. It counters the evil person's earlier bent towards contention (v. 11). The poet frames it with two sayings addressing a single theme – ethical upset ('return[ing] evil for good' in v. 13, and 'justif[ying] the guilty' in v. 15).

Closure concerning family, with reversal (17:6, 13, content-based). Closure results from mention of family ('his house') in 17:13, near the conclusion of Section I (17:4–15), since family featured prominently in v. 6. Reversal is at work since family members in v. 6 epitomized mutual encouragement, while the evil actor of v. 13 will bring misfortune to his kin.

Closure concerning divine justice (17:5, 15, content-based). Mention of divine assessment contributes closure in 17:15 (final verse of Section I), since the divine as creator was referenced early in that section (v. 5).

Section II (17:16–26). *Wisdom commendation (17:16, content-based).* Section II opens with a wisdom commendation concerning a stupid person who pointlessly seeks after wisdom (17:16). Wisdom content follows in the next saying, a dual-theme introduction of friends and family (v. 17).

Dual-theme verse (17:17, content-based). The wisdom content in 17:17 presents a dual-theme saying introducing two groups of people generally meriting trust: one's friends (v. 17a) and family members (v. 17b). Subsequently, the theme of friends develops in Block II. B (vv. 18–20), while that of family members develops in Block II.C (vv. 21–26).

The assumed trustworthiness of a friend the sage announces by this statement: 'At all times a friend loves' (17:17a). However, as the sage points out in Block II.B, not all seeming friends prove to be trustworthy (vv. 18–20). For the 'friend' of v. 18 manages to persuade his senseless comrade to co-sign his loan. Waltke similarly recognizes the continuity of 'friend' in vv. 17a and 18 (2005: 57). Although the term 'friend' does not recur in vv. 19 or 20, the shift to the second theme thereafter (family members) implies that the nefarious conduct described in vv. 19–20 extends the description of a friend in v. 18.

After Block II.B, the term 'friend' appears in this lecture four more times, each with a negative connotation (18:17, 24; 19:4, 6). A related term, 'close friend', similarly associates with disappointment when used in 19:7. The term 'friend' (not including 'close friend') occurs roughly three times more frequently within this lecture, when compared with the balance of Proverbs. The fact that each use connotes either unexpected harm or superficial adulation reinforces concern raised in Section II regarding issuing indiscriminate trust.

Like the category of 'friend', one would expect family members to remain loyal despite adverse circumstances (note 'brother' and 'be born', 17:17b). Yet even a family member may create distress (Block II.C, vv. 21–26). Family-related expressions in Block II.C include 'to father [an offspring]', 'a father' (twice), 'son' and 'she who gave birth'.

After Block II.C, the theme of family relations appears four more times in this lecture, all with the term 'brother' (in 18:9, 19, 24; 19:7). 'Brother' occurs roughly seventeen times more frequently in this lecture, when compared with the balance of Proverbs.

Assonance involving 'friend' and 'evil' (17:17, 18, 20, form-based). Assonance links *rēʿa*, 'friend' (17:17, 18), with *rāʿâ*, 'evil' (v. 20). The link generates tension, since friend and evil form ethical opposites. This tension fits well the sage's point concerning evil arising from unexpected sources (Section II).

Thematic continuity concerning ill-managed wealth (17:16, 18, 23, 26, content-based). Misuse of wealth recurs as a theme in Section II. In the opening saying, someone seeks to purchase wisdom, despite lacking sense enough to use it (17:16). Block II.B opens as someone foolishly guarantees a loan to a supposed friend (17:18). Both units of Block II.C close with wealth wrongly used, whether to bribe (v. 23) or to fine unfairly (v. 26). Thus each mention of misused wealth either opens or closes a portion in Section II.

Thematic continuity concerning (a) lack of sense and (b) ill-managed wealth (17:16, 18, content-based). As observed above, ill-managed wealth joins 17:16 and 18. In addition, the negative fellow in these verses is either 'missing sense' (v. 16) or 'lacking sense' (v. 18), supplying a second link between these sayings.

Inclusio involving lēb *('mind' or 'sense'), with assonance of 'friend' and 'evil' (17:18, 20, form-based).* Two elements contribute to an inclusio involving the first and last lines of Block II.B. First, both refer negatively to *lēb*, 'sense' or 'mind', in their first cola (17:18a, 20a).

The second link is assonantal. The first saying ends with the expression *rē 'ēhû*, 'his friend' (line-terminal in 17:18), while the last ends with *rā 'â*, 'evil' (line-terminal in v. 20).

Reversal concerning 'love' (17:17, 19, form- and content-based). Through reversal the sage teaches that by noticing what a person loves one may distinguish between authentic and counterfeit friends. A 'friend' should be characterized by extending 'love' at all times (17:17a). When instead that 'love' focuses on brawling (v. 19), one should realize that this individual is not a 'friend'.

Repetition of 'joy' (17:21, 22, form-based). In addition to sharing vocabulary for wisdom, 17:21 and 22 repeat the root *smḥ*, 'joy' or 'rejoice', tantalizing the parent of v. 21 to experience the emotions of v. 22.

Repetition of 'stupid' (17:24, 25, form-based). 'Stupid' joins 17:24 with 25, implying that one's unwise behaviour in v. 24b would distress his parents (v. 25).

Two-plus-one verse-trios, wisdom commendation and focal instruction, with theme of family (17:21–23, 24–26, content-based). Another double trio of adjacent sayings (two sayings with a connected theme, followed by one with a contrasting theme) appears in 17:21–23, 24–26 (see 17:4–6, 7–9, above). Initial verse-pairs (vv. 21–22, 24–25) present wisdom commendations, followed by single-saying focal instructions (vv. 23, 26).

Outer sayings of wisdom commendations establish the theme of family (17:21, 25). This creates an AB-C, BA-C pattern (A = family saying, B = verse paired with A, and C = focal instruction). Waltke also notes that *yld* links v. 21 ('to father') and v. 25 ('to give birth'), and observes intensification in v. 25 by adding mother, and by escalating 'grief' to 'bitterness' (2005: 59, 62–63). Heim observes the thematic link between 17:23 and 26 (2001: 237–239). However, by regarding vv. 21 and 25 as forming an inclusio (rather than each belonging to separate introductory wisdom commendations spanning vv. 21–22, 24–25), he infers a major separation after v. 25, rather than treating vv. 24–25 as introductory to the wisdom content in v. 26, just as vv. 21–22 introduce wisdom content in v. 23.

Thematic escalation surrounding abuse of power (17:23, 26, content-based). The theme of abuse of power intensifies from manipulative generosity (bribery, 17:23) to unwarranted intimidation (unjust fines, v. 26a), even reaching physical violence (striking, v. 26b). Since each saying supplies wisdom content, together they trace thematic escalation of evil, a strategic contribution of Block II.C (vv. 21–26). Waltke similarly observes evil behaviour escalating from v. 23 to v. 26 (2005: 60, 63).

Assonance linking 'to divert' and 'to strike' (17:23, 26, form-based). Assonance among opening verbs joins the second colon of 17:23 (*lĕhaṭṭōt*, 'to divert') with the second colon of v. 26 (*lĕhakōt*, 'to strike') – the two wisdom-content sayings of Block II.C.

Repetition of 'not . . . good' at a block's close (17:20, 26, form-based). Each saying closing Blocks II.B and II.C issues a negative evaluation, whether 'not finding good' or 'not being good' (17:20 and 26, respectively). Like a refrain, this helps to mark the close of these blocks.

Section III (17:27 – 18:22). *Wisdom commendation (17:27–28, content-based).* Section III opens with a two-verse wisdom commendation associating wisdom with self-control in speech (17:27–28). Waltke also regards these verses as a pair (2005: 64). Wisdom content follows in 18:1, describing the litigious nature of one pursuing his cravings.

Wisdom commendation followed by wisdom content (18:2, 3, content-based). Unit III.B.1 begins with a wisdom commendation about a stupid fellow (18:2), leading to wisdom content regarding a guilty person's litigation tactics (v. 3).

Wisdom commendation followed by wisdom content (18:4, 5, content-based). Unit III.B.2 similarly begins with a wisdom commendation, this time concerning subtle and sinister speech (18:4). This leads to wisdom content censuring partiality (v. 5).

Wisdom commendation followed by wisdom content (18:6–7, 8–9, content-based). Unit III.B.3 opens with a wisdom commendation concerning unwise litigation (18:6–7), leading to wisdom content concerning abuse of the legal system, whether actively or passively (vv. 8–9).

Thematic escalation of litigious strategies (18:2–9, content-based). Block III.B consists of three units, each of which presents a despicable strategy for swaying a court (18:2–9). The first uses reviling speech to cast aspersions on the defendant (Unit III.B.1, vv. 2–3). The second shifts attention from defendant to judiciary, envisioning a judge who practises unethical partiality (Unit III.B.2, vv. 4–5). The third strategy deals with both defendant and judiciary. Initial reviling intensifies to slander (Unit III.B.3; esp. v. 8). Although v. 9 does not name judges, the context envisions the judiciary that earlier showed partiality but now descending to ennui, too preoccupied to be bothered with the plight of the unjustly accused.

As with content, length also escalates. Single sayings (whether for wisdom commendation in 18:2 and 4, or wisdom content in vv. 3 and 5) expand to verse-pairs: two of commendation (vv. 6–7) and two of content (vv. 8–9).

Thematic continuity of protection from damage (18:10–19, content-based). 'Strong tower', 'perched on high', 'strong city', 'high town wall' and 'breakage' – these expressions establish a theme of protection from metaphoric damage in 18:10–12 (a cluster also noted by the medieval Jewish commentator Ramaq [d. AD 1190; in Fox 2009: 642]). Metaphor gives way to concrete damage from malicious litigation, against which a diligent and impartial judiciary should supply protection (18:13–19). Meinhold similarly observes a portion spanning vv. 10–19 (1991: 301–302).

Progression in specificity, concerning carelessness (18:9, 13, content-based). When the sage cautioned against carelessness in 18:9, only the preceding context (v. 5) lent to that saying a judicial connotation. By v. 13 the judiciary is indicted explicitly.

Wisdom commendation followed by wisdom content (18:13, 14, content-based). Unit III.C.3 begins with a wisdom commendation concerning judicial laziness (18:13), leading to wisdom content depicting the heavy weight of justice denied (v. 14).

Wisdom commendation followed by wisdom content (18:15, 16, content-based). The next segment begins with a wisdom commendation urging judicial diligence (18:15). This is followed by wisdom content concerning judicial impartiality (vv. 16–19).

Thematic continuity concerning justice (18:13–19, content-based). The following contribute to a judicial theme for Unit III.C.3 (18:13–19): 'verdict' (18:13), 'lawsuit' and 'cross-examine' (both v. 17). Related are expressions of dispute ('investing in information' and 'searching for information' in v. 15, 'strife' and 'opponents' in v. 18 and 'strivings' in v. 19), expressions of victimization ('crushed spirit' in v. 14, and 'a brother . . . suffered transgression by a "strong city"' in v. 19), and expressions of unjust influence (a 'gift' [bribe] in v. 16).

Framing involving caution concerning subversion of judiciary (18:16, 18, content-based). The caution against jumping to judicial conclusions (18:17) is framed by sayings that fortify the judiciary against caving to influence, whether succumbing to seduction through bribes (v. 16) or by succumbing to intimidation by the mighty (v. 18).

Repetition of 'strife' (18:18, 19, form-based). 'Strife' appears in both 18:18 and 19, joining v. 19 to the rest of Unit III.C.3 with its theme of the loner's predatory litigation. The first offers a strategy (casting lots) when powerful litigants threaten judicial impartiality (v. 18). The second cautions that damage from miscarriage of justice may become irreversible (v. 19).

Thematic escalation of strife (18:18, 19, content-based). The sayings concerning 'strife' escalate from 'mighty opponents' (18:18), intensifying to antipathy as metaphorically impenetrable as a 'citadel bar' (v. 19).

Framing with 'fruit' (18:20–21, form-based). Aside from elements necessarily prefixed (as a prep.) or suffixed (as an object suff.), 'fruit' frames 18:20–21 by appearing line-initial in the first verse and line-terminal in the second.

Wisdom commendation dealing with speech (18:20–21, content-based). The poet associates wisdom with speech at several points in Section III (17:27–28; 18:2, 4, 6–7). Each operates as a wisdom commendation, paving the way for wisdom content. Since 18:20–21 deals with speech and leads to wisdom content in v. 22, these verses may also operate as a wisdom commendation, despite lacking terms such as 'wisdom' or 'folly'.

The fact that the problem appearing directly after the section-opening wisdom commendation of 17:27–28 (the malevolent loner, 18:1) resolves in the section-closing wisdom content that follows 18:20–21 (finding a wife, 18:22) – this problem-and-solution link located in section-framing positions – further endorses classification of 18:20–21 as a wisdom commendation (see 'Section-level framing', below).

Two-plus-one verse-trios framing a section, involving a theme of speech restraint (17:27 – 18:1, 18:20–22, content-based). The three sayings spanning 17:27 – 18:1 consist of a wisdom commendation urging speech restraint (two sayings), plus one saying presenting the malevolent loner (18:1). The three sayings spanning 18:20–22 consist of a wisdom commendation urging speech restraint (two sayings), plus one saying presenting a solution for the loner (v. 22). These two verse-trios frame Section III (17:27 – 18:22). For additional two-plus-one verse-trios, see above under 'What to watch for'.

Section-level framing with problem-and-solution (18:1, 22, content-based). The problem of the malevolent loner appears in the wisdom content of Block III.A (18:1). A solution for this problem follows in the wisdom content of Block III.D (18:22). These blocks frame Section III.

Section IV (18:23 – 19:9). *Problem-and-solution (18:23–24, content-based).* Problem-and-solution joins 18:23 with v. 24. Isolation comprises the problem (fostered by poverty, v. 23). A shallow solution aims merely to multiply one's friends (v. 24a). A better solution would value even a solitary friend, if that friend exhibits loyal character (v. 24b).

Wisdom commendation followed by wisdom content (19:1, 2–9, content-based). The palistrophe comprising the lecture's final block begins with a commendation concerning the wisdom of integrity (19:1). The balance of the palistrophe supplies the wisdom content – a strategy for success despite isolation caused by poverty (vv. 2–9).

Emphasis through length and opacity (19:7). In 19:7 the sage at last reveals the commendable person who, despite poverty, remains wise. The length of this saying retards the rate of reading (cf. 1:22, 27; 5:18; 6:8; 22:29). Opacity also slows the reading, especially in the third colon. Literally, it states, 'he is pursuing sayings, not they' (19:7c). Whereas some would index friendship by wealth, the exemplary person, though poor, prioritizes the pursuit of wisdom.

Thematic continuity involving investment, with contrast (19:4, 6, 8). A theme of investment appears in 19:4, 6, 8. To obtain friends, one may opt to invest wealth and gifts (vv. 4, 6). Sadly, such friends last only as long as the wealth (v. 7). Contrastingly, through 'acquiring sense' one may achieve 'good' that will endure (v. 8).

Palistrophe (19:1–9, form- and content-based). The sayings spanning 19:1–9 form a palistrophe pivoting on v. 5. The outermost pair of sayings deal in integrity, explicitly named in 19:1, and portrayed by its inverse in v. 9 ('perjurer'). The second step combines 'appetite' (named in vv. 2, 8) with either ignorance (v. 2) or its opposite ('perception', v. 8). In the third step, 'rage' (v. 3) links with 'hate' (v. 7). The lost fool through rage alienates himself from the LORD (v. 3), while brothers and so-called friend through hatred alienate themselves from the poor (v. 7). Disappointment and wisdom also link the third step. His own failure (loss of direction) fosters disappointment (v. 3) for one who has abandoned integrity (v. 1). Suffering abandonment by family and friend would bring disappointment to the poor person (v. 7). 'Wisdom' appears negatively through 'folly' in v. 3, and positively in v. 7. The fourth step registers 'friends' in a large quantity ('many') in both branches (vv. 4, 6). Here one's quantity of friends increases with one's wealth, betraying insincerity.

The fourth step flanks the palistrophe's core, with its emphasis on integrity (19:5). Integrity also marked the first palistrophic step, in both v. 1 and v. 9 (Waltke similarly links vv. 1, 5, 9 [2005: 101]). In fact, the close (v. 9) quotes the palistrophic core (v. 5), only exchanging the expression 'will not be rescued' with the more ominous 'will perish', achieving intensification.

Comment

Section I (**17:4–15**). *Block I.A (17:4–9).* The evildoer longs for splendour and popularity. In quest of splendour, through deceit he scans for disaster so he may capitalize on another's misfortune to accelerate his own promotion (17:4). Instead of assisting those in need, with cruel words he mocks them, finding perverse glee in their disaster (v. 5). Yet he fails to realize that genuine splendour resides richly within a family marked by reciprocal honour routinely bridging generational divides (v. 6).

In quest of popularity, he lavishly bestows flattering words (17:7) and gifts with strings attached (v. 8). He fails to realize that true friends will be drawn to gifts of uncalculating mercy (v. 9a). His erstwhile closest friends will jettison him, once they discover he has traded publicly the secrets they entrusted to his safekeeping. (v. 9b).

Block I.B (17:10–15). After introducing the evildoer with his intended destiny (splendour and popularity), the sage reveals what this figure achieves, and issues a warning to dissuade him from that path (Block I.B, 17:10–15). In reality he accumulates a concentration of contention (v. 11a) that will consolidate over time, eventually circling back to his own doorstep in the form of retributive cruelty (note that localized pain of 'a hundred blows' in v. 10b expands to pervasive 'cruelty' in v. 11b).

By sequencing 17:11 after v. 10, the sage implies that the evildoer of v. 11, against whom 'a cruel messenger' will be sent, is more hazardous even than the 'stupid fellow' who displays insensibility to 'a hundred blows' of corporal reproof (v. 10).

The sage proceeds to caution the evildoer: both a fool excelling in folly and a rampaging bear enjoy more popularity than an evildoer. A fool at the height of his folly ranks worse than a raging bear (17:12, a wisdom commendation).

The wisdom content of 17:13–15 decries the community-collapsing behaviour of the evildoer. By positioning this directly after the shocking wisdom commendation of v. 12, the sage fairly shouts his warning to dissuade the malevolent member from his universally damaging destiny.

For the evildoer would rend the community fabric by rewarding good with evil (17:13a). Since the evildoer will both inflict and inherit indelible misery (v. 13b), the sage pointedly directs him to desist from his self-destructive path, before it unleashes an irreversible flash flood of retributive litigation (v. 14, this lecture's sole imperative). The poet underscores his singular command (v. 14), positioning it at the core of a three-verse palistrophe (vv. 13–15).

Lest the troublemaker may counter, claiming the gains of mischief would more than offset the pains of retribution, the sage adds in 17:15 a caution paralleling v. 13. For, to subvert the judicial system, declaring the guilty to be 'just' and the just 'guilty' (v. 15a), will incite severest censure of a divine dimension (v. 15b).

17:5. An insult launched at a poor person indirectly taunts his Maker since he assesses the Maker's handiwork as inferior (medieval Jewish commentator Radaq [AD 1160–c. 1235], in Fox 2009: 627). Thus the sage's doctrine of the Creator dictates esteem for others.

'Joy over calamity' presents a striking and sinister counterfeit of the preceding lecture's portrayal of a robust mind, characterized by joy arising from ethically responsible strategies that come to fruition (15:13, 21, 23, 30, with v. 26 ensuring the moral dimension).

17:6. Despite parallels between 16:31 and 17:6 ('splendid' or 'splendour' and 'crown', and a connection between longevity with morality), these sayings belong to separate lectures with distinct themes. In 16:31, longevity argues for the importance of discernment, while in 17:6 longevity argues against a life focused on doing evil (*pace* Waltke, who regards these two verses as a frame [2005: 35–36]).

17:8. While 17:8 appears value-neutral, later this lecture disapproves of bribery (e.g. 17:23).

17:9. The sage commended covering another's trespass in 12:16b also.

Section II (17:16–26). After describing in Section I how the evildoer employs subterfuge to achieve splendour and popularity, and after exposing the demise he inevitably suffers, in Section II the sage alerts the pupil concerning two circles whence the evildoer may unexpectedly emerge (17:16–26): friends and family.

Block II.A (17:16–17). A wisdom commendation cast as a ridiculous rhetorical question signals the start of a fresh section. How strange, if one 'missing sense' should one day, with tuition in hand, apply for wisdom training (17:16)! (The theme of lacking sense returns two sayings later in v. 18.) Then follow in v. 17 the dual-themes of friends and family. By their very nature, true friends and family will cultivate love and diminish distress, not stir it up (so different from the evildoer's conduct in 17:4, 5, 9b). However, not all friends prove true, and even family may produce malefactors. So the youth must beware.

Block II.B (17:18–20). Friends – the first of dual-themes introduced in 17:17 – the sage unfolds next (Block II.B, vv. 18–20). On behalf of a supposed 'friend' only a fool would co-sign a loan, proving he lacks sense (v. 18, a wisdom commendation with close links to surrounding content).

The sage makes his point with two sayings of wisdom content. When friendship factors in a loan, one must examine motives carefully. Does the applicant genuinely love the pupil as friend ('at all times a friend loves', 17:17a)? Or has an ignoble fascination seized his affection ('one who loves trespass loves a brawl', v. 19a)?

And why does this 'friend' need the loan? Does the applicant seek essentials, or excess? If excess, beware! Here the poet imagines a loan to fund construction of an ostentatious gateway, hazardously overextended, supported neither by sound architecture nor by the applicant's character (17:19b). This façade one day will come crashing down – leaving the unwise co-signer on the hook for the cost of its catastrophic collapse.

The so-called friend's misplaced love (17:19a) stems from bent thinking (v. 20a). So he spins clever yarns (worthless financial pledges), nimbly pivoting to misdirect the inattentive (v. 20bα).

Life does not end well for the counterfeit friend. Unable to attain ultimate satisfaction (17:20bβ), he careens headlong into the misery he so carefully contrived.

Block II.C (17:21–26). After so-called friends, family comprises the second group that unexpectedly may give rise to evildoers. The sage treats family in two units (17:21–23, 24–26). The first specifies family relationships through a wisdom commendation portraying a good-for-nothing son who distresses his father (v. 21).

That parent may respond to his son in one of two ways. He may (a) remain resilient in personal joy, refusing to tether his emotional state to whether his son inspires pride. Grounded in joy, he will be able to render appealing counsel his son requires to escape stupidity (17:22a). Or (b) the son's behaviour may crush his father's spirit. In that condition, whatever advice the parent offers risks 'desiccating the bones' of the son, failing to administer the intended cure (17:22b).

Following the wisdom commendation of 17:21–22, the evildoer's specific conduct emerges – perpetrated, evidently, by the 'son' of v. 21. That conduct consists of subverting justice through graft (v. 23).

In the second unit, through another wisdom commendation a stupid son pains parents to the point of bitterness, greedily longing after things (his 'eyes are on the ends of the earth', 17:24–25). Instead of distributing money (bribery, 17:23), he now schemes to seize money (illicit fines, v. 26a), covering his tracks by punishing any moral whistleblower (v. 26b).

17:16. The stupid fellow errs by supposing that wisdom can be purchased like so many dry goods (Fox 2009: 633).

17:17. Also the psalmist knows of a 'friend' and 'brother' who no longer merit customary trust (Ps. 35:14).

17:18. In a longer caution against guaranteeing a loan, the sage identifies the 'friend' also as 'stranger' (Prov. 6:1–5).

17:16–26. Caution against evil arising from family and from supposed friends would be especially pertinent for pupils with connections to royalty. Competition for the throne led to rivalries with fatal consequences among royal officials and members of the Israelite royal family (e.g. Absalom, Jehu and Ahab's sons, Athaliah and Zimri).

17:22, 23, 26. The utter demoralization resulting from overturning justice resembles modern countries where graft, rife in law enforcement, accuses victims of crimes for which they themselves sought redress.

Section III (17:27 – 18:22). After introducing the evildoer (Section I), after exposing circles whence, unexpectedly, he may emerge (Section II), the sage now grapples with the evildoer's underlying nature and the strategy he employs (Section III, 17:27 – 18:22). His nature and strategy appear briefly by introduction (Block III.A, 17:27 – 18:1), followed by a more thorough exposure of strategy (litigious speech, Block III.B, 18:2–9). Recommended safeguards offer a beacon of hope to offset so ominous a warning (Block III.C, 18:10–19). Section III closes with assurances of retribution and a prescription for cure, both of which correspond uniquely to the malevolent and misguided loner (Block III.D, 18:20–22).

Block III.A (17:27 – 18:1). The evildoer – the focus of this lecture – emerges as the sage's evil twin. For he, too, chooses words so carefully (17:27) that others conclude he must be rather perceptive (v. 28). But behind this veneer of verbal restraint lurks a counterfeit who by nature is a loner, intent on satisfying personal cravings (18:1a; cf. 17:11a and contrast 17:9a). In reality, verbal restraint merely cloaks his strategy of finely honed predatory litigation, patiently awaiting an opportune moment (18:1b). Waltke similarly notes the theme-introductory function of the character in 18:1, who 'alienates himself from society by his self-indulgent pursuit' (2005: 69).

Block III.B (18:2–9). The litigious strategies of this loner the sage now exposes in depth. As stated before (17:27–28), the evildoer is not stupid, for he can hold his tongue (18:2). At the opportune moment he (now labelled 'guilty person') will enter the court setting to commence his accusations, putting his opponent on the defensive through initial tactics of scorn-filled speech (v. 3).

Unlike the 'rushing stream' of genuinely wise speech, pristine in its clarity, one must measure carefully the loner's language (18:4b). Deep and deceptive, it can conceal hidden hazards (v. 4a), declaring the guilty 'innocent', while handing down a verdict of 'guilty' against the moral (v. 5).

This litigious loner must not be confused with the loquacious stupid fellow, who here exceeds his earlier habit of merely 'laying bare his mind' (18:2). Now he rashly brandishes litigation as a cudgel, with this outcome: he reaps judicial punishment (v. 6). Longing to be proved right, he goes wrong – ultimately trapped by his own talk (v. 7).

In contrast, after initial tactics of scorn (18:3) the loner employs a second tactic. Now he serves up dainty morsels of mortal slander, exuding the aroma of exotic pastries (18:8).

Such a cunning evildoer earns the unenviable title of 'master-destroyer' (18:9b). Paradoxically, to qualify as runner-up for this ignominious award requires far less effort. A hearty dose of carelessness will suffice (v. 9a).

By withholding the identity of this 'careless person' of 18:9a, the poet crafts a rhetorical riddle, fostering curiosity in the reader. Who could this be? The answer will appear in the next block, as the sage teaches that a judge must exercise (a) vigilance against graft, and (b) diligence in gathering all information pertinent to a case (Unit III.C.3, 18:13–19).

Block III.C (18:10–19). After exposing the loner's predatory, litigious strategies, Block III.C offers safeguards to protect against his tactics (18:10–19). In the immediate wake of substantial hazard posed by the master-destroyer (v. 9b), the sage swiftly assures the pupil that the LORD himself stands ready to shield any moral person who hurries to him for help, secluding him as if in a high tower, out of predation's reach (v. 10). Recourse to the divine forms the premier safeguard against the evildoer.

Next, the sage measures the extent of protection provided by monetary wealth (18:11). Read in isolation, this saying seems to praise wealth. But when read in the light of negative remarks about riches found earlier in this lecture, the picture is not so rosy. Thus far, wealth has served as a vantage point from which to mock the poor (17:5a) and a tool of bribery (17:8), especially within the judicial system (17:23). Consequently ominous klaxons should sound when the pupil learns that the rich regard their wealth as their 'strong city', 'a high town wall'. These rich rest serenely, for the courts are in their pocket. As 18:19 will show, the expression 'strong city' may carry a negative flavour as well.

Despite seeming safety, a fissure fragments the rich person's arrogant security (18:12). Though in his imagination his metaphoric wall may tower loftily, yet it will crumble, having been founded on presumptuous values wherein the LORD is noticeable only by his absence.

Unlike the momentary security of monetary wealth, judicial diligence and impartiality supply a durable defence. Judicial diligence begins with a commitment to hear all arguments before rendering a decision (18:13a). Anything less would amount to disgraceful folly (v. 13b), compounding unconscionably the victimization suffered by the innocent (v. 14).

In place of lassitude, the devoted judge will spare no effort to discover evidence relevant to a case (18:15), resisting all offers of bribery (v. 16). Nor may shortcuts be entertained, as they would circumvent fairness (v. 17).

Having said that, a situation may unfold where, after preliminary hearings, contesting players may attempt to overwhelm justice by dint of force. For a judge then to refer the case to the divine (by casting lots) constitutes no shortcut, but a sage manoeuvre (18:18).

But the judge who allows bribery or power to skew justice (recall 18:16 and 18b, respectively), will, in effect, imprison the victimized as surely as if confined behind a citadel bar (v. 19). For, wealth that funds bribes will, like a 'strong city', forge the victim's prison as a high citadel (recall the connection between wealth and 'strong city', 18:11, and see 'Notes' for v. 19). And 'strivings' (v. 19b) by 'mighty opponents' (v. 18b), if unresolved, will erect a barrier impenetrable as a stout beam. In consequence, the wronged 'brother' becomes isolated.

Such alienation comprises the very material of which the 'loner' consists (18:1a). This means that, by his dereliction of duty, the lazy judge achieves what even the evildoer-loner could not (18:13–19). He has franchised isolation, populating its potentially sociopathic group with fresh recruits consisting of novice malevolent loners. Thus the negligent judge proves the answer to the riddle of 18:9: it is the delinquent judge who is a close relation of the master-destroyer.

Block III.D (18:20–22). Section III began by observing that restrained speech masquerades as wisdom (17:27–28). Then appeared the loner, motivated by deep longings (18:1). Now at the section's close appear two more sayings about speech (18:20–21). This time, however, no amount of verbal restraint will prevent retribution, returning to the speaker either death or life, according to his or her words.

Also, now at the section's close, the sage presents a cure for the loner with his longings. For him to remain alone is not good. As in Eden, a spouse's companionship comprises the loner's perfect solution, a provision that gives proof of divine approval (18:22; cf. Gen. 2:18). Herein lies the foundation both for authentic friendship and for supportive family relationships, correcting the two circles from which evildoers may unexpectedly arise (17:16–26). Whereas the manipulative mind that used friends for monetary gain was powerless to 'find good' (17:20), the married man has at last 'found what is good' (18:22b).

18:19. Perhaps the poet had in mind the long-simmering revenge of Absalom against his brother Amnon after Amnon's rape of Tamar, Absalom's sister (and Amnon's half-sister, 2 Sam. 13).

18:20. Unlike close parallels in 12:14 and 13:2, one need not be 'good' in order to receive 'fruit' or 'revenue'. Consequently this saying teaches comprehensive retribution, assuring alike positive and negative rewards corresponding to conduct.

Section IV (18:23 – 19:9). In his final section the sage further explores the experience of loneliness (Section IV, 18:23 – 19:9). For the evildoer, isolation represents the outworking of his sinister inner nature (18:1). Yet not all isolation is chosen, arising from evil inclinations. Consider the rejected-poor, for example. Cast aside by society due to economic inferiority, they suffer isolation involuntarily.

Block IV.A (18:23–24). The dilemma of the rejected-poor is not new to this poem. As early as the lecture's second verse, the poor suffered disdain from evildoers (17:5). Rejection resurfaces in the final section's first saying, 'A poor person keeps on uttering pleas for help, but a rich person keeps on replying stridently' (18:23).

To assist the rejected-poor, the sage will engage three implicit questions. First, to what extent does wealth determine worth? Second, under what circumstances should appetite trump integrity? Third, what constitutes true friendship? The poet's answers will not unfold sequentially, one after another. Instead they interweave, generating a cumulative impact as forceful as it is artful.

Surrounded by the rich, the poor feel invisible, friendless (18:23). To respond by hastily accumulating a host of shallow friends, at any cost – such a cure would only worsen the wound (18:24a; see assonance in 'Notes').

In contrast stands a solitary figure with depth of character. His loyalty surpasses superficial 'friends', and even family members (18:24b). Not till the poem's close will the sage reveal the identity of this one who loves so faithfully (see 'Comment' on 19:8, under Block IV.B, below).

The quatrain opening Section IV (18:23–24) engages each of the implicit questions posed above. First, though discounted by the rich, the poor possess great worth. Second, the poor must not sacrifice integrity in pursuit of superficial friends. Third, true friendship consists of loyalty.

Block IV.B (19:1–9). The theme of isolation arising from poverty continues in the remainder of Section IV (esp. 19:1, 4, 6, 7). Should one abandon integrity in order to escape poverty? 'Never!' responds the sage. For moral failure confirms membership among fools (v. 1).

Furthermore, the sort of folly displayed by moral failure indicates ignorance about the proper role of appetites (19:2). Appetites excel at motivation, but fail miserably at navigation (16:25–30). By opting for moral compromise, the fool has entrusted appetites with navigation.

Upon discovering that appetites misled him, the fool compounds his catastrophe. Loath to own his error, he rails against the divine (19:3). 'Instead of repenting . . . , the earthbound creature is so convinced that his sinful way of life is right that he storms against the LORD, holding him accountable for not granting what he thought, planned, and willed' (Waltke 2005: 99–100).

Exactly how did the deluded fellow of 19:3 lose his way? He suffered friendlessness because he wove those friendships of the frail and fraying fabric of riches. Surrounded by wealth, he would be surrounded by friends. But when through reversal of fortunes he became 'helpless', those so-called friends were nowhere to be found (v. 4).

Like a perjurer, he played the deceiver as he financed friendships (19:5a). But in the end, only the fool was fooled. So, reminiscent of one who ridiculously rages against the divine (v. 3), he 'will breathe out violence' but 'will not be rescued' (v. 5b). For his fair-weather friends flatter him only so long as gifts drip from his hands (v. 6).

Although close friend and even family may abandon the poor, if he will, the materially poor can distinguish himself above them all. For, despite economic poverty, he can still persist in 'pursuing words of wisdom' – a path less travelled by fair-weather friends (19:7). And high among wise counsels would be to quest after integrity: 'Better a poor person who walks in his integrity, than if he were to operate with twisted lips – and so would prove to be a stupid person' (v. 1).

So wisely to prioritize integrity wisely amounts to 'acquiring sense' (19:8a). Such an investment appears to forget appetites, declining to feed the felt-need of gaining friends. Instead of funding counterfeit friendship through gifts, the path of wisdom insists on honesty. By navigating according to ethics instead of appetites, this one – though seemingly poor – will attain 'what is good' (v. 8b), a goodness where all licit appetites (for a time forgotten) now achieve true satisfaction. In this fashion, that earlier-mentioned 'loving person who clings more loyally than a brother' (18:24) proves not to be an external friend, but one's own self – provided one has pursued wisdom in 19:7b and 8a (evidenced by pursuing integrity in 19:1, instead of duplicitously purchasing friends in 19:4, 6, 9).

Not so the deceptive person, who remains powerless to shed the shackles forged of his own lies (19:9; cf. v. 5a). He will perish, ever muttering out resentful threats, with none to blame but his own insecure self.

Through this closing section the sage imparts to the poor his gifts of insight, earlier suggested by three implicit questions. First, the poor may learn not to measure worth – neither of self, nor of others – by tangible wealth. Second, navigating by integrity, not by an elusive appetite for more 'friends', one eventually will achieve what is genuinely 'good'. Third, no level of destitution should alienate an authentic friend (18:24). And the individual who, despite poverty, still clings to integrity proves to be his or her own best friend. Such a one truly 'loves his appetite' and will 'find what is good' in life (19:8).

18:23. The sage corrects a callous attitude towards the poor also in 14:20–21.

19:5. Although mention of 'perjury' (19:5, 9) raises the possibility of a judicial theme for all of vv. 4–7 (so Waltke 2005: 100–102), the larger concept of uninvited isolation that characterizes 18:23 – 19:9 more probably colours 19:5, particularly since 'uninvited isolation' complements the concept of isolation as a trait of loners and of evildoers, a concept that appeared earlier in this lecture (17:27 – 18:22; esp. 18:1). Viewed from this vantage point, perjury (an expression of deceit) vividly underscores deception as the evildoer's fundamental flaw. Deceit opens and closes this lecture, producing an inclusio (*šeqer*, rendered 'falsehood' in 17:4, is also embedded in 'perjury' [lit. 'witness of falsehoods'] in 19:9; for other indications of deceit, cf. 17:4, 7, 15, 20, 28; 18:8; 19:1).

19:7. Whereas 17:17 describes how family and friends ought to behave and sometimes do, 19:7 'exposes a seamier reality, and both are valid' (Fox 2009: 651).

19:9. It is instructive to observe that the Masoretes sensed a major disjunction following 19:9. Here the Ben Asher text, preserved in Codex Leningradensius, displays a *pĕtuḥâ*, 'open[-ended space]', so that the next verse (19:10) begins uncharacteristically on a fresh line. *Pĕtuḥôt* comprised the most substantial separators of textual material, exceeded only by a colophon (scribal notes at the close of an individual book within the Bible). A *pĕtuḥâ* generally coincides with a transition from one topic to another, as here. Ten *pĕtuḥôt* appear across Prov. 10 – 24. The most recent appeared immediately before 14:1. The next follows 21:30.

Explanation

Section I. Introduction of evildoers (17:4–15)
Simply to avoid folly will not suffice. We must train ourselves to be alert to those who 'perpetrate evil' (17:4).

How may we recognize the evildoer? Notice those who seek to get ahead by demeaning others (17:4–5) and by distributing manipulative gifts (vv. 7–8). Observe those who discount the inestimable worth of family relationships strengthened by forgiveness (vv. 6, 9), supposing that they exhibit superiority by disclosing confidences entrusted to them (v. 9b). Sadly, the contention and cruelty they dole out will find its way home to them, fuelled by divine disappointment (vv. 10–15).

That is why with vigilance we must counteract the brambles of contention that insinuate themselves in the soil of our relationships. Differences there will be. But contention born of selfish ambition must be uprooted, and that quickly (17:14).

Section II. Evil arising from unexpected sources (17:16–26)
The effectiveness of evildoers owes, in part, to the fact that they emerge from unexpected quarters. Our natural inclination to trust family and friends renders us more vulnerable. We must train ourselves to exercise discretion, gauging our relationships according to the adverse conditions they can withstand, not content with fair-weather friends (17:17).

To pledge our resources to another based on a superficial friendship, without studying the validity of the request – this is perilous (17:18, 20). We must pause to examine where this so-called friend's affections truly lie (v. 19). Does he resort to unethical practices (v. 23) or twist fairness to make a profit (v. 26)? Even if he is a family member, be on your guard (vv. 21, 25). Do your best to correct such a one, fashioning your appeal out of joy (not condemnation, 17:22). Help him or her realize that the loneliness he seeks to assuage can be satisfied only by other, moral means (cf. 18:1 in Section III).

Section III. The evildoer's nature and strategy, with safeguards against them (17:27 – 18:22)

To understand the evildoer, we must realize that his world orbits around his own cravings. Externally, he exhibits restraint of speech, appearing rather wise (17:27–28). But this must not fool us. What matters most, what he ultimately drives towards, is the satisfaction of his own appetites (18:1). People around him function merely as means to that end. Such an ambition inevitably fosters contention, leading to isolation. James similarly observes that appetites for what one does not have will lead to divisive contentions (Jas 4:1–2). This insight provides an incisive point for personal examination: Where do other persons factor in the grand scheme of our personal goals? Do they serve merely as stepping stones in our ascent to supposed success (Prov. 18:1b)?

We must beware when we, or others with whom we deal, resort to tactics of scorn (18:3) or – worse yet – slander (v. 8) in an effort to get ahead. Even though we may manage to conceal predatory litigation behind a curtain of seeming legality (swaying the opinion of decision makers), such strategies will not ultimately succeed. Ostentation will collapse (v. 12), while those relying on the LORD will be lifted to safety (v. 10).

Have we been entrusted with privilege as decision makers, whether judicial or otherwise? We must not yield to unethical influence, whether by laziness (18:13), bribes (18:16) or threat of conflict (v. 18).

When dealing with the evildoer, it is critical to realize that what he lacks – that craving he labours so craftily to satisfy – is a faithful, trusting relationship. In this lecture it appeared first with the winsomeness of intergenerational honour (17:6). The picture of 'one who covers transgression', who does not violate confidences (17:9a, 9b) further portrays such a rich relationship. The friend who 'at all times . . . loves', the brother who 'for distress will be born' – these add still more portraits to the album of faithful friendship (17:17). And here, at the close of Section III, the sage presents God's most fundamental provision to satisfy man's loneliness. As in the Garden of Eden, marriage between a man and a woman brings a degree of wholeness like nothing else, thereby making a new personage far exceeding the mere sum of its parts (18:22).

Section IV. Loneliness: the problem of uninvited isolation, with strategies for success (18:23 – 19:9)

We must not conclude that isolation always signals an evildoer, a loner by choice. Some cry for escape from the isolation of their poverty. Woe to us if, having more resources, with indifference we walk by on the other side (18:23).

If we discover ourselves suffering isolation, we must respond insightfully. Merely to add superficial friends (18:24), or to dispense with integrity in an effort to get rich (19:1) – these tactics will fail (19:4, 6–7). Instead we must become aware of our appetites, discovering what is driving us (19:2). Only by choosing to pursue integrity (19:5), by cultivating an appetite for sense (v. 8), will we attain what is truly 'good'. Instead to maintain a life of lies and brutality will prove suicidal (19:9).

PROVERBS 19:10 – 20:4
'Will not wealth and power consistently lead to satisfaction?'

Overview of Proverbs 19:10 – 20:4

From the lecture just ended, the youth would have noticed wealth's capacity to bring a measure of benefit. A bribe seems to secure favour (17:8), whereas poverty may leave one quite abandoned (19:4). Against such a backdrop the youth might have pressed, 'Will not assets of wealth and power reliably lead to satisfaction, regardless of how one may acquire those assets?' Such is the implicit question addressed by this lecture (19:10 – 20:4; Heim recognizes borders at 19:11 – 20:4 [2001: 268]).

The sage begins by explaining that, although wealth and power do have roles to play in achieving satisfaction, their roles are not so robust and reliable as the pupil may imagine (Section I, 19:10–17). After addressing the youth concerning (a) the deficiencies inherent in power, and (b) the inferiority of wealth in contrast to nourishing relationships, the sage turns to address parents. He challenges them to assume the responsibility to reprove a youth who exhibits (a) entitlement to anger, (b) a tendency towards miserliness in relationships or (c) an inclination towards scoffing. Otherwise he will be powerless to achieve genuine satisfaction (Section II, 19:18 – 20:1). In the closing three sayings he summarizes the lecture's themes of power and generosity in relationships, combined with individual industry requisite for satisfaction (Section III, 20:2–4).

Position of this poem within Proverbs

Preceding context. The preceding lecture concentrated on evil and its practitioners, with frequent reference to the concept of *rāʿaʿ*, 'to be evil' (17:4 – 19:9). In contrast, the present poem mentions *rāʿaʿ* only once (19:23). *Šeqer*, 'false', a term associated with *rāʿaʿ* in the previous poem, does not appear in this lecture. In their place, the twin themes of authentic wealth (i.e. relationships) and power feature prominently here, as the sage explains how to secure authentic satisfaction.

Ensuing context. The present lecture (19:10 – 20:4) emphasizes cultivation of character marked by faithful love (19:22). The next lecture extends the study of faithful love, as evident in its second saying, 'Many a mortal may proclaim, "A person consists of his faithful love." But a person characterized by faithfulness, who can find?' (20:6). The balance of that lecture (20:5 – 21:4) outlines the nature of true greatness in three periods of life: during youth, life's prime and later years.

What to watch for
Notice references to power, relationships and satisfaction. Distinguish between power over others (including anger) and power over self (including restraint of anger). Observe that wealth and power fail to achieve satisfaction independent of healthy relationships. Watch what the sage teaches concerning appetite, craving and satisfaction. Notice recurring references to indolence, and where those references appear within a given portion.

Distinguish between (a) sayings that address pupils, (b) sayings that address parents and (c) sayings that provide parents with a script for use when (like the sage) they address their children. As a corollary, consider what the sage teaches concerning reproof. Distinguish between verbal and corporal forms of reproof, and consider the rationale for this distinction.

Finally, study with care the final three verses (20:2–4). Then reread the entire lecture, attentive to prior mention of any expressions or concepts lodged in those last lines.

Translation and outline

Verse	*Translation*	*Outline*
		I. How wealth and power pertain to achieving satisfaction (19:10–17)
19:10	It is not pretty when a stupid person has luxury; how much less, when a servant rules over princes!	A. Dual-theme introduction: wealth and power in some forms are undesirable (19:10)
		B. Royal power: sometimes desirable, sometimes not (19:11–12)
19:11	A mortal's good sense will have curbed his anger, and his splendour consists of passing over an offence.	1. Restraint of anger is desirable (19:11)
19:12	Roaring like a young lion is a king's angry storming, but like light rain upon grassland is his approval.	2. Since royal power is variable, it needs restraint (19:12)
		C. Domestic wealth: more desirable than wealth is the enrichment of relationships (19:13–14)

Verse	*Translation*	*Outline*
19:13	The demise of his father is a stupid son, and a constant dripping are a wife's contentions.	1. Folly and strife undermine domestic wealth (19:13)
19:14	House and wealth are parents' inheritance, but from the LORD is a wife with good sense.	2. Superior to wealth is the worth of a wise wife (19:14)
		D. Satisfaction falls with indolence, and rises with industry (19:15–16)
19:15	Laziness will cast a deep sleep, and a misleading appetite will go hungry.	1. Indolence prevents satisfaction by insisting on autonomy (19:15)
19:16	One who guards a command guards his appetite; one who despises his ways will be put to death.	2. Industry supports satisfaction by submitting to obedience (19:16)
19:17	He lends to the LORD who treats the helpless with grace; and as he treated others, so will the LORD repay him.	E. Section conclusion: gracious relationships can govern wealth and power, bringing satisfaction (19:17)
		II. Guidance for parents of children who lack anger-restraint and who scoff (19:18 – 20:1)
		A. The dilemma of children lacking in anger-restraint calls for verbal reproof (19:18–24)
		1. A wisdom commendation with summons to parents and a rationale for parents of angry children (19:18–19)
19:18	Reprove your son since there is hope, and do not long to bring about his death!	a. Wisdom commendation with summons to parents: reprove swiftly, if you care at all (19:18)!
19:19	Entitlement-to-anger pays a fine; indeed – if you were to rescue, then you would need to do so repeatedly.	b. Wisdom content with rationale: coddling his anger will earn you a co-dependent career of posting bail (19:19)
		2. Script for reproving children lacking in anger restraint (19:20–24)

19:20 Listen to counsel and gather reproof, in order that you may wind up wise. 19:21 Many are the plans in a person's mind, but the LORD's counsel – that is what will stand firm.	a. Positive wisdom commendation: summons to, and divine source of, 'counsel', *'ēṣâ* (19:20–21)
19:22 The core longing of a mortal consists of his faithful love, and better to be poor than deceptive.	b. Principal counsel concerning satisfaction: practising faithful love satisfies deepest human desire (start of wisdom content, 19:22)
19:23 Reverence for the LORD tends towards life, so that satisfaction may spend the night, undisrupted by misery. 19:24 A lazy fellow hid his hand in a dish; he is not willing even to make it return to his mouth.	c. The importance of satisfaction (19:23–24) i. The LORD: the source of enduring satisfaction (19:23) ii. 'Indolence', *'āṣēl'*: the enemy of satisfaction (19:24)
19:25 A scoffer you should strike, so that a naive person may grow shrewd; whereas, when applied to a perceptive person, a reprimand will bring knowledge to light. 19:26 One who treats a father with violence will chase a mother away, such is a son who causes shame and disgrace.	B. The dilemma of children who scoff calls for physical reproof (19:25–29) 1. A wisdom commendation with summons to parents, and a negative assessment of children who scoff (19:25–26) a. Wisdom commendation with summons, to parents of children who scoff (19:25) b. Wisdom content: a negative assessment of violently disrespectful children (19:26)
19:27 Refuse, my son, to listen to reproof, in order to wander away from words of knowledge!	2. Script for reproving children who scoff (19:27–29) a. A negative, sarcastic wisdom commendation with summons (19:27)

Verse	*Translation*	*Outline*
		b. Wisdom content: the problem with scoffing at penalties (19:28–29)
19:28	A worthless witness will scoff at justice, while the mouth of guilty folk will swallow disaster whole.	i. The hazard of advisors who scoff at just penalty (19:28)
19:29	Just penalties have been scheduled for the scoffers, and beatings for backs of stupid folk.	ii. Certitude of penalties awaiting scoffers and stupid folk (19:29)
20:1	A scoffer amounts to wine; a growler – strong drink; and anyone who wanders away in this manner cannot grow wise.	C. Dual-theme conclusion with summation: scoffers and angry persons altogether amount to drunken fools (20:1)
		III. Recap: how to harness power and manage relationships to reach satisfaction, with warning (20:2–4)
		A. How to harness power and manage relationships to reach satisfaction (20:2–3)
20:2	Roaring like a young lion is a king's terror; one who works himself into a rage sins against his own appetite.	1. The wrong approach: responding with unrestrained angry power prevents satisfaction (20:2)
20:3	Glory belongs to the person ceasing from litigation, but any fool can lose his temper.	2. The right approach: managing relationships with self-restraint yields dividends surpassing wealth (20:3)
20:4	After the rainy season a lazy fellow is unwilling to plough; he will beg during the harvest, but – none!	B. A final warning: indolence concerning self-restraint prevents satisfaction (20:4)

Notes on the text

19:11. 'good sense', *śēkel*: sound-and-sense inversion contrasts 'good sense', *śēkel*, with 'stupid person', *kĕsîl*, in 19:10.

'will have curbed his anger': lit. 'lengthened his nose' (idiom for anger-restraint). Choice of ind. 'will have curbed' in the first colon (in contrast to infin. 'passing over' in the second) attributes to 'good sense' a higher degree of initiative. The verse-pair in 19:11–12 implies an offence has been committed. Good sense will already have responded by restraining anger (fut. pf. inferred from the qat.), in contrast to an insensitive, roaring monarch (v. 12).

19:12. 'Roaring', *naham*: based on a contrast with 'roar', *šʾg*, in Isa. 5:29–30, *nhm* may describe the relatively quieter sound emitted by a lion, such as after seizing its prey.

19:13. 'The demise': since 'wife' links 19:13 and 14, the topic of wealth in v. 14a may give an economic colour to 'demise' in v. 13a. Similarly relational strife of v. 13b may trace to financial tensions.

'a constant dripping . . . a wife's contentions': cf. 27:15.

19:14. 'House': or 'household'.

'parents': lit. 'fathers'. Hebr. lacks a separate term encompassing mother and father.

'good sense', *maśkālet*: closely related to *śēkel*, 'good sense', in 19:11.

19:15. 'will cast a deep sleep', *tapîl tardēmâ*: this expression occurs elsewhere only in connection with Adam's sleep before God formed Eve (Gen. 2:21).

'misleading', *rĕmiyyâ*: this term may be rendered either 'misleading' or 'lazy'. Since the poet already established 'laziness', *ʿaṣlâ*, in the first colon, one should detect the added connotation of deceit in *rĕmiyyâ* (similarly, in 12:27; see 'Comment', below).

19:16. 'his appetite', *napšô*: as in 19:15, *nepeš* is rendered 'appetite'. The alternative meaning 'life' must be borne in mind, sharpening the contrast with 'death' in the second colon.

'his ways': i.e. the ways of 'one who despises' (just as '[one who] guards' supplies a pronominal antecedent for 'his appetite' in 19:16a). As the converse of 'guarding one's appetite' in v. 16a, to 'despise one's ways' in v. 16b would imply giving free rein to one's appetites.

'will be put to death', *yûmāt*: following the pass. voice (hoph.) of K, rather than the act. voice (qal) of Q, 'will die'. The pass. voice matches the Torah's penalty for rebellious children (Exod. 21:15, 17). Also the caus. tone of the hoph. in Prov. 19:16 (causing, not simply experiencing, death) continues with the same verb in v. 18b: 'do not long to bring about his death' (caus., as opposed to 'do not long for him to die').

19:17. 'He lends . . . who treats . . . with grace': the same person is the subject of both verbs.

'and as he treated others': lit. 'and his responsive deed'; i.e. how he responded when he encountered a helpless person.

'so will the LORD repay him': lit. 'he will repay to him'. While the entity issuing repayment may be his deed (treating others kindly, 19:17a), more likely the sage intends the LORD as actor here. It is from the LORD that one obtains a sensible wife (v. 14b), and the LORD is in debt to a youth who treats the helpless with grace (v. 17a). Thus it is the LORD who 'will repay' the youth for his benevolent responsive deed.

19:18. 'since there is hope', *kî-yēš tiqwâ*: Waltke (2005: 91) and Fox (2009: 565) observe that the particle *kî* expresses certitude that while a youth yet lives, hope remains for a positive response to reproof.

'do not long', *al-tiśā napšō*: lit. 'do not lift up your appetite' or 'soul'.

19:19. 'Entitlement-to-anger', *gōral-ḥēmâ*: lit. 'a lot-allocation of wrath' (K). With this expression the sage envisions one who declares, in effect, 'Due to real or perceived offences committed against me or my ancestors, anger comprises my rightful and perpetual inheritance'. Q needlessly simplifies to read *gĕdŏl-ḥēmâ*, 'great of anger'.

'indeed – if', *kî 'im*: the sense of 19:19b indicates that the component meanings (*kî*, 'indeed', and *'im*, 'if') should be retained (cf. 1 Sam. 14:39), not rendered as a compound meaning 'except'.

'then you would need to do so repeatedly', *wĕ'ôd tôsip*: lit. 'and again you would repeat' (necessity inferred from yiq.). Laziness (implied by the recurring need for bailout, 19:19b) may comprise a passive–aggressive manifestation of anger.

19:20. 'you may wind up wise': lit. 'you may become wise in your conclusion'.

19:21. 'but the LORD's counsel – that is what will stand firm', *wa'ăṣat-yhwh hî' tāqûm*: lit. 'but the LORD's counsel, it will stand firm', with emphatic use of pronoun.

19:22. 'core longing', *ta'ăwat*: rendered 'what he craves' in 18:1. To emend with LXX *karpos*, reading *tĕbû'at*, 'fruit', is unnecessary, diminishing significantly the sage's teaching concerning human nature (*pace* Fox 2009: 658–659).

'his faithful love', *ḥaśdô*: since 'mortal' supplies the nearest antecedent, this refers to the mortal's faithful love. Bertheau comments, 'Man's desire and joy is to show kindness' (in Toy 1902: 378). Toy renders, 'The desire of a man is his kindness.' According to the second colon, such altruism must be genuine, not deceptively self-serving (19:22b).

Versions routinely misrepresent this saying. Some cast the mortal as desiring love from others ('What a person desires is unfailing love', NIV). Others connect the love with the mortal, but overlook the fact that he will find personal satisfaction as an agent of love ('What is desirable in a person is his kindness', NASB; similarly, NRSV and ESV).

19:23. 'satisfaction', *śābêa'*: lit. 'satisfied' (adj. as substantive). In 19:22 the sage explained how one's core longing may be satisfied. Now, by personifying satisfaction, he portrays its continuance as it consents to 'spend the night' as the pupil's honoured guest. This understanding fits the context better than treating *śābêa'* as a person (such as the pupil) who now enjoys repose in another's house.

'undisrupted by misery': lit. 'misery (or evil) will not be visited' (inflicted) upon this personified satisfaction.

19:24. 'he is not willing even to make it return': lit. 'also to his mouth he will not make it return' ([un]willingness inferred from yiq.; cf. imperfective of desire, *IBHS* §31.4.h).

19:25. 'you should strike', *takeh*: obligation inferred from yiq. (similarly, potentiality in 'may grow shrewd', *yarîm*).

'whereas, when applied to a perceptive person, a reprimand will bring knowledge to light', *wěhôkîaḥ lěnābōn yābîn dāʿat*: lit. 'and to reprimand a perceptive person, it will issue perception regarding knowledge'. Both cola of this verse answer the implied question 'What happens when reproof is applied to a particular sort of person?' The act of 'giving reprimand' (infin. abs. *hôkîaḥ*) serves as the subject of the finite verb *yābîn*, 'it will bring to light' (reading *yābîn* as hiph. meaning 'to foster perception', not as homonymous qal, which would mean 'it will perceive'). Whereas the process of striking a scoffer (corporal discipline) will benefit the scoffer not at all (19:25a), the process of delivering a verbal reprimand to a perceptive person will cause that person to grasp knowledge even better than before (v. 25b). Note that 'perceptive person' and 'bring to light' both trace to the root *byn*.

19:27. 'Refuse', *ḥadal*: lit. 'cease'. This verse fairly drips with irony, especially in view of the message of 19:20, which is also cast as an imperative and similarly uses the terms 'listen' and 'reproof'. To 'refuse' (to listen) evidently comprises the Hebr. antonym contrasting 'receptive listening', based on the pairing of these two words elsewhere (cf. Ezek. 2:5, 7; 3:11, 27). In view of the irony transparent in 19:27b, to render *ḥadal* in v. 27a as 'be successful' (and so remove the irony of v. 27a) would ignore the context (*pace HALOT*).

19:28. 'while the mouth': lit. 'and the mouth'. By rendering 'while', one may detect more readily that the propaganda peddled by the worthless witness (i.e. that the accountability inherent in justice is laughable) comprises the disaster the guilty folk, in turn, swallow whole. To the extent that the son of 19:27 behaves as a guilty person of v. 28b, he will gullibly devour this misinformation, as if gleefully swallowing poison against which he presumes immunity.

'will swallow . . . whole', *yěballaʿ*: lit. 'will engulf'. Notice assonance with 'worthless', *běliyyaʿal*.

19:29. 'have been scheduled': lit. 'have been established'.

20:1. 'A scoffer amounts to wine; a growler – strong drink', *lēṣ hayyayn hōmeh šēkār*: lit. 'A scoffer [is] wine, a growler [is] strong drink'. It has been customary to understand this teaching as attributing to alcoholic beverages the traits of scoffing and anger, rather than characterizing the scoffer and growler as inebriated, not sound of mind (cf. NRSV, NIV, among others). However, such an interpretation does not reflect our best understanding of Hebr. syntax for verbless clauses (Muraoka 1999: 205; Niccacci 1999: 218–220). In unmarked syntax, a verbless clause will present known or anticipated information first, followed by new information. Thus in the verbless Hebr. clause 'Dame Folly makes a lot of racket', *'ēšet kĕsîlût ḥōmiyyâ*, 'Dame Folly' is the anticipated character contrasting Lady Wisdom, and so appears first in this phrase (9:13a). New information about that anticipated character that would be unknown to the audience then follows – Dame Folly is one who 'makes a lot of racket'.

Within the present lecture, verbless syntax appears in 19:22a. The statement 'The core longing of a mortal consists of his faithful love' consists of two nominal parts: 'The core longing of a mortal' and 'his faithful love' ('consists of' is supplied to reflect the implied verb 'to be' that joins the two nominal parts of a Hebr. verbless expression). What appears second supplies the new or unexpected information. By this syntax the sage is saying that most in the audience would not realize the fact that, as far as mortals' core longings are concerned, to become an agent of faithful love is what they truly crave.

By the time the reader reaches 20:1, the topic of 'scoffer' or 'scoffing' already has been established as a theme (19:25, 28, 29). The scoffer is not new information. Therefore it appears first: 'A scoffer [is] wine' (not 'Wine [is] a scoffer').

What is new (unknown by the reader) is this: a scoffer shares a trait in common with wine (and similarly a growler shares a trait in common with strong drink). Just as intoxicating beverages may influence someone to lose his or her way, so also may the scoffer and growler (20:1b). Persons who let themselves fall under the heady influence of a scoffer or the self-righteous influence of a growler will, like the inebriated, discover themselves travelling a path they did not consciously choose.

Thus it is the misleading influence of scoffer and growler (not the misleading influence of alcohol) against which the sage cautions in 20:1b. For a passage where the sage cautions specifically against the harmful effects of drunkenness, see Prov. 23:29–35.

'a growler', *ḥōmeḥ*: note assonantal link with 'anger', *ḥēmâ*, 'growler' sharing a measure of semantic overlap (19:19).

'cannot grow wise': 'will not be (or become) wise'. (In)capability inferred from yiq.

20:2. 'one who works himself into a rage', *mit'abĕrô*: reflexive action (hith. stem). Unbridled anger ultimately brings harm to oneself. Versions such as NASB, NRSV and NIV alter the meaning, treating *mit'abĕrô* as act., not reflexive (provoking another to become angry, rather than stirring oneself to become angry).

'his own appetite', *napšô*: recent emphasis on appetite (19:15, 16), craving (19:22) and of failure to self-feed (19:24) favour *nepeš* as 'appetite' (not 'life' or 'self').

20:3. 'can lose his temper', *yitgallā'*: lit. 'will burst out [in strife]' (capability inferred from yiq.). Like *mit'abĕrô*, 'one who works himself into a rage', 20:2, *yitgallā'* is a hith. form, focusing on action performed to or for oneself. Each accents lack of self-restraint.

20:4. 'After the rainy season': soil conditions favour planting following the rainy season (October to March; Fox 2009: 664).

'is unwilling to plough': lit. 'will not plough'. As with 'he is not willing' in 19:24b (un)willingness is inferred from yiq.

'he will beg', *yišʾal*: K presents the two actions of 20:4 as indivisible sides of a single coin (two yiq. verbs), as if the indolent were gambling on later begging, even when he initially refrained from ploughing. By rendering them sequential (weqat. for the second form), Q softens the connection, as if excusing the second (begging) as an unforeseen consequence of the first (not ploughing).

'but – none!': lit. 'but there is none'. An abrupt sense of emptiness accompanies the Hebr. syntax chosen to conclude this lecture.

Form and structure

Borders

After examining evildoers (preceding poem, 17:4 – 19:9), the present lecture explores the intersection of wealth, power and satisfaction. The sage references wealth and power in a dual-theme saying at the poem's upper border (19:10).

Recap, closure, inclusio and a climactic finish combine to indicate 20:4 as the lower border (additional structures listed under 'Macrostructural features' and 'Microstructural features' also apply, if focus encompasses those sayings leading up to v. 4). After ranking relationships above wealth (19:13–14, 17), after commending industry above indolence (vv. 15–16), a recap encompassing power, relationships and indolence concludes the poem (20:2–4).

Recurrence of 'lazy' produces closure. Towards the close of Section I laziness emerges as the enemy of satisfaction (19:15). 'Lazy' next associates with children lacking anger-restraint (v. 24, closing Block II.A). 'Lazy' occurs once more at the lecture's last line, where indolence produces emptiness at harvest (20:4).

The lecture's first and last sayings negate by means of *lōʿ* (rendered 'not' in 19:10 and 'unwilling' in 20:4), creating an inclusio. *Lōʿ* occurs only twice more within this lecture, each marking the end of a portion (19:24 marks the end of the first cycle of reproof, spanning 19:18–24, while 20:1 marks the close of Section II, spanning 19:18 – 20:1). The sense of negation intensifies in 20:4 as that saying closes with *ʾāyin*, 'none'. The decision in 19:23 not to negate with *lōʾ* may stem from a desire to reserve *lōʾ* for the final line of a portion (19:23 negates with *bal*, in 'undisrupted').

A climactic finish concludes the lecture as the sage portrays lack of food resulting from indolence (20:4). When viewed in isolation, it offers general counsel for industry. But when read in concert with vv. 2–3, that tragic scenario of lethargic starvation could supply the motivational difference, convincing a monarch to seek lasting honour by abandoning resentful rage that only proves he or she lacks self-restraint (for progression of thought, see below under 'Comment' for Section III).

Macrostructural features

Thematic continuity involving harmful power (Sections I–III, content-based). Power operating harmfully, whether as irresponsible anger or violent aggression, appears in each section. In Section I, a sensible person knows how to curb his anger (19:11). A king's powerful, leonine anger instils dread among any nearby (v. 12). In Section II, smug, self-justified anger on the part of a youth calls for reproof (v. 19). Violent aggression towards one's parents may be explained (not excused) as anger gone to seed (v. 26). In Section III, a monarch's rage proves self-destructive (20:2), indicative rather of folly than of royalty (v. 3).

Thematic continuity concerning wealth (Sections I–III, content-based). The theme of wealth operates in each section. In the opening saying, wealth comprises no unconditional asset since luxury in the hands of a stupid person is not pretty (19:10a). Continuing in Section I, a son may cause a father's 'demise', *hawwōt*, a term that can include loss of material assets (19:13). Riches become explicit in the next saying: 'House and wealth are parents' inheritance' (v. 14a). An economic expression describes how the LORD keeps record of kindness displayed to a helpless person ('He lends to the LORD who treats the helpless with grace', v. 17a).

In Section II, the arrogant-angry youth suffers a financial penalty (19:19). Tangible wealth fades before the superior worth of integrity (v. 22b).

The term 'glory' continues the concept of wealth in Section III. To quit litigation results in 'glory' in 20:3a, a sublime degree of wealth.

Thematic continuity of indolence and hunger (Sections I and II, form- and content-based). In Section I the sage links laziness with insufficient food (19:15). In Section II indolence is personified in a lazy person (same root as 'laziness'), who suffers hunger (v. 24).

Thematic continuity of deadly hazard (Sections I and II, form-based). Towards the close of Section I the pupil learns the mortal cost of despising divine commands (19:16). The first line of Section II cautions parents against entertaining for their child a death-wish masquerading as leniency (v. 18). These expressions employ the root *mwt*, 'to die', in a caus. stem.

Inclusio with phrase repetition (Sections I and III, form-based). The phrase 'roaring like a young lion' appears in 19:12a and 20:2. Both vividly portray harmful royal power. The first phrase appears three verses from the poem's beginning, closing a two-verse portion dealing with the need to restrain anger (19:11–12). The second appears three verses from the poem's end, opening a two-verse portion underscoring the need to restrain anger (20:2–3). Escalation marks the second instance, intensifying from the king's 'angry storming' to his 'terror'.

Inclusio involving the magnificence of anger-restrained (Sections I and III, content-based). Self-restraint supplies the solution to harmful power expressed as anger. It first appears as 'curbing one's anger' and 'passing over an offence' in 19:11, where it earns the designation 'splendour'.

Self-restraint appears again towards the lecture's close, in the expression 'ceasing from litigation'. Such self-control earns the lofty designation of 'glory', and contrasts the fact that 'any fool can lose his temper' (both in 20:3). Since 19:11 and 20:3 are located one verse from the lecture's outer edges, these form an inclusio.

Inclusio involving root *ʿbr* (Sections I and III, form-based). Twice in this lecture the root *ʿbr* occurs. It appears as 'passing over' in the statement 'his splendour consists of passing over an offence' (19:11b). With a sense of reversal, it appears again as 'to work into a rage' (20:2).

Palistrophe of inclusios (Sections I and III, form-based). The initial three sayings of this lecture link to its last three sayings, nested so that they form a palistrophic inclusio. For the innermost step, a roaring lion appears in 19:12 and 20:2 (and not elsewhere in this lecture). The middle step consists of restrained anger. It appears in 19:11 (curbing anger and overlooking an offence) and 20:3 (refraining from pursuit of litigation).

The outermost steps are universally negative. It is negative when both luxury (19:10a) and authority (v. 10b) fail to enhance beauty. Similarly negative are agricultural indolence (20:4a) and panhandling (v. 4b), when neither generates any useful return. Heim similarly observes the chiastic pairing of 19:11–12 with 20:2–3 (2001: 258).

Microstructural features

Section I (19:10–17). *Dual-theme introduction of wealth and power (19:10, content-based).* The twin themes of wealth and power initially appear in the first and second cola of 19:10, respectively. Wealth is signified by 'luxury', *taʿănûg*, and by 'pretty', *nāʾweh*. Power is signified by 'rule', 'princes' and negatively by 'servant'. The sage expands on the second (power) by comments concerning anger in vv. 11–12. In vv. 13–14 he expands on the first (wealth) by sayings comparing the relative value of one's house and estate, when contrasted with the value of a spouse who has 'good sense'.

Thematic continuity involving wealth (19:13–14, content-based). Mention of 'demise' (which can describe loss of wealth) in 19:13 together with 'house', 'wealth' and 'inheritance' in v. 14 fosters a theme of tangible riches. A wife with good sense exceeds tangible riches as an asset of superior worth.

Thematic continuity concerning power (19:11–12, content-based). Power in the form of self-control appears in 19:11, while 'a young lion' describes a monarch's power (v. 12).

Thematic continuity involving household (19:13–14, form- and content-based). Mention of father, son, wife, house and parents joins 19:13 with v. 14 in a theme of household.

Contrast of scopes – dynastic and domestic (19:10b, 11–12, 13–14, content-based). A royal or dynastic scope in 19:10b and 11–12 is indicated by mention of servants, princes and king. Mention of father, parents, son, wife, house and inheritance indicate a more domestic scene in vv. 13–14 (so also Waltke 2005: 107). 'Pretty' in v. 10a may connect with 'wife' in the domestic portion (vv. 13–14), since the adj. 'pretty' (root *nwh*) may describe a woman's beauty (e.g. Song 1:5; 6:4).

Inclusio of 'good sense' (19:11–14, form-based). The dual-theme topics of power and wealth from 19:10 find their expansion in vv. 11–14. The first word of v. 11 and the last of v. 14 trace to the root *śkl*, 'good sense', creating an inclusio.

Repetition of 'appetite' (19:15–16, form-based). The verse-pair in 19:15–16 coheres by repetition of 'appetite'. With this term the sage shifts attention from ostensible sources of well-being (wealth and power), focusing instead on sources of authentic satisfaction. While it is tempting to infer that the indolence of v. 15 describes (and links to) the unwise son of v. 13a (just as v. 14 linked to the contentious wife of v. 13b), v. 15 does not mention the son (as v. 14 did mention the wife; *pace* Waltke 2005: 108–109). Consequently the repetition of 'appetite' in vv. 15, 16 comprises the clearer indication of structure.

Assonantal inclusio with lō' *and* lô *(19:10, 17, form-based).* In Hebr. the first word of Section I is pronounced *lō*ʾ, 'not' (19:10a), a sound fairly indistinguishable from the last word of Section I, *lô*, '[to] him' (19:17b). Although pronunciation in ancient times might have differentiated the two, their sounds would have been quite similar, resulting in a first-word and last-word inclusio precisely spanning Section I. Incidentally, the phoneme *lô* occurs a second time in that closing colon (v. 17b), ending the expression 'and as he treated others', *ûgĕmulô*.

The same general sound (whether *lō*ʾ, 'not', or *lô*, 'to him', or any other *lo* phoneme) recurs only twice more in this entire lecture, appearing as *lō*ʾ, 'not'. It coincides with portion conclusions (19:24; 20:1).

Threefold section-closure (19:17, content-based). Three themes of Section I effect closure in its final verse (19:17). Mention of the LORD in a highly active role re-establishes the theme of power (cf. vv. 11–12). Mention of lending and repaying pertains to the theme of wealth (cf. vv. 13–14). Mention of kindness towards the helpless revisits the earlier encouragement to restrain impulses of revenge against subordinates (cf. vv. 10b–12).

Section II (19:18 – 20:1). *Wisdom commendations with summons (19:18, 20–21, 25, 27, form-based).* Four times in Section II the sage incorporates a command with a commendation of wisdom, producing a wisdom summons (19:18, 20–21, 25, 27). Each wisdom summons paves the way for wisdom content (19:19, 22–24, 26, 28–29).

The first reinforces the importance of reproof by a charge addressed to parents (19:18). This is not the start of a new lecture, since mention of anger in the next saying (v. 19) builds on that topic from vv. 11, 12. Rather, in v. 18 the sage rivets his gaze on listeners able to aid youths, who need what he has been teaching in vv. 10–17. The wisdom summons in v. 18 paves the way for wisdom content concerning anger in v. 19.

In the second (19:20–21), the sage directs the wisdom summons to the youths who were named when addressing parents in v. 18. Youths must 'listen to counsel and gather reproof'.

The third wisdom summons again addresses parents, recommending sterner measures of reprimand in the case of a scoffer (19:25). The next saying accounts for the more confrontational approach, since a child openly belligerent towards parents earns the double castigation as shameful and disgraceful (v. 26).

In the fourth, the sage addresses the youth for the second time, hoping sarcasm will jolt him to alertness (19:27). This negative wisdom summons paves the way for two teachings that warn against the self-harming folly of arrogance that defies punishment for criminal behaviour (vv. 28–29).

Two cycles of script for youths prefaced by a charge to parents (19:18–24, 25–29, form- and content-based). Twice in Section II (19:18 – 20:1) the sage supplies parents with a script for reproving youths. The first script addresses children with unrestrained anger (19:20–24). The second, children who scoff (19:27–29). Each begins with an imperative (vv. 20, 27).

A charge to parents precedes each script (19:18–19, 25–26). The first colon of each exhortation presents a command, whether an imperative form ('Reprove!', 19:18) or a yiq. form expressing an obligation ('you should strike', 19:25).

Repetition of 'counsel' (19:20–21, form-based). 'Counsel' appears in 19:20, 21. The first commends receptivity to counsel (and to reproof). The second elevates divine counsel above mortals' advice.

Thematic continuity concerning plenty (19:23–24, content-based). 'Satisfaction' signals the theme of plenty in 19:23. An abundance of food appears in v. 24 also, although with a negative connotation since the lazy fellow refuses to move his handful of food to his mouth, leaving him unsatisfied (Waltke links vv. 23–24 similarly [2005: 121]).

Palistrophe involving themes of counsel and satisfaction, centring on a mortal's core longing (19:20–24, form- and content-based). The LORD is mentioned in 19:21, 23 creating one level of a palistrophic frame. Another involves assonance of 'counsel', *ʿēṣâ*, in v. 20 and 'lazy fellow', *ʿāṣēl*, in v. 24. Admittedly, the fact that 'counsel' appears in v. 21 as well as in v. 20 weakens the uniqueness of the link with *ʿāṣēl* in v. 24.

Centred in this five-verse span lies a solitary teaching identifying what a mortal most longs for, namely to be a sincere agent of faithful love (19:22). The two preceding verses underscore the importance of receptivity to counsel, especially divine counsel. This solitary saying of v. 22 comprises the counsel referred to in vv. 20–21.

The two verses following that counsel (a) commend reverence since it leads to satisfaction (19:23), and (b) dismiss indolence since it fails to satisfy (v. 24). The solitary teaching at the palistrophe's core identifies faithful love as that behaviour particularly consistent with reverence and leading to satisfaction. Thus the palistrophe spanning vv. 20–24 showcases in v. 22 a pivotal teaching concerning the satisfaction of a mortal's core longing.

Repetition of 'scoff' (19:25, 28, 29; 20:1, content-based). The portion spanning 19:25 – 20:1 (Blocks II.B and II.C) coheres by repetition of verbs and nouns involving 'scoff' (so also Waltke 2005: 121). In 19:25 parents are instructed how to reprove a scoffer. In v. 28 the sage describes how 'a worthless witness will scoff at justice'. And the final punishment of scoffers appears in v. 29. The scoffer reappears in the following verse as part of a dual-theme conclusion to Section II (20:1).

Reversal concerning receptivity to reproof (19:20, 27, form-based). In 19:20 the sage urges receptivity to reproof. In v. 27 he urges the opposite, suggesting this saying must involve sarcasm.

Repetition of 'justice' or 'just penalties' (19:28, 29, form-based). Both 'justice' and 'just penalties' represent the term *mišpāṭ* (sg. and pl., respectively). Their appearance in 19:28, 29 creates a verse-pair portraying the hazard of discounting the consequences of unlawful conduct (so also Waltke 2005: 124).

Block-level inclusio involving corporal punishment (19:25, 29, content-based). Mention of corporal punishment in 19:25, 29 operates as a block-level inclusio. Those lines mark the outer boundaries of the Block II.B.

Dual-theme conclusion to Section II involving scoffing and angry behaviour (20:1, form- and content-based). By mention of scoffer, the final verse of Section II (20:1) recalls the signature attitude of 19:25–29 (Block II.B), which comprised the second counsel given to parents ('scoffer' or 'scoff' appear in vv. 25, 28, 29). By mention of 'growler' in 20:1 the sage recalls the theme of anger that typified the youthful error in the first counsel to parents (Block II.A, 19:18–24; esp. v. 19).

Summation contributing to climax (20:1, form-based). By modifying the final colon of Section II with 'anyone', the sage intensifies to a universal scale the spectrum of hazard threatening those who indulge in scoffing or anger ('anyone who wanders', 20:1).

Section-level closure, with reversal, concerning attaining wisdom (19:20; 20:1, form-based). Early in Section II the sage urges behaviour that would lead his son to 'wind up wise' (19:20b). In the section's final colon the picture is reversed. As if drunk with their arrogant and incorrigible attitudes, the scoffer and angry fellow lose their way. They 'cannot grow wise' (20:1b).

Section III (20:2–4). *Problem–solution sequence (20:2–3, content-based).* The verse-pair in 20:2–3 begins with a problem – an angry, self-destructive leonine king. That problem would find an answer – with noteworthy splendour – if that character could restrain himself enough to discontinue strife (20:3).

Comment

Progression across entire lecture. Before examining specific portions, it is instructive to note how thought progresses from one section to the next across the entire lecture. Three major themes recur through this lecture: power, relationships and satisfaction. The sage begins by analysing the problem (Section I), and presenting a solution (Section II). The lecture closes by recapping the three themes (Section III).

Section I analyses the problem (19:10–17). Power becomes a problem when it gives rise to abuse, expressed as anger. Relationships suffer when wealth outweighs the worth of family members. Finally, satisfaction suffers when laziness deprives legitimate supply of needs.

Section II presents a solution in the form of reproof a parent may employ when helping a youth who struggles with the three focal areas of power, relationships and satisfaction (19:18 – 20:1). In particular, that reproof should address the theme of power, for this young person exhibits excessive anger, symptomatic of his abusing power within a family context (19:19). Further, that reproof should address relationships with persons in authority over him, for this youth scoffs at his parents (v. 25) and at justice (vv. 28–29). He may go so far as to treat parents violently (v. 26). Finally, that reproof should address true satisfaction, since the youth needs to realize that satisfaction results from becoming an agent of faithful love (v. 22), and from reverence mixed with diligence (vv. 23–24).

Section III recaps the three themes (20:2–4). As to power, one must guard against its abuse (venting anger, v. 2a). As to relationships, more splendid than fighting for one's rights is the decision to leave off litigating (v. 3). As to satisfaction: rage (v. 2b) and indolence (v. 4) will deprive one of the opportunity for satisfaction. Having surveyed progression of thought across the entire lecture, next consider progression within successive sections.

Progression within sections. *Section I (19:10–17).* <u>Block I.A (19:10)</u>. The sage introduces wealth and power in Section I by presenting a negative example of each in the opening verse (19:10, dual-theme). When paraded by a stupid fellow, wealth lacks lustre (v. 10a). Even less attractive is power, when wielded by one accustomed to a subordinate role (v. 10b). Wealth and power share this in common: their worth ultimately depends not on static valuation, whether sheer quantity of assets, or one's rank on an organizational chart.

<u>Block I.B (19:11–12)</u>. Power, second of the dual-themes, occupies the sage's attention in 19:11–12. From the negative picture of power-over-others exercised by one who had been a servant (dual-theme introduction, v. 10b), the sage turns to a positive picture of power over one's own self in v. 11. In contrast to the ugliness of v. 10b, it is beautiful when a person in power treats an offender with mercy, not with customary retribution (v. 11). Evidently, the servant's authority in v. 10b lacks mercy. It is not

inexperience, but his bent towards revengeful tyranny that disqualifies him for rule ('his rulership will develop into unbearable despotism', Waltke 2005: 105). In contrast, power ruled by self-restraint exhibits 'good sense' (v. 11).

The theme of power escalates with the appearance of the monarch (19:12). The need for self-restraint (v. 11) swells since royal whims land on his subjects with amplified impact, whether menacing harm (v. 12a) or ministering benefit (v. 12b).

From 19:10–12 the pupil would learn that power carries neither inherent justification nor its own moral compass. Power may either be hurtful and vindictive (vv. 10b, 12a) or helpful and mercy-filled (vv. 11, 12b). One wielding power must ensure that might is managed aright.

Block I.C (19:13–14). Wealth – the first of the dual-themes in 19:10 – the sage expands in vv. 13–14. 'Demise' (v. 13), 'house', 'wealth' and 'parents' inheritance' (v. 14) indicate wealth. Nevertheless, expanding tangible wealth is not the sage's main objective in this quatrain. Rather, material riches serve as a platform for presenting a treasure of greater worth – the treasure of relationships. That treasure is a wife who exhibits 'good sense' (v. 14b). Since 'good sense' contrasts the 'constant dripping' of contention (v. 13b), and since the sage already associated 'good sense' with mercy that overcomes a reflex of retribution (v. 11), the wife portrayed here neither nags nor works revenge in the face of disappointment or offence (Heim also recognizes merciful forbearance as this wife's primary trait [2001: 259]). With self-control she extends the mercy needed to maintain and strengthen a relationship. She constitutes a divine gift whose worth exceeds even great tangible wealth (v. 14).

It is instructive to note that in Block I.B. the principal figure is the king (19:11–12), while the wife is the principal figure in Block I.C (19:13–14). Thus the sage distinguishes contributions its male and female partners bring to a marriage.

A strategic shift occurs with the next quatrain, signalled by repeating 'appetite' in 19:15, 16. Thus the sage turns the discussion from lesser goals of wealth and power, focusing instead on the ultimate objective those goals aim to secure, namely deep inner satisfaction.

Block I.D (19:15–16). Two routes compete for travellers, both promising satisfaction. First is the unreliable route of indolence – a route that advertises satisfaction while never producing it (19:15). Indolence stands as the antithesis of power. In view of the sage's careful teaching that the optimal expression of power consists of power over self for the purpose of replacing vindictive urges with mercy (which displays good sense, vv. 11, 14), the indolence of v. 15 amounts to a 'misleading appetite' for vindication that refuses to lift a finger in restraint of its own tendency to answer offence with resentment and rage.

Second is the route leading reliably to satisfaction. In contrast to lazy autonomy, the individual travelling on this second route submits willingly to 'a command' and so exerts the self-governing power needed to 'guard' his appetite (19:16). An appetite thus guarded (a) will be restrained from wantonly devouring (as in restraining an appetite for revenge), and (b) will be assured a supply of nourishment.

It is critical that the traveller would choose wisely between the route of indolence and the route receptive to a superior's command. Fatal consequences befall the careless choice (19:16b).

To this point the sage has specified neither (a) who is one's rightful superior, nor (b) to what sort of 'command' one should submit (19:16a). The answers appear in the next verse. The identity of that superior, ultimately, is none other than the LORD (19:17aα). Based on the behaviour commended in v. 17aβ, one may infer that his directive would call for gracious treatment of the helpless – that is, kindness towards any possessing power or wealth relatively less than oneself. This conduct recalls the restraint-of-anger urged in vv. 10b–12.

Block I.E (19:17). So highly does the divine value kindness towards the helpless that any practitioners will receive a veritable promissory note signed, as it were, by the LORD himself (19:17b). One's own generosities will be repaid by the most powerful person of all. Thus the three themes of power, relationship (expending wealth to aid the helpless) and satisfaction (receiving repayment from the LORD himself) merge in this final saying of Section I.

19:10–12. Egyptian sages similarly registered concern when inexperienced persons acquired wealth and power. *The Admonitions of Ipuwer* (Twelfth Dynasty, 1991–1786 BC) preserves this lament:

> All say, 'We don't know what has happened in the land . . .
> Lo, poor men have become men of wealth,
> He who could not afford sandals owns riches.
> Lo, men's slaves, their hearts are greedy,
> The great do not mingle with their people.
> Lo, hearts are violent, storm sweeps the land,
> There's blood everywhere, no shortage of dead.
> (Lichtheim 1973, 1:151)

The contrast between usurped power in Prov. 19:10 and restrained power in v. 11 implies that the defect inherent in usurped power lies in its tendency towards tyranny – a trend attested by vindictive purges that tend to follow a violent overthrow.

Section II (19:18 – 20:1). Block II.A (19:18–24). The crescendo of intensity marking the end of Section I does not dissipate as that section closes, but flows swiftly into the wisdom commendation opening Section II (19:18). In evidence, notice the continuity linking these expressions: 'one who despises his ways will be put to death' (v. 16b in Section I), and 'do not long to bring about his death!' (i.e. the death of one's child who needs reproof, v. 18b).

A survey of Section II shows that the sage here dispenses with merely offering observations regarding power and relationships. Now he issues two layers of commands – a cycle that occurs twice. The first layer addresses parents, challenging them to reprove their children (Units II.A.1 and II.B.1). The second layer addresses the children, as if supplying a script for use by parents (Units II.A.2 and II.B.2).

Using a twofold rationale, the sage motivates parents to reprove their children. The first rationale is positive. The sage observes that it is never too late to issue reproof. If the child is alive, there remains hope of receptive response (19:18a; see 'Notes').

The second is negative. The sage exposes the deadly consequences when a parent refuses to reprove. Such a parent, the sage implies, should be charged with negligent homicide (19:18b).

Following the section-opening wisdom commendation commissioning parents to issue reproof (19:18), in Block II.A the sage counsels parents concerning children inclined to display arrogant anger, who embrace entitlement-to-rage as their rightful identity (v. 19a). The child who claims his or her anger has been titled 'by lot-allocation' renders his anger unimpeachable, exempt from indictment (see 'Notes').

Whether the child's anger stems from an offence (as in 19:11) or simply from an ungoverned exploitation of superior station (as with the monarch in v. 12), the sage does not specify. What he does indicate is the cost of such anger. Any who through pity may shield the youth from the costly consequences of his anger must be prepared to bail him out not only once, but over and again (v. 19b). The sage envisions co-dependency where a doting parent enables a child's tantrums, even into adulthood.

After counselling parents concerning children with anger issues (19:18–19), the sage proceeds to supply those parents with a virtual script for use when issuing reproof (vv. 20–24). This five-verse script unfolds as a palistrophe, with a core in v. 22 (see 'Microstructural features', above).

The script begins with a wisdom commendation intended for the youth, underscoring the importance of receptivity (19:20a). Without external critique, the youth would stand little chance of 'wind[ing] up wise' (v. 20b).

If receptive to reproof, the youth must then choose wisely which sources may speak into his life with authority. Although human counsel may abound (19:21a), its value pales in comparison with divine counsel (v. 21b).

At the palistrophic core the sage reveals what constitutes the fundamental divine counsel for the youth – or for anyone, for that matter (19:22). That counsel centres on correctly identifying (and thus satisfying) a human's deepest longing. 'The core longing of a mortal consists of his faithful love,' the sage explains (v. 22a). Deepest satisfaction results not from an inward focus that pursues self-centred appetites for power, for wealth at the expense of relationships or for pleasure. Rather, satisfaction emerges as one learns to treat others with faithful love (recall restraint of anger in v. 11).

With the second colon (19:22b) the sage explores more deeply the nature of faithful love. Although acts of kindness will ultimately benefit the benefactor (he or she will achieve deep satisfaction), those acts must not conceal selfish motives. For it would be better to remain poor than to acquire advantage at the cost of deception (ostensible generosity despite selfishness, v. 22b). To borrow Paul's words, 'Love must not be inauthentic' (Rom. 12:9a).

After establishing faithful love as the youth's most worthy goal (19:22), the sage reinforces the divine primacy of that goal by reminding the youth that reverence for the divine is what will lead to abundant life (v. 23a) and lasting satisfaction (v. 23b). To disregard the priority of cultivating faithful love (v. 22) would court irreverence (v. 23) and thereby ruin any prospect of ever achieving durable personal fulfilment.

The sage closes this first script supplied to parents by portraying a youth who, although amply informed, fails to act on what he has learned. He holds in his hand the 'food' that will satisfy him (19:24a). That is, he now knows that his deepest cravings will find satisfaction only as he cultivates faithful and sincere love towards others (v. 22). A comical scene laced with sorrow portrays one whose indolence prevents him or her from bringing a food-filled hand to his own hungry mouth (v. 24b). How tragic to starve while seated so near a table sagging under an abundance of food!

Block II.B (19:25–29). In Block II.A the sage began by addressing parents (19:18–19), then supplied them with a script to use with youths (vv. 20–24). Similarly, in Block II.B remarks directed to parents (vv. 25–26) are followed by a script for use with youths (19:27–29).

The preface to parents in Block II.B sounds a more sombre note than that in Block II.A. Earlier, the son exhibited anger, meriting reproof (19:18). Now the target individual is more rebellious – a scoffer (v. 25) – who violently chases his parents away (v. 26). The prescribed reproof grows commensurately more forceful, involving physical discipline ('strike', v. 25).

The principle of scaling of reproof according to the recipient's needs is also attested for a perceptive person. For him, a merely verbal reprimand will suffice to impart knowledge (19:25b; Waltke 2005: 122).

Like the preface to parents, the second script intended for the youth is similarly more sobering than the first. The youth now teeters at the brink of ruin (19:28–29). The sage consequently recommends the shock value of sarcasm when parents first address their son: 'Refuse, my son, to listen to reproof, in order to wander away from words of knowledge!' (v. 27).

To class the sage's words in 19:27 simply as irony is inadequate. While the sage's aim is indeed the opposite of what he says (as would be the case with irony), he intends also to mock the scoffer, turning against him his own tool of mockery in the form of sarcasm (so also Waltke 2005: 117, n.).

It is instructive to observe that the opening colon of 19:27 ('Refuse, my son, to listen to reproof') reverses the opening colon of earlier advice for the son ('Listen to counsel and gather reproof', v. 20a; observed also by Heim 2001: 269). Reversal accentuates the extent of sarcasm.

No longer is the youth merely attending to inferior, humanistic counsel (19:21b), feeding his cravings with deceptive and unsatisfying strategies of indolence (vv. 22b, 24). Instead he now attends to patently worthless advice that brazenly mocks the prospect of criminal punishment (v. 28a). He fills his appetite, consciously consuming self-destructive disaster (v. 28b). The sage moves to discredit that source of misleading advice, discarding the scoffer as 'a worthless witness' (v. 28). Not only are such advisors 'worthless witnesses'; they and their followers brashly consume the very wickedness that will eventually spell their ruin (v. 28b).

Predictably, such scoffing will not end well. No amount of mocking at just penalties will make them go away (19:29a; note link with 'justice' in v. 28). In fact, such a mocker is neither so bold nor so courageous as his arrogant deconstructions would imply. In reality, this sorry fellow is simply so stupid that he schedules a beating for his own back (v. 29b).

Block II.C (20:1). The sage closes his advice to parents with a single saying that encompasses the youthful errors both of anger and of scoffing (20:1). Anyone (note the climactic summation in 20:1b) who through scoffing (recalling 19:28) or hostility ('growler' recalls 19:19) succumbs to false and heady notions will thereby lose his way, never to arrive at wisdom. For the sage, such a dismal conclusion represents the worst possible outcome.

19:19, 24. The traits of anger (19:19) and indolence (v. 24) ironically may be connected, since anger over suffering injustice may become so preoccupied with pinning blame on another that the offended party may stall, paralysed, failing to lay hold of a better future that still remains within the reach of his initiative. Following a period of justifiable anger, persistent refusal to take reasonable initiative evidences laziness.

19:22. Earlier the sage commended concern for others:

> The core longing of moral folk is strictly good; the hope of guilty folk is an angry outburst. There is one who scatters generously yet gains still more, while one who holds back from straight dealing surely winds up in want. An appetite for blessing others will itself be made fat, just as one who waters thoroughly will himself be watered. (11:23–25)

Concerning 19:22b, see 19:1, where the sage ranks poverty-with-integrity above subterfuge.

19:24. 'Orientals dispensed with spoons and forks, dipping their hand into the dish to take their portion' (Waltke 2005: 121).

Section III (20:2–4). Block III.A (20:2–3). As the sage nears the lecture's close, he reiterates his earlier caution: power unleashed as unrestrained anger wreaks terrible damage. By repeating in 20:2a the phrase 'roaring like a young lion' from 19:12a, the sage reminds the pupil how important is self-restraint when inclined to angry outbursts of disappointment. This is especially true as one rises to royal positions, where commoners and even nobles may hesitate to reprove a person so powerful.

Bystanders are not the only victims of royal outbursts. In the final analysis, though he be king, the enraged person harms himself (20:2b). One who lazily refuses to corral his angry reactions supposes that by giving free rein to rage he will more rapidly bluster his way to the front of the line, positioning himself to seize satisfaction. But he fails to reckon with this fact: unchecked anger leads reliably in the opposite direction. Anger unrestrained storms out on a suicidal mission, always leading away from authentic satisfaction of one's core longing. This holds true because that sole commodity for which one most profoundly longs is this: to become an agent of love that remains loyal (19:22).

One who instead de-escalates strife – who refuses to seek revenge for every real or perceived offence – that one will win lasting esteem in the community (20:3a). Instead to go about losing one's temper merely guarantees a place of ignominy in a hall of fools (v. 3b).

Block III.B (20:4). At lecture's close the sage returns to the principle of indolence. For the entire teaching concerning achieving true satisfaction (by restraining anger so as to become a person of faithful love) will have no effect unless the pupil replaces native indolence with conscious industry. Only then will he lay hold of glory (a superlative expression within the theme of wealth, 20:3a) in place of the shame associated with the lazy fellow and his lack of self-control (v. 4). Such shame recalls the arrogant ignorance of the lazy fellow who has yet to master self-feeding (19:24).

True satisfaction will elude the lazy fellow because, at the point when he should have been ploughing and planting, he opted instead to indulge his appetite-for-ease. Later on when he should be gathering, for him there will be no harvest (20:4b). Even his begging will turn up empty. Like the drowning fools who delayed calling to Lady Wisdom until too late (1:26–28), it will never work to delay planting until the day before harvest. Failure to surmount one's own inertia works its own results, some with devastatingly irremediable consequences.

20:3. Earlier the sage counselled to abandon strife: 'Water escaping is the start of strife. So before the dispute breaks out, give it up' (17:14).

Explanation

Like the author of Ecclesiastes, here the sage seeks to correct the misguided assumption that wealth and power can deliver authentic satisfaction. The correction unfolds in the first section as he challenges fallacies concerning wealth and power (19:10–17). In the second section he stirs the parent to instil these corrections within youth (19:18 – 20:1). The third section reviews the entire lecture, observing again the immense value that derives from power exerted to restrain one's own tendency towards angry retaliation in relationships (20:2–4).

Section I. How wealth and power pertain to achieving satisfaction (19:10–17)

With his opening saying the sage challenges the misleading allure of both wealth and power (19:10). He does not indict luxury categorically, only opulence in the hands of stupid folk. Similarly not all power is bad. But problems arise when yesterday's servants today gain power over their masters.

The problem with power lies in its need of moderation by mercy (19:11). Since persons migrating from the repressed to the powerful tend towards revenge, their newly minted power easily sours into poison. In Herbert Spencer's words, 'The tyrant is nothing but a slave turned inside out' (1869: 118). For evidence that elevation from repressed to powerful need not result in revenge, consider the role of mercy in Nelson Mandela's leadership of South Africa, as chronicled in *No Future Without Forgiveness* (Tutu 2000).

In contrast, seasoned leaders have sense enough not to take offence easily (19:11a). A Malawian saying captures the flame-retardant quality desirable in a leader: 'A chief is like a swamp where the fire ceases to burn.'

However, a novice leader ascending from either servitude or youthful status typically lacks the strength of character required to rule over his own anger. Instead of dismissing offences (19:11), he wreaks havoc with abusive outbursts. The greater his power, the greater the havoc. For power in itself is value-neutral, requiring a strong and moral governing hand (v. 12).

The problem with wealth, for two reasons, lies in its failure to assure familial security. First, domestic well-being is not immune to erosion at the hands of family members (cf. the effect of a foolish son or a contentious wife in 19:13). Second, wealth is powerless to procure what the youth most needs – supportive relationships epitomized by a sensible wife (19:14). Only God can provide such a spouse. Like power, wealth proves a poor panacea.

Better than both wealth and power is an inclination towards industry (implied by the rejection of lassitude in 19:15) and self-denial (bowing to divine instruction in 19:16). Chief among those divine instructions is the strategy to 'treat the helpless with grace' (v. 17a). Better than resting in luxury's lap (v. 10), such a strategy puts one in the path of divine reward (v. 17b). To disregard this strategy hastens death (v. 16b).

Section II. Guidance for parents of children who lack anger-restraint and who scoff (19:18 – 20:1)

So hazardous is youthful deception associated with wealth and power, that parents and others having influence must be stirred to their responsibility as trainers (19:18). Idly to stand by while our children indulge in arrogant anger (v. 19a) or pursue wealth at the expense of integrity (v. 22b) will consign us always to foot the bill for the next generation's fines (v. 19b). Worse still, such negligence is tantamount to a parental death wish for one's child (v. 18b)!

When nurturing their children, parents should discover what sources of influence each child regards most highly (19:20). Then discern where the child ranks counsel issued by the LORD. After all else has collapsed, it is divine counsel that will produce durability (cf. Ps. 1).

Then help the youth grasp this profound but counter-intuitive insight concerning human flourishing. The overarching mortal quest for core longings will be met through neither wealth nor power. Rather, what a mortal craves is to operate as an agent of faithful love (19:22a) – a love strong enough to overlook an offence (19:11b), a love rich enough to share what little it may have to help the helpless (19:22b). Such conduct proves divine reverence (19:23a), which alone will yield a robust and rewarding life – a life flourishing with authentic and sustained satisfaction, not relying on ephemeral wealth (v. 23b).

Agents of such love remain loyal despite adverse circumstances. They prefer not to punish the offender, but to reconcile. These traits describe the deepest character of the divine (Exod. 34:6–7). Predictably, they surface most lavishly in the divine Son (Mark 10:45). Such profound divine character cannot consistently be manifest in mortals apart from the inworking of the divine (Gal. 5:22–26).

Mere awareness of this advice will not suffice, any more than a hand immobile in the food bowl can satisfy hunger (19:24). The youth who discovers himself inclined towards anger or miserliness must overcome lazy inertia by converting the sage's advice into action.

After addressing the angry and indolent son (19:18–24), one might be inclined to bypass the incorrigible scoffing son. Since he resists correction so categorically, why waste time trying to reprove him? There are two reasons. First, ignoring the scoffer would give onlookers the impression that scoffing is excusable. Instead we must make conditions unpleasant for the scoffer, thereby instilling a deterrent in the naive onlooker, the secondary learner (19:25a). Ugandan wisdom similarly cautions, 'If the man in front falls into a hole, do not follow him.' Second, one should impose discipline on a scoffer because, left unchallenged, a scoffer may go so far as to bring violence and disgrace to his parents' home (v. 26).

Just as one may be disinclined to discipline a scoffer, so also one may be hesitant to reprove a perceptive son (19:25b). However, he constitutes the most fruitful investment of reproof. From it he will derive great benefit

(v. 25b). One should reprove the scoffer and the perceptive son alike, although not necessarily using the same tone.

Sarcasm offers the tone of reproof suitable for a scoffer. To paraphrase the script supplied to parents in 19:27:

> If desisting from reproof is what you desire, then, by all means, have nothing more to do with it! In that way you may be sure to secure what you seem so intent on acquiring: a life marked by straying far from any intelligent discourse.

As with the angry and miserly sons of 19:18–24, so also with the scoffer the parent must expose those sources-of-counsel on which the scoffer depends (v. 28). In his counsel-of-folly there is no wisdom, only bold-faced stupidity that eventually must bare its back for the inevitable beating it pretends will never come (v. 29). In the final analysis, the angry, miserly and scoffing sons alike are blundering onwards into a foolishly intoxicating moral free-fall from which they may never awaken, like disgraced drunkards who perpetually stumble in their self-induced stupor (20:1). By preferring wealth and power above wisdom, integrity and mercy, scoffing and angry sons will miss everything worthwhile.

Section III. Recap: how to harness power and manage relationships to reach satisfaction, with warning (20:2–4)

With deliberate repetition that recalls the poem's third verse ('Roaring like a young lion is a king's angry storming', 19:12a), the sage begins the recap of his entire lecture ('Roaring like a young lion is a king's terror', 20:2a). We must not lose sight of the fact that, without self-restraint, power inflicts harm not merely on others, but upon oneself as well (20:2).

Superior to the power of angry abuse is the power of self-control employed to de-escalate and disarm angry reactions (20:3a, recalling 19:11b). From this heroic act emerges a measure of magnificence far superior to the tawdry glitter of superficial luxury (20:3). This splendour belongs to those who, although they may have a winning case, can discern when greater gain will arise, not by prosecuting, but by declining to press charges. Such conduct characterizes the wise person, since any mere fool may burst out angrily, determined to litigate at any cost (v. 3b). By pursuing splendour instead of merely tangible riches, the wise attain authentic wealth of a most durable sort.

But neither the power of self-control that enables one to overlook an offence nor the durable splendour that emerges from such de-escalation will result from wishful daydreaming, any more than a surplus harvest will appear magically without the hard work of planting. Lacking initiative, the wishful wind up only in want (20:4). All the teaching in the world will do us no good if we refuse to stir ourselves to act upon it. As with the indolent wedding-attendants who lack fuel in a story told by Jesus, the sage's indolent beggars will receive the same response: 'None!' (cf. Matt. 25:7–10; 2 Thess. 3:10).

PROVERBS 20:5 – 21:4
'What is the loftiest expression of human flourishing?'

Overview of Proverbs 20:5 – 21:4

An image of 'deep water' – with difficulty drawn from a well – opens the lecture spanning Prov. 20:5 – 21:4. Thus the sage indicates that this poem will be exceptional – both in its worth and in terms of skill required to discern its message (20:5a). Energies invested when studying this treatise will yield uncommon insights, illuminating the loftiest flourishing of human personhood. For 'a person with perception may draw it out' (v. 5b).

While others agree that a new portion begins at 20:5 (Krispenz, Whybray and Heim, cited in Heim 2001: 272), the compositional subtlety suggested by 'deep water' (v. 5) may explain why verse-groupings vary greatly among scholars (274, n.).

After announcing his lecture's topic (what it means to reach full human potential), the sage concludes the introduction by indicating three dimensions of human flourishing (Section I, 20:5–9). Each dimension subsequently expands in a section of its own (Section II, 20:10–23; Section III, 20:24–28; Section IV, 20:29 – 21:1). Along the way the sage associates each with a distinct stage in life, from youth to old age. With a two-verse character summary he closes the lecture, leaving the pupil to choose between integrity that secures divine favour, and an arrogant outlook that will devolve into a twilight of misdirection (Section V, 21:3–4).

Position of this poem within Proverbs

Preceding context. From the previous lecture (19:10 – 20:4) the youth learned that wealth and power cannot deliver as one might have supposed. Ungoverned, wealth and power fail to guarantee satisfaction. If not wealth and power, what can elevate a human to attain maximal fulfilment? It is to this question that the sage turns his attention in the lecture of 20:5 – 21:4.

Ensuing context. With the next lecture (21:5 – 22:16) the sage will refrain from introducing any new objectives or 'ends'. Instead he will concentrate on persuading the youth to employ worthy 'means', noble strategies in pursuit of those ends. Strategies should not presumptuously favour selfish pursuit of wealth or self-centred use of power. Instead they should abandon pretence, revere the divine and embrace humility.

What to watch for

From the outset, it will be important to consider carefully the axiom embedded in 20:6. Next, examine the varied realms requiring integrity, whether interior or exterior (in relationships). Attention to wisdom commendations will reveal boundaries of many portions, although not all (e.g. 20:5, 15, 18, 24). Blatant repetitions (as in 20:10, 23) and patterns created by double appearance of words in a single saying (e.g. 20:10, 14) comprise some of this poem's structural signals. Notice who is being addressed, whether pupil/youth or youth's advisor. Finally, observe the varied stages of life signalled by terms such as 'youth', 'robust man' and 'elderly'.

Translation and outline

Verse	*Translation*	*Outline*
		I. Introduction to faithful love as the loftiest human flourishing (20:5–9)
20:5	'Deep water' is counsel in a person's mind, but a person with perception may draw it out.	A. Wisdom commendation: profound counsel, and its cost (20:5)
		B. Wisdom content: identifying and achieving faithful love as the loftiest human flourishing (20:6–9)
20:6	Many a mortal may proclaim, 'A person consists of his faithful love.' But a person characterized by faithfulness, who can find?	1. Identifying faithful love: the elusive core of human flourishing (20:6)
		2. Triple-theme introduction: achieving faithful love through three behaviours (20:7–9)
20:7	One who, of his own accord, consistently behaves with personal integrity – he is moral; how fortunate are his children who come after him!	a. Cultivating integrity within (20:7)
20:8	A king who sits on a throne of justice scatters with his eyes all that is wrong.	b. Vanquishing evil without (20:8)
20:9	Who can say, 'I have cleansed my motives; I have become purified from my sin'?	c. Pursuing purity within (20:9)
		II. Cultivating integrity within: the quest to exhibit faithful love during one's youth (20:10–23)

	A. Advice offered to youth tempted by economic shortcuts (20:10–14)
20:10 One weight for selling, another weight for buying; one scoop for selling, another scoop for buying: abhorrent to the Lord are both of them together.	1. Illicit gain: among sellers (20:10)
20:11 Furthermore, it is through his deeds that a youth may distinguish himself, showing his work to be clean and honest.	2. Industry: the evidence of integrity (20:11)
20:12 A listening ear and a seeing eye, the Lord made both of them together.	3. Divine origin of integrity-alertness (20:12)
20:13 Do not love sleep, lest you may be dispossessed. Open your eyes! Be satiated with food!	2'. Industry (non-sloth): protect against loss (20:13)!
20:14 'Bad! Bad!' the buyer keeps saying. But once he is out of sight, then he will brag.	1'. Illicit gain: among buyers (20:14)
	B. Advice offered to those who counsel youth tempted by economic shortcuts (20:15–23)
	1. Encouragement and an imperative for counsellors of youth (20:15–17)
20:15 Gold and an abundance of corals there may be, but lips of knowledge are a precious vessel.	a. Wisdom commendation: encouragement concerning the superior value of a counsellor's seasoned advice (20:15)
	b. Wisdom content: imperative and rationale for rescuing a youth tempted by economic shortcuts (20:16–17)
20:16 Take his garment, if he has guaranteed a stranger's loan; and, in place of foreigners, tie him up!	i. Imperative: accelerate eventual penalties, to deter from a hazardous greedy alliance (20:16)
20:17 Seemingly sweet is deceptive food, but later on his mouth will be filled with gravel.	ii. Rationale: initial deceptive delight will turn to disappointment (20:17)

Verse	*Translation*	*Outline*
20:18	Plans through counsel may be laid, but to conduct a battle you must use hands-on skill.	2. Script for counselling youth attracted by economic shortcuts (20:18–23) a. Wisdom commendation: explanation concerning the superior value of counsellor's experiential advice (20:18)
20:19	One who leaks secret counsel goes about as a slanderer, and with one who talks indiscriminately you must never enter into partnership.	b. Wisdom content: two imperatives to discourage ill-advised economic partnerships (20:19–23) i. First imperative and rationale, concerning partnership with those who blame others (20:19–21) α. Imperative: do not partner with those who specialize in smearing others (20:19)
20:20	One who curses his father and his mother, his lamp will go out during the most profound darkness.	β. Rationale: utter disorientation awaits those who blame those deserving respect and gratitude (20:20–21)
20:21	When an inheritance is despised early on, then its ensuing development cannot be blessed.	
20:22	Do not say, 'I am determined to repay wrong!' Wait for the LORD, so may he rescue you!	ii. Second imperative and rationale, concerning sympathy towards unfounded claims of economic injustice (20:22–23) α. Imperatives concerning claims of injustice: refrain from reflex-retribution; await divine rescue (20:22)
20:23	Abhorrent to the LORD is one weight for selling, another weight for buying; and deceptive small scales are not good.	β. Rationale: economic injustice matters deeply to God (20:23)

Translation	Outline
	III. Vanquishing evil without: the quest to exhibit faithful love during life's prime (20:24–28)
20:24 From the LORD are the steps of a robust man. How can a mere mortal perceive which way he should go?	A. Dual-theme wisdom commendation: decisive divine direction or mortal aimlessness (20:24)
	B. Wisdom content: two opposing strategies to achieve faithful love (20:25–28)
20:25 The snare of a mortal rapidly and repeatedly declares, 'It is consecrated!', but then after making those vows, tries to rescind them.	1. The drifting strategy of vacillating piety: a picture of mortal aimlessness (20:25)
	2. The decisive strategy of evicting evil: a picture of divine direction (20:26–28)
20:26 One who has scattered guilty folk is a wise king, who then has made the wheel go back over them.	a. Evicting societal evil (20:26)
20:27 The lamp of the LORD is a mortal's breath; it examines all chambers deep within.	b. Deep divine detection of duplicity (20:27)
20:28 Faithful love and constancy can protect a king, and he can through faithful love sustain his throne.	a'. Effecting faithful love (20:28)
	IV. Pursuing purity within: the quest to exhibit faithful love during later years (20:29 – 21:2)
	A. For those in later years: the audience's worth, aim and outcome (20:29 – 21:1)
20:29 A splendour for capable men is their strength, but magnificence for elders is grey hair.	1. The audience: the worth of mature community members (20:29)
20:30 Beatings that cut in may scrub clean from wrong, and blows – chambers deep within.	2. The aim: the deep human need for deep cleansing (20:30)
21:1 Streams of water – that is what a king's motives are in the LORD's hand; he can steer them wherever he may please.	3. The maximal outcome: increased coöperation with the divine, for increased divine benefit (21:1)

Verse	*Translation*	*Outline*
21:2	Every way of a person is honest in his own eyes, but the one who weighs motives is the LORD.	B. The need for divine insight in the pursuit of purity (21:2)
		V. Concluding character summary: the contrasting outcomes of integrity and pretence (21:3–4)
21:3	Executing morality and justice is more preferable to the LORD than sacrifice.	A. Integrity secures divine favour better than ritual (21:3)
21:4	With its lofty eyes and expansive mind, the lamp of guilty folk is sin.	B. The arrogantly liberal outlook of the immoral parades misdirection as trustworthy guidance (21:4)

Notes on the text

20:5. 'Deep water': as in 18:4, depth indicates a well or cistern, not a deep portion of a river or lake.

20:6. 'Many a mortal may proclaim, "A person consists of his faithful love,"' *rŏb-ʾādām yiqrāʾ ʾîš ḥasdô*: lit. 'A multitude of mortals will proclaim, "A person is his faithful love"' (potentiality inferred from yiq. conjugation). According to the simplest syntax, this saying distinguishes between the frequency with which people outwardly subscribe to a noble axiom (expressed by the verbless clause 'A person consists of [or amounts to] his faithful love,' 20:6a) and the infrequency with which people embody that principle ('But a person characterized by faithfulness, who can find?', v. 6b). 'Proclaim' is attested elsewhere introducing quotations (cf. Gen. 41:43; Exod. 34:6; 1 Sam. 3:6; Prov. 9:15, 16). The poet will embed another quotation later in this lecture (20:22a, introduced by *ʾāmar*, 'to say').

It is unnecessary to emend the act. verb *yiqrāʾ*, 'to proclaim or call', making it pass. *yiqqārēʾ*, 'to be called' (*pace* Fox, who also deletes 'his' in 'his faithful love', and so renders, 'Many a one is called a kind man' [2009: 665]). This also rules out the reflexive emendation 'Many proclaim themselves loyal' (cf. NRSV, NASB, NIV, and ESV). While remaining closer to the Hebr., to render 'As for many human beings, each person proclaims his unfailing kindness' is also problematic, due to requiring supply of 'as for' to accommodate 'many human beings', and due to treating 'each person' (not 'many human beings') as the subject of 'proclaim' (*pace* Waltke 2005: 119).

With a disjunctive *deḥi* accent placing a pause after 'proclaim', and with a conjunctive *munaḥ* mark joining 'a person' with 'his faithful love',

Masoretic cantillation supports the translation 'Many a mortal may proclaim, "A person consists of his faithful love."' For further discussion of embedded epigrams, see under 'Comment', below.

20:7. 'One who, of his own accord, consistently behaves with personal integrity', *mithallēk bĕtummô*: lit. 'one who walks back and forth in his integrity'. The hith. stem of the verb *hlk*, 'to walk', conveys repeated action ('back and forth') engaged in one's own interest. Even when concerned to please none but himself, this individual will reliably behave with integrity.

'who come after him': lit. 'after him'. To be 'after' encompasses both temporal succession and imitative behaviour (cf. Ps. 49:14).

20:9. 'motives', *lēb*: lit. 'mind' or 'heart'. Scheming marketplace deception (20:10, 14) recommends rendering *lēb* as 'motives' (cf. 21:2).

20:10. 'One weight for selling, another weight for buying; one scoop for selling, another scoop for buying': lit. 'a stone and a stone, a dry-measure and a dry-measure'. These expressions describe a deceptive, double set of weights and measures. One set would be used for buying (light weight, large scoop), another for selling (heavy weight, small scoop).

'together': lit. 'also'. *Gam* also appears in 20:11, 12, producing a rare concentration of this particle in three adjacent verses. Across twenty-three occurrences of *gam* in Proverbs, nowhere else does *gam* appear in adjacent verses.

20:14. 'But once he is out of sight', *wĕʾōzēl lô*: lit. 'but going away for himself', i.e. removing himself to a place where the seller cannot overhear him congratulating himself for his shrewd bargaining.

20:15. 'there may be': lit. 'there are'. The sage admits that raw, glittering gems do constitute material riches. But he hastens to caution that they pale in comparison to the worth of a wisdom source – an exquisitely crafted container that dependably pours out wisdom as an invigorating draught. Raw minerals in the first colon advance to a skilfully fashioned vessel in the second.

'corals': see 'Notes' for 3:15.

20:16. 'foreigners', *nŏkrîm*: following K, rather than replacing with the Q expression *nŏkriyyâ*, 'a foreign woman'. While the f. sg. form *nŏkriyyâ* is more common (2:16; 5:20; 6:24; 7:4; 23:27; 27:13), it is not required here. With the shift from 'stranger' to 'foreigners' in 20:16 the sage appears more interested in escalating from sg. to pl. (K) than from m. ('stranger') to f. ('foreign woman', as proposed by Q). Concerning 'in place of foreigners, tie him up', see 'Comment'.

20:17. 'Seemingly sweet': lit. 'sweet to a person'. The initial positive impression will fade.

'sweet', *ʿārēb*: note homophonous link with 'to guarantee a loan', *ʿārab* (20:16a). The deception associated with sweetness in v. 17a suggests by homophony that similarly the incentive to guarantee a loan is deceptive (so also Fox 2009: 670). The root *ʿrb* rendered in v. 16a 'to guarantee a loan' recurs in v. 19b, there rendered 'to enter into partnership with someone', *hitʿārāb*.

20:18. 'may be laid', *tikôn*: lit. 'may be prepared'. In the absence of any 3 f. sg. subject (and since to render *tikôn* as 2 m. sg. 'you may be prepared' cannot fit 'plans' and 'counsel'), the 3 f. pl. noun 'plans' governs the 3 f. sg. verb 'be laid' (concerning Hebrew writers' tendency to employ a f. sg. verb with a f. pl. subj., see Joüon §150g). Potentiality ('may') inferred from yiq.

'hands-on skill', *ûbĕtaḥbulôt*: lit. 'rope-work', from the root *ḥbl* – as is 'tie him up' (20:16b), registering a shift from benevolent restraint (v. 16) to thoughtful advancement (v. 18).

20:19. 'and with one who talks indiscriminately': lit. 'and for one who is gullible regarding his lips'.

'you must never enter into partnership', *lōʾ titʿārāb*: in the hith. stem, lit. 'you must never get involved with' (*HALOT*) or 'exchange pledges' (BDB). In the qal stem, the same root is rendered 'guarantee a loan' (20:16). The legislative prohibition found here (*lōʾ* plus yiq.) is especially solemn.

20:20. 'during the most profound darkness': lit. 'in the [eye's] pupil of darkness', the Hebr. idiom for pitch blackness of night.

20:21. 'When . . . then': the adverb 'when' is inferred due to the consequential tone of the second colon.

'despised', *mĕbuḥelet*: the qal stem of *bḥl* is attested three times, meaning 'to loathe'. *Mĕbuḥelet* is the pu. stem (pass. voice) of the same root, attested only here. The most likely meaning is 'to be despised, loathed'. To render as 'in haste' (Waltke 2005: 148) or 'in a rush' (Fox 2009: 673) requires reading *mĕbôhelet*, 'to be hurried' (from *bhl*), in place of *mĕbuḥelet*, 'to be despised'. This substitution is both unnecessary and breaks the link with the arrogant attitude of cursing one's parents (20:20), who supply the despised inheritance of v. 21.

'then its ensuing development': lit. 'then its afterness'.

'cannot be blessed': lit. 'will not be blessed'. (In)ability is inferred from the yiq. Note the synonymy of 'cursing' in 20:20a and 'not blessed' in v. 21b. To curse the generation before (one's parents) amounts to cursing also the generation to come (one's children).

20:22. 'I am determined to repay', *ʾăšallĕmâ*: the first-person cohort. summons the self to action, conveying resolve.

'so may he rescue', *wĕyōšaʿ*: after an imperative ('wait!'), a weyiq. form (such as *wĕyōšaʿ*) conveys a wish ('so may he rescue', known as an indirect volitive).

20:23. 'small scales', *mōʾzĕnê*: this refers to a highly portable, hand-held scale, in contrast to *peles*, a floor-mounted balance (*HALOT*).

20:24. 'a robust man . . . a mere mortal', *gāber . . . ʾādām*: lit. 'a man, a robust male' in contrast to 'man, mortal'. *ʾĀdām* connotes frailty before the divine.

'How can a mere mortal perceive which way he should go?': lit. 'and a mortal, how can he perceive his way'. The antecedent of 'his' in 'his way' is 'mortal' (not the LORD). Capability inferred from yiq.

20:25. 'rapidly and repeatedly declares': lit. 'he will stammer'. The durative connotation of yiq. is inferred from the fact that the vows in 20:25b are pl. This individual is so eager to make a good impression that he nervously ('hastily', LXX) devotes to God one possession after another.

'but then after making those vows, tries to rescind them', *wĕʾaḥar nĕdārîm lĕbaqqēr*: lit. 'but after vows, to seek for'. One who initiated multiple acts of dedication now endeavours to reverse them. As evident from the same verb *bqr* used to describe retrieval of sheep (Ezek. 34:11–12), the worshipper's actions are far more decisive than merely 'begin[ning] to reflect' (NRSV) or 'consider[ing]' (NIV).

20:27, 30. 'chambers deep within': lit. 'chambers of belly'.

20:28. 'Faithful love and constancy', *ḥesed wĕʾĕmet*: lit. 'faithful love and truth'. To preserve a link with the pairing of these roots in 20:6 (where the second term *ʾĕmûnîm* is rendered 'faithfulness'), *ʾĕmet* here is rendered 'constancy' rather than 'truth'.

20:29. 'capable men', *baḥûrîm*: lit. 'ones who are chosen', men in the prime of life, between the category of youth (20:11) and the elderly (20:29b).

'magnificence', *hădar*: assonance links this term with 'chambers deep within', *ḥadrê-bāṭen*, in 20:27b and again in 30b.

20:30. 'Beatings that cut in', *ḥabburôt peṣaʿ*: lit. 'beatings of a wound'.

'may scrub clean', *tamrîq*: reading with K the hiph. of *mrq*, 'to cleanse', a root distinct from but semantically related to 'cleanse', *zkh* (20:9).

'and blows – chambers': i.e. 'and blows [may scrub clean those] chambers [that are located] deep within' (by ellipsis from 20:30a).

21:1. 'Streams of water – that is what a king's motives are in the LORD's hand', *palgê-mayim leb-melek beyad-yhwh*: unlike rivers or intermittent wadis, 'streams' can refer to irrigation canals manually constructed (Ps. 1:3). When channelled by the LORD, the king's motives result in refreshing metaphoric hydration, as does a well-engineered irrigation canal. Concerning *leb* as 'motives', see 20:9.

'he can steer them': lit. 'he will steer it' (capability inferred from yiq.). Once the king places his motives under the LORD's direction, the LORD is able to direct them.

21:2. 'motives', *libbôt*: lit. 'minds' or 'hearts'. Not intellect ('mind'), but intent ('motive') is under divine evaluation (see 20:9).

21:4. 'With its lofty eyes and expansive mind': lit. 'a pair of lofty eyes and spaciousness of mind'. The first expression conveys proud presumption (cf. 6:17), while the second connotes a wide-ranging outlook on life (the opposite of parochialism). Taken together, they portray guilty folk exuding an arrogance that would dismiss as narrow-minded any not so progressive as they. In consequence, the direction they confidently propound as moral (their 'lamp') leads astray ('is sin').

'lamp', *nir*: lit. 'lamp', alternatively 'a field recently cultivated' (13:23) or 'descendants' (1 Kgs 11:36; 15:4). These alternative meanings invite the hearer to consider that, when possessed by the guilty, even customarily beneficial, hope-generating assets will miscarry.

Form and structure

Borders

After discussing the intersection of wealth, power and satisfaction (preceding poem), the sage turns to explore faithful love as the loftiest expression of human flourishing (present poem). An initial wisdom commendation (20:5) leads to wisdom content launching the human-flourishing theme in v. 6. Thus 20:5 serves as the upper border.

A character summary, inclusio and seven instances of closure mark the final quatrain as the lower border (21:3–4; also Heim recognizes a portion closing with 21:4 [2001: 282–284]). Concerning character summary, vv. 3–4 confront the reader with a striking contrast between two behaviour options, whether humbly moral or arrogantly guilty.

Concerning inclusio, *lēb*, 'mind', appears in the lecture's first and last verses (20:5; 21:4). Unlike the mysterious depth associated with a mind concealing valuable counsel (in the poem's first colon, 20:5a), in the last saying the 'mind' of the guilty exchanges profound depth for shallow breadth (21:4). The fact that what they do perceive leads them astray ('the lamp of the guilty is sin') suggests that through indiscriminate open-mindedness they forfeited the capacity for moral evaluation (cf. 21:2).

Concerning closure, the first of seven closural elements involves the concept of morality expressed by the root *ṣdq* in 20:7, the first of three sayings, each of which introduces a separate subsequent section (vv. 7, 8 and 9, introduce Sections II, III and IV, respectively). The root *ṣdq* returns in Section V, contributing to closure (21:3). Second, the poet establishes the importance of 'justice' in 20:8, the second of three introductory sayings linked to subsequent sections. Like 'morality', 'justice' fosters closure when it returns in 21:3. Third, the notion of securing divine favour first appeared (negatively) in Section III (20:25). It operates positively in Section V, with behaviour 'more preferable to the LORD than sacrifice' (21:3). Fourth, 'eye' occurs five times in this poem, whether to detect evil (20:8, 12; 21:2) or to combat sleepy indolence (20:13). In the lecture's last verse, 'eyes' that are 'lofty' portray arrogance (21:4). Fifth, 'guilty folk' appears twice in this lecture. Those persons were scattered by a responsible monarch in 20:26. At the close they derive misleading illumination from a lamp comprised of sinful acts or attitudes (21:4). Sixth, 'lamp', *nēr*, occurs twice, referring to (loss of) hope amid deep distress (20:20), and the LORD's capacity to shine light on hidden human motives (20:27). When the near-synonym *nir* (also rendered 'lamp') appears in 21:4, the sage teaches that what light the guilty possess cannot guide them aright. As a seventh closural feature, in 21:4 the lecture's last word, 'sin', recalls the closing word of Section I, 'Who can say, "I have cleansed my motives; I have become purified from my sin"?' (20:9). The quest for purity introduced in Section I proves unachievable by those who cling to sin as their source of direction.

Macrostructural features

Triple-theme introduction regarding faithful love (Sections I–IV, content-based). Directly after the lecture-opening wisdom commendation (20:5), the poet presents his implicit objective: to describe how one may recognize – and become – a person characterized by 'faithful love' (v. 6). Each of the remaining three sayings of Section I introduces a behaviour the poet will expand later, distributed across three corresponding sections (vv. 7, 8, 9, corresponding respectively to Sections II, III and IV; also Weeks notices unity in vv. 7–9 [1994: 22]). Although the term 'faithful love' from v. 6 does not recur in vv. 7–9, the programmatic nature of v. 6, combined with the introduction-and-expansion structure extending from vv. 7–9 to the close of Section IV, together with double repetition of 'faithful love' at the close of Section III (20:28), combine to suggest that the sage regards the three behaviours of vv. 7–9 as exemplifying faithful love.

The first of three behaviours involves cultivation of integrity within (20:7), expanded in Section II by cautioning against illicit gain in the marketplace (20:10–14), and by cautioning against lazy economic shortcuts (such as loan-guarantee deals, vv. 16–17). A target audience of youth is indicated by mention of 'youth' (v. 11), and by a script provided to aid their teachers (vv. 18–23).

The second behaviour involves vanquishing evil without – a mission particularly (not exclusively) befitting a monarch (20:8). Ridding wrongdoing from the realm resurfaces in Section III (vv. 24–28), again referencing the monarch (vv. 26, 28). Mention of 'a robust man' in the first verse of Section III (v. 24) together with energetic actions taken by the king (chasing evildoers from his territory) suggests a target audience of adults in their prime.

The third behaviour involves pursuit of purity within, at the level of one's motives (*lēb*, 20:9). The poet expands the need for purity with a call in Section IV (20:29 – 21:2) for metaphoric scrubbing of inner chambers. *Lēb*, 'motives', are specified in 21:1, 2 (elsewhere in this lecture *lēb* connotes 'mind' [20:5; 21:4]). Section IV closes by recalling the futility of human attempts to self-assess (21:2; cf. 20:9).

In Section IV the transition from 'capable men' (recalling the target audience of Section III) to 'elders' with their 'grey hair' indicates a target audience of elders (20:29). Reappearance of 'king' in Section IV (21:1) suggests that even in later years, after having banished evildoers (20:26), the monarch must – through cooperation with the divine – diligently exhibit faithful love.

Reversal involving supply of water, with *lēb*, 'mind' or 'motives' (Sections I and IV, form-based). 'Water' occurs twice in this lecture (20:5; 21:1). Each time it appears with *lēb* ('mind' or 'motives', respectively). In the first, counsel resembles 'deep water' since it may be retrieved from the sage's 'mind', *lēb*, only with difficulty. In the second, when the king's 'motives', *lēb*, cooperate with divine direction, they operate as refreshing waters, freely flowing. The bleak picture of scarcity in 20:5 (also v. 6) transforms to abundance in 21:1.

Dynamic progression of chronological age (Sections II, III and IV, content-based). Each of sections II, III and IV deals with a different age group, progressing from young to old. 'Youth' (20:11) and children who disregard their parents (20:20) appear in Section II. Section III opens with reference to 'a robust man' (20:24). Section IV mentions 'elders' with grey hair in the first saying, in contrast to younger, 'capable men' (20:29).

Thematic continuity involving profound divine perception (Sections II, III and IV, content-based). At three points the sage associates the divine with perception. He formed human organs of perception (20:12 in Section II). He engages in perception, since he 'examines all chambers deep within' humans (v. 27 in Section III). He perceives better than can humans, assessing motives (21:2 in Section IV). As to structure, the sayings in Sections II and III occur at the core of palistrophes (20:10–14, vv. 26–28), while the last saying closes Section IV (20:29 – 21:2).

Section-level closure (Section III, with Section I, form-based). Double mention of 'faithful love' in the final saying of Section III (20:28) recalls the only other use of that expression, appearing in the lecture's second saying (v. 6).

Section-level closure (Section IV, with Sections I, II and III, form- and content-based). Section IV closes with this saying: 'Every way of a person is honest in his own eyes, but the one who weighs motives is the LORD' (21:2). Six terms or concepts in 21:2 occurred earlier in the lecture, resulting in section-level closure. These include 'honest (20:11), 'person' (20:5–6, 17), 'eye' (20:8, 12, 13), the concept of weighing (20:10, 23), 'mind/motives' (20:5, 9; 21:1) and 'the LORD' (20:10, 12, 22, 23, 24, 27; 21:1).

Microstructural features

Section I (20:5–9). *Wisdom commendation followed by wisdom content (20:5, content-based).* A wisdom commendation opens this lecture, accenting the effort and skill required to extract wisdom from its purveyor (20:5). Thus the poet may imply that, though the present lecture may appear impenetrable, it will reward those who apply themselves to its study.

Wisdom content follows in 20:6–9, beginning with the lecture's thesis: one attains maximal human flourishing to the extent that he or she exhibits faithful love (v. 6). Three specific behaviours or aims worthy of emulation cluster in vv. 7–9.

Repetition of 'person' (20:5–6, form-based). *'îš*, 'person', appears four times in 20:5–6, twice in each verse. Such a repetition befits the sage's unveiling of his thesis concerning human flourishing: 'A person consists of his faithful love' (20:6a). While 'person' will appear twice more in this lecture (20:17a; 21:2a), double use of this term occurs only once more in all of Proverbs (29:9). Weeks also joins vv. 5–6, based on unspecified 'verbal and/or literal links' (1994: 22).

Inclusio involving 'mind' or 'motives' (20:5, 9, form-based). The term *lēb*, 'mind' or 'motives', appears in the first and last sayings of Section I, fostering section-level closure (20:5, 9).

Thematic continuity concerning virtuous behaviour (20:7–9, content-based). Each saying within the cluster spanning 20:7–9 specifies a distinct virtue, whether cultivating integrity within (v. 7), safeguarding justice for one's community (v. 8) or pursuing inner purity (v. 9). In view of other microstructures lending cohesion to vv. 5–9, these three suggest how the sage understands the overarching virtue of 'faithful love' (v. 6). The fact that each saying within vv. 7–9 connects with a subsequent section further supports thematic continuity joining these sayings (see 'Triple-theme introduction', above).

Closure involving rhetorical questions of impossibility (20:6, 9, form-based). Impossibility colours the rhetorical question of 20:6b: 'But a person characterized by faithfulness, who can find?' Closure results when another rhetorical question tinged with the impossible concludes Section I: 'Who can say, "I have cleansed my motives; I have become purified from my sin"?' (v. 9).

Section II (vv. 10–23). *Inclusio of 'one weight for selling, another weight for buying' (20:10, 23, form-based).* Mention of 'one weight for selling, another weight for buying' (20:10, 23) creates an inclusio for Section II.

Palistrophe deterring economic shortcuts (20:10–14, form- and content-based). A palistrophe unites 20:10–14. The outermost pair of sayings call attention to duplicity in the marketplace, whether on the part of seller (v. 10) or buyer (v. 14). Both sayings employ words doubly. 'Weight' and 'scoop' appear twice in v. 10, while 'bad' appears twice in v. 14. The second palistrophic step urges honest industry in place of indolence (20:11, 13).

At the third step the LORD appears as the fashioner of organs that detect duplicity (eye and ear, 20:12, the palistrophic pivot). By implication, divine capacity to detect wrongdoing exceeds that of humans. This divine intensification suitably locates at the palistrophe's core.

Wisdom commendations leading to wisdom content (20:15, 18, content-based). A wisdom commendation in 20:15 affirms the worth of counsel provided by the wise. Wisdom content follows in vv. 16–17, charging pupils to intercept youth intent on opportunistic, ill-advised economic partnerships.

Another wisdom commendation in 20:18 observes that, in a contest of ideas, counsel must escalate to employ 'hands-on skill'. Wisdom content follows, concerning unwise economic partnerships (vv. 19–23).

Address to parents, followed by a script for parents (20:15–17, 18–23, content-based). When the sage instructs, 'Take his garment' (20:16), he addresses parents. Adjacent sayings presenting wisdom commendation (v. 15) and incentive (v. 17) similarly address parents.

In contrast, youth are addressed by the instruction 'With one who talks indiscriminately you must never enter into partnership' (20:19b, extending through v. 23). These sayings comprise a script for use by parents or those who counsel youth. The wisdom commendation of v. 18 (preceding the youth address of vv. 19–23) would fortify counsellors who must confront erring youth. Those teachers must leave off merely 'laying plans'. They now must wage a metaphoric 'battle', using 'hands-on skill' in an effort to rescue youth. (A script for parents and counsellors also appeared in 19:20–24 and 19:27 – 20:1).

Imperative-plus-rationale sequences (20:19–21, 22–23, form- and content-based). The script supplied to counsellors consists of imperative-plus-rationale, in two cycles. Commands in 20:19b and 22 are followed by rationales in vv. 20–21 and in 23.

Thematic continuity concerning ungrateful children (20:20–21, content-based). As others also have observed, the character of an ungrateful child links 20:20 and v. 21 (Heim 2001: 284, n.).

Recurring root ʻrb *(20:16, 17, 19, form-based).* In 20:16 the expression, 'to guarantee a loan' uses a verb from the root *ʿrb*. That root recurs in 'to enter into partnership' (v. 19).

In 20:17 appears a root meaning 'to be sweet', incidentally spelled *ʿrb*. Thus the sage links a caution concerning deceptive food at first seeming 'sweet' (v. 17) to a caution against ill-advised partnerships (vv. 16, 19).

Closure concerning 'ears' and 'scales' (20:12, 23, form- and content-based). The term 'small scales', *mōʾzēnê* (20:23), derives from the root also found in 'ear', *ʾōzen* (20:12, a form-based link). Evidently the two pans on opposite ends of a small balance beam called to mind two 'ears' flanking a face. Just as 'ears' in v. 12 associate with the divine capacity for detection or assessment, so also the 'small scales' in v. 23 signify divine evaluation of human behaviour (a content-based link). Closure results since Section II spans 20:10–23.

Section III (20:24–28). *Wisdom commendation followed by wisdom content (20:24, content-based).* Mention of 'perception' concerning one's direction in life ('steps', 'which way he should go') identifies 20:24 as a wisdom commendation. Wisdom content outlining alternative behaviours follows in vv. 25–28.

Dual-theme introduction (20:24, content-based). The sage contrasts two characters in the first verse of Section III (20:24). The first is robust, stepping decisively forward along a path marked by divine direction. The second, a mere 'mortal' (suggesting he operates in a humanistic manner apart from divine direction), does not know which way to proceed. He suffers from indirection.

By repeating 'mortal' in the next saying (20:25), the sage signals expansion of the second individual (suffering indirection). Now his remoteness from divine direction grows explicit. For after consecrating something to God, he vacillates, retrieving it for personal use.

In contrast, the divinely directed fellow of 20:24a returns in vv. 26–28. As he energetically enforces ethical standards, he functions as a monarch safeguarding his community (vv. 26, 28). As in v. 24a, here again he operates under divine accountability – an accountability defying mortal concealment (v. 27). Thus the dual-theme introduction in vv. 24a and 24b find chiastic expansion in vv. 26–28 and v. 25, respectively.

Framing structure concerning 'king' (20:26, 28, form-based). Mention of 'king' in 20:26, 28 frames a saying concerning the LORD's ability to probe human motives profoundly (v. 27; so also Waltke 2005: 157).

Section IV (20:29 – 21:2). *Thematic continuity concerning inner purity (20:30, 21:2, content-based).* The expression 'to scrub clean' and the contrast of self-assessed honesty (versus motives divinely weighed) contribute to a theme of inner purity (20:30; 21:2).

Assonantal link (20:29, 30, form-based). Assonance joins 20:29a with v. 30. Transposition of sounds links initial syllables of *baḥûrîm*, 'capable men' (v. 29a) with *ḥabburôt*, 'beatings' (v. 30a).

Repetition of 'motives' (21:1–2, form-based). Repetition of human 'motives', supervised by the divine, links 21:1 and v. 2.

Summation (21:2, form-based). A summation ('every way of a person') intensifies the final saying of Section IV (21:2). As he approaches this lecture's close, with the expression 'every way' the poet recalls various strategies previously discussed – alternative schemes for economic or religious advantage (cf. 20:10, 14, 25).

Section V (21:3–4). *Thematic continuity surrounding theological orientation (21:3–4, content-based).* Both character portraits of 21:3–4 are distinguished by theological orientation. The first pleases the LORD (v. 3), while the second is guided by 'sin' (v. 4). Character summaries more typically deal in wisdom or general morality, without such explicitly theological vocabulary (cf. 1:32–33; 2:21–22; 11:31; 13:25; 15:6; 19:8–9).

Grammatical contrast (21:3–4, form-based). Character summaries typically employ nominal expressions (e.g. 'a moral person' in 15:6a) or ptcs. (e.g. 'one who acquires sense' in 19:8a). Such is the case with the nominal expression 'guilty folk' in 21:4.

In contrast, 'executing morality and justice' employs an infin. in 21:3a (*ʿăśōh*, reflected by infin. *poiein* in LXX) creating a grammatical contrast with v. 4. By preferring action (an infin.) over static traits (nominal expressions) the sage commends concrete conduct over hollow claims (cf. 20:14, 25).

Comment

The middle three sections (Sections II, III and IV) present three seasons of life (youth, prime of life, seniority). An overview of this three-part theme appears below, following Section I.

Section I (20:5–9). An arresting wisdom commendation opens the lecture spanning 20:5 – 21:4. Typically, such a commendation will posit the worth of wisdom and urge receptivity (cf. 2:1; 3:1; 12:1; 13:1; 14:1; 15:7). By this point, however, the sage evidently assumes the youth no longer needs persuasion concerning wisdom's worth. Rather, what he wants now is motivation, a stirring up to pursue and acquire that counsel whose value by now lies beyond dispute. So the sage tantalizes the pupil at the start of this lecture by saying, in effect, 'Wisdom is yours for the taking, provided you desire it so deeply that with determination you will coax it from those within whom it deeply resides' (see 20:5).

Also through that initial wisdom commendation the sage serves notice that this lecture will deal with deeper reaches of sapience. To grasp this lecture will require greater intentionality on the part of the pupil (20:5). The ensuing wisdom content unfolds the lecture's theme, a treatise answering the implicit question 'What is the loftiest expression of human flourishing?' (v. 6). The sage responds that humans reach their highest potential as they become exponents of faithful love – a trait widely valued (v. 6a) but seldom encountered (v. 6b).

The remaining three verses of Section I line out three dimensions of faithful love: cultivating integrity within (20:7), vanquishing evil without (v. 8) and pursuing purity within (v. 9; note escalation to theological level with mention of 'sin'). As explained below, the sage correlates each behaviour with a successive period of life: youth, the prime of life and advanced age (Sections II, III and IV, respectively). Taken together, all three advocate moral conduct. Their distinguishing features enable the pupil to pursue moral conduct with ever-sharpening focus, rather than with bland assent.

Overview of three seasons of life in Sections II, III and IV. Three seasons of life unfold through the lecture. A 'youth' is named in 20:11 (Section II), a 'robust man' in 20:24 (Section III) and grey-haired 'elders' in 20:29 (in Section IV, in contrast to young men). It is instructive that mention of 'robust man' (Section III) and of grey-haired 'elders' (Section IV) occur in section-initial lines, respectively.

The sage associates a distinct, positive behaviour with each age group. Thus the youth of Section II operates with integrity (20:11) and industry

(v. 13, palistrophically linked to v. 11), in contrast to deceptive marketplace practices that surround him (vv. 10, 14). Integrity and industry will help him to discredit the siren call of greed associated with the stranger who comes applying for a loan (vv. 15–23). By devoting a longer section to youth than to the remaining two life-seasons, the sage indicates his primary audience.

The robust man of Section III is characterized as purposeful, with marching orders deriving from the LORD (20:24). Armed with this sense of direction, he tackles evil head-on, leveraging his position (particularly in the capacity of a monarchy) to vanquish wrongdoing from his realm (v. 26). Through faithful love his young reign will become a long reign (v. 28; note double mention of 'faithful love', recalling the foundational principle of v. 6).

What the elders of Section IV may lack in youthful vigour (20:29a), they make up for in wisdom long-accumulated (implied by 'grey hair', v. 29b). And while younger folk energetically apply direct force to cleanse wrong (v. 30), elders pursue inner purity by a different strategy. They practise the deeper wisdom of alliance with the divine, operating at the level of inner motives (21:1). By tracing the seasons of life through this poem, one discovers the sage mapping a path for character development that matures over time, addressing challenges unique to each season.

20:6. An epigram is embedded within the larger proverbial saying of 20:6. Epigrams that have been embedded or deployed within other compositions may be detected by one of three criteria (Hallo 1990: 212–213). First, notice content incongruous with surrounding context, as it may indicate that the proverb has been included for persuasive effect (e.g. a fowler saying embedded towards the close of a father's warning to his son, Prov. 1:17). Second, notice recurrence of a saying within the literature of the same culture or in the literature of another culture, as multiple use may identify independent proverbs. Finally, notice introductory attribution, such as, 'people are always saying this'. Such is the case in Prov. 20:6 when the sage uses the attribution 'Many a mortal may proclaim' to preface the saying 'A person consists of his faithful love.'

The saying 'A person consists of his faithful love' builds on the statement in 19:22 'The yearning of a mortal consists of his faithful love,' since both showcase the character trait of faithful love, whether as a mortal's core longing (19:22) or as a fundamental trait (20:6). Linking these two expressions illumines layering of the sage's insights concerning faithful love. The two may be paraphrased 'What a mortal most deeply longs for is to become a person characterized by faithful love,' and 'A mortal reaches his or her ultimate potential only to the extent that he or she embodies faithful love' (19:22a; 20:6a).

Idealism wrestles with realism in the axiom of 20:6. Initially, the sage discloses the widely held ideal: faithful love comprises human flourishing at its best. A realistic, rhetorical lament follows: 'But a person characterized by faithfulness, who can find?' (20:6b; cf. 'A resourceful wife, who can find . . . ?', 31:10).

Section II (20:10–23). *Block II.A (20:10–14).* Section II addresses the quest to exhibit faithful love during one's youth (first of three life-seasons). A twofold strategy organizes this section. The sage first addresses youth directly, fortifying against the allure of the marketplace's economic shortcuts (Block II.A, 20:10–14; note 'youth' in v. 11). With a palistrophe the sage exposes deceptive selling (v. 10) and buying (v. 14). Vendor and consumer mutually seek to defraud. In contrast, with steady industry the youth must pursue an ethical course (vv. 11, 13). Three imperatives underscore urgency (v. 13). The sage highly recommends integrity since the divine himself will detect its absence (v. 12, the palistrophic core).

Block II.B (20:15–23). After addressing the youth directly (Block II.A), the sage turns to those with influence over youth (Block II.B, 20:15–23). He stresses the worth of wisdom that they alone can supply (wisdom commendations, vv. 15, 18). His first counsel to influencers (parents, teachers) urges them incisively to disrupt the youth's descent into a loan-guaranteeing partnership (v. 16). Without delay they must inflict on the youth the sort of penalties he eventually will suffer (such as being deprived of his garment or being bound), were his shady partner to default on the loan. Such intervention is a kindness, for the seemingly sweet strategy of guaranteeing a loan soon will devolve into a mouthful of gravel (v. 17; both 'sweet' in v. 17 and 'to guarantee a loan' in v. 16 involve roots spelled *'rb*).

The sage's second counsel to parents comprises a script they may deliver to youth (Unit II.B.2, 20:18–23). Here the sage exposes faulty character traits typical of strangers appealing for a loan guarantee. They take up slander against those who disappoint (v. 19), even smearing the reputation of those most deserving of respect (their own parents, v. 20), and despising as worthless anything of value they may have inherited (v. 21).

Since the root meaning 'to guarantee a loan' in 20:16a appears also in 'to enter into partnership' (v. 19b), one may infer that it is the stranger of v. 16 who also 'talks indiscriminately' in v. 19 (see 'Notes'). He is content to convert confidential disclosures into manipulative weapons he then wields against those who made the mistake of trusting him.

The youth must forego financial partnership with such a one, because of how that stranger has treated those who trusted him in the past. What is to prevent the stranger from slandering this loan-guaranteeing youth, just as he slandered those who earlier relied on him (including his own parents)? His feeble excuse for slandering his parents stems from resentment over the inheritance they allotted to him (20:21).

From these hints concerning the stranger's base character the following portrait emerges. Evidently his appeal for a loan guarantee took this form: 'I am seeking this loan owing to the fact that my own wretched parents cheated me, awarding me a paltry inheritance! Had they not treated me so cheaply, I would not be in such straits, today.' In the sage's words, that person 'cursed his father and his mother' and 'despised his inheritance' (20:20–21a). Given the tightly knit family structure of biblical times, one should puzzle why the stranger would not apply first to his own family for financial assistance. Are they bankrupt? Likely not, since a larger, more enviable portion of the inheritance went to a recipient other than this stranger – perhaps allotted to a more worthy sibling. So one must conclude that here is a stranger who has ruined the trust of those who know him best. Parents could have bequeathed to him more, but chose not to, based on inferior character observed in him during years past. Only a fool would disregard so glaring a non-endorsement by the stranger's own family. Only the wilfully ignorant would insist on engaging such a stranger as a financial partner.

Given his history as one who curses parents (20:20a) and despises what they gave him (v. 21a), this stranger (v. 16a) appears bound for a dark and dismal conclusion (vv. 20b, 21b). Having ill-treated his own family, he would be even less honour-bound to deal nobly with the youth, as one outside his clan. All indicators converge, confirming he poses a thoroughly unreliable business risk.

Section II closes with a second instruction for the youth (20:22–23), one that cannot be understood apart from the first (vv. 19–21). In the second instruction the sage is concerned that, while the youth may consent not to enter into business dealings with the loan-applicant stranger, the stranger's sob story (ostensibly cheated by parents) may evoke compassion on the part of the youth, even spawning a desire to avenge him. This would explain the sage's caution: 'Do not say, "I am determined to repay wrong!"' (v. 22a). The 'wrong' here in view is not an offence suffered by the youth himself, but one the stranger claims to have suffered. He complains of having received a lesser inheritance than what he supposed was his due (vv. 19–21). The youth must guard against succumbing to the stranger's story of ostensible offence, becoming recruited to his agenda of revenge.

So hypnotic are the deceptive powers of rhetoric falsely claiming injustice, that only divine insight can protect the youth by unmasking the stranger's lie. So the sage counsels, 'Wait for the LORD, so may he rescue you!' (20:22b). Here again the sage guards his pupil against victimization (cf. v. 16).

A second mention of deceptive weights and the LORD's deep aversion to such trickery establishes that the entire enterprise presented by the loan-applying stranger with his woeful tale is no more than a clever scheme calculated to drain the gullible youth of financial resources, a calamity the sage works desperately to prevent (20:23 recalls v. 10). Although the loan applicant may argue that it would 'not be good' if the youth were callously to dismiss his pleas for help, what in fact is 'not good' are the 'deceptive small scales' the loan applicant figuratively employs to disguise his financial ruse (v. 23b).

The loan applicant of Block II.B illustrates the very marketplace duplicity warned against in Block II.A. Like the merchant with dishonest weights, the loan applicant advertises deceptive advantages he hopes the youth will 'buy', perhaps crassly promising to thank the youth with one of ten silver pieces he may seek to borrow.

20:12. To describe eyes fashioned by the LORD as 'seeing' (and ears as 'hearing') implies that the Fashioner similarly can see and hear: 'Cannot the one who installed the ear himself hear? If he fashioned the eye, will he lack the power of sight?' (Ps. 94:9). God can be fooled neither by empty affirmations of faithful love (Prov. 20:6) nor by claims of clean motives tainted by greed (vv. 9–10, 14). His 'lamp' peers more deeply than will any medical imaging device (v. 27).

20:15. By comparing less glamorous (a vessel) with more (gold and many corals), this saying resembles the disputation genre, a form well attested in Mesopotamian wisdom literature, which compares silver to copper, ox to horse, tamarisk to palm tree. The less glamorous routinely emerges with superior worth. Here, the mere 'vessel' (lips speaking knowledge) exceeds in value gold and even heaps of coral.

The lecture's opening saying implies a vessel-like instrument, required for drawing water from a deep well (20:5). After mentioning a 'precious vessel' in v. 15 the sage pours out a torrent of six imperatives (vv. 16–23).

20:16. Since the foolish youth agreed to forfeit freedoms if his business partner should default, the sage advises shocking the youth to his senses by tying him up now, in place of the defaulting foreigner (who deserves punishment, 20:16b).

20:20–23. Baseless complaints about unfair treatment belie assumptions of entitlement and an unwillingness either to assume personal responsibility or to take initiative (see discussion under 'Comment'). That the complaints are baseless is implied by the fact that they spin a web of deception so subtle that extrication will require the LORD's assistance (20:22). Reliance on deception locates the loan applicant's ploys with those of merchants with deceptive weights (v. 10). Refusal to assume responsibility pits the loan applicant against earlier counsel advocating industry and initiative (vv. 11, 13). It is no wonder that the stranger's rhetoric (projecting blame on to others) sounds a klaxon in the sage's ears – an alarm he trains the youth to detect.

Section III (20:24–28). Section III describes the goal to which one should aspire during the prime of life. Whereas Section II focused on youth, impressing on them the cultivation of integrity within (20:7 of Section I, expanded in Section II), Section III envisions a 'robust man' in life's prime, seeking a meaningful life-direction (v. 24).

For optimal life-direction, the wise will appeal to the LORD (20:24a). However, that very desire for divine direction may lure one to barter with God, making spiritual-sounding promises in exchange for guidance (v. 25a). The sage decries the hypocrisy of this tactic, since that fellow, 'after making those vows, tries to rescind them' (v. 25b).

Instead of trying artificially to impress God, one should focus on evicting evil (20:26). Recalling v. 8 (the second of three topic verses in vv. 7–9), the sage assesses as 'wise' that monarch who aggressively scatters the guilty, instituting a painful incentive so miscreants will depart his realm.

Lest any still wonder, the sage underscores the futility of artificial efforts to impress God. After all, one who formed organs of perception (20:12) surely can probe human motives (v. 27).

Instead of spiritual pretence, a responsible king will pursue a policy of 'faithful love and constancy' (20:28; note double use of 'faithful love'). Herein lies a human's flourishing (cf. 'faithful love' in v. 6; 'constancy' in v. 28 links etymologically to 'faithfulness' in v. 6b).

20:26. Despite being scattered (20:26a), some of the guilty evidently refuse to quit either their wrong or the realm, requiring the monarch's metaphoric threshing. Threshing carts were outfitted with rollers having sharp iron cutters. By repeatedly driving the threshing cart across the sheaves, the husks would fall away from kernels of grain (Waltke 2005: 156–157).

Section IV (20:29 – 21:2). Distinct from the priority for youths (cultivating integrity within, 20:7 and Section II), and distinct from the priority for those in life's prime (vanquishing evil without, v. 8 and Section III), for persons in later years the sage stresses pursuit of purity within (v. 9 and Section IV).

The audience of persons in their later years the poet specifies by contrasting a younger group ('capable men' who are strong, v. 29a) with a senior group ('magnificence for elders is grey hair', v. 29b). This emerges in the section's initial saying.

The aim (pursuit of inner purity) appears next. To achieve loftiest flourishing, humans require aggressive cleansing, reaching to the extent of 'chambers deep within' (20:30). Such depth encompasses one's 'motives' (21:1, 2).

As to outcome, cleansing will locate the individual more fully under divine direction, especially regarding motives. As a result, he or she will enjoy deployment as an agent of life-giving refreshment wherever the LORD may choose (21:1). Such a one may embody the answer to the earlier problem of wisdom's inaccessibly deep 'water' (20:5). He or she epitomizes human flourishing as an agent of divine beneficence (faithful love), resoundingly resolving the lecture's original dilemma: 'But a person characterized by faithfulness, who can find?' (20:6).

The sage closes Section IV reflectively, observing (like 20:9) that no mortal can pursue inner purity to the level of motives (21:2). The LORD alone is equal to this task.

20:29. Wisdom, though not explicitly named, may be inferred for elders and their grey hair, as is evident from elders who advised monarchs such as Solomon and Rehoboam (1 Kgs 12:6), and from the consternation befalling a community when its elders prove unable to dispense wisdom (Job 12:20; Ezek. 7:26).

21:1. Whereas Israel depended on dry farming, Egypt and Mesopotamia practised irrigation. Perhaps Jesus alluded to Prov. 21:1 when he spoke of those trusting in him, from whose inner being would 'flow rivers of living water' (John 7:38).

21:2. This verse closely resembles 16:2 (see 'Comment' for 16:2).

Section V (21:3–4). The final section recaps central themes through a character summary quatrain with theological overtones. For the positive character, integrity ('executing morality and justice') constitutes a divine priority, ranking above religious ritual (21:3).

For the negative character, to dismiss such integrity only betrays arrogance masquerading as open-mindedness ('lofty eyes and expansive mind', 21:4). Since these persons share with all humankind the inability to detect inner wrong (21:2), and since they refuse divine direction by embracing what is 'guilty', the lone light left to them can never lead to their desired destination (to 'sin' is to miss the way, v. 4).

21:4. The reputable conduct of one's children comprised one of the most indisputable witnesses to a parent's worth. In contrast, when one's 'lamp' (progeny) amounts to 'sin', the resulting failure swells to staggering proportions.

Explanation

A section-by-section consideration of moral and spiritual implications of this lecture appears first. Then follows a summary of how the sage portrays the divine across this lecture.

Section I. Introduction to faithful love as the loftiest human flourishing (20:5–9)

How shall we measure individual greatness? What trait should we examine? The sage responds that, more than any other trait, the extent of a person's faithful love best reveals his or her genuine greatness (20:6a). This insight ranks as one of the sage's 'deepest' disclosures across the whole of Proverbs (20:5). Yet how few of us flourish to this extent (v. 6b)! In the Messiah and his self-sacrifice this trait would be manifested most fully (Mark 10:45; John 15:13).

Those who would thus flourish may mature in three stages. The foundational stage calls for conduct that cultivates integrity within (Prov. 20:7a) – a strategy that rewards even generations to come (v. 7b; cf. Section II). In the second stage, faithful love consists of contributing stability to the community by executing justice and evicting wrongdoers (v. 8; cf. Section III). In the third stage, faithful love consists of inner purity (v. 9; cf. Section IV).

Section II. Cultivating integrity within: the quest to exhibit faithful love during one's youth (20:10–23)

The exhortation to cultivate inner integrity especially (but not exclusively) addresses youth. They must resist the temptation for quick-but-shady gains, applying honest industry instead (20:10–11, 13–14). For just as they can see and expose marketplace cheats, so also can the LORD (v. 12).

Also those who truly care about youths must remain alert, issuing precious counsel (20:15). Beyond counsel, they must intervene to rescue from disaster if the youth has succumbed to sly and ruinous plots (vv. 16–17). Be ready to step in (v. 18) if you notice attitudes that (a) blame those deserving honour (v. 19–21), or (b) issue sympathy in response to unfounded perceptions of economic injustice that would spawn revenge (vv. 22–23; see 'Comment'). God's unequivocal opposition to injustice does not authorize revenge.

Section III. Vanquishing evil without: the quest to exhibit faithful love during life's prime (20:24–28)

As a youth transitions into adulthood, he or she enters broader spheres of influence. He will either squander them aimlessly (20:24b) or appeal to God for guidance (v. 24a). Some aim for a non-existent middle realm, on the one hand thinking to flatter God, while inwardly maintaining private control (v. 25). Only a fool can convince himself that such a strategy can fool God (v. 27).

Instead one who behaves as a responsible adult will work energetically to evict evil (20:26). This strategy marks the pathway to genuine human flourishing – that path paved with durable love, leading to a durable reign (20:28).

Section IV. Pursuing purity within: the quest to exhibit faithful love during later years (20:29 – 21:2)

According to a proverb from Nigeria, 'Strategy is better than strength.' Thus venerable wisdom ('grey hair') outpaces youthful strength in the sage's last counsel for human flourishing (20:29). Beyond wrestling to achieve integrity within (Section II), beyond striving to vanquish evil without (Section III), the sage urges mature readers to prize above all purity within, even to the depth of one's motives (v. 30). The Master Teacher much later would similarly urge devotion reaching to the level of motives: 'You have heard that it has been said . . . but I say to you . . .' (Matt. 5:21–22, 27–28, 31–32, 33–34, 38–39, 43–44).

Yet purity is not purity's end, but only a means to the far richer destination of divine presence (cf. Ps. 15). The mortal described in Prov. 21:1 has so thoroughly located his will within the LORD's that he now liberally enjoys divine direction. Since this third scenario (Section IV) marks the summit of human flourishing, it comes as no surprise that the sage calls that human whose will has merged with his Maker's a 'king'. Here is the ideal monarch, an example to which all should aspire, regardless of station or pedigree.

The quest for flourishing resolves in one of two alternatives. Either we will deceive ourselves into supposing that our every behaviour is ethically adequate (21:2a recalls 20:9), or we will bow before the Divine Assessor, whose scales weigh even inner character, hidden far from human view (21:2b).

Section V. Concluding character summary: the contrasting outcomes of integrity and pretence (21:3–4)

What steps should we take to become the persons intended by our Maker? Choose small steps in the direction of morality and justice, for they mark the path of faithful love. Let youths with industry concentrate on cultivating personal integrity, not deception (Section II). Let robust adults evict evil instead of trying to buy divine favour (Section III). Let the more mature through purity pursue divine presence (Section IV). Herein lies divine approval, the ultimate metric of human flourishing (21:3).

If instead I cavalierly dismiss the sage's counsel, I prove myself a pompous empty-head. What I claim as superior insight will leave me stumbling blindly towards a destination without divine favour (21:4; cf. 20:24).

Portrayal of the divine across this lecture

It is instructive to observe progressive development of a human's involvement with the divine across the three stages of life. Initially, it is important for a youth to realize that God notices and cares how people treat each other (avoid duplicity, embrace integrity, 20:10, 12).

As a person matures into robust adulthood, he or she will begin to seek divine direction even when not facing an ethical dilemma (20:24). The mature continue to deepen their awareness of divine assessment (v. 27).

Advanced maturity will display eager surrender to divine control. He or she embraces the discovery that faithful love towards others finds richest fulfilment in the life under greatest divine guidance (21:1), satisfied with divine assessment (v. 2). In such a life the dependable steps of fairness regularly disarm any temptation to religious pretence (v. 3).

PROVERBS 21:5 – 22:16
'What strategies will lead to worthy wealth and proper power?'

Overview of Proverbs 21:5 – 22:16

In the lecture of Prov. 21:5 – 22:16 the sage again considers twin goals of wealth and power (cf. 10:1–22; 19:10 – 20:4). Unlike earlier exploration of these goals, here he shows how flawed means (strategies) render fatally toxic the attainment of those ends.

Section I (21:5–10) introduces (a) the principal topic (strategies), (b) twin goals (pursuit of wealth and power) and (c) the secret to successful strategies (relationships characterized by morality and grace). Section II exposes failed strategies, showing how selfishness undermines the goal of wealth (Block II.A, 21:11–21), while abuse undermines the goal of power (Block II.B, 21:22–29). Section III resolves failed strategies of Section II, outlining successful strategies that centre in reverence (21:30 – 22:5).

Before leaving the twin goals of wealth and power, the sage turns to address instructors – a focus increasingly evident in recent lectures (cf. 15:20–24; 19:20–24, 27–29; 20:15–23). Section IV coaches instructors to train youth for wise use of worthy wealth and proper power (22:6–16).

Position of this poem within Proverbs

Preceding context. In the previous lecture (20:5 – 21:4), the sage answered the implied question 'What is the loftiest expression of human flourishing?' He counselled faithful love (a) by cultivating integrity within (choosing honest industry rather than marketplace shortcuts), (b) by vanquishing evil without (ridding the kingdom of evildoers) and (c) by pursuing purity within (maintaining motives that operate thoroughly under divine direction; see 20:6 and the triple-theme structure that grows out of 20:7–9).

Following a wisdom commendation in 21:5, the present lecture revisits the same triple themes in 21:6, 7, 8, even matching the same sequence. Thus the temptation to angle for wealth by means of shortcuts (21:6) recalls (a) the theme of marketplace integrity, found in the preceding lecture (cf. 20:7). The picture of retribution descending on violent guilty folk (21:7) recalls (b) the king who cleared his realm of evildoers (cf. 20:8). And when the sage contrasts the straight work of the clean person with the crooked criminal (21:8), he recalls (c) the need for inner purity (cf. 20:9) – even to the extent of recycling from 21:2 the term 'straight' (21:2 belongs to the third of the triple themes in the preceding lecture).

Distinct in this lecture is the concept signalled by its opening word, 'strategies'. The concept of strategy recurs at pivotal points in the poem, often through the term 'way' (cf. 21:8, 16, 29; 22:5, 6).

This poem also resembles the last in its quantity of references to 'the LORD'. 'The LORD' appeared nine times across thirty sayings in the last lecture with seven appearing in the last thirteen verses (20:22 – 21:4). In the present lecture 'the LORD' is mentioned six times, all within the final eighteen sayings (21:30 – 22:16).

Ensuing context. After this poem a combination of imperatives and first-person address begins in 22:17. This marks the start of an extended wisdom commendation or apologia (vv. 17–21) that initiates the next lecture. That lecture acknowledges prior instructions (v. 20).

What to watch for

Attention to form and content discloses this lecture's structure. Concerning form, the sage makes strategic use of wisdom commendations (21:5, 11, 16, 20, 22, 30; 22:6, 10, 15) and character summaries (21:8, 29; 22:5). Also salient are palistrophes. Roughly three-quarters of the lecture's forty-three sayings reside within one of four palistrophes (21:5–8, 11–21, 22–29; 22:6–14).

Regarding content, this lecture revolves around the themes of wealth, power and grace. At times an entire portion is devoted either to wealth (Block II.A, 21:11–21) or to power (Block II.B, 21:22–29). At other times those two themes operate in tandem (e.g. 21:31 – 22:1, 2–3, 4–5).

The third theme, grace, surfaces at strategic points, correcting abusive pursuit of power and selfish pursuit of wealth, though never dominating an entire portion. Twice 'grace' follows a discussion of wealth or power, drawing to a close either a section or a block (21:10 and 22:1, respectively).

At times grace is implied without explicit mention, through expressions such as 'equity and faithful love' (at the climactic close of Block II.A, 21:21) and by extolling generosity (at the pivot point of a palistrophe in 21:26b, and again in 22:9). As grace grows in clarity, depictions of contentious relationships advance even further the indisputable need for kindness (e.g. 21:9, 19; 22:16).

Translation and outline

Verse	*Translation*	*Outline*
		I. Introduction: consider dual-theme of goals that fail, and the strategies that account for their failure (21:5–10) A. Faulty strategies account for the failure of two goals (21:5–8)
21:5	Strategies of a diligent person surely result in plenty, but anyone in a hurry surely winds up in need.	1. Wisdom commendation: strategies determine a goal's success or failure (21:5)
21:6	Generating treasures with a lying tongue amounts to a scattered vapour: they are seeking death.	2. First failed goal: wealth fails due to a strategy of deceit (start of wisdom content, 21:6)
21:7	Violence of guilty folk will drag them off, for they refused to do justice.	2'. Second failed goal: power fails due to a strategy of abuse (21:7)

Translation	Outline
21:8 Crooked is the way of a criminal, but as for a clean person – his work is straight.	1'. Character summary: personal morality determines strategy, which in turn determines a goal's success or failure (21:8)
	B. Grace constitutes the corrective for faulty strategies (21:9–10)
21:9 It is better to live on the corner of a roof than with a woman disposed to contention, and a shared house.	1. A contentious marriage: clear evidence of a faulty strategy (21:9)
21:10 The appetite of a guilty person has longed for misery; his neighbour cannot – in his eyes – be treated with grace.	2. Hoarded grace: the root cause of faulty strategies (21:10)
	II. Principal teaching: consider the dual-themes of faulty strategies more closely (21:11–29) A. First, concerning wealth: selfishness is a poor strategy, amassing only illusory wealth (21:11–21) 1. From the outset, wisdom connects destructive relationships with loss (21:11–12)
21:11 When a scoffer is fined, a naive person can grow wise, and by carefully observing a wise person he can acquire knowledge.	a. Wisdom commendation: wisdom points the way (21:11)
21:12 A moral person carefully observes the house of a guilty person; it overturns guilty folk, resulting in ruin.	b. Family relationships that devalue others lead to ruin (start of wisdom content, 21:12)
21:13 One who plugs his ears at the cry of the helpless, even he will call but will not be answered.	2. Devaluing others will lead to friendless isolation (21:13)
21:14 A gift in secret mollifies anger, and a bribe in a breast pocket – strong wrath.	3. Anger-inducing behaviour forfeits resources through mandatory generosity (paying a bribe, 21:14)
21:15 Joy for a moral person is execution of justice, but it is dread for those who practise disaster.	4. The arrival of justice breeds joy for the moral, but terror for miscreants (21:15)

Verse	*Translation*	*Outline*
21:16	A mortal who wanders from the way of careful observation, in the assembly of shades he will rest.	5. To drift from careful observation leads to deadly loss (21:16)
21:17	A person routinely lacking something loves joy; one who loves wine and perfume cannot grow wealthy.	4'. Discontentment about opulence results when joy is the goal (21:17)
21:18	Ransom for the moral is a guilty person, and in place of honest folk is a treacherous one.	3'. Guilty behaviour forfeits resources through mandatory and wholesale generosity (becoming ransom, 21:18)
21:19	It is better to live in a wilderness region than with a wife who is contentious and incensed.	2'. Devaluing others will lead to impoverished isolation (21:19)
		1'. In the end, wisdom connects supportive relationships with gain (21:20–21)
21:20	Delightful treasure and perfume are in the grazing place of wisdom, but a mortal's folly can swallow it up.	a'. Wisdom commendation: wisdom points the way to wealth (21:20)
21:21	One who pursues equity and faithful love, he will find life, equity and honour.	b'. Wisdom content: relationships that value others lead to prosperity that surpasses wealth (21:21)
		B. Second, concerning power: abuse is a feeble strategy, securing only momentary power (21:22–29)
21:22	A city of warriors a wise man scaled; next he dismantled its confident fortification.	1. Wisdom commendation: wisdom, not abusive power, determines long-term security (21:22)
21:23	One who restrains his mouth and his tongue is one who restrains his appetite from troubles.	2. Power involving words: a guarded speaker guards self from harm (start of wisdom content, 21:23)
21:24	An insolent person is presumptuous; Scoffer is his name; he operates with insolent overreach.	3. Overt schemes to lord it over others are arrogant (21:24)

Translation	Outline
21:25 The longing of a lazy fellow will put him to death, for his hands have refused to work.	4. With deadly effectiveness, the craving of laziness overpowers healthy initiative (21:25)
21:26 All day long he was consumed with longing, but a moral person will keep on giving and cannot hold back.	4'. The self-centred power of continual craving starkly contrasts the self-denying power of relentless generosity (21:26)
21:27 The sacrifice of guilty folk is an abomination: how much more when he would present it in a manipulative manner!	3'. Covert schemes to manipulate the divine are disgusting (21:27)
21:28 A deceitful witness will perish, but a person who listens endlessly will be able to issue right verdicts.	2'. Power involving words: manipulative words return harm, while careful listening restores justice (21:28)
21:29 A guilty person fortified his image, but it is the honest person who will make his ways solid.	1'. Character summary: morality, not a mask of power, ultimately determines long-term security (21:29)
	III. Conclusion: reverence – the ultimate strategy for power and wealth – begins with admission of inadequacies (21:30 – 22:5)
21:30 Wisdom does not exist, perception does not exist and counsel does not exist – when appearing before the LORD.	A. Wisdom commendation: divine exposure of wisdom's limitations, opposite the LORD (21:30)
	B. Divine exposure of power's weakness, also the inferiority of wealth (start of wisdom content, 21:31 – 22:1)
21:31 A horse is readied for battle day, but to the LORD belongs rescue.	1. Power must concede its weakness when encountering the grace of divine rescue (21:31)
22:1 A good name is preferable to great wealth; when compared with silver and gold, grace is better.	2. Wealth must concede its inferiority when encountering grace (22:1)
	C. Divine exposure of wealth's insufficiency, also the inferiority of power (22:2–3)

Verse	Translation	Outline
22:2	A rich person and a poor person were encountered: the maker of them all is the LORD.	1. All lack wealth, on a day of divine encounter (22:2)
22:3	The shrewd fellow noticed misery and so took cover, but naive fellows kept on going and will be fined.	2. On that day, only those who realize their lack of power will avoid forfeiting wealth (22:3)
		D. Reverence for the divine constitutes the supreme strategy, leading to true wealth and effectual power (22:4–5)
22:4	Humility's reward is reverence for the LORD: wealth and honour and life.	1. Because a strategy of humility leads to reverence, it leads to benefits exceeding mere wealth (22:4)
22:5	Barbs, bird traps occur in the way of a twisted person; one who restrains his appetite will keep far from them.	2. Character summary: power over desires brings freedom from imprisonment (22:5)
		IV. Advice for instructors: train youth in the worthy use of wealth and the proper use of power (22:6–16) A. Teach youth to employ wealth for generosity, and power for gracious treatment of others (22:6–14)
22:6	Train a youth at the outset of his way; even when he may grow older he will not turn from it.	1. Wisdom commendation: let your speech train youth early, so later they may not lose their way (22:6)!
22:7	A wealthy fellow may rule over poor folk, and one who borrows is servant of the person who lends.	2. Wealth may beget power (a truism, start of wisdom content, 22:7)
22:8	One who sows injustice will harvest disaster, and his overreaching rod will come to an end.	3. However, cruel power is bound to crumble (22:8)
22:9	A generous person – it is he who will become blessed, for he gave some of his food to the helpless.	4. In contrast, the generous gain favour (22:9)

22:10 Drive out a scoffer! So may quarrelling leave, and so may counterarguments and insults cease! 22:11 One who loves purity of motives: his lips are graciousness itself, his friend is a king. 22:12 The LORD's eyes kept watch over knowledge, so he overturned the threats of a treacherous fellow. 22:13 A lazy person said, 'A lion is without. Within the marketplace I will be murdered!' 22:14 A deep pit is the mouth of strange women, one cursed of the LORD will fall into it.	5. Disruptive mockers must leave (22:10)! 4'. In contrast, sincere and gracious speech gains access to monarchial power (22:11) 3'. Speech that conveys abusive power will crumble, due to attentive divine power (22:12) 2'. Lack of power (insecurity) may prevent wealth-generation (a false pretext, 22:13) 1'. By listening to illicit speech, those who incur divine disfavour hazardously lose their way (22:14)
22:15 Folly is tightly tied to the motives of a youth; a rod of reproof will put it far from him. 22:16 One who oppresses a helpless person makes him increase; one who gives to a wealthy person surely winds up in need.	B. Conclusion: training of youth can enable them to break free from self-centred delusions of power and wealth (22:15–16) 1. Wisdom commendation: effective training of youth will require reproof (22:15) 2. Wisdom content: dual-theme recap of twin failed strategies (abusive power, selfish pursuit of wealth, 22:16)

Notes on the text

21:5. '[they] result in plenty . . . [he] winds up in need', *lĕmôtār . . . lĕmaḥsōr*: lit. '[they tend] to plenty, [he tends] to lack'. Note assonance. The expression *lĕmaḥsōr* will return in 22:16b, closing the lecture.

21:6. 'Generating treasures . . . amounts to a scattered vapour: they are seeking death', *pōʿal ʾôṣārôt . . . hebel niddap mĕbaqĕšê māwet*: lit. 'making treasures . . . [is] a scattering vapour: they are ones who seek death'. The m. pl. 'treasures' provides the simplest antecedent for the ptc. 'they are seeking'. It is unnecessary to emend to sg. the pl.

expression *mĕbaqĕšê*, 'ones who seek', since the hazard of treasures-by-deceit lies in their pursuit of death (*pace* Fox 2009: 681, n.).

21:6, 8. 'Generating' (21:6), 'his work' (v. 8), *pōʿal, poʿŏlô*: the first word of 21:6 and the last word of v. 8 derive from the root *pʿl*.

21:8. 'a criminal, but as for a clean person', *wāzār wĕzak*: lit. 'criminal, and clean'. Adjacent in Hebr., the assonance of 'criminal and clean' sharpens their contrast in meaning (so also McCreesh [1991: 58–59]). *Wāzār* appears only here in the HB.

'straight', *yāšār*: elsewhere rendered 'honest', here *yāšār* contrasts 'crooked'.

21:10. 'misery; his neighbour', *rāʿ . . . rēʿēhû*: assonance again draws attention to these words with their semantic contrast. Although adjacent in English, in Hebr. each concludes its colon.

'his neighbour cannot – in his eyes – be treated with grace', *lōʾ yuḥan bĕʿênāyw rēʿēhû*: the guilty person's strategic flaw consists of his unwillingness to be an agent of grace towards others (contrast 19:22 and 20:6). This flaw would be deflected were we to emend *bĕʿênāyw rēʿēhû* to *bĕʿênê rēʿēhû*, yielding 'he will find no forgiveness in the eyes of others' (*pace* Fox 2009: 683–684, following the Syriac).

21:11. 'and by carefully observing', *ûbĕhaśkîl*: although *śkl* in the hiph. stem often means 'to be (or make) successful', mention of 'growing wise' in 21:11a recommends *śkl* as 'carefully observing' in v. 11b (also in vv. 12a, 16).

21:12. 'it overturns guilty folk': the nearest antecedent of 'it' in 21:12b is the 'house of a guilty person' at the close of v. 12a. As the self-absorbed values of vv. 9–10 would foreshadow, the enterprise of the guilty collapses from within. Instead to regard 'moral person' (v. 12a) as the agent of overturning would be doubly inferior, as grammatically it is more remote and removes the reflexive, retributive dimension (*pace* Fox 2009: 684).

21:14. 'gift', *mattān*: this gift is manipulative since it parallels 'bribe' in 21:14b.

21:16. 'from the way of careful observation', *miderek haśkēl*: the connotation of *śkl* as 'to carefully observe' continues from 21:11, 12. Also the connotation of *śkl* as 'to make successful' should be noted, since the wanderer's inattention will deprive him of success.

21:17. 'joy': unlike other sayings, the mention of love for wine and perfume contributes to 'joy' a preoccupation with frivolous parties and vanishing pleasures (contrast 'joy' in 12:20 and 15:13).

21:18. 'a guilty person . . . honest folk', *rāšāʿ . . . yĕšārîm*: reversal of sounds (*r*, *š*) mirrors ethical inversion joining these terms.

21:21. 'equity', *ṣĕdāqâ*: this term connotes faithful community relationships and shares with 'moral' in 21:12, 18 the root *ṣdq*. With the LXX to delete 'equity' from the second colon (presuming dittography) would weaken the climactic impact of this block-closing saying (*pace* Fox 2009: 689).

21:22. '[he] scaled; next he dismantled', *ʿālâ wayyōred*: lit. 'he ascended, then he pulled down'. Outside Prov. 1 – 9 and 31, the qat. . . . wayyiq. syntax of narrative sequence is rare, appearing in only three other sayings (18:22; 21:12; 30:4).

'its confident fortification': lit. 'its strength (or rampart) of confidence'.

21:23. 'restrains': lit. 'one who guards'.

'his appetite', *napšô*: mention of 'his mouth and his tongue' recommend rendering *nepeš* as 'appetite'. Yet the translation 'life' also pertains here, since it would be desirable to 'restrain (or guard) his life [*napšô*] from troubles'. Recurrence of the phoneme *šō* renders this entire verse highly alliterative: *šōmēr pîw ûlĕšônô šōmēr miṣṣārôt napšō* (Fox 2009: 689).

21:24. 'insolent overreach', *ʿebrat zādôn*: lit. 'an excess of insolence'. *ʿEbrâ* conveys overflowing amounts of whatever commodity the context may specify. Here the commodity is insolence. It need not be restricted to an excess of rage (*pace* Fox 2009: 690).

21:24, 25. 'operates', 'to work', *ʿôśeh, ʿăśôt*: both expressions derive from the root *ʿśh*, meaning to 'do', 'work' or 'make'.

21:26. 'he was consumed with longing', *hiʾtawwâ taʾăwâ*: lit. 'he was longing after a longing'. Assonance links this phrase in 21:26 with *tôʿēbâ*, 'abomination', v. 27.

'will keep on giving': lit. 'will give'. Durative connotation is inferred from yiq.

'cannot hold back': lit. 'will not hold back'. (In)capability is inferred from yiq.

21:27. 'guilty folk . . . he would present': the shift from pl. ('guilty folk') to sg. ('he') sharpens focus.

21:28. 'endlessly': Masoretic cantillation groups 'endlessly' with the ensuing phrase 'he endlessly will be able to issue verdicts'. Connection with the preceding phrase also is possible, suggesting doubled connotation: 'a person who listens endlessly, endlessly will be able to issue right verdicts'.

'will be able to issue right verdicts', *yĕdabbēr*: lit. 'will declare'; similarly *lalēsei*, 'will say', LXX. Capability is inferred from the yiq. The verb *dabbēr* can describe the handing down of judicial decisions (e.g. Jer. 1:16; 4:12), which connotation fits well the present use (also inferred by Heim 2001: 302). It is not necessary with *HALOT* to posit here a hapax legomenon meaning 'to have descendants'.

21:29. 'A guilty person fortified his image', *hēʿēz ʾîš rāšāʿ bipānāyw*: lit. 'a guilty person made his countenance strong' (compare *hēʿēzâ*, describing the seductress's brazen attitude in 7:13).

'honest person': this expression connotes both the traveller's moral rectitude and the straightness of the route travelled (cf. 21:8).

'will make his ways solid', *yakîn dĕrākāyw*: this reading follows the K, both for the expression 'will make solid' (not *yabîn*, 'will understand')

and for 'ways' (not sg. *darkô*, 'way'). To read 'will understand' would weaken the semantic reversal contrasting 'fortify' (undesirable) in the first colon and 'make solid' (desirable) in the second (*pace* Fox 2009: 692).

21:30. 'when appearing before': lit. 'before' or 'directly in front of'.

22:1. 'name', *šēm*: in this context *šēm* connotes 'a good reputation'. Literal translation 'name' is retained to preserve connection with 21:24.

'grace': generous and respectful regard for others. 'Grace' parallels 'name', since gracious behaviour fosters a good reputation among one's neighbours. 'Grace' here describes a generous regard conveyed to others (not kindness received from others), evident from the priority that already in this lecture the sage placed on exercising a gracious outlook towards others (the opposite is rejected in 21:10b) – a priority he will underscore again in 22:9 (though without naming 'grace'). Perhaps it is due to reading 'grace' in 22:1 apart from what the poet says concerning gracious conduct in 21:10 and 22:9 (which belong to the same lecture as 22:1) that others have regarded 'grace' in 21:10 as emanating from the subject, while regarding 'grace' in 22:1 as being received by the subject (Heim 2001: 304, 306; Waltke 2005: 176, 193; Fox 2009: 683, 694). While doubtless to garner grace from others is better than heaping up stores of silver and gold, when read in the context of this lecture the sage rather teaches in 22:1b that the generous disbursal of unmerited favour towards others is better than accumulating stores of silver and gold.

'when compared with silver and gold': lit. 'than silver and gold'. The inferiority of silver and gold is emphasized by appearing first in the colon.

'grace is better', *ḥēn ṭôb*: a comparative expression, as recognized by the LXX, parallel to 'preferable' in the first colon (so also Waltke 2005: 193; not 'good grace' or 'good favour', *pace* Fox 2009: 694).

22:2. 'A rich person and a poor person were encountered', *ʿāšîr wārāš nipgāšû*: as a niph. conjugation, the verb *nipgāšû* may be (a) mid. (they experienced an encounter), (b) pass. (without precipitating it, they were encountered by someone else), (c) reflexive (they encountered themselves) or (d) reciprocal (they encountered each other). Most often niph. yields a pass. meaning (*IBHS* §23.2.1, 2). Thus the poet conveys that the rich and poor – with no initiative of their own – one day found themselves jointly encountered by someone else. The encountering person was the LORD (22:2b). The sage described a similar divine encounter only three sayings earlier (21:30). Such an encounter would arrest the presumptuous arrogance of 21:24 and the manipulative religiosity of 21:27. Towards the end of Proverbs the violent and the poor similarly experience a 'divine encounter', *nipgāšû* (29:13).

Thus it is neither necessary nor preferable to regard *nipgāšû* as reciprocal (*pace* LXX '[they] encountered each other', ESV '[they] meet together', and NRSV, NIV to 'have [something] in common'). For an instance of *nipgāšû* as reciprocal, with no third party to be encountered, see Ps. 85:11 (ET v. 10).

The poet's choice of the qat. (*nipgāšû*) conveys certitude (rendered here as past tense, 'were encountered'). A yiq. form would have allowed a connotation of potentiality ('may be encountered').

'of them all', *kullām*: LXX understandably reads, 'of both of them', since only two humans are present (rich and poor persons). Here, however, by indicating that he made *kullām*, 'all of them' (rather than *šĕnêhem*, 'both of them'), the sage collects all present and future audiences under a canopy of divine accountability.

22:3. 'noticed misery', *rāʾâ rāʿâ*: lit. 'saw misery'. Assonance closely binds these words.

'and so took cover', *wayyissātēr*: since noticing misery (22:3aα) leads logically to taking cover (v. 3aβ), the K option *wayyissātēr*, 'and so took cover' (wayyiq.), fits better than either *wĕyissātēr*, 'and may he take cover' (indirect juss.), or the Q alternative *wĕnistār*, 'and will take cover'. See 27:12 for a close parallel.

22:4. 'Humility's reward is reverence for the LORD': lit. 'reward of humility [is] reverence of the LORD'. Fox similarly interpolates the verb 'to be' for this verbless expression (2009: 697). Instead to interpolate a conj. ('The reward for humility *and* fear of the LORD', NRSV and similarly ESV and NASB) weakens the causal role of humility in producing reverence.

22:5. 'the way of a twisted person; one who restrains his appetite': lit. 'a way of a twisted person' and 'one who guards his appetite'. Since the commendable person restrains his desires, conversely to be 'twisted' would suggest erratic, hedonistic pursuit of whatever one may desire.

'his appetite', *napšô*: since earlier the poet established that flawed life strategies trace to flawed appetites (21:10b), *nepeš* here should be rendered 'appetite' (not 'life').

22:6. 'Train', *ḥănōk*: this term occurs only here with the meaning 'train' (elsewhere 'dedicate', 'consecrate'). In Arab. this root refers to rubbing the palate of a newborn with oil or date juice, evidently to coax sucking (note mention of 'mouth' in Hebr. of the expression 'at the outset of his way', 22:6a). Elsewhere the root *ḥnk* refers to dedicating a building (house or temple). Semantic overlap with 'dedicate' suggests encouraging a young person to give singular concentration to one's energies, as a vintner would 'train' a vine to follow a trellis (in contrast to 'training' in the sense of 'transmitting information').

'at the outset of his way': lit. 'according to the mouth of his way'. To grasp the connotation of 'mouth' when construed with 'way', it is instructive to observe three parallel uses of 'mouth'. When construed with years, 'mouth' refers to the start of a span of years (Lev. 27:18). With a city gate, 'mouth' describes the point where one begins to enter that city (Prov. 8:3). With a sack, 'mouth' again indicates the opening (Gen. 42:27). Consequently 'mouth' construed with 'way' would indicate where that path begins – a trailhead (so also Barucq, cited in Heim 2001: 308). This interpretation fits 22:6b, where the sage contrasts chronological beginning ('youth') with later age (growing old).

Thus, as an NET translator's note appropriately observes, 'This phrase does not describe the concept perpetuated by a modern psychological interpretation of the verse: Train a child according to his personality trait.' Rather, it urges the teacher to help the youth cultivate an appetite for what will be wholesome and nourishing. When it recurs in Prov. 22:14, 'mouth' contributes to the palistrophic link joining that saying with v. 6.

22:7. 'may rule': possibility is inferred from the yiq.

22:8. 'One who sows', *zôrēʿa*: wordplay may operate here since *zôrēʿa*, 'one who sows', is phonetically similar to *zĕrôʿa*, 'arm'. Since 'arm' connotes 'force' or 'power', and since the 'sower' of 22:8 spreads injustice, hearers may have fused a wordplay surrounding this cruel member of the community. 'Sowing injustice' would then bear the connotation of 'inflicting unfairness through the application of unwarranted force'.

'his overreaching rod': lit. 'his rod of excess' or 'of outburst'. One's rod (a symbol of power imposed on inferiors) here angrily violates healthy boundaries.

22:9. 'A generous person': lit. 'good-of-eye' (the opposite – miserliness – is 'bad-of-eye', Prov. 23:6; 28:22). This idiom is attested in the first century AD (Matt. 6:22–23). At the close of Section I the poet associated eyes with negative treatment of one's neighbour (21:10).

'will become blessed': whether this 'blessing' issues from God or from grateful neighbours the poet leaves open to interpretation. Both are likely (Murphy 1998: 165).

22:10. 'So may . . . leave' and 'so may . . . cease', *wĕyēṣēʾ* and *wĕyišbôt*: after the imperative 'Drive out!', the two weyiq. forms involving 'leave' and 'cease' operate as indirect jussives, extending the volitive tone.

'counterarguments and insults': escalation from thoughtful reasoning to unfounded libel.

22:11. 'purity of motives': lit. 'purity of mind'. Earlier the sage disparaged tainted motives evident in schemes to manipulate God (21:27). In 22:9 and v. 11 he presents the epitome of laudable behaviour: generosity free from hidden agendas. 'Motives' captures this context better than 'mind'.

'his friend is a king': one who can count a king as friend would enjoy even more access to power than the royal counsellor (known as the 'friend of the king', 1 Chr. 27:33).

22:12. 'threats': lit. 'words'. Since the one speaking is 'a treacherous fellow', his 'words' would convey abusive power; hence 'threats'.

'so he overturned': lit. 'and he overturned' (see earlier note on 21:22).

22:13. 'without': lit. 'outside'.

'marketplace': lit. 'plazas', often refers to the area near the city gates, serving economic and political commerce.

22:14. 'strange women', *zārôt*: since the author elsewhere employs the m. equivalent *zārîm*, 'strangers' (5:10, 17), use of the f. here is intentional.

Mention of 'mouth' implies seduction, whether metaphoric (a word, 7:5) or literal (a kiss, 7:13). Fox understands 'strange women' to designate any woman not one's wife (2009: 702; for an impersonal use of *zārôt*, see 23:33).

22:15. 'motives', *lēb*: see 'Notes' for 'purity of motives' in 22:11, above. Mention of 'folly' shows that, in addition to being impure, exploitive motives are patently unwise.

22:16. 'makes him increase', *lĕharbôt lô*: i.e. the oppressed person paradoxically gains ascendency as a result of the oppression that he suffers. The antecedent of 'him' is the person suffering oppression (Heim 2001: 308; Fox 2009: 703; *pace* Waltke 2005: 196 and many versions).

'helpless', *dāl*: although a person signified by *dāl* may be penniless, this term primarily indicates powerlessness.

'winds up in need', *lĕmaḥsōr*: lit. '[tends] to lack'. *Lĕmaḥsōr* opened this lecture (21:5b).

Form and structure

Borders

After establishing faithful love as index of loftiest human flourishing (preceding poem), the theme shifts to strategies for wealth and power that shun abusive greed (present poem). A wisdom commendation about 'strategies' that contrasts 'plenty' and 'need' marks the upper border (21:5).

Structures that locate a lower border in the verse-pair spanning 22:15–16 include three elements of closure and one of inclusio. The first closural device involves the theme of abuse of power (oppressing a helpless person, 22:16a). The sage introduced abuse of power in Section I (21:8), then expanded it in Block II.B (21:22–29). Second is the theme of wealth deviously acquired or manipulatively distributed (giving to a wealthy person, 22:16b). This theme featured earlier in Section I (21:6a) and Section II (21:14). Third involves the verb *rāḥaq*, 'to remain [or to place something] far away' ('a rod of reproof will put [folly] far from [the youth]', 22:15b). *Rāḥaq* appeared earlier in 22:5 (Section III). Since it occurs only ten other times in Proverbs, recurrence in this lecture reinforces closure.

Inclusio results when the expression 'surely winds up in need' appears in the lecture's first and last sayings (21:5; 22:16). It occurs only twice more in the book (11:24; 14:23).

Macrostructural features

Section-opening wisdom commendations (Sections I–IV, content-based). Each section opens with a wisdom commendation. The first introduces the theme of 'strategy' (21:5). The second seeds the character of the scoffer (21:11), who reappears in 22:10 at a palistrophic core of Section IV. The third launches the admission of inadequacies by modelling shortcomings of wisdom (21:30; Heim also recognizes a new portion beginning in 21:30 [2001: 303]). The fourth sets out the teacher perspective, as trainer-of-youth (22:6).

Repetition of 'way' (Sections I–IV, form-based). The term 'way' appears in each section with structural significance, whether closing a portion (21:8 in Block I.A, 21:29 in Section II, and 22:5 in Section III), opening a portion (22:6 in Section IV), or bringing a palistrophe to its climactic pivot point (21:16, within the palistrophe spanning II.A 21:11–21). As a synonym of 'strategy' (21:5), 'way' contributes to a primary theme of this lecture.

Thematic continuity involving wealth and power (Sections I–IV, content-based). The themes of wealth and power feature prominently in each section, beginning with adjacent sayings in the first (wealth in 21:6, and power in v. 7). Section II expands on wealth in its first block (a fine in 21:11, gift and bribe in v. 14, growing wealthy in v. 17, ransom in v. 18, and treasure in v. 20). The second block focuses on power (conquering a city in 21:22, exercising self-restraint in v. 23, hands that should exert labour but do not in v. 25).

Wealth and power intertwine in Section III. Wealth is indicated by silver and gold (22:1), rich and poor (v. 2), suffering a fine (v. 3), and 'wealth' (v. 4). Power is implicit in a war horse (21:31), in the LORD as sovereign maker of great and small (22:2), in humility and reverence (which acknowledge the superior power of another, v. 4), and in self-control (power over self, v. 5).

In Section IV wealth and power again intertwine. Wealth (or poverty) is connoted by wealthy and poor folk (22:7; cf. v. 16), by borrowing and lending (also 22:7), and the helpless (vv. 9, 16). Power appears in rule (conversely in serving, 22:7), an overreaching rod (v. 8), overturning someone (v. 12), and a lion's menace (v. 13).

Continuity of three-theme cluster (Sections I, III and IV, content-based). In a refinement of basic wealth-and-power themes noted above, three sections present the following trio, closely clustered: the inadequacy of wealth, the weakness of power, and gracious regard for others (antidote to the trio's first two). Section I clusters them thus: poverty of wealth (21:6), weakness of power (v. 7), and gracious regard for others (vv. 9–10).

In Section III they appear thus: weakness of power (21:31), relative poverty of wealth (directly following in 22:1), and 'grace' (also 22:1). Since in this lecture the term 'grace' does not occur outside 21:10 and 22:1, its mention in 21:10 colours 22:1 with a connotation of favour extended from the individual, radiating outward to the community (not approval obtained from the community, as 'name'/reputation in 22:1a might imply).

In Section IV the threefold cluster appears thus: wealth as an amoral and therefore insufficient sole qualification for superiority (22:7), abusive power (v. 8), and a portrait of one who gains favour in the community through his generosity towards the helpless (v. 9). Although the term 'grace' does not appear in Section IV, the picture of generosity in v. 9 illustrates what sort of behaviour the sage envisioned earlier for the term 'grace'.

Wordplay involving 'mouth' and 'appetite' (Sections I–IV, content-based). Due to the semantic overlap of appetite and mouth, mention of 'mouth' in 22:6 (within the expression 'outset of his way') builds on earlier teaching concerning 'appetite' within this poem (see 'Notes' for 22:6). Section I concludes by cautioning that an 'appetite' that has 'longed for' misery constitutes the guilty person's fundamental flaw (21:10). Conversely, in Section II, a 'mouth' (also tongue) and 'appetite' that are wisely restrained exempt one from 'troubles' (21:23). Similarly, at the close of Section III, one who 'restrains his appetite' will successfully avoid entrapment (22:5).

When 'mouth' subsequently appears at the opening of Section IV in 22:6 (within the phrase 'outset of his way'), wordplay reasonably is involved. From the 'outset' of a youth's life, teachers should cultivate in him or her an appetite for displaying grace (21:10), together with restraint of speech (21:23) and longings (22:5).

Closure regarding straight or crooked way (Sections I, II and III, form- and content-based). The first block concludes: 'Crooked is the way of a criminal, but as for a clean person – his work is straight' (21:8). Closure results when 'way' and *yāšār* (rendered 'straight' or 'honest') return in the conclusion of Section II (21:29), and when 'way' and 'twisted' (opposite of straight) appear in the conclusion of Section III (22:5). 'Way' appears only twice more within this lecture, one of which opens the final section in 22:6 ('way' also appears in 21:16).

Section-level closure regarding 'restraint of appetite' (Sections II and III, form-based). The expression 'to restrain one's appetite', first occurring in 21:23 (within Section II), fosters closure, reappearing in 22:5 (the final saying of Section III). While the verb 'to restrain', *šāmar*, occurs often in Proverbs (in twenty-eight other sayings), within this poem it appears only in these two instances.

Contrast of audience in Section IV, differing from Sections I–III (content-based). Advice appearing in the first three sections envisions the sage's typical audience (youthful pupils). In Section IV he addresses fellow teachers (or parents), signalled by that portion's opening saying: 'Train a youth at the outset of his way; even when he may grow older he will not turn from it' (22:6). The charge, 'Drive out a scoffer!' similarly addresses teachers, whose effectiveness would suffer if a scorner among the pupils were to disrupt. Teachers similarly comprise the audience when the sage explains that, 'Folly is tightly tied to the motives of a youth; a rod of reproof will put it far from him' (22:15, within the final verse-pair of Section IV).

Heightened urgency in Section IV (content-based). Three factors in Section IV signal a heightened sense of urgency, when compared with Sections I–III. First, this lecture's sole imperatives appear in Section IV:

'Train a youth at the outset of his way' (22:6, the opening line of Section IV), and 'Drive out a scoffer!' (v. 10).

Second, the sage advocates measures in Section IV that connote urgency. The scoffer, earlier encountered in 21:24, now is not patiently to be reprimanded, but aggressively driven out (22:10). Regarding the youthful pupil, if he exhibits deeply ingrained folly, persuasive techniques of discipline should escalate to allow application of the rod (implying that lesser measures proved insufficient to change behaviour, 22:15; 'rod' in 22:8 is unrelated since it was a weapon of the unjust, not a teacher's corrective tool).

Third, consider the profound hazard indicated by a deep pit and by suffering a divine curse in 22:14: 'A deep pit is the mouth of strange women, one cursed of the LORD will fall into it'. Since only a two-verse conclusion (22:15–16, Block IV.B) separates it from the lecture's close, this saying conveys a sobering sense of urgency.

Microstructural features

Section I (21:5–10). *Wisdom commendation at section boundary (21:5, content-based).* As observed among 'Macrostructural features', Section I opens with a wisdom commendation (21:5) at the start of a four-verse palistrophe. The balance of the palistrophe comprises the wisdom content (vv. 6–8).

Thematic continuity involving strategies (21:5–8, content-based). Block I.A coheres in the theme of strategies, launched with the poem's opening word ('strategies', 21:5). The next two sayings illustrate harmful strategies (wealth by deceit and power by abuse, vv. 6 and 7, respectively). The block's last saying introduces the yardstick of morality to evaluate strategies ('crooked is the way', contrasting 'straight', v. 8). Garrett similarly groups vv. 5–8, regarding vv. 6–7 as examples of a wrongful strategy seen in v. 5b, with v. 8 serving as a summary (1993: 180).

Dual-theme introduction (21:6–7, content-based). The verse-pair spanning 21:6–7 coheres since those sayings introduce themes of wealth and power (respectively) that will feature prominently across most of this lecture (see Thematic continuity involving wealth and power, under 'Macrostructural features').

Palistrophe concerning strategies (21:5–8, content-based). As indicated immediately above, 21:6–7 form an introductory verse-pair, evident from how prominent their themes (strategies associated with wealth and power) will become through the balance of the poem. Note that both sayings are wholly negative. In contrast, the flanking sayings (also dealing in strategies) each contain both positive and negative cola (vv. 5, 8). Thus vv. 5–8 form a brief palistrophe.

Character-summary conclusion (21:8, content-based). Block I.A. closes with a character summary contrasting a 'criminal' and a 'clean person' (21:8). Thus the sage traces to personal character the morality of one's strategy.

Thematic continuity concerning relationships (21:9–10, content-based). Both 21:9 and 10 deal in relationships, whether in a marriage relationship or with a neighbour devoid of grace. The second saying (v. 10) illumines the ingredient missing from the first (v. 9): the husband was unable to regard his 'neighbour' (i.e. his wife) with 'grace'.

Section II (21:11–29). *Wisdom commendations strategically positioned (21:11, 20, 22, content-based).* The three wisdom commendations in Section II are strategically positioned. They appear at boundaries, whether beginning a block (21:11, 22), or ending a block by inclusio (21:20–21 mirror vv. 11–12 palistrophically). Wisdom content follows each (cf. 21:12, 21, and the balance of the palistrophe in 21:23–29).

Thematic continuity concerning wealth (21:11–20, content-based). A theme of wealth (and conversely impoverishment) binds together Block II.A (21:11–21). This theme is indicated by a fine (loss of wealth, v. 11), ruin (v. 12), the helpless (v. 13), a gift (v. 14), disaster (v. 15), the shades (mortal disaster, v. 16), lack, wealth, and perfume (all in v. 17), ransom (v. 18), wilderness (suggesting impoverishment, v. 19), and treasure and perfume (both in v. 20).

Repetition of 'observe' (21:11–12, 16, form-based). Through repetition, 'observe', *śkl*, joins 21:11–12. The root *śkl* will appear only once more within this lecture – at the pivot (21:16) of a palistrophe that began with the quatrain containing *śkl* (21:11–12).

Continuity of loss, with contrasting cause (21:11–12, content-based). Both 21:11, 12 present reversals of fortune. The first, a fine, is imposed on the scoffer from without. The second is perpetrated by a guilty person's own house, as if it turns against him.

Palistrophe concerning selfish pursuit of wealth (21:11–21, content-based). A five-level palistrophe concerning selfish wealth unfolds in Block II.A (21:11–21). The core (Level 5) appears in v. 16, showcasing the importance of 'careful observation' (seen earlier in vv. 11, 12).

At Level 4, 'joy', *śimḥâ*, links 21:15 and 17, a term not appearing elsewhere in this lecture (so also Heim 2001: 294).

Both sayings at Level 3 deal with forced generosity that forfeits wealth. In 21:14 a wealthy person must feign generosity ('gift' and 'bribe') to mollify anger he has incited. Worse yet, in v. 18 he must forfeit his life to benefit a moral person.

Callous behaviour (eventually yielding loss) characterizes both sayings at Level 2, either explicitly or implicitly (21:13, 19). Explicitly, the cry of the helpless goes unheeded in v. 13. Implicitly, such insensitivity would explain why the wife of v. 19 grew 'contentious and incensed' (cf. discussion of thematic continuity in 21:9–10, above).

The first palistrophic level connects two verse-pairs. Each pair consists of a wisdom commendation followed by a message linking relationships with either loss or gain. Wisdom commendations appear in 21:11, 20. The first deals with wealth-forfeiture (a fine), and is followed by a caution against the self-destructive nature of relationships in a guilty person's household (v. 12). The second deals with wealth acquisition ('delightful treasure and perfume'), followed by affirmation of supportive relationships (marked by 'equity and faithful love'), due to the 'life, equity, and honour' that they bring (v. 21). Concerning the second verse-pair, Waltke similarly observes a content-based link joining vv. 20–21, with v. 21 elaborating the benefits accruing to the wise in v. 20 (2005: 184).

Block-level closure (21:20–21, form- and content-based). Several elements in 21:20–21 foster closure for Block II.A. 'Wise' (v. 11) and 'perfume' (v. 17) relate to 'wisdom' and 'perfume' in v. 20. A living space (whether wilderness or home, v. 19) relates to 'grazing place' (v. 20; Waltke 2005: 183). Relationships implied by 'house' (v. 12), 'the cry of the helpless' (v. 13), and marriage (v. 19) pertain to relational traits of 'equity and faithful love' (v. 21). The root *ṣdq* appears in vv. 12, 15, 18 ('moral'), and again in v. 21 ('equity').

Thematic continuity involving power (Block II.B, 21:22–29, content-based). With expressions, 'A city of warriors', 'dismantled', and 'confident fortification (*ʿzz*)', the first saying of Block II.B presents a theme of power (21:22). 'Warriors' in this case use power immorally, opposing the liberating-wise. Waltke similarly regards this saying as depicting the victory of the wise and moral over evil and wicked persons (2005: 184).

The sage commends power as self-control over words and wants in 21:23 (see 'mouth' under 'Notes'). Power as negative psychological pressure emerges with the insolent scoffer and his agenda of 'overreach' (21:24).

The lazy fellow's resolute refusal – 'all day long' – to exert effort portrays a perverse sort of power over self (21:25–26a). Power over self reverses in 21:26b, as irrepressible generosity replaces indolence.

The absence of explicit power vocabulary in 21:27 underscores the guilty person's cunning-but-flawed strategy, contributing sacrifices to manipulate (overpower) God. Similarly cunning is the perjurer's imperceptible use of power parading as truth, to inflict judicial harm, evident to none but the victim (21:28a). Conversely, the judge who listens 'endlessly' exhibits stamina of an internal sort (v. 28b).

Recycling 'fortify' from the block's opening saying, the final saying of Section II cautions against power exerted for pretence: '[he] fortified (*ʿzz*) his image' (21:29a; cf. v. 22). In contrast, the 'honest person' displays productive power by 'mak[ing] his ways solid' (v. 29b). Without isolating power as a theme, Waltke regards v. 29a as the climactic conclusion of negative characters starting with v. 24 (2005: 190).

Palistrophe concerning power (Block II.B, 21:22–29, content-based). A four-level palistrophe organizes Block II.B (21:22–29). Beginning with a quatrain at the palistrophic core, Levels 4 and 4' cohere through the character of the lazy fellow (vv. 25–26a), and through the root *ʾwh* ('longing' in vv. 25, 26, 'consumed with' in v. 26). Others also observe the link involving *ʾwh* (Heim 2001: 299; Waltke 2005: 186–187; Fox 2009: 690).

That root appears once more in this poem, in the theme-rich conclusion to Section I (21:10). As to power, the indolent make a studied effort to prevent gainful employ, while the moral person overcomes self-centredness with persistent generosity (v. 26b).

If at Level 4 the indolent exerts power over self to resist productivity, the scoffer of Level 3 exerts malicious power over others, through insolent overreach (21:24). Undesirable power over others appears in Level 3', as the guilty seek to manipulate the divine through superficial religiosity (v. 27).

Power in Level 2 involves words, especially words that go unspoken through self-control (21:23). Negatively, powerful words of the perjurer in Level 2' convict the innocent (v. 28).

Level 1 of the palistrophe introduces power through 'warriors' and 'fortification', *ʿzz* (21:22). Level 1' refers to 'fortif[ying] (*ʿzz*) his image' (21:29). The fact that, aside from vv. 22, 29, the root *ʿzz* recurs only once more in this lecture (21:14b) increases the likelihood that vv. 22 and 29 are linked. Both sayings contrast presumptuous strength in colon A and prevailing strength in colon B.

Section III (21:30 – 22:5). *Wisdom commendation at section boundary (21:30, content-based).* Like Sections I and II, a wisdom commendation begins Section III (21:30). This commendation anchors inadequacy (theme of Section III) within wisdom. Ensuing wisdom content continues that theme (21:31 – 22:5).

Recurrent pairing of wealth with power (21:31 – 22:1, 2–3, 4–5, content-based). Very early in Section I the twin topics of wealth and power were set forth (21:6, 7). Now in Section III, after the section-opening wisdom commendation (21:30), the balance of Section III breaks into verse-pairs, with each pair referencing both wealth and power. Thus the pair spanning 21:31 – 22:1 describe a 'horse' and 'battle' (power) in the first verse, and 'great wealth', 'silver', and 'gold' in the second (wealth).

The verse-pair spanning 22:2–3 treats 'rich' and 'poor' (wealth) in v. 2, followed in v. 3 by someone who realizes that he will be powerless to deflect impending misery. A financial penalty (wealth) also appears in v. 3.

The verse-pair spanning 22:4–5 refers to 'wealth' in the first, and, in the second verse, power operates both negatively (restraint by 'barbs' and 'traps') and positively (self-restraint involving one's appetite). Attention to the theme of wealth (while overlooking power) yields a rather different verse grouping (e.g. Waltke 2005: 198–203).

Block-initial repetition of 'LORD' (21:30, 31; 22:2, 4, form-based). Grouping of verses according to wealth and power (21:31 – 22:1, 2–3, 4–5) is further reinforced by mention of the LORD in the first verse of each pair (at 21:31; 22:2, 4). It is fitting for the initial saying of Section III similarly to mention the LORD: 'Wisdom does not exist, perception does not exist, and counsel does not exist – when appearing before the LORD' (21:30).

Thematic continuity concerning inadequacy (21:30 – 22:5, content-based). Inadequacy courses as a theme through Section III. Human wisdom fails, opposite the divine (21:30). Military power proves weak, opposite divine capacity to emancipate (21:31). 'Great wealth' cannot measure up to a gracious reputation (22:1). 'Rich[es]' avail not, opposite the divine (v. 2; Kugel may be correct, inferring death as leveller of rich and poor alike [2017: 25–26]). Instead of presuming self-sufficiency, the pupil must meekly admit inadequacy in the face of looming misery, thus enabling a strategic retreat (22:3).

The intimation of meekness in 22:3 grows explicit in v. 4. 'Humility' (an admission of inadequacy) alone can escort the pupil into 'wealth and honour and life'. Humility will safeguard the youth from falling prey to 'barbs' and 'traps' set by his own unwillingness to curb appetites through self-control (v. 5).

Section IV (22:6–16). *Block-initial wisdom commendations (22:6, 15 content-based).* As with Sections I, II and III, a wisdom commendation opens Section IV as well (22:6). With an imperative this saying begins the portion directed to teachers of youth. Wisdom content follows in 22:7–14.

This section's second block similarly opens with a wisdom commendation designed for teachers (22:15). Wisdom content concerning wealth and power follows in v. 16, concluding the entire lecture. Waltke also groups vv. 15–16 as a conclusion (2005: 215).

Palistrophe teaching right use of wealth and power (22:6–14, content-based). A five-level palistrophe unifies 22:6–14. Levels 1 and 1' are linked by repeating the term *peh* ('outset' in v. 6, 'mouth' in v. 14). Reversal will transmute that innocent 'outset', *peh*, which commenced as the youth ventured into life with great expectations (22:6). At the palistrophe's close, *peh* (referring to the pit-like 'mouth of strange women' in v. 14) dismally signals the wayward youth's final and fatal destination. Since *peh* occurs only once elsewhere in this lecture ('mouth', 21:23), its repetition in 22:6 and 14 indicates connectedness (Block IV.A).

Levels 2 and 2' speak to wealth in terms of power. The first (22:7) observes wealth generating power, virtually holding the poor hostage in a caste system. The second (v. 13) nuances the first, observing that some who claim inability to escape poverty (lack of wealth), in reality are held hostage by their own indolence (lack of power over self). Imaginary lions paralyse these whose poverty traces to sloth, deterring them from venturing into the plaza of gainful employ.

Eventual triumph of justice over abusive power joins Levels 3 and 3'. Ruthless injustice ultimately will fail (22:8). The LORD himself will upend 'the threats of a treacherous fellow' (v. 12).

At Levels 4 and 4' the sage most lucidly discloses right strategies for wealth and power (offsetting the flawed strategies so studiously exposed across this lecture). Wealth must be managed through generosity (22:9). And power must derive – not from manipulative schemes – but from pure and gracious motives (v. 11; lit. 'purity of motives' and 'lips' that are the epitome of 'graciousness').

A strikingly strident imperative fairly explodes at the palistrophe's core (Level 5): 'Drive out a scoffer! So may quarrelling leave, and so may counterarguments and insults cease!' (22:10). By indicting the scoffer, the sage telegraphs the fundamental requirement of receptivity. Here at the zenith of his lesson concerning motives (vv. 9, 11) no scoffer must be permitted to undermine, disrupt, or smear with scurrilous slurs the sage's precious insights. Owing to the scoffer's record of non-responsiveness when punished (21:11) for culpable conduct (v. 24), ejection would strike the pupil as the wisest response to a scoffer.

Contrast of blessed and cursed (22:9, 14, content-based). The four ascending steps (22:6–9) of the palistrophe described above conclude by describing the success of the admirable person as being 'blessed': 'A generous person – it is he who will become blessed' (v. 9a). In contrast, the four descending steps (vv. 11–14) conclude by describing the demise of the dishonourable person in terms of being 'cursed': 'A deep pit is the mouth of strange women, one cursed of the LORD will fall into it' (v. 14).

Reversal of hazards: perceptibility and authenticity (22:13–14, content-based). Contrasting hazards appear in 22:13, 14. The first (a lion in the marketplace) is vividly perceived by the lazy fellow, while posing no authentic threat. The second (pit-like mouth of strange women) poses an authentic threat, all the more hazardous because its victims fail to perceive it.

Four structures linking linear portions in 22:6–14 (form- and content-based). In evidence of compositional sophistication, the poet intertwined a linear scheme alongside the palistrophic structure for 22:6–14 described above. This secondary scheme groups sayings sequentially as follows: (a) a wisdom commendation (22:6), (b) a distillation of teachings on wealth and power (vv. 7–9), (c) a challenge to evict the scoffer (v. 10) and (d) observations about speech (vv. 11–14). Four structures link these sequential groups, as follows (the structures do not equate to the four portions, but stitch them together).

First linear structure: distillation of teachings on wealth and power (22:7–9, content-based). The sayings spanning 22:7–9 provide a condensed version of this lecture's primary principles (also Waltke clusters vv. 7–9 together [2005: 206–210]). Wealth and power appear in an initial, rather colourless truism (v. 7). Then follow alternative avenues, either navigating power negatively through abuse (v. 8), or navigating wealth positively through generosity (v. 9; wealth in terms of food). Through the teaching spanning vv. 7–9 the sage recaps this lecture's entire teaching.

Second linear structure: imperatives as bookends (22:6, 10, form-based). Due to thematic coherence of 22:7–9 (wealth and power), and due to the rarity of imperatives in this lecture (only in 22:6, 10), those two imperatives serve vv. 7–9 as structural bookends.

Third linear structure: thematic continuity concerning speech (22:11–14, content-based). A theme of speech threads through 22:11–14. Lips may speak graciously (v. 11). Or speech may take the form of treacherous threats (v. 12), indolent excuses (v. 13), enticements from the 'mouth of strange women' (v. 14a), or a divinely uttered curse (v. 14b).

Speech also operates in the commands to teachers (22:6) and to scoffers (v. 10). Yet these rather direct what transpires in the sage's 'classroom'. They do not dictate what one should or should not say.

Fourth linear structure: inclusio involving lips and mouth (22:11, 14, content-based). Mention of 'lips' in 22:11 and 'mouth' in v. 14 creates an inclusio enveloping the speech-themed verses spanning 22:11–14. 'Lips' in v. 11 are positive, delivering gracious messages, while 'mouth' in v. 14 is negative, concealing a hazardous trap.

Dual-theme recap (22:16, content-based). The sage summarizes twin failed strategies of abusive power and selfish pursuit of wealth in the lecture's closing saying (22:16). Oppression of a helpless person depicts abusive power (22:16a), earlier implicated in 22:7–8. Assets 'giv[en] to a wealthy person' (22:16b) recall riches paid out as anger-mollifying bribes (21:14).

Comment

Section I (21:5–10). From this poem's first word the sage accents the importance of 'strategies', and the perseverance they require (21:5, a wisdom commendation). Not all strategies merit pursuit, however. Two in particular the youth must disqualify: a strategy of deceit in pursuit of wealth (v. 6), and a strategy that dismisses justice in pursuit of power (v. 7). Wealth and power are amoral. But when achieved through an immoral 'way', when not attained in a 'clean' fashion, through 'work' that is 'straight', wealth poisons and power corrupts (v. 8). Moral strategy is indispensable.

To sharpen the need for morality in one's strategies, the sage specifies further. Strategies fail morally when they devalue persons in relationship. To illustrate, the sage describes a strained marriage (21:9). The pupil should respond by probing, 'Why? What caused this marriage to sour?'

The sage explains. Presumably this marriage did not begin in strife. Curved inward, the husband's 'appetite' took no thought of his wife, predictably acquiring the 'misery' for which he unwittingly longed (20:10a). (With Waltke to group vv. 10–12 together due to recurrence of 'guilty' in outer verses would overlook the division introduced by a wisdom commendation in 20:11, and would diminish the way that callousness in v. 10 may explain the marital tension in v. 9 [2005: 174–176].)

The husband failed due to voluntary vision impairment. His eyes were unable to see in his 'neighbour' (i.e. his wife) someone meriting 'grace' (20:10b). If only he had regarded her more generously, he could have avoided rooftop exile. As it was, his indifference forced her to resort to bickering and contention, simply to overcome her callous husband's inattention. By devaluing his wife as disposable, the husband proved how bankrupt were his strategies in pursuit of wealth (v. 6) and power (v. 7).

21:5. 'Haste makes waste'.

21:6–8. Integrity (21:6), justice (v. 7) and purity (v. 8) featured prominently near the outset of the preceding lecture (20:7, 8 and 9, respectively).

21:6. To introduce death so early in a lecture is unusual, suggesting the solemnity of this poem weighed heavily on the sage's mind. Of the sage's thirty-five lectures identified in this commentary, only five others mention 'death' (root *mwt*) within the first seven verses (5:5; 10:2; 11:4; 15:10; 19:16).

21:9. Since a virtually identical saying appears in 25:24, this proverb may have enjoyed independent circulation.

21:10. This verse exposes misery-loving motives of a 'guilty person'. In relationships he proves parsimonious. Subsequent references to 'guilty' round out his or her portrait (he employs violent strategies in 21:7, is unable to retain wealth in 21:18, is cultically manipulative in 21:27, and presents a confident façade in 21:29).

Section II (21:11–29). *Block II.A (21:11–21).* After initially critiquing misguided strategies for wealth and power in Section I, in Section II the sage considers each in greater detail. He begins with wealth, pursued through a strategy of selfishness (21:11–21, a palistrophe).

There are two characters who, instead of amassing wealth, must forfeit: the scoffer and the guilty. The scoffer is 'fined', with wealth-loss imposed by an external authority (21:11). 'Ruin' describes the demise of the guilty, inflicted by his own household – a case of internal collapse (v. 12).

These losses occurred because they determined to devalue others (21:13). They will experience ruin without rescue.

Financial loss accelerates, for selfish conduct has provoked another to anger (21:14). Only a bribe will silence the offended. Else his angry protest over injustice may reach the ears of the authorities.

In fact, the angry resentment of 21:14 escalates to file legal complaint against the perpetrator of 'disaster' (v. 15). If only he had been more observant, the guilty could have avoided mortal penalty – the sign of total loss (v. 16, a palistrophic core; cf. v. 11).

Next the sage explores what launches so selfish a pursuit of wealth. The pursuer has detected an inner void – a deficit of joy (21:17a). So he invests in shallow consumables ('wine and perfume', v. 17b). But all they generate is a drain on personal wealth.

As if financial loss were not bad enough, ultimately the guilty will forfeit his own person (21:18). Such is the eventual price of devaluing persons, epitomized by a contentious marriage (v. 19; caused by a self-absorbed husband as in vv. 9–10).

Instead of devaluing persons, 'treasure and perfume' can be obtained along a wiser route (21:20). That route consists of 'pursu[ing] equity and faithful love', and leads to prosperity far exceeding tangible wealth ('life, equity and honour', v. 21).

Block II.B (21:22–29). After elaborating wealth pursued through a strategy of selfishness (21:11–21, a palistrophe), in the next block the sage expands on power, when pursued through a strategy of abuse (21:22–29, also palistrophic).

With an initial wisdom commendation the poet shows that the wise can breach security that relies exclusively on military power (21:22). They achieve superiority by exerting the power of verbal self-control and restraint of appetites (v. 23). In contrast, power-abusers earn a reputation for spouting ridicule and for lording it over others (v. 24).

In reality, power-abusers cower as mortal captives of their own longings, strong only in their resolute refusal to exert effectual restraint over their wants-run-wild (21:25). Eventually their laziness will kill them.

Not so the moral. They display a winsome weakness, generously – even helplessly – meeting the needs of others (21:26b). Such is the paradoxical power of self-sacrifice.

When the guilty occasionally parade religious generosity, manipulative motives convert sweetness to stench. They imagine they can bribe God (21:27).

In addition to manipulating the divine, they presume through perjury to manipulate human judges, with deadly repercussions (21:28a). However, a judiciary characterized by attentive listening will not be fooled (v. 28b).

The exposition of momentary power that began in 21:22 concludes by confronting the pupil with a choice between two contrasting characters. The youth may emulate the guilty person (v. 29a), epitomized by the insolent scoffer (v. 24) who lazily (vv. 25–26) presumes to manipulate God and deceive others (vv. 27–28).

Or the youth may emulate the honest person (21:29b) who corresponds to victorious wisdom (v. 22), self-restraint combined with generosity (vv. 23, 26b), and trustworthy adjudication (v. 28b). Instead of inflicting fleeting power, such an individual constructs a durable highway – a life-route impervious to erosive floodwaters of moral compromise (v. 29bβ).

21:21. The trio of benefits 'life, equity and honour' is reminiscent of a stock description of well-being in Egyptian literature: *ankh*, *wedja*, *seneb*, 'life, prosperity and health'.

21:23. Mention of 'tongue' and 'appetite' in 21:23 telescopes and corrects mistakes and misfortune associated with these terms, found earlier in this lecture (cf. 21:6, 10).

21:24. Humility as reverence (22:4) resoundingly offsets the scoffer's attitude, who eventually will suffer expulsion (22:10).

21:25–26. By locating at the palistrophic core such a redundant description of the lazy person's myopic self-centredness, the sage implies that the fatal flaw of abused power (this block's theme) lies in its insipid preoccupation with self. Such a person amounts to a community parasite, a cosmic black hole of greedy narcissism.

Brueggemann insightfully analyses the existential error underlying greed:

> At the root of reality is a *limitless generosity* that intends an extravagant abundance. This claim is exposited in Israel's creation texts, sapiential traditions and hymnic exuberances. This insistence flies in the face of the theory of scarcity on which the modern world is built. An *ideology of scarcity* produces a competitiveness that issues in brutality, justifies policies of wars and aggression, authorizes an acute individualism, and provides endless anxiety about money, sexuality, physical fitness, beauty, work achievements, and finally mortality. It seems to me that, in the end, all of these anxieties are rooted in an ideology that resists a notion of limitless generosity and extravagant abundance. (1997: 559, emphasis original)

Section III (21:30 – 22:5). In Section III the sage concludes his evaluation of strategies in pursuit of wealth and power (Section IV will issue an afterword for instructors). The concept unifying this section is inadequacy. The poet begins by admitting that even wisdom proves inadequate, when 'appearing before the LORD' (21:30, a wisdom commendation).

Power and wealth (twin topics of this lecture) similarly prove inadequate. Even the mightiest of human powers – battle-ready chariotry – will fail when arrayed against the LORD (21:31). Immense wealth similarly falls short, surpassed by the worth of one's reputation (22:1a). Especially superior is a reputation infused with grace – the finest agent of robust and resilient relationships (22:1b; cf. 'grace' in 21:10 and generosity in 26). With arresting concision the sage declares simply, 'Grace is better' (22:1b).

Like the inadequacy of wisdom and power when encountering the LORD (21:30, 31), similarly wealth counts for naught before the divine (22:2). Yet one thread of wisdom may help – when one 'shrewd[ly]' observes that to oppose the LORD will bring 'misery'. That bit of insight should propel one humbly to seek safety (v. 3a). Instead to blunder naively onwards against the divine only forfeits wealth (v. 3b).

Returning to the lecture's study of right strategies, humility (illustrated by the safety-seeking shrewd person) constitutes the sole legitimate strategy. For humility marks the first step towards reverence, the true source of wealth (22:4). Beyond wealth, reverence also brings honour, together with the supreme good – life itself (v. 4b).

If, by disdaining humility, the youth foregoes 'wealth' (22:4), he will forfeit power as well. For, by pursuing instead a morally 'twisted' path, he will find himself powerless – hopelessly hooked and trapped (v. 5a). Only those strong enough to overpower their own appetites will successfully refuse the bait, thus steering clear of hook and trap, thereby preserving true freedom (v. 5b).

21:30. 'By the triple anaphoric hammer blows "there is no" [here rendered 'does not exist'], the proverb drives home the vast and unbridgeable gulf between the best of human wisdom and the LORD's sovereignty' (Waltke 2005: 191). Manipulative sacrifices illustrate presumptuous wisdom, so foolish before the divine (21:27).

21:31. Candidates for rescue referenced in this poem include victims of the violent (21:7), the overlooked helpless (21:13), city-dwellers whom warriors hold captive (21:22), persons suffering injustice (22:8) and violence (22:12b), and the oppressed (22:16).

22:1. The sage's recent esteem for generosity (21:26b) suggests that grace in 22:1 connotes favour extended to others, not received from others. When such an asset adorns one's reputation it will vastly surpass wealth of a merely material sort.

22:3. Shrewdness enabling evasive action recalls the importance of 'carefully observing', commended in 21:11, 12, 16.

22:4. Seldom in all of Proverbs does the trait of humility appear with such lucidity (compare Prov. 30:1–9). Humility leads to reverence, that supreme sapiential prize. Conversely, this lecture presents with unparalleled clarity the character of the scoffer (21:24). A strategy of humility upends the bankrupt scheme of abusive power (21:8, 22), cloaked in angry, presumptuous arrogance (21:24, 29a). By elevating humility to so high a rank, the sage reveals how hazardous is scoffing. So it follows that it is the scoffer (not the guilty person or false witness) who must be expelled (22:10).

Section IV (22:6–16). After presenting reverence as the sole effective strategy (22:4–5 in Section III), Section IV will turn from teaching youth, now to address teachers of youth (22:6–16).

Block IV.A (22:6–14). Opening with a wisdom commendation expressed as a command, the sage charges teachers (and parents) to begin training youth early (22:6). The curriculum should address wealth and power, starting with an axiom widely affirmed: wealth typically begets power (v. 7).

Such wealth-driven power exerted over the community will weaken and disappear, if wielded ruthlessly (22:8). If instead one channels wealth into generosity, then community affirmation will only grow stronger (v. 9; see 'Notes').

The next saying – a command – appears alarmingly out of place. The sage announces that his audience of fellow teachers must 'Drive out a scoffer!' (22:10; a palistrophic core). Drive him out? Who even noticed the scoffer had come in?

The scoffer is no stranger to this lecture. Early on, when levied a fine, he showed others how not to behave (21:11). Later he grew bolder, spouting insolence like an illegitimate overlord (21:24).

With the saying of 22:10 the lecture imagines the scoffer has now strategically reinserted himself, directly on the heels of the sage's clearest expression of this poem's supreme aim. In place of selfishly pursuing wealth and power, one should embrace a life strategy of generous acts (v. 9), stirred by pure motives, and conveyed by words gracious to the core (v. 11; the palistrophic partner to v. 9).

For the sage in 22:10 so stridently to warn against the scoffer can only mean that, precisely between these two climactic sayings (vv. 9, 11), the scoffer began launching a counter-campaign, employing his signature technique of ridicule to undermine the sage's closing appeal for grace and humility as the only effective strategies in life.

Alert to the scoffer's sedition (and aware that neither reprimand nor reprisal will avail against his strategy of derision), the sage cuts off the scoffer midstride, charging his fellow teachers forcibly to remove that troublemaker (22:10a). Only then can the lecture continue, uninterrupted by counterarguments of contempt (22:10b).

Now rid of the scoffer with his slanderous speech, the sage resumes his core counsel. Just as selfish pursuit of wealth must be displaced by generosity that generates favour (22:9), so teachers must train youths to embrace untainted motives and gracious words as the right route to rare human power (friendship-access to royalty, v. 11).

Those who, rejecting gracious words (22:11), prefer to brandish power through intimidating words will discover their 'threats' tossed harmlessly aside by the divine. For 'the LORD's eyes' safeguard 'knowledge'. Since none can fool the divine through simulated knowledge, he will neutralize their petty protests in the light of inexorable facts (v. 12).

As if overhearing the mention of hazard (22:12), the indolent proposes that the safest strategy would not take him beyond his own threshold (v. 13). Thus he renounces all power, even healthy personal initiative to engage wealth-generating marketplace activity. The sage does not even dignify with a response such a flimsy pretext. He trusts the audience will recall his earlier exposé of never-satisfied laziness (21:25–26; the palistrophic pinnacle of Block II.B).

With a stern warning the sage draws to a close his primary charge to teachers (22:6–14). A formidable catastrophe (tumbling into a treacherous pit) awaits those whose behaviour earns a divine curse (v. 14). Unlike v. 13, this report of hazard is not a concocted excuse.

Cleverly the sage labels the metaphoric opening of the trapper's pit as a 'mouth', a threefold organ of speech, appetite and – when belonging to 'strange women' – seduction. The concepts of hazardous speech and appetite appeared earlier in this lecture (speech in 21:6, 28 and 22:12, 13; appetite in 21:10, 17, 20, 23 [positive], 26). The seductive strange woman has not been seen since 7:5. Waltke regards her return in 22:14 as recalling Prov. 1 – 9, here at the close of 10:1 – 22:16 (2005: 210–211, 214). Propelled by their own values, the cursed fall into this pit.

In terms of persuasive impact, it is difficult to conceive of a threat more stirring than this risk of suicidal destruction (22:14). Such is the end of those who selfishly pursue wealth and power – a deadly demise resembling the foolish young man's fate in Prov. 7.

Block IV.B (22:15–16). Closing words to teachers admit that convincing youth to embrace right 'motives' may be difficult (22:15; right motives here are synonymous with right strategies). By escalating from 'training' youth (v. 6) to applying a 'rod of reproof' (v. 15), the sage intensifies the sense of urgency surrounding this task.

Dual-themes of power and wealth return in the lecture's last saying. Abusive power will not advance the abuser, but will backfire, causing the victim to 'increase' (22:16a). Conversely, bribery (giving to a wealthy person) will not help the donor acquire wealth. It will only reduce him to poverty (22:16b).

22:13. The adjacent terms 'without' and 'within' betray the confused excuse offered by the indolent. Although he claims his problem lies outside, beyond his control, in actuality his problem lies within (cf. 26:13).

22:14. Repeatedly in this lecture the sage has commended grace-laden relationships as the corrective to faulty strategies (21:9–10, 20–21; 22:9, 11). When at last this poem's unwise candidate takes an interest in relationships, he sadly succumbs to 'strange women' (22:14). Since 'deep pit' later describes a prostitute (23:27), also here it may warn against the hazard of illicit amorous attraction.

22:15. 'The father must not underestimate the difficulty of his task, for he does battle with an innate recalcitrance and perversity. He must both tear down and build up; eradicate and implant' (Waltke 2005: 216).

Explanation

Suitable means or 'strategies' in pursuit of worthy wealth and proper power comprise the thrust of this lecture. To begin with, the sage cautions against strategies that defeat the goals they seek to achieve.

Section I. Introduction: consider dual-theme of goals that fail, and the strategies that account for their failure (21:5–10)

The two presumptuous strategies most liable to defeat goals are selfish pursuit of wealth and self-centred use of power (21:6–7). Not only do they fail to deliver – they drag away their practitioners to death. The reason is simple: they devalue human relationships.

Section II. Principal teaching: consider the dual-themes of faulty strategies more closely (21:11–29)

Are we reluctant to decline a strategy of selfishly pursuing wealth (Block II.A, 21:11–21)? Then we must consider carefully the conduct and outcome of such a strategy. It is characterized by turning a deaf ear to the helpless. Those it has angered by unethical expedience, it silences with hush money. On the inevitable day of reckoning it must forfeit both wealth and life itself as a ransom to benefit the moral. Fragrance, life, equity and honour could have been theirs, if only they had rejected their self-centred strategy.

Do we subscribe to an abusive strategy in pursuit of power (Block II.B, 21:22–29)? If so, we must let the sage expose its fatal flaws. Power exerted to control others (instead of restraining our own selfish desires) fails to realize that one day it will atrophy to a sickly mass of wants with neither muscle nor spine to satisfy its own needs. Self-serving power amounts to a pretentious and pitiful black hole of narcissism.

But those with the power of self-control, who rule their appetites instead of the reverse – these flex the power required to take from their plenty and contribute to the needs of others, and incessantly so. The progress of the generous-moral person grows increasingly unassailable, day by day (21:29). Just as wealth gained by devious means brings no lasting prosperity, so also power brandished selfishly is powerless to supply security.

Section III. Conclusion: reverence – the ultimate strategy for power and wealth – begins with admission of inadequacies (21:30 – 22:5)

If we insist on selfish pursuit of wealth and self-centred use of power, then we ourselves are numbered among those seduced into supposing that our wisdom and power reign supreme. We have forgotten that 'grace is better', and superlatively so (22:1b).

If the sage's warning awakens any spark of hesitancy, any fear lest our wealth in the final analysis might prove insufficient, lest our power ultimately might prove inadequate – then the sage counsels us to replace our scoffer-like mentality, embracing a new strategy instead.

What strategy, we ask? It is this: abandoning all self-assured pretence, and aware of the divine, we must embrace the strategy of humility. With appetites thus in check we will remain truly free from otherwise-inevitable traps. Then we will enjoy genuine wealth, authentic honour and a life most deeply fulfilling (22:4).

Section IV. Advice for instructors: train youth in the worthy use of wealth and the proper use of power (22:6–16)

Aware that his career as discipler-of-youth one day will draw to a close, and aware that even while he lives he cannot reach all the youth who need his counsel, the sage concludes with a challenge issued to any entrusted with influence over the next generation. We must waste no time impressing on them the importance of exercising care when choosing life strategies. If a youth is fortunate enough to gain wealth and power, he must take care not to slip into self-destructive patterns of power abuse. He must train himself to recognize the other as a guest worthy of kindness (cf. 21:10b, 22:9, 11).

Do some of our pupils respond with scoffing? Set them outside (22:10). Do not allow their ridicule to recruit even one more to their arrogant and incorrigible ignorance.

Do any fear the force of another's false testimony? Assure them that the LORD knows and safeguards the truth (22:12).

Do any fear the risk attending healthy personal initiative? Confront them with the fact that such fear is only indolence masquerading as caution (22:13). Do any still love their laziness? Show them the cunning trap into which their appetites will sweetly lead them – a delicious pit of no return (v. 14).

Do not shrink from such confrontation, for certain sorts of folly will not release their young prisoners except by concerted intervention. Remind the youth that faulty strategies fail equally, whether by ruthless treatment of the helpless (22:16a; cf. 21:7), or through selfish pursuit of wealth (22:16b; cf. 21:6).

Remind them that strategies of oppressive power and selfish pursuit of wealth can be counted on never to satisfy. Instead challenge them to gather wealth so as to give, as though their very life depended on graciousness (22:1b)! And urge them to demonstrate the superiority of their power by controlling themselves so much that they are able to bow deeply before the supreme power of their Maker.

The sage's cautions concerning the absolute poverty of selfish wealth and the utter impotence of self-serving power offer teachings profoundly needed in a modern culture conditioned by self-centred materialism and Western individualism. Only humility before the divine and gracious regard for our neighbour will yield the rich and fulfilling lives for which all long. For neither the accumulation of wealth nor the aggregation of power, but gracious investment in relationships alone, will safeguard against lack.

PROVERBS 22:17 – 24:34
'As I now venture out, what objective must I pursue, above all?'

Overview of Proverbs 22:17 – 24:34

The lecture spanning Prov. 22:17 – 24:34 draws to a close the teachings that began in Prov. 10 (Division II). The next division of lectures begins in 25:1 with an authorship attribution on a par with 1:1 and 10:1, extending until Agur is introduced as the author in 30:1.

Whereas lectures beginning in Prov. 25 will envision pupils already employed as royalty or as councillors in the royal court, the poem spanning 22:17 – 24:34 pictures pupils standing on the brink of such a career. Soon they will be commissioned to discover facts about judicial cases (22:21; 24:23–26). Privileges previously unavailable will now present themselves (22:22–25). Onlookers will begin to envy their new wealth (22:26–27) due to new employment (22:29) in positions accompanied by upscale social events (23:1–3, 6–8) hosted in lavish settings – scenes quite novel for the youth, and potentially intoxicating, whether metaphorically (23:4–5) or literally (23:29–35).

To guard against the heady influences of forthcoming privileges, in this lecture the sage carefully reinforces character boundaries. Confidence must remain anchored in the LORD rather than relying on career advancement (22:19). Twice the sage warns against manipulating moral margins: 'Do not move an ancient boundary' (22:28a; 23:10a). It appears that with this lecture the sage responds to the pupil's implicit question 'As I now venture out, what objective must I pursue, above all?'

Position of this poem within Proverbs

Preceding context. The previous lecture (Prov. 22:5 – 22:16) cautioned against selfishly pursuing wealth and abusively wielding power, urging humility, grace and generosity instead. By safeguarding society's 'helpless' (22:16), the final sentiment of that previous lecture anticipates the first wisdom content of the present (v. 22; after wisdom commendations comprising Section I, vv. 17–21).

Ensuing context. After the present lecture, there commence four poems comprising a master lecture extending through Prov. 29, opening with the authorship statement 'These, too, are Solomonic proverbs, which the men of Hezekiah, king of Judah, arranged' (25:1). That four-poem series will address the implicit question 'How may a monarchy attain magnificence?'

Similarities to The Instruction of Amenemope

Several parallels between Proverbs and the Egyptian sapiential composition *The Instruction of Amenemope* have been observed since the latter's English translation appeared in 1922. The poet of *Amenemope* designed that work from the outset with thirty theme-related chapters (plus an introduction and brief colophon).

My examination of hieratic palaeography preserved on the Cairo Ostracon EM 1840-4 (the earliest attestation of *Amenemope*), courtesy of the staff of the Egyptian Museum, confirms preliminary conclusions of Georges Posener, who dated the inscribed potsherd to the Nineteenth or Twentieth Dynasties of the Ramesside era (1295–1069 BC; Posener 1975: 195). Statistical evidence finds the closest correlation to palaeographic samples from the era of Ramesses IV (1153–1147 BC).

The Cairo Ostracon was a practice copy written on a somewhat rectangular, convex fragment of pottery measuring 14.5 cm by 14.5 cm (6 in. by 6 in.), with a handle in the lower left corner. It was inscribed after being broken. The fragment was discovered by Howard Carter in the Valley of the Kings during his 1917–18 excavation season, while searching for the tomb of King Tutankhamun. Attestation in this form helps classify *Amenemope* as a schoolboy text – one of several compositions routinely assigned for copying by pupils to train in literacy and grammar, while also transmitting moral values.

As a schoolboy text, *Amenemope* must have been composed, initially, decades before the Cairo Ostracon – consequently originating over two centuries before the time of Solomon. This dating together with the Hebr. poet's attentiveness to *Amenemope*'s structure (evident from the selective parallels in Proverbs) combine to suggest that the Hebr. sage studied truths found in the Egyptian work for adaptation and inclusion in the inspired Hebr. canon (Overland 1996; for adaptations, see 22:23 and 23:5 under 'Comment', below). Further, the fact that it was copied repeatedly as a schoolboy text adds to the diffusion and portability of this Egyptian composition. Like the Hebr. poet, the apostle Paul in Athens similarly would draw from the literature of a neighbouring culture (Acts 17:28).

Unless otherwise indicated, translations of *Amenemope* found here are my own. For an excellent summary of theories connecting Proverbs and *Amenemope*, see Fox 2009: 753–769. For further discussion of the sage's use of *Amenemope*, see §5.11 in the 'Introduction'. Concerning inclusion of non-Israelites among biblical authors, see §6 in the 'Introduction'.

What to watch for

Seven features distinguish the structure and themes of this lecture. First, watch for wisdom commendations and the sectioning they may signal. Second, in Sections I and III notice references to truth in connection with durability and reverence, in contrast to ephemeral pleasures associated with dissipation. Third, beginning in Section II notice references to literal and metaphoric shifting of boundaries. Mention of fields (bounded regions) in Section IV adds to this theme. Fourth, in Sections II and III consider the theme of rescue. Fifth, in Section III observe multiple 'my son' vocatives. Consider what these may indicate concerning the intended audience, in concert with reproof in that section's initial three sayings. Sixth, also in Section III notice mention and placement of sayings concerning reverence. Seventh, observe dual-theme structures, whether narrow, broad or even operating as a recap (24:19–20; cf. 22:16).

Translation and outline

Verse	*Translation*	*Outline*
		I. Introductory wisdom commendations: for learners, for teachers (22:17–21) A. Wisdom commendation and rationale for wisdom learners (22:17–19)

22:17 Incline your ear and listen to sayings of the wise, and let your mind take note of my knowledge, 22:18 Since it is delightful when you preserve them in your belly, let them be arranged together on your lips. 22:19 So that in the LORD your confidence may lie, I have made known to you today, especially you.	1. Wisdom commendation for wisdom learners (22:17–18) 2. Rationale for learning wisdom: trust in the divine (22:19)
22:20 Have I not written for you, for some time, concerning counsels and knowledge, 22:21 To make known to you verity, words of truth, so you may return words – truth to those who send you?	B. Wisdom commendation and rationale for wisdom teachers (wisdom transmitters, 22:20–21) 1. Wisdom commendation concerning wisdom teachers (wisdom transmitters, 22:20) 2. Rationale for teaching wisdom: to train a truthful respondent (22:21)
22:22 Do not rob the helpless because he is helpless, and do not crush the oppressed in court. 22:23 For the LORD will argue their case, and will steal from those who would steal from them – life. 22:24 Do not befriend a master-of-anger, and with a person known for wrath you must never venture.	II. Wisdom content: instructions for pupil as wisdom learner, to counteract the allure of boundary-shifting (22:22 – 23:11) A. The allure of flawed boundary-shifting pursuits, and a positive alternative (22:22–29) 1. Three flawed boundary-shifting pursuits, with summary (22:22–28) a. The hazard of shifting boundaries that protect against abuse of legal power, with rationale (22:22–23) b. The hazard of shifting boundaries that protect others against over-retaliation, with rationale (22:24–25)

Verse	*Translation*	*Outline*
22:25	Lest you learn his path and consequently snatch for yourself a life-threatening snare.	
22:26	Do not be among those who shake hands, among those who guarantee loans.	c. The hazard of shifting boundaries that protect oneself against economic insolvency, with rationale (22:26–27)
22:27	If you have no means of repaying, why should he snatch your bed out from under you?	
22:28	Do not move an ancient boundary, that your ancestors had made.	d. Summary concerning boundaries: shifting time-tested boundaries invokes dishonour (22:28)
22:29	You have observed, no doubt, a person efficient in his occupation: before kings he will become stationed; he will not become stationed before obscure folk.	2. The positive alternative to boundary-shifting: diligent industry (22:29)
		B. The defect inherent within boundary-shifting pursuits, with summary (23:1–11) 1. The defect within boundary-shifting pursuits: illusive and elusive gains (23:1–8)
23:1	If you sit down to dine along with a ruler, be very perceptive concerning what is before you.	a. Don't let illusive morsels tantalize you (23:1–3)
23:2	And put a knife to your throat if you are a master-of-appetite.	
23:3	Do not crave his dainty morsels, given that they are deceptive food.	
23:4	Do not wear yourself out to generate wealth; stop supposing that your insight is adequate.	b. Don't let elusive wealth captivate you (23:4–5)
23:5	Do your eyes soar after it? But it is nowhere, for it most certainly will produce for itself wings like an eagle and a sense of exhaustion stretching to the heavens.	

23:6 Do not dine along with food of a miserly fellow, and do not crave his dainty morsels. 23:7 For, just as he has calculated according to his own appetite, that is the sort of person he is. 'Eat and drink!' he may say to you, but his motives are not in league with you. 23:8 Your morsel you ate – you will vomit it up, and you will have wasted your delightful comments.	c. Don't let illusive generosity poison you (23:6–8)
23:9 Into the ears of a stupid fellow do not speak, for he will despise the common sense of your remarks. 23:10 Do not move an ancient boundary, and into orphans' fields do not even enter. 23:11 For their redeemer is strong; he it is who will argue their case against you.	2. Summary about boundaries: the inviolability of boundaries, with rationale (23:9–11) a. Wisdom commendation: wasted effort in teaching (23:9) b. Wisdom content: wasted, hazardous effort in shifting boundaries (23:10–11)
23:12 Present your mind for reproof and your ears for words of knowledge. 23:13 Do not withhold reproof from a youth, for although you may strike him with a rod, he will not die. 23:14 Take responsibility yourself to strike him with a stick, and you will rescue his life from Sheol.	III. Wisdom content: instructions for pupil as wisdom teacher, concerning the sole objective worthy of youth's pursuit (23:12 – 24:22) A. Introductory charge to wisdom teachers: the urgency of reproof, for rescue (23:12–14) 1. Wisdom commendation for wisdom teacher: model personal receptivity to reproof (23:12) 2. Dual-theme wisdom content for wisdom teacher: administer reproof, so as to secure rescue (23:13–14)

Verse	*Translation*	*Outline*
		B. Scripts to use when training learners about longings (23:15 – 24:22) 1. A script to restrain from longing after the way of dissipation, choosing reverence instead (23:15 – 24:14) a. Introduction to competing longings, whether for dissipation or for reverence (23:15–25)
23:15	My son, if your mind is wise, my own mind will rejoice as well.	i. Introductory wisdom commendation: parental joy due to wisdom (23:15–16)
23:16	And my inner being will celebrate when your lips speak what is honest.	
		ii. Wisdom content: behave with the future in view, not to achieve short-term gains (23:17–23)
23:17	May your mind not long after sinners, but rather long after reverence for the Lord, all the day long.	α. Dual-theme introduction: let not longings take the 'immediate view' (dissipation), but the 'future view' (wisdom as reverence, 23:17–18)
23:18	Most certainly there is a future, and then your hope will not be cut off.	
23:19	You, my son: listen and be wise! And lead your mind straight in the way.	β. First theme: do not take the 'immediate view', longing after dissipation (wisdom commendation and content, 23:19–21)
23:20	Do not be among those who drink wine to excess; with those who squander flesh for their own use.	
23:21	For a drunkard and a glutton will be bankrupted, and drowsiness will clothe with rags.	
23:22	Listen to your father: it is he who begot you; and do not despise your mother since she is elderly.	γ. Second theme: instead take the 'future view', longing for wisdom (wisdom commendation and content, 23:22–23)
23:23	Truth is what you must acquire and not sell – wisdom and reproof and insight.	

23:24 The father of a moral fellow will be overjoyed; he begot a wise fellow and so rejoices in him. 23:25 May your father and your mother rejoice, and may she who bore you be joyful.	i'. Concluding wisdom commendation: parental joy due to morality of child (23:24–25)
23:26 My son, give your mind to me, and may mine be the ways in which your eyes take pleasure. 23:27 For a prostitute is a trapper's deep pit, and a foreign woman is a narrow well. 23:28 In fact, as a robber she lies in ambush, and she will proliferate the treacherous among mortals. 23:29 Who exclaims, 'Alas!'? Who exclaims, 'Woe!'? Who has a hankering for a fight? Who has complaints? Who has unexplained bruises? Who has bloodshot eyes? 23:30 Those who linger over the wine, those who go in quest of spiced wine. 23:31 Do not look at wine when it glows rose-coloured, when it sparkles the cup; it will encounter no resistance as it makes its way down. 23:32 In its future – like a serpent it will bite, and like an adder will sting. 23:33 Your eyes will see strange things, and your mind will make seditious statements. 23:34 And you will be like one who lies down in the heart of the sea, and like one who lies down, high in the rigging.	b. By longing after dissipation, you will suffer captivity (23:26 – 24:2) i. Dual-theme wisdom commendation: buttressing mind and eyes (23:26) ii. First wisdom content: from the captivity of dissipation in sexual appetites you will require rescue (23:27–28) iii. Second wisdom content: from the captivity of dissipation in alcoholic appetites you will require rescue (23:29–35)

Verse	*Translation*	*Outline*
23:35	'They struck me – I didn't get hurt; they pummelled me – I was oblivious. When will I come around? I will do it again: I am going to hunt for it, yet again!'	
24:1	Do not long after people disposed to evil, and do not desire to be with them.	iv. Recap imperative: longing for dissipation leads to destruction (24:1–2)
24:2	For devastation is what their mind will contemplate, and harm is what their lips will speak.	
		c. By longing after wisdom instead, you will free others from captivity (24:3–14) i. Sincere wisdom brings security, enabling rescue of others (24:3–6)
24:3	By wisdom a house will be built, and by perception it will be firmly established.	α. Wisdom commendation: wisdom brings stability and riches (24:3–4)
24:4	And through knowledge rooms will become filled with all sorts of valuable treasure and delightful things.	
24:5	It is the warrior who is wise, who embodies authentic strength, and it is a knowledgeable person who amasses power.	β. Wisdom content: wisdom enables one to rescue others (24:5–6)
24:6	For through practical experience you can wage your own war, and you can bring about deliverance through an abundance of counsel.	
		ii. Counterfeit wisdom (similarly ignorance) inflicts harm and thwarts rescue (24:7–12)

24:7 Lofty is wisdom, for a fool; in court he cannot open his mouth. 24:8 He strategizes to do himself harm; 'Master-of-scheming!' they will call out. 24:9 A fool's scheming is a sin, but abhorrent to humankind is a scoffer. 24:10 You proved feeble in a day of calamity: your power is constricted. 24:11 Rescue those who are being carried off to death, and those who would be tottering towards slaughter, if you were to keep to yourself! 24:12 Suppose you say, 'Look: we did not know about this!' He who weighs motives, can he not perceive? He who watches over your life, will he not know? Further, will he not repay to a mortal according to his deed?	α. Negative wisdom commendation: the harm of counterfeit wisdom (24:7–9) β. Negative wisdom content: a cowardly counterfeit of ignorance thwarts rescue of others (24:10–12)
24:13 My son, eat honey for it is good, for a honeycomb is sweet in your mouth. 24:14 In the same fashion, know wisdom experientially, as if your life depended on it; if you have discovered it, then there is a future and your hope will not be cut off.	iii. Recap imperative and conclusion: freely indulge wisdom longings, as if for survival, to attain hoped-for future (24:13–14)
	2. A script to restrain longings inspired by the guilty, choosing reverence instead (24:15–22) a. Focus not on longings regarding the guilty, whether of envy or revenge (24:15–20)

Verse *Translation*	*Outline*
24:15 Do set an ambush, O guilty person, for the residence of a moral person. Do not destroy his resting place. 24:16 For seven times a moral fellow will fall and will keep on getting up; but guilty folk will get tripped up by wickedness.	i. Refrain from longings of envy that would imitate advantages of the guilty, since they will fall permanently (24:15–16)
24:17 When your enemies fall, do not rejoice, and when he is tripped up, keep your mind from celebrating. 24:18 Lest the LORD would see and regard it as wicked, and divert his anger from against him.	ii. Refrain from longings of revenge that celebrate demise of guilty, since that would incur divine displeasure (24:17–18)
24:19 Refrain from rising anger about wicked folk. Do not long after guilty folk. 24:20 Because a future cannot materialize for the wicked person; the lamp of guilty folk will go out.	iii. Dual-theme recap: refrain both from longings against the guilty (revenge) and from longings towards them (envy), since their future is dark (24:19–20)
	b. Focus instead on reverence (24:21–22)
24:21 Revere the LORD, my son, and the king; do not get mixed up with people who shift.	i. Imperative: revere superiors, withdraw from changelings (24:21)
24:22 For suddenly their disaster will arise; and the ruin associated with both of them, who can know?	ii. Rationale: certitude of sudden demise by superiors (24:22)
	IV. Recap concerning boundaries: cautions against trespassing, and exhortations to industry (24:23–34) A. Cautions against trespassing, and a call to industry within boundaries (24:23–27) 1. Take care how you respond to enticements to trespass outside boundaries (24:23–26)

24:23 These, too, pertain to the wise. To show favouritism in court proceedings is not good. 24:24 One who says to a guilty person, 'You are moral,' kin will curse him; nations will denounce him. 24:25 But for those who issue reprimands it will be delightful, and to them will come a blessing of goodness. 24:26 He would kiss the lips – who returns sayings that are straight. 24:27 Prepare your occupation outside, and for your own benefit make it ready in the field belonging to you; then, afterwards, build your house.	a. Do not respond with collusion, relabelling immoral conduct in court (for wisdom learners, 24:23–24) b. Rather, respond with confrontation, issuing reproof (for wisdom teachers, 24:25–26) 2. Take care to venture outside, cultivating a crop within your boundaries (24:27)
24:28 Do not witness against your neighbour without cause. Now, have you persuaded with your lips? 24:29 Do not say, 'Just as he did to me, I will do to him. I will repay the man according to his deed.'	B. The insufficiency of boundary-observance, without industry (24:28–34) 1. Do not respond to trespass-enticement with envy or revenge (24:28–29) a. Do not respond with unprovoked litigious envy (24:28) b. Do not respond with revenge (24:29)
24:30 I walked through a field belonging to a person given to laziness, and through the vineyard of a mortal who lacked sense. 24:31 Look! All over it, thistles had sprung up, weeds covered its surface; and its perimeter wall of stones was broken down.	2. Instead plough your field: a negative story about indolence, despite boundaries (24:30–34) a. Registering a wisdom observation: an autobiographical chronicle of uncovering wisdom (24:30–31)

Verse *Translation*	*Outline*
24:32 Then I myself observed, my mind began to take note; I saw, I gained reproof. 24:33 A little sleep, a little slumber, a little folding of the hands to lie down, 24:34 So your poverty will come prowling, and your insolvency – like an armed man.	b. Converting that wisdom observation into a wisdom expression: without industry, respecting boundaries cannot prevent poverty (24:32–34)

Notes on the text

For *Amenemope* parallels, please see under 'Comment', below.

22:17. 'take note': lit. 'place'. The imperative mood of 'incline' and 'listen' in 22:17a continues with this yiq. verb.

22:18. 'let them be arranged', *yikkōnû*: juss. indicated by phrase-initial syntax (contrast phrase-terminal ind. *yikkōnû*, 4:26b).

22:20–21. 'Have I not written for you, for some time', *hălōʾ kātabtî lĕkâ šilšôm*: instead of K *šilšôm*, 'for some time', NRSV, NIV, ESV prefer Q *šālišîm*, 'thirty'. NJPS renders, 'a threefold lore', evidently following *trissōs*, 'threefold', of LXX. The K spelling *šilšôm* (with waw representing a *holem*-waw vowel) indicates that the earliest preserved vocalization understood this term as 'for some time', 'recently', 'in the past', 'previously' (*DCH*, s.v. '*šilšôm*'; cf. 1 Sam. 3:17; 2 Sam. 5:2). Prior to the provision of vowel letters the text remained ambiguous, conveying either 'for some time' or 'thirty'. Adding the vowel letter waw removed that ambiguity. When vowel points were subsequently supplied, they testified to *šālišîm* as a later reading tradition, preserved in the Q.

The rhetorical question 'Have I not written for you?' illumines the K–Q variant. That question retrospectively urges the pupil to notice that his training has been progressing over a considerable span of time, leading up to this point in Proverbs (so also Whybray 1994a: 134). That training would trace at least to its beginning in Prov. 10 (Division II, Prov. 10 – 24), and perhaps to Prov. 1. The pupil's training has indeed progressed 'for some time'.

Since several sayings in Prov. 22 – 24 resemble portions of the Egyptian *Amenemope* with its thirty theme-cohesive chapters, the similarity between the K *šilšôm*, 'for some time', and *šālišîm*, 'thirty' (preferred by Q) may comprise a wordplay designed by the Israelite author. For, Amenemope (who composed his text before 1150 BC) inventoried his 'thirty' sayings at a retrospective point, at the outset of his final chapter: 'You see for yourself these thirty chapters – they please, they educate' (*Amenemope* col. 27, lines

7–8 [ch. 30.1–2]; Overland 1996: 282). The numeral thirty epitomized justice – the domain of Ma'at, goddess of wisdom in the culture of ancient Egypt (Ray 1995: 23). By using the Hebr. expression *šilšôm*, 'for some time', with its close resemblance to *šālišîm*, 'thirty', and by using it at a retrospective point comparable to when *Amenemope* refers to 'thirty', was likely the Israelite sage's way of subtly acknowledging awareness of – even indebtedness to – the Egyptian document, without implying that his own collection would number thirty teachings.

Therefore it seems unwise to continue past attempts to isolate and enumerate thirty teachings within this lecture. Assuming the word in question was *šālišîm*, several have proposed various clusters of sayings that total thirty (e.g. Fox, who divides 22:17 – 24:22 into thirty teachings [2009: 705], and Waltke [2005: 217–286]). Yet this interpretation dismisses the retrospective pause plainly signalled by *šilšôm* (Whybray 1994c: 88). Further, the quest to isolate thirty sayings (without internal prioritization) weakens the text by causing wisdom commendations (generally introductory in nature) to be elevated to the same priority as wisdom content (which routinely carries more weight than its corresponding commendation). For example, some prioritize the introductory wisdom commendation in 23:15–16 as an isolated instruction, while artificially bundling the concluding wisdom commendation of 23:24–25 with the commendation-and-content of 23:22–23 (so Waltke 2005: 253–254, 258–259). Instead to accept *šilšôm* as written ('for some time') frees interpreters from the obligation to force the lecture into exactly thirty teachings. Only then can one experience the lecture's native texture, allowing it to speak as it will, distinguishing wisdom commendations from content, which content consists of multiple-but-related themes and recaps.

The retrospective intent of *šilšôm*, meaning 'for some time [past]' (22:20), is reinforced by the fact that in the MT a major break appears only one verse later (following v. 21). Thus 22:21 is separated from v. 22 by a *pětuḥâ*, 'open [space]' – a blank portion extending from the last word in the Hebr. of v. 21, all the way to the left margin (Hebr. reads right-to-left). In the MT preserved in Codex Leningradensius this *pětuḥâ* is unmistakable, occupying an entire line. Verse 22 begins on the next line.

Since no space (whether a shorter *sětumâ*, 'closed [space]', or the longer *pětuḥâ*) appears between (a) the lecture-concluding sayings of 22:15–16 and (b) the lecture-opening wisdom commendation of vv. 17–21, this suggests that the Masoretes regarded 22:17–21 (grouped in the outline as Section I) as more closely connected with what preceded, rather than connecting to what would follow in v. 22 (which begins Section II, extending through 23:11). Such would fit with *šilšôm* meaning 'for some time [prior]', by focusing attention on the teaching delivered up to this point. For the writer of Prov. 10 – 24 in this fashion to begin the last lecture (22:17 – 24:34) by referencing earlier material lends a seamless cohesion to the whole of Division II (Prov. 10 – 24).

22:21. 'so you may return words', *lĕhāšîb ʾămārîm*: 'to return words' (or 'sayings', 24:26) connotes a judicial environment (cf. 'in the gate' in 22:22, 'to argue a case' in 22:23, 'court proceedings' in 24:23). 'Verity', *qōšṭ*, reinforces a judicial framework (22:21). In Arab. *qōšṭ*, 'equity, justice', may describe a verdict or sentence based on truth that has been unearthed during the discovery phase of judicial proceedings. So one may paraphrase 22:21b, 'so that in court cases you may recognize what is the truth when confronted with conflicting testimonies, and so you may return a fair verdict to the one who sent or applied for it'. In case the judicial accusation is unfounded, the verdict/words-returned would constitute a reproof (see under 'Comment' for 22:21). Thus those 'senders' (22:21b) anticipate persons who in the future may seek the pupil's help in ascertaining what is fair.

'verity, words of truth, so you may return words – truth to those who send you', *qōšṭ ʾimrê ʾĕmet lĕhāšîb ʾămārîm lĕšōlĕḥeykā*: again to specify 'truth' after the phrase 'you may return words' is syntactically jarring, intentionally underscoring the high priority the sage places on avoiding duplicity. The priority surrounding truth is underscored with redundancy in 23:23. With Fox to delete the second mention of 'truth' in 22:21 may achieve smoothness, but comes at the expense of pungency (2009: 713).

22:22. 'Do not rob the helpless because he is helpless', *ʾal-tigzāl-dāl kî dal-hûʾ*: considerable assonance unifies v. 22a. As in English, so in Hebr., 'because he is helpless' may explain both the ease of such exploitation and its inexcusability (similarly 23:22).

'in court': lit. 'in the gate', where judicial proceedings would transpire.

22:23. 'life', *nāpeš*: of seven references to *nepeš* in this lecture, twice the context recommends rendering 'appetite' (23:2, 7), with 'life' or 'life-threatening' better-fitting the remainder (22:23, 25; 23:14; 24:12, 14). By delaying 'life' until the end of 22:23, it describes both what the aggressors steal (victim's life) and what they will forfeit (aggressors' life; Waltke 2005: 231–232).

22:24b. 'you must never venture', *lōʾ tābôʾ*: this legislative negation is more far-reaching than the more urgent but scope-limited juss. negated in v. 24a ('Do not befriend').

22:25. 'his path': rather than pl. 'his paths' (Q), the sg. 'his path' (K) communicates a more finely delineated character trait of habitual anger.

'a life-threatening snare', *môqēš lĕnapšekā*: lit. 'a snare for your life' (see 'Notes' for 22:23 concerning *nāpeš*).

22:26. 'Do not be among those who shake hands': 'to be among' describes shared identity, not mere proximity (cf. Prov. 23:20a; Amos 1:1). To 'shake hands' sealed an agreement (cf. 6:1).

22:27. 'why should he snatch': one who would snatch may be the creditor, or even the defaulting borrower, come to claim pledged collateral before surrendering it to his creditor.

22:28. 'Do not move': this refers to boundary relocation, not removal (as also Waltke 2005: 226, NASB, NIV; *pace* NRSV). Complete removal would surely be faulted. But subtle encroachment may go unnoticed (Fox 2009: 718; cf. 23:10).

'your ancestors': lit. 'your fathers'.

'had made': plpf. inferred from context of antiquity implied by 'ancestors'.

22:29. 'You have observed, no doubt', *ḥāzîtā*: lit. 'you have observed'. Hebr. can express polar questions (yes/no) without the interrogative particle *hă* (Joüon §161a and *IBHS* §40.3b). On that basis it has been customary to render the literal Hebr. 'You have observed' in Prov. 22:29 as 'Have you observed . . . ?' When embedded within a speech or teaching (as here, rather than reporting a question–answer exchange), such a question would be rhetorical, with an affirmative answer assumed. The net result conveys a forceful declaration, 'I am sure that you have observed . . . !'; hence, 'You have seen, no doubt' (cf. 26:12; 29:20).

'efficient', *māhîr*: connotes speed. When associated with an occupation, *māhîr* envisions one who, upon receiving an assignment, executes it with optimal skill, without grumbling.

23:2. 'a master-of-appetite', *baʿal nepeš*: *baʿal* may indicate either control or proficiency. As control, it implies, 'If you truly are in control of your appetite, then you will be able to apply self-restraint.' As proficiency, it implies, 'If you have become one proficient at eating, then you had better change your ways and begin to apply self-restraint!' Reference to eating in 23:1–3 recommends *nepeš* as 'appetite' (as in v. 7) rather than 'life' (as in 22:25; 23:14; 24:12, 14). The 'master-of' idiom was earlier associated with fowl (1:17) and more recently with persons inclined to anger (22:24a).

23:3. 'given that they are', *wĕhûʾ*: lit. 'and that is'. The two cola of this verse are concomitant (paratactic), exposing the host's sinister nature.

23:4. 'stop supposing that your insight is adequate', *mibbînātĕkā ḥădāl*: lit. 'from your insight, desist'. Since the sage recently urged cultivation of insight (23:1b), the flaw here must involve overestimating one's powers of perception. Waltke renders, 'stop trusting in your own insight' (2005: 226; cf. 3:5).

23:5. 'Do your eyes soar . . . ?', *hătāʿôp ʿêneykā*: reading with K, so that a f. pl. noun ('your eyes') serves as the subject for a f. sg. verb ('it soars', not the expected 'they soar'). This sg./pl. disparity is attested elsewhere in the HB (Joüon §150b). Q proposes smoothing by vocalizing the verb as 2 m. sg. hiph. (*hătāʿîp ʿêneykā*, 'Do you cause your eyes to soar . . . ?'), while diminishing the K sense of eyes soaring involuntarily.

'your eyes . . . But it is nowhere', *ʿêneykā wĕʾênennû*: assonance joins these expressions, located nearer each other in Hebr. than in English.

'and a sense of exhaustion stretching to the heavens', *wĕʿāyēp haššāmāyim*: lit. 'and the weariness of the heavens'. As a substantive, the adj. *ʿāyēp*, 'weary', is in const. with 'the heavens', conveying colossal fatigue (cf. *ʿăyēpâ* in 25:25). Since the exact expression *wĕʿāyēp* occurs twice elsewhere with the meaning 'weary', it is unclear why some regard it 'an impossible form' (*pace* Fox 2009: 724; 2 Sam. 17:29; Ps. 63:1 [MT v. 2]).

The Q alternative with its proposed emendation of *yāʿûp* would surely yield a phrase easily fitting the context. *Yāʿûp haššāmāyim* would mean 'it will fly [to] the heavens' (resembling *tāʿûp bāššāmāyim* in Deut. 4:17, though lacking the customary prep. 'towards', whether *bĕ* as in Deut. 4:17, or *ʾel* as in Isa. 6:6). The nominal expression *ʿôp haššāmāyim*, 'birds of the sky', occurs twenty times (e.g. Job 12:7; Ezek. 38:20).

Yet the spelling *ʿāyēp*, which the sage provided, does not mean 'it will fly', *yāʿûp*, but 'weariness [of]'. The concept of 'weariness' fits the context since it links the quatrain's closing expression (weariness) with its first and foundational thought ('Do not wear yourself out', 23:4a). By assonance with 'it will fly' (*yāʿûp* proposed in Q), *ʿāyēp* also links the soaring of one's eyes towards wealth ('Do your eyes soar [*tāwûp*] after it?' in v. 5a), with the elusiveness of wing-sprouting wealth ('it most certainly will produce for itself wings like an eagle', v. 5b).

Thus 23:5 teaches that to obsess over wealth-generation will 'certainly produce' two results (not one). In the first, it will produce a pair of metaphoric wings sprouting from the wealth, removing it beyond reach, thereby defeating the entire enterprise of wealth acquisition. Second, obsessing over wealth-generation will produce a towering sense of weariness ('stretching to the heavens'), due to the futility of the enterprise. Such an obsession will surely deplete anyone thus preoccupied, consigning him or her to a consuming sense of exhaustion. The alternative spelling proposed by the Q (*yāʿûp*, 'it will fly', in place of *wĕʿāyēp*, 'and the weariness of'), while fitting smoothly with the notion of 'making wings', would forfeit the skilfully orchestrated wordplay and imagery of colossal weariness conveyed by the original (the K).

23:6. 'Do not dine along with food of a miserly fellow', *ʾal-tilĕḥōm ʾet leḥem raʿ ʿāyin*: the redundancy of the Hebr. idiom (root *lḥm* in both 'dine' and 'food') clarifies that this segment (23:6–9) resumes the topic of consumption-restraint already introduced in an earlier segment (vv. 1–3).

It is possible that the particle *ʾet* in *ʾet leḥem*, 'with food', is not the prep. 'with', but the particle marking a direct object, despite absence of the customary definite article (cf. *IBHS* §10.3.1.b). However, the poet's sophisticated compositional skills, together with his penchant for issuing intentionally jarring expressions (cf. §5.7 in the 'Introduction'), recommends treating this phrase as customary grammar (*ʾet* as 'with'), parallel to dining 'along with [*ʾet*] a ruler' in 23:1. In v. 6, we expect the host as a dining companion. Instead the dining companion jarringly consists of food offered by that host (a stingy person, incidentally). Fixation with food (cf. vv. 2–3) has thus rendered the eater oblivious to the presence of the host. Such food-fixation fits precisely the message of vv. 6–9, where one risks a bad reaction after blindly devouring savoury morsels, heedless of the malevolent character of the host who spread the alluring table.

As may be expected, one Hebr. manuscript (also LXX) replaced the jarring expression with a simpler reading, 'Do not dine along with a miserly fellow' (similarly NRSV, NASB, NIV). The more difficult MT reading is preferable.

23:7. 'according to his own appetite', *bĕnapšô*: as in 23:2, the context of dining in 23:6–8 recommends *nepeš* as 'appetite', not 'life' (contrast 22:25; 23:14; 24:12, 14).

23:8. 'and you will have wasted your delightful comments', *wĕšiḥattā dĕbāreykā hannĕʿîmîm*: lit. 'and you will waste your delightful sayings'. Fut. pf. connotation available to qat. conjugation (understanding *wĕšiḥattā* as cop. weqat.) conveys that the guest's compliments, issued before falling ill, will prove in retrospect to have been wasted (cf. *IBHS* §30.3.b).

23:9. 'remarks', *milleykā*: lit. 'words, speeches' (distinct from *dābār*, 'saying', 22:17, and *ʾāmār*, 'word', 22:21).

23:10. 'Do not move': see note on 22:28.

'do not even enter': lit. 'do not enter'. 'Even' is inferred from escalating protection, since in addition to boundary-moving (23:10a), even less egregious trespassing is prohibited (v. 10b).

23:13a. 'Do not withhold reproof from a youth', *ʾal-timnaʿ minnaʿar mûsār*: assonance unifies this colon.

23:14. 'Take responsibility yourself to strike him with a stick', *ʾattâ baššēbeṭ takkennû*: lit. 'You, with a stick strike him' (yiq. as imperative after command in 23:13a). 'Yourself' reflects the redundant pronoun 'you' (i.e. the nascent wisdom teacher whom the sage is training).

'his life', *napšô*: as in 22:23, 25; 24:12, 14, the context of mortal threat recommends rendering *nepeš* as 'life' rather than 'appetite' (as is found in 23:2, 7).

23:17. 'but rather, long after reverence for the LORD': lit. 'but rather, the reverence for the LORD' ('to long after' supplied by ellipsis from 23:17a).

'all the day long': lit. 'all the day' (only in English does 'long' in 'all the day long' link with 'to long after').

23:18. 'Most certainly there is a future', *kî ʾim-yēš ʾaḥărît*: in 23:17b *kî ʾim* appears at the juncture between opposites, rendered 'but rather'. In v. 18 *kî ʾim* does not contrast opposites, establishing instead an assertion with high certitude (Joüon §173c). The durable hope of 23:18b relies on the fact that 'there is a future'.

23:19. 'You, my son: listen', *šĕmaʿ-ʾattâ bĕnî*: lit. 'listen-you, my son'. This redundant voc. elevates intensity that recurringly marks this division-closing lecture (closing Prov. 10 – 24). Intensity is evident also in the pronouns of 22:19 and 23:14, and in the confrontations of 23:11b and 24:10.

23:20. 'those who squander', *zôlĕlê*: rendered 'glutton' in 23:21. Apart from food consumption, *zll* refers to approaching life in a rash, presumptuous, unthinking manner (they 'brush aside' the Law, 28:7).

'flesh', *bāśār*: this term encompasses meanings that include 'body', 'meat' and 'pubic region'.

23:21. 'a drunkard', *sōbē'*: this participle is rendered 'those who drink to excess' when appearing in 23:20.

'a glutton', *zôlēl*: this participle is rendered 'those who squander' when appearing in 23:20.

23:22. 'since she is elderly', *kî-zāqnâ*: with sapiential concision, this explanation accounts for both respect and a lack of respect (cf. double meaning in 22:22).

'Since she is elderly', the receptive son will treat his mother with respect. But an irresponsible son might treat the same mother with disrespect, owing to her advanced age.

23:24. 'he begot a wise fellow and so rejoices in him', *yôlēd ḥākām wayyismaḥ bô*: reading the K as a wayyiq. form (not the weyiq. form inferred by *BHS* notes [*wĕyismaḥ*, 'so may he rejoice']).

The combination found in K of ptc. (*yôlēd*, 'one who begets') followed by wayyiq. (*wayyismaḥ*, 'and so rejoices') expresses a past event (begetting a son) leading to a consequence (deriving joy, *IBHS* §33.3.5.c). In contrast, the Q *yismaḥ* lessens sense of consequence: 'he who begets a wise fellow will rejoice in him'.

23:26. 'My son, give your mind to me', *tĕnâ-bĕnî libbĕkā lî*: this unprecedented call for surrender of the son's mind to the father (as if for guardianship) indicates how sinister is the capacity of substance addiction (23:20–21, 29–35) and sexual captivity (vv. 27–28) to overwhelm the son's defences. A similar sentiment stirs in Division I: 'Against every imprisonment protect your mind' (4:23a).

23:27. 'trapper's . . . pit', *šûḥâ*: or 'gorge', 'precipice' (*HALOT*).

23:29. 'Who exclaims, "Alas!"? Who exclaims, "Woe!"?', *lĕmî 'ôy lĕmî 'ăbôy*: lit. 'Who has "alas!"? Who has "woe!"?' Both 'alas' and 'woe' are interjections, not abstract nouns.

'complaints', *śîaḥ*: by rendering as *aēdia kai leschai*, 'nausea and scandals', LXX infers both the hangover's physical discomfort and gossip evoked by the alcoholic's conduct.

'bloodshot eyes', *ḥaklilût 'ênāyim*: lit. 'darkened, dullness of eyes' (BDB).

23:32. 'In its future', *'aḥărîtô*: lit. 'its future', a nominal expression here serving adverbially (Waltke 2005: 248, n.). The subject of m. verbs 'bite' and 'sting' is 'wine' (23:31), not the f. noun *'aḥărît*, 'future'.

24:3. 'perception': derives from the same root as 'insight'. Thus 'by wisdom . . . and by perception' in 24:3 recalls 'wisdom . . . and insight' from 23:23.

24:5. 'It is the warrior who is wise, who embodies authentic strength', *geber-ḥākām ba'ôz*: lit. 'a warrior-wise in the strength'. 'Authentic' reflects the abstract sense of 'strength', signalled by definite article. The prep. *bĕ*, 'in', introduces a verbless predicate, indicating that capacity (strength) of which the subject (a wise warrior) consists (BDB, p. 88, *Beth essentiae*). Wisdom, not brute force, will be the measure of a warrior's strength (so NIV and NASB; cf. parallel in 24:5b).

While to render as comparative conveys the sense, yet it sacrifices pungency ('better is wisdom than strength', LXX; similarly NRSV and Fox 2009: 744). To infer agency from *bĕ* requires a verb lacking in Hebr., resulting in a rather different meaning ('a wise man prevails by might', Waltke 2005: 269).

24:7. 'in court': lit. 'in the gate' (see 'Notes' for 22:22).

24:12. 'will he not know? . . . will he not repay . . . ?', *yēdāʾ . . . wĕhēšîb*: lit. 'he will know . . . he will repay'. The negative interrogative in 24:12c and v. 12d is inferred from v. 12b: 'can he not perceive . . . ?'

'your life', *napšĕkā*: as in 22:23, 25; 23:14; and 24:14, the context of mortal threat in 24:11 recommends rendering *nepeš* as 'life' rather than 'appetite' (contrast 23:2, 7).

24:12, 18. 'repay', *hēšîb*, and 'divert', *hēšîb*: the words are identical in Hebr. In the first, the divine causes one's actions to rebound in retribution. In the second, if the divine observes a victim rejoicing over the defeat of an enemy, such warped glee may influence God to repeal ('divert') his retributive anger from against the enemy.

24:14. 'as if your life depended on it', *lĕnapšekā*: lit. 'for your life'. While mortal threat (hope being 'cut off') recommends *nepeš* as 'life' (as also in 22:23, 25; 23:14; 24:12), mention of eating in 24:13 also indicates wordplay concerning *nepeš* as 'appetite' (as in 23:2, 7).

'if you have discovered it': lit. 'if you have discovered'. The object 'it' is implied, referring to 'wisdom' (specified in 24:14a).

24:15. 'Do set an ambush, O guilty person, for the residence of a moral person', *ʾal-teʾerōb rāšāʿ linwê ṣaddîq*: this is one of five instances in this lecture when the poet follows a verb in the first colon with a voc., such as 'O guilty person' (cf. 23:19, 26; 24:13, 21; cf. NASB). By addressing his pupil, 'O guilty person', the sage shocks his audience into realizing the culpability of any inclination to trip up an innocent victim. Destruction of his 'resting place' further amplifies the sense of violation (24:15b). The ensuing saying exposes the folly of such an abusive strategy, for, unlike the moral, the guilty cannot bounce back after 'stumbling' (v. 16). To preserve the pungency of this reproof, the voc. in v. 15 should neither be omitted (*pace* Fox 2009: 749) nor rendered as a simile (e.g. 'Do not lurk like a thief' [NIV] and similarly NRSV).

24:16. 'and will keep on getting up': durative inferred from weqat.

24:18, 21. 'the LORD would see' and 'Revere the LORD', *yirʾeh yhwh* and *yerāʾ-ʾet-yhwh*: while the roots 'to see' and 'to revere' are distinct, assonance would have registered with native hearers.

24:20. 'a future cannot materialize', *lōʾ-tihyeh ʾaḥărît*: lit. 'there will not be a future'. Since the sage expresses the positive as *yēš ʾaḥărît*, 'there is a future' (23:18; 24:14), one would expect the negative in 24:20 to read *ʾên*

ʾaḥărît, 'there is no future'. Instead to negate a finite verb as *tihyeh*, 'there will (not) be', excludes even the hope of a desirable tomorrow emerging for the wicked person, so long as he or she remains wicked. (In)capability is inferred from the yiq.

24:21. 'people who shift', *šônîm*: the root *šnh* occurs only once more in Proverbs, where it describes overturning justice by denying what the oppressed should receive (31:5).

24:21–22. 'people who shift' and 'both of them', *šônîm* and *šĕnêhem*: assonance links these terms, located in parallel cola.

24:22. 'their disaster . . . the ruin associated with both of them', *ʾêdām . . . ûpîd šĕnêhem*: a double meaning operates in this saying, arising from two considerations. First, what are the antecedents of 'their' and 'them'? The previous saying offers two groups: the alliance of the Lord and king (24:21a), and 'people who shift' (v. 21b). Both may associate with disaster, yet in differing ways.

The second consideration involves the disaster/ruin itself. Is it reflexive, afflicting their own selves? Or do they inflict it upon others? Waltke observes that both are possible (2005: 280, 287). This yields two equally reasonable scenarios, given the subjects identified from 24:21. On the one hand, the Lord and the king bring disaster on those deserving punishment. At the same time, 'people who shift', by virtue of their duplicitous conduct receive disaster they deserve. Thus v. 22 may be paraphrased doubly, 'For suddenly the Lord-and-king may dispense disaster on miscreants, just as suddenly as disaster may befall people-who-shift. For, who can fathom the extent of ruin the Lord-and-king can inflict on deserving persons, and who can fathom the extent of ruin people-who-shift are destined to suffer?'

24:25–26. '[those who] issue reprimands' and '[sayings that] are straight', *môkîḥîm* and *nĕkōḥîm*: though tracing to differing roots (*ykḥ* and *nkḥ*), assonance evokes the notion that those who issue 'reprimands' (*môkîḥîm*) are behaving in an ethically straight fashion (corresponding to *nĕkōḥîm*).

24:25. 'a blessing of goodness': since by nature any blessing is beneficial, to further specify a blessing as 'good' intensifies the degree of benefit it will bring (attested elsewhere only in Ps. 21:4 [v. 3, ET]).

24:26. 'He would kiss the lips': Herodotus reports of Persian culture in the fifth century BC that a kiss on the lips signalled honour among equals, whereas an inferior would kiss the other's cheek, or, if much inferior, would prostrate himself instead of offering a kiss (Herodotus 1:134, 1954: 69). Such a gesture signified friendship without sexual overtones (Jones 2019: 117–119).

'[one] who returns sayings': as suggested in the note on 22:21, 'to return sayings' may connote handing down a verdict in response to a proposal or dilemma. By casting truthful speech as synonymous with a kiss, the sage teaches that reproof (24:25) is a sign of genuine affection (Fox 2009: 771; cf. 3:11–12).

24:27. 'Prepare your occupation outside': lit. 'establish your work outside'. The sage portrays an agrarian economy where houses were located within the city, while fields lay outside it (Waltke 2005: 294–295).

'in the field belonging to you', *baśśādeh lāk*: the emphasis on taking care to operate only in one's rightful field (in contrast to simpler *biśdekā*, 'in your field') fortifies the prohibition against manipulation of boundaries, mentioned previously in connection with orphans' fields (23:10).

24:28. 'Now, have you persuaded': lit. 'and have you persuaded?' The persuasion in 24:28b offers an instance of the sort of voluntary negative testimony already censured in v. 28a. To probe with this question ('Have you persuaded?') so soon after the censure implies suspicion, expressed colloquially in English by asserting 'now', followed by a dramatic pause. The enquirer's unstated follow-on would be 'I certainly hope you have not!' Waltke thoughtfully renders, 'you would not convince with your lips, would you?' (2005: 289).

24:30. 'lacked sense', *ḥăsar-lēb*: lit. 'lacking mind'. *Lēb* as 'mind' will return in 24:32: 'my mind began to take note'.

24:32. 'take note': lit. 'place' or 'put' (cf. 22:17).

24:33–34. The saying fashioned here was deployed in 6:10–11, with two minor variations. 'Like a vagabond', *kimĕhallēk*, in 6:11 corresponds to 'prowling', *mithallēk*, in 24:34. 'Your poverty' in 24:34 is spelled with tsere yod (*rêšĕkā*) rather than tsere aleph (*rēšēkā*).

'So your poverty will come prowling', *ûbāʾ-mithallēk rêšĕkā*: lit. 'so will come walking forth and back, your poverty'. Poverty's repeated movement in 24:34a contrasts the immobility of laziness (v. 33). Mere 'prowling' for valuables (v. 34a) escalates to a menacing invasion as poverty becomes armed (v. 34b).

Form and structure

Borders

After addressing strategies for wealth and power that shun abusive greed (preceding poem, Prov. 21:5 – 22:16), the theme shifts, focusing on character boundaries and the importance of industry instead of dissipation (present poem). A pair of wisdom commendations begins this lecture (each followed by a rationale), thus fixing the upper boundary at 22:17–21.

Despite an unnamed authorship note in 24:23a, previous themes concerning boundary-observance and industry extend through 24:34. A named authorship note in the next saying (25:1) together with a new theme for that poem (25:1–12) join with (a) recap, (b) closure and (c) inclusio in the present poem to locate its lower border in 24:34. Recap operates in 24:23–34, reviewing the importance of respecting boundaries and diligent labour.

Closure emerges when earlier lessons about industry (22:19; 24:3–4) reappear in the final section as the sage advocates field cultivation (24:27) and cautions concerning the high cost of non-cultivation (24:30–34). Closure also obtains from repetition of 'observe' in 22:29 and 24:32. Since this root (*ḥzh*) occurs in Proverbs only twice more (29:18, 20), double use in the present lecture is noteworthy.

Concerning inclusio, the lecture's opening saying urges the pupil to 'let your mind take note of my knowledge' (22:17). Three verses from the lecture's end the sage reports, 'my mind began to take note' (24:32; Waltke 2005: 299–300).

Macrostructural features

Wisdom commendation followed by wisdom content (Sections I, II and III, content-based). Section I consists of two wisdom commendations (22:17–18, 20), each supported by a rationale (22:19, 21). Section II follows with wisdom content (22:22 – 23:11), as does Section III (23:12 – 24:22).

Distinct pupil roles, whether as wisdom learners or as prospective wisdom teachers (Sections I, II, III and IV, form- and content-based). At times this lecture addresses pupils personally, as learners needing wisdom. At other times the sage looks ahead to their career as sages – prospective wisdom teachers (or trusted advisors).

Section I refers to pupils both as learners and as trusted advisors. The poet regards them as learners when he explains the lecture's purpose with this statement: 'So that in the LORD your confidence may lie, I have made known to you today, especially you' (22:19). In a nearby purpose statement (still within Section I), he pictures pupils as trusted advisors, dispatched by their employer: 'so you may return words – truth to those who send you' (v. 21b).

By its focus on the pupil's need to cultivate moral character, Section II regards the pupil as a learner. Rather than shifting boundaries, it is moral diligence that ensures career advancement (22:22–29). Instead of heedlessly devouring delicacies at an employer's feast, one should exercise restraint and assess the host's motives (23:1–8). Aside from a wisdom commendation not to waste time with disinterested hearers (23:9), this section lacks advice for pupils as teachers.

In contrast, from its outset Section III envisions pupils as teachers. They must receive reproof (23:12) so that they in turn may reprove youth under their care (vv. 13–14; Waltke similarly observes the sage here preparing his maturing pupil 'to become himself an instructor' [2005: 251]). Then follow two scripts for teachers to use when training youth (23:15 – 24:14, 15–22). These scripts repeatedly refer to the youth as 'my son' (only within Section III, 23:15, 19, 26; 24:13, 21).

Section IV begins by discouraging immoral conduct in court – counsel resembling Section II with its focus on learners (24:23–24). The poet then transitions to advocate reprimand (restraining another's immoral conduct) – counsel resembling Section III with its focus on teachers (vv. 25–26).

In sum, Section I introduces both pupil roles. Section II addresses the pupil as learner, while Section III concentrates on his role as teacher. Like Section I, Section IV addresses both.

Repetition of 'LORD' (Sections I, II and III, form-based). Of this lecture's five references to 'LORD', four display structural significance. The first (22:19) fuels the lecture's primary objective (vv. 17–19). Emphasis rests on the expression 'in the LORD', since it appears before the nominal phrase 'your trust' (Fox 2009: 708).

The second and third mentions of 'LORD' occur in quatrains appearing early in their respective sections, whether as first incentive (22:23) or as first wisdom content (23:17). A fourth leads its section's closing quatrain (24:21). One instance conveys only minimal structural influence (24:18). Together these five foster divine accountability and respect.

Repetition of 'ear', 'mind' and 'knowledge' (Sections I and III, form-based). 'Ear', 'mind' and 'knowledge' appear in the lecture's initial saying (22:17), and again at the start of Section III (23:12). This trio is rare in Proverbs (again only in 18:15), increasing the likelihood that 23:12, like 22:17 marks the beginning of a major portion.

Repetition of imperative 'listen' (Sections I and III, form-based). Three times the imperative 'listen' occurs within this lecture, beginning with the first saying (22:17). The second and third appear in Section III. After the dual-themes involving 'immediate view' and 'future view' are introduced in 23:17–18, 'listen' begins each portion expanding those respective themes. Thus the 'immediate view' expansion in vv. 19–21 begins, 'You, my son: listen', while the 'future view' expansion in vv. 22–23 begins, 'Listen to your father'.

Repetition of 'truth' (Sections I and III, form-based). 'Truth' occurs three times in this lecture, twice in the initial section's final saying (22:21). By adding 'verity' (unique in the HB; see 'Notes' for v. 21), the poet underscores the foundational nature of truthfulness in the curriculum (vv. 17–19) and career (vv. 20–21) of a sage.

The last mention of 'truth' in this poem exhibits similar intensity, both by pairing positive and negative commands, and by wisdom concomitants: 'Truth is what you must acquire and not sell – wisdom and reproof and insight' (23:23). This saying rounds out two portions (vv. 19–21, 22–23) that elaborate on two themes (short-range versus long-range gains) introduced in vv. 17–18. Standing at the end of those two theme-elaborations, v. 23 enjoys prominent positioning. (Those themes are expanded still further in 23:26 – 24:2 and 24:3–14, respectively.)

Thematic continuity surrounding right and wrong longing or acquisition (Sections II and III, content-based). Training concerning longing or acquisition (of either a right or wrong sort) features prominently in Sections II and III, sometimes significantly positioned at the start or close of a portion. In Section II the sage trains the pupil to keep in check his own longings for food and wealth, when hosted by a ruler (23:1–8). Related expressions include 'dine' (23:1, 6), 'master-of-appetite' (v. 2), 'crave' (vv. 3, 6), 'wear yourself out [to achieve an objective]' (v. 4), 'eyes soar after it [longingly]' and 'exhaustion [due to pursuit]' (v. 5), 'appetite' and 'eat and drink' (v. 7), 'morsel', 'ate' and 'vomit up' (v. 8).

Five times Section III deals with longing or acquiring, with four located at either the start or the close of a portion of sayings. The initial script for teachers (23:15 – 24:14) presents as its first wisdom content these negative and positive instructions about longings: 'May your mind not long after sinners, but rather long after reverence for the LORD, all the day long' (23:17).

Negative and positive sayings ensue. Emphatically positive is an instruction concerning truth: 'Truth is what you must acquire and not sell – wisdom and reproof and insight' (23:23, ending 23:17–23). Negative sayings include two warnings against consuming alcohol in excess (23:20–21, 29–35). Notice longing in the quatrain closing a twelve-saying connected segment (23:26 – 24:2): 'Do not long after people disposed to evil' (24:1–2).

Two related quatrains close Section III. The first warns against 'long[ing] after guilty folk' (24:19–20). The second urges the youth to 'Revere the LORD, my son, and the king' (vv. 21–22). They are related, since those same sentiments (do not long after sinners, but revere the LORD) appeared in the saying that opened the wisdom content of this block (23:17 within Block III.B, 23:15 – 24:22).

Thematic continuity involving rescue (Sections II and III, content-based). Through five sayings spread across Sections II and III the poet develops a theme of rescue. Initially, it is the LORD who rescues, arguing in court on behalf of the helpless (22:22–23), and again as orphans' 'redeemer' (23:10–11; Waltke infers a supernatural 'Defender' [2005: 245]). Those two quatrains foster an inclusio for Section II.

For his part, the teacher through reproof and corporal punishment can 'rescue' the pupil's 'life from Sheol' (23:13–14, first wisdom content of Section III). Then the teacher, using the first script (23:15 – 24:22), advises the pupil to prioritize wisdom (not dissipation) so that through 'an abundance of counsel' he may 'bring about deliverance' for others (24:6).

The youth's charge to 'rescue those who are being carried off to death' ranks as no elective whim (24:11). The Divine Observer will hold accountable any who fail to act as an agent of intervention, brushing aside any agnostic excuse (24:12).

Thematic continuity concerning boundaries (Sections II, III and IV, content-based). At various points across Sections II, III and IV the sage teaches concerning boundaries, literal and figurative, often closing a section.

To start with, literal, longstanding land boundaries must not be tampered with (22:28). Instead of intruding on another's territory, to gain promotion one should concentrate efforts on one's own occupation (v. 29).

Similarly the next saying teaches that when enjoying the hospitality of one's superior, attention should concentrate on food 'before you', rather than being led by unbridled appetite (23:1). Section II ends its second and final block much as the first, cautioning against boundary-shifting of a literal sort (23:10–11; cf. 22:28–29).

Again in Section III, figurative 'shifting' appears in its closing quatrain (24:21–22). Now it is not merely boundaries that are subject to relocation, but the inner character of persons bound for disaster and ruin.

Literal boundaries return in Section IV, implicit in the exhortation to cultivate 'the field belonging to you' (as opposed to slyly appropriating a neighbour's plot, 24:27). However, merely to refrain from infringing on another's property will not guarantee a harvest. As he closes the lecture, the sage points out that one also must apply industry, diligently cultivating one's own farm (24:30–34).

Closural devices. Section IV begins, 'These, too, pertain to the wise' (24:23a). This suggests that at some point in the process of composition or editing, the lecture stopped at 24:22 (the close of Section III). For that reason, closural devices for this poem should be studied relative both to Section III and Section IV.

Closure in Section III. Five elements that began in earlier portions continue in Section III. First, the lecture's initial wisdom teaching cautioned against getting ahead by oppressing the helpless (Section II, 22:22–23). Section III similarly cautions against setting an ambush to harm the unsuspecting innocent (24:15–16).

Second, in Section II the poet warns against victims who angrily seek revenge (22:24–25). This lecture's only other mention of anger occurs in the final unit of Section III. There the sage cautions against glee over harm befalling an offender, lest it blunt the LORD's retributive anger intended for that offender (24:17–18).

Third, the sage argues against faulty pursuits by providing two sorts of rationales: (a) divine opposition, and (b) wasted effort. In Section II divine opposition appears in 22:23; 23:11, with wasted effort in 23:5, 8, 9–11. In Section III wasted effort appears in 24:15–16a, with divine opposition in 24:17–18.

Fourth, the sage refers to the LORD in Section I (22:19), Section II (22:23), as well as in Section III (23:17; 24:18, 21). First, third and fifth describe appropriate attitudes towards the divine, whether trust (22:19) or reverence (23:17; 24:21).

Fifth, several scenarios prepare the reader for the warning against getting 'mixed up with people who shift' (24:21). First, the person seeking a loan guarantee may shift, defaulting on his loan (22:26–27). Second, the miserly host pretends generosity, while inwardly scheming with devious motives (23:6–8). Third, the adulteress appears attractive outwardly, but later turns deadly (23:27–28). Fourth, the red-sparkling wine glows with initial appeal, but in excess produces a hangover (23:29–35). Fifth, schemers who relocate property boundaries to their advantage shift land ownership surreptitiously (22:28; 23:10). The background created by these five amplifies the warning against 'people who shift' in the last prohibition of Section III (24:21). To emend *šônîm*, 'people who shift', to *šĕnêhem*, 'both of them', would severely weaken the rhetorical impact of this topic, so central to the message of this lecture (*pace* Fox 2009: 751–752).

Closure in Section IV. Seven elements in Section IV link to prior portions of the lecture, fostering closure. First, the initial teaching of Section II warns against 'crush[ing] the oppressed in court' (22:22–23). The initial teaching of Section IV similarly cautions against judicial abuse: 'To show favouritism in court proceedings is not good' (24:23b).

Second, Section II warned against shifting moral boundaries (22:22–27), property boundaries (22:28; 23:10–11) or boundaries of appetite (23:1–8). Section III cautions against association with people who 'shift' (24:21). Section IV cautions against shifting moral values by relabelling immoral behaviour: 'One who says to a guilty person, "You are moral," kin will curse him; nations will denounce him' (24:24).

Third, Section III showed that administering reproof features prominently in a teacher's role (cf. 23:12–14). Section IV describes how nations will reprove ('denounce') one who relabels moral values (24:24).

Fourth, in Section IV the exemplary trait of 'return[ing] sayings that are straight' (24:26) recalls one of the sage's objectives for this lecture. He purposed to train the pupil so that he 'may return words – truth to those who send you' (22:21, Section I).

Fifth, in Section II a saying concerning career advancement includes the term 'occupation' (22:29). A saying in Section IV similarly honouring industry again mentions 'occupation' (24:27). That term occurs only once more in Proverbs (18:9).

Sixth, in Section III the sage prohibited ambushing an innocent person (24:15–16). Section IV prohibits predatory legal proceedings against one's neighbour: 'Do not witness against your neighbour without cause' (24:28a).

Seventh, consider cautions against fixating either on retribution or on delight when enemies suffer. These appear in Section III (24:17–18) and again in Section IV (24:29; for additional closural features, see 'Borders', above).

Microstructural features

Section I (22:17–21). *Two wisdom commendations plus rationales (22:17–19, 20–21, content-based).* Block I.A consists of a wisdom commendation (22:17–18) followed by a rationale (v. 19). In Block I.B another wisdom commendation is followed by a rationale (vv. 20–21). Distinguishing these blocks is cultivation of the individual pupil's character (Block I.A), in contrast to preparation for employment as a teacher or transmitter of wisdom (Block I.B).

Section-level inclusio concerning speech (22:17, 21, content-based). Mention of 'sayings' in 22:17 and 'words' in v. 21 forms an inclusio enveloping Section I (Waltke 2005: 221).

Section II (22:22 – 23:11). *Section-level inclusio involving divine protection for the disadvantaged (22:22–23; 23:10–11, form- and content-based).* The quatrain that opens Section II prohibits oppressing the disadvantaged, with this incentive: the LORD will avenge the helpless (he will 'argue their case', 22:22–23).

The quatrain that closes Section II similarly prohibits oppressing the disadvantaged, warning that 'their redeemer' will 'argue their case' (23:10–11). Since the avenger in 22:23 is explicitly divine, 'their redeemer' in 23:11 also would be supernatural. The caution expressed against a third-person offender in 22:23 intensifies by shifting to second person in 23:11: 'Their redeemer . . . will argue their case against you.' This inclusio has also been observed by Niccacci ('*Proverbi* 22,17–23,11', *Studii Biblici Franciscani Liber Annus* [Jerusalem], 29 [1979]: 42–72, cited in Whybray 1994c: 90) and by Waltke (2005: 228, 244).

Block-terminal repetition of 'boundary' (22:28; 23:10, form-based). The term 'boundary' occurs three times in Proverbs. Two occur in this lecture (22:28; 23:10; the third appears in 15:25). Both blocks of Section II mention 'boundary', each time in a saying located one verse from that block's terminal verse.

Four prohibitions plus positive alternative (22:22–29, form- and content-based). Four evenly spaced prohibitions unify the sayings spanning 22:22–28, with rationales following the first three. One must avoid taking advantage of the weak (vv. 22–23), taking revenge (vv. 24–25), guaranteeing an unstable business proposition (vv. 26–27) or manipulating boundaries (v. 28). The last (boundary-shifting) functions as a summary, by metaphor subsuming the previous three. Waltke similarly observes coherence in vv. 22–28 (2005: 234).

One positive alternative then appears in 22:29, offsetting and completing these prohibitions. To secure advancement, an individual must execute diligently his or her own responsibilities.

Thematic coherence cautioning against elusive gains (23:1–8, content-based). Three segments comprise 23:1–8. The appeal of foods appears in the first and third (23:1–3, 6–8). The appeal of wealth occupies the middle segment (vv. 4–5). The elusive nature of both objectives (food and wealth) renders them unwise goals. Wealth will fly away (v. 5). Food served by a manipulative host will cause indigestion (v. 8).

Section-level prohibition-and-rationale structure (22:22–29; 23:1–11, content-based). The two blocks comprising Section II join as a series of prohibitions (plus alternative) (22:22–29, Block II.A) followed by a rationale revealing the defect inherent within those prohibitions (23:1–11, Block II.B). In sum, the practices of Block II.A must be avoided because the gains they promise will mislead (23:1–3), will remain elusive (vv. 4–5) or may even harm the pupil (vv. 6–8). Parallel cautions against boundary-shifting located towards the end of each block (22:28; 23:10–11) recommend reading these adjacent blocks in concert.

Wisdom commendation followed by wisdom content (23:9, 10–11, content-based). Section II closes with a wisdom commendation concerning judicious issuance of counsel (23:9), which introduces wisdom content reinforcing the caution against manipulating boundaries (vv. 10–11).

Section III (23:12 – 24:22). *Wisdom commendation followed by wisdom content (23:12, 13–14, content-based).* Section III begins with a wisdom commendation urging the pupil to embrace a mental attitude receptive to 'reproof' and 'knowledge' (23:12). Wisdom content follows, advocating administering reproof (vv. 13–14).

Thematic continuity involving reproof (23:12–14, content-based). Reproof unifies the first block of Section III. The teacher must submit to 'reproof' (23:12). To rescue youth from death, the teacher must not shrink from administering 'reproof', 'striking with a rod' or a 'stick' when necessary (vv. 13–14).

Dual-themes of reproof and rescue (23:13–14, form- and content-based). In the first block of Section III the poet introduces dual-themes concerning administering reproof and executing rescue (23:13 and v. 14, respectively; in contrast, reproof in v. 12 is received, not administered).

Reproof unfolds through warnings concerning dissipation through sexual promiscuity and alcoholism in Segment III.B.1.b (23:26 – 24:2). Rescue is expanded in Segment III.B.1.c (24:3–14). A pupil who has grown secure through wisdom (24:3–4) will be able to bring 'deliverance' to others (vv. 5–6). If he shirks his duty to 'rescue' others, he proves to be an uncompassionate coward (vv. 10–12). 'Rescue' and 'deliverance' do not occur in this lecture aside from these sayings.

Thematic continuity concerning death (23:13–14, content-based). The hazards of death and Sheol unify 23:13–14.

Wisdom commendation followed by wisdom content (23:15–16, content-based). Block III.B opens with a wisdom commendation quatrain regarding parental joy (23:15–16). The sage advocates taking a long view of life through the wisdom content that follows in vv. 17–23.

Repetition of 'my son', with closure (23:15, 19, 26; 24:13, 21, form-based). Within scripts supplied to teachers (Block III.B), the audience intended by those scripts is addressed as 'my son' five times (23:15, 19, 26; 24:13, 21). Often these mark beginnings or endings of portions (23:15, 26; 24:13), with section-level closure operating in 24:21.

Repetition of ʾḥr, *a root associated with 'future' (23:18, 30, 32; 24:14, 20, form-based).* The root *ʾḥr* (which underlies the term 'future') occurs five times in Section III. These foster a level of coherence for this section, reorienting the pupil's longings away from the near term, encouraging instead a long view. The first occurs early within the first script supplied to teachers (23:15–25): 'Most certainly there is a future, and then your hope will not be cut off' (23:18).

A warning against inebriation contains the second and third instances of the root *ʾḥr*. The pupil should not imitate 'those who linger [*ʾḥr*] over the wine' (23:30a). For 'in its future – like a serpent [the wine] will bite' (v. 32a).

The fourth mention of 'future' appears strategically in the final saying of a unit: 'In the same fashion, know wisdom experientially, as if your life depended on it; if you have discovered it, then there is a future and your hope will not be cut off' (24:14, closing Unit III.B.1, 23:15 – 24:14). By positing a 'future' and reassuring that 'your hope will not be cut off', 24:14 recalls 23:18.

The final mention of 'future' in Section III is negative. Solemnly the sage warns that 'a future cannot materialize for the wicked person' (24:20, two sayings before the close of Section III).

Dual-theme introduction concerning longings, negative and positive (23:17, extending to 24:14, content-based). The first wisdom content of Block II.B contrasts longings. It cautions against 'long[ing] after sinners', urging the pupil instead to 'long after reverence for the LORD, all the day long' (23:17).

The negative and positive parts of 23:17 form a dual-theme introduction, since the sage will later expand on negative longings (dissipation through consumption, vv. 19–21), expanding immediately thereafter on the positive pursuit of wisdom (analogous to reverence) (vv. 22–23).

This contrast between negative and positive longings persists in the balance of Block III.B. Thus, after a quatrain about joy (23:24–25) that completes the teaching containing the initial expansions (vv. 19–21, 22–23), the sage issues a second expansion of negative longings through a segment cautioning against dissipation that stems from longings that are sexually immoral and excessively alcoholic, cautioning concerning the captivity they set in motion (23:26 – 24:2). An exhortation warning against longing after evilly inclined persons closes this second negative expansion (24:1–2).

A second positive expansion follows directly, showing that wise conduct offers a noble goal for one's longings (24:3–14). Through wisdom one may grow personally secure, while also rescuing others. Two sapiential terms or roots found in the first positive expansion (23:23–24) recur at the start of the second positive expansion (24:3). They are *ḥokmâ*, 'wisdom', and *byn* (rendered 'insight' in 23:23 and 'perception' in 24:3). An encouraging exhortation that urges consuming wisdom like honey closes this second positive expansion (24:13–14).

While parallel segment-length does not universally indicate structure, it may endorse structures otherwise attested. Each of the 'second' expansions above spans twelve sayings (23:26 – 24:2; 24:3–14).

Inclusio regarding wisdom commendations with parental joy (23:15–16, 24–25, content-based). A theme of parental joy dominates the quatrain spanning 23:15–16, and again in vv. 24–25. This results in an inclusio for

23:15–25 (Segment III.B.1.a). Each quatrain presents a wisdom commendation, framing the wisdom content of 23:17–23 (see 10:8–13 for another portion with opening and closing wisdom commendations).

Nested inclusios concerning reverence (23:17 and 24:21–22) and expressions about a hopeful future (23:18 and 24:14, form-based). An exhortation to prioritize 'reverence for the LORD' in 23:17 presents the first wisdom content of Block III.B (23:15 – 24:22), a block consisting of scripts for apprentice sages or parents to use when training others about longings. Since 'reverence' does not reappear until the quatrain in 24:21–22, this forms an inclusio for Block III.B (excluding only the wisdom commendation opening the block in 23:15–16).

In 23:18 (the saying directly after the first part of that inclusio) there appear the two expressions 'future' and 'your hope will not be cut off'. These two appear together only once more in all of Proverbs, in 24:14. This forms an inclusio whose upper member is adjacent to the earliest wisdom content of Unit III.B.1 (wisdom content begins in 23:17), with its lower member forming the close of that unit (24:14). This inclusio (23:18; 24:14) nests within the earlier inclusio (23:17; 24:21–22).

Successive wisdom commendations followed by wisdom content (23:19–21, 22–23, content-based). The trio of sayings spanning 23:19–21 separate into a voc. wisdom commendation in 23:19 ('You, my son: listen and be wise!') followed by wisdom content cautioning against gustatory excess (vv. 20–21). The ensuing quatrain similarly segments into a voc. wisdom commendation ('Listen to your father . . . and do not despise your mother', 23:22), followed by wisdom content charging the pupil to pursue truth, which will consist of 'wisdom and reproof and insight' (v. 23).

Dual-theme introduction contrasting dissipation and wisdom (23:19–23, content-based). The script to restrain youths from longing after dissipation (Unit III.B.1, 23:15 – 24:14) begins with an introduction (23:15–25) initiating two themes the sage subsequently expands. Those themes are (a) a warning against dissipation (the 'immediate view', 23:19–21) and (b) an exhortation to choose wisdom instead (the 'future view', 23:22–23). The first (against the 'immediate view') the sage will expand in 23:26 – 24:2, while the second (favouring the 'future view') he will expand in 24:3–14, concluding Unit III.B.1.

Dual-theme introduction concerning immediate and future view (23:17–18, 19–23, content-based). Both the initial teaching against the 'immediate view' of dissipation described above (23:19–21) and the initial exhortation towards the 'future view' of wisdom (23:22–23) are prefigured in the quatrain preceding those two portions (23:17–18). In 23:17, by urging the youth not to let his 'mind long after sinners' but to pursue reverence instead, the sage argued against allowing his longings to take the 'immediate view' (short-term gratification). In 23:18 by emphasizing that 'most certainly there is a future', the sage argued in favour of longings oriented towards the 'future view' (deferred gratification of longings).

Thus 23:17–18 provides a dual-theme introduction to 23:19–21 and 22–23, respectively.

Dual-theme introduction concerning inebriation and promiscuity (23:19–21, form- and content-based). As described earlier, a warning against dissipation is introduced in 23:19–21, with corresponding expansion in 23:26 – 24:2. That expansion portion itemizes two harmful attractions: sexual promiscuity (23:27–28) and alcoholic addiction (23:29–35). Closer examination shows that alcoholism specifically appeared also in the introduction to dissipation, as the sage cautioned against consuming excessive alcohol, referring to 'drink[ing] wine' and 'drunkard' in vv. 20a, 21a.

It is likely that, in addition to anticipating alcoholic addiction in the introduction, the poet also alluded to promiscuity (the second particular found in the expansion of dissipation) within the introduction spanning 23:19–21. Although to 'squander flesh' (23:20b) principally describes gluttonous consumption of meat, that expression may also connote sexual activity (cf. 'flesh' in Ezek. 16:26; 23:20).

Repeated exhortation to 'listen' (23:19, 22, form-based). As the dual-themes introduced in 23:17–18 expand in vv. 19–21 and 22–23, respectively, each expansion begins with an exhortation for the child to 'listen' (vv. 19a, 22a).

Wisdom commendation, wisdom content, and recap (23:26, 27–35 and 24:1–2, content-based). The segment spanning 23:26 – 24:2 consists of a wisdom commendation (23:26) followed by two portions of wisdom content (vv. 27–28, 29–35). A recap consisting of imperative and rationale closes the segment in 24:1–2.

Recap and continuity concerning destruction (24:1–2, 22, content-based). The segment spanning 23:26 – 24:2 describes personal destruction following involvement with a prostitute (23:27–28) and excessive alcohol consumption (23:29–35). That segment closes with a verse-pair recapping how imitative association with evil persons brings destruction (24:1–2). The entire section within which the segment spanning 23:26 – 24:2 appears similarly will close with a warning against 'getting mixed up with' persons who instigate 'disaster' (24:21–22, ending Section III).

Dual-theme introduction concerning alcoholism and promiscuity (23:26, form- and content-based). The saying in 23:26 presents a dual-theme introduction concerning alcoholism and promiscuity. Regarding alcoholism, mention of 'eyes' in 23:26b anticipates three later instances when warning against this addiction (vv. 29, 31 [in 'sparkles'], and 33). While 'eye' occurs in this lecture three more times (23:5, 6; 24:18), since the additional three operate at some distance from the immediate portion, there remains a link joining 'eye' in 23:26b with the teaching about alcoholism in vv. 29–35.

Regarding promiscuity, the exhortation in 23:26a for the pupil to 'give your mind [*lēb*] to me' involves this second dual-theme. Earlier in Proverbs the sage associated 'mind' with defence against promiscuity. Shortage of 'sense', *lēb*, explained why the youth failed to turn away from the adulteress (6:32; 7:7). For her part, the adulteress was clever of 'mind', *lēb* (7:10), so that the youth's 'mind', *lēb*, was diverted to her ways in 7:25. Buttressing the youth's mind (23:26a) would safeguard him against the prostitute's allurement (vv. 27–28).

Thematic continuity of entrapment and rescue (23:26 – 24:12, content-based). With expressions such as 'a trapper's deep pit', 'a narrow well' and 'as a robber she lies in ambush', the theme of entrapment emerges from the warning against promiscuity (23:27–28). The alcoholic similarly evidences entrapment by chemical dependency (23:29–35). These teachings isolate captivity as a principal theme for the segment spanning 23:26 – 24:2.

Appropriately, after a segment-recap in 24:1–2, the portions warning about captivity (23:27–35) are followed by a segment concentrating on rescue (24:3–14). The wise will possess 'strength' and 'power', able to 'wage . . . war' so as to 'bring about deliverance' on behalf of captives (24:5–6). A fool, in contrast, cannot even keep from harming himself, let alone rescue others (vv. 7–9).

This priority of rescuing others constitutes no optional pastime (24:10–12). The wise must 'Rescue those who are being carried off to death, and those who would be tottering towards slaughter, if you were to keep to yourself!' (24:11).

If, denying their resources of strength and power (24:5–6), the pupils were to plead ignorance concerning a victim's clear and lethal plight ('Look: we did not know about this!', v. 12a), the divine (on whom the youths depend for safeguarding) would not be duped. He would hold them accountable (v. 12b).

Wisdom commendation followed by wisdom content regarding security (24:3–4, 5–6, content-based). The theme of rescue characterizing Segment III.B.1.c (24:3–14) launches with a wisdom commendation featuring the security of a soundly built and well-furnished house (23:3–4). Then follows wisdom content advocating use of wisdom to escort others into security (vv. 5–6).

Thematic contrast of longings, restrained or indulged (23:17a; 24:1; 24:13–14, content-based). In Unit III.B.1 misguided longings in the form of unbridled consumption (sexual and alcoholic) pose a problem against which the pupil must be on guard (esp. 23:17a; 24:1; 23:26–35). In contrast, the sage places no limit on another consumption, located at the unit's close. Like consuming beneficial honey, the youth should indulge in wisdom without restraint (24:13–14; since this directive to consume wisdom like honey epitomizes the thrust of its portion [24:3–14], it does not function as a wisdom commendation).

Negative wisdom commendation followed by negative wisdom content (24:7–9, 10–12, content-based). When cautioning against the attempt of counterfeit wisdom to thwart rescue, the sage begins with a negative wisdom commendation. When the fool engages in supposed wisdom activities of strategizing and scheming, he only harms himself (24:7–9). The ensuing wisdom content decries those who protest ignorance as an excuse for refusing to intercept wrongful harm about to befall the innocent (vv. 10–12).

Thematic continuity surrounding 'longing' and 'guilty' (24:15–20, form- and content-based). The concepts of 'longing' and 'the guilty' create a dynamic coherence for the three quatrains comprising 24:15–20. The 'guilty' are named expressly in the first and last quatrains (vv. 15, 16, 19b). 'Your enemies' represents the guilty in the middle quatrain (v. 17); also called 'wicked' (vv. 19a, 20).

The last quatrain provides the interpretive key to these six sayings. When the sage cautions, 'Do not long after guilty folk' (24:19b), the pupil will realize that the sage is circling back to what may constitute the prevailing theme of this section (Section III, 23:12 – 24:22), now towards the section's close (recall esp. 23:17; 24:1–2). Consequently all of 24:15–20 should be viewed through a lens of 'longings'.

Since the sage found it necessary at the start of this portion (24:15) to address as 'O guilty person' someone in his audience (which consisted of 'My son' as recently as the recap in 24:13–14), evidently some among his pupils had covertly begun to long after gains of the guilty (24:15). So the poet exposes that those supposed gains will be short-lived, returning misfortune on the perpetrators' heads (v. 16). Reinforcing 23:17 and 24:1–2, youths must steel themselves against envying supposed gains of the guilty.

At the other extreme, youths also must not celebrate when misfortune befalls enemies who inflicted harm (24:17). By longing after their deserved demise, by rejoicing when it arrives, youths would fall into divine disfavour (v. 18).

Both hazards combine in the third quatrain. Neither should one indulge in revengeful anger over harm caused by the guilty (24:19a), nor should one long to be like them, envying their hollow gains (v. 19b). For their desired 'future' never will arrive. Instead their sputtering lamp will only extinguish in darkness (v. 20).

Thematic contrast between negative and positive instructions (24:15–20, 21–22, content-based). A positive segment encouraging reverence (one in 24:21–22) that closes Unit II.B.2 (vv. 15–22) completes and balances the preceding negative segment cautioning against employing tactics of the guilty (three quatrains in vv. 15–20). Reverence ranks not merely as one more good idea the pupil must add to his lengthy to-do list. It constitutes a fundamentally curative reorientation, preventing one's attention from being either consumed by envy over the success of the guilty or from being corroded by seemingly righteous resentment over their offences, eager for their demise.

Unit-level inclusio of assonance and kî*-rationale (24:15–16, 21–22, form-based).* The first quatrain of Unit III.B.2 begins with the prohibition

ʾal-teʾĕrōb, 'Do not set an ambush' (24:15a). That unit's last quatrain presents the prohibition *ʾal-titʿārāb*, 'do not get mixed up [with]' (24:21b). Assonance thus fosters an inclusio enveloping Unit III.B.2, combined with the fact that each verse is followed by a rationale introduced by *kî*, 'for' (vv. 16, 22).

Section IV (24:23–34). *Repetition of 'good', with thematic continuity (24:23–26, form- and content-based).* Repetition of *ṭôb*, 'good(ness)', in initial sayings of adjacent quatrains (24:23, 25) combines with a shared theme of 'how to respond to trespass-enticements', unifying vv. 23–26 (Unit IV.A.1).

Thematic contrast concerning responses to evil (24:23–24, 25–26, content-based). The two quatrains comprising 24:23–26 offer alternative responses to evil. One may either collude with evil, giving preferential treatment in court and relabelling immorality, consequently earning universal denunciation (vv. 23–24), or one may condemn such evil conduct, gaining hearty approval ('a blessing of goodness') as a result (vv. 25–26).

Two cycles contrasting evil and industry (24:23–34, content-based). Section IV consists of two blocks, each of which begins by addressing wrongdoing and ends by urging industry. Block IV.A reviews alternative responses to evil (24:23–26), while endorsing industry explicitly in v. 27. Block IV.B evaluates alternative responses to evil (vv. 28–29), while endorsing industry implicitly in vv. 30–34 by exposing the harm of indolence.

Each time the sage raises the need for justice (24:23–26, 28–29) he follows with an encouragement to diligent labour (vv. 27, 30–34). By following justice with industry the sage teaches that industry, not justice, should persist as one's default strategy. Justice, while vital, is necessitated only by the periodic eruption of evil. Industry, in contrast, is perennially needful. In the absence of ongoing industry, a preoccupation with justice consigns one to a life of rootless righteousness (24:27). Only to dismantle wrong fails to construct sustainable community.

Thematic contrast concerning farming – diligent and negligent (24:27, 30–34, form- and content-based). Section IV introduces two teachings about industry (24:27, 30–34). 'Field' appears in both, whether positive (diligent farming, 24:27), or negative (negligent farming, vv. 30–34).

The first presents farming as preparatory, enabling erection of a richer asset – a dwelling place ('then, afterwards, build your house', encompassing both literal and metaphoric connotations of 'house', 24:27). The second laments the indolent's failure to farm, with no mention of a house (vv. 30–34).

By omitting mention of a house from the second teaching, the sage implies that some measure of career success should precede energies invested in homebuilding. Without a resource-generating career, how can one sustain home and family?

Contrast of responses to evil, envy or revenge (24:28, 29, content-based). Both sayings in 24:28–29 counsel how not to respond to evil. One must not respond enviously to the gains of wrongdoing, imitating such tactics as perjury (v. 28). Conversely, one must not respond resentfully to the wounds of evil, scheming revenge (v. 29).

Comment

The theme of boundaries (explicit and implied) extends pervasively within this lecture, both early and late. Consequently the following discussion will call attention to this concept, whether stated or implied.

Section I (22:17–21). The initial section urges attention to wisdom, with supporting rationales (Section I, 22:17–21). This will benefit the pupil both as one learning wisdom personally (Block I.A, vv. 17–19), and as one maturing to the point of transmitting (teaching) wisdom to others (Block I.B, vv. 20–21).

These twin perspectives (wisdom learner, wisdom transmitter/teacher) correspond to Sections II and III, respectively. Section II cultivates the pupil's own character (22:22 – 23:11), while Section III prepares him as one who teaches wisdom to others (23:12 – 24:22).

22:18. *Amenemope* parallel reads, 'Place [them] in the treasure house of your heart . . . they will be a mooring post for your tongue' (*Amenemope* col. 3, lines 13, 16 [ch. 1.5, 8]).

22:20. Mention of wisdom sayings reduced to writing discloses that by this point wisdom was transmitted both orally and in written form. Wisdom writings such as Proverbs may have supplied the curriculum for scribal literacy training (see §5.12 in the 'Introduction').

By referring to past teachings (22:20), the sage foreshadows that the present lecture will draw to a close the series of teachings that began in Prov. 10. Both the emphasis on reverence at the close of Section III (24:21–22) and the poignant story warning against the high cost of indolence at the close of Section IV (24:30–34) resemble the emphasis on reverence (9:10) and example of lassitude (Dame Folly's indolent and injurious hospitality in 9:13–18) that concluded Division I, and conspire to draw Division II to a climactic conclusion.

22:21. The second purpose statement accounting for the sage's teaching reads, 'To make known to you verity, words of truth, so you may return words – truth to those who send you' (22:21). Note especially the expression 'so you may return words', resembling 'To know how to return an answer to the one who has addressed him', in the first line of this excerpt from the prologue in *Amenemope*:

> To know how to return an answer to the one who has addressed him,
> To carry back a report to him who dispatches him,
> To enable him to enter the ways of life,

> To enable him to prosper upon the earth,
> To allow his heart to descend into its chapel,
> To enable him to steer away from evil,
> To rescue him from the mouth of ones who then shall conspire,
> To be praised in the mouth of humankind.
> (*Amenemope* col. 1, lines 5–12 [prologue lines 5–12])

In *Amenemope*, it is an unfounded accusation that would prompt one to 'return an answer to the one who has addressed him' (col. 1, line 5). Consequently that answer would constitute a refutation. Similarly in the present Proverbs lecture, one who 'returns sayings' may refer to one who issues a reprimand (Prov. 24:25–26). In *Amenemope*, 'praise' accrues to those who oppose evil and experience rescue from conspirators (col. 1, lines 10–12). Similarly in Proverbs, 'blessing' accrues to those who refuse to join in approving evil, who respond instead with reprimands to reinforce what is right (also Prov. 24:25–26).

Section II (22:22 – 23:11). *Block II.A (22:22–29).* Section II addresses the pupil as a wisdom learner, cultivating the pupil's character through three scenarios that entice towards unethical conduct (Block II.A, 22:22–29). First is the temptation to abuse the helpless by manipulating the judicial system (v. 22). Divine defence of the oppressed renders this enticement ill-advised (v. 23).

Second is the temptation to respond with well-rehearsed anger when offended (22:24). Though more justifiable than initiating abuse (vv. 22–23), companionship with such a reactionary may incline the pupil to imitation's deadly trap (v. 25).

Third is an invitation to profit financially through loan guaranteeing (22:26). Though more benign than abuse (vv. 22–23) or revenge (vv. 24–25), the guarantor may suffer destitution, left with naught but a worthless note (v. 27).

If the youth would but recognize that pursuits of abuse, revenge and unwise financial advantage require manipulation of moral boundaries, he could draw upon ancestors' counsel and resist such deceptive overtures (22:28). Instead of manipulating, he must with excellence complete his current and legitimately assigned tasks. Reliable service leads to promotion (v. 29).

Introduction of reliable service and promotion in 22:29 is not 'somewhat out of place', since it offsets negative allurements of 22:22–28 (*pace* Fox 2009: 719). The sage employs this pattern of positive offsetting negative twice more in Block III.B (negative in 23:17–21 and positive in vv. 22–23; negative in 23:26 – 24:2 and positive in 24:3–6).

Block II.B (23:1–11). After issuing cautions against boundary-shifting, the sage probes more deeply, exposing the defective engine that inclines the pupil towards boundary-shifting. It is his own longings that lure him out of bounds. To dramatize the dilemma, the sage invites the pupil to imagine appetites that would awaken when hosted by his employer ('ruler') at a sumptuous feast (23:1–8).

Three enticements would attract the wide-eyed dinner guest. First is an abundance of exquisite food – a temptation to overstep boundaries of hospitality and health. If perceptive (23:1), the new-hire will realize that only rigorous self-denial of appetites (v. 2) will prevent delicacies from overpowering him (v. 3).

Second is the appeal of glittering riches – perhaps adorning the host's home. He must resist the temptation to redraw boundaries of life's wiser priorities in order to pursue wealth (23:4). For wealth's satisfaction lies perpetually beyond reach, delivering only exhaustion (v. 5, see 'Notes').

Exquisite food returns in the third enticement. The pupil must not overlook the host's motives, for mouth-watering desserts served with miserliness make for indigestion. The youth must resist the temptation to redraw character-assessment boundaries, through confirmation bias presuming his host will be above using his menu to manipulate (23:6–8).

As Block II.B closes, the sage warns learners not to sidestep the plain prohibition against bending boundaries. The categorical caution near the close of Unit II.A.1 ('Do not move an ancient boundary', 22:28) he rephrases in the unit closing Block II.B: 'Do not move an ancient boundary, and into orphans' fields do not even enter', 23:10). Else they must answer to those orphans' redeemer (v. 11, alluding to the LORD himself; cf. 22:23).

22:22. *Amenemope* parallel reads, 'Guard yourself against robbing the poor, against being valorous against the man with a broken arm' (*Amenemope* col. 1, lines 5–6 [prologue lines 5–6]).

22:23. *Amenemope* parallel reads, 'Thou Moon, bring forward his crime!' (*Amenemope* col. 4, line 19 [ch. 2.16]). The Hebr. sage replaced the moon deity (Thoth) with Yahweh, the LORD of Israel: 'For the LORD will argue their case'.

22:24. The *Amenemope* parallel reads, 'Do not make friends with the hot-headed man, nor approach him for conversation' (*Amenemope* col. 11, lines 13–14 [ch. 9.1–2]). If the 'master-of-anger' in 22:24 is the victim of v. 22a or v. 22b, counsel not to befriend someone who has been wronged may lead to the incorrect inference that the sage cares not for victims. Yet his scathing indictment against passivity found later in this lecture disallows that inference (24:10–12). Rather, it is the savage sense of revenge against which the sage here warns (cf. censure of glee over an enemy's demise in 24:17–18, and prohibition against revenge in 24:29).

22:25. The *Amenemope* parallel reads, 'Do not leap to cleave to that [fellow], lest a terror carry you away' (*Amenemope* col. 13, lines 8–9 [ch. 9.35–36]). This closes ch. 9 in *Amenemope*. Thus two related teachings adjacent in Proverbs (22:24–25) telescope an expanse of material from within a single chapter of *Amenemope*, ending on its chapter's closing verses (9.35–36; Overland 1996: 285). Unwilling to entrust vindication to God, the master-of-anger in Proverbs forfeits freedom, enslaved by his own vindication-agenda.

22:27. Generating income by pledging a loan guarantee is, in the sage's estimation, the labour of one with too much leisure in bed – which explains his warning against the pupil losing his bed. After the grandfather-sage's forceful exhortation against loan guaranteeing (6:1–5), he urges the youth to roust himself from bed and get moving (6:6–11; cf. 24:33–34).

22:28. *Amenemope* parallel reads:

> Do not move a landmark on the boundaries of sown land, nor shift the position of the measuring cords.
> Do not be greedy concerning a cubit of land, nor throw down the boundaries of a widow.
> (*Amenemope* col. 7, lines 12–15 [ch. 6:1–4])

Land possession comprised an inviolable economic security in Israelite society, a cross-generational asset reverting to the originating family each Jubilee Year (every fifty years), terminating temporary forfeiture due to debt. Manipulating boundaries offered an insidious strategy whereby the powerful (who might repel infringement suits) could erode even this calendarized reset of a poor family's depleted assets. A similar protection was provided in Deut. 19:14 (leading to speculation concerning influence between Proverbs and Deuteronomy; cf. Fox 2009: 732–733).

22:29. *Amenemope* parallel reads, 'As for a scribe who is experienced in his offices, he will find himself worthy of being a courtier' (the last saying before the colophon, *Amenemope* col. 27, lines 15–16 [ch. 30.9–10]; see also Simpson 1973: 265). Elevation to serve monarchs marked careers of Joseph and Daniel (Longman 2017: 79–93). Earlier in Proverbs, advancement to royal association rewarded pure motives and gracious speech (22:11).

23:1–8. *Amenemope* parallel reads:

> Do not eat food before an official; may your mouth wait at the beginning.
> If you are full, chewing is unlawful; it will travel back in your vomit.
> Focus attention on the drink before you; cause it to supply your needs.
> (*Amenemope* col. 23, lines 13–18 [ch. 23:1–6])

The Egyptian wisdom composition *The Instruction of the Vizier Ptah-hotep* (or Ptahhotpe) similarly counsels, 'If you are one of the guests at the table of one who is greater than you, accept what he gives you when it is set before you. Look at what is before you and do not pierce him with much staring, for to annoy him is an abomination of the spirit' (seventh maxim, *The Maxims of Ptahhotpe*; Faulkner 1973: 162). Ptah-hotep served King Izezi (c. 2450 BC). The earliest copy of his instructions dates to Egypt's Middle Kingdom (c. 2080–1759 BC).

23:3. Earlier, 'deceptive food' described how gains from guaranteeing a loan would turn to gravel in one's mouth (20:17).

23:4–5. *Amenemope* parallels read, 'Do not cast your heart after wealth' (*Amenemope* col. 9, line 10 [ch. 7.1]), 'Day dawns and they [riches gained by robbery] are not in your house. / One sees their place but they are not there' (*Amenemope* col. 9, lines 18–19 [ch. 7.9–10]), and 'They have made themselves wings like geese; they have flown heavenward' (*Amenemope* col. 10, lines 4–5 [ch. 7.15–16]). The Hebr. sage replaces 'geese' with 'eagle', since aquatic fowl would be less common in Israel than along the Nile.

23:6–8. *Amenemope* parallels read:

> When you are undone in the presence of your supervisor, you will not be acclaimed in your speeches. Your obsequious swaying they will reject with cursing, your homage [will call] for a beating.
> This mouth, full of much bread: you swallow it, you vomit it up. You will be emptied of your good things.
> (*Amenemope* col. 14, lines 13–18 [ch. 11.9–14])

23:8–9. Though referring to different communications (compliments in 23:8 and counsel in v. 9), both sayings deal in wasted messages (Waltke 2005: 244–245).

23:10–11. *Amenemope* parallels read, 'Do not remove the landmark on boundaries of the sown field' (*Amenemope* col. 7, line 12 [ch. 6.1]), 'nor throw down the boundaries of a widow' (*Amenemope* col. 7, line 15 [ch. 6.4]), and 'he [the aggressor] will be lassoed by the power of the Moon' (*Amenemope* col. 7, line 19 [ch. 6.8]). The Nile's routine flooding kept scribes occupied year after year, re-establishing boundaries of riverside fields. This custom easily created a temptation to profit by repositioning stone-marked boundary lines (Fox 2009: 732).

Section III (23:12 – 24:22). At Section III the sage transitions from training the pupil as wisdom learner (Section II) to now training him as wisdom teacher (23:12 – 24:22; cf. esp. 23:13–14). The poet anticipated this transition from this lecture's second block (Block I.B, 22:20–21).

Block III.A (23:12–14). Teacher-training, the sage explains, begins with reproof. Before administering reproof, the novice teacher himself must first welcome reproof (23:12). Subsequently, though their charges may protest, novice teachers must not shrink from inflicting penalties to disincentivize reproof-worthy behaviour (23:13). The youth's very life is at stake (v. 14).

Block III.B (23:15 – 24:22). The balance of Section III (Block III.B) supplies wisdom teachers with two scripts for training pupils. The first counters longings leading to dissipation, counselling reverence instead (Unit III.B.1, 23:15 – 24:14, with reverence in 23:17). The second cautions against preoccupation with the guilty, counselling reverence instead (Unit III.B.2, 24:15–22, with reverence in 24:21). Novice teachers receiving this counsel would address their pupils as 'my son', an expression that for this lecture occurs only within these two scripts (23:15, 19, 26; 24:13, 21).

Block III.B, Unit 1 (23:15 – 24:14). Dissipation masquerades as momentary joy. So the script against dissipation begins (also ends) urging youths to bring joy to their wisdom teachers and parents (23:15–16, 24–25). Parental affirmation will doubtless result, returning lasting joy to the youth.

At issue is whether the youth will prefer short-sighted or future-oriented longings (23:17–18). Dissipation of drunkenness illustrates instant gratification, resulting in poverty (vv. 19–21). Future-oriented longings will relentlessly pursue what is authentic ('truth', described as 'wisdom and reproof and insight', vv. 22–23). This moral-wise route produces authentic joy – not of a fleeting narcissistic sort, but generating joy among those whom the youth should value most (vv. 24–25).

Those competing longings (destructive, fleeting dissipation, versus productive, durable wisdom) the sage proceeds to expand in 23:26 – 24:2 and 24:3–14, respectively. To withstand the appeals of fleeting dissipation the pupil must begin by fixing attention receptively upon (strategically termed 'taking pleasure in') the wisdom teacher's counsel (23:26). Against two dissipation-traps the youth must be on guard: erotic and alcoholic (23:27–28 and 29–35, respectively). For like a thief the prostitute ambushes and then franchises treachery, while alcohol makes injured idiots of its willing addicts.

Before advocating pursuit of wisdom (dissipation's alternative), the sage pointedly charges the youth neither to 'long after people disposed to evil', nor to 'desire to be with them' (24:1). For their type can produce only 'devastation' and 'harm' (v. 2).

Having dispatched dissipation with its impoverishment and imprisonment, the script explores wisdom – that alternative longing – with its consequences (24:3–14). Instead of destruction and poverty, wisdom will yield security and wealth (vv. 3–4). Instead of inflicting harm (v. 2b), wisdom's adherents liberate captives (vv. 5–6).

In contrast (and despite lofty claims), a fool generates self-harm, not security (24:7–8). In moral rank he eclipses only the loud-mouthed scoffer (v. 9).

Lest the youth congratulate himself for being neither fool nor scoffer, with their counterfeit claims of wisdom, the sage issues a reprimand about counterfeit claims of ignorance (24:10–12). He asks, in effect, 'What of those you know who suffer victimization, who even now are being dragged to wrongful death, tottering to their own slaughter?' (cf. Fox 2009: 747). 'Has your strength (24:5) matured to the point of bringing deliverance to hostages (24:6)? Or is your strength only for show – inwardly spineless when calamity strikes captives (24:10)? Do not presume to hide behind hollow claims of ignorance as you protest, "Look: we knew nothing of their victimization!"' (24:12a).

'Do not cower before my trivial censure,' the sage persists. 'The one you truly should be concerned about is the divine, who observes your life. Though you claim not to know, he most surely does, and will "reward" you for what you, mere mortal, have done or have left undone (24:12b).'

Waltke observes, 'To the injustice of not helping the defendant (v. 11), v. 12a adds the injustice of lying' (2005: 277).

Before advancing to the script concerning preoccupation with the guilty (24:15–22), the sage encourages 'my son' to indulge longings for sweet wisdom, just as he must deny longings erotic and alcoholic (vv. 13–14). Thus he will achieve no less than 'a future' marked by 'hope that will not be cut off' (recall 'future' in 23:18). 'The outcome of internalizing the revealed moral order is nothing less than unending eternal delight' (Waltke 2005: 282).

Block III.B, Unit 2 (24:15–22). After the longing after dissipation (Unit III.B.1), twin longings from a new source may derail the youth's pursuit of wisdom (Unit III.B.2, 24:15–22). That source is the guilty. The twin longings appear most clearly in two prohibitions of v. 19. On the one hand, one may long for revenge against the guilty, due to crimes suffered at their hands ('Refrain from rising anger about wicked folk', v. 19a). Alternatively, one may long after their guilty gains ('Do not long after guilty folk,' v. 19b).

To discourage the youth from longing for supposed gains of the guilty, the sage warns at this unit's start that they will not last (24:15–16). Against longing for revenge the sage warns next that to celebrate enemies' demise incurs divine disfavour (24:17–18).

Assuredly, no 'future' awaits the wicked (24:20; cf. 23:18; 24:14). The LORD and the king will see to that. Therefore, instead of envy or revenge, one should concentrate on rendering due reverence (in 24:21a, directly after mention of 'future' in 24:20; also in 23:17, directly before mention of 'future' in 23:18).

Reminiscent of shifting boundary lines for personal gain (22:28; 23:10), it makes no sense to find common cause 'with people who shift' (24:21b). They will suffer ambush by immeasurable ruin (v. 22).

23:13–14. Ironically, although administering reproof will not cause death, withholding it will (by non-rescue from Sheol).

23:17–18. The quatrain spanning 23:17–18 ranks among the most central and solemn of this lecture, advocating unrelenting divine reverence (v. 17b), and affirming the prospect of undying hope (v. 18b). These richly displace misguided longings (v. 17a) by riveting one's reverential focus 'all day long' (v. 17b).

23:23. As an Egyptian vizier observed long ago, the worth of truth derives from its durable, trustworthy nature: 'The strength of *maʿat* [truth/justice] is that it lasts' (*The Instruction of the Vizier Ptah-hotep*; Wilson 1969: 412).

23:29–35. In an ancient Egyptian school-letter a father cautions his son against drunkenness with these words: 'Beer makes (you) stop being a man. It makes your soul to wander, and you are like a crooked steering oar in a boat that obeys on neither side' (Papyrus Anastasi IV 11.9–11, quoted in Fox 2009: 743).

24:1. To infer that the sayings spanning 24:1–22 comprise an alphabetic acrostic (the Hebr. alphabet has twenty-two letters) overlooks structural evidence indicating that the first two verses (24:1–2) do not mark the start of a composition, but join to what precedes. They recap the theme cautioning against longing for dissipation leading to destruction, a theme that began in 23:17. Fox refutes inference of an acrostic (only in v. 1 does the first word match the alphabet sequence), yet maintains that 24:1–22 'is clearly demarcated as a unit', based on alphabetic quantity (2009: 743).

24:3. Towards the close of lectures that began in Prov. 1 the sage portrayed Lady Wisdom building a lavish house (9:1a). As lectures beginning in Prov. 10 approach their close, again the poet attributes to wisdom a sturdy house.

24:6b. This expression appeared in 11:14.

24:14. Solemnity marks this tricolon. Both drawn to wisdom by appetite (24:13), and driven to wisdom by necessity ('as if your life depended on it', v. 14), the youth must 'know wisdom experientially'. Only thereby will he gain a future. Failing wisdom, the future will fail (cf. 24:20).

24:20. The expression 'the lamp of guilty folk will go out' appears also in 13:9b.

24:21–22. A hazard exceeding the penalty associated with boundary-shifting (22:28; 23:10) attaches to persons who themselves 'shift'. The opening portion of the next section will indict the related practice of moral relabelling, a specific example of boundary-shifting (24:23–26).

Section IV (24:23–34). Although the incisive exhortation to reverence concluding Section III delivers a potent climax ('Revere the LORD, my son, and the king,' 24:21–22), and despite the distinct division marked by the next sentence ('These, too, pertain to the wise', 24:23a), the lecture that began in 22:17 will not reach its carefully composed close apart from Section IV (24:23–34).

Recalling the earlier caution not to 'crush the oppressed in court' (22:22b), again in conclusion the sage warns against colluding with evil enticement by redrawing moral boundaries in a judicial setting ('show[ing] favouritism in court proceedings' in 24:23b–24). Such counsel for moral formation would be especially suitable for a wisdom learner (cf. 22:22–28). Suitable for a wisdom teacher would be the exhortation to administer reprimand in order to reaffirm boundaries that distinguish right from wrong (24:25–26; cf. 23:12–14).

Better still than either respecting or even reaffirming moral boundaries is the strategy of industry. Instead of shifting boundaries so as to encroach on another's field, one should invest energies in 'the field belonging to you; then, afterwards, build your house' (24:27; cf. 22:29; 24:3). Here is a wholesome formula to secure a sustainable income and a resilient family.

The sage proceeds to reinforce these two points (refraining from trespassing moral boundaries, and urging industry). Regarding the first, one must resist any temptation enviously to smear another with baseless indictments (24:28a). (Unprovoked malice [24:28] implies envy due to the link with revenge in v. 29, based on the general theme of longings spanning 23:15 – 24:22, and based more specifically on the sage's earlier pairing of envy with revenge in 24:15–20.) One must carefully review what might already have passed his or her lips – sly words of suspicion or statements of overt slander (v. 28b). Even after offence, one must disallow revenge (v. 29).

Better still than refraining from tearing down another is the initiative that invests energies within the legitimate boundaries of one's own 'field' (24:27; contrast 23:10 and 24:30–31). Instead to slumber uninterrupted will slowly compound, morphing into a menacing marauder who will relieve the sleeper of all assets (vv. 32–34). It is insufficient merely to remain respectfully within the boundaries of one's own field (admirably refusing to shift another's boundaries). For without industry no harvest will result – a fact persuasively argued by the crop of useless weeds overflowing the lazy fellow's untilled field.

This call to implementation strategically concludes Division II. For, without activation all the sage's past lectures will remain fruitless. Jesus similarly closed three chapters of teaching (Matt. 5 – 7) with a story about implementation (Two houses, Matt. 7:24–27; esp. vv. 24a and 26a).

By the story about the indolent fellow's field, the sage introduces a sapiential dimension not previously seen in Proverbs. Here at last the sage divulges how he goes about fashioning a proverb. Observation (strolling past the field of the lazy fellow, 24:32aα) leads to reflection ('my mind began to take note', v. 32aβ), which crystallizes in a 'reproof' (24:32b–34). Now the way is open for the wisdom learners to begin crafting and transmitting apophthegms of their own.

24:23–34. In the LXX the material that begins 'These also pertain to the wise' (24:23–34) appears directly after 30:14 of the Hebr. text (see discussion of LXX in §4.2 of the 'Introduction').

24:23. Deut. 1:17 expresses an equivalent caution against preferential treatment in judicial proceedings.

24:24. The sage earlier indicted reversal of the moral values of guilt and honesty (17:15).

24:30–34. Proverbs seldom discloses the context for a single saying, let alone a complete origin story. As an exception, the father-sage relates in 4:1–4 how as a child he received legacy wisdom from his own father. Similarly King Lemuel recalled a time when he was the target of his mother's reproof – which reproof he then transmits to his hearers or readers (31:1).

Explanation

Section I. Introductory wisdom commendations: for learners, for teachers (22:17–21)

In the masterful lecture concluding Division II (Prov. 10 – 24), the sage gathers climactic thoughts as he prepares his pupils for leadership careers of service (a transition realized in Division III). Anticipating the twofold concern expressed by a later biblical mentor, here the sage urges youths to 'let drift neither yourself nor your teaching' (paraphrase of 1 Tim. 4:16a).

To prevent drifting personally the sage charges us – regardless of our age or station – rigorously to practise receptivity to counsel offered by others (22:17–18). High-grade counsel will cultivate unrivalled reliance on the LORD (v. 19; cf. 3:5–6; also Acts 16:31; 1 Peter 1:7).

To prevent our teaching from drifting, the sage points back to the foundation found in truth. Truth he has faithfully transmitted to us (22:20–21a). And it is truth that we, in turn, reliably must transmit to others (v. 21b).

Section II. Wisdom content: instructions for pupil as wisdom learner, to counteract the allure of boundary-shifting (22:22 – 23:11)

Consider more fully the first instruction – how to guard ourselves against drifting from stalwart confidence in the divine. Drift grows noticeable as our perspective alters relative to stable moral points of reference. As we manipulate moral boundaries, we betray the erosion of our trust in the sufficiency of divine supply (22:28; 23:10–11).

Boundary-shifting may take the shape of encroaching on another's rights by manipulating rules and regulations to our advantage (22:22–23), or by suing for reasonable retribution while blinded by anger (vv. 24–25). It may take the shape of seeking lazy gain by foolishly lending our credit, whether in currency or character (vv. 26–27).

None of these will pan out, since attempting to achieve satisfaction through illicit gains will remain hopelessly elusive. For navigating by appetites (not morals) will blind us to their addictive and deceptive enslavement (23:1–3). Chasing after the ever-receding glitter of wealth will achieve only immeasurable exhaustion (vv. 4–5). Those whom we may admire for advancing further along this crumbling route will only disappoint, using and then disposing of us (vv. 6–8).

Supposing to get ahead by abusively manipulating boundaries makes as much sense as bestowing precious counsel on someone determined not to hear (23:9–10). God will avenge the helpless boundary-victim (v. 11). Instead we must focus diligently on our own legitimate labour. Only such a strategy yields advancement (22:29).

Section III. Wisdom content: instructions for pupil as wisdom teacher, concerning the sole objective worthy of youth's pursuit (23:12 – 24:22)

Then we must consider more fully the second instruction – how to keep our teaching from drifting. As teachers, we must first model receptivity to reproof (23:12). How much do we value caution or correction offered by others?

Then we must be willing to transmit reproof (23:13–14a). Instead to shrink from caring confrontation only coddles and consigns to destruction those we would mentor (v. 14b).

Concerning the content of our teaching, how can we keep it from shifting? As foreshadowed in the introduction, our teaching must be founded on the bedrock of truth and integrity (22:20–21; 23:16). Foundational to truth is an outlook that ranks and reveres God as high above all, from start (23:17) to finish (24:21–22). A reverential outlook alone will be able to navigate the future in a way that attains durable hope (23:18). An early lesson in the curriculum of truth will expose the false advertising concerning dissipation, such as illicit sex or gluttony (23:19–20). Instead of satisfaction, these bring only impoverishment (v. 21).

Beyond embracing truth ourselves, we will impress on our pupils the centrality of pursuing truth (23:22–23). For it is a life marked by morality that will generously instil authentic joy (vv. 24–25) – not the counterfeit joy of promiscuity (vv. 26–28) or chemical imprisonment (vv. 29–35). That is why we must envy neither the attainments nor the companionship of the evil (24:1–2).

When trained by wisdom and truth, not only will our pupils enjoy rich personal security (24:3–4). From that secure foundation, through their courageous labours they will rescue those who have become trapped (24:5–6, 10–12). 'It is not enough to refrain from committing wrongs; you must actively try to prevent them' (Fox 2009: 747). Instead merely to boast of our wise strategizing (without practical wisdom to back it up) will earn communal rejection (24:7–9).

Unlike addictive dissipations, to long after wisdom (like truth) remains a noble, rewarding appetite, preparing us and those we train to venture into the future with durable hope (24:13–14; cf. 23:23). Instead to long after the guilty (envious of their advances) or to cherish longings against the guilty (resentful of their offences) will divert a pupil from the optimal route – a path marked by reverence for God and respect for leaders (24:15–22). For eventually the guilty will suffer irreparable disaster, brought about by those whom their arrogance refused to revere (v. 22). Simply put, 'a future cannot materialize for the wicked person; the lamp of guilty folk will go out' (v. 20).

Section IV. Recap concerning boundaries: cautions against trespassing, and exhortations to industry (24:23–34)

In conclusion, we must guard ourselves against the temptation to trespass ethical boundaries by awarding a free pass to immoral conduct, whether the misbehaviour of someone we may envy (24:23–24), or our own misbehaviour – even when offences we have suffered may seem to justify revenge (vv. 28–29). We must steel ourselves against culture's cry to relabel moral values (v. 24), courageously reprimanding ethically transgressive behaviour (vv. 25–26).

Yet simply to preserve boundaries will bring home no harvest. Merely to refrain from trespassing into another's field will never sow our own. We must take initiative to venture outside, energetically cultivating whatever productive field is rightfully ours (24:27a). Even noble goals such as providing a comfortable dwelling should defer to the priority of establishing a stable income (v. 27b). Authentic productivity requires both integrity (operating within bounds) and initiative (24:30–34). Else, like a robber, our own indolence will leave us with nothing but a field overrun with empty regrets (vv. 30–34).

Finally, we should train ourselves to walk through life observantly (24:30–34). By paying attention to what works and what does not, we may harvest wisdom insights. Those insights, in turn, will enable us as wisdom teachers to help others achieve a flourishing life.

DIVISION III (PROV. 25 – 29): ADVICE FOR THE JOURNEYMAN SAGE, SERVING THE ROYAL COURT

Division III (Prov. 25 – 29) consists of Solomonic material edited by King Hezekiah's staff. Regarding form, a wisdom commendation marks the upper boundary of this division (25:1–3), while the last lecture (and lower boundary of Division III) coheres in a sevenfold refrain (28:1 – 29:27).

Regarding content, Division III serves kings and courtiers. Both are treated in Lecture One – a dual-theme introduction to the division. Lecture Two serves courtiers, while Lecture Three deals with both courtiers and kings. Division III closes by concentrating attention on kings in Lecture Four. Taken together, these poems form a master lecture suitable for journeyman sages (including monarchs) who aspire to lead their community to magnificence (cf. 'glory' in 25:2, 27; 26:8; 27:18; 29:23 [inclusio with 25:2]). Millar observes that 'the king and courtier might be idealized figures, *pedagogically* designed as standards for evaluation or paradigms for emulation' (2020: 189; emphasis original). For a fuller discussion of inter-poem progression, inter-division progression and the audience intended for this division of Proverbs, see the 'Introduction', §3.3.

Advice for the journeyman sage (to achieve a magnificent monarchy)	
Lecture One:	How may a monarchy (king and courtier) attain magnificence? (25:1–12)
Lecture Two:	What counsel may guide courtiers who aspire to magnificence? (25:13 – 27:22)
Lecture Three:	What may courtier and king learn from a farmer? (27:23–27)
Lecture Four:	What counsel may guide kings who aspire to magnificence? (28:1 – 29:27)

PROVERBS 25:1–12
'Lecture one (introduction): How may a monarchy attain magnificence?'

Overview of Proverbs 25:1–12

In Division III the first lecture (25:1–12) provides a dual-theme introduction to the master lecture's principal audiences – kings and courtiers – in their quest for magnificence. Subsequent lectures concentrate on courtiers and kings, in turn (Lectures Two and Four, respectively). This first lecture even previews particular counsel the sage later will direct towards these distinct groups. Towards its close the sage launches reproof, a theme that returns towards the close of Lectures Two and Four.

Position of this poem within Proverbs

Preceding context. The preceding lecture closed Division II with guidance for youths on the verge of assuming leadership positions. In contrast, the present lecture envisions an audience serving within the monarchy, whether as courtiers or as king.

The previous lecture's injunction to 'Revere the LORD, my son, and the king' (24:21a) anticipates two roles that feature in the first wisdom saying of the present lecture. Deity and monarch hold a keen interest in wisdom, whether to craft or to uncover it (25:2).

Ensuing context. The second lecture of Division III offers counsel to courtiers (25:13 – 27:22). After a brief poem pertaining to both kings and courtiers (Lecture Three, 27:23–27), the sage concludes with counsel primarily for kings (Lecture Four, 28:1 – 29:27).

What to watch for

Topics of splendour (including the term 'glory') and refining are key to this lecture. Certain counsel will apply to kings, other counsel to courtiers. Note sayings involving wisdom generally, or reproof specifically. Observe the distinction between wisdom dispensed in 25:11, and wisdom received in v. 12.

Translation and outline

Verse	*Translation*	*Outline*
		I. Wisdom commendation: the connection between wisdom, monarchs, the divine and magnificence (25:1–3)
25:1	These, too, are Solomonic proverbs, which the men of Hezekiah, king of Judah, arranged.	A. Editorial note concerning monarchs and wisdom (25:1)

Verse	*Translation*	*Outline*
		B. Wisdom as essence of magnificence, and those who purvey it (25:2–3)
25:2	The glory of God is to conceal a saying, while the glory of kings is to search out a saying.	1. The essence of magnificence consists of wisdom – the domain of God and kings (25:2)
25:3	Skies extend to the heights, the earth extends to the depth, but the mind of kings is unsearchable.	2. The king's unique qualification to deal in wisdom (25:3)
		II. Wisdom content: counsel for king and courtier, to achieve magnificence (25:4–12)
25:4	Remove dross from the silver: thus a vessel has emerged for the refiner.	A. Counsel for kings: justice in the quest for magnificence (25:4–5)
25:5	Remove a guilty person who is before a king: so that through morality his throne may be established.	
		B. Counsel for courtiers (dual-theme*): self-control concerning greed, and shrewdness concerning generosity, in the quest for magnificence (25:6–10)
		1. Self-control concerning greed: when inclined to advocate for self (25:6–7)
25:6	Do not put on airs before a king, and in the place reserved for people of prominence do not stand.	a. Prohibition: restrain boastful promotion of greed (25:6)
25:7	For it would be better if he were to say to you, 'Come up here,' rather than bringing you low in the presence of a prince, someone whom your eyes regarded.	b. Incentive: to gain honour, not insult (25:7)
		2. Shrewdness concerning indiscriminate generosity: when inclined to advocate for others (25:8–10)

25:8 Do not be in a hurry to argue a case. What can you do afterwards, when your neighbour puts you to shame? 25:9 It is your own case which you must litigate against your own neighbour. You must not take up in public someone else's personal concern.	a. Prohibition: restrain impulses of judicial helpfulness (25:8–9)
25:10 Otherwise, one who hears may shame you, and the evil report about you would not go away.	b. Incentive: to avoid gaining a bad reputation (25:10)
	C. The worth of wisdom, and especially reproof: counsel for kings and courtiers alike (25:11–12)
25:11 Golden apples within silver carvings – such is a saying said in the setting proper for it.	1. The worth of wisdom properly dispensed (25:11)
25:12 A golden ring and an inlay of rare gold – such is one who wisely reprimands a listening ear.	2. The worth of reproof properly received (25:12)

*The 'dual-theme' concerning greed and generosity in the lives of courtiers introduced in Block II.B will be expanded in the first and last of seven characters presented in 25:13 – 27:4 of Lecture Two.

Notes on the text

25:1. '[they] arranged': lit. '[they] moved'. Likely this connotes more than copying material from one manuscript to another, since copying generally was completed not by a group, but by a single individual (Fox 2009: 777).

25:2. 'to search out a saying', *ḥăqōr dābār*: lit. 'to search out a saying' or 'matter'. Two connotations combine here: (a) king as sage crafting insightful sayings, and (b) king as judge testing the validity of allegations. Mention of 'proverbs' in 25:1a recommends the first. Mention of the king ridding the realm of the guilty persons in vv. 4–5 favours the second (cf. 29:3–14; esp. vv. 4, 14). When used in connection with *ḥqr*, 'to search out', the term *dābār*, 'saying', takes on the connotation of 'allegation' (e.g. Deut. 13:14 [v. 15 MT]; cf. Waltke 2005: 311).

25:3. 'Skies extend to the heights': lit. 'skies for height' ('extend to' is inferred in both cola of 25:3).

25:4. 'Remove . . . : thus [it] has emerged', *ḥāgô . . . wayyēṣēʾ*: the infin. abs. *ḥāgô*, 'remove', operates as an emphatic imperative (GKC §113.bb; *IBHS* §35.5.1; cf. 5:5; 12:7; 13:20). Use of a wayyiq. form (*wayyēṣēʾ*) conveys a consequence that transpired in the past (a beautiful vessel 'has emerged', in consequence of dross having been removed).

25:5. 'Remove . . . : so that [it] may be established', *ḥāgô . . . wĕyikkôn*: here again an infin. abs. operating as an imperative (as in 25:4a) leads to a weyiq. form to express purpose (*wĕyikkôn*, 'so that it may be established'; *IBHS* §39.2.2.a).

25:7. 'someone whom your eyes regarded': the context of upward aspiration (25:6) implies longing eyes, not mere observation (cf. 27:20).

25:9. 'your own case . . . your own neighbour', *rîbkā . . . rēʿekā*: repetition of poss. pronoun stresses the need to focus attention on one's own concerns, not those of another.

'You must not take up in public', *ʾal-tĕgāl*: lit. 'do not disclose'. In connection with a legal suit this refers to taking a case before a judge (Jer. 11:20; 20:12).

'someone else's personal concern', *sôd ʾaḥēr*: lit. 'another's confidential matter.' Given the legal context, *sôd*, 'personal concern', here refers to a private legal complaint. While it is true that one should not openly disclose another's confidential information, that counsel is not the point of this colon (*pace* NIV ['do not betray another's confidence'] and NRSV ['do not disclose another's secret']). The next lecture will clarify when one must refrain from endorsing another's personal concern (26:17–28). In contrast, the sage elsewhere mandates advocacy when death threatens innocents (24:10–12).

Form and structure

Borders

A named authorship attribution establishes the upper border (25:1). Then follows a wisdom commendation set in a divine and monarchial arena (vv. 2–3).

Two inclusios indicate 25:11–12 as the lower border. At the macro level, an inclusio involving the root *dbr* anchors in 'saying', appearing twice in 25:2 (which forms a quatrain with v. 3). That root returns in 'saying' and 'said' (v. 11, which forms a quatrain with v. 12). Within Section II, metallurgy links the first and last quatrains (vv. 4–5, 11–12), confirming the poem's lower border.

Macrostructural features

Wisdom commendation followed by wisdom content (Sections I and II, content-based). The first section forms a wisdom commendation, fostered by references to 'saying' (twice in 25:2), 'to search out' (also v. 2) and 'mind' (v. 3). The first verse also enhances the reputation of wisdom, announcing a collection of 'proverbs' with royal roots. The balance of this lecture consists of wisdom content (Section II, vv. 4–12).

Repetition of 'king' (Sections I and II, form-based). Repetition of 'king' focuses attention on the monarchy in Section I and in the first block of Section II (25:1, 2, 3, 5). Mention by noun and pronoun in Block II.B shows that the courtiers operate in a royal environment (vv. 6, 7). In retrospect, even the naming of two monarchs in the authorship credits contributes to a royal atmosphere.

Microstructural features

Repetition of 'searching out' and 'kings' (25:2–3, form-based). Repetition of the expression 'search' (or 'unsearchable') with 'kings' joins 25:2, 3.

Thematic continuity concerning refinement (25:4–5, form- and content-based). 'Removal' of something impure or undesirable in 25:4, 5 establishes a theme of refinement for those sayings, forming a quatrain.

Prohibition-plus-incentive pattern (25:6–7, 8–10, form-based). The verse-clusters spanning 25:6–7 and 8–10 begin with prohibitions (vv. 6, 8–9), followed by incentives (vv. 7, 10). These adjacent portions of imperative-plus-incentive join to form a block (Block II.B, vv. 6–10).

Contrasting prohibitions (25:6–7, 8–10, content-based). Courtiers must guard against greed: presumptuously boasting before one's superiors (25: 6–7). They must also beware of irresponsible generosity: hastily advocating for others in the context of litigation (vv. 8–10). Greed and generosity form a contrasting pair.

Thematic continuity comparing wisdom to jewellery (25:11, 12, form- and content-based). The sage likens wisdom to jewellery with the term 'golden' in both 25:11 and 12.

Progression in wisdom labels (25:11–12, content-based). Although both 25:11 and 12 deal with wisdom, the first uses the general label 'saying', while the second specifies 'reprimand' – a more specific form of wisdom.

Contrast between giving and receiving wisdom (25:11–12, content-based). Although both 25:11 and 12 deal with wisdom, the first focuses on how it should be given ('a saying [which was] said'). The second emphasizes how it should be received ('a listening ear').

Comment

Section I (25:1–3). After crediting these sayings to Solomon (with the help of King Hezekiah's staff, 25:1), the sage anchors magnificence in neither opulence nor influence, but in wisdom divinely deposited, recovered by monarchs (v. 2). In view of vv. 4–5, the royal proclivity for ferreting-out wisdom relates to the king's duty to root out criminal activity from the realm (see 'Notes' for v. 2, above).

With their divinely appointed role of discovering wisdom, kings operate without human peer (25:3). Waltke observes that vv. 2–3 serve to establish the descending hierarchy of God, king and subjects (2005: 310).

LXX follows Prov. 24 with 31:1–9. Then appears Prov. 25 – 29, followed by the balance of Prov. 31.

25:1. Hezekiah's reign (728–687 BC) began two centuries after the close of Solomon's.

25:2. By initially referring to God as Elohim, the sage sets wisdom in a global framework. Later the master lecture will refer specifically to Yahweh, the God of Israel (cf. 25:22; 28:5, 25; 29:13, 25, 26).

Since it is concealed, wisdom may initially be counterintuitive. Since it must be uncovered (not fashioned), the sage implies that one ought not so much to 'make sense' of life than to 'find sense' divinely concealed within life.

25:3. Directed to courtiers, this saying may alert them to the fact that their monarch's 'quirky mind and changing whims' at times may be inscrutable to subordinates (Fox 2009: 779).

Section II (25:4–12). After establishing that magnificence derives from wisdom, in Section II the sage counsels the king (Block II.A, 25:4–5) and courtiers (Block II. B, vv. 6–10) in pursuit of magnificence. The importance of wisdom as reproof closes the lecture (Block II.C, vv. 11–12).

A monarch intent on expanding magnificence must confront and eradicate wrongdoing (Block II.A, 25:4–5). Like removing impurities from silver ore, this will improve the lustre of the realm.

For their part, courtiers' dreams of greatness may go wrong in two ways (Block II.B, 25:6–10). First, greed may prompt empty boasts calculated to impress those whom they envy (vv. 6–7) – a hazard that grows clearer in Lecture Two (cf. 25:13–28). Second, indiscriminate generosity may cause courtiers to lend influence to another's unworthy claim (25:8–10) – a hazard that similarly grows clearer in Lecture Two (cf. 26:1–28).

The lecture closes with counsel applicable to king and courtier alike. Since wisdom is the true currency of magnificence (25:2), like a goldsmith's glittering craftsmanship the route to genuine splendour will be marked by wisdom, both unveiled in timely circumstances (v. 11), and admired by persons receptive to its priceless message – especially a message of reproof (v. 12).

25:7. Jesus similarly counselled guests in deferential conduct, including the motivation of avoiding disgrace or gaining honour (Luke 14:7–11).

Explanation

Four key principles unfold within this poem regarding magnificence in leadership.

First principle: the nature of true magnificence
The sage begins by defining the nature of true magnificence. Magnificence consists of the ability to uncover wisdom that God has cached within the universe (25:2). One must not be misled by the glitter of wealth, prestige or power. Wisdom alone can lead to magnificence since only wisdom enables a life aligned with the divine, who remains the sole source of immeasurable splendour.

Second principle: the chief responsibility of leaders
The second principle defines the foremost responsibility for leaders intent on magnificence. Such a leader must focus his or her authority on weeding out immoral conduct. Equity will characterize the resulting environment – a realm in which morality will thrive naturally. Such a focus yields the reward of a durable dynasty (25:4–5).

Third principle: the responsibilities of subordinate persons
For their part, subordinates must guard against greed that chases after advancement. Presumptuous self-promotion will result in humiliation (25:6–7). Similarly unwise is generosity in the form of hair-trigger advocacy – lending reflex-like support to another's untested claim of victimization (vv. 8–10). Where genuine offence has been suffered, it should be settled methodically and directly, between the principal parties.

Fourth principle: the critical role of reproof in attaining magnificence
This introductory lecture concludes by stressing that any intent on magnificence – whether as leader or as subordinate – must reckon with the indisputable value of wisdom. Those positioned to dispense wisdom must take care lest wisdom spoil due to poorly timed transmission (25:11). Conversely, those who should receive wisdom must take care not to bristle at reproof. Instead they must deeply embrace it, until the raw material of personal character gleams with refined magnificence – as a 'ring' beautifully adorning the listening ear (v. 12).

PROVERBS 25:13 – 27:22
'Lecture two: What counsel may guide courtiers who aspire to magnificence?'

Overview of Proverbs 25:13 – 27:22
Lecture One took up the implicit question 'How may a monarchy attain magnificence?' (25:1–12). Now the sage focuses on courtiers, as if responding to the question 'What counsel may guide courtiers who aspire to magnificence?' (Lecture Two, 25:13 – 27:22).

The poet advises against the twin hazards of greed (25:13–28) and indiscriminate generosity (26:1–28) by considering a series of seven persons towards whom the pupil may be inclined to respond with either greed (four relationships) or ill-advised generosity (three relationships). After a recap concerning greed and generosity (27:1–4), the sage teaches courtiers concerning reproof, both receiving it (vv. 5–10) and dispensing it (vv. 11–16). Here again relationships form the vehicle of instruction (vv. 17–18). These three topics (greed, generosity and reproof) comprise Section II.

After stressing the importance of personal reflection in order to discern one's own motives (27:19), Lecture Two closes by reviewing – in the same sequence – the three topics of Section II: greed, generosity and reproof (27:20, 21 and 22, respectively). This comprises Section III.

Position of this poem within Proverbs

Preceding context. In preliminary fashion Lecture One cautioned courtiers against greed and indiscriminate generosity (25:6–10). Now the sage develops each more fully, in the same sequence.

Lecture One closed with a quatrain concerning reproof, showing both how to dispense it effectively and how to receive it properly (25:11–12). In Lecture Two, Section II similarly closes with lessons on reproof, whether received (27:5–10) or dispensed (27:11–18).

Ensuing context. Lecture Three presents an agricultural illustration of effective management (27:23–27), forming a bridge linking courtiers in Lecture Two (25:13 – 27:22) with monarchs in Lecture Four (28:1 – 29:27).

Lecture Two shares with Lecture Four a rhetorical technique wherein paradoxical counsel concerning a lesson is delayed until its close. In Lecture Two, the avenue to attain glory for oneself paradoxically lies not in burnishing one's own reputation, but in pursuing the glory of another (in 25:27b, near the close of Block I.A [25:13–28]).

Two delayed paradoxes appear in Lecture Four. First, the path to becoming well-nourished paradoxically passes not through expanding one's appetite, but rather by relying on the LORD (28:25, near the close of Section I in Lecture Four [28:1–28]). Second, the path to improving one's lot lies not in anxiously scheming strategies of abuse spurred by greed (29:25a; cf. 29:5, 6). Instead the sage paradoxically advocates divine trust (29:25b; located two verses from the close of Lecture Four).

What to watch for

Note indications of greed and generosity associated with various characters. Note references to reproof, observing both concepts and relationships involving reproof. Mark when a key term appears twice in a single verse, considering whether these may be strategically positioned. Observe also the concept of refining raw materials. Watch for the return of principal themes (greed, generosity, reproof) in the closing verses.

Translation and outline

Verse	*Translation*	*Outline*
		I. Counsel for courtiers: lessons concerning greed and generosity, in seven relationships (25:13 – 27:4) A. Restraining the hazard of greed through self-control in four relationships, with recap (25:13–28) 1. Restraining promotion-greed in relation to one's employer (25:13–15)
25:13	As snow's chill on harvest day, so is a faithful envoy to his senders; and the soul of his master will he revive.	a. A dependable subordinate is refreshing (25:13)
25:14	Mist and wind, but no rain! Such is a person given to boasting about a false gift.	b. A subordinate who sacrifices integrity to gain advancement is disappointing (25:14)
25:15	Through patience a leader may be persuaded, and a soft tongue can crack a bone.	c. A self-controlled subordinate eventually advances (25:15)
		2. Restraining guest-greed in relation to one's neighbours (25:16–20)
25:16	You found some honey? Eat what you need, lest you eat your fill of it and vomit it up.	a. Self-control towards the generous neighbour (25:16–17)
25:17	Rarely may your feet be in your neighbour's house, lest he have his fill of you and start to hate you.	
25:18	A scatterer and a sword and a sharpened arrow is a person inclined to respond with false testimony against his neighbour.	b. Self-control towards the vulnerable neighbour (25:18–19)
25:19	A bad tooth and an unsteady foot – such is confidence in a treacherous person on a day of distress –	
25:20	One who pulls off a garment on a cold day, vinegar on soda, and one who sings songs to the tune of 'Wrong Motives'.	c. Core principle: wrong motives ruin an ostensibly generous deed (25:20)

Verse	Translation	Outline
25:21 25:22	If one who hates you is hungry, feed him some bread, and if he is thirsty, give him a drink of water. For, burning coals you are scooping on to his head, and the LORD himself will repay you.	3. Restraining revenge-greed in relation to one's adversaries (25:21–22)
25:23 25:24	A north wind will give birth to rain, and an indignant face – a sly tongue. It is better to live on the corner of a roof than with a wife disposed to contention, and a shared house.	4. Restraining the greed of self-centredness in relation to one's spouse (25:23–24)
25:25 25:26	Cool waters over a weary soul, such is a good report from a distant land. Muddied headwaters and a ruined spring, such is a moral person who loses his footing in the presence of a guilty person.	5. Block-level recap (25:25–28) a. Positive and negative recap of greed (25:25–26) i. Positive: remember to refresh your employer (25:25) ii. Negative: remember to remain morally grounded despite guilty opposition (25:26)
25:27 25:28	To eat a large quantity of honey is not good, but to search out their glory is glory. A city which has been breached has no wall, such is a person who has no restraint over his spirit.	b. Overarching principle concerning greed: self-control (25:27–28) i. Remember to prefer another's fame above greedy indulgence (25:27) ii. Remember the necessity of self-control (25:28)
		B. Refining the hazard of indiscriminate generosity through shrewdness, in three relationships (26:1–28) 1. Indiscriminate generosity towards the patently stupid is ill-advised (26:1–12)

26:1	As the snow in the summer and the rain at harvest, so for a stupid fellow glory is not fitting.	a. The harm of glory when indiscriminately awarded to the stupid (26:1)
26:2	As the bird is disposed to flutter, as the swallow is disposed to fly, so a groundless curse cannot alight.	b. Ineffective communication: a baseless curse poses no threat (26:2)
26:3	A whip for the horse, a bridle for the donkey, but a rod is for the back of stupid folk.	c. Unsuitable as a labourer; the stupid requires bodily harm (corporal discipline, 26:3)
26:4	Do not reply to a stupid fellow in a manner corresponding to his folly, lest you become like him – even you!	d. How not to answer a stupid person, to prevent imitation (26:4)
26:5	Reply to a stupid fellow in a manner corresponding to his folly, lest he become wise in his own estimation.	d'. How to answer a stupid person, to prevent 'know-it-all' (26:5)
26:6	He amputates both feet; he drinks violence – whoever sends messages by the hand of a stupid fellow.	c'. Unsuitable as a messenger; a stupid person's boss self-inflicts bodily harm (26:6)
26:7	Thighs were dangling on account of lameness, and a proverb was in the mouth of stupid folk.	b'. Ineffective communicator: a stupid person's proverb is useless (26:7)
26:8	As binding a stone into a catapult, so is one who gives glory to a stupid person.	a'. The harm of glory when indiscriminately awarded to the stupid (26:8)
26:9	A briar has come into the hand of a drunkard, and a proverb into the mouth of stupid folk.	b". Harmful communicator: a stupid person's proverb (26:9)
26:10	An archer who wounds everyone – such is one who hires a stupid fellow, and one who hires transients.	c". Unsuitable as an employee; the stupid person's boss inflicts bodily harm all on others (26:10)
26:11	As a dog returns to its vomit, a stupid person repeats his folly.	d". A stupid person perpetuates a self-imitation loop (26:11)

Verse	*Translation*	*Outline*
26:12	You have seen, no doubt, a person who is wise in his own estimation. A stupid person has more hope than he.	d'''. Yet a stupid person is not yet a know-it-all (26:12)
		2. Indiscriminate generosity towards the incurably lazy is ill-advised (26:13–16)
26:13	A lazy fellow said, 'A young lion is in the street – a lion is in the middle of the marketplace!'	a. Laziness presents immobility, camouflaged by caution (26:13)
26:14	The door pivots on its hinges, and a lazy fellow on his bed.	b. Laziness presents motion without advancement, camouflaged by exertion (26:14)
26:15	A lazy fellow hid his hand in the bowl; he is too weary to return it to his mouth.	c. Laziness presents motion with advancement, thwarted by non-completion (26:15)
26:16	In his own estimation, the lazy fellow is wiser than seven who respond with sound discernment.	d. Analysis of lazy person's failure: myopic arrogance, with no use for external advice (26:16)
		3. Indiscriminate generosity towards the seductively litigious is ill-advised (26:17–28)
26:17	As one who grasps a dog's ears, so is he who becomes enraged concerning a litigation not his.	a. Introducing the problem: advocacy ill-advised (26:17)
26:18	As a deranged fellow shooting flaming missiles, arrows with death,	b. What disqualifies a plea for advocacy as illegitimate: deception (26:18–19)
26:19	So it was that a certain individual deceived his neighbour and then would say, 'Am I not merely making a joke?'	
26:20	For want of wood a fire will die out, and when there is no slanderer strife will grow silent.	c. How to verify a litigant's claims: remove him from the equation, then see whether the problem vanishes (26:20–21)

Translation	Outline
26:21 Charcoal fuel is to red-hot coals and wood is to fire as a contentious person is to the kindling of litigation.	
26:22 Words of a slanderer are like delicacies, so it is they that have descended deep within. 26:23 Silver consisting merely of silver-dross overlaid on earthenware: such are persons who set lips on fire with wrong motives.	d. Why unfounded litigation (slander) will not succeed (26:22–23) i. Because a longing to elevate self fuels an appetite for another's demotion (26:22) ii. Because confirmation bias is attracted to a glittering veneer, while ignoring the pernicious core (26:23)
26:24 By means of his lips one who hates may go undetected, but deep within he will be set on deception. 26:25 Although he may make his voice sound gracious, do not trust him, for there are innumerable abominations in his motives.	e. What truly motivates the seductive litigant, and how one should respond (26:24–25) i. They are motivated by an engine of revenge (26:24) ii. One should respond with a healthy suspicion, due to their sinister motives (26:25)
26:26 Hatred may cover itself with guile; its wickedness can be uncovered through a juridical assembly. 26:27 One who digs a pit – into it he will fall, and one who rolls a stone – to him it will return.	f. Will the seductive litigant ultimately succeed (26:26–27)? i. No, the community will expose his hatred (26:26) ii. For, as everyone knows, through retribution he will self-destruct (26:27)
26:28 A false tongue keeps on hating those whom it crushes, and a slick mouth will fashion an opportunity for stumbling.	g. Summary: deceptive revenge-seekers are intent on their own demise (26:28)

Verse	*Translation*	*Outline*
		C. Section recap (27:1–4)
27:1	Do not boast about yourself regarding tomorrow, for you cannot know what a day may bring forth.	1. Self-praise (boasting) exposes presumptuous greed (27:1–2; cf. 25:14)
27:2	May a stranger boast about you and never your own mouth, a foreigner, and not your own lips.	
27:3	A stone is a heavy load, and sand is a burden, but a fool's angry response is heavier than both.	2. The fool's anger over a request-refused will expose him (27:3–4; cf. 26:1–5)
27:4	Rage is cruel and anger is a flood, but who can remain standing in the face of revengeful wrath?	
		II. Lessons concerning reproof, both received and dispensed (27:5–18)
		A. Receiving reproof: the importance of relationships and receptivity (27:5–10)
27:5	Better is reproof revealed than love kept secret.	1. The comparative worth of reproof (27:5)
27:6	To be trusted are wounds from one who loves; but manipulative are kisses from one who hates.	2. Faithful relationships: the source for reproof (27:6)
27:7	A satisfied appetite will trample on a honeycomb. But as for a hungry appetite – anything bitter is sweet!	3. Receptivity: the requirement for reproof 27:7)
27:8	As a bird wandering from its nest, so is a person inclined to wander from his place.	4. The high cost of relationships rendered remote (27:8)
27:9	Perfume and incense may delight the mind, but sweetness of its friend issues from advice regarding appetite.	3'. Receptivity: optimized by fragrance and faithfulness (27:9)
27:10 a–b	Do not abandon your friend and your father's friend, and do not enter your brother's house when you experience distress;	2'. Faithful relationships: a priority meriting cultivation (27:10a–b)

Translation	Outline
27:10c Better is one who dwells nearby than a brother far away.	1'. The comparative worth of relationships that can offer reproof (27:10c)
27:11 Be wise, my son, and make my mind joyful; so may I have something to reply to one who reproaches me.	B. Dispensing reproof: a positive analysis and failed models (27:11–16) 1. A positive analysis of dispensing reproof: a maturity-milestone, rationale and urgency (27:11–13) a. Wisdom commendation: how a maturing son brings a father joy (27:11)
27:12 A shrewd fellow observed misery, he took cover; a naive fellow blundered forward, he was fined. 27:13 Grasp his garment, if he guarantees a loan for a stranger; and if he goes so far as to a foreign woman, tie him up!	b. Wisdom content: rationale and urgency of dispensing reproof (27:12–13) i. The rationale undergirding reproof: to enable early warning (27:12) ii. The urgency of dispensing reproof: intervention (27:13)
27:14 One who blesses his neighbour with a loud voice, rising early in the morning: a curse will be reckoned to him. 27:15 An incessant dripping on a persistently rainy day – that is what a contentious wife is like. 27:16 Those who hide her hide the wind, and oil will accidently get on his right hand.	2. Failed models for dispensing reproof (27:14–16) a. Men fail who employ words poorly timed (27:14) b. Women fail who employ words poorly metred (27:15) c. Dual-theme conclusion: she cannot be restrained (27:16a), while he loses his grip (27:16b)
27:17 May iron by iron grow sharp, and may a person sharpen the face of his friend.	C. Two relationships that successfully foster reproof (27:17–18) 1. A mutual relationship of reproof benefits both parties (27:17)

Verse	*Translation*	*Outline*
27:18	One who guards a fig tree will eat its fruit, and one who guards his master will be given glory.	2. A mentor relationship of reproof achieves glory (27:18)
		III. Recap: motives determine one's capacity through reproof to refine generosity by displacing greed, in quest of magnificence (27:19–22)
27:19	Just as water reveals the face to that face, so the motives reveal the mortal to that mortal.	A. Preface: thoughtful reflection will yield a realistic picture of one's own motives (27:19)
		B. Recap of counsel concerning greed and generosity (27:20–21)
27:20	Sheol and the underworld will not be satisfied, and the eyes of a mortal will not be satisfied.	1. Greed: when appetites drive behaviour, a person will be doomed to perilous dissatisfaction (27:20)
27:21	A smelting pot corresponds to silver, and a small smelting furnace corresponds to gold; and each individual corresponds to the sort of praise issuing from his mouth.	2. Generosity: magnificence manifests when reproof's crucible results in praise (27:21)
27:22	If you were to pulverize a fool in a mortar with a pestle, together with hulled barley, his folly would not leave him.	C. Recap of reproof: without receptivity, reproof concerning greed and generosity would be wasted (27:22)

Notes on the text

25:13. 'soul', *nepeš*: to convey the master's need for psychological refreshment, 'soul' fits better than 'appetite' (cf. 25:25).

25:16. 'You found some honey?', *dĕbaš māṣā ʾtā*: interrogative inferred from context, not marked by interrogative particle (cf. Joüon §161a).

25:19–20. 'unsteady' and 'pulls off', *mû ʿādeh* and *maʿădeh*: these join assonantally, although roots differ (*m ʿd* and *ʿdh*, respectively). Assonance also joins 'treacherous', *bôgēd*, in 25:19 and 'garment', *beged*, in v. 20 (divergent meanings from homonymous roots, both spelled *bgd*). The collection of three scenarios in v. 20 extends the list of two undesirable features in 25:19 ('a bad tooth and an unsteady foot') to form a single sentence. Since v. 20 reveals a core principle it merits separation in the outline.

25:20. 'One who pulls off a garment on a cold day': this describes the first of three ostensibly generous actions that harm due to deceptive motives (helping someone remove his garment when frigid weather advises against it, pouring out a gift of vinegar when the target of that gift [soda] will produce a ruinous reaction, and performing a supposedly cheery song set to a tune that undermines the message of its lyrics). Deceptive motives re-enter the lecture at 26:23, 25; 27:19.

'vinegar on soda', *ḥōmeṣ ʿal-nāter*: combining these two ingredients results in effervescence ('soda' refers to natron, sodium carbonate; Fox 2009: 786). If instead the LXX is correct in understanding *nāter* as 'wound', that meaning would endorse the understanding that this verse cautions against ostensible generosity (a pouring out of antiseptic vinegar) that inflicts pain.

'Wrong Motives', *leb-rāʿ*: lit. 'heart of evil' (here capitalized to represent modern convention that capitalizes the title of a musical composition, on which see below). When this same phrase appears later in this lecture, its malicious connotation is widely recognized (both Waltke and Fox render *leb-rāʿ* as 'evil heart' in 26:23 [2005: 342 and 2009: 800, respectively]). That sense of malice (not sadness) also fits 25:20 remarkably well. Instead to render *leb-rāʿ* in 25:20 as 'heavy heart' (Waltke 2005: 306) or 'sad heart' (Fox 2009: 786) misses the later link with *lēb*, 'motives', 27:19. The sage there elevates to climactic prominence the diagnostic value of *lēb*, 'motives' – with closural impact deriving from prior cautions against *leb-rāʿ*, 'wrong motives', in 25:20 and 26:23.

'and one who sings songs to the tune of "Wrong Motives"', *wĕšār bašširîm ʿal leb-rāʿ*: lit. 'and one who sings upon wrong motives'. When associated with song, a prep. phrase beginning with *ʿal* may indicate the name of a tune or the sort of musical instrument intended for that song (cf. superscriptions for Pss 6, 8, 9, 12, 45, 46, 53, 56).

25:22. 'and the LORD himself': lit. 'and the LORD'. Emphatic 'himself' reflects frontal extrapositioning of the subject.

25:23. 'and an indignant face – a sly tongue': the husband's indignant face generates the wife's sly tongue, just as in the previous colon the north wind gives birth to rain. The sage clarifies this generative relationship in the next verse by revealing the penalty the self-centred husband reaps from his now-contentious wife (25:24).

25:25. 'soul', *nepeš*: see 'Notes' for 25:13.

25:27. 'their glory', *kĕbōdām*: with Bryce to emend as *kĕbōd[î]m*, 'difficult things', would undermine the link operating at the level of the master lecture. 'Their glory' recalls the glory of God and of kings in 25:2 (note pl. in 'their' and 'kings'; 1972: 153).

26:2. 'alight': lit. 'enter, come'.

26:8. 'catapult': a handheld weapon of artillery, sometimes referred to as a 'slingshot'.

26:12. 'You have seen, no doubt', *rāʾîtā*: lit. 'you have seen'. Concerning the tendency to infer a question despite lack of the interrogative particle *hă* (as in NASB, NRSV and NIV), see 'Notes' for 22:29.

26:18. 'flaming missiles, arrows with death': lit. 'flaming missiles, arrows and death'.

26:23. 'with wrong motives', *wĕleb-rāʿ*: lit. 'with a bad mind' (cf. 25:20). Recent mention of duplicity (26:19), slander (vv. 20, 22) and sham (v. 23a), together with concealed hatred (vv. 24a, 26a) reinforce the connotation of *lēb* in v. 23 as 'motives' rather than 'heart' or 'feelings'.

26:25. 'innumerable': lit. 'seven'. Completeness connoted by the number 'seven' suggests limitlessness.

'in his motives', *bĕlibbô*: lit. 'in his mind' or 'heart'. As in 26:23, a context of concealed intent recommends *lēb* as 'motives'.

27:2. 'and never your own mouth . . . and not your own lips', *wĕlōʾ-pîkā . . . wĕʾal-śĕpāteykā*: through ellipsis the verb 'boast' is implied as the activity of both 'mouth' and 'lips'. Since negation with *lōʾ* is more comprehensive than with *ʾal*, they are rendered 'never' and 'not', respectively.

27:3. 'A stone is a heavy load': lit. 'a stone is heaviness'. Despite the *maqqef* joining these two words, it seems best to render the first as an absolute form, resulting in a verbless clause ('a stone is a heavy load'), not a const. chain ('a heavy load of stone').

'load . . . burden . . . heavier': a threefold progression of increasing heaviness. 'Burden' indicates a weight that has become more onerous, due to being moved from a static position (such as lying on the ground) to being imposed on a person or animal.

'angry response': lit. 'vexation'. Since this term can describe how one reacts with anger when treated wrongfully, it links to the theme of vengeful litigation that began in 26:17.

27:4b. 'revengeful wrath', *qinʾâ*: often rendered 'jealousy', *qinĕʾâ*, in connection with vengeful and sly litigation (26:17–22) implies a sort of wrath that, beyond the 'rage' and 'anger' of 27:4a, has escalated to a cruelly calculated response to real or perceived injustice.

27:6. 'manipulative': lit. 'being entreated, pertaining to supplication'. Such kisses are devoid of friendship, only signalling a supplicant's bribe, a prelude to petition (cf. Jones 2019: 117–118).

27:8. 'its nest', *qinnâ*: this expression is highly assonantal with 'revengeful wrath', *qinʾâ*, at the close of 27:4, although without structural connection.

27:9. 'Perfume and incense may delight': by coordinating a m. sg. verb ('[he/it] may delight') with a compound subject, the sage indicates that 'perfume and incense' function as a single idea (Joüon §150p; cf. 29:15a). Potentiality inferred from yiq.

'its friend': the antecedent of 'its' is 'mind'. Although one's mind may experience delight, even euphoria, as a result of aromatic stimuli (perfume and incense), that mind's authentic friend consists of one speaking sound – even confrontational – counsel concerning that same appetite for fragrance (cf. 27:13).

'issues from advice': lit. '[is] from advice'. As Waltke observes, the prep. *min* here signals source ('from'), not comparison ('sweeter than'), since comparison would require an adj. ('sweet') instead of the noun ('sweetness') that appears here (2005: 368).

27:16. 'those who hide her hide the wind', *ṣōpneyhā ṣāpan rûaḥ*: the first verb (a ptc.) is pl.; the second is sg., so that the second describes all members comprising the first. For the connection between 27:16a and 15, see under 'Comment' for these sayings. 'Hide' in 27:16 and 'north' in 25:23–24 share the same root. Both sayings refer to 'wind' and deal in marriage dynamics.

'will accidently get on': lit. 'will encounter by chance, by accident'. Whether during cooking or refilling lamps, people in ancient times often would transfer olive oil. Presumably then, as now, oil coating one's hands was deemed undesirable. For the connection between 27:16b and 14, see 'Microstructural features'.

27:19. 'reveals . . . reveal': 'to reveal' is inferred from the depiction of water's reflective quality.

'to that face . . . to that mortal': lit. 'to the face . . . to the mortal'. 'That' (in place of 'the') is inferred in each case.

'so the motives reveal the mortal to that mortal', *kēn lēb hāʾādām lāʾādām*: at the pre-Masoretic stage, no *maqqef* would have joined *lēb*, 'motives', to *hāʾādām*, 'mortal'. Consequently the first instance of 'mortal' could function as the object of the implicit verb 'to reveal' ('motives [reveal] the mortal', not 'motives of the mortal'). This pre-Masoretic reading is preferable since the resulting second colon ('motives reveal the mortal') more closely parallels the syntax of the first colon. That is, just as 'water' is absolute (yielding 'water reveals the face', not as a const. form, 'water of the face'), so also 'motives' should be read as absolute (yielding 'motives reveal the mortal', not in const., 'motives of the mortal').

In each phrase there is a reflective, revealing agent, whether 'water' or 'motives'. The visage thereby revealed is reflexive, so that an image of that person reflects back for the originator to see. A person peering into a calm pool sees his own likeness (not that of another), and a person peering into his motives discovers his own true character (not the character of another). The necessity of such self-awareness is consistent with the degree of prominence the sage accords self-control in this lecture.

27:21. 'corresponds to', *lĕ*: essential for careful reading of this verse is strict attention to the parallel structure of three Hebr. phrases. Three times the sage asserts that a first element (Item A) corresponds to a second element (Item B), connecting the two simply by *lĕ*, a prep. here best rendered ‘for’ or ‘corresponds to’: pot-to-silver, furnace-to-gold, individual-to-his-praise.

In each case, ‘Item A’ enables its respective ‘Item B’. That is, the smelting pot and small smelting furnace enable the processes that issue in refined silver or gold, respectively.

In the third pair, Item A is an ‘individual’. It is that individual (not praise) who, like smelting pot and furnace, constitutes the equipment from which raw material emerges with greater refinement and hence greater magnificence than in its unrefined state. LXX (and with it, most translations) unfortunately inverts the order of the third pair, incorrectly regarding ‘praise’ as the crucible-like refining agent, and the ‘person’ as the raw material towards which this praise is focused. This inversion incorrectly gives rise to a question such as this, for personal inventory: ‘How does a person respond, when subjected to praise?’ However, this diverges from what the sage wrote.

Instead the sage likens gold (issuing from the refining process) to praise, issuing from the mouth of the individual. Personal magnificence escalates as the praise one issues towards others grows increasingly sincere.

‘corresponds to the sort of praise issuing from his mouth’, *lĕpî lĕmahălālô*: lit. ‘corresponds to the mouth of the praise of him’. Due to the indivisible const. link joining ‘mouth of’ and ‘praise’, Hebr. requires that the poss. pronominal suff. ‘of him’ must be delayed till the end of the const. chain (i.e. it must follow ‘praise’), even when the intended meaning is ‘the mouth of him’; i.e. ‘his mouth’ (cf. 12:8, where *lĕpî-śiklô* means ‘according to his insightful statement [or mouth]’, not ‘according to the statement [or mouth] of his insight’). Another example may be helpful. The expression *kĕlê milḥamtô* woodenly would be rendered ‘the implements of the battle of him’, which one might suppose would mean ‘the implements of his battle’. But it means ‘his implements of battle’ (Deut. 1:41; Joüon §129kb). Again following LXX, modern translations routinely overlook the better alternative, resulting in wooden renditions that suppose that the praise issues from others who are lauding the ‘individual’ in this verse. To continue the error noted above, the recipient of praise then is ‘tested’ by how he responds to praise originating from others. However appealing this scenario may seem, it does not reflect the clear meaning of the Hebr.

The better translation (‘each individual corresponds to the sort of praise issuing from his mouth’) is supported by the fact that, earlier within this same lecture, the sage has already taken up this topic, namely the praise that one’s own mouth utters. At that point this praise was of a reflexive sort, wherein the person’s own mouth was employed in self-praise or boasting. The sage declared his opposition to this faulty route to magnificence: ‘May a stranger boast about you and never your own mouth, a foreigner and not your own lips’ (27:2). The fact that this warning appears within a section-recap amplifies its importance (within Block I.C, 27:1–4, closing Section I).

The sage's offsetting model – self-control seeking to expand the fame of someone else – he expressed even earlier in the lecture: 'To eat a large quantity of honey is not good, but to search out their glory is glory' (25:27; where 'their glory' recalls the glory of God and the king of 25:2, on which see above). Once again, the fact that this verse appears within a recap amplifies its importance (within Unit I.A.5, 25:25–28, closing Block I.A). For these reasons, the context leading up to 27:21 calls for *pî lĕmahălālô* to be rendered 'the sort of praise issuing from his mouth'. Given the context of refinement (contrasting the reproof-resistance of 27:22), this praise would be directed nobly towards others, not self.

To summarize: by setting 'each individual' parallel to the smelting equipment in 27:21, the sage teaches that each person possesses the capacity to refine 'the sort of praise issuing from his mouth' – choosing whether (a) he will posture his words for self-promotion (disregarding the sage's warning in 27:2), or whether (b) he will use his words to build the reputation of others (in keeping with the sage's counsel of 25:27). This choice goes to the heart of this entire lecture. Will the courtier eventually attain the magnificence he desires?

27:22. 'in a mortar . . . with a pestle': according to Num. 11:8, either mortar or millstones might be used to process grain. The word for 'pestle' occurs only here within the HB.

Form and structure

Borders

Concerning theme, the preceding poem introduced king and courtier in their quest for magnificence. The present poem concentrates on the courtier's contribution.

Recap of topics and six closural features indicate that this poem concludes with Section III (27:19–22). As to recap, earlier topics of magnificence, greed and generosity, and reproof combine in Section III. The recap comprising Section III spans four verses, resembling a pattern of recaps seen earlier in this lecture. In Block I.A, the first series of relationships (25:13–24) leads to a four-verse recap (Unit I.A.5, 25:25–28). All of Section I closes with another four-verse recap (Block I.C, 27:1–4).

The first of six closural features involves 'fool' and 'folly'. Foolish behaviour associates with indiscriminate generosity (26:4, 5, 11). 'Fool' resurfaces in the block recapping that section (27:3). The lecture's final verse recycles 'fool' and 'folly': 'If you were to pulverize a fool in a mortar with a pestle, together with hulled barley, his folly would not leave him' (27:22).

Second, closure results from expressions pertaining to metallurgic refinement – a metaphor introduced as early as the preceding poem as a metaphor for magnificence (cf. 25:4–5, 11–12). In Section I of the present lecture, metallurgy appears in the duplicity of skim-coating a cheap earthenware vessel with low-grade silver (26:23).

A few verses later minerals return with mention of 'stone' and 'sand': 'A stone is a heavy load, and sand is a burden, but a fool's angry response is heavier than both' (27:3). These are 'heavy', *kbd*, but not 'glorious' ('glory' also traces to *kbd*; cf. 25:2a, 2b, 27bα, 27bβ; 26:1, 8). No amount of refining can extract gold or silver from mere fieldstone or sand. Nor can folly be converted to wisdom or integrity. For, in response to generosity-denied or some manner of reproof, the fool reliably responds, not with receptivity, but with an angry outburst (27:3–4).

Refinement intensifies in the lecture's closing verses with mention of 'smelting pot', 'smelting furnace', 'silver', 'gold', 'pulverize', 'mortar' and 'pestle' (27:21–22). Like a refiner's fire, reproof offers the potential for fostering personal improvement that will evoke grateful praise from the reproof-recipient (27:21; see 'Notes'). However, no amount of corrective pressure can coax character from a fool (27:22). Like grain that refuses to separate from its hull, the fool remains impervious even to the impact of mortar and pestle. Like weighty-but-worthless fieldstone and sand, no alchemy exists to transform that raw material into anything even remotely glorious (27:3).

Third, closure results from recurrence of *hll*, to 'boast' or 'praise'. 'Boast' appears twice in the recap of Section I (27:1, 2). 'Praise' appears near the lecture's close in Section III (27:21).

Fourth, recurrence of 'face' fosters closure. 'Face' appears in connection with peer-to-peer candour in Section II (27:17), and twice in Section III (both in 27:19).

Fifth, repetition of 'satisfied' contributes to closure. In Section II, 'A satisfied appetite will trample on a honeycomb. But as for a hungry appetite – anything bitter is sweet!' (27:7). 'Satisfied' appears twice in Section III: 'Sheol and the underworld will not be satisfied, and the eyes of a mortal will not be satisfied' (27:20).

Sixth, closure arises from repetition of 'motives'. The sage refers to 'wrong motives', *leb rāʿ*, in Sections I and II (25:20; 26:23). Near the lecture's conclusion he isolates the importance of discerning one's own 'motives', *lēb* (27:19 in Section III). Nothing more effectively reveals to people their true character than an unvarnished view of their inner motives (27:19).

Macrostructural features

Two devices join sections of this lecture, in addition to the elements of recap and closure described above. Those devices involve repetition of 'glory' and opposing attitudes towards reproof.

Repetition of 'glory' (Sections I and II, form-based). Contributing to the master-lecture theme of magnificence, the term 'glory' appears in four sayings within this poem, strategically positioned. Containing 'glory' twice, the first such saying is located penultimately in Block I.A: 'To eat a large quantity of honey is not good, but to search out their glory is glory' (25:27). The second begins Block I.B (26:1). The third occupies a palistrophic pivot (26:8), while the fourth concludes Section II: 'One who guards a fig tree will eat its fruit, and one who guards his master will be given glory' (27:18). In addition to strategic positioning within respective portions, in the Hebr. text 'glory' in each saying appears line-terminal.

Opposing attitudes towards reproof (Sections I and II, form- and content-based). Within the first section's warning against indiscriminate generosity, the first two characters earn the designation 'wise in his own estimation' (twice for the stupid person in 26:5, 12, and once for the lazy person in 26:16). By dismissing these characters with their disinterest in reproof, the sage fosters esteem for any who would welcome reproof. This leads seamlessly to Section II with its extensive teaching about reproof (27:5–18).

Microstructural features

Section I (25:13 – 27:4). *Block I.A (25:13–28).* Thematic continuity surrounding greed (25:13–28, content-based). As indicated in Lecture One, courtiers must beware of greed and indiscriminate generosity (25:6–10). The first four of seven character-scenes in Lecture Two share a trait of self-centredness, corresponding to greed (25:14, 16, 17, 18, 19, 23). Rejection of greed is implied also by honouring its antithesis (25:21).

The first character angles (futilely) to impress and persuade a supervisor with a 'false gift' (25:13–15). Against this sort of advancement-greed the sage cautioned in Lecture One (25:5–6).

In the second scenario, greed emerges when self-control is dismissed in favour of overindulgence (25:16–17) and rapacious slander (vv. 18–19). Wrong motives will poison seeming kindnesses.

The third scenario challenges one not to hoard food and water greedily, even when the needy person is one's enemy. Generosity (25:21) and justice (v. 22) are not mutually exclusive.

The fourth scenario depicts the marriage relationship (25:23–24). A husband who treats his wife with cool self-preoccupation or with stormy disregard (25:23) will eventually attain the isolation he evidently desires (v. 24). Such self-centred indifference betrays greed.

To combat greed will require self-control. Lacking self-control, the courtier's life will prove as insecure as a city with ruined revetments – an open invitation to any marauding bands that chance may bring (25:27–28).

Thematic continuity concerning subordinate–supervisor relationships (25:13–15, content-based). A subordinate–supervisor relationship in 25:13–15 is indicated by mention of a 'faithful envoy' in the service of 'his senders' and 'his master' (v. 13), and by one who patiently persuades a leader (v. 15). Given this context, the 'false gift' of v. 14 aims to impress and persuade one's supervisor. Patience and quiet speech persuade better than empty promises (v. 15).

Thematic continuity concerning neighbour relations (25:16–20, form- and content-based). Mention of 'neighbour' in both 25:17 and 18 indicates the theme unifying vv. 16–19. The wise will let self-control govern neighbour relations, preventing both abuse of hospitality (vv. 16–17) and abuse of trust (vv. 18–19). Right motives would prevent kindness from serving as a front for manipulation (v. 20).

Thematic continuity concerning enemy relationships (25:21–22, content-based). The quatrain of 25:21–22 coheres in enemy relationships. When the pupil encounters hatred, he should respond with humanitarian compassion (v. 21). Paradoxically, this will effect a sort of revenge, earning divine reward (v. 22).

Repetition of 'eat' (25:16, 21, form-based). The root *ʾkl*, 'to eat' or 'feed', appears in the first sayings of adjacent characters in the greed group. When hosted by a neighbour (25:16–20), one should 'eat' only what is needed (v. 16). When encountering an enemy (vv. 21–22) in need of food, one should 'feed' him (v. 21).

Thematic continuity concerning marital relationships (25:23–24, content-based). An atmosphere of hostility unifies the quatrain spanning 25:23–24, evident in 'an indignant face', 'a sly tongue' and 'contention'. Consequently the marriage relationship explicit in v. 24 applies to v. 23 as well, forming a cause–effect verse-pair. Like the north wind's chill, a husband characterized by angry indifference will condition his wife to respond with sly, snide remarks. As this toxic atmosphere escalates and grows habitual, the husband will discover himself evicted, heir to the isolation he strove to attain.

Block-level closure (25:25–28, content-based). Six elements effect closure in 25:25–28 (recap to Block I.A). First, a 'good report' from 'a distant land', refreshing like 'cool waters' (25:25), recalls the message from an 'envoy' that 'revive[s]' one's 'master' like 'snow's chill' on a hot 'harvest day' (25:13).

Second, a 'moral person' who feebly forsakes integrity 'in the presence of a guilty person' and thus can no longer supply clear 'spring[water]' (25:26) recalls the converse: a person who clung to integrity in the presence of 'one who hate[d]' him, who supplied him with 'a drink of water' (25:21).

Third, binge-eating honey (25:27) recalls overeating honey to the point of nausea (25:16). 'Honey' does not appear elsewhere in this lecture.

Fourth, 'a person who has no restraint over his spirit' (25:28) recalls the fundamental flaw underlying each relationship governed by greed, whether in work relationships, neighbour relationships, adversarial relationships or in marital relationships (25:13–24). Each lacks self-control, inviting plunder by any passers-by.

Fifth, 'soul' appears at the start of this block (25:13) and at the start of its recap (25:25). 'Soul' does not appear elsewhere in Section I.

Sixth, 'wind/spirit' frames the first four units of Block I.A (in 25:14a of Unit I.A.1, and line-initial in v. 23, opening Unit I.A.4). 'Wind/spirit' contributes to closure for Block I.A when it appears only once more in this block, as the block's final word (25:28b).

Block-level closure (25:25–28, content-based). The verse-pairs in 25:25–26, 27–28 combine to recap Block I.A (25:13–28). Regarding 25:25–26, three concepts correspond to the 'employee' character in 25:13–15 (the first of four greed-themed characters). Both portions envision (a) an employee serving as an envoy, (b) a refreshing report and (c) a comparison to moisture, whether refreshing or disappointing ('snow', 'rain', 'cool waters', 'muddied headwaters' or 'a ruined spring').

Regarding 25:27–28, a theme of self-control unifies this verse-pair and connects it with preceding sayings. Self-control would moderate one's consumption of honey (25:16, 28). More broadly, self-control would prevent an employee from filing a falsely glowing report (25:13–14), and would calm his impatience towards an unreasonable supervisor (25:15). Self-control would deter taking indulgent advantage of his neighbour's hospitality (25:16–17) or abusing his neighbour's relative powerlessness (25:18–19, summarized in v. 20). An offended courtier must show considerable self-control towards those who hate him, replacing revenge with benevolent care (25:21–22). Finally, the married courtier must keep in check any inclination to treat his wife roughly, if he would avoid sparse and solitary accommodations (25:23–24). Thus the verse-pairs in 25:25–26, 27–28 combine to recap Block I.A (25:13–28).

Block-initial repetition of 'snow' and 'harvest' (25:13a; 26:1a, form-based). Both 'snow' and 'harvest' appear in 25:13a and 26:1a. These mark the initial sayings of Blocks I.A (25:13–28) and I.B (26:1–28). Nowhere else in the HB does this pair occur in a single verse.

Block I.B (26:1–28). Thematic continuity surrounding indiscriminate generosity (26:1–28, content-based). As indicated in Lecture One, courtiers must beware of both greed and indiscriminate generosity (25:6–10). Of the seven character-scenes in Lecture Two, the first four taught concerning greed (25:13–28, Block I.A). The remaining three introduce characters who may apply to the pupil, hoping to receive indiscriminate generosity (26:1–28, Block I.B): the patently stupid, the incurably lazy and the seductively litigious (appearing first in Lecture One, 25:9). It is the seductively litigious who most clearly distinguish indiscriminate generosity as the theme unifying the three characters of Block I.B.

Among this remaining set of three, the first to appear is the 'stupid' fellow (named in each saying of 26:1–12, except v. 2). Since the sage cautions against entrusting him with various privileges, he implies that the stupid fellow is the sort of character who may be inclined to approach the pupil-as-courtier, asking him generously to grant various favours. Those favours may include employing him as a messenger (26:6, 10), training him with proverbial sayings (vv. 7, 9) and granting him glory (v. 8).

Against such appeals for indiscriminate generosity the pupil must steel himself, ready judiciously to 'reply' (vv. 4–5).

Second is the incurably lazy fellow (26:13–16). Upon hearing his opening protest ('A young lion is in the street', v. 13), the pupil would deduce that, immediately prior, this indolent fellow appealed to someone (such as a well-to-do courtier) for aid not requiring labour – a handout. The person appealed to would have responded, 'You seem capable enough. Why are you not working to support yourself?' To which the lazy fellow would respond with the excuse appearing in v. 13. As with the stupid fellow, also against the lazy fellow's appeals for indiscriminate generosity, the pupil must steel himself. To do otherwise would only enable the indolent's cycle of dependence. Instead the pupil should reserve his aid for the truly needy (28:27).

The third and final character may appeal to the courtier for unwarranted advocacy, likely because the courtier would be in a position to influence a judicial outcome, perhaps as a local adjudicator (26:17–28). As indicated in Lecture One (25:9), lending support in another's court case can backfire (26:17), due to tainted motives on the part of the litigant (26:19a, 23b, 25b). Innocent bystanders may be harmed in the process (26:18).

Thematic continuity concerning the stupid person (26:1–12, form-based). With the exception of 26:2, the term 'stupid' appears in each saying of 26:1–12.

Thematic continuity concerning how to relate to the lazy person (26:13–16, form-based). 'Lazy' appears in each saying of 26:13–16. In all of Prov. 25 – 29 the root for 'lazy', *ʿzl*, does not appear again.

Thematic continuity concerning the seductively litigious person (26:17–28, content-based). Three terms or concepts combine in 26:17–28 (Unit I.B.3) to portray one who is seductively litigious, hijacking the judicial process for selfish aims: 'litigation' (26:17 [first saying of this unit] and 26:21), 'slander' (used to discredit a plaintiff or defendant in 26:20, 22) and deceptive speech (26:19, 24, 25, 26, 28). Instead to identify within this portion a variety of antisocial characters (rather than various aspects of the litigious character) would not sufficiently account for the commonality shared in 'litigation', *rîb* (26:17, 21; *pace* Waltke 2005: 343–344, 358–366).

Unit-level closure (26:28, form- and content-based). Three terms or concepts reappear in the last saying of Unit I.B.3 (26:17–28), creating closure for that unit. First is slander ('slander' in vv. 20, 22, 'lips' with concealed motives in vv. 23, 24, 'false tongue' and 'slick mouth' in v. 28). Second is 'hating' (vv. 24, 26, 28). Third is stumbling ('falling' into a pit in v. 27, 'stumbling' in v. 28).

Progression from stupid to lazy, concerning wisdom (26:5, 12, 16, form-based). Worse than the stupid fellow (26:1–12) is the lazy fellow (vv. 13–16), based on how each regards his own wisdom. The stupid fellow risks becoming 'wise in his own estimation' (26:5), although he has not yet reached that self-assessment (v. 12). In contrast, 'In his own estimation, the lazy fellow is wiser than seven who respond with sound discernment' (v. 16).

Overlapping palistrophes (26:1–12, form- and content-based). Coherence of Unit I.B.1 (26:1–12) derives from repetition of 'stupid' (noted above), and from a pair of overlapping palistrophes, summarized in the tables below. The first palistrophe spans 26:1–8, framed by 'glory' in vv. 1, 8. Then follow paired steps concerning misappropriated communication (vv. 2, 7), suffering bodily harm (vv. 3, 6) and 'do (or do not) reply to a stupid fellow in a manner corresponding to his folly' (vv. 4, 5).

A second palistrophe incorporates the last five sayings of the first palistrophe (26:4–8), then continues for four more verses (26:9–12). It is framed by 'his folly' (vv. 4, 11). 'His folly' appears in v. 5 as well, so that vv. 4–5 form a verse-pair (as will vv. 11, 12). The palistrophe continues with 'wise in his own estimation' (vv. 5, 12), suffering bodily harm (vv. 6, 10), and misappropriated communication (vv. 7, 9). The palistrophe features 'glory' at the pivot (v. 8), recalling the master-lecture theme of magnificence. Garrett also observed a palistrophe in vv. 6–10 (1993: 212).

First palistrophe (26:1–8)

v. 1 'Glory' in line-terminal position			
	v. 2 Misappropriated communication: a curse that will not come to pass		
		v. 3 Suffering of bodily harm: a whip, bridle, and beating	
			v. 4 'Do not answer a stupid person in a manner corresponding to . . .'
			v. 5 'Do answer a stupid person in a manner corresponding to . . .'
		v. 6 Suffering of bodily harm: leg amputation and poisoning	
	v. 7 Misappropriated communication: 'a proverb in the mouth of stupid folk'		
v. 8 'Glory' in line-terminal position			

Second palistrophe (26:4–12)

			v. 4 'His folly'
			v. 5 'Wise in his own estimation'
		v. 6 Suffering of bodily harm: leg amputation and poisoning	
	v. 7 Misappropriated communication: 'a proverb in the mouth of stupid folk'		
v. 8 'Glory' in line-terminal position			
	v. 9 Misappropriated communication: 'a proverb in the mouth of stupid folk'		
		v. 10 Suffering of bodily harm: an archer who wounds everyone	
			v. 11 'His folly'
			v. 12 'Wise in his own estimation'

Block I.C (27:1–4). Section-level closure (27:1–4, content-based). Four elements foster closure for the final unit of Section I (27:1–4, Block I.C). First, the caution against presumptuous boasting (27:1–2) recalls self-centred greed that characterized the series of four relationships of Block I.A (25:13–28).

Second, 'fool' in 27:3 recalls three other occurrences of 'fool' or 'folly' in this lecture (26:4, 5, 11) – all within the 'stupid' character portion (first of four individuals who may appeal to the courtier for indiscriminate generosity, 26:1–12). Neither 'fool' nor 'folly' will reoccur until both appear in this lecture's final line (27:22).

Third, the root *kbd* (underlying 'glorious' and 'heavy') appears twice in 27:3. Like 'fool/folly', 'glory' appeared earlier in connection with the stupid fellow (26:1, 8).

Fourth, cruelty motivated by revenge (27:4) recalls the seductive litigant. Intent on revenge, murderously he fires 'flaming missiles, arrows with death' (26:18).

Within the recap of 27:1–4, the first verse-pair links to greed, corresponding to Block I.A (25:13–28). The second verse-pair (27:3–4) links to elements in the block concerning indiscriminate generosity (Block I.B, 26:1–28). Thus the recap (Block I.C) summarizes both preceding blocks of Section I.

A recurring four-verse recap (25:25–28; 27:1–4, form-based). As noted above in the discussion on 'Borders', the first block of Section I closes with a four-verse recap (Unit I.A.5, 25:25–28), as does all of Section I (Block I.C, 27:1–4).

Section II (27:5–18). *Thematic continuity involving reproof (27:5–18, content-based).* A theme of reproof develops across the three blocks comprising Section II (27:5–18). The first block establishes the worth of reproof and outlines how to obtain it (vv. 5–10). The second explains how to dispense reproof, illustrating with two failed models (vv. 11–16). The closing block showcases two relationships where reproof operates optimally (vv. 17–18).

Palistrophe concerning relationships fostering reproof (27:5–10, form- and content-based). A four-level palistrophe teaches the importance of both receptivity and relationships as a context for reproof (27:5–10, Block II.A). Steps 1 and 1' begin with 'better' statements: better is reproof, and better is a near-neighbour when help (including reproof) is needed (vv. 5, 10c). Steps 2 and 2' underscore the necessity of supportive ('loving'), time-tested relationships, if reproof is to function healthily (vv. 6, 10a–b). Steps 3 and 3' accent how vital it is for the recipient of reproof to welcome it with a receptive 'appetite', valuing a friend's counsel as fragrant perfume (vv. 7, 9).

The pivot in step 4 (the palistrophic zenith) warns the courtier, whose youthful wanderlust may incline him to discard webs of trustworthy relationships long-cultivated by generations past (v. 8). Without this trove of

wise friends, how can he hope to access the treasure, which is loving reproof?

Palistrophe (27:5–10c)

27:5	'Better' in line-initial position (concerning value of reproof)
27:6	Dependable relationships are essential for reproof
27:7	Reproof requires receptivity
27:8	Wanderlust at the cost of relationships earns a net loss
27:9	Reproof should generate receptivity
27:10a–b	Don't discard dependable relationships
27:10c	'Better' in line-initial position (concerning value of neighbour, source of reproof)

Wisdom commendation followed by content (27:11, 12–13, content-based). A wisdom commendation describing parental joy over a wise son (27:11) is followed by wisdom content teaching the rationale and urgency of dispensing reproof (vv. 12–13).

Dual-theme conclusion, chiastic conclusion (27:14–16, content-based). Two negative repercussions of failed reproof appear in 27:16, forming a dual-theme conclusion, summarizing vv. 14, 15 chiastically. The futility of 'hid[ing] the wind' expresses the first (v. 16a). This refers to the contentious wife with her incessant reproving, introduced in the preceding saying (v. 15).

'Oil . . . on his right hand' expresses the second (27:16b). As fuel, food product or costly perfume, oil would normally be an asset. But in the wrong place it becomes a liability, preventing the hand from gripping. This parallels closely the misguided blessing of v. 14. Normally an asset, in the wrong place (shouted loudly to a neighbour too early in the day), a blessing becomes a liability.

Gender indicators further link 27:16a with v. 15, and v. 16b with v. 14. 'Her' in v. 16a corresponds to 'wife' in v. 15, while 'his' in v. 16b fits m. ptc. 'one who blesses' and the pronoun 'him' in v. 14.

Section-level climax associating reproof with attaining glory (27:18, content-based). From its opening saying, reproof forms the dominant theme of Section II: 'Better is reproof revealed than love kept secret' (27:5). After failed models for dispensing reproof (27:14–16), near the section's close the sage depicts a mutual relationship of reproof ('May iron by iron grow sharp', 27:17). Then, in the section's final saying, the sage portrays a supreme and implicitly reproof-rich relationship: master–pupil (27:18). Here one achieves the climactic goal of 'glory' (v. 18b), recalling the fundamental quest of the entire master lecture, to achieve a monarchy characterized by magnificence ('glory', 25:2).

Section III (27:19–22). *Double terms or roots within a single verse (27:19, 20, 22, form-based).* Earlier in this lecture, doubled words or roots signalled structurally strategic sayings (e.g. 'glory', *kbd*, in 25:27 [penultimate in Block I.A] and 27:3 [penultimate in Section I]; cf. 25:2 [start of master lecture]). Doubling intensifies in the lecture's final section, operating four times across three of four sayings in that section. Both 'face' and 'mortal' appear twice in 27:19. 'Be satisfied' occurs twice in 27:20. Two roots repeat in 27:22, the lecture's final saying. The root *ktš* yields *tiktôš*, 'pulverize', and *maktēš*, 'mortar'. The root *ʾwl* yields *ʾĕwîl*, 'fool', and *ʾiwwaltô*, 'his folly'. This device lends coherence of form to Section III.

Comment

Section I (25:13 – 27:4). *Block I.A (25:13–28).* Section I advises courtiers to refrain from both greed (Block I.A) and, paradoxically, from its seeming inverse, indiscriminate generosity (Block I.B). The sage begins by presenting four characters towards whom the pupil may be inclined to respond with greed. These four relationships progress along a vector beginning with professional acquaintances, ending with intimately personal associations.

First to appear is one's supervisor (Unit I.A.1, 25:13–15). What a supervisor seeks most in an employee is dependability (v. 13). Conversely, a supervisor learns to dismiss as unreliable that courtier who thinks to curry favour by promising desirable things ('gifts'), even though they may never come to pass (v. 14). The temptation to curry favour may seem reasonable when one's supervisor is contrary. But the best counsel in such a scenario is to practise soft-spoken patience. This strategy will prove more persuasive than a verbal frontal assault (v. 15).

Neighbours form the second acquaintance group – one step removed from the formality of supervisor–employee relationships (25:16–20, Unit I.A.2). The first two sayings envision cordial neighbour relations (vv. 16–17). This quatrain revolves around the idea of 'having one's fill' – exercising self-control over one's appetite when enjoying another's hospitality, lest greed on the part of the guest (i.e. the pupil) might cause the host to 'have his fill' of that self-centred neighbour (vv. 16–17).

Neighbour relations persist in 25:18–19, now exposing the harm of treacherous opportunism perpetrated against a vulnerable neighbour. Even when ostensibly justified to offset personal setbacks ('on a day of distress'), treating neighbours with treachery will result only in net loss and self-inflicted pain. Following as it does the caution against behaving as a self-centred, greedy guest (vv. 16–17), the warning of vv. 18–19 implies that, left unchecked, what begins as naive self-centredness may mature into treacherous greed.

Neighbour relations, both cordial (25:16–17) and hostile (vv. 18–19), coalesce in 25:20 as the sage discloses a core principle summarizing neighbour relations. In sum, one should beware when self-indulgent motives drive neighbour relations. When one performs a neighbourly act of ostensible generosity (such as helping remove another's cloak) in a manner that causes discomfort (during frigid weather), or when seeming generosity (such as contributing a condiment such as vinegar; cf. Ruth 2:14) is performed to inflict damage – when such actions are executed with wrong motives, at best they leave neighbours feeling cold or, at worst, leave them frothing with resentment (foaming as vinegar encountering soda; regarding a song titled 'Wrong Motives', see 'Notes' for v. 20). Recurrence of the phrase 'on a . . . day' in vv. 19b and 20a indicates that v. 20 shares the theme of neighbour relations governing vv. 16–19.

After supervisor and neighbour, third is the character 'who hates you' (25:21–22). Due to his fundamentally malicious animus, the 'hater' surpasses in malevolence one who exhibits periodic treachery (vv. 18–20). To counteract the revenge-greed such hatred would naturally provoke in the courtier, the sage calls for radical kindness – supplying that mean-spirited person's basic needs, irrespective of his or her malignant attitude towards the courtier. Motivating such radical kindness is the incentive of divine reward (25:22). Whereas counterfeit kindness earned censure (v. 20), to heap up 'burning coals' in the form of kindness earns commendation.

The 'greed' relationships (25:13–28) progress from professional to personal, culminating in marriage – the fourth and final relationship (vv. 23–24) before the block-level recap in vv. 25–28. Elements indicating marriage include 'giving birth' (metaphoric, v. 23), 'wife' and 'shared house' (v. 24).

The courtier-husband who persistently behaves towards his wife with chilling, self-centred conduct (25:23) foolishly precipitates 'rain' (metaphor for tears). So he will consign himself to sparse and solitary accommodations (v. 24; for another marriage saying implying preventative steps for the husband, cf. 21:9).

After four 'greed' characters (Units I.A.1–4, 25:13–24), a four-verse unit recaps the hazard of greed (Unit I.A.5, 25:25–28). The poet reminds the pupil that a 'good [truthful] report' brings refreshment (25:25; recalling the trustworthy envoy of 25:13–15). Since a truthful report may expose corruption, the faithful courtier must steel himself not to alter his account under the pressure of guilty colleagues who may demand that he falsify his report. Else 'waters', otherwise refreshing, thereby would grow morally muddied, unpotable, incapable of reinvigorating one's supervisor (v. 26).

A final quatrain crystallizes this block's core problem and solution (25:27–28). Greed identifies the problem (an unrestrained appetite, 25:27a). The solution consists of a self-control so mature that it would sooner advance another's reputation than focus on self (v. 27b). Narcissistically to abdicate self-control would amount to trusting in a fortress wall in ruins (v. 28).

Block I.B (26:1–28). Progression from one character to the next. In Block I.B the sage turns from greed to generosity. Three characters appear, who may ply the pupil for indiscriminate generosity. The progression moves from greater to lesser worth (or increasing threat) to the community.

First is the patently stupid (26:1–12). Though deserving neither trust nor honour, he yet ranks one step above 'a person who is wise in his own estimation' (26:12).

Who, then, ranks more hopeless than the stupid fellow? It is the incurably lazy (26:13–16). He epitomizes myopic arrogance. By his rejection of external advice (v. 16) he illustrates the very person warned against in v. 12a.

Third is the seditiously litigious (26:17–28). Against this character the sage unleashes as lengthy a discourse as was devoted to the stupid fellow (twelve verses). His penchant for deception and strife determines to destroy others in his single-minded quest for ascendancy. As to eventual demise, in contrast to the stupid who will not rise above their perpetual folly (26:11), and in contrast to the lazy who may go hungry (v. 15), through retribution the litigious will find himself exposed, ensnared and crushed (vv. 26–27) – a demise more deadly by far than what the stupid and lazy suffer.

Progression within individual characters: the stupid fellow (26:1–12). Consider next the progression operating within the first of those three: the stupid fellow (26:1–12). The sage posits first an overarching principle warning against indiscriminate generosity (v. 1). To refuse to lavish glory on an undeserving person such as the stupid fellow does not amount to miserliness. Rather, carelessly to issue honours would inflict damage by upsetting community values. It would prove as harmful as untimely precipitation at harvest.

Upon discovering his wrongful request for glory has been refused, the stupid fellow will call down supernatural revenge on the careful courtier (26:2). Baseless, the curses will not stick.

If not a candidate for glory, perhaps a stupid fellow should be hired as a manual labourer (like a draught animal). Yet horses and donkeys respond more cooperatively than he (26:3).

Double mention of 'reply[ing] to a stupid fellow' (26:4–5) renders explicit what vv. 1–3 implied: the stupid fellow has applied to the courtier for special consideration. Having issued the overarching principle that indiscriminate honour may harm, having explained that his curses will fall harmless, and having disqualified the stupid even for manual labour (vv. 1–3), in vv. 4–5 the sage coaches the pupil concerning how to respond properly. With paradoxical reversal he advises first not to respond in the style of the stupid fellow (v. 4), then advises just the opposite (v. 5)! This clever quatrain appears on the surface to mimic the sort of nonsensical thinking one would expect from a foolish person. This verse-pair teaches that, just as one must refrain from indiscriminate generosity, so also one must refrain from an indiscriminate approach when wording rejections. A response must adapt to the respective applicant's frame of mind.

But perhaps the stupid should be considered for other positions. What if he offered to serve as a messenger (26:6)? Such trust amounts metaphorically to 'shooting oneself in the foot', to borrow a modern equivalence.

If not a messenger, what if the role awarded a stupid person interacted only with the courtier – perhaps as an advisor (26:7)? Even this will not do. Though he may master many wise sayings, the stupid person will be useless, not grasping how to employ them.

Not only is a stupid fellow unfit for glory (26:1); to bestow glory on him arms him with a weapon (v. 8). Furthermore, teaching him proverbs amounts to putting bullets in his bandolier (v. 9).

Thus, to hire such a one only places innocent targets within range (26:10). The 'archer' responsible for this crime is the employer who hired the stupid fellow.

Is not such categorical rejection of the stupid fellow too severe? It is not, for it reckons with the stupid fellow's consistent nature – not wishfully, but honestly (26:11).

To prevent the pupil from writing off the stupid fellow as utterly incorrigible, and to transition to the second character (who ranks still worse), the sage adopts a more personal tone at the close of this unit: 'You have seen, no doubt, a person who is wise in his own estimation' (26:12a; cf. v. 16). Fortunately, the stupid fellow has not descended to that level.

Progression within individual characters: the lazy fellow (26:13–16). Progression of thought concerning the lazy fellow emerges through stages of increased motion. Self-imposed paralysis is first. This fellow fears a pseudo-hazard, should he brave the arena of commerce and potential profit (26:13). Second, he makes back-and-forth motion like a hinge: indications of movement, despite never leaving his bed (v. 14). Finally, muscular activity with potential benefit displays at the dinner table (v. 15). Alas, the hand, laden with nourishment, aborts its mission partway, leaving him hungry still.

What can explain such profound indolence? By a factor of seven he thinks himself wiser than any who dare offer advice (26:16).

Progression within individual characters: the seductively litigious fellow (26:17–28). With the phrase 'so is he who becomes enraged concerning a litigation not his' the sage introduces the third character who may prey on the pupil's sense of generosity (26:17b). A judicial context is implied by 'litigation', 'slander', 'lips on fire', 'juridical assembly' and 'false tongue' (cf. 26:17, 19, 21, 23, 24, 25, 26, 27, 28).

The litigious fellow seeks the courtier's support 'concerning a litigation not his' (i.e. not directly impinging on the courtier). If the courtier were to comply, he might as well attempt to aid a dog by grasping its ears – a strategy bound to backfire (v. 17a).

The injurious dog of 26:17a (biting the well-intentioned courtier-figure because he reached for his ears) represents the litigious fellow, as does the injurious, mentally unstable archer indiscriminately firing deadly missiles at bystanders who otherwise might be won to his cause (vv. 18–19).

The litigant's flaw consists of deception (26:19a). This distinguishes him from those with a legitimate claim on the courtier's compassion (cf. 24:10–12). When pressed to prove claims of victimization, he will evade with a nervous laugh, excusing the entire episode as a mere prank (v. 19b).

There is a way to test whether the litigant's claims are valid: remove him from the equation. If he has hurled only empty, contentious slander, his case will fade away (26:20–21). If others verify his complaints, his case has merit.

When litigation proves spurious (collapsing on close examination), why does he gain traction in the first place? Because, explains the sage, like a fine pastry, slander appeals to rudimentary appetites – especially it appeals to the innate longing to appear superior to others (26:22). Fiery lips, seemingly so passionate for justice, subtly seek to convince onlookers that their shiny, sanctimonious glaze extends more than skin deep (v. 23).

However, too often a litigant's glaze of justice-rhetoric thinly conceals an ugly engine of revenge, rooted in hatred (26:24). That explains why, in exceptionally strident tones, the sage forbids the youths from trusting their sweet talk (v. 25). Hidden motives rank their schemes as perfectly vile (v. 25b)!

Given the nearly irresistible appeal of slander, will the seductive litigant ultimately succeed? 'Not at all!' comes the sage's confident reply. The community will eventually expose the litigant's schemes (26:26), leading to his downfall, at his own hands (v. 27).

The sage closes the unit concerning the seductive litigant by revealing that, in reality, he seeks not justice, but perpetual revenge (he 'keeps on hating', 26:28). Sadly, the ultimate target of his hatred proves to be himself. He is the one whom his tongue 'crushes' (v. 28a) as if by a stone he has rolled (v. 27). Thinking to trip others, he it is who ultimately will 'stumble' (v. 28b).

Block I.C (27:1–4). Just as two verse-pairs recapped Block I.A (25:25–28), two verse-pairs also recap all of Section I (Block I.C, 27:1–4). Mention of boasting in both v. 1 and v. 2 recalls the first of four greedy characters, similarly known for boasting (25:14). The root for 'boasting', *hll*, occurs only once more in this lecture (27:21, near its close). Mention of anger, rage and revengeful wrath in the recap's second verse-pair (27:3–4) recalls the seductive litigant – that final of three characters seeking indiscriminate generosity (notice 'litigation', 'strife', 'fire' and 'hatred' in 26:17, 20–21, 23, 26). Thus in the recap the sage reviews counsel against both greed and careless generosity.

Those greedy for acclaim should corral their boasting, since today's achievements tomorrow may evaporate (27:1). External acclaim matters much more than internal accolades (v. 2).

For the generous courtier who weighs whether to lend influence to an applicant, the sage advises to assess how, if refused, the applicant will respond. If rejection unleashes an angry flood, the applicant is unworthy (27:3–4). Like a stone he is 'heavy', but amounts only to a sand-filled 'burden' (v. 3). He lacks any trace elements of precious (glory-producing) metals (v. 3; 'heavy', 'heavier' and 'glory' come from the root *kbd*; cf. 'glory' in 26:1, 8, and silver-refining in v. 23).

25:22. Scooping coals on to a person's head served as a method of punishment in some societies of the ANE (*HALOT*, s.v. '*ḥth*'). Paul draws from Prov. 25:21–22 in Rom. 12:20.

25:23–24. The sage will associate rain, wind and concealment (same root as 'north') with a contentious marriage in 27:15–16.

25:27. 'Their glory' recalls glory of God and of the king in the previous lecture (25:2). To search out the glory of one's king amounts to giving respect. To search out the glory of God is to engage in worship.

It is tempting to conclude Block I.A with 25:27 due to the double use of 'glory' in the expression 'search out glory', since that would form an exact inclusio with 25:2 (so Waltke, who regards 25:28 as a Janus verse, bridging what precedes with what follows [2005: 337]). However, the remarkable extent to which the content of 25:28 crystallizes the self-control theme specifically spanning Block I.A (25:13–28) recommends joining v. 28 to that block. At times a formal device (such as inclusio) may be subordinated to cohesion created by a feature derived from content.

26:1. Unlike the refreshing of 'snow's chill' in 25:13, a summer snowfall or rain at harvest brings damage.

26:9. A briar 'coming into the hand' portrays an aggressor wielding a weapon (similar to a catapult in 26:8).

26:13. Lion-induced paralysis appeared also in 22:13.

26:27. This deployed proverb about pits and moving stones constitutes a classic apophthegm of retribution. Consequently the person crushed in 26:28 is not only the victim, but the lying victimizer as well, thus exposed as a self-hater.

27:1. A New Testament wisdom writer sounds a similar caution concerning boasting about tomorrow (Jas 4:13–16).

Section II (27:5–18). *Overview of Section II.* After explaining in Section I the counterbalanced hazards of selfish greed (Block I.A) and indiscriminate generosity (Block I.B), in Section II the sage addresses reproof, again in counterbalanced parts. Reproof must both be eagerly received (Block II.A) and insightfully dispensed (Block II.B). By this sequence the sage suggests that, before presuming to offer reproof, one must excel in embracing it. Two reproof-rich relationships close this section (Block II.C).

Block II.A (27:5–10). Covert love, or caring criticism – which is worth more? 'Choose criticism,' urges the sage (27:5). Despite its pain, caring reproof can be trusted (v. 6a). Conversely, learn to suspect as superficial any love with strings attached (v. 6b). Despite its bitter flavour, reproof will not repel a wise person, so ravenous is his or her appetite for improvement (v. 7).

Sadly, one who aimlessly drifts from native territory forfeits reproof that deep friendships may offer (27:8). Such a wanderer may be drawn away by enticing aromas, forgetting that friends left behind could have supplied invaluable reproof, correcting his misguided longing after the exotic (v. 9). So vital are these friendship-sources of reproof that the sage charges the pupil not to forsake them (v. 10a–b). They are more valuable even than family (v. 10c)!

Block II.B (27:11–16). After excelling in receiving reproof, the courtier may – even must – excel in dispensing it (II.B, 27:11–16). A son who exhibits this extent of wisdom enables his parent to debunk baseless insults hurled by opponents (v. 11).

When dispensing reproof, one must not lose sight of its objective: to benefit the recipient by supplying foresight (making him 'shrewd'), so he or she may avoid impending 'misery' (27:12).

Does the pupil timidly shrink from intervening, confronting a friend with much-needed reproof? Then 'Grasp his garment!' urges the sage, lest that friend tumble into a financial trap (27:13a). Is the friend succumbing to an appetite for illicit sexual pleasure? Then, without delay, 'Tie him up!' insists the sage (v. 13b).

Next the poet anticipates the hesitation to dispense reproof out of fear lest that communication backfire. He admits that communication can go awry, and cites two failures, teaching by negative example. In the first, even a message of compliment can work harm, when poorly timed (27:14, a man's message). How much more, if an ill-timed message were to convey reproof!

In the second example, a message of confrontation ('contentious') fails, when it knows not when to stop (27:15, a woman's message). Unwisely, 'her' strident message defies containment (v. 16a). Equally unwisely, 'his' sweet message will spill, spoiling his grip (v. 16b).

Block II.C (27:17–18). Such models of failed communication (poorly timed, lacking moderation) would incline a pupil to probe, 'What, then, would effective reproof look like?' So the sage closes with two reproof-rich relationships (Block II.C, 27:17–18). In the first, the sage heartily commends a reciprocal relationship where both members derive benefit from reproof (v. 17, note the impact of juss. in 'may . . . grow sharp' and 'may . . . sharpen').

In the second, the sage concedes that not all reproof relationships will be confined to peers. To access wisdom beyond one's years, the wise courtier will nourish ties with a senior sage. This, too, marks the path to magnificence ('glory', 27:18).

27:5. The tendency to refrain from disclosing helpful reproof constitutes 'love kept secret'.

27:9. 'Appetite' significantly comprises the topic of the friend's advice. Whether commending noble appetites, or cautioning against misleading appetites, we are not told. James similarly underscores the importance of receiving advice concerning one's desires (Jas 1:14–16).

27:12. The paradigmatic centrality of this saying as an encapsulation of the entire wisdom enterprise is reinforced by the fact that it appeared nearly verbatim in 22:3, differing only in conjs.

27:13. A close parallel appears in 20:16.

27:14–15. Just as 27:14 does not describe all men in general, neither does v. 15 describe all women in general. Rather, each saying teaches one principle concerning the effective administration of reproof. Taken in context, the example of 'blessing' in v. 14 operates as an argument from less to more. If even a blessing may be misconstrued through poor timing, how much more will a message of reproof be rejected through poorly timed delivery?

Section III (27:19–22). In closing, the sage urges awareness of inner motives. Motives will determine whether reproof will successfully refine greed and indiscriminate generosity, leaving magnificence of character (27:19). For, like the netherworld's unslaked lust for victims, a person unrefined, who remains enslaved by greedy appetites, never can rest content (v. 20; cf. Block I.A, 25:13–28).

Instead one should exhibit judicious generosity that affirms others, even during personal distress (27:21; Shafer-Elliott 2018: 288; cf. 'Notes' and Deut. 25:4; Isa. 41:15). When distress issues in generous praise (not litigious accusations or angry revenge), this demonstrates that the crucible of reproof's confrontation has successfully refined the pupil's character, leaving magnificence in its wake.

Is the crucible's heat or the pestle's pressure alone sufficient to convert any stone or sand to gold or silver (27:22; recall v. 3)? No, even resorting to extreme measures in threshing (mortar and pestle, in place of ox-drawn threshing sledge) cannot achieve the impossible – divesting the fool of his folly. If the hull-removing service of reproof would succeed, the subject must be receptive, willing to shed unwise ways. Refusing receptivity, no amount of reproof-pressure can reform someone stubbornly clinging to folly.

27:19. One's motives offer the best predictor of future behaviour.

27:20. Given the prominence of creation principles in the sage's world view, mention of 'eyes' and 'mortal', *ʾādām*, associated with satisfying one's appetite, may recall the Edenic garden (Gen. 3:6). 'Eyes' are mentioned in Gen. 3:5, 7 as well, while *ʾādām* as 'Adam' occurs nearby in Gen. 3:8, 9, 12.

Explanation

This lecture initially counselled courtiers intent on leading their monarchy to magnificence. That same counsel can serve today's managers, public and private, who long to help their organization to prosper genuinely.

Section I, Block A. Restraining the hazard of greed through self-control in four relationships, with recap (25:13–28)
Managing with excellence begins by reckoning our native inclination towards greed. To fortify ourselves against such gaping vulnerability we must cultivate self-control (25:28), specifically in four relationships: towards superiors, peers, opponents and our spouse. First, towards superiors: exercise sufficient self-control to prioritize honesty and faithfulness, rather than succumbing to the temptation to submit progress reports padded with unreasonable sales or production promises, calculated merely to please. Through dependable conduct, seek to refresh those who labour over you (25:13–15, 25).

Second, towards peers: self-control takes the shape of moderation, reining in our appetite when enjoying another's hospitality, not overstaying our welcome (25:16–17). Never participate in a smear campaign against peers. Just as our superiors should be able to rely on us, so should our neighbours (25:18–19). Before offering a supposed kindness, we must check our motives. Are we doing it to make ourselves feel better, or truly to benefit our neighbour (v. 20)?

Third, towards opponents: self-control prevents us from forgetting that they, like us, are human beings with great worth. Do they lack basic humanitarian necessities, such as food and water? Let us stop what we are doing in order to meet those needs. God will repay us (25:21–22).

Fourth, towards our spouse: especially husbands must exercise self-control that restrains the chill of indifference and the heat of anger – unless, of course, they wish to live in the 'dog house'. Husbands who choose to cultivate caring instead, will discover their wives will have less cause to resort to contention (25:23–24).

A manager is in a position to refresh both superiors (25:25) and subordinates downstream from him or her (v. 26). Stalwart integrity (not 'losing our footing in the presence of a guilty person', v. 26), self-control concerning greed (v. 27a) and a genuine interest in the success of others (v. 27b) offer waymarkers along the path leading to excellence in management.

Section I, Blocks B–C. Refining the hazard of indiscriminate generosity through shrewdness in three relationships, with recap (26:1 – 27:4)
Greed is not the only hazard threatening to undermine a manager's success. Offsetting the risks attending self-centredness is the hazard of excessive generosity – routinely approving every appeal for help that comes

our way. In three relationships the manager must exercise particular care – towards the stupid fellow, the incurably lazy and the seductive litigant. First, consider the fellow whom the sage labels 'stupid'. The sage does not here refer to a person with genuine mental deficiencies. Rather, he designates as 'stupid' one who manifests wilful and recurring irresponsibility (26:3, 11), who contributes no productive employee skill set (26:7), yet who nevertheless complains of compensation incommensurate with his worth to the company (26:1b). His or her primary contribution to group life is to make others run for cover, once he has gained a promotion (26:8).

When such a one, appealing to the manager's generosity, applies for special honours and privileges, the manager must choose carefully how he responds (26:4–5). He must realize that to approve the stupid fellow's request would countermand the company's overall mission and impair its productivity. To authorize such an appeal would make as much sense as a farmer hoping for a hurricane, just as his crew readies to harvest the fields (26:1a). That is why, when the stupid fellow asks for honours or for employment in a task for which he is ill-suited, the manager must politely but firmly decline. For, generously to hire the stupid fellow would derail the company's operation and jeopardize his own managerial position (26:6).

Second, consider the incurably lazy fellow (26:13–16). A manager must learn to probe the excuses offered by the lazy to paper-over indolence (including trumped-up excuses of peril, 26:13). Do not be fooled by illusions of his industry, when all he labours so hard to refine is his nap time (26:14). Learn to restrain your words of congratulation until after he has crossed the finish line. Beware of his inclination to leave a job half-done (26:15). And notice how he responds to advice. Too often lazy people arrogantly presume they know it all (26:16). Any manager who bestows generosity indiscriminately on the lazy only perpetuates his habit of indolence.

Third, consider the seductive litigant (26:17–28). Here is an employee who complains of unjust treatment. Out of a manager's commitment to ensure an ethical work culture, he or she naturally feels inclined, even obligated, to advocate for the complainer's cause, hoping to restore fairness. But before we pick up placards and join the protest, the sage warns us we must examine the claims of injustice. For example, does the claimant tend to go berserk, then excuse his own harmful behaviour as a prank (26:18–19)? Or consider how the atmosphere changes when the complainer is removed from the conversations surrounding the complaint controversy. Even in his absence, is moral concern sustained by irrefutable evidence, or does the complaint largely dissipate when he leaves the room, collapsing under its own weight? If moral concern persists despite his absence, that grievance is likely valid (26:20–21). If not, it may be a case of superficial concern driven by ulterior motives (26:22–28). In summary, to counteract greed we must remain focused on the well-being of others, not ourselves (27:1–2). And to safeguard against bestowing generosity indiscriminately, we must carefully probe the character of one filing a grievance, claiming to labour under a load of injustice. If he or she is motivated by rage, anger or revenge, beware (27:3–4)!

Section II. Reproof received and dispensed (27:5–18)
In addition to navigating relationships (a) by cultivating self-control concerning our own greed, and (b) by deepening shrewdness concerning our generosity, as managers intent on magnificence we must excel in reproof, both receiving and dispensing it. Even when offered critique that is bitter, we must learn to treat it as a treasure (27:7). We must go out of our way to cultivate a cadre of caring and candid mentors (27:5–6, 8, 10), particularly those bold enough to counsel concerning disordered appetites of all sorts (vv. 9–10).

In addition to benefiting from reproof, a wise manager will consent boldly to intervene with reproof – and without superiority – when a friend careens towards entrapment (27:12–13). We must monitor carefully both the timing and amplitude of reproof we offer (vv. 14–16). Best is reproof delivered organically within a sustained and mutual relationship (v. 17). Even better is reproof received mentor-to-disciple, crafted with unquestionable concern. Reproof received, delivered in this manner, guides managers to lead towards magnificence (v. 18).

Section III. Recap: motives determine one's capacity through reproof to refine generosity by displacing greed, in quest of magnificence (27:19–22)
In our quest for magnificence, we must choose between two routes. Which we choose will be determined by interior motives to which, already, we have entrusted the privilege of piloting our life. Take time to become still enough so you may recognize your true character in the mirror of your motives (27:19).

Either we will choose the low route of greed, navigating by our appetites, blind to the fact that they are sadly, hopelessly insatiable (27:20). Or, if wise, we will choose the high route of generosity, allowing fiery experiences of reproof to refine the praise of others (not of self) that by default we issue (v. 21). For it is generosity, not greed, that leads to magnificence of metaphoric 'silver' and 'gold'. If instead we resist the benevolent – though painful – impact of reproof, we only confirm our identity as fools (v. 22). In the next lecture the sage offers a winsome model of management, engaging both courtiers and kings (27:23–27).

PROVERBS 27:23–27
'Lecture three: What may courtier and king learn from a farmer?'

Overview of Proverbs 27:23–27
The poem spanning Prov. 27:23–27 introduces a model of excellence in management, drawn from the world of animal husbandry. Both courtiers

and kings (the two audiences indicated for Prov. 25 – 29) would benefit by fixing in mind this concrete image of leadership.

Position of this poem within Proverbs

Preceding context. Within the master lecture spanning Prov. 25 – 29, Lecture Two cautioned courtiers against the reciprocal hazards of self-centred greed and indiscriminate generosity (25:13 – 27:22). Towards its close, Lecture Two emphasized the need to shift from self-promotion, cultivating instead a self-awareness concerning inner motives (with the help of a friend's reproof, 27:17, 19). Reproof that reveals one's own motives will escort a courtier towards magnificence. In Lecture Three the sage encourages awareness of a different sort – not of self, but of the 'flock' under one's care (27:23).

Ensuing context. After a study in leadership drawn from animal husbandry (Lecture Three), Lecture Four supplies the sage's last answer to the overarching master-lecture question 'How may a monarchy attain magnificence?' That answer focuses on the monarch – accenting his role in assuring justice for the wider community (28:1 – 29:27).

A scene of escalating crime begins Lecture Four – a condition calling precisely for the help of a judge-king who, like the attentive shepherd of Lecture Three, cares more for 'the face of [his] flock' (27:23) than for burnishing his own image (or 'face'; cf. 27:19). Such a monarch will rid negative elements from his realm (as prefigured in 25:5 of Lecture One).

What to watch for

Notice the pattern of imperative (or strategy statement) followed by rationale. Observe any development in the objects occupying the farmer's concern.

Translation and outline

Verse	*Translation*	*Outline*
		I. Introduction: imperative and rationale concerning asset-management (27:23–24)
27:23	Know thoroughly the face of your flock. Focus your mind on your herd.	A. Urgent imperative: shift attention from greed and boastful image-management to asset-management (v. 23)
27:24	For treasure does not last for ever, and even though it be a crown, from one generation to the next.	B. Dual-theme rationale: because, if untended, assets of both courtier and king will fade (v. 24)

Verse	Translation	Outline
		II. Strategy and rationale for successful asset-management (27:25–27)
27:25	Grasses had vanished, yet new growth appeared, and the luscious mountain vegetation was gathered.	A. Strategy: persistent care of wealth-producers (v. 25)
		B. Rationale: benefits of such care (vv. 26–27)
27:26	Lambs are for your clothing, and he-goats for purchase of a field,	1. Economic benefits both for self and business expansion (v. 26)
27:27	And she-goats' milk is sufficient for food for you and food for your household, bringing life to your young maidens.	2. Life-giving benefits for self and dependants (v. 27)

Notes on the text

27:23. 'Know thoroughly', *yādōaʿ tēdaʿ*: lit. 'knowing, you must know'. Within Proverbs, intensification by reduplicating a verb (paronomastic infin. abs.) occurs only once more, again with a verb of knowing: *bîn tābîn*, 'perceiving, you must perceive' or 'be very perceptive' (23:1).

27:24. 'and even though it be a crown', *wĕʾim-nēzer*: lit. 'and if a crown' (for concessive, see *HALOT*, s.v. 'ʾ*im*'). Negation in the first colon extends to the second: 'even though it be a crown [it will not last] from one generation to the next'. Multiple references to 'king' at the outset of the master lecture (cf. 25:1, 2, 3, 5, 6) connect 'crown' with monarchy (not high priest).

27:25. 'Grasses had vanished, yet new growth appeared', *gālâ ḥāṣîr wĕnirʾâ-dešeʾ*: these phrases portray two scenes or seasons: one barren, the other fruitful. The grammar of the second scene (a weqat. form) indicates that it unfolds independent of the first. Otherwise the second scene would be expressed by a consequential wayyiq. form. Despite prior barrenness, the pasture now bursts with new growth. Verdure of spring emerges of its own initiative. Current discouraging conditions are not a conclusive indicator of future fruitlessness. Instead to render 27:25a as a protasis would infer either conditionality ('If the grass is removed') or causation ('[When] grass disappears') – connotations not supported by the sage's choice of grammar, therefore disrupting his intended point (*pace* Waltke 2005: 389 and Fox 2009: 814, respectively).

27:26. 'and he-goats for purchase of a field': lit. 'and a field's price, he-goats'.

27:27. 'is sufficient', *dê*: the same noun (plus pronominal suff.) described moderate honey consumption in 25:16, rendered 'what you need', *dayyekā*.

Form and structure

Borders

The last poem counselled courtiers aspiring after magnificence, closing with a lecture recap (27:19–22). In contrast, the present lecture coheres in an agrarian metaphor for effective management, pertinent for courtiers and kings alike (resembling the double emphasis of Lecture One, 25:1–12). A pair of urgent, agrarian imperatives marks its upper border (27:23). The preceding poem contained only one imperative, found ten verses earlier (27:13).

Thematically, the farmer's attainment of sufficiency marks the lower border (27:27). Assonantal inclusio and two elements of closure also indicate the lower border. Concerning assonantal inclusio, notice *d-ē/ê* sounds as this lecture begins (*yādōaʿ-tēdaʿ*, 'Know thoroughly ', 27:23a) and ends (*wĕdê*, 'So, sufficient is ', 27:27a).

Content-based closure results when animals appear in the first block of Section I and again in the last block of Section II. 'Flock' and 'herd' appear in 27:23, while 'lambs', 'he-goats' and 'she-goats' appear in vv. 26–27.

Content-based closure operates again, since concern for the well-being of farm animals begins this lecture (27:23, 25). Concern for well-being returns at the poem's conclusion, this time directed towards the farmer's own family (vv. 26–27).

Macrostructural features

As discussed above in connection with borders, assonantal inclusio and two elements of closure operate as macrostructures.

Microstructural features

Section I (27:23–24). *Imperative-plus-rationale (27:23–24, content-based).* The poem's first saying issues two imperatives calling for attentiveness, supported by a rationale in the second saying (27:23–24).

Dual-theme concerning courtier and king (27:24, content-based). 'Treasure' in 27:24a and 'crown' in v. 24b form a dual-theme: 'For treasure does not last for ever, and even though it be a crown, from one generation to the next.' 'Crown' links to monarchy, one of two primary roles in the master lecture (e.g. 25:2–5). Since 'crown' represents the monarchy, and since the master lecture counsels both kings and courtiers (cf. 25:6–10), it seems likely the lesser asset of 'treasure' connotes courtiers, forming a dual-theme verse in 27:24. Thus the dual-theme saying joins a prior lecture concerning courtiers (Lecture Two, 25:13 – 27:22), and an ensuing lecture concerning monarchs (Lecture Four, 28:1 – 29:27). Of this pair, 'treasure' appears first in 27:24, linking to the courtier poem just past (Lecture Two). 'Crown' appears second, linking to the ensuing poem concentrating on monarchs (Lecture Four).

Section II (27:25–27). *Strategy-plus-rationale (27:25–27, content-based).* Section II begins with a strategy for fruitful farming (diligently providing food for flocks, 27:25). Strategy is supported by rationale – benefits following diligent labour (clothing, enterprise-expansion, food, vitality for family, vv. 26–27).

Word-pair involving livestock (27:26–27, content-based). The poet refers to he-goats in 27:26 and she-goats in v. 27. This word-pair endorses treating these as a verse-pair, otherwise thematically joined as rationale (Waltke 2005: 394).

Comment

Master-lecture features of progression involving Lecture Three

Three features bridging to other lectures substantially influence this poem's meaning. They involve (a) progression in the repetition of 'face', (b) progression among illustrations of productivity and (c) progression from greed to generosity.

Progression in the repetition of 'face' (Lectures Two and Three, form- and content-based). Although occurring only once in Lecture Three, the term 'face' features prominently in the opening imperative 'Know thoroughly the face of your flock' (27:23a).

Three mentions of 'face' in Lecture Two create a background for this term. The first is negative, inwardly focused. By his 'face' the husband communicated hostile attitudes ('an indignant face', 25:23). The second is positive, as by mutual reproof one friend 'sharpens the face' of another (27:17). The third connotes healthy self-awareness. One should monitor self-motives, as if studying one's own 'face', reflected on the water's surface (27:19). Thus 'face' in Lecture Two begins in self-centredness, progresses to self-reform, ending in ongoing self-awareness. In contrast, in Lecture Three to know 'the face of your flock' encourages outward-awareness.

Progression among illustrations of productivity (Lectures One, Two and Three, content-based). The sage employs four industrial illustrations of productivity in the first three lectures – two from metallurgy and two from agriculture. Regarding metallurgy, silversmithing (especially refining ore) describes the monarch's duty to remove evil elements from society (25:4–5). Later the sage likens skilful dispensing of reproof to a jeweller's artistic composition (25:11–12). Regarding agriculture, caring for one's master resembles caring for a fig tree, since both reward with valuable fruit (27:18a). Subsequently the sage observes that attentive care of livestock will reward a farmer with food, clothing and funds for expanded productivity (27:23, 25–27).

Progression emerges from contrasting the benefits deriving from metallurgy with those from agriculture. Benefits from metallurgy result directly. Efforts exerted in refining ore or shaping a piece of jewellery yield noticeably beautiful products in a straightforward manner. In contrast, benefits from agricultural efforts emerge only indirectly. Pruning a fig tree produces fruit indirectly, and feeding a flock produces milk, wool and revenue indirectly. Unlike the metalworker, it is the tree or flock (not the farmer) that generates the desirable product.

When applied to leaders, on the direct level they must metaphorically refine and carve away undesirable elements from the community. On a grander, indirect level, they must 'feed' (by supplying compensation and an appealing work environment) those who in turn will produce desired products.

Progression from greed to generosity (Lectures One, Two, Three and Four, concept-based). Over the course of this master lecture the sage guides the pupil from greed to generosity through a four-step passage. Greed first emerges in the courtier's lust for advancement in Lecture One (25:6–7), followed by extensive exposure of greed in Lecture Two (25:13–28).

Step two reveals dissatisfaction – the engine driving greed. Towards the close of Lecture Two the sage introduces a haunting comparison, tracing greed to its source in dissatisfaction: 'Sheol and the underworld will not be satisfied, and the eyes of a mortal will not be satisfied' (27:20).

Step three showcases sufficiency (not abundance) as dissatisfaction's cure. This turning point emerges in Lecture Three through the shepherd who focuses attention not on himself but on his flock. Consequently 'she-goats' milk is sufficient for food for you' (27:27). Sufficiency continues in Lecture Four with another agricultural illustration: 'The one who works his soil, food will satisfy; but the one who chases after emptiness, poverty will satisfy' (28:19).

Sufficiency leads to generosity (step four): 'One who gives to the poor has no lack, while one who averts his eyes is an abundance of curses' (28:27, Lecture Four). Thus the metaphor in Lecture Three of a shepherd's diligent labour leading to sufficiency plays a decisive role in the master-lecture progression from greed to generosity.

Progression of thought particular to this poem

Section I (27:23–24). The pupil must devote attention to what is under his care and responsibility (metaphorically his flock, 27:23). The reason is plain. Neither courtier (who possesses 'treasure') nor monarch (who wears a 'crown') may risk indolence, supposing their store of wealth or status as royalty guarantees perpetual support (27:24).

27:23–27. Also in 24:30–34 the sage drew a teaching illustration from agriculture.

Section II (27:25–27). Section II explains how (strategy) and why (rationale) the pupil should attend to his 'flock'. A shepherding strategy requires supplying the flock with food (27:25). When the 'grasses [have] vanished' (v. 25aα), one must not despair. In time the field routinely flourishes, yielding fresh vegetation (v. 25aβ-b; see 'Notes', above).

A rationale for shepherding looks to the rewards that healthy flocks bring: clothing and surplus funds to expand operations (27:26). Beyond this, the farmer can feed himself and his family. Best of all, his young maidens – the tenderest who depend on his care – will attain exuberant vitality ('life', v. 27).

27:27. The milk of goats was preferred for its nutritional value (Waltke 2005: 394).

Explanation

Moving beyond the caution against image-management (Lecture Two, Prov. 25:13 – 27:22), Lecture Three counsels asset-management (27:23–27). This requires a leader to shift attention away from self, studying instead the well-being of others. Especially he should attend to the well-being of all under his leadership – those on whose labours he depends for wealth-generation.

Such a shift of attention comprises no incidental obligation appended to a leader's crowded to-do list. Rather, routinely to assess his subordinates' well-being must rank foremost of any data that an effective manager should gather ('Know thoroughly'; see 'Notes' for 27:23a).

Such knowledge derives neither from impersonal polls nor from hearsay surveys. We must study compassionately the 'face' of our 'flock'. Do they register weariness? We may be driving them too hard. Do they appear gaunt? Perhaps we have grown inattentive to their need for 'nourishment'. Or, knowing their need, are we slow to meet it (cf. Ezek. 34)? Are they bruised, literally or psychologically? If so, what lies within our power to ensure an environment free from physical, social, psychological or spiritual hazard?

What may influence leaders to lose sight of their 'flock's' well-being? A tyrannical longing-for-more (discredited by the sage in 25:6–7, 16, 27; 27:20) may seduce us into valuing productivity above people.

Escaping bonds forged by insatiable greed, the sage commends a strategy of sufficiency. So long as the farmer truly knows his flock and faithfully nourishes it, resulting production (wool and milk) will be 'sufficient' (27:27a). Although he may sacrifice short-term prestige or ease, the results will prove 'enough': food-enough, clothing-enough, mixed with robust health enjoyed by those depending on his care. Such sufficiencies will earn him or her a place among the most magnificent of managers (27:26–27).

When training disciples centuries later, Jesus and his followers would draw from animal husbandry. Shepherding both described Jesus' own leadership (John 10; Matt. 9:36), and outlined how his followers should treat individuals entrusted to their care (John 21:15–17; Acts 20:28).

PROVERBS 28:1 – 29:27
'Lecture four: What counsel may guide kings who aspire to magnificence?'

Overview of Proverbs 28 – 29
As early as the first instalment of the master lecture spanning Prov. 25 – 29 (Lecture One, 25:1–12), the sage has signalled kings' responsibility in a monarchy's quest for magnificence. Lecture Four (28:1 – 29:27) now details that role (esp. 29:3–14, early in Section II).

To set the scene for the monarch's role, the sage depicts in Section I a disturbing societal scene – a land whose residents have been put to flight (28:1). This portrayed the diametric opposite of what the sage desired for his community. So he explores first why they fled (Block I.A, vv. 1–18), then probes how to reverse such severe destabilization (Block I.B, vv. 19–28).

Against this backdrop of unnamed intimidation and societal disintegration, in Section II the sage casts the monarch's role as the ultimate human agent of justice (29:3–14, Block II.B). Joining the monarch, parents and lesser rulers also must intercept and reprove insolence wherever it may spring up (Block II.C, 29:15–23).

Section III concludes Lecture Four with a recap of dual societal perils (greed and erosion of justice, 29:24), followed by supreme responses to each (29:25–26). As this master lecture draws to a close, the sage steels the pupil to stay the course, never to abandon the struggle. Those struggling for moral right must reject the counsel of fatigue that would press for peace at any price (29:27).

Position of this poem within Proverbs
Preceding context. Approaching Lecture Four (Prov. 28 – 29), the pupil has (a) learned that monarch and courtier share responsibility for achieving a magnificent monarchy (Lecture One, 25:1–12), (b) studied courtiers' counterbalanced hazards of selfish greed and indiscriminate generosity (Lecture Two, 25:13 – 27:22), and (c) considered a winsome model of management drawn from animal husbandry (Lecture Three, 27:23–27). All that lacks in the counsel for king and courtier is instruction for monarchs (together with parents and lesser rulers, who share responsibility for reproving insolence).

Ensuing context. Following the master lecture edited by Hezekiah's staff (Prov. 25 – 29), advice from two new wisdom contributors awaits the pupil. In Prov. 30 Agur ben Yaqeh will counsel (a) reverence for the divine and

(b) contentment, correctives countering the greed that spawned societal strife in Prov. 28.

The monarch's role (prominent in Prov. 28 – 29) will resurface towards the close of Agur's lecture, confronting abusive greed (30:30–31). Thereafter King Lemuel's mother will urge her monarch-son in his capacity as judge to advocate diligently for the oppressed (31:4–9) – echoing the call for kings to impose justice (25:4–5 in Lecture One; 29:3–14 in Lecture Four).

What to watch for

Observe abusive greed and lawlessness, also generosity and integrity. Examine mention of king and princes. Notice awareness of community extending beyond the family unit. Observe varied operations of reproof. Be aware of the refrain-like insistence that, despite immorality's substantial force, the moral will both endure and emerge victorious. Notice how the sage showcases the right approach to magnificence (29:23). Observe when both 'guilty' and 'moral' appear in a single saying, especially at the lecture's close (29:27).

Translation and outline

Verse	*Translation*	*Outline*
		I. Greed and generosity: the struggle for magnificence in the monarchy (28:1–28) A. Greed: the false route to national magnificence (28:1–18) 1. Symptoms, diagnosis and prognosis of greed – that conventional route to magnificence (28:1–10) a. Symptoms and diagnosis of greed (28:1–6) i. Symptoms of greed (28:1–3)
28:1	They had fled since no one was pursuing the guilty person, but moral folk are like a young lion capable of confidence.	α. State of affairs: intimidation-unrestrained, yet failing to menace universally (first guilty–moral refrain, 28:1)
28:2	By means of a land's transgression, many are its officials; but by means of an insightful mortal alert to this fact, it will be able to last long.	β. Transgressive rule may expand, yet morality will outlast (28:2)

Translation	Outline
28:3 A strong man is poor and therefore oppresses helpless folk. Rain comes like a flash flood so there is no food.	γ. Core symptom: greed prompted by poverty, generating fruitless abuse (28:3)
	ii. Diagnosis of greed's root cause (28:4–6)
28:4 Those who abandon the Law are able to praise a guilty person, but those who keep the Law will enter the fray against them.	α. Orientation to Moral Code reveals root values (28:4)
28:5 Persons inclined to wickedness are unable to perceive impending judgement, but those who seek the LORD can perceive everything.	β. (Dis)orientation to source of moral values determines (un)awareness of approaching disaster (28:5)
28:6 Better a person who is poor, walking in his integrity, than one who is twisted both ways, even though he may be rich.	γ. Core diagnosis: a failure to grasp moral nature of wealth is root cause of greed (28:6)
	b. Prognosis, if greed continues untreated (28:7–10)
28:7 One who preserves the Law is an insightful son, but one who gets himself mixed up with those who brush it aside will disgrace his father.	i. Wisdom commendation: insight is determined by orientation to Moral Code (28:7)
	ii. Wisdom content, with response (28:8–9)
28:8 As for one who multiplies his wealth by charging exorbitant interest and by profiteering, it is for one who is gracious to the helpless that he will collect it.	α. Content: greed leads ironically to involuntary generosity (28:8)
28:9 One who turns his ear away from listening to the Law, even his prayer will be something loathsome.	β. Response: callous response towards Moral Code spells spiritual doom (28:9)
28:10 One who misleads straight folk into a wicked way will himself fall into his pit, but those with integrity will inherit what is good.	iii. Core of prognosis: moral misdirection brings ruin, not satisfaction (character summary, 28:10)

Verse	*Translation*	*Outline*
		2. Humility: a preliminary cure for greed (28:11–14)
28:11	Wise in his own eyes is a person who is rich, but a helpless person who is insightful will be able to discover his error.	a. Wisdom commendation: insight is not determined by wealth (28:11)
		b. Wisdom content, with response (28:12–13)
28:12	When moral folk exult, splendour abounds; but when guilty folk rise up, a mortal will be hunted down.	i. Content: magnificence consists of morality, not tangible wealth (second guilty–moral refrain, 28:12)
28:13	One who covers his transgressions will not succeed, but one who confesses and abandons them will be treated with compassion.	ii. Response: personal response to guilt concerning Moral Code determines future success (28:13)
28:14	How fortunate is the mortal who trembles continually! But one who renders his mind stubborn will fall into misery.	c. Core of cure: a humble response constitutes greatest good (character summary, 28:14)
		3. Final assessment of greed's methods and outcomes (28:15–18)
28:15	A roaring lion, an attacking bear: such is a guilty person who rules over helpless people,	a. The futility of greed, ruling with escalating abuse (28:15–16)
28:16	such is a prince with a shortage of perception but an abundance of extortions. As for those who hate treachery, he will lengthen days.	
28:17	A mortal who experiences oppression for having taken a life will flee to a pit-grave. May no one hold him back!	b. Ultimate demise of oppressor, ultimate rescue of moral person (28:17–18, character summary)
28:18	One who walks in integrity will be rescued, but one who is twisted both ways will fall summarily.	

	B. Satisfaction, trust and generosity: the cures for greed (28:19–28) 1. Replace greed with inner satisfaction (28:19–22) a. Instead of chasing riches, seek satisfaction through faithfulness . . . (28:19–20)
28:19 The one who works his soil, food will satisfy; but the one who chases after emptiness, poverty will satisfy.	i. Food satisfaction follows faithful industry, not hollow schemes (28:19)
28:20 A person characterized by faithfulness is an abundance of blessings, but one who rushes to gain riches will not be exonerated.	ii. Social satisfaction follows faithful relationships, not sacrificing relationships to greed (28:20)
	b. . . . For greed only depletes (28:21–22)
28:21 Giving preferential treatment is not good, yet for a crust of bread a strong man will trespass.	i. Greed depletes relationships (28:21)
28:22 One who hurries after wealth is a miserly person, and he knows not that lack will come to him.	ii. Greed depletes resources (28:22)
	2. Replace greed with trust and generosity towards others, for eventual success (28:23–28) a. Reproof . . . and the paradox of divine trust (28:23–25)
28:23 One who reprimands a mortal may afterwards discover favour, more than one who flatters.	i. Wisdom commendation: reproof wins favour, eventually (28:23)
28:24 One who robs his father and his mother, and then says, 'there was no transgression' – he is a companion to one who destroys.	ii. Exposing the by-product of greed: destruction (start of wisdom content, 28:24)
28:25 One with an expansive appetite will spread strife, but one who places his confidence in the LORD will be nourished abundantly.	iii. Character summary: the paradox of greed that fails, and trust that nourishes (28:25)

Verse *Translation*	*Outline*
	b. Receptivity . . . and the paradox of neighbourly generosity, with refrain of struggle (28:26–28)
28:26 One who places confidence in his mind – he is stupid; but one who walks in wisdom – he will be delivered.	i. Wisdom commendation: receptivity, not self-reliance, leads to rescue (28:26)
28:27 One who gives to the poor has no lack, while one who averts his eyes is an abundance of curses.	ii. Character summary exposing the by-product of generosity: generosity paradoxically yields sufficiency (start of wisdom content, 28:27)
28:28 When guilty folk rise up, a mortal must be hidden, but when they perish, moral folk may multiply.	iii. The moral contest: guilt may menace now, but the moral eventually will flourish (third guilty–moral refrain, 28:28)
	II. Lesser and greater agents reproving greed in the monarchy (29:1–23) A. Dual-theme introduction about reproving greed: reproof through lesser and greater agents (29:1–2)
29:1 A reprimand-resistant person is a neck rendered stubborn; suddenly it will be snapped, and without recovery.	1. Individual liability following routinized rejection of reproof (lesser agents of reproof, 29:1)
29:2 When moral folk multiply, the people will rejoice; but when a guilty person rules, people will groan.	2. Corporate asset or liability depending on ruler's morality (greater agents of reproof, fourth guilty–moral refrain, 29:2)
	B. Greater agents of reproof: kings and rulers (29:3–14) 1. A king must reject the seduction of internal greed (29:3–6)
29:3 A person inclined to love wisdom will make his father joyful, but one who gets himself mixed up with prostitutes will destroy wealth.	a. Wisdom commendation: greed traces to an appetite for seductive pleasures (29:3)

Verse	Translation	Outline
29:4	A king by administering justice will make a land stand firm, while a person known for demanding contributions will decimate it.	b. Abusive greed excuses graft and depletes communities (start of wisdom content, 29:4)
29:5	A strong man who operates in a slippery fashion towards his friend is spreading a net for his steps.	c. Abusive greed that deceives friends snares self (29:5)
29:6	Within a wicked person's transgression is a snare, but a moral person will shout aloud and be joyful.	d. Concluding principle: the deception of self-ensnarement thwarts joy (29:6)
		2. A king must counter external greed that would manipulate justice (29:7–11)
29:7	A moral person is knowledgeable concerning a legal claim of helpless folk; a guilty person cannot perceive knowledge.	a. Personal morality anchors public morality (fifth guilty–moral refrain, wisdom commendation, 29:7)
		b. Three-phase strategy to hijack justice (start of wisdom content, 29:8–10)
29:8	Persons inclined to scoff will inflame a city, but wise folk will reverse anger.	i. Phase one: inflammatory ridicule, reversed by the wise (29:8)
29:9	A wise person went to court against a foolish person; and he was excited, and he ridiculed, and was not quiet.	ii. Phase two: passionate but unfounded litigation, countered by the wise (29:9)
29:10	Persons inclined to shed blood will hate a person of integrity, but honest folk will seek the life of each.	iii. Phase three: murderous malevolence, vindicated by honest folk (29:10)
29:11	A stupid person vents all his emotion, but a wise person can calm it later on.	c. Summary: the wise neutralize attempts to hijack justice (29:11)
		3. Recap: the truth about moral kings (29:12–14)
29:12	A ruler who subscribes to false talk, all his officers are guilty folk.	a. A monarch must embrace truth, or suffer devious staff (29:12)

Verse *Translation*	*Outline*
29:13 A poor person and a person inclined to violence were encountered: the one who illumines the eyes of them both is the Lord.	b. A warning truth: victimizers enjoy no security before their Maker (29:13)
29:14 A king who faithfully administers justice for helpless folk, his throne will be established permanently.	c. A reassuring truth: a monarch who secures the vulnerable enjoys security (29:14)
	C. Lesser agents of reproof: parents and supervisors (29:15–23) 1. Reproving children (29:15–17)
29:15 Rod and reprimand may impart wisdom; but a youth who is given free rein shames his mother.	a. Parents may administer reproof, or suffer shame (29:15)
29:16 When guilty folk multiply, transgression will multiply; but moral folk will observe their downfall.	b. Consequences of exponential societal immorality (sixth guilty–moral refrain, 29:16)
29:17 Reprove your son! So may he bring you rest! So may he supply your appetite with delicacies!	a'. An urgent call to administer reproof (29:17)
	2. Reproving adults (29:18–20)
29:18 For want of a divinely revelatory message, a people will run wild; but one who keeps the Law – he is fortunate.	a. Adults attentive to the Law need no further reproof (29:18)
29:19 It is not through words that a servant will be reproved, if he perceives what you are saying; yet nothing you say generates any affliction.	b. But subordinates who resist divine words require incentive more compelling than merely compounded words of human reproof (29:19–20)
29:20 You have observed, no doubt, a person who is quick with words. A stupid fellow has more hope than he.	
	3. Recap of reproof, with climax of magnificence (29:21–23) a. The high cost of non-reproof (29:21–22)

29:21 A person pampers his servant from youth; so in the end he will get insolence. 29:22 A person inclined to anger will stir up strife, and a master-of-wrath will stir up an abundance of transgression.	i. Initial cost: impertinence towards supervisor who withholds reproof (29:21) ii. Exponential cost: community agitation and flood of offences (29:22)
29:23 A mortal's loftiness will bring him low, but it is lowness of spirit that will lay hold of glory.	b. The secret to magnificence: humility, not arrogance, achieves glory (character summary, 29:23)
	III. Conclusion: recap of perils within greed, with responses and refrain (29:24–27) A. Recap of perils, with responses (29:24–26)
29:24 One who divides portions with a thief hates his very life; he can hear the solemn summons for witnesses, but he will not give evidence.	1. Dual-theme summary of perils: greed that harms self (29:24a), and passive injustice (29:24b)
	2. Response to dual perils (29:25–26)
29:25 A snare yields anxiety for a mortal, but one who places his confidence in the LORD will be lifted up.	a. Response to greed that harms self: depend on the LORD's aid (29:25)
29:26 Many seek a ruler's face, but it is from the LORD that a person's justice derives.	b. Response to peril of passive injustice: remain confident of divine justice (29:26)
29:27 Loathsome to moral folk is a person inclined to dishonesty; and loathsome to a guilty person is a person whose way is straight.	B. Seventh refrain: the moral struggle will persist, requiring persistent courage (character summary, final guilty–moral refrain, 29:27)

Notes on the text

28:1. 'They had fled since no one was pursuing the guilty person', *nāsû wĕʾên rōdēp rāšāʿ*: lit. 'they fled and none was pursuing a guilty person'. An unnamed populace (pl.) had been set to flight because no one was bothering (or dared) to challenge the aggressor (sg.). For parallel syntax, see Lev. 26:17b: *wĕnastem wĕʾên rōdēp ʾetkem*, 'then you will flee though none pursues you'. In each case the unpursued object follows the verb 'to [not] pursue'.

Instead to render as 'guilty persons fled though none pursues' requires treating a sg. noun appearing last in the colon (*rāšāʿ*, 'guilty person') as subject of a pl. verb appearing first in the colon (*nāsû*, 'they had fled'; so LXX; Waltke 2005: 395; Fox 2009: 819). However, if 'guilty' had been intended as subject, the pl. form *rĕšāʿîm*, 'guilty folk', should have been used (attested thirty-five times in Proverbs). Simply to treat 'guilty person' as object (not subject) is preferable, both syntactically and rhetorically, since it casts in bolder relief the leonine confidence of moral folk (28:1b) who, by their resoluteness, would fortify those driven into hiding by the guilty (28:12), and who stand as stalwart prototypes for the monarch who, 'by administering justice will make a land stand firm' (29:4a).

'moral folk are like a young lion capable of confidence', *ṣaddîqîm kikĕpîr yibĕṭāḥ*: not 'moral folk remain confident like a young lion', since the verb 'to be confident' requires a sg. subject, 'lion', not the pl. 'moral folk'. Capability is inferred from the poet's choice of a yiq. form (*yibĕṭāḥ*) where one would expect a ptc. (*bōṭēaḥ*).

28:2b. 'but by means of an insightful mortal alert to this fact, it will be able to last long', *ûbĕādām mēbîn yōdēaʿ kēn yaʾărîk*: lit. 'but by a mortal who is insightful, one who knows thus, it will last long'. The expression *yōdēaʿ kēn* means '[he] realizes that this is so' (cf. 1 Sam. 23:17b; this interpretation departs from the disjunctive trope separating *yōdēaʿ*, 'knows', from *kēn*, 'thus'). This apophthegm sets in parallel two circumstances generating independent results. A transgressive land fosters multiplied bureaucrats (28:2a). Conversely, an insightful person (especially one cognizant of the principle that 'transgression proliferates bureaucrats') fosters a land that endures (note reference to 'land' by pronoun 'its' in first colon; for 'land' as m., cf. Ezek. 21:24). The desire for a stable land returns in 29:4. Since the 'insightful mortal' has not been presented as a subject, the likelihood reduces that he (not land) is the entity to 'last long'.

28:3. 'A strong man is poor and therefore oppresses': lit. 'A strong man poor and oppresses'. 'Poor' serves as verbless predicate (not 'a poor strong man'). It is his poverty that stirs the strong man greedily to oppress the helpless.

28:4. 'are able to praise': capability inferred from yiq.

'Law', *tôrâ*: lit. 'law' or 'instruction'. In Prov. 28 – 29, *tôrâ* connects closely with divine direction (not mere human advice). Note the parallel between *tôrâ* in 28:4a and 'those who seek the LORD' in v. 5b. *Tôrâ* connects with divinely revelatory communication in 29:18 (cf. Fox 2009: 821). Thus to 'abandon the Law' (28:4a), to 'keep the Law' (28:4b; 29:18) and to 'listen to the Law' (28:9) portray responses to divine direction, epitomized by the Torah ('Law'; i.e. the Pentateuch). Consequently *tôrâ* is rendered 'Law' (capitalized) in these two chapters.

28:5. 'are unable to perceive impending judgement', *lōʾ-yābînû mišpāṭ*: lit. 'will not perceive judgement' ([in]capability inferred from yiq.).

'Impending' is supplied to clarify that 'judgement' refers to forthcoming retribution, not a desirable skill of discernment. 'In the legal sense they do not realize that divine justice will catch up with them' (Waltke 2005: 410).

'can perceive': capability inferred from yiq.

28:6. 'both ways', *dĕrākayim*: lit. 'a pair of ways' (only here and 28:18). Both here and in 28:18, travel along 'both ways' contrasts 'walking in integrity', suggesting that 'both ways' refers not to any particular pair of ways, but to moral deficit encompassing vacillation, double-mindedness, ethical indecision and duplicity.

28:7. 'those who brush it aside': lit. 'those who despise', or 'treat lightly' or 'are rash'. The object 'it' (the Law) is inferred from the first colon.

28:8. 'his wealth' and 'gracious', *hônô* and *ḥônēn*: assonance links these words with opposing meaning (economic abuse versus generosity).

28:15. 'lion', *ărî*: distinct from *kepîr*, 'young lion' (28:1).

28:15–16. 'such is . . . such is': the expression 'such is' is implied by the Hebr. The metaphor of menacing animals in 28:15a corresponds both to the guilty ruler of v. 15b and to the abusive prince of v. 16a.

28:16. 'perception', *tĕbûnôt*: LXX renders as 'A king who lacks income [*prosodōn*] is a great extortioner' (as if the exemplar read *tĕbû'ôt* in place of *tĕbûnôt*). The Hebr. teaches that extortion traces not to income deficit, but to ignorance concerning wise rule.

'As for those who hate treachery, he will lengthen days', *śōne'ê beṣa' ya'ărîk yāmîm*: lit. 'haters of treachery – he will lengthen days' (following K). The verb 'he will lengthen' requires a sg. antecedent as subject. To emend pl. *śōne'ê*, 'those who hate', to sg. *śōnē'*, 'one who hates', would solve that anomaly (so Q). However, this obscures the intimation that an individual other than the 'treachery-haters' supplies that longevity. Longevity first appeared in 28:2 as a benefit enjoyed by the insightful person, without mention of its source (whether human or divine). The divine dimension appeared soon after, implicit in the Law (v. 4; cf. vv. 7, 9), and explicit in the expression 'those who seek the LORD' (v. 5). The attitude of 'trembling continually' may imply reverent awareness of the divine (v. 14a; perhaps also the rescue from a pit-grave for those with integrity in vv. 17–18). The next express mention of 'the LORD' occurs in 28:25. Thus it seems best to recognize the divine as the sg. subject of 'he will lengthen' in 28:16.

28:17. 'oppression', *'āšaq*: from the root *'šq*, as also 'extortions' (28:16).

'pit-grave', *bôr*: lit. 'pit', here implying a grave (distinct from 'pit', *šĕḥut*, in 28:10).

28:18. 'both ways', *dĕrākayim*: see 'Notes' for 28:6.

'summarily', *bĕ'eḥāt*: lit. 'in one'. This expression unifies 'both ways' into a sudden and single whole (cf. *bĕ'aḥat* in Jer. 10:8 and *kĕ'eḥād* in Eccles. 11:6). Ruin will befall one who rejects integrity. Lacking integrity, it matters not which of various 'ways' he subsequently may choose.

28:20. 'is an abundance of blessings', *rab-bĕrākôt*: beyond gaining benefit for himself (28:19a), a faithful person embodies much blessing, enriching those with whom he or she associates (contrast 28:27b).

28:23. 'than one who flatters': lit. 'than a slippery-tongued person'.

28:25. 'nourished abundantly': lit. 'made fat'.

28:27. 'is an abundance of curses', *rab-mĕʾērôt*: parallels 'is an abundance of blessings' (see 'Notes' for 28:20).

28:28. 'must be hidden . . . may multiply': lit. 'will be hidden . . . will multiply' (obligation and possibility inferred from yiq.).

'a mortal . . . but when they perish', *ʾādām ûbĕʾābĕdām*: assonance links these expressions, adjacent in Hebr.

29:1. 'A reprimand-resistant person', *ʾîš tôkaḥōt*: lit. 'a person of reprimands'; i.e. a person often in need of reproof (Waltke 2005: 398; Fox 2009: 833). Sg. *tôkaḥat* reappears in 29:15.

'is a neck rendered stubborn', *maqšēh-ʿōref*: the neck was not initially stubborn, but has been made so (hiph.). The sage discloses the true character of the subject ('a reprimand-resistant person') by blunt, verbless colocation with the predicate ('a neck rendered stubborn').

29:2. 'rejoice . . . groan': these roots form an antonymous pair in Isa. 24:7; 35:10 (= Isa. 51:11).

29:4. 'a person known for demanding contributions', *ʾîš tĕrûmôt*: lit. 'a person of contributions'. This envisions a leader who depletes his country through exorbitant expectations for contributions, whether to the temple or, more likely, to fill royal coffers (cf. BDB and *HALOT*, s.v. '*tĕrûmâ*').

29:5. '[one] who operates in a slippery fashion', *maḥălîq*: lit. 'one who is slippery', implying deception (cf. *maḥălîq lāšôn*, 'slippery-tongued', 28:23).

'for his steps': initially the friend's steps are implied. Yet the malevolent 'strong man' retributively traps himself (so also Fox 2009: 835).

29:6. 'a snare': the snare latent within transgression retributively traps also the wicked person (cf. 29:5).

29:7. '[he] cannot perceive knowledge': lit. '[he] will not perceive knowledge' ([in]capability inferred from yiq.).

29:8. 'inflame': lit. 'breathe out, utter', associated with anger in 29:8b (LXX renders, 'kindle a fire').

'will reverse': the wise will redirect scoffers' anger, so it recoils against its originators.

29:9. 'went to court', *nišpāṭ*: lit. 'engaged a judicial dispute' (shares root *špṭ* with 'justice' in 29:4, and 'administer justice' in v. 14).

'and he ridiculed': resorting to the rhetoric of ridicule, the fool concedes his case lacks rational grounds for persuasion (for an exploration of ridicule in persuasion, see Grewell 2013).

29:10b. 'but honest folk will seek the life of each', *wîšārîm yĕbaqšû napšô*: Hebr. syntax of 29:10b parallels v. 10a (pl. subject, pl. verb and sg. object). Since in the nearby context, positive persons repeatedly counteract negative persons (cf. vv. 7, 8, 9 and 11), the simplest interpretation recognizes the same dynamic in v. 10 (immoral action in v. 10a precipitates moral reaction in v. 10b). Honest folk in v. 10b will return the effects of bloodshed upon each perpetrator of murder in v. 10a (for *napšô* as 'the life of each', cf. GKC §145.5; not *napšām*, 'the life of them', as in Jer. 21:7 and 34:20, 21).

'life': as object of 'to seek', *npš* denotes 'life', not 'appetite'.

29:13. 'were encountered': see 'Notes' for 22:2.

'the one who illumines the eyes of them both': 'to supply light for the eyes' connotes (a) restoration of energy or enjoyment during life (1 Sam. 14:27, 29; Ps. 19:8 [v. 9 MT]; Ezra 9:8) and (b) supply of mortal existence itself, the converse of 'sleeping the sleep of death' (Ps. 13:3 [v. 4 MT]; cf. Eccles. 11:7–8).

29:15. 'Rod and reprimand may impart wisdom', *šēbeṭ wĕtôkaḥat yittēn ḥokmâ*: with m. sg. verb 'impart', 'rod and reprimand' form a single concept (similarly 'perfume and incense may delight' in 27:9; Joüon §150p).

'and reprimand', *wĕtôkaḥat*: see 'Notes' for 'reprimand-resistant' in 29:1.

29:17. 'So may he bring you rest!', *wînîḥekā*: 'quiet' (29:9) shares root *nwḥ* with 'rest'.

29:18. 'divinely revelatory message', *ḥāzôn*: lit. 'vision', a term principally referring to divine night revelations, conveying symbolic information or specific instructions to a prophet or nation (cf. Fox 2009: 841). If 'vision' in the modern sense of corporate planning were intended, a term such as *maḥăšābâ*, 'plan, purpose', would likely have been selected (cf. Jer. 29:11).

'will run wild', *yippāraʿ*: lit. 'will be unrestrained'. Twice this term describes Israel's idolatrous frolicking about the golden calf, even as God on Mount Sinai was in the process of revealing to Moses the Law designed to restrain them (Exod. 32:25).

'but one who keeps the Law – he is fortunate': lit. 'the keeper of the law, he/it is blessed' (cf. pl. 'those who keep' in 28:4).

29:19. 'if he perceives what you are saying; yet nothing you say generates any affliction', *kî-yābîn wĕʾên maʿăneh*: lit. 'if he perceives, but none causes affliction'. Though the servant comprehends fully the meaning of your reproof, your efforts will be pointless if he knows that non-compliance will bring no negative consequences. Without penalties, warnings are wasted. Since *maʿăneh*, 'generates affliction', can alternatively mean 'response', NASB renders, 'For though he understands, there will be no response' from the servant. Yet the emphasis on effective reproof in the surrounding context (even applying a 'rod', 29:15) recommends *maʿăneh* as 'generating affliction', since absence of affliction would explain why merely verbal reproof is insufficient (v. 19a). The medieval Jewish commentator Hame'iri (1249–c. 1316) similarly rendered 'humiliate' or 'afflict'

(Fox 2009: 843). A wordplay overlapping lack-of-affliction with lack-of-response is also possible.

29:20. 'You have observed, no doubt', *ḥāzîtā*: lit. 'you have observed'. Concerning the emphatic 'no doubt', and the tendency to infer a question in this expression despite the lack of the interrogative particle *hă*, see 'Notes' for 22:29.

29:21. 'so in the end he will get insolence', *wĕʾaḥărîtô yihyeh mānôn*: lit. 'and his latter part, insolence will comprise'; i.e. the pampered servant will reward his benefactor with insolence. In place of 'pampering', this saying implies the importance of administering reproof (29:17), not with words alone (29:19). The indication of outcome ('in the end') describes what will befall the lenient master, not the pampered servant (*pace* NRSV, 'A slave pampered from childhood will come to a bad end'). To translate, 'He . . . will in the end find him to be a son' presumes a connection between *mānôn* (here rendered 'insolence') and the root *nîn*, 'offspring' (cf. Fox 2009: 844), a meaning not supported by the LXX, which renders with *odynēthēsetai*, 'to suffer pain'.

29:22. 'and a master-of-wrath will stir up an abundance of transgression', *ûbaʿal ḥēmâ rab-pāšaʿ*: lit. 'and a master-of-wrath, an abundance of transgression'. The verb 'will stir up' extends by ellipsis from *yĕgāreh* in the first colon.

29:24. 'One who divides portions with': distribution of loot from a collaborative theft.

'he can hear the solemn summons for witnesses', *yišmaʿ ʾālâ*: lit. 'he will hear an oath'. The expression 'to hear an oath', followed by 'not give evidence', *lōʾ yaggîd*, reflects the community requirement to present testimony when summoned (Lev. 5:1). The thief of Prov. 29:24 excuses himself without warrant, undermining the justice system on which the community depends.

29:25. 'A snare yields anxiety for a mortal', *ḥerdat ʾādām yittēn môqēš*: m. 'snare' (not f. 'anxiety') serves as subject of *yittēn*, 'he/it yields' (similarly Rashi, a medieval Jewish scholar [AD 1040–1105], noted by Fox [2009: 847]; not 'The fear of man brings a snare' [NASB]).

Form and structure

Borders

Following an agrarian metaphor (preceding poem), the present lecture opens with a crisis of community intimidation and fruitless abuse of power (28:1–3). This marks the upper border for a lecture especially designed for monarchs aspiring to magnificence.

The lower border is marked by a character summary with a transparently parallel structure (29:27) and by a seventh and final moral/guilty refrain (also 29:27; see under 'Macrostructural features', below). Commensurate with the conclusion of a master lecture, multiple closural elements operate in Section III (29:24–27), described next.

Closure in 29:24 (content-based). Three themes signal closure in the first saying of Section III (29:24): the hazard of abusive greed, the need for communal justice and the harm of reproof-resistance. First, the initial colon cautions against greedy abuse: 'One who divides portions with a thief hates his very life' (29:24a). This theme (counterbalanced with the need for generosity) occupied much of Section I (cf. 28:3, 8a, 15–16, 20, 22, 24 concerning greed, and vv. 8b, 27 concerning generosity).

Second, the solemn and public call for witnesses (29:24bα) indicates a judicial perspective, recalling the community's fundamental need for just rule. The sage addressed this in the first block of Section II (cf. 29:4a, 7, 9, 13, 14).

Third, the greedy character's apathetic reaction to a public summons for witnesses (29:24bβ) was foreshadowed in the reproof-resistant character of Section II. Parent and ruler must reprove such an individual (cf. 29:15, 17–19, 21).

Closure in 29:25 (form- and content-based). 'Snare', 'confidence' and the metaphor of elevation contribute to closure in 29:25. As a form-based closural feature, 'snare' earlier appeared in 29:6.

'Confidence' appears three times in Section I. The resilience of moral folk manifests 'confidence' (28:1). Moral folk place their 'confidence' in the LORD (28:25), not in their own mind (v. 26). Form-based closure results when in Section III the sage again commends those whose 'confidence' is in the LORD (29:25).

A picture of honour achieved through abasement appears at the close of Section II: 'A mortal's loftiness will bring him low, but it is lowness of spirit that will lay hold of glory' (29:23). Content-based closure obtains two sayings later in Section III when, instead of abasement, 'one who places his confidence in the LORD will be lifted up' (29:25b). Metaphoric elevation appeared in the master lecture as early as 25:7, contributing to the quest for magnificence.

Closure in 29:26 (form-based). Closure results from repetition in 29:26 of four terms encountered in 28:5: 'person', 'judgement/justice', 'seek' and 'the LORD'. By comparing these, it proves better to 'seek the LORD' than to 'seek a ruler's face', since 'it is from the LORD that a person's justice derives' (29:26).

Closure in 29:27 (form- and content-based). Doubled terms, the connotation of 'loathsome' and repetition of 'way' contribute to closure in 29:27. As described under 'Macrostructural features', doubled words appear in each section. Thus double use of 'loathsome' in 29:27 generates form-based closure.

On a content level, 'loathsome' indicates intense negative assessment (29:27). A similar sentiment appeared earlier, with hatred directed against treachery (28:16).

'Way' appears four times in this lecture, each marking the close of a portion successively superior in outline subordination. The first use of 'way' ends a mere segment (28:6, ending vv. 1–6). The second closes a unit (v. 10, ending vv. 1–10). The third closes a block (v. 18, ending vv. 1–18). The last instance of 'way' closes a section, and with it the entire lecture (also the master lecture as well, 29:27). 'Way' is saying-terminal in the Hebr. of that saying: 'and loathsome to a guilty person is a person who is straight-of-way'.

Macrostructural features

Repetition of 'rule(r)' (Sections I, II and III, form-based). The root *mšl*, 'rule' or 'ruler', appears in Section I (28:15) and Section II (29:2, 12). In each case, 'rule' is tainted by 'guilt'. Consequently when in Section III the sage remarks that 'many seek a ruler's face' (29:26a), the pupil will realize that the ruler may be susceptible to bribes (29:4b; cf. 28:21), rendering the Lord's guarantee of ultimate justice all the more prized (29:26b).

A sevenfold 'guilty–moral' refrain (Sections I, II and III, form-based). Seven sayings contain the pair 'guilty' and 'moral' (28:1, 12, 28; 29:2, 7, 16, 27; each is designated 'refrain' in outline). Outside the present poem, this word-pair appears only twice in the master lecture (25:5, 26). Structural significance emerges from the positioning and progression evident in these seven sayings, as follows.

Positioning of refrains. By prominently locating the seven moral–guilty refrains, the poet underscores the importance of morality for a monarch aspiring to magnificence. Three contribute to two overlapping inclusios. Lecture Four spans 28:1 – 29:27, with a refrain in first and last sayings (so also Malchow 1985: 239). Section I spans 28:1–28, with a refrain in its first and last sayings. The remaining four display prominence, appearing as either first or second saying in their respective portions (first saying in 29:7–11, and second saying in each of 28:11–14; 29:1–23, 15–23).

Progression of refrains. A progression of thought becomes apparent through the series of seven refrains.

First step (28:1). As Lecture Four opens, the guilty put the general populace to flight, with impunity. But not all is lost. Moral folk remain robustly confident.

Second step (28:12). The contest between guilt and morality forms no minor issue, since on it hinges the overarching quest for magnificence ('splendour'). Burgeoning guilt not only puts to flight people in general; it also takes singular aim at the moral, 'hunt[ing them] down'.

Third step (28:28). Pursued and hunted-down, the moral respond by retreating to seclusion. But once the guilty perish (as assuredly they will), the moral will both reappear and proliferate.

Fourth step (29:2). Indeed, the moral consequently will proliferate, spreading joy across the realm – a splendid metric of a magnificent monarchy. Conversely, anguish seizes the land when the guilty gain ascendancy.

Fifth step (29:7). When, instead, moral folk occupy positions of judicial power, then the helpless obtain justice. For the guilty do not grasp the first thing about advocating for others.

Sixth step (29:16). If the helpless do not obtain justice – if, instead, the guilty evade and proliferate – then criminal activity will spread exponentially. Nevertheless, their reign of terror is unsustainable. When they fall (and they will), the moral will remain standing.

Seventh step (29:27). Although the guilty eventually will fall, at present the moral and guilty remain grimly deadlocked. Anchored in realism, the sage will not countenance a retreat into fantasies of negotiated compromise. Through this closing character summary he fortifies the pupil's resolve. Now to relax one's guard would spell capitulation, surrendering the community's safety and forfeiting all hopes of magnificence. Thus across seven guilty–moral refrains the sage displays a persuasive progression of thought.

Meinhold (1991, 2: 464) and Waltke (2005: 404–405) also comment on various of these seven refrains. Meinhold overlooks certain structural indicators since (a) he omits 29:7 from the collection of seven (due to sg. 'moral person' instead of pl. 'moral folk'), (b) he groups 29:15 with what precedes it (rather than as a wisdom commendation leading to the refrain in v. 16), and (c) he does not regard 29:25–27 as a conclusion. Waltke, by assuming the guilty–moral refrains operate only in Janus positions, discounts some appearing in section-opening wisdom commendations, and thus obscures elements of the poem's structure.

Double use of a word (Sections I, II and III, form-based). Each section contains sayings with double use of words. These words include 'Law' (28:4), 'perceive' (28:5), 'satisfy' (28:19), 'people' (29:2), 'low' (29:23) and 'loathsome' (29:27).

Several double usages occur at structurally significant points. Thus in Section I the double use of 'Law' in 28:4 opens a three-verse segment (vv. 4–6). 'Satisfy', twice in 28:19, opens a ten-verse block (vv. 19–28). Double use of 'perceive' in 28:5, while not structurally significant in itself, may by its proximity to the first doubling ('Law' in 28:4), alert the pupil to be on the lookout for additional doublings as potentially signifying structure. In Section II the double use of 'people' (29:2) belongs to a dual-theme introduction (29:1–2), which dual-themes determine the remainder of that section (vv. 1–23). That section closes with another double-term saying ('low[ness]', 29:23). In Section III, 'loathsome' appears twice (29:27). The lecture concludes with this saying.

Other poems within Prov. 25 – 29 employ word-doubling as well, sometimes at structurally significant points. Thus 'glory' in 25:2 occurs twice within the master lecture's first saying (aside from the authorial note in 25:1). In the second lecture, its final section (27:19–22) begins with a saying that repeats both 'face' and 'mortal' (27:19). The next verse of that section contains a double use of 'to be satisfied' (27:20). In the same poem, however, doubled use of 'appetite' in 27:7 is not structurally significant.

Problem–solution (Sections I and II, content-based). The problem of abuse escalates across Section I: 'they had fled [before the guilty]' (28:1), 'A strong man . . . oppresses helpless folk' (v. 3a), 'A roaring lion, an attacking bear: such is a guilty person who rules over helpless people' (v. 15) and 'When guilty folk rise up, a mortal must be hidden' (v. 28a). This fosters a longing for a champion to restrain the guilty.

As a solution, that champion arrives in Section II – a just and courageous king, who by executing equity restores joy to the realm (29:3–14). Other influential persons also assist (vv. 15–23).

Repetition of 'transgression' (Sections I and II, form-based). 'Transgression(s)' occurs seven times in Lecture Four, in Sections I and II (28:2, 13, 21, 24; 29:6, 16, 22). The first and last frame these combined sections, appearing one saying from their collective first and last borders (28:2; 29:22). They teach that permissiveness towards transgression proliferates bureaucracy (28:2), and that permissive rearing of youth proliferates transgression (29:21–22). The sage thus implies a causal connection between child-rearing practices and the extent of criminality.

Remaining sayings teach that transgression is irreducible. Attempts at hiding or denying it only bring failure to self and destruction to others (28:13 and 24, respectively; also 29:6). Transgressors finally lose their footing (29:16).

Thematic continuity concerning reproof (Sections I and II, content-based). Section I refers to reproof once, towards its close: 'One who reprimands a mortal may afterwards discover favour, more than one who flatters' (28:23). Evidently some demurred, needing reassurance they would gain by dispensing reproof.

Reproof headlines Section II, warning from its first saying that those who repel reproof will suffer irreparable damage (29:1). To refrain from giving reproof amounts to withholding wisdom, while inviting shame and denying rest for oneself (vv. 15, 17). If one pampers a subordinate (instead of administering needed reproof), the resulting insolence should come as no surprise (vv. 19, 21). Given this context, the sage recognizes in 'the Law' a reproof-styled restraint, divinely sourced (v. 18).

Thematic continuity concerning ultimate demise (Sections I and II, content-based). The last saying of Section I and the first of Section II warn of ultimate demise: 'but when [guilty folk] perish' (28:28), and 'suddenly [a stubborn neck] will be snapped, and without recovery' (29:1).

Microstructural features

Section I (28:1–28). *Inclusio involving predation (28:1, 28, content-based).* Section I opens as people have 'fled' (28:1), and ends as the moral withdraw into hiding (v. 28). Thus a theme of predation forms a section-level inclusio.

Sequence of repeated terms (28:1–3, 4–6, form-based). The trio of sayings spanning 28:1–3 parallels vv. 4–6, due to a matching sequence of terms in each trio. 'The guilty person' occurs in vv. 1 and 4. Terms from the root *byn* appear in vv. 2 and 5 ('insightful' and 'perceive', respectively). 'Poor' appears in vv. 3 and 6.

These recurring terms are not coincidental, but outline a principle that is fundamental to this lecture. It is his inability to 'perceive' (28:2, 5) the true nature of 'poverty' (vv. 3, 6) that distinguishes the 'guilty' (vv. 1, 4) from his nemesis. When he notices a neighbour acquiring more than he (thus assessing himself as relatively poor), due to his inability to perceive he infers that his gnawing sense of deficiency will be resolved by acquiring more, even at the expense of ethical behaviour.

As the sage will caution, such an acquisitive strategy will only condition insatiability (28:25a). This and other oft-overlooked dynamics of poverty, together with their solution, the sage unfolds in Block I.B (28:19–28; see esp. v. 27).

Conflict-plus-analysis pattern (28:1–3, 4–6, content-based). A consistent pattern governs 28:1–3, 4–6. In each case two verses depicting conflict (vv. 1–2, 4–5) are followed by one verse of analysis (vv. 3, 6). Each of the four conflict sayings presents the disapproved party in the first colon, followed by the approved party in the second.

Assonance involving the roots 'šq *and* 'qš *(28:3, 6, 16–18, form-based).* Twice the poet located the roots *'šq*, oppress, and *'qš*, twisted, near enough to create assonantal links.

The first involves 28:3, 6 (*'ōšēq*, 'oppresses', and *'iqqēš*, 'twisted', respectively). Each occurs in the last line of its three-verse portion (vv. 1–3, 4–6), and so may help to mark conclusions. In addition, v. 6 marks the close of a six-verse segment (I.A.1.a).

The second involves 28:16–17, 18. The root *'šq*, oppress, appears in vv. 16, 17 (*ma'ăšaqôt*, 'extortions', and *'āšāq*, 'oppression', respectively). The root *'qš*, 'twisted', follows in v. 18, which, like *'iqqēš* in v. 6, appears at the close of a portion (ending Block I.A).

Coherence by parallel wisdom commendations and by particulars within wisdom content (28:7–10, 11–14, form-based). The sequence of wisdom forms in the four sayings spanning 28:7–10 matches the sequence found in vv. 11–14. First, a wisdom commendation leads each group (vv. 7, 11; note 'insightful' in each). Second, wisdom content follows the commendations (vv. 8–9, 12–13). Third, within the wisdom content, each second saying cautions how one should (or should not) respond to that content (vv. 9, 13). Fourth, character summaries conclude each portion (vv. 10, 14).

Repetition of 'fall', closing three contiguous units (28:10, 14, 18, form-based). Block I.A (28:1–18) consists of three units (vv. 1–10, 11–14, 15–18). The verb 'to fall' appears in the last saying of each unit (vv. 10, 14, 18). Reference to 'pit-grave' as a fatal destination in v. 17 sharpens the mention of 'fall' in v. 18 ('pit-grave' recalls 'pit', from the initial mention of 'fall' in v. 10). Since the root *npl*, 'fall', appears only twice more within Prov. 25 – 29 (in 26:27; 29:16), the likelihood increases that this repetition marks unit boundaries in 28:1–18.

Character summary (28:18, content-based). A character summary in 28:18 helps to mark the close of Block I.A (vv. 1–18).

Continuity of three topics (28:1–10, 15–18, content-based). Three topics addressed in 28:15–18 resemble the three topics organizing vv. 1–10: (a) symptoms of greed, (b) diagnosis of greed and (c) prognosis of unchecked greed. (In addition, synonyms for 'lion' appear in the first saying of each portion [*kepîr* in v. 1; and *ărî* in v. 15], and only once more in Prov. 25 – 29 [*ărî*, 26:13].)

Symptoms (or evidence) of greed's threat in 28:15–18 include hazard (lion, bear and extortions) and vulnerability (helplessness of victims, vv. 15–16). These correspond to earlier effects of greed, where people are put to flight, the helpless are oppressed and crops are washed out (vv. 1–3).

Diagnoses in 28:15–18 trace to their source those symptoms of greed. Greed springs from 'guilty' rule characterized by a 'shortage of perception' (foolishly supposing that oppression will reap gain) and 'an abundance of extortions' (vv. 15–16). These correspond in vv. 4–6 to 'those who abandon the Law' (v. 4), who consequently lack 'perception' (v. 5). The amassed wealth (resulting from an 'abundance of extortions', v. 16) corresponds to the doubly 'twisted' person who is 'rich' (28:6).

Prognosis (inevitable consequences, if greed is left unchecked) in 28:17–18 envisions a swift and fatal fall. This corresponds to the demise of the greedy fellow described in vv. 7–10. He will shame parents, forfeit his ill-gotten gain, suffer divine indifference and finally fall into the very pit in which he planned to trap others.

Framing by 'abundance of blessings/curses' (28:20, 27, form-based). The expression 'an abundance of blessings' in 28:20 contrasts 'an abundance of curses' in v. 27. These create a frame, appearing one saying removed from the outer boundaries of their block (Block I. B, vv. 19–28). Contrasting behaviour that treats others with either faithfulness (v. 20) or miserliness (v. 27) accounts for the response of blessings or curses.

Wisdom commendation followed by wisdom content (28:23–25, content-based). Unit I.B.2 begins with a wisdom commendation about administering reproof (28:23), leading to wisdom content contrasting greed with divine trust (vv. 24–25).

Wisdom commendation followed by wisdom content (28:26–28, content-based). The second segment of Unit I.B.2 begins with a wisdom commendation about valuing others' input (28:26), leading to wisdom content linking generosity with morality (vv. 27–28).

Framing of character summary (28:27, form-based). The poet highlights the importance of the character summary in 28:27 by framing it with a wisdom commendation (v. 26) and with one of this lecture's seven guilty–moral refrains (v. 28). The wisdom commendation in v. 26 prepares for the character summary in v. 27 that advocates generosity, by cautioning against relying on one's own wisdom (contrast reliance on the Lord in v. 25). Indeed, one's native insight would question the wisdom of generosity, erroneously concluding that kindness would deplete resources. But generosity, evidence of an appetite under control (contrast 28:25a), comprises the character-summary counsel of 28:27. Due to its prominence in the closing segment of Section I, this saying may encapsulate the entire anti-greed teaching of Section I.

Closure for Section I (28:23–28, form- and content-based). Ten elements within the last unit of Section I (Unit I.B.2, 28:23–28) contribute to section-level closure. First, abusive wealth-pursuit that appeared in 28:1, 3, 15–16 now resurfaces in one who protests his innocence after robbing father and mother (v. 24).

Second, in 28:19, 22 the sage inveighed against greedily questing after more. Again in the last unit of Section I the sage cautions against 'one with an expansive appetite' (v. 25).

Third, at the outset the sage described as 'capable of confidence' those moral persons not intimidated by guilty abusers (28:1). When describing in Unit I.B.2 the corrective for a greedy appetite and strife, 'confidence' again appears: 'but one who places his confidence in the Lord will be nourished abundantly' (v. 25b). Instead to 'place confidence' in one's own 'mind' amounts to stupidity (v. 26).

Fourth, 'rescue', *yšʿ*, marks the advantage enjoyed by persons of integrity (28:18), a necessary solution since people were obliged to flee (v. 1) as prey (v. 12). In Unit I.B.2, 'deliverance', *mlṭ* (a synonym of *yšʿ*), will come to the wise (28:26).

Closural elements five to eight concentrate in 28:27. The fifth, generosity towards the poor, earlier appeared in v. 8b. Sixth, freedom from insufficiency, recalls both the attainment of adequate nourishment (v. 19a) and the risk of insufficiency (v. 22). Seventh, averting one's eyes from someone in need, recalls the miser (lit. bad-of-eye, v. 22). Eighth, an abundance of curses garnered by the pernicious, contrasts the abundance of blessings accruing to the faithful (v. 20). Such a concentration of closural elements in v. 27 underscores the pivotal nature of this saying for Section I (see 'Framing of character summary', above).

Ninth, the guilty–moral refrain in 28:28 recalls two earlier iterations of this refrain (28:1, 12). No mere repetition, here the pupil learns that the deceptive, stubborn and twisted will not only 'fall' (28:10, 14, 18) but also 'perish' (v. 28).

Tenth, while transgressions should not be 'covered', *ksh* (28:13), during the ascendancy of the guilty, mortals must 'hide', *str*, themselves (28b).

Section II (29:1–23). *Section-level inclusio involving reproof (29:1, 21–23, content-based).* Reproof forms an inclusio around Section II (29:1–23). Its opening saying refers to a 'reprimand-resistant' person (v. 1). The section's final unit describes one who refrains from reproving his servant, pampering him instead (v. 21). Resistance and receptivity towards reproof are implied by 'loftiness' and 'lowness of spirit', respectively (v. 23a, b).

Thematic continuity concerning reproof (29:1–23, content-based). Reproof as the theme unifying Section II (29:1–23) anchors in its initial saying 'A reprimand-resistant person is a neck rendered stubborn; suddenly it will be snapped, and without recovery' (v. 1). Reproof will resurface with urgency in v. 15 ('Rod and reprimand may impart wisdom; but a youth who is given free rein shames his mother') and v. 17 ('Reprove your son!'). Also named in v. 19 ('It is not through words that a servant will be reproved'), reproof is implied in v. 18 ('a divinely revelatory message' and 'the Law'), v. 20 ('quick with words [of reproof]') and v. 21 by 'pampering' (failure to reprove). Consequently the topic of reproof constitutes the lens through which each saying in Section II should be viewed.

Dual-theme introduction concerning reproof (29:1–2, content-based). The opening two sayings of Section II (29:1–23) present a dual-theme introduction concerning lesser (individual) and greater (corporate) agents delivering reproof. As described below, lesser agents involve parents and supervisors. This theme begins in v. 1 with expansion in Block II.C (29:15–23). The theme of greater agents involves kings and rulers. It begins in v. 2 with expansion in Block II.B (vv. 3–14).

First consider 29:2. Double mention of 'people' establishes a greater, corporate (not individual) context. In order for 'moral folk' to be able to 'multiply' so that 'the people will rejoice', moral rule must be in place, restraining criminality through judicial reproof (v. 2a). Instead 'when a guilty person [one who indulges criminality instead of reproving it] rules, people will groan' (v. 2b). (The term 'people' also appears in v. 18, indicating the community-wide influence served by divine revelation.)

The greater, corporate dimension of reproof introduced in 29:2 is expanded in the next block (Block II.B, 29:3–14). The king (vv. 4 and 14) bears judicial responsibility to reprove greed, as do 'ruler' and 'officer' as well (both in v. 12). *Špṭ*, a root referring to judicial decisions, appears in three expressions ('justice', 'going to court' and 'administering justice', vv. 4, 9 and 14, respectively).

Next consider 29:1. Within this lecture, 'reprimand', *ykḥ*, occurs only in 29:1, 15. In 29:15 the reproving agent is not the king, but a lesser individual within the community – a mother. Several such lesser agents of reproof appear in the block beginning with v. 15 (Block II.C, vv. 15–23), including parents (vv. 15, 17) and supervisors (vv. 19, 21). (A parent appears also at the start of the 'greater agents' portion ['father', v. 3], but, unlike the 'lesser agents' portion in Block II.C, it is not reinforced by 'youth' or 'son' [contrast vv. 15, 17], or by direct address to a parent, as in v. 17.) While the king must set a corporate example of judicial reproof, the community relies on parents and supervisors to begin the process much earlier, so that only those who develop a reputation as 'reproof-resistant'

(v. 1) will graduate (sadly) to require ultimate accountability before the monarch as corporate reprover.

Inclusio involving 'joy' for (29:3, 6, form-based). 'Joy' appears in the opening and closing lines of Unit II.B.1 (29:3, 6), forming a unit-level inclusio (so also Waltke 2005: 431). ('Joy' also joins 29:2 with the corporate reproof agent portion [vv. 3–14], since the root *śmḥ*, 'joy', appears only in vv. 2, 3, 6 within this lecture.)

'Father' and 'mother', 'joy' and 'shame', in block-initial wisdom commendations (29:3, 15, content-based). A contrast of father–mother and joy–shame joins block-initial commendations in 29:3, 15. Given the shift from greater agents of reproof in Block II.B (29:3–14) to lesser agents in Block II.C (vv. 15–23), it appears that parental references initiate their respective blocks, rather than framing vv. 3–15 (*pace* Waltke 2005: 442).

Wisdom commendations, followed by wisdom content (29:3–6, 7–11, content-based). The first two units of Block II.B each begin with a wisdom commendation (29:3, 7). The first teaches that misplaced affections (literal or metaphoric) drain wealth – a deficit of magnificence (v. 3). The ensuing wisdom content explains that graft undermines one's rule, leading to entrapment (vv. 4–6).

A second wisdom commendation identifies the moral person as one able to issue impartial judicial decisions, even for the helpless (29:7). The ensuing wisdom content describes scenarios where wise, moral people uphold judicial standards when opposed by angry, excitable and murderous opponents (vv. 8–11).

Unit-level closure concerning transgression (29:6, content-based). Various transgressions appear in the first three verses of Unit II.B.1: sexual promiscuity (29:3), graft (v. 4) and deception (v. 5). Closure results when the unit's fourth and final saying cautions against 'transgression', generally (v. 6).

Summation yielding unit-level climax (29:11, form-based). After indicating a judicial scenario in a unit-initial saying (29:7, Unit II.B.2), the next three sayings describe escalating levels of unfounded litigation (vv. 8–10). This negative series reaches a zenith with a summation, as the stupid litigant proceeds to vent 'all his emotion' (v. 11).

Block-level closure (29:12–14, content-based). Block II.B (29:3–14) ends with a three-verse unit (vv. 12–14), each verse of which lends closure to that block. 'A ruler who subscribes to false talk', whose entire staff is composed of 'guilty folk' (v. 12), recalls governmental graft in vv. 3–6. Mention of persons accountable before the LORD (v. 13) is reminiscent of prior litigation (vv. 7–11). By describing 'a king who faithfully administers justice for helpless folk' (v. 14), the sage recalls the 'king [who] by administering justice will make a land stand firm' (v. 4).

Framing involving parents and reproof (29:15, 17, content-based). Sayings that encourage parents to administer reproof in 29:15, 17 (notice 'reprimand' and 'reprove', also 'youth', 'his mother' and 'your son') frame and thus highlight an apophthegm in 29:16 that describes what happens when a society fails to restrain immoral behaviour.

Repetition of 'words' (29:19–20, form-based). Both 29:19 and 20 teach that 'words' alone may be ineffective for reproof. 'Words' stands line-initial in the Hebr. of v. 19, while 'quick with words' appears in the first colon of v. 20. By adding 'quick with', the sage teaches that mere acceleration will not increase reproof's persuasiveness.

Inclusio involving the root ḥzh *(29:18–20, form-based).* Two of Proverbs's four occurrences of *ḥzh* appear in this lecture, at the outer edges of Unit II.C.2 (29:18–20). The first saying begins that unit (*ḥāzôn*, 'divinely revelatory message', 29:18), while the second closes it (*ḥāzîtā*, 'you have observed', 29:20). (Remaining instances occur in 22:29; 24:32.) This forms an inclusio around a portion dealing with reproving adults (vv. 18–20), in contrast to reproving one's children (vv. 15–17).

Block-level closure in Unit II.C.3 (29:21–23, content-based). Six aspects in its final unit (29:21–23) contribute closure to Block II.C (vv. 15–23). First, one who 'pampers his servant' in v. 21 recalls the supervisor as agent of reproof (cf. v. 19). Second, pampering a servant (v. 21) also recalls non-reproof practised by a mother (v. 15), as well as those who behave without restraint (v. 18). Third, the expression 'an abundance of transgression', *rab pāšaʿ* (v. 22b) resembles 'transgression will multiply', *yirbeh-pāšaʿ* (v. 16a).

A fourth involves a malevolent maturation in the characters needing reproof. These appear as early as the reprimand-resistant fellow of 29:1, also a youth 'given free rein' in v. 15, escalating to a larger group that behaves in an unruly manner in v. 18, and even a royal official who rejects reproof in v. 19. Surpassing all these is the enraged person who stirs up strife and masterminds transgression (v. 22).

A fifth involves assonance of *m-n* sounds in adjacent verses, beginning with *maʿăneh*, 'affliction', in v. 19, and *minnennû*, 'than he', in v. 20. Assonance continues in Unit II.C.3 with *mānôn*, 'insolence' (v. 21), and *mādôn*, 'strife' (29:22a). The first three end their respective sayings, while the fourth ('strife') ends the first colon of v. 22.

A sixth closural element involves abasement ('downfall', 29:16), which returns in the block's last saying: 'A mortal's loftiness will bring him low, but it is lowness of spirit that will lay hold of glory' (v. 23).

Character summary (29:23, content-based). A character summary closing Section II associates magnificence with humility and ignominy with arrogance (29:23). Since the aim of Section II is to stir to action the community's greater and lesser agents of reproof, the section-closing saying in v. 23 warns those agents to pamper their subordinates no longer (v. 21). Instead they must humbly assume their responsibility as agents of reproof.

Section III (29:24–27). *Dual-theme introduction (29:24, content-based).* The two cola of 29:24 respectively introduce vv. 25 and 26 in the following manner. The picture of a greedy thief harming himself in 29:24a resembles one who hopes to gain by setting a trap, yet captures only anxiety for himself (v. 25a). The picture of passively derailing the justice system by refusing to give evidence in v. 24b resembles the ruler who passively accepts the appeals (perhaps accompanied by gifts) of those who seek a favour from him (v. 26a), even though it falls short of the justice the LORD intends (v. 26b).

Repetition of 'LORD' (29:25–26, form-based). Repetition of 'LORD' links 29:25 with 26.

Parallel structure of problem-and-solution (29:25–26, content-based). A parallel problem-and-solution structure joins 29:25–26. The first colon of each presents a problem (anxiety concerning human oppression in v. 25a, and the difficulty of securing justice from a human ruler in v. 26a). Each second colon provides a solution (vv. 25b, 26b).

Comment

For progression of thought particularly in the sevenfold guilty–moral refrains, see 'Macrostructural features', above.

Section I (28:1–28). *Block I.A (28:1–18).* After counselling courtiers aspiring to magnificence (Lecture Two), now in Lecture Four the sage turns to kings (and others with influence). He begins by outlining oppressive conditions that thwart magnificence (28:1–3) – especially the horror of a populace put to flight by persons enjoying impunity (v. 1a). Yet not everyone has fled in terror. A moral-wise remnant will not be bullied, a harbinger of justice's ultimate triumph (v. 1b; the seven guilty–moral refrains begin here). That remnant with irrepressible resilience will keep resurfacing in this lecture, subject to and fortified by the divine (cf. 28:2b, 4b, 5b, 12a, 16b, 18a, 20a, 25b, 26b, 27a, 28b; 29:2a, 4a, 8b, 10b, 13b, 14, 16b, 18b, 25b, 26b).

Society's accelerating moral decay spawned increased regulation and regulators (28:2a). Yet those who perceive why this came about will endure – they know who wins in the end (v. 2b). They understand both the engine of greed that fuels power's abuse, and its powerlessness to achieve such self-centred objectives (v. 3). No nourishing moisture, this oppressive 'rain' delivers a devastating flash flood.

The root cause underlying destructive greed the sage unveils next (28:4–6). Adhering to the Law had become inconvenient – interfering with individual appetites (v. 4a). So the guilty were elevated as paragons of virtue. But not everyone slavishly conformed to this trend. Some kept hold of the Law and took opponents to task (v. 4b).

Those who played loose with the Law lost sight of the fact that their shifting opinions would alter neither the Law nor the dire consequences cautioned by the Lawgiver (28:5a). But those whose gaze remained fixed on the LORD (not on their appetite for more) knew exactly how this would turn out (v. 5b). They knew that less ultimately is more, mixed with integrity (v. 6).

Building on the hazard of 'impending judgement' (28:5), the sage further clarifies the undesirable prognosis awaiting unchecked greed (vv. 7–10). For the greedy, disregard for the Law (v. 7) may express itself as charging 'exorbitant interest' or reaping unconscionable profits, a glaring contrast to gracious regard for those unable to help themselves (v. 7). Paradoxically, gains of the greedy will fall to the gracious. Worse yet, the God whose Law the greedy refuses to hear, will himself refuse to hear the greedy's eventual cries for help (v. 8). Thinking to waylay the honest, they ensnare themselves, inflicting no lasting harm on the upright (v. 9).

If the foolish-guilty catch wind of this prognosis and wish to escape judgement, their first corrective step must involve humility (28:11–14). By admitting their poverty, the rich will discover the escape route (v. 11). For the monarchy grows magnificent by morality, not by riches (v. 12a). Abandon morality, and the nation will disintegrate into the abusive chaos pictured in this lecture's first saying (v. 12b; cf. v. 1). So the first corrective step consists of humble confession and repentance (v. 13). And one should embrace humility continually, not merely as a 'foxhole faith' to barter for momentary relief (v. 14).

To review: when the guilty who possess power think they are poor, they will viciously crush the helpless, insisting on 'protection money' (28:15–16a). But those who refuse such abusive tactics will outlast them (v. 16b). Here is why: upon incurring blood-guilt, the perpetrator unwittingly buys himself a one-way ticket to destruction. No one should slow his downward slide (v. 17). In contrast, someone will come to the rescue of the innocent who get tripped up (v. 18a). But wherever the 'twisted' turn, they will be doomed (v. 18b).

Block I.B (28:19–28). Humility supplies the first step to escape greed's grim prognosis, but not the last. A second step retrains focus from a desire for more (greed) to the desire for enough (satisfaction, 28:19b). Replacing idle abuse, faithfulness unlocks the door to satisfaction, whether through honest industry (v. 19a), or in dependable relationships (v. 20a). Instead to rush about after riches, manipulating base appetites of the mighty, only damns and depletes (vv. 20b–22).

After bracing to administer reproof (evidently confronting greed, 28:23), the sage discloses that appetites cannot be satisfied by brazen, abusive theft. For greed, though an adept destroyer, fails utterly at preserving and building (28:24).

For the third step out of greed, the sage plots an oblique approach. One wishing to shed past greed should resolve to anchor his confidence in the LORD. Therein lies the paradoxical path to abundant nourishment (28:25).

Once again advocating outside counsel (28:26), the sage commends a fourth step to reprogramme greed. For those who choose generosity, plenty paradoxically will follow (v. 27).

In sum, moral-magnanimous folk will resurge as the guilty-greedy are weeded out (note the guilty–moral refrain concluding Section I in v. 28). The need to weed out the guilty-greedy fosters a longing for personnel willing to confront the scourge of greed, who – in the words of v. 4b – 'will enter the fray against them'. To these personnel the sage turns in Section II.

28:3. Just as excessive rain destroys, satisfaction comes not through force wielded against the helpless by the self-perceived poor.

28:4. Relabelling of moral values earns a curse (24:24).

28:5. As a child who covers her eyes and supposes she can no longer be seen, so are those who suppose discounting the Law cancels its consequences. It marks a grave perception-deficit.

28:6. Cf. 19:1.

28:8. Reminiscent of Pentateuchal regulations, caution against exorbitant interest rates follows directly after a wisdom commendation underscoring the importance of Law-adherence (28:7; cf. Exod. 22:25; Lev. 25:36; Deut. 23:20).

28:19. Agricultural sufficiency recalls 27:27.

28:20. Perhaps this caution inspired Paul's warning:

> But those who want to be rich fall into temptation and are trapped by many senseless and harmful desires that plunge people into ruin and destruction. For the love of money is a root of all kinds of evil, and in their eagerness to be rich some have wandered away from the faith and pierced themselves with many pains. (1 Tim. 6:9–10, NRSV)

'Wandering away' corresponds to losing one's way (Prov. 28:10), while 'pierced' and 'pains' correspond to destruction (Prov. 28:28) and snares (29:25).

28:24. To quest after wealth may spawn an addictive tendency that breaks down filial restraint, producing an indiscriminate destroyer.

28:25. Competition for limited resources may explain strife engendered by the voracious person.

28:26. Misplaced confidence (in one's own mind) recalls 3:5.

28:27. Sufficiency (i.e. absence of lack) traces to attitude, not accumulations. Ironically, the avaricious suffer no lack of curses.

Section II (29:1–23). Section II (29:1–23) presents the personnel for whom Section I led the pupil to hope: agents within the community who would counter the scourge of greed. The sage distinguishes two levels – greater and lesser agents of reproof.

The monarch operates as chief among the greater agents for confronting greed. After a two-verse introduction (29:1–2, Block II.A), the sage outlines the king's responsibility to intercept greed judicially (Block II.B, 29:3–14). Note the leadership labels 'king' in vv. 4, 14, 'rule' and 'officers' in v. 12.

The king is not alone in opposing greed. A healthy community should reprove budding greed multiple times through lesser agents (parents and supervisors), before an inveterate abuser eventually must be halted by the monarch. The sage focuses on parents and supervisors in Block II.C (29:15–23).

Block II.A (29:1–2). The ruin of the rebellious comes about only after resisting countless reprimands (29:1a). This colon envisions a community of persons who, upon observing early indications of greed, responded with concerned reproof. Their efforts will not always succeed. Those who routinely resist reproof (the stiff-necked) may perish (from a snapped neck, v. 1b).

The community will experience joy only to the extent that its rulers abstain from guilty conduct (29:2). Such monarchs will also serve as court of last resort to protect the victimized, consequently punishing the reproof-resistant greedy.

Block II.B (29:3–14). As chief among the greater agents for confronting greed, the monarch must embrace two strategies. First, before opposing the abuse of external greed, he must confront greed within his or her own self (29:3–6, Unit II.B.1). That greed may begin in the form of sensuous appetites that masquerade as love, while only depleting resources (v. 3). The need to restore drained resources leads one to wring 'contributions' from the community (v. 4). Having engaged such graft, what is to prohibit deceiving even one's 'friends' (v. 5)? Tragically, none of these ploys generate the desired joy. They lead only to self-entrapment, while the moral find joy unrestrained (v. 6).

After confronting greed within, the monarch's second strategy must shield the community against predatory greed (29:7–11). As this scene opens, someone has greedily abused the helpless, moving the victim to seek redress from the courts (v. 7a). Since the ruler/judge embraces morality personally (vv. 3–4), he understands how to aid the oppressed.

The abusers begin with a campaign of incendiary bluster, trying to sway public opinion (29:8a). The wise are on to them, knowing how to 'reverse anger' (v. 8b).

Realizing they cannot vandalize the helpless in court without overcoming their protectors (the wise and just judges), these fiery fools take the wise to court (29:9a). They redouble litigious noise, hoping that a concussive blast will mask their unsubstantiated case (v. 9b). If that strategy fails, they escalate commotion, now issuing murderous contracts against key opponents (v. 10a).

Despite all this, the surviving honest folk remain unintimidated. They vindicate murder with due process that results in capital punishment for the convicted (29:10b). The sage resolves such attempts to overwhelm the judicial system in this way: after the dust has settled (and a stupid fellow will indeed raise all the wind-driven commotion he can, v. 11a), the wise will succeed in restoring calm (v. 11b). Thus Unit II.B.2 ends in successful resolution (resembling how 29:6 concluded Unit II.B.1).

Before turning to lesser, individual agents of reproof (parents and persons of influence, 29:15–23), the poet recaps the responsibility of monarchs. First, they must themselves embrace truth, unless they wish to be surrounded by councillors who conspire (29:12). Then follow two truth statements designed for a king – one of warning and another of reassurance (29:13–14). Any ruler supposing he can get away with violent abuse (as if might makes right) should be warned. Ultimately, he will stand defenceless before the one giving him sight (i.e. life) – before the divine whose perception penetrates every deception (v. 13).

In addition to warning, truth can reassure a king. The monarch who secures the vulnerable will himself gain security (29:14).

Block II.C (29:15–23). Having expanded in Block II.B (29:3–14) the need for greater agents of reproof (second of the dual-themes introduced in vv. 1–2), in Block II.C (vv. 15–23) the sage focuses on lesser agents of reproof (first dual-theme). While the monarch must stand ready as greater agent of reproof to confront miscreants in the courts, the community relies on others to reprove greed at two earlier stages: as youths are under parental care (vv. 15–17) and then as they enter adulthood (vv. 18–20).

'Youth', 'his mother' and 'son' (29:15, 17) mark the parental stage of reproof. A parent will either assume the responsibility as lesser agent of reproof or (to her shame) will let her son do as he wishes (v. 15). If the latter, then society will bear the cost of burgeoning lawlessness (v. 16). Consequently parental discipline is imperative. Else rest will elude the parent (v. 17).

'People' and 'servant' (29:18, 19) mark the second stage, where adults receive reproof. Ideally, adults will welcome and heed the Law's divinely revealed reproof (v. 18). But some resist, determined to careen about, harming bystanders.

When reproving such an adult subordinate ('servant'), if he already refuses to bow to divine Law, one must not suppose that mere words will change his mind. The supervisor must incentivize compliance through negative reinforcement ('generating affliction', 29:19). He is worse than stupid who presumes that sheer volume, a flood of reproving words, will restrain community-harming conduct (v. 20; note the shift to second-person address).

Before a lecture-wide conclusion in 29:24–27, the poet recaps the community's role in reproof (29:21–23). Echoing the first saying about community-sourced reproof (v. 15), failure to reprove initially will disappoint only the individual responsible for reproof (v. 21). However, as insolence mushrooms into full-blown rage, casualties will multiply community-wide (v. 22).

To achieve magnificence (the master lecture's grand goal), one must reject presumptuous pride. It only humiliates. Paradoxically, humility marks the gateway to the desired goal of glory (29:23).

29:3. The contrast between 'loving wisdom' and 'prostitutes' suggests the issue is not whether to love, but what or whom to love.

29:6. Since the moral person does not slyly manipulate, he is free joyfully to 'shout aloud', using words without calculation, except as required by norms of civility (contrast the speech of scoffer, fool and stupid fellow in 29:8, 9 and 11, respectively).

29:13. By observing that their power of sight originates from the LORD, the sage implies that the LORD is even more able than they to observe when the violent are abusing the poor (cf. 20:12). The psalmist renders explicit the connection between Creator and capability: 'He who planted the ear, will he be unable to hear? If he forms the eye, will he be unable to see?' (Ps. 94:9).

29:14. 'Throughout the ANE, protecting the rights of the poor was a royal duty and not a matter of charity' (Fox 2009: 839).

29:15. For the sage, wisdom will not be attained but by 'rod-and-reproof'. Coddling cannot deliver (29:15b, 21).

29:17. For another injunction directed to instructors, see 22:6–16, closing the lecture spanning 21:5 – 22:16.

29:18. 'Running wild' in 29:18a overlaps with 'abandoning the Law' and 'praising a guilty person' in 28:4a, since both passages contrast 'keeping the Law' (28:4b; 29:18b).

29:19–20. By combining 'reprimand' with 'rod' in 29:15, the sage corrects the mistaken assumption that behaviour may be changed by words alone.

Section III (29:24–27). In conclusion, Section III (29:24–27) reviews two of this lecture's more prominent perils. First, greedy abuse, typified by 'divid[ing] portions with a thief', rather than escorting out of relative poverty, only perpetrates mortal self-harm ('hates his very life', v. 24a; recall Section I).

Second, for the community to escape such abusive greed, its system of justice must be intact. This is imperilled through passivity when persons who, despite the fact that they 'hear the solemn summons for witnesses, [do] not give evidence' (29:24b; recall Section II).

One should respond to the first peril (the appeal of abusive greed) by rejecting gain-by-snare. Traps capture nothing but anxiety. Instead depend on the divine for ultimate protection and promotion ('lifted up', 29:25).

One should respond to the second peril (failed justice system) by allowing that human courts are not impervious to manipulative ploys. Instead one must depend on the divine as dependable guarantor of ultimate justice (29:26).

With a seventh guilty–moral refrain, the sage concludes this master lecture. Ethical opponents oppose one another in irreconcilable array (29:27), an implicit call to moral courage.

29:24. Contrary to its claims, thievery is powerless to bring satisfaction. It only multiplies self-loathing, a picture of suicidal despair. Resolving instead to resist the temptation to trespass ethical boundaries will reinforce personal worth and core dignity.

Explanation

Four principal lessons emerge from this lecture. The first three focus on the harm of greed and the benefit of generosity and just rule. The fourth fortifies persons of influence to remain persistent in administering reproof.

Lesson 1. Abusive greed is self-destructive (Block 1.A, 28:1–18)
Those with power – who suppose themselves to be not rich enough and so greedily oppress the helpless – will be shocked to discover it is themselves they are destroying (28:1a, 3). Although for a time the rising tide of transgression (28:2a) may let them get away with price-gouging, loan-sharking (28:8a) and graft (28:21; 29:4b), eventually it will catch up with them, with disastrous effects (28:3b, 10, 14, 18). Since they chase after emptiness, they will fill themselves with poverty (28:19b).

Where did they go wrong? Their strategies began to crumble the moment they abandoned the Law in order to acquire more wealth (28:4). While they might succeed in ignoring the Law, yet they will remain powerless to postpone their appointment with judgement (28:5). Instead of subscribing to the mantra 'Wealth, at any cost!', they should have clung to the principle 'Integrity is not for sale' (28:6).

Is there hope for the greedy? Yes, but it comes at the price of humility. If they admit their wrong, if they replace headstrong arrogance with respectful reverence, they will discover compassion (28:13, 14).

Those who insist on vicious and murderous tactics will fall with unexpected suddenness. But those who insist on integrity will enjoy rescue (28:15–18).

Lesson 2. Overcome greed with industry, relationships, satisfaction, reliance and generosity (Block I.B, 28:19–28)
How ought one to respond when tempted by greed or envy? First, begin by cultivating a combination of honest industry (work your own land; do not steal from another's) and enriched relationships (cultivate community ties marked by faithfulness, 28:19–20). Shortcuts that hurry after wealth while ignoring industry and relational health will return a loss (28:19b, 22).

Second, displace envy-for-more with satisfaction. Make sufficiency (not endless expansion) your goal (28:19a). When appetites rule (instead of being ruled), strife swells and will consume even closest relationships (vv. 24–25).

A third solution reaches beyond satisfaction to cultivate reliance on the LORD (28:25). This is why, even in the face of unchecked abuse of power, some were able to respond with quiet leonine confidence, even after others had fled in fear (28:1b).

Finally, a posture of reliance on the divine will position one to overcome greed with generosity. Notice those with less, and share. For the generous there will be no lack (28:27).

Lesson 3. Spread joy through just rule (Block II.B, 29:3–14)

Beyond conquering personal greed, we must also stir ourselves to intervene on behalf of the helpless oppressed. As a leader pursues integrity (29:7; contrast 29:12), he or she will pave the way for dynastic longevity (29:4a, 14). One who instead compromises integrity will find himself surrounded by ignoble subordinates who may be quite happy to dispatch their ruler as he sleeps (29:12).

Just rule aims not merely to foster an atmosphere of fairness or even of peace. Justice serves a higher aim – to make possible a realm characterized by joy (29:2a, 3a, 6b), the diametric opposite of flight-inducing fear (28:1a).

Superior to any leader there rules a supreme sovereign to whom violent and poor alike must answer (29:13). His power of perception (and the certitude of accountability) encourages careful attention to his Law (cf. 28:5).

Lesson 4 (to parents and leaders). Persist in administering reproof (Block II.C, 29:15–23)

It will not suffice simply (a) to expose the futility of abusive strategies and point out an escape through repentance, (b) to show a better response to disparity through industry, faithfulness, trust and generosity, and (c) to describe the moral leadership required to arrest wrong and restore societal joy. For, persons of influence must be fortified to persist in administering reproof. Otherwise, youths given free rein (29:15b) and pampered (v. 21a) will grow insolent (v. 21b), inclined to anger and being socially maladjusted (v. 22a), ultimately contributing to the rising tide of transgression (v. 22b). By fostering humility instead, parents and teachers will enable youths to achieve highest success (v. 23).

What sort of discipline will prove effectual? It must be grounded in precepts that trace to a divine source (29:18). Multiplied and hurried words of a merely human sort may be dispensed, but will effect no change (29:19–20).

To this task parents and teachers must carefully devote themselves, if only for self-serving motives. For it is the disciplined youth who will supply the parent with rest and refreshment (29:17), a highly desirable alternative to disgrace inflicted by the unrestrained (v. 15b).

Conclusion: recap of perils within greed, with responses and a resolute refrain (Section III, 29:24–27)
In closing, the sage reviews three principles. First, consider the failed strategy that seeks to solve poverty through abusive acquisition of wealth. Such a plan amounts to self-hatred (29:24a). Only by placing confidence in the LORD may we escape our strategy of setting snares, with their attendant anxiety (v. 25).

Second, consider the importance of just rule. For us to withdraw from the judicial process depletes the rule of law in the community – a depletion on which predators depend (29:24b). Whereas human powers may delay or disappoint regarding justice, the LORD's judgements remain reliable (v. 26).

Third, the sage concludes by implying that since good and evil will endlessly oppose each other, so also parents and leaders must commit themselves to the unstinting labour of moral formation (29:27). Prematurely to quit the field of ethical contest would amount to capitulation: ceding to marauders the moral citadel, and abandoning to victimization all who took refuge there.

DIVISION IV (PROV. 30 – 31): CONCLUDING ADVICE FOR BOTH COMMONER AND KING

Proverbs achieves closure in both form and content through the lectures of chs. 30–31. Concerning form, the clearly delineated poems of Division IV would remind the pupil of borders distinguishing poems in Division I (Prov. 1 – 9).

Concerning content, Agur's exhortation to reverence recalls Division I from its start (1:7) to its finish (9:10). In addition, advice in Division IV often targets the monarch, resembling the last lecture of Division III.

The sage-mother has the last word in Proverbs (the queen mother of Lemuel, ch. 31), balancing the sage-father at the outset (chs. 1–3). By this meristic inclusio the poet underscores the parental unit as the fundamental agent of counsel for the next generation. For a fuller discussion of inter-poem progression, inter-division progression and the audience intended for this division of Proverbs, see the 'Introduction', §3.4.

PROVERBS 30:1–33
'What must one come to know above all else?'

Overview of Proverbs 30:1–33
Standing as it does in the shadow of Solomonic wisdom, the wisdom of Agur mistakenly may be treated as a casually appended supplement.

However, awareness of the topics addressed through lectures in Divisions I–III would not support that conclusion. Agur's mention of weariness (twice in 30:1b) as he anticipates death (v. 7b) casts this lecture as a sage's grand finale. Such a senior perspective suitably appears in the latter chapters of this book.

Agur's teaching answers the implicit question 'In order to become wise, what must one come to know above all else?' (cf. 30:2–3). His reply involves theology and anthropology. Concerning theology, Agur portrays God not only as creator, but also as personal communicator – even conversational interlocutor. God speaks to humans (30:5), and a human speaks to God (vv. 7–9). Agur preserves the only prayer within Proverbs (other wisdom prayers appear in the dialogues of Job, Ps. 73 and Solomon's petition [1 Kgs 3:4–15]). Concerning anthropology, Agur explores the human tendency towards abusive greed (30:10–17, 18–31). Such mistreatment of others will not go unanswered, for retribution will rise up, vindicating the abused and judging the oppressor.

Position of this poem within Proverbs

Preceding context. The Hezekian master lecture just concluded (Prov. 25 – 29) counselled kings and courtiers intent on developing a magnificent monarchy, concentrating on (a) restraint of greed, (b) judicious generosity, (c) just rule and (d) vigilant reproof. Contentment as the antidote to greed comprises the greatest overlap with Agur's teachings in the present poem.

A narrower point of connection involves the weariness evident in Agur's opening (30:1). This is reminiscent of the protracted struggle between good and evil in the last saying of the Hezekian material (29:27).

Ensuing context. After Agur's lecture there appears a poem contributed by yet another non-Israelite wisdom teacher, a ruler over Massa (to which group Agur likely belonged; see 'Notes' for 30:1). This teacher was a king named Lemuel, who preserved his mother's instruction (31:1–9). The monarch's role in maintaining justice (see 30:28, 31 in Agur's material) provides a segue to similar lessons in the Lemuel material (31:4–5).

Noteworthy aspects of Agur's lecture

Three features distinguish Agur's lecture. These involve its source, its extent and wisdom operating as oracle.

The source of Proverbs 30. An authorship statement resembling 1:1, 10:1 and 25:1 begins Prov. 30. However, instead of crediting a known figure from Israelite history, Agur likely belonged to the Massa people (perhaps associated with northern Arabia; see 'Notes' for 30:1). Nevertheless, this sage subscribes to Israelite theology, referring to God as 'the LORD' (30:9). Inclusion of a foreigner's lecture among inspired scriptures attests the global scope of divine interest as well as the transcultural nature of wisdom.

The extent of Agur's composition. The authorship formula beginning Prov. 30 and the continuity of content found there recommend crediting all of this chapter to Agur. A new author appears in 31:1 (King Lemuel's mother), which further suggests that all material in the previous chapter was composed by Agur.

Continuity of content also supports Agur as the author throughout Prov. 30. Thematically, the entire chapter recommends respect and contentment in place of arrogance and greed. Stylistically, across the chapter there emerge instances of second-person address (e.g. vv. 1, 4, 6, 7–9, 32) and numerical tallies (e.g. vv. 7, 15, 18, 24, 29).

Wisdom as oracle. Agur categorizes his teaching as an 'oracle', *nĕʾum* (30:1) – a remarkable claim within wisdom literature of the HB. Oracles generally indicate a source other than the speaker, and carry an aura of solemnity.

As to source, an oracle generally derives from the divine. When King David issued a *nĕʾum* (2 Sam. 23:1), he credited God as the source: 'the LORD speaks through me' (v. 2). Prophets would often transmit messages designated 'an oracle of the LORD' (e.g. Isa. 1:24; Jer. 1:8; Ezek. 5:11). But for a sage to imply he or she speaks for God is highly unusual (cf. Job 33:14–18).

Early on Agur stresses the superior nature of divine communication: 'Every declaration of God is fire-refined' (30:5a). This, too, suggests that by 'oracle' Agur implies a divine source for his message.

In addition to its generally divine source, an oracle carries an aura of solemnity. The above oracle by David exudes solemnity since it constitutes the monarch's final words (2 Sam. 23:1). Agur similarly alludes to personal weariness and his impending death (Prov. 30:1, 7).

What to watch for

Notice these sequential topics: reverence, contentment, greed, victimization and resolution through retribution. Observe clusters of sayings, whether joined by repeated initial words (e.g. interrogative 'who', or 'generation'), or by a numerical tally. Pay particular attention to the last item in each cluster.

Translation and outline

Verse	*Translation*	*Outline*
		I. A personal introduction to wisdom: the author, his paradoxical message, and his paradoxical success (30:1–3)
30:1a	The words of Agur, son of Yaqeh, the pronouncement, the oracle of the strong man:	A. Introduction of author and his paradoxically oracular message (v. 1a)

Verse	*Translation*	*Outline*
		B. Wisdom commendation: the author's paradoxical success and its paradoxical explanation (vv. 1b–3)
30:1b	I have grown weary, O God, I have grown weary, O God, yet I will prevail.	1. Paradox of success despite weakness (v. 1b)
30:2	For denser am I than all humankind, yet it is not a mortal's insight that I possess.	2. Paradoxical explanation of success: achieving divine knowledge, despite lack of mortal wisdom (vv. 2–3)
30:3	Similarly I have not learned wisdom, yet knowledge of the Holy One I do know.	
		II. Wisdom about God and wisdom about humankind (start of wisdom content, vv. 4–17)
		A. Wisdom about God: teaching and caution result in two petitions with consequences (vv. 4–9)
		1. Teaching about divine nature, followed by caution (vv. 4–6)
30:4	Who has ascended the celestial skies and then descended? Who has collected the wind in the hollow of his hands? Who has confined waters in a cloak? Who has established all the ends of the earth? What is his name, and what is the name of his son, if you know?	a. Divine nature expressed by creative deeds ('Who is . . . ?' cluster, v. 4)
30:5	Every declaration of God is fire-refined; a shield is he to those who take refuge in him.	b. Divine nature expressed by declarations (v. 5)
30:6	Do not add to what he has said lest he reprimand you and you become exposed as a liar.	c. Caution: beware of human addenda, expanding divine declarations (v. 6)
		2. Two resulting petitions, with related consequences (vv. 7–9)

Verse	Translation	Outline
		a. Twin petitions of restraint, with mortal urgency: integrity in human speech and contentment with divine provision (vv. 7–8)
30:7	Two things I have asked of you; do not refuse me before I die.	i. Mortal urgency concerning petitions (v. 7)
30:8	Pretence and lying words – keep them far from me; poverty and wealth – give them not to me; tear off for me my allotted portion of food.	ii. Twin petitions: integrity in human speech and contentment with divine provision (v. 8)
		b. Risk of harmful consequences that argue in favour of Agur's petitions (v. 9)
30:9a	Lest I grow satiated and would disavow, and say, 'Who is the LORD?',	i. Surfeit may induce arrogant speech that alienates God from Agur (v. 9a)
30:9b	or lest I grow poor and would steal and lay hold of the name of my God.	ii. Poverty may induce actions that arrogantly alienate Agur from God (v. 9b)
		B. Wisdom about humankind: caution and teaching result in two petitions with consequences (vv. 10–17)
		1. Teaching about human nature, preceded by caution (vv. 10–14)
30:10	Do not slander a servant in front of his master, lest he declare you accursed and then you are found guilty.	a. Caution: beware of abusive communication, incurring retribution (v. 10)
		b. Teaching about human nature: declarations and deeds of greed ('generation' cluster, vv. 11–14)
30:11	A generation can declare its father accursed, and cannot bless its mother.	i. Initial arrogant declarations that abuse one's parents (v. 11)
30:12	A generation – pure in its own eyes, yet from its filth has not been washed.	ii. An eye for excusing self (v. 12)

Verse	*Translation*	*Outline*
30:13	A generation – how lofty their eyes, and their eyelashes keep on being lifted up!	ii'. An eye for exalting self (v. 13)
30:14	A generation – swords are their teeth, daggers are their incisors, to devour oppressed folk from the earth, and needy from among mortals.	i'. Ultimate cruel deeds that greedily devour the weak (v. 14)
		2. Two resulting petitions with related consequences (vv. 15–17) a. Twin petitions of greed, with mortal finality ('insatiable' cluster, vv. 15–16)
30:15a	The leech has two daughters: Give! Give!	i. Two duplicate petitions: to feed greed (v. 15a)
30:15b	Three there are that cannot be satisfied, four that have not said, 'Plenty!'	ii. Conclusion of petitions, with mortal finality (vv. 15b–16)
30:16	Sheol and a denied womb, a land – it is not satisfied with water, and fire – it does not say, 'Plenty!'	
		b. Risk of harmful consequences that argue against leeches' petitions (retribution, v. 17)
30:17a	An eye which derides father and shows contempt for obeying mother,	i. Eyes that refuse to respect parents . . . (v. 17a)
30:17b	Ravens of the valley shall peck it out, and the eagle's sons will devour them.	ii. . . . will forfeit sight altogether (v. 17b)
		III. Expansion of earlier teaching about human nature: the inclination towards abusive greed, and its remedy in retribution (vv. 18–31) A. Two steps that escalate the harm inflicted on others through abusive greed (vv. 18–23)

		1. Greed: as incomprehensible as an adulteress with no conscience ('incomprehensible' cluster, vv. 18–20)
30:18	Three things there are that are incomprehensible to me, and four – I have been unable to know:	a. Wisdom commendation (through unknowing, v. 18)
30:19	The eagle's way in the celestial skies, a snake's way upon a rock, a ship's way far from land, and a strong man's way with a maiden.	b. Wisdom content: illustrations of things incomprehensible (vv. 19–20)
30:20	Such is the way of an adulterous woman: she devours, she wipes her mouth as she says, 'I have not committed a sin'.	
30:21	Under three things the earth has shuddered, and under four it will be unable to bear up:	2. Greed: as unbearable as a handmaiden who executes a hostile takeover ('unbearable' cluster, vv. 21–23)
30:22	Beneath a servant when he begins to rule, and a senseless person when he becomes sated with food,	
30:23	Beneath a hated woman when she becomes married, and a handmaiden when she dispossesses her mistress.	
		B. Two steps that escalate the remedy in retribution (vv. 24–31) 1. Retribution: it begins through audience with the king ('small-yet-wise' cluster, vv. 24–28)
30:24	Four they are – small ones of the earth, yet they are exceptional wisdom apprentices.	a. Wisdom commendation (v. 24)
30:25	The ants were a community which is not strong, yet in the summer they prepared their food.	b. Wisdom content: illustrations of things small-yet-wise (vv. 25–28)

Verse	Translation	Outline
30:26	Rock badgers were a community which was not numerous, yet they located their houses in the cliffs.	
30:27	Kingless is the migratory locust, yet it set out by division, without exception.	
30:28	A gecko you can capture with two hands, yet it is in palaces of a king.	
30:29	Three there are with stately stride, and four with stately transit.	2. Retribution: it arrives through justice executed by the king ('invincible' cluster, vv. 29–31)
30:30	A lion is mighty among animals, and will not turn aside for anyone!	
30:31	A war horse with thighs, or a he-goat, and a king accompanied by a band of soldiers.	
		IV. Conclusion: caution against arrogance and greed, with harmful consequences (vv. 32–33)
30:32	If you have behaved senselessly in lifting yourself up, and if you have been scheming – hand to mouth!	A. Caution: a directive regarding the danger of arrogance and greed (v. 32)
30:33	For pressing milk will bring forth cream, but pressing a nose will bring forth blood, and pressing anger will bring forth litigation.	B. Harmful consequences: incentive concerning litigation ('pressing' cluster, v. 33)

Notes on the text

30:1a. 'Agur', *ʾāgûr*: meaning, 'I am in awe' (root *gûr*). This root connotes reverence towards the LORD in Pss 22:23 (MT v. 24) and 33:8. Reverence features prominently in Agur's teaching (Prov. 30:4–6, 9). 'To foment strife', an alternative meaning of *gûr*, is less suitable here. *Gûr* meaning 'sojourn' is feasible, yet would not parallel the poem's content so closely as 'awe'.

'Yaqeh', *yāqeh*: the root *yqh/i* can mean in Arab. 'to be pious, careful of one's religious duties' (BDB, s.v. '*yqh*') – an attitude consistent with Agur's teachings. If the name traces to the root *yqh*, it would connote 'obedient'. The noun 'obedience' later in this lecture (30:17) derives from *yqh* (elsewhere only in Gen. 49:10). 'Agur' and 'Jakeh' are names attested in languages cognate to Hebrew (Waltke 2005: 465, n.).

'the pronouncement', *hammaśśāʾ*: *maśśāʾ* (lit. 'burden') refers to a solemn proclamation, generally of a prophetic sort, often attributed to divine influence or inspiration (e.g. Isa. 13:1; 15:1; 21:13; Jer. 23:33; Ezek. 12:10; Hab. 1:1). *Maśśāʾ*, 'pronouncement', and *nĕʾum*, 'oracle' (adjacent in Prov. 30:1), are synonyms. Agur thus doubly credits his composition to divine influence.

Many treat *hammaśśāʾ* (with definite article) in 30:1 as designating the Massaite people group of North Arabia (cf. Gen. 25:14; 1 Chr. 1:30; Mas'aia in late eighth-century BC Assyrian sources, Perdue 2000: 251), as in the phrase *melek maśśāʾ*, 'King of Massa', in const. without article (31:1). Such nationality information would reasonably appear following lineage information ('The words of Agur, son of Yaqeh', then, 'the Massaite'), especially given the definite article *hammaśśāʾ*, '*the* Massaite' (Plöger 1984: 353; similarly Meinhold 1991: 496; Whybray 1994b: 407; Murphy 1998: 225, 226, n.; Clifford 1999: 259, 260, n.). However, if indicating a people group, the syntax in 30:1 should add *-î* (gentilic suff. *maśśāʾî*, 'a Massaite'), or should supply a prep. *mimmaśśāʾ*, 'from Massa' (*BHS* notes). Lacking both of these, *hammaśśāʾ* means 'a pronouncement', reinforcing *nĕʾum*, 'oracle' (Waltke 2005: 454; Fox 2009: 852–853).

Since when taken alone *maśśāʾ* can mean either 'pronouncement' or 'Massa', it is highly likely that the sage author (or sage editor) intended a wordplay by *maśśāʾ* in 30:1. According to its primary meaning, Agur's literary contribution consists of a solemn 'pronouncement', which he regarded as oracular in its supernatural influence. According to the second meaning of *maśśāʾ*, Agur resembles Balaam as another non-Israelite whose oracles merited inclusion with inspired Scripture (Num. 22 – 24, see under 'Comment', below).

'the oracle of the strong man', *nĕʾum haggeber*: *nĕʾum*, 'oracle', is normally followed by 'of God' or 'of the LORD', thus introducing a divine message. By calling his poem an 'oracle', Agur credits it with theological significance – a perspective consistent with his high regard for 'every declaration of God', to which nothing may be appended (30:5–6). Fox observes that 'a *nĕʾum* claims divine origin without necessarily recording God's words' (2009: 853; see further under 'Comment').

30:1b. 'I have grown weary, O God, I have grown weary, O God, yet I will prevail', *lĕʾîtîʾēl lĕʾîtîʾēl wĕʾukāl*: the two-part contrast established here (incapability twice, followed by capability) returns as 30:2a contrasts v. 2b, and v. 3a contrasts v. 3b. In each case the inadequacy appears first, followed by adequacy.

While it is possible that the phrase rendered ‘I have grown weary, O God, I have grown weary, O God, yet I will prevail’ discloses the names of recipients for whom this teaching was initially intended (‘to Itiel, to Itiel and Ukal’), for the author twice to have repeated the name of a recipient seems unlikely (the name ‘Itiel’ occurs in Neh. 11:7). Various scholars suspect that these are verbal forms from *lʾh*, ‘to grow weary’, and from *ykl*, ‘to prevail’ (cf. Plöger 1984: 351; Murphy 1998: 225; Fox 2009: 850). Coincidentally, the consonants comprising *lĕʾîtîʾēl* form a palindrome, both before and after the yods were supplied as *matres lectionis*: *lʾitiʾl*.

The marginal Masorah observes that *wĕʾukāl* is spelled defectively, presumably representing *wĕʾûkāl*. The same combination of roots occurs in the context of a supplication at the close of Isaiah’s oracle against Moab (Isa. 16:12). Though Moab may ‘weary itself’ (from *lʾh*) in prayer, it will not ‘prevail’ (from *ykl*). Agur is confident of a different result from his prayer, perhaps because, unlike Moab, he displays humility (contrast Isa. 16:6).

30:2. ‘For denser am I than all humankind’, *kî baʿar ʾānôkî mēʾîš*: lit. ‘For denser am I than humankind’. By associating no qualifier with ‘humankind’, the sage implies ‘all humankind’ (similarly Isa. 52:14; contrast Prov. 19:22, which employs a qualifier, where *mēʾîš kāzāb* means ‘than a deceptive person’). LXX supplies ‘all’, and a superlative: ‘For most ignorant am I among all humankind.’

‘yet it is not a mortal’s insight which I possess’, *wĕlōʾ-bînat ʾādām lî*: adversative ‘yet’ is inferred from contrast between inferior value in 30:2a (‘denser’) and superior value in v. 2b (‘not a mortal’s insight’ implies a measure of insight exceeding what a mere mortal would naturally grasp). The same obtains with ‘yet’ at the start of v. 3b.

What is negated here is the sort of wisdom possessed, not the possession of wisdom universally (which latter meaning would better have been expressed as *ʾên lî-bînat ʾādām*, ‘I do not possess a mortal’s insight’). In this way the sage leaves open the door for disclosure of a different sort of wisdom Agur *does* possess. This possession he will disclose as ‘knowledge of the Holy One’ (30:3b).

30:3a. ‘Similarly I have not learned wisdom’: lit. ‘And I have not learned wisdom.’ This parallels the sentiment of 30:2b ‘yet it is not a mortal’s insight that I possess’. Since in v. 3b Agur will assert that he does possess knowledge of a non-mortal sort, the salient information in the admission ‘I have not learned wisdom’ (v. 3a) resides in the term ‘learned’, suggesting training acquired through merely human instruction. ‘The wisdom in which Agur is deficient must be [human] *erudition*’ (Fox 2009: 861; emphasis original). Despite his lack of human tutoring, Agur nevertheless has acquired ‘knowledge of the Holy One’ (v. 3b). This accents a marked contrast that shifts from ‘mortal’ of v. 2b (extending by implication into v. 3a), transitioning to ‘the Holy One’ in v. 3b.

30:3b. 'yet knowledge of the Holy One', *wĕdaʿat qĕdōšîm*: as a substantive, 'One' is inferred with the adj. *qĕdōšîm*, 'holy' (cf. 9:10, where the sage recommends *daʿat qĕdōšîm*, 'knowledge of the Holy One', parallel to 'reverence for the LORD'). *Qĕdōšîm* is pl. of abstract, an intensive designating sovereignty, and thus rendered sg. (not 'holy ones'; cf. GKC §124h).

The question whether 'knowledge of the Holy One' in 30:3b refers to information possessed by the divine, or acquaintance with the divine person, resolves in the contrasting grammar of the parallel in v. 2b. There the sage describes 'mortal's insight' in terms not of acquaintance with mortals, but 'possession' of insight belonging to mortals: 'yet it is not a mortal's insight that I possess'. In contrast, 'knowledge of the Holy One' is not 'possessed', but 'known', suggesting acquaintance with a person.

The inference that 'knowledge of the Holy One' refers to personal acquaintance is further reinforced by the only other instance of 'knowledge of the Holy One' within Proverbs: 'The starting point of wisdom is reverence for the LORD; and knowledge of the Holy One is insight' (9:10). Since knowledge here is parallel to 'reverence for the LORD', and since that reverence involves a personal attitude (not a body of information), therefore knowledge of a person (i.e. of the Holy One) would similarly involve acquaintance (cf. Num. 24:16).

'I do know', *ʾēdāʿ*: the negation from 30:3a should not be inferred by ellipsis for v. 3b (do not infer, 'I do [not] know'). This follows from the fact that vv. 2–3 form a chiastic quatrain, unified on the theme of an autobiographical wisdom commendation. In the first verse of this quatrain (v. 2), the affirmative 'For denser am I than all humankind' does not carry over by ellipsis any information into the second colon: 'yet it is not a mortal's insight that I possess', which is negative. The affirmative appears in the first colon (v. 2a). In v. 3 the positive and negative chiastically reverse (negative in v. 3a; positive in v. 3b). As in v. 2, the positive and negative should still be regarded as independent of each other in v. 3. For this reason v. 3b reads (closely following the Hebr.), 'yet knowledge of the Holy One I do know' (a positive affirmation), rather than 'yet knowledge of the Holy One I do [not] know' (with negation inferred). The LXX concurs, so that in v. 3b Agur claims to possess this knowledge: 'and knowledge of holy things I have come to know'. Waltke concurs with the positive reading: 'but I want to experience the knowledge of the Holy One' (2005: 456). Fox initially concurred (rendering 30:3b positive when commenting on *qĕdōšîm* in 9:10, Fox 2000: 309); then later reversed his opinion (Fox 2009: 855).

By way of comparison, in Ps. 44:19 (v. 18 ET) a negation in the first colon should not be inferred for the second. The expression in Ps. 44:19b should be rendered, 'but you [the divine] have turned our steps from your path', implying a perceived loss of divine protection, despite the speaker's innocence (cf. Ps. 44:9–12 [vv. 10–13, MT]). This translation concurs with

LXX, which renders *wĕttēṭ* as 2 m. sg. 'but you have turned' [referring to God], not 3 f. sg. 'but [they] have [not] turned', referring to 3 f. pl. 'our steps' and inferring negation). Thus Ps. 44:19b should not be rendered, 'but our steps have not turned from your path'.

30:4. 'the celestial skies': lit. 'skies' or 'heavens'. This denotes not the afterlife, but the region of clouds and stars.

'all the ends of the earth': when contrasted with creation's 'waters', 'earth' refers particularly to dry land (not the entire planet conceived by moderns). 'The ends of the earth' often describes the remotest extent of human habitation (e.g. Pss 2:8; 22:27 [v. 28 MT]; 67:7 [v. 8, MT]). Thus the final of four elements describing divine activity in the cosmos focuses on regions inhabited by humans.

'if you know', *kî tēdāʿ*: some render *kî* forcefully, with a tone of presumption: 'Surely you know!' (NRSV). Yet this tone is out of character with Agur's humble sense of awe, favouring *kî* as 'if'.

30:5. 'declaration of', *ʾimrat*: lit. 'utterance', 'saying' or 'speech' (only here in Proverbs, with thirty-six occurrences outside Proverbs).

'God', *ʾĕlôah*: appearing also in 30:9, this designation for the divine is less common than *ʾĕlōhîm*.

30:6. 'what he has said': lit. 'his words'.

30:9. 'Lest I grow satiated and would disavow', *pen ʾešbaʿ wĕkiḥaštî*: a paradoxical wordplay underlies these two expressions. The root *kḥš* in the pi. means 'to disavow' (as found here). In the qal stem *kḥš* would mean 'to grow lean', the antithesis of 'growing satiated'.

'Who is the LORD?': the fact that Pharaoh defiantly voiced the same question amplifies its hubris here (Exod. 5:2).

'and [would] lay hold of the name', *wĕtāpaśtî*: the verb *tpś*, 'to lay hold of', connotes wielding for one's own purposes (as with a musical instrument or a shield, Gen. 4:21 and Jer. 46:9, respectively). The closest parallel describes God's faulting leaders who 'handle the Law' without 'knowing' its divine Author (Jer. 2:8). Applied to individuals, the verb *tpś* means 'to coerce' (Isa. 3:6) or 'to arrest in order to kill' (Jer. 26:8; 37:13). Applied to a city, it means 'capture' (2 Kgs 18:13). Here in relation to the divine name, it conveys a manipulative attitude of hubris.

'my God', *ʾĕlōhāy*: see 'Notes' for 30:5.

30:10. 'in front of his master, lest he declare you accursed': 'his master' is a nearer antecedent than 'servant', so serves as the subject of 'declare'. By insulting a servant, one collaterally insults his master, provoking that master to come to his servant's defence.

30:11. 'can declare . . . accursed' and 'cannot bless': (in)capability inferred from yiq. conjugations. If a generation brashly utters declarations of filial dishonour (cursing, not blessing, parents, 30:11), in time they will advance to performing deeds of violence (v. 14).

30:12. 'yet from its filth has not been washed': 'its filth' refers to personal excrement. Passive voice pictures an infant who, after defecating, requires assistance for cleansing. Despite the revolting depth of its putridity, this 'generation' has the temerity to self-assess as 'pure'.

30:13. 'keep on being lifted up': durative 'keep on', inferred from yiq.

30:15. 'Give! Give!', *hab hab*: from root *yhb* (not *ntn*, the commoner root meaning 'to give'). The poet may have chosen *yhb* over *ntn* since *yhb* might call to mind *ʾhb*, 'to love'. In fact, that is how LXX translators understood *hab hab*, as seen in their double mention of 'love' in their rendition 'it [i.e. the leech] will love the beloved [daughters]'. By artful word choice, the Hebr. poet implies that whereas 'love' should characterize the parent–child relationship, leech-daughters greedily have degraded it to 'Give! Give!'

30:16. 'denied': lit. 'restrained', 'denied' or 'closed'; not limited to infertility.

30:17. 'the eagle's sons': lit. 'sons [or 'children'] of an eagle'. 'Sons' contrast with leech's 'daughters' (30:15) in retributive reversal.

30:19. 'far from land': lit. 'in [the] heart of [the] sea', meaning remote from shore. Since mariners of this era travelled generally within sight of land, to navigate 'far from land' was wondrous.

'a strong man', *geber*: a capable, robust male in his prime.

'maiden', *ʿalmâ*: refers here to a marriageable young woman (e.g. Rebekah in Gen. 24:43; also Isa. 7:14), sometimes a younger girl (Exod. 2:8).

30:20. 'Such': lit. 'thus', 'so' or 'in the same manner'. The adulteress's ethical misconduct is as inexplicable as the four mysteries of 30:19.

'she devours, she wipes . . . as she says', *ʾākĕlâ ûmāḥătâ . . . wĕʾāmĕrâ*: lit. 'she eats, and she wipes . . . and she says'. As qat., *ʾākĕlâ*, 'she eats', describes a customary pattern (not 'she ate'). By following this qat. with waw-cop. weqat. forms (*ûmāḥătâ . . . wĕʾāmĕrâ*) the sage portrays the adulteress's pattern as routine (*IBHS* §32.1.1.a). The trio 'eat–wipe–excuse herself' forms a cohesive, repeated behaviour, to which the adulteress attaches no more ethical import than hedonistic satisfaction of gustatory appetite. 'This would be a deliberately crude jibe aimed at the adulteress' (Fox 2009: 873). With such vivid imagery the sage left pupils in no doubt concerning how hazardous is the satisfaction of sexual appetites by illicit means.

'sin', *ʾāwen*: or 'disaster'. *ʾĀwen* combines connotations of transgression with impending hazard.

30:24. 'exceptional wisdom apprentices', *ḥăkāmîm mĕḥukkāmîm*: lit. 'wise ones who have been taught wisdom'.

30:26. 'rock badgers', *šepannîm*: or simply 'badgers' (hyraxes). 'Rock' derives from this mammal's English designation.

30:28. 'you can capture', *tĕtappēś*: capability derives from yiq.

30:31. 'A war horse with thighs', *zarzîr mātĕnayîm*: mention of powerful 'thighs', *mātĕnayîm*, recommends rendering *zarzîr* as 'war horse', although this animal's identity confounds lexicographers. Proposals also include greyhound, raven (Talmud) or rooster (LXX). Cognate language options range from starling to locust or cricket.

'and a king accompanied by a band of soldiers', *wĕmelek ʾalqûm ʿimmô*: *ʾalqûm* is a hapax legomenon (not attested elsewhere in biblical Hebr.).

30:32. 'hand to mouth!', *yād lĕpeh*: best understood as a command, abruptly delivered as an apodosis following the two protases ('If you have been senseless . . . and if you have been scheming – [then you must place your] hand to [your] mouth!'). A fuller form appears in Job: 'my hand I have placed on my mouth', *yādî śamtî lĕmô-pî* (Job 40:4). Elsewhere the prep. *ʿal*, 'upon', appears in place of *lĕ*, 'to': 'place your hand upon your mouth', *śîm yādekā ʿal-pîkā* (Judg. 18:19; cf. Job 21:5; Mic. 7:16). Fox paraphrases, 'Shut up!' (2009: 882; cf. Jones 2019: 146). In contrast, when expressed with the prep. *ʾel*, 'to', 'hand-to-mouth' implies feeding (*yādô ʾel-pîw*, 1 Sam. 14:26–27).

30:33. 'anger', *ʾappaîm*: 'anger' is the dual form of *ʾap*, 'nose' (note sg. *ʾap*, 'nose', 30:33b). While both sg. and dual may mean either 'nose' or 'anger' (so sg. could have been employed for 'anger' in v. 33c), by expanding from sg. in v. 33b (rendered 'nose') to dual in v. 33c (rendered 'anger') the poet parallels the escalation from initial injury ('bringing forth blood', v. 33b) to consequent legal reprisal ('bringing forth litigation', v. 33c).

Form and structure

Borders

Authorship notes in 30:1 (Agur) and 31:1 (King Lemuel's mother) provide upper borders for this lecture and the next. Continuity of Agur's composition extending through 30:33 is indicated by themes of respect and contentment, by second-person address and by numerical tallies (see 'The extent of Agur's composition', under 'Noteworthy aspects of Agur's lecture', above). In addition, four features described next contribute to closure in the final section (Section IV, 30:32–33). By virtue of continuity and closure, 30:33 comprises the lower border.

Closure involving arrogance (Sections II, III and IV, content-based). Arrogance has featured prominently in Agur's lecture prior to this point (cf. 30:6, 9, 10, 11, 12, 13, 17, 20). Arrogance returns in the final section (30:32–33), by attitude ('lifting yourself up'), by strategizing ('scheming') or through action ('pressing' the nose of another, and 'pressing anger').

Closure involving problem–solution concerning speech (Sections II and IV, content-based). A problem at the opening of Section II involved slanderous speech (30:10). The final section presents a solution: '[Place your] hand to [your] mouth' (v. 32b).

Closure involving repetition with assonance (Sections II and IV, form-based). The fourfold questions pointing to divine sovereignty in 30:4 read, '*mî . . . mî . . . mî . . . mî . . .*, 'Who . . . ?', 'Who . . . ?', 'Who . . . ?',

'Who . . . ?' Three statements in the lecture's closing saying read, '*mîṣ . . . mîṣ . . . mîṣ* . . . , 'Churning . . .', 'Churning . . .', 'Churning . . .' (v. 33). Given that vv. 4 and 33 constitute, respectively, the first and last wisdom-content sayings of Agur's lecture (in contrast to vv. 1–3, which present a wisdom commendation with its explanation), this assonance generates a high degree of inclusio.

Closure involving problem–solution regarding litigation against injustice (Sections II and IV, content-based). In Section II the slanderer is proven guilty (30:10b). Yet no penalty is prescribed. That problem resolves as the lecture's final saying announces that litigation is about to begin (v. 33b).

Macrostructural features

Wisdom commendation followed by wisdom content (Sections I and II–IV, content-based). Following an author note in 30:1a, Section I consists of an atypical wisdom commendation. Instead of contrasting wisdom with folly, Agur distinguishes two sorts of wisdom: mortal wisdom (30:2b) and knowledge of the Holy One (v. 3). Skill in the latter more than makes up for ineptitude in the former. The poem's remaining three sections comprise wisdom content (30:4–33).

Thematic continuity involving success despite weakness (Sections I–IV, content-based). On seven occasions Agur demonstrates concern for the plight of the weak, often demonstrating how they can overcome liabilities to gain success. First, Agur acknowledges his own weakness: 'I have grown weary' (30:1, Section I). Despite weakness he remains confident: 'yet I will prevail' (also v. 1). His weakness involves wisdom deficiencies (vv. 2–3a). His confidence rests in knowing the Holy One (v. 3b).

Second, all humankind is weak, in need of refuge (30:5, Section II). The divine offers the needed refuge. The ensuing prayer of Agur models how a person aware of inner weakness may find refuge by appealing to God (vv. 7–9).

Third, someone in a weaker position ('servant') may suffer slander (30:10a, Section II). The weak achieves success as the master vindicates him (v. 10b).

Fourth, the oppressed and needy are victimized by an abusive group called simply 'a generation' (30:14, Section II). They gain success through vindication at the close of that section (v. 17).

Fifth, a mistress suffers injustice when displaced by her handmaiden (30:23b, Section III). Although she receives no direct vindication, the retribution portion of Section III begins immediately thereafter (Block III.B, vv. 24–31).

Sixth, the gecko is subject to capture (30:28a, Section III). Success lies in the initially innocuous observation that, despite its susceptibility to victimization ('a gecko you can capture with two hands'), this insignificant reptile gained access to the king's chambers. As a metaphor for human victimization, the victim-gecko's proximity to the king implies access to robust retribution.

Seventh, the poet focuses on 'success-despite-weakness' in the final verse (30:33, Section IV). The victim's nose, bloodied, indicates the victim (v. 33b). Success emerges as an unnamed figure (likely the king of v. 31b) calls that conduct to account before a court (v. 33c).

A dialogic tone (Sections I–IV, form-based). Agur's use of a dialogic tone, as if conversing with an audience of wisdom pupils, spans the various sections of his lecture (so also Waltke 2005: 464). The dialogic setting is evident through (a) first-person forms, (b) second-person forms, (c) commands and (d) questions. First-person forms characterize 30:1–3, 7–9, 18, lending an autobiographical flavour (Sections I, II and III).

Second-person forms near the close further indicate a dialogic tone. There the sage virtually interrogates the pupil (30:32a, Section IV; though the second-person expression 'you can capture with two hands' in v. 28 is impersonal).

Commands indicate an implicit audience. They appear in 30:6, 7, 8, 10, 32b (Sections II and IV; the leeches' pleas 'Give! Give!' imply a figurative audience).

Finally, questions indicate dialogue. Six appear early in Section II (30:4a–e). Though no reply is given, the last of these is real, and not rhetorical.

Portion-opening wisdom expressions (Sections I–IV, content-based). The poet establishes the primacy of wisdom for the lecture as a whole by seeding the introductory Section I with five wisdom expressions. These include 'mortal's insight', 'I have not learned', 'wisdom', 'knowledge' and 'I do know' (30:2, 3).

Thereafter four sayings containing wisdom expressions are positioned at the outset of a portion (30:4 opens Section II, v. 18 opens Section III, v. 24 opens Block III.B, and v. 32 opens Section IV). An exception occurs in v. 22 (though a wisdom saying, it does not open a portion).

Thematic continuity concerning knowledge of the divine (Sections I and II, content-based). Agur affirms his knowledge of the divine at the close of Section I (30:3). Section II opens as Agur quizzes the pupil concerning his knowledge of the divine (v. 4).

Thematic contrast of wisdom deficiency versus wisdom competence (Sections I and III, content-based). Twice Agur pairs an admission of wisdom deficiency with a statement of wisdom competence. First, within the quatrain of 30:2–3 he admits his wisdom deficiency (Section I). He follows with wisdom competence: 'yet knowledge of the Holy One I do know' (v. 3b).

Second, Agur admits wisdom deficiency with the admission 'Three things there are that are incomprehensible to me, and four – I have been unable to know' (opening the 'incomprehensibles' cluster, 30:18–20, Block III.A). Wisdom competence appears at the start of the next block: 'Four they are – small ones of the earth, yet they are exceptional wisdom apprentices' (opening the 'small-yet-wise' cluster, 30:24–28).

Thematic continuity involving greed (Sections II, III and IV, content-based). Greed forms the single theme most thoroughly unifying Sections II, III and IV. In Section II, Agur prays for protection from inner greed, desiring contentment with divine sufficiency (30:8b–9). The 'generation' devours the oppressed greedily (v. 14). Greed characterizes the blood-sucking leeches (v. 15a), and each of the four remaining elements of the 'insatiables' cluster (30:15b–16). In a metaphor of retribution, birds of prey greedily devour the eyes of aggressors (v. 17).

In Section III, greed emerges with the adulteress: 'she devours, she wipes her mouth as she says, "I have not committed a sin"' (30:20). Among the 'unbearables' cluster, the handmaiden displays greed as she schemes to displace the wife of the house, who is her supervisor (v. 23b). When the gecko suffers capture, presumably it would occur at the hands of one greedily exerting power (v. 28).

In Section IV, cautions against 'pressing a nose' and 'pressing anger' are the sage's way to restrain greedy conduct (30:33). The abuse the pugilist supposed would satisfy his greed will instead be the cause of his own demise.

Numbered and unnumbered sayings (Sections I, II and III, form-based). Agur's wisdom is characterized by related elements grouped together. These include double admission of fatigue in 30:1b, questions in v. 4, petitions in v. 8, 'a generation' in vv. 11–14, and what may be termed 'insatiables' in vv. 15–16, 'incomprehensibles' in vv. 18–20, 'unbearables' in vv. 21–23, 'small-yet-wise' in vv. 24–38 and 'invincibles' in vv. 29–31.

Some lists are unnumbered. Others announce a fixed number (static-numbered), while still others state an initial number, and then increase it by one (dynamic-numbered) or two. Unnumbered lists include 30:1b, 4, 11–14. Static-numbered include vv. 7–8, 24–28 (the leech's two daughters resemble this group, though occupying only a colon in v. 15a).

Dynamic-numbered lists begin with an escalation from two leech daughters, then three 'that cannot be satisfied', raised to 'four that have not said, "Plenty!"' (30:15–16). The balance advance from three to four (vv. 18–20, 21–23, 29–31).

Unnumbered lists introduce new topics. The first discloses Agur's profound exhaustion (30:1b). The second introduces the incomparable grandeur of the divine (v. 4). The third introduces destructively acquisitive tendencies of humankind (vv. 11–14).

Identification of the divine 'son' with the monarch (Sections II, III and IV, content-based). Agur closes his series of questions about the divine by asking, 'What is the name of his son, if you know?' (30:4e, Section II). No answer is given, though the divine's capacity to give refuge would reasonably characterize the son as well (v. 5).

In Section III Agur introduces the 'king'. He appears as an implicit champion for the beleaguered gecko (30:28), then as explicit agent of justice at the climax of the 'invincibles' cluster (v. 31). The lecture soon ends, warning of ineluctable litigation that will befall the greedy aggressor (v. 33 in Section IV). The monarch of v. 31 reasonably stands ready to enforce that threat. As a source of refuge, and as the metaphoric son of the divine, the human king was likely implied by the question 'What is the name of his son?' in v. 4e (for human royalty designated as God's son, see 2 Sam. 7:14).

Intensification within clusters (Sections II, III and IV, content-based). The final element within each cluster of sayings registers a heightened level of intensity. Thus among the questions that open the teaching portion of Agur's lecture, the last, a compound question, presses the hearer quite directly: 'What is his name, and what is the name of his son, if you know?' (30:4).

Among the four antisocial behaviours exhibited by the arrogant 'generation' (30:11–14), cruelty reaches a zenith in the concluding step. At this point they ferociously devour the defenceless (v. 14).

Among the cluster of 'insatiables' (30:15–16), the greediest is reserved for last: the fire that refuses to decline the offer of additional fuel (v. 16b). For fire alone stakes its very existence on its ability to consume fuel ceaselessly. If ever it ceases to consume, at that point it ceases to exist.

Among the 'incomprehensibles' (30:18–20), the last to appear is the adulteress (v. 20). With this element the cluster transitions from admiration to horror due to her unfathomable lack of moral scruples.

Among the 'unbearables' (30:21–23), the last to appear is a handmaiden who displaces her mistress (v. 23b). Her conduct draws that list to a nadir of reprehensible conduct.

Among things 'small-yet-wise' (30:24–28), the last to appear is an unimposing gecko (v. 28). He exceeds in wisdom the others in his cluster, since he gains audience with one so powerful as the monarch.

Last among the 'invincibles' is the king (30:31b). By travelling in the company of a band of warriors, his might exceeds all others in his cluster.

Among the trio of 'consequences of pressing' that comprises 30:33, the final consequence presents a maximal hazard. 'Pressed anger' is the only element producing a response of litigation.

Microstructural features

Section I (30:1–3). *Paradoxical oscillation concerning capability (30:1a, 1b–3, content-based).* The sage initially claims capability, calling himself a 'strong man', *geber*, rather than 'mortal', *ʾādām*, in 30:1a. This gives way to an admission of weakness ('I have grown weary, O God') twice in the next colon. Despite that weariness, he paradoxically remains confident ('yet I will prevail', v. 1b).

Incapability returns in 30:2–3a, when assessing his prowess in terrestrial wisdom (wisdom of *ʾādām*, 'mortal'). However, this deficiency is outweighed by another sort of knowledge: 'yet knowledge of the Holy

One I do know' (v. 3b). This 'knowledge of the Holy One' accounts for Agur's paradoxical confidence, a principle reinforced by the way he quizzes his pupil concerning his own knowledge of the Creator (v. 4). Thus Agur condenses that foundational principle of wisdom: 'the starting point of wisdom is reverence for the LORD, and knowledge of the Holy One is insight' (9:10).

Section II (30:4–17). *Continuity of parallel elements (Block II.A and Block II.B, content-based).* Section II (30:4–17) divides into two blocks: Block II.A (vv. 4–9), and Block II.B (vv. 10–17). The first teaches concerning the divine nature, with the second focusing on human nature. Each block consists of four elements: focal teachings (vv. 4–6, 10–14), a cautionary statement (vv. 6, 10), a twofold petition (vv. 7–8, 15a) and consequences associated with those petitions (vv. 9, 17).

The four elements appear in the same sequence in Block II.A and Block II.B, except that in Block II.B (human nature) the cautionary statement begins the focal teaching (30:10–14), while in Block II.A it concludes the focal teaching (vv. 4–6). The length of corresponding elements is roughly equivalent (allowing for subdividing long verses such as v. 4), except that in Block II.B the twofold petition is petulantly brief ('Give! Give!' in v. 15a), launching the 'insatiable' cluster (extending through v. 16). The overall continuity of parallel elements in Blocks II.A and II.B fosters cohesion unifying all of Section II (vv. 4–17), distinguishing it from the numerical sayings that comprise Section III (vv. 18–31).

Repetition of 'accursed' (30:10, 11, form-based). The caution in 30:10 links with the start of the 'generation' cluster in v. 11 by repeating 'accursed', *qll*.

Palistrophe (30:11–14, form- and content-based). The 'generation' cluster forms a brief palistrophe (30:11–14). 'Eyes' repeats at the core (30:12, 13). Flanking these sayings is the logical pair consisting of declarations (v. 11) and deeds (v. 14). The poet used this pair earlier in vv. 4, 5.

Repetition of 'plenty' (30:15b, 16, form-based). The closing exclamation 'Plenty!' joins 30:15b, 16.

Chiasm concerning destruction and creation (30:16, content-based). The last four components of the 'insatiable' cluster as ordered in 30:16 form a destruction–creation chiasm (a-b-b-a). The first and last elements involve destruction (Sheol and fire). The middle two nourish life (womb and soil).

Block-level closure (30:17, form- and content-based). Block II.B (30:10–17) achieves closure through four features. First, retribution appearing initially in v. 10 (being declared accursed and found guilty) returns through carrion birds in v. 17. By involving the outer sayings of the block, this feature fosters an inclusio. Second, 'father' and 'mother' appear in vv. 11, 17 (Waltke 2005: 484). Neither 'father' nor 'mother' occurs elsewhere in this lecture. Third, 'eye' appears in 30:12, 13, 17. As with 'father' and 'mother', this term does not appear again in this poem. Fourth, the cannibalistic generation would 'devour' others (30:14). As observed earlier, in v. 17 birds retributively 'devour', *'kl*, guilty aggressors (v. 17).

Section III (30:18–31). *Wisdom commendations, followed by wisdom content (30:18, 24, content-based).* Both blocks in Section III divide into two units, each of which presents a numerical teaching. The first unit of each block is introduced by a wisdom commendation (30:18, 24). Then follows wisdom content in the form of numerical teachings, whether a list of 'incomprehensibles' (vv. 19–20), or a list of the 'small-but-wise' (vv. 25–28).

Correlation and intensification at the close of paired clusters (30:18–23, 24–31, content-based). Two clusters are paired within Block III.A – 'incomprehensibles' (30:18–20) and 'unbearables' (vv. 21–23). Final elements in each correlate, dealing with marital promiscuity (an adulteress in v. 20, and a usurping handmaiden in v. 23). Intensity escalates from v. 20 to v. 23, since the adulteress's infringement on a marriage may be one-time, while the handmaiden permanently 'dispossesses her mistress'.

Likewise, two clusters are paired within Block III.B – 'small-yet-wise' ones (30:24–28) and 'invincibles' (vv. 29–31). Final elements in each correlate, referring to a 'king' (vv. 28, 31). Intensity escalates from first to second, since the gecko (representing a vulnerable person in v. 28) is merely near the king (as an agent of vindication), while the 'king accompanied by a band of soldiers' manifests invincible strength that would strike terror into the heart of any victimizer (v. 31).

Section IV (30:32–33). *Command-plus-incentive (30:32–33, content-based).* The exclamation 'Hand to mouth!' forms an implicit command, arresting arrogant conduct (30:32). The next saying begins with an explanatory 'for', *kî*, supplying an incentive for the command (v. 33). If the pupil does not heed the warning, retributive litigation will follow (v. 33).

Comment

Section I (30:1–3). With names that connote awe (Agur) and piety (Yaqeh), and by associating this message with a prophetic burden (*maśśā'*, 'pronouncement'), the author embraces humility. Though a sage, paradoxically he issues an 'oracle'. He oscillates between strength and weakness. Although a 'strong man' (v. 1a), paradoxically he feels deep fatigue (v. 1b). Yet he remains confident of eventual success (v. 1b).

Also he oscillates between wisdom poles of knowing and unknowing. While he lacks mortal insight (30:2a, 3a), paradoxically he succeeds because he achieves a superior knowledge – personal acquaintance with the Holy One (vv. 2b, 3b; see 'Notes').

30:1. Prov. 30:1 is one of six instances where *nĕ'um*, 'oracle', associates with someone other than the divine. Yet even with these the underlying message is divine. Four involve Balaam, who, likely similar to Agur, was not of Israel (Num. 24:3, 4, 15, 16). Two of Balaam's messages employ a phrase found in Prov. 30:1 ('the oracle of the strong man', Num. 24:3, 15b).

Like Agur, Balaam notes divine faithfulness. God may be depended on to bring his promises to pass. Terms for 'speech', *ʾmr* and *dbr*, and 'deception', *kzb*, appear in material from both Balaam (Num. 23:19) and Agur (Prov. 30:5–6). These similarities suggest that Agur might have employed a formulaic preamble to authenticate his credentials.

Another oracle of interest traces to King David. Like Agur's, David's occurs towards the close of his life (2 Sam. 23:1; cf. Prov. 30:7). Like Agur and Balaam, it employs the expression 'oracle of the strong man', *nĕʾum haggeber* (2 Sam. 23:1).

Agur's disclosure of weariness ('I have grown weary, O God', *lĕʾîtîʾēl*), together with the reference 'before I die' (30:7b), suggests he was elderly. Seniority in that culture would enhance credibility, evident in Sumerian *Instructions of Shuruppak*: 'The instructions of an old man are precious' (Alster 2005: 58).

30:2–3. Like Agur, the sage-poet of Ps. 73 classes himself as 'dense': 'I was a dense fellow and unable to comprehend, an unthinking beast was I towards you' (Ps. 73:22). Waltke observes, 'By confessing that he has no wisdom apart from revelation (30:5–6), [Agur] displays his wisdom and his becoming a true human being. His confession implicitly polemicizes against sages who claim wisdom through their own efforts' (2005: 470).

Section II (30:4–17). *Block II.A (30:4–9).* The theme of knowing the Holy One bridges from wisdom commendation (30:3, Section I) to wisdom content beginning in Section II. After professing to know the divine, now Agur enquires whether his pupil also has come to know him (v. 4). The sage's knowledge consists not of human 'erudition, but an untutored awareness of divinity' (Fox 2000: 309).

Agur comes to know God through divine deeds and declarations. Divine deeds anchor in creation, whether celestial (30:4a–b) or terrestrial (v. 4c–d). If the pupil aspires after his mentor, he must above all excel in the knowledge of this mighty creator (v. 4e).

Divine declarations also enable Agur to know God (30:5–6). As awe-inspiring as are the acts of God, they fade before 'every' sterling and secure affirmation of God. And just as divine deeds inspire awe, so also do his declarations. Hence the caution 'Do not add . . . lest he reprimand you and you become exposed as a liar' (30:6).

This sort of caution appears elsewhere only in connection with the Sinai Covenant (Deut. 4:2; 13:1). 'Agur . . . must have in mind a defined corpus of revealed instruction, though he does not identify it further. It could be the Pentateuch . . . or Deuteronomy' (Fox 2009: 858).

Agur's statements in 30:4–6 concerning divine deeds and declarations prompt him to appeal to God concerning his own declarations and deeds (vv. 7–9). He requests, first, that authenticity may characterize his own declarations (v. 8a). Second, he asks for sufficiency, that by divine disbursement he may receive neither too little nor too much (v. 8b). If supplied with too much, his declarations may grow arrogant (v. 9a; note inversion of multiple awestruck queries of 'Who . . . ?' in v. 4). And if supplied with too little, his thieving deeds irreverently, manipulatively may 'lay hold of' the divine name (v. 9b). Paradoxically, poverty and wealth threaten equally what Agur wisely values most: a personal and respectful relationship with the divine.

Agur's thoughtful appeal for sufficiency (30:8b) initiates the topic that will dominate the balance of the lecture: vanquishing the temptation of greed. For Agur, arrogance-laced-greed constitutes the supreme pitfall threatening human nature. After an emphasis on the divine in vv. 1–9, the poet spends the balance of Section II addressing human nature. Section III (vv. 18–31) will expand on aspects of human nature introduced in Block II.B (vv. 10–17).

Block II.B (30:10–17). In the next block Agur addresses the human tendency towards arrogance and greed (30:10–17). Speech that arrogantly slanders another's servant (v. 10) may stoop to curse one's own parents (v. 11). Through conceit, blind to his own wrong (vv. 12–13), such a self-centred person will attain a cannibalistic climax of greedy deeds, devouring and even exterminating the disadvantaged (v. 14).

Such a 'generation' begets 'daughters' who give voice to collective greed. So the leech sisters insist with escalating intensity, 'Give! Give!' (30:15a).

Absent from the vocabulary of the 'insatiables' is the exclamation 'I have plenty!' (cf. 30:15b). Beginning with the greedy leeches and ending with fire, by definition the 'insatiables' suffer perpetual insufficiency (vv. 15–16).

Retribution will descend on contemptuous children (30:17a, recalling v. 11). As they devoured others (v. 14), so will they be devoured (v. 17b).

30:4–6. As with Ps. 19, Agur's remarks divide between the deeds of God (Prov. 30:4; Ps. 19:1–6) and the declarations of God (Ps. 19:7–13; Prov. 30:5).

30:4. The Epic of Gilgamesh observes, 'man, the tallest, cannot reach to heaven; man, the widest cannot cover the earth' (lines 28–29; Hallo 1990: 216). The Mesopotamian Dialogue of Pessimism enquires, 'Who is so tall as to reach to heaven? Who is so broad as to encompass the netherworld?' (Fox 2009: 857).

Agur's initial four rhetorical questions employ sapiential methods (observation and reflection) to study the divine (cf. 24:30–34). The fifth question shifts to identity, asking this supreme being's name (30:4). To enquire concerning his 'son' infers a dynasty, not a solitary supreme figure.

30:5. While this affirmation concerning the worth of divine declaration may be expected among the prophets, to encounter it among the sages is quite striking. This verse resembles part of David's victory song (2 Sam. 22:31; Ps. 18:30 [MT v. 31]; Waltke 2005: 476).

30:7. Numerical specificity ('Two things I have asked') suggests that Agur has given considerable thought to his petitions, ultimately settling on only these.

30:9. Several elements of Agur's teaching correspond to a prayer taught by Jesus (the Lord's Prayer, Matt. 6:9–13). They include reverence (Prov. 30:3–4), petitions for sufficient supply (v. 8) and the petition for protection against temptation (v. 9; cf. Byargeon 1998: 353–365).

30:11. To curse father or mother was a mortal offence (Exod. 21:17).

30:14–15. LXX locates 24:23–34 ('These also pertain to the wise') between the 'generation' cluster (30:11–14) and the 'insatiable' cluster (30:15–16), demonstrating awareness of a shift in content at that point. LXX also inserts Prov. 25 – 29 after 31:9, between the two poems by the queen mother.

30:15a. The leech's two 'daughters' may refer to its two suckers. One secured it to the host so the other might siphon the host's blood (Waltke 2005: 487).

Section III (30:18–31). After introducing wisdom about humankind in Block II.B (30:10–17), in Section III the sage expands on the human inclination towards abusive greed, together with the remedy found in retribution (vv. 18–31).

Block III.A (30:18–23). Before expanding on the retribution for greed indicated in 30:17 (vv. 24–31), Agur presents two clusters escalating the harm inflicted on others through greed (vv. 18–23).

The first cluster begins by portraying several incomprehensible scenarios of progress, characterized by leaving no trace (Waltke 2005: 491). They encompass progress both literal (moving across a trackless sky, rock or sea) and metaphoric (a wholesome friendship budding between a man in his prime and a marriageable young woman, 30:18–19). To object that the 'without trace' theme cannot unify these since the fourth (friendship between a man and a woman) could not but leave evidence (if romance, then a marriage might become evident; if sex, then a birth might become evident) – this objection indicates that interpreters' imaginations have exceeded the riddle's intent (*pace* Fox 2009: 871–872; cf. Waltke 2005: 490). Just as the progress of reptile, bird and ship forms general images, so also the wonder of relational progress between man and maiden fits with this trio, so long as not pressed to extremes of imagination. While sex will emerge explicitly in v. 20, to infer it for v. 19 is premature.

Announced as a four-part cluster (30:18a), the pupil would expect it to end with the man and maiden (v. 19bβ). Yet there follows a fifth, that crest of argumentation towards which the sage has been moving since the outset of this 'incomprehensible' cluster: the 'way of an adulterous woman' (v. 20). Like the first three intriguing but harmless sorts of transit, she begins innocently enough. And like the fourth, hers involves a 'way' between a man and a woman. She 'wipes' herself, giving the impression that, like the previous four, her activities also leave no trace. What remains incomprehensible about the adulteress consists not of how she manages to progress promiscuously. Rather, the sage finds staggeringly incomprehensible her self-assessment after finishing her meal of sensuous and harmful greed, after devouring men and marriages. For, presuming her actions leave no transgressive trace, astonishingly she exclaims, 'I have not committed a sin' (v. 20b).

After the 'incomprehensibles', the second cluster of escalating greed catalogues four individuals who attain unexpected privileges, who proceed to make life unbearable for the community (30:21–23). First, a servant vaults to a position of authority (v. 22a). An ensuing purge may indeed cause the land to 'shudder' (v. 21a).

The second scenario appears benign – a senseless person who gorges himself (30:22b). Yet his appetite is reminiscent of the devouring adulteress (v. 20).

With the third and fourth 'unbearable' characters (30:23) the poet deepens the marital dissolution introduced by the adulteress (v. 20). A hated woman gains a husband, and a handmaiden (perhaps the same woman, hated by her mistress) manages to overthrow her mistress, reminiscent of 'a servant when he begins to rule' (v. 22a). Thus the final element drags the cluster of 'unbearables' down to its nadir.

With the 'handmaiden' (the fourth 'unbearable' character, 30:23b) the sage bridges to the next topic: retribution (30:24–31). For only the handmaiden scenario explicitly indicates a victim needing redress. The rightful wife was deposed and dispossessed by the handmaiden's greedy stratagems.

Block III.B (30:24–31). The two clusters that follow (30:24–31) seek to remedy injustice, such as caused by greed in the preceding two clusters (vv. 18–23). The first focuses on 'small-yet-wise' characters (vv. 24–28), initially praising the collaborative efforts of insects stockpiling food (v. 25). Beyond food, a community of small mammals can collaborate to secure their home (v. 26). Collective effort continues as locusts model coordinated migration without any monarch (v. 27).

A monarch reappears strategically with the gecko, the last 'small-but-wise' character (30:28). The gecko's vulnerability (easily captured) groups it with prior victims, whether of a vicious generation, victims of blood-sucking leeches, of a devouring fire, of a remorseless adulteress or of a dispossessing handmaiden.

Yet the gecko is not without recourse. Wisely he penetrates royal chambers, gaining access to the king, the nation's chief agent of retribution. If ants encourage humans to gather food with forethought, if badgers encourage humans to build secure houses, if locusts encourage collaborative operations, then a lone gecko in the palace encourages even the solitary weak to appeal to the monarch for retributive justice. By placing 'king' first in 30:27 and last in v. 28 the sage underscores recourse to the monarch as a retributive resource.

As Section III closes, the poet specifies retribution more explicitly. A cavalcade of 'invincible' characters passes by, climaxing with a king in the company of his troops (30:29–31). As the ultimate human agent of justice, the monarch stands ready to vindicate the victimized, invincibly.

30:20. The adulteress epitomizes wanton hedonism – the antithesis of measured contentment advocated across Agur's lecture (for an extended warning against sexual hedonism, see Prov. 7).

30:22b. According to the Egyptian prophecy of Neferti, widespread societal chaos unfolded as irresponsible people gained inordinate access to food (Fox 2009: 874–875).

30:23. A handmaiden rivalling her mistress is reminiscent of tensions surrounding Hagar and Sarai (Gen. 16, 21). The Babylonian Counsels of Wisdom warns against a handmaiden who gains ascendency: 'The household that a slave-girl rules, she will break up' (Fox 2009: 877).

30:30–31. A lion's threat is transparent. Yet mountain goats also can kill, as in 2010 a hiker sadly discovered in the Olympic National Forest.

Section IV (30:32–33). Agur's lecture closes as decisive litigation descends on those who dared to bloody the nose of the innocent-helpless (30:32–33). Shifting to direct address, the sage cautions against arrogance ('lifting yourself up') and greed ('scheming', v. 32). Both proud declarations and greedy appetites must promptly be arrested ('Hand to mouth!').

A final 'pressing' cluster consolidates the threat of retribution, further propelling the youth to desist from proud words and greedy deeds (30:33). Pressing milk may yield something desirable (cream), but not so when cruelly 'pressing a nose'. 'Pressing anger' (stirring up the righteous wrath of the judicial system) will bring down retributive litigation upon the aggressor.

So ends Agur's lecture against arrogance and abusive greed. Any who resist the route of humility and contentment before the divine will reap ineluctable retribution.

Explanation

In this lecture a seasoned sage distils what likely represents his most prized counsel for successful living. Issued during the waning days of his life, it displays the fruit of long refinement.

With spiritual transparency uncommon among sages, Agur acknowledges that, once one ventures beyond the shallow waters of common-sense advice, wisdom disallows theological neutrality. When probing the depths of life's paradoxes, one's presuppositions concerning the divine soon dictate what becomes admissible as wisdom, and what one will dismiss as folly (centuries later the apostle Paul would take up the intersection of wisdom and theological presuppositions in 1 Cor. 1:18–31).

Section I. A personal introduction to wisdom: the author, his paradoxical message and his paradoxical success (30:1–3)

Wisdom, which in Proverbs initially operated as human observation of order instilled by the Creator, now towards the book's close achieves status among 'oracles'. How suitable, then, for a poem credited to the names 'Agur' ('I am in awe') and 'Yaqeh' ('pious'), and associated with the solemn term *maśśā'* (pronouncement), to escort us into an inspired lecture whose message cultivates awe and piety (30:1a).

Do we feel unequal to the challenge before us, dwarfed by intellectual giants? So long as we have 'knowledge of the Holy One', like Agur with his admission of shortcomings, we can succeed (30:1b–3).

Section II. Wisdom about God and wisdom about humankind (30:4–17)

After modelling admission of personal weaknesses, after stressing acquaintance with the divine, Agur would enquire about our concept of God. How frequently does divine grandeur overwhelm us (30:4a–d)? Beyond remote reverence, do we know him personally (vv. 3b, 4e)?

And what is our esteem for the declarations of God? Are they to us the fine and finished gifts from a shielding divine (30:5)? Or do we tool them as raw materials, rough ideas requiring clever refinement by self-appointed revisionists? If the latter, beware – lest we emerge as fabricators of falsehood (v. 6).

How free are we of pretence? Will we follow Agur's lead, making thoroughgoing truthfulness our primary petition (30:8a)? Or are we intoxicated by the lure of personal posturing and deceptive speech calculated to burnish our image?

And what of greed? Are we determined that in all things God will determine our supply – granting neither too much nor too little (30:8b)? Else reverence is forfeit (v. 9), and wisdom will deteriorate into folly. Right regard for God must remain supreme. Combined with contentment, it constitutes immense gain (cf. Phil. 4:11–13; 1 Tim. 6:6).

After examining our regard for God, Agur reviews how we treat others. Do we think to improve our standing by insulting others, even family members who deserve our respect (30:10–11)? If so, we prove only how repulsive (v. 12) and vicious (v. 14) we have grown. Such strategies proliferate a grade of greed that will turn to devour its hosts (v. 15a). Ultimately our addiction to consumption will itself consume and destroy us (vv. 15b–17).

Section III. Expansion of earlier teaching about human nature: the inclination towards abusive greed, and its remedy in retribution (30:18–31)

Do we respond to Agur's conviction of our greed by protesting innocence (30:20)? We must beware, for eventually the very earth will shudder under our audacious intrigues (vv. 21–23), ensuring that regal resources of justice redress victimization of the weak (vv. 24–28). And who can remain standing when justice, flanked by reinforcements, mightily strides forth (vv. 29–31)?

Section IV. Conclusion: caution against arrogance and greed, with harmful consequences (30:32–33)
In closing, do we remain ambivalent, even after Agur has exposed within us any patterns of arrogance or greed? He pleads with us to stop at once, before intractable litigation deservedly catches us in its clutches (30:32–33).

CONCLUSION: A MOTHER'S WISDOM (PROV. 31)

Two poems comprise Prov. 31, attributed to Lemuel, king of Massa. He, in turn, credits them to his mother (31:1). In the first poem she answers his implicit question 'How should a king spend his resources?' (vv. 1–9). Since her answer, in part, cautions against improper conduct with women, it leads to a second question: 'Who can possibly find a resourceful wife?' Her second poem addresses this question (vv. 10–31).

Three factors recommend the mother of King Lemuel as the poetess for all of Prov. 31 (not only vv. 1–9). First, *ḥayil* (rendered 'resources' or 'resourcefulness') appears in both poems: once in the first (31:3), and twice in the second (at the beginning in 31:10 and near the close in 31:29). Across Proverbs *ḥayil* appears only two other times (12:4; 13:22).

Second, both poems supply the young man with counsel concerning male–female relationships. In the first that advice is brief, negative (cautionary) and ranks before any other advice for a king (31:3). The second poem gives extensive, positive advice. It is wholly devoted to helping the young man find and properly esteem a woman worthy of marriage. Thus the second poem balances and substantially extends the first poem's counsel.

Third, the editors of Proverbs made a practice of carefully indicating transitions in authorship, whether named (10:1; 25:1; 30:1) or unnamed (24:23a). The absence of any authorship notice at the start of the Resourceful Wife poem (31:10–31) suggests a single sage composed all of Prov. 31.

Female wisdom authorship as attested in Prov. 31 is unique not only within Proverbs, but within the entire corpus of ANE wisdom literature (Fox 2009: 883). By ending the book with a sage-mother's voice, the editor complements the sage-father's voice presented at its beginning (Prov. 1 – 3). This produces a bookwide meristic inclusio underscoring the foundational role of both parents for training the next generation.

PROVERBS 31:1–9
'How should a king spend his resources?'

Overview of Proverbs 31:1–9

The queen mother's first lecture responds to an implicit question, 'How should a king spend his resources?' (31:1–9). She responds with alarm (v. 2), urgently arresting her son's natural inclination towards self-gratification, both romantic and alcoholic (vv. 3–4). Instead of serving self, he must use his position to alleviate pain for the dying (vv. 6–7) and to restore justice for the victimized (vv. 8–9).

Position of this poem within Proverbs

Preceding context. Towards the close of the last lecture, Agur (likely a non-Israelite of Massa; see 'Notes' for 30:1) focused on the role of a monarch. The king must support victims ('small ones', 30:24) as their chief advocate (v. 28), launching his irresistible force (vv. 29–31) to intercept and prosecute greedy oppressors (vv. 32–33).

The present lecture (attributed clearly to a Massaite) similarly focuses on a monarch's duties. Threefold use of the interrogative 'what' (31:2, exclamatory) resembles the fourfold use of the interrogative 'who', early on in Agur's lecture (30:4, rhetorical).

Ensuing context. As observed earlier, both lectures of Prov. 31 employ the term *ḥayil* (rendered 'resources' or 'resourcefulness', vv. 3, 10, 29). Both poems advise concerning male–female relationships, whether negative in the first (v. 3) or positive in the second (vv. 10–31). All indications point to King Lemuel's mother as authoress for both compositions.

What to watch for

It is helpful to note the succession of victims, aggressors, harms inflicted and recourses for recovery. This lecture challenges the royal pupil to assume a steadily expanding scope of responsibility for those under his care.

Translation and outline

Verse	*Translation*	*Outline*
		I. Authorial introduction and summons (31:1–2)
31:1	The sayings of Lemuel, king of Massa, with which his mother reproved him.	A. Introduction: a note attributing maternal, royal authorship (v. 1)
31:2	What, my son! And what, son of my womb! And what, son of my vows!	B. Summons: exclamation of maternal alarm (v. 2)

	II. Two behaviours to avoid (vv. 3–5) A. First scenario: do not squander resources on amorous pleasures (v. 3)
31:3a Do not give to women your resources, 31:3b nor your behaviour to what is responsible for destroying kings.	1. Imperative: do not engage in sexual promiscuity (v. 3a) 2. Rationale: promiscuity destroys even the mighty (v. 3b)
	B. Second scenario: do not squander resources on sedative pleasures (vv. 4–5)
31:4 Let not kings – who belong to God, let not kings drink wine, and dignitaries must not desire intoxicating drink.	1. Imperative: leaders and liquor should not mix (v. 4)
31:5 Lest he may drink and forget what has been decreed, and sabotage the legal claim of all the descendants of the oppressed.	2. Rationale: for liquor may incite abuse (v. 5)
	III. Two behaviours to embrace (vv. 6–9) A. First scenario: instead, alleviate pain for those near death (vv. 6–7)
31:6 Give intoxicating drink to one who is perishing, and wine to those in mortal anguish.	1. Imperative: what you earlier refrained from consuming, now contribute (v. 6)
31:7 May he drink so as to forget his destitution, so his hardship he may remember no more.	2. Rationale: for the perishing, it can sedate pain (v. 7)
	B. Second scenario: alleviate victimization for the marginalized (vv. 8–9)
31:8 Open your mouth for one with no voice, for the legal claim of all the routinely transient ones.	1. Imperative: as an attorney, amplify the claim of the marginalized (v. 8)
31:9 Open your mouth! Render just verdicts! And fulfil legal claims on behalf of the oppressed and poor!	2. Imperative: as a judge, vindicate the victimized (v. 9)

Notes on the text

31:1. 'Lemuel, king of Massa', *lĕmûēl melek maśśâ*: 'Lemuel' appears only here within the HB. While medieval commentators supposed 'Lemuel' represented Solomon (Fox 2009: 884), here he rules the non-Israelite Massa people, with whom Agur may have been associated (see 'Notes' for 30:1). To render *maśśâ* as 'an inspired utterance' (NIV), 'the pronouncement' (NASB) or 'an oracle' (NRSV), while representing the Masoretic accents (a disjunction after 'king'), would require a definite article before 'king' (Fox 2009: 884).

31:2. 'What . . . ? What . . . ? What . . . ?', *mâ . . . mâ . . . mâ . . .* : generally introducing a literal question, the interrogative particle *mâ* can convey incredulity or rebuke, as in, 'Whatever were you thinking?' Fox renders, 'No . . . no . . . no' (2009: 882, 884).

'son', *bar*: each mention of 'son' in 31:2 employs Aram. *bar* (alternatively, Moabite, Fox 2009: 883–884), rather than Hebr. *bēn* (cf. Ps. 2:12, the only other use of *bar* aside from Aram. portions of the HB). Aram. (or Moabite) influence in the present lecture is evident also in 'kings', *mĕlākîn* in v. 3b (contrast customary Hebr. *mĕlākîm*, v. 4a). These suggest Aram. influence either originating within Massa composition, or occurring later when Israel experienced greater contact with Assyrian cultures.

31:3. 'your resources', *ḥêlekā*: the noun *ḥayil* routinely is rendered 'strength' (NASB, NIV, ESV, NRSV; NJPS 'vigor'). The term encompasses personal assets, competence, wealth, strength, effectiveness, prowess, skill, effort or ability, whether of a material, intellectual, or moral sort. *Ḥayil* may be associated with plants, animals, and people. An orchard characterized by *ḥayil* would be rich in fruitfulness (Joel 2:22). A horse with *ḥayil* possesses superior strength and endurance needed for battle (Ps. 33:17). *Ḥayil* complements women in Prov. 12:4; 31:10. A king's *ḥayil* may indicate military assets (2 Kgs 25:1 or Esth. 1:3). Since Prov. 31:3 is the sole passage where *HALOT* and *DCH* infer a sexual sort of power for *ḥayil*, that connotation, while possible, lacks strong independent evidence.

Corresponding to *ḥayil* in Prov. 31:3 is the scenario where a vanquished population must surrender material assets to a conqueror (cf. Num. 31:9; Jer. 15:13; 17:3). For Lemuel similarly to surrender his *ḥayil* to women would imply allowing women (or, more accurately, allowing his own passion for pleasure) to vanquish him. By such conduct he would shrink to the stature of a puppet-king. Wiser than squandering his 'resources' on multiple women in 31:3 is this: to find a woman who would invest her 'resourcefulness', *ḥayil*, into their marriage, yielding lasting enrichment (31:10).

'nor your behaviour': lit. 'and your ways'. Beyond 'resources' of a more material sort, Lemuel must guard against surrendering his sense of moral direction.

'to what is responsible for destroying', *lamḥôt*: lit. 'for causing something to be wiped out'. If the poetess here narrowly warned against 'destructive women', we would expect *lĕmōḥôt* (qal f. pl. ptc., as emended by Fox 2009: 886; Waltke renders, 'those who destroy' [2005: 504]). Instead to use *lamḥôt* (hiph. infin. const.) censures promiscuous conduct more broadly.

'kings', *mĕlākîn*: see note on 'son' in 31:2.

31:4. 'Let not kings', *ʾal lamĕlākîm*: lit. 'not for the kings', with emphatic negation *ʾal* (*HALOT*, s.v., '*ʾal*', cf. 2 Sam. 1:21; Ps. 83:1).

'who belong to God', *lĕmô ʾēl*: although employing the same consonants as the name 'Lemuel', *lĕmû ʾēl*, in 31:1, Masoretes understood this word in v. 4 to be vocalized differently, meaning 'belonging to God', *lĕmô* and *ēl*; perhaps the meaning signified by the name 'Lemuel' (cf. 'Lael', Num. 3:24; Waltke 1995: 502–503). LXX similarly renders *lĕmû ʾēl* in v. 1 as *hypo theou*, 'by God' (though rendering *lĕmô ʾēl* in v. 4 *meta boulēs*, 'judiciously'). Perhaps as an infant, Lemuel's mother dedicated him as 'belonging to God' in connection with her 'vows' concerning him (v. 2c).

'and dignitaries must not desire intoxicating drink', *ûlĕrôzĕnîm ʾô šēkār*: ellipsis extends the negation established by two prohibitions earlier in this verse ('let not . . . let not', 31:4a).

'desire', *ʾô*: reading with K, the const. of *ʾaw*, a hapax legomenon meaning 'a desire' (from root *ʾwh/i*, 'to desire'; BDB, s.v. '*ʾāwâ*'). To caution against 'a desire' for 'intoxicating drink' fits the context better than understanding *ʾô* as 'or', or reading *ʾê* 'where' with Q. It is not necessary to posit a lost consonant '*r*', yielding *rĕʾô*, 'to imbibe' (although the resulting meaning would be smoothly parallel: 'nor for rulers to imbibe strong drink'; *pace* Thomas 1962: 499–500).

31:5. 'drink and forget . . . and sabotage', *yišteh wĕyiškaḥ . . . wîšanneh*: lit. 'drink and forget . . . and change'. Assonance creates a cascading effect.

31:6. 'Give', *tĕnû*: pl. imperative here may extend from 'kings' and 'dignitaries' in 31:4. The remaining command forms in this poem are sg.

'to one who is perishing': this condition leads the list, governing how 'mortal anguish' and 'destitution' are to be understood. Consequently the instruction to administer a sedative beverage as an anodyne would extend mercy to the dying (with Fox 2009: 887; *pace* Waltke, who regards it as a sarcastic directive not intending fulfilment [2005: 508–509]).

'to those in mortal anguish', *lĕmārê nāpeš*: lit. 'to persons who are bitter of life'. Mention of 'perishing' favours *nepeš* as 'life', not 'appetite'.

31:7. 'destitution', *rîš*: lit. 'severe poverty'.

31:8, 9. 'Open your mouth': since this expression characteristically signals the onset of speech after a period of silence, it connotes, 'You must no longer passively maintain your silence! Find your tongue and speak out!' (cf. Num. 22:28; Job 3:1; Ezek. 24:27; 33:22; Dan. 10:15–16). Conversely, 'one with no voice' cannot speak out, due either to physical impairment or social intimidation (Ps. 38:13 [MT v. 14]).

31:8. 'for one with no voice': lit. 'for a dumb [unspeaking] person'. Beyond the speech-impaired, this designation would encompass any whose just claim fails to secure the attention of those in power (cf. Waltke 2005: 509; Fox 2009: 888).

'all the routinely transient ones': lit. 'all the children of transience'. Since the poetess and her audience are distinct from the 'transient ones', the expression cannot refer to human frailty in general. Instead lack of rootedness characterizing these owes to their occupational custom (such as nomadic Bedouin) or uninvited misfortune (refugees). Their lack of community connection must not jeopardize access to justice.

Form and structure

Borders

Authorship attribution crediting King Lemuel's mother sets the upper border (31:1). The lower border is marked by an inclusio consisting of threefold exclamations in v. 2 and threefold imperatives in v. 9. Additional features demonstrating coherence leading up to v. 9 are described under 'Macrostructural features'.

Macrostructural features

Personal address (Sections I, II and III, form-based). The sage-mother specifically addresses her audience five times. She employs a voc. three times in 31:2 (Section I), then uses second-person address in 31:3, 6, 8, 9 (Sections II and III).

Repetition of 'king[s]' (Sections I and II, form-based). Both the authorship note in 31:1 and the instructions of vv. 3, 4 refer to 'king[s]', linking Sections I and II.

Imperative-plus-rationale (Sections II and III, content-based). Sections II and III present imperatives supported by rationales. In Section II a single verse issues both an imperative (not to squander resources on women) and a rationale (lest destruction ensue, 31:3).

A rationale similarly follows a second imperative in Section II. The sage cautions the son concerning consumption of alcohol (31:4). For intoxication may cause dereliction of duty to the point of perpetrating oppression against the disadvantaged (v. 5).

An imperative in Section III urges the son to contribute sedative to the dying who are in pain (31:6). The rationale anticipates alleviation of discomfort (v. 7).

The final verse-pair noticeably breaks with this pattern. An imperative (31:8) is followed, not with rationale, but with three more imperatives (v. 9), resulting in a highly charged conclusion.

Reversals (Sections II and III, content-based). The poet employs a double-layered reversal linking Sections II and III. Consuming alcoholic beverages at first is proscribed (31:4 in Section II). Later on such beverages are prescribed, as an anodyne (v. 7 in Section III).

A second layer operates within these opposing instructions. Alcohol should be declined (by rulers) due to the forgetfulness it may induce (31:5). On the other hand, alcohol is to be administered (to the suffering), precisely because of the forgetfulness it may induce (v. 7).

A third reversal may be at work here. When prohibiting intoxication, the sage implicitly instructs her son not to open his mouth (to consume alcohol, 31:4). In both sayings of the closing quatrain he is charged, 'Open your mouth!', so he may rightfully advocate for the victimized (vv. 8–9, so also Fox 2009: 888).

Chiasm involving beverages (Sections II and III, form-based). The sequence of beverages in Section II lists 'wine', followed by 'intoxicating drink' (31:4). The same beverages are repeated in reverse order in Section III (v. 6). These verses appear at the start of their respective sections.

Microstructural features

Thematic continuity of reproof (31:1–2, content-based). The threefold expressions of astonishment in 31:2 convey reproof. This fits with the author's announcement that the whole of this lecture serves to 'reprove' (v. 1).

Thematic continuity of parent–child relationship (31:1–2, content-based). Within Section I, both the introduction (31:1) and the summons (v. 2) refer to the parent–child relationship ('mother' and 'my son', respectively).

Repetition of 'open your mouth' (31:8–9, form-based). Both 31:8 and 9 begin with the charge: 'Open your mouth!', creating a form-based link.

Comment

Section I (31:1–2). This poem delivers a royal, maternal rebuke (31:1). Three exclamations underscore the poetess's high level of alarm: 'What, my son! And what, son of my womb! And what, son of my vows!' (v. 2). From this Fox infers that Lemuel's culpability is a foregone conclusion. It is too late to prevent his wrongdoing. The best his mother can do now is to keep him from proceeding further down a harmful path (2009: 885).

The three exclamations escalate intensity (31:2). 'My son' in the first gives way to the more emphatic, 'son of my womb' in the second, stressing the child's indebtedness. The third phrase, 'son of my vows', expands to include the divine. Like Hannah, the mother evidently engaged sacred commitments before his birth (cf. 1 Sam. 1:11).

Unlike the HB, LXX locates the Hezekiah material (Prov. 25 – 29) between 31:9 and 10 (see 'Comment' on 30:14–15). Early readers recognized seams within the literary tapestry, distinguishing one lecture from another.

31:1. Attribution to a specific mother renders this lecture especially noteworthy (contrast general maternal influence in 1:8; 6:20).

31:2. Unlike past references to 'my son(s)', which envisioned youth beyond the speaker's own offspring (e.g. 2:1; 7:24; 8:32; 19:27; 23:15, 19), the expression 'son of my womb' indicates this lecture initially was composed for King Lemuel by his birth mother. As a wisdom teacher she exemplifies the Resourceful Wife (31:26).

The depth of concern evident in the queen mother's summons in 31:2 signals a unique intimacy that can join birth mother to child. Though muted by some modern cultures, mothers possess a profound and timeless capacity wisely, compassionately, and insistently to influence their child's life.

Section II (31:3–5). *Block II.A (31:3).* Having established her genuine concern, the sage-mother issues two cautions. The first prohibits self-indulgence involving women (31:3). The expression, 'giv[ing] to women your resources [*ḥayîl*]', may range from gifts to sexual encounters (see 'Notes' for 31:3).

The sage's rationale is pointed. Not even a monarch can evade the destruction resulting from promiscuous conduct (31:3b). 'Obsession with women has the same effect as obsession with liquor' (Waltke 2005: 507).

Block II.B (31:4–5). Liquor is a second self-indulgence against which the sage-mother cautions (31:4).

A rationale again follows. Intoxication risks dulling and thus diverting the monarch from his duty to avenge the victimized in court (31:5a). Worse yet, he may begin personally to participate in 'sabotaging the legal claim of all the descendants of the oppressed' (v. 5b). The queen mother is determined to prevent him from harming the beleaguered by perverting laws to turn a royal profit.

31:3. The queen mother's first instruction pointedly cautions her son against amorous dissipation with female friends. Yet she is no misogynist. Worthy women merit exceptional honour, evident from her treatise in the ensuing, carefully composed acrostic lecture (31:10–31).

31:4. 'Intoxicating drink' designated by *šēkār* would primarily be made from fruit and/or barley beer, with from seven to ten percent alcoholic content (contrasting *śōbe'*, made from wheat). Lack of distillation techniques precluded production of hard liquor in ancient times (Waltke 2005: 505).

31:5. Whereas the liability associated with drunkenness in an earlier lecture would harm the youth himself (23:35), here the harm would befall an innocent, abused bystander. This echoes Sumerian Shuruppak's advice 'When you are drunk, do not judge!' (Shuruppak 1.131, in Fox 2009: 887).

The fact that a drinking event may sabotage another's legal claim suggests that some may seek to lobby or bribe the king by hosting him to an alcoholic party. This would disadvantage the poor, as they could not fund so lavish an event.

The Code of Hammurabi (5:13–16) illumines *mḥqq* (what has been decreed) and *yšnh dyn* (sabotage the legal claim), neither of which expressions appear elsewhere in the HB: 'If a judge renders a verdict, gives a decision, deposits a sealed tablet, but later alters his verdict, they shall prove that judge of having altered the verdict he has given.' Such judicial misconduct would lead to a twelvefold financial penalty and dismissal (Paul 1979: 233).

Section III (31:6–9). *Block III.A (31:6–7).* The sage balances two negative counsels (Section II, 31:3–5) with two that are positive (Section III, vv. 6–9).

The first cleverly reverses components of the sobriety counsel. Whereas the monarch should not imbibe-to-intoxication, lest he forget his duty to advocate for victims in court, others, in contrast, should use alcohol in order to forget, and the king should assist that process. He should administer alcohol to those suffering extreme pain (v. 6), so they may forget their difficult circumstances (v. 7).

Block III.B (31:8–9). The lecture concludes with a second positive counsel (31:8–9). Building on the duty to advocate (v. 5), the sage-mother pointedly charges her son to utilize his resources to alleviate the victimization suffered by 'one with no voice', and by 'all the routinely transient ones' (v. 8). While to sedate the pain of a dying person extends compassion for a brief time (vv. 6–7), rectifying injustice yields benefits that last a lifetime, extending even to successive generations.

Reminiscent of the initial alarm that sounded with three indicting exclamations (31:2), the poetess closes with three staccato imperatives. King Lemuel must vindicate the victimized (v. 9).

Explanation

Escalating persuasiveness marks successive sections of the queen mother's lecture. Each component offers enduring relevance for the modern reader.

Section I. Authorial introduction and summons (31: 1–2)

The queen mother's pointed and passionate reproof shows she has paid close attention to, and cares deeply about, her son's behaviour and well-being. Attentiveness anchored in caring forms an essential foundation for counsel we would dispense to others, especially to family members. Both Samuel and Paul modelled these priorities (1 Sam. 12; Gal. 4:19).

Block II.A. First scenario to avoid: do not squander resources on amorous pleasures (31:3)

If we may infer from his mother's cautions, Lemuel has ventured to navigate by appetite – catering to his sexual appetites, in particular (31:3). This will be his undoing, unless he manages his resources with moral responsibility.

Still today momentary exploits of sexual pleasure, purchased at the expense of moral character, work to unmake kings, not to mention lesser mortals. How can any who, like King Lemuel's mother, care about their children, refrain from warning of impending self-destruction?

Block II.B. Second scenario to avoid: do not squander resources on sedative pleasures (31:4–5)

Together with women, wine loomed too large among Lemuel's diversions (31:4–5). Strikingly, it was not his personal well-being that concerned his mother. As king, he shouldered a profound, even sacred duty on behalf of the oppressed. Sorry enough it would be, were he to ruin his own life. But to sacrifice protection due the vulnerable – merely for an alcohol-induced dopamine hit – this would be unconscionable.

Whom are we sacrificing on the altar of our pleasure or pain-avoidance? While the literal hazard of alcohol abuse remains pertinent today, it would be a mistake to discount unwholesome addiction of any sort, whether chemical or visual, emotional or relational. Have we so curved inward towards self that we feel no shame for abandoning those who should be able to count on our aid?

Block III.A. First scenario to embrace: instead, alleviate pain for those near death (31:6–7)

Beyond challenging her son to refrain from passively causing harm (dereliction of duty by drunkenness), she also urged him to alleviate suffering (31:6–7). Does Lemuel notice the destitute, literally at death's door? Without denouncing his relative prosperity, she points out that they deserve a merciful anodyne – a palliative draught that he can deliver.

We, too, must watch for ways to serve those in desperate straits of a material, social, emotional, or spiritual sort. From our plenty it is our privilege and duty to serve as agents of mercy in temporary and tactical, non-enabling ways.

Block III.B. Second scenario to embrace: alleviate victimization for the marginalized (31:8–9)

While to alleviate pain of the dying brings focused, individual aid, to raise up reliable justice would bring benefit to many for years to come (31:8–9). Such a mission will bring us alongside the rootless poor and oppressed, whose lack of resources (relational, educational, or financial) thwarts initial steps towards self-sufficiency. On such a mission we must renounce apathetic silence. We must engage the courts, arguing an irrefutable case for those whose voices cannot be heard.

PROVERBS 31:10–31
'Who can possibly find a resourceful wife?'

Overview of Proverbs 31:10–31

Similar to the poem just concluded (31:1–9), the final poem in Proverbs was evidently composed for King Lemuel by his mother (31:10–31; concerning authorship, see 'Conclusion: a mother's wisdom', above). This poem boasts a complete alphabetic acrostic, unique within Proverbs (see 'Macrostructural features', below).

Unlike past lectures, the question inspiring this composition appears transparently, with no need for conjecture. In its opening line the youth voices his despairing dilemma: 'A resourceful wife, who can find – since her purchase price exceeds corals?' (31:10).

In reply, the queen mother composed this poem to train her son to become a man who could recognize a marriage-worthy woman. While women also may benefit by studying this character inventory, they do not comprise the poem's primary audience. The wording of the dilemma (31:10) indicates that man (suitor), not the woman, is the audience intended for this lecture.

Among the traits Lemuel should watch for, trustworthiness is foundational (31:11). Trustworthiness may be observed from the way a woman (a) invests in her household (Section II), (b) models caring for others (Section III), and (c) durably sustains these desirable traits (Section IV).

As the poem closes, the family of such a woman honours her for her achievements and contributions (31:28–31, also Section IV). A 'resourceful wife' will bring to her fortunate husband such considerable benefit, tangible and intangible, that the youth would be a fool to let himself be swayed by the appeal of merely superficial charm – the best that lesser women have to offer (v. 30).

Given the sage's earlier personification of wisdom and folly as female characters (e.g. Prov. 8 – 9), one should consider whether a metaphoric dimension may operate here, alongside advice literally to guide a young man in search of a wife. The metaphoric possibility will be discussed below (see after 'What to watch for').

Position of this poem within Proverbs

Preceding context. The queen mother's first lecture disapproved of her son's conduct towards women (31:3). Likely stung by the forcefulness of her rebuke (v. 1b), he may have countered, 'But Mother: how can I ever find a wife that would please you?' The present poem explains what sort of wife she would approve.

As observed earlier, *ḥayil* (rendered 'resources' or 'resourcefulness') appears in both poems of Prov. 31. The first cautioned against diminishing the prince's *ḥayil*, 'resources', squandering them among multiple women (31:3). Now the sage examines those assets by which a 'resourceful' (*ḥayil*) wife will augment a marriage (v. 10; cf. vv. 15–17, 23–24).

Ensuing context. In the HB, Ruth appears following the Resourceful Wife lecture of Proverbs. Among Naomi's marriage counsel to Ruth, she affirms her by observing, 'For all of my people who assemble at the gate realize that you are a resourceful [*ḥayil*] woman' (Ruth 3:11b; ['woman' and 'wife' translate a single Hebr. term, *ʾiššâ*]). Since the expression 'resourceful woman/wife' appears only twice more in the HB (Prov. 12:4; 31:10), for biblical editors to position Ruth after Prov. 31 seems more than coincidental. Further, Naomi's mention of acclaim for Ruth at the 'city gate' resembles the last phrase of Prov. 31: 'may what she has produced praise her in the gates' (Prov. 31:31).

What to watch for
To detect divisions in this poem, distinguish between activities involving the fabric industry, in contrast to food preparation. Towards the close, observe how mention of the husband seems to intrude into the flow of thought, suggesting a shift of topic. Finally, listen for crescendo in the honour shown this woman by three successive groups or individuals, concluding with a sense of overwhelming acclaim.

The Resourceful Wife: literal or metaphoric?
The array of accomplishments achieved by this resourceful woman raises the question, whether the poetess envisions a woman who is literal (a marriage candidate for the prince), or figurative (such as Lady Wisdom). Admittedly some of the actions of this woman (such as buying a field and planting it in grape vines) would have been unthinkable for poorer women in the community.

Yet the sage-mother is not addressing all young men eligible for marriage. She focuses her attention on her son, destined for the throne (31:1–2). In a culture of arranged marriages, a bride suitable for a prince would likely come from upper echelons of society, whose families might deal in real estate and planting new fields, with experience in marketing textile products and managing servants. Fox observes, 'The original readers of the poem would not have found it outlandish for a woman to deal with merchants, buy land, plant vineyards' (2009: 901). Thus the poem of the Resourceful Wife should be read at face value, aware that it targeted a narrow socio-economic sector. To apply the advice of this poem beyond that sector requires one to extrapolate universal principles not restricted to a particular social class, such as faithfulness, industry, and selflessness.

At the same time, certain indicators suggest that, on a metaphoric level, the queen mother counsels her son to engage Lady Wisdom as a permanent partner in his enterprise. The metaphoric line of thinking is discussed further under 'Explanation', below (under the final heading 'Counsel for all').

Translation and outline

Verse	*Translation*	*Outline*
		I. A despairing question and an initial reply (31:10–12)
31:10	A resourceful wife, who can find – since her purchase price exceeds corals?	A. The despairing question: Who can possibly find a resourceful wife? (v. 10)

31:11 Her husband's mind has trusted in her, and no loot will he lack. 31:12 She rewarded him with good and not evil, all the days of her life.	B. Initial reply with triple-theme introduction: watch for trustworthiness (vv. 11–12) 1. Watch for trustworthiness, evidenced (first) by deeds that invest in her household (v. 11) 2. And evidenced (second) by an attitude that genuinely cares about her family, and (third) by behaving thus durably (v. 12)
31:13 She sought out wool and flax, then her palms worked with delight. 31:14 She was like a merchant's ships; from afar she would bring her food.	II. First in-depth reply: she invests in her household (vv. 13–24) A. Two illustrations of investing in her household: fabric industry and food preparation (vv. 13–22) 1. Dual-theme introduction: investing through fabric industry and food preparation (vv. 13–14) a. Fabric industry: starting with raw materials (v. 13) b. Food preparation: starting with raw materials (v. 14)
31:15 Then she would rise while it was still night, and would give a portion to her household and an allotment to her maidservants. 31:16 She considered a field, then acquired it; by the fruit of her palms a vineyard was planted. 31:17 She girded her waist with strength, and made her arms strong. 31:18 She savoured the fact that her profit was good; her light will not be extinguished in the night.	2. Diligence and service in food preparation (vv. 15–18) a. Before sunrise she serves others in her household first (v. 15) b. She cultivates an independent food source (vv. 16–17) i. Planning and planting a vine (v. 16) ii. Cultivating what was planted (v. 17) a'. After sunset she evaluates the quality of her labours (v. 18)

Verse	*Translation*	*Outline*
		3. Diligence and service in fabric industry (vv. 19–22)
31:19	She laid her hands on the distaff, and her palms will grasp a spindle-whorl.	a. Labouring by hand to spin yarn (v. 19)
		b. Distributing finished products (vv. 20–21)
31:20	She spread out her palms towards oppressed folk, and her hands she stretched out to the poor.	i. Contributing to meet the need of the oppressed (v. 20)
31:21	She will not be afraid for her household when it snows, for her entire household is clothed in scarlet.	ii. Clothing her household to provide climate security (v. 21)
31:22	She has made covers for herself; her clothing is of fine linen and purple-dyed fabric.	c. Afterwards, serving self last, one may observe the quality of her work (v. 22)
		B. Still wider benefits for household: recognition and revenue (vv. 23–24)
31:23	Known in the gates – such is her husband, as he is seated with the elders of the land.	1. Recognition: husband gains prestige in community (v. 23)
31:24	She has made a vest of fine linen, sold it and gave a sash to the merchants.	2. Revenue: wife makes and sells garments (v. 24)
		III. Second in-depth reply: she is a genuinely caring person (vv. 25–27)
31:25	Strength and splendour are her clothing, so she laughed about the future.	A. Stamina, regality and readiness for the future is the 'fabric' that clothes her character (v. 25)
31:26	She opened her mouth in wisdom, and instruction concerning faithful love is on her tongue.	B. Focal point: she has become an acclaimed wisdom teacher, in the curriculum of caring (v. 26)
31:27	She keeps watch over the journeys of her household, and the bread of sluggishness she will not eat.	A'. Watchful care over her household is the 'food' that nourishes her character (v. 27)
		IV. In conclusion, a third in-depth reply: she displays durable character, bringing highest accolades (vv. 28–31)

31:28 Her sons stood up and proclaimed her supremely fortunate; then her husband praised her:	A. Her family, from children to husband, assembles to honour her (v. 28)
31:29 'Many daughters have performed resourcefully, but you have risen above them all. 31:30 '"Faulty is charm, and fleeting is beauty; a woman who reveres the Lord – she it is who can boast." 31:31 'Give her some of the fruit of her hands, and may what she has produced praise her in the gates'.	B. Her husband ranks her achievements, discloses her secret, and calls for public praise (vv. 29–31) 1. Explanation (for later exhortation): because her performance has outpaced all others . . . (v. 29) 2. Focal principle: the secret of her success (v. 30) 1'. Exhortation (for previous explanation): . . . Therefore, the wider community must reward and praise her publicly (v. 31)

Notes on the text

31:10. 'resourceful', *ḥayil*: see 'Notes' for 31:3.

'since her purchase price', *wĕmikrâh*: lit. 'and her purchase price'. Drawn from the realm of trade, this term might have reminded hearers of 'bride price', *mōhar* (cf. Exod. 22:15). Desperation marks the transition from initial discovery of this remarkable woman (30:10a) to securing her hand in marriage. Even if she could be found, her worth (bride price) exceeds what any suitor could afford.

'exceeds corals': a wife with great capability would be worth whatever bride price she might require, and more (Fox 2009: 892). In four of six mentions of corals, wisdom (like the Resourceful Wife) compares favourably to them (Job 28:18; Prov. 3:15; 8:11; 20:15; see 'Notes' for 3:15).

31:12. 'She rewarded him', *gĕmālathû*: lit. 'she treats him', 'deals with him', 'responds to him' or 'looks after him'. This term describes an ongoing relationship, not an isolated action.

'her life', *ḥayyeyh[â]*: normally 'her life' closes with a *qamets* vowel (Lev. 18:18).

31:15. 'a portion', *ṭerep*: a serving of food one distributes to another.

31:16. 'was planted', *niṭṭa*ʿ: unvocalized, the K (*nṭ*ʿ) supports several forms, with niph. 3 m. sg. ind. *niṭṭa*ʿ, 'it [the vineyard] was planted', as most probable (cf. Isa. 40:24). Masoretes vocalized *nāṭĕʾā[h]* (Q) on the assumption that a final he is missing, yielding the smooth (but unnecessary) reading 'she planted'.

31:18. 'She savoured the fact': lit. 'she tasted'.

31:19. 'distaff', *kîšôr*: a rod loosely wrapped with the unspun supply of wool or flax fibres, from which the spinner would draw off strands, twisting them together with the help of a drop spindle. The spindle served as the receptacle around which the finished (spun) yarn or thread would then be wrapped.

'spindle-whorl', *pālek*: a small disk-weight with a hole centre-bored, through which the spindle was passed. When fixed to a spindle, the whorl's mass helped sustain the momentum of the spindle's revolutions, aiding production of thread or yarn.

31:22. 'purple-dyed fabric', *ʾargāmān*: a sign of luxury. Purple dye from the *Murex brandaris* and *Murex trunculus* molluscs was exported by Syro-Phoenicia at considerable cost (Boraas 1985: 844).

31:25. 'about the future': lit. 'about the future day', referring to the future generally.

31:27. 'She keeps watch over', *ṣôpiyyâ*: a f. sg. ptc. meaning 'a woman watching over', this term uncannily resembles the sound pattern of *sophia*, a Greek word meaning 'wisdom'. The fact that this word is line-initial in the verse immediately after this lecture's only mention of 'wisdom', *ḥokmâ*, increases the likelihood that the sage composed an inter-language assonantal link (cf. Wolters 1985).

'journeys': lit. 'goings'. This term refers to a person's progress or travel, whether literal or metaphorical.

31:28. 'and [they] proclaimed her supremely fortunate', *wayĕʾaššĕrûhā*: often translated as to be 'blessed', 'fortunate', 'happy', the root *ʾšr* identifies one who has achieved a supreme level of worth or success.

31:29. 'performed resourcefully', *ʿāśû ḥāyil*: lit. 'produced resource' or 'strength'. *Ḥāyil* appeared earlier in 31:3, 10.

31:30. 'charm', *haḥēn*: lit. the 'approval', 'grace', 'elegance'. Since *ḥēn* is here not to be trusted (parallel to ephemeral beauty), it connotes superficial elegance or insincere charm (cf. Nah. 3:4), not a priceless inner quality of kindness (Prov. 11:16).

'a woman . . . she', *ʾiššā . . . hîʾ*: this entire saying is enclosed in double quotation marks since it constitutes an apophthegm quoted by the husband to his wife, in the hearing of other family community members (whom he addresses in 31:31). This explains the shift from addressing his wife with 'you' in v. 29, and now referring to reverent women generally with 'she' in v. 30. This contrasts Waltke, who infers from the pronoun shift that it is the poet who speaks in v. 30, not the husband (2005: 535). It is similarly unnecessary with Fox to assign these lines to the poet, on grounds that they would sound 'pompous and patronizing', if spoken by the husband (2009: 898). The Resourceful Wife's remarkable achievements lead naturally to her husband's unabashed expression of admiration – a considered and crucial climax to this lecture's message.

'a woman who reveres the LORD', *ʾiššâ yirat-yhwh*: within this phrase, *yirat* is a f. adj. describing the woman: she is a 'reverential woman, with regard to the LORD'. Yet in the phrase *yirat-yhwh* the listener would have heard that foundational principle undergirding all of Israelite wisdom – 'reverence for the LORD' (with *yirat* as f. noun in const.). Reverence for the LORD appears suitably near the book's close as this woman's crowning asset. Very early it emerged as wisdom's foundation (1:7; Fox 2009: 898).

'she it is who can boast', *hîʾ tithallāl*: like the twenty-two other occurrences of the root *hll* in the hith. stem, this should be rendered with the act. voice (not pass. '[she] is to be praised'; *pace* NRSV, NIV and GKC §54.g, perhaps influenced by pass. *eulogeitai* in LXX). Simultaneously to revere and boast (both in 31:30b) fits the sage's penchant for paradox. What the Resourceful Wife brags about is the grandeur of the LORD, whom she reveres.

31:31. 'what she has produced': lit. 'her deeds, products' (pl.). In the Hebr. idiom, this refers to achievements aside from children she may have borne.

Form and structure

Borders

The upper border is marked by the aleph-word in this alphabetic acrostic (*ʾēšet*, 'wife', begins 31:10 in Hebr.). The alphabet's final letter, taw, begins *tĕnû*, 'give', in v. 31, indicating the lower border of this alphabetic acrostic poem (also the book's final saying). Multiple elements of closure coalesce in the final section (vv. 28–31), further consolidating this poem's completion (see under 'Microstructural features', below).

Macrostructural features

Alphabetic acrostic (Sections I–IV, form-based). As indicated above, this poem presents a complete acrostic of the Hebr. alphabet, with one verse assigned to each of the successive twenty-two letters. Other alphabetic acrostics include Pss 34 and 119, and each of the first four chapters of Lamentations. Other poems in Proverbs may preserve partial alphabetic acrostics (2:1–22; 10:1–22; 12:1–22).

The flexibility of Hebr. syntax ensures that a poet's decision to follow an acrostic structure need not pre-empt sequencing sayings to convey progression of thought. For example, with a simple rearrangement of word order, 31:17 could have supplied the 'B' verse (by advancing *bāh*, 'in her', to the start of v. 17), in place of v. 11, the actual 'B' verse (which begins with *bāṭaḥ*, '[he] trusts').

Triple-theme introduction (Sections I–IV, content-based). After establishing trustworthiness as the overarching quality desirable in a bride (31:11a), by a triple-theme introduction the sage-mother presents three traits demonstrating trustworthiness. First, the Resourceful Wife generously invests in her household, rather than enriching herself ('no loot will [her husband] lack', v. 11b). This will be expanded in Section II (vv. 13–24). She invests in her household through prowess in food preparation and fabric industry.

Second, she genuinely cares for others. When offences might incline her to seek revenge, she chooses instead to 'reward' her husband 'with good and not evil' (31:12a). This will be expanded in Section III (vv. 25–27). Beyond exhibiting such 'faithful love', she also expounds on it (v. 26).

Third, she demonstrates these qualities (investing in her household and caring for others) not sporadically, but durably ('all the days of her life', 31:12b). This will be expanded in Section IV (vv. 28–31), as her family reviews the generosity and caring they have received from her over the years. Thus the triple-introduction of vv. 11b–12 anticipates the balance of this lecture.

Inclusio by repetition of 'resourceful(ly)' (Sections I and IV, form-based). The term *ḥayil* ('resourceful' or 'resourcefully') appears in the first block (31:10) and opens the last block (v. 29), effecting an inclusio.

Reversal concerning resourceful women (Sections I and IV, content-based). Based on the youth's initial question, one would conclude that resourceful women are few in number (31:10). This inference reverses towards the close when the husband declares, 'Many daughters have performed resourcefully' (v. 29a). Evidently the youth of v. 10 had overlooked them, not yet knowing what traits to watch for.

Thematic continuity involving fabric (Sections II and III, content-based). Within Section II, the poetess introduces fabric in 31:13, then develops that theme across vv. 19–22 (esp. vv. 19, 21, 22) and again in v. 24. Fabric returns figuratively in v. 25 (within Section III), especially instilling confidence regarding the future (as did clothing in v. 21).

Thematic continuity involving food (Sections II and III, content-based). The theme of food joins Section II with Section III. Within Section II, food is introduced in 31:14. The poetess develops that theme across vv. 15–18 (esp. vv. 15, 16, 18). Within Section III, food returns figuratively in v. 27.

Closure through repetition (Section IV, with Section II, form-based). The lecture's final verse (31:31) creates a high degree of closure, linking to words or roots found earlier. These include the following: 'give', *ntn* (vv. 15, 24), 'fruit', *pri* (v. 16), 'hand', *yd* (vv. 19, 20), 'praise', *hll* (vv. 28, 30), 'gate', *šʿr* (v. 23), 'produced', *ʿśh* (including to 'work', 'make', 'perform', vv. 13, 22, 24, 29).

Microstructural features

Section I (31:10–12). *Summation (31:12b, form-based).* The expression 'all the days of her life' presents a chronological summation, bringing to a climax the final colon of the verse-pair about trustworthiness (31:11–12).

Section II (31:13–24). *Dual-theme introduction of fabric and food (31:13–14, content-based).* The first verse-pair of Section II introduces the Resourceful Wife's initiative in the fabric industry and in food preparation (31:13–14). This verse-pair forms a dual-theme introduction, since the poet will expand on food preparation in vv. 15–18, and will detail the Resourceful Wife's garment production in vv. 19–22.

Chiasm of fabric and food topics (31:13–22, content-based). Chiasm results when the fabric industry appears before food preparation in the dual-theme introduction (31:13–14), whereas food preparation appears first when the topics are expanded (food in vv. 15–18, and fabric in vv. 19–22).

Palistrophe of darkness and planting (31:15–18, form- and content-based). 'Night' appears in 31:15, 18. Planting occurs between those sayings (in vv. 16, 17), creating an a-b-b-a palistrophe across vv. 15–18.

Continuity of serving self last (31:18, 22). During food production, the woman serves others (31:15) before taking time for herself (v. 18; though used metaphorically, 'savouring' evokes the notion that she ate after others). In fabric production, she served others (vv. 20–21) before clothing herself (v. 22).

Continuity of labour followed by evaluation (13:15–18, 19–22, content-based). The four sayings concerning food production begin with labour (31:15–17) and end with evaluation (v. 18). Similarly the four sayings concerning fabric industry begin with labour (vv. 19–21) and end with evaluation (v. 22).

Section III (31:25–27). *Compact palistrophe involving fabric and food (31:25–27, content-based).* The three verses comprising Section III form a compact palistrophe. Outer lines refer metaphorically to fabric (31:25) and food production (v. 27) – themes identified in Section II, in the same sequence. The palistrophe showcases the woman as a wisdom teacher at the pivot point (v. 26).

Section IV (31:28–31). *Thematic cohesion surrounding the source of honour (31:28–31, content-based).* Section IV coheres by describing how other family members regard with honour the Resourceful Wife and mother (31:28–31).

Explanation-plus-imperative palistrophe (31:29–31, content-based). Frequently, the sage follows an imperative with an explanation (or incentive; cf. 31:6–7). In Section IV the explanation appears first (v. 29), allowing the poem to conclude with a directive (v. 31). These logically connected parts form a concise palistrophe. At the palistrophic pivot they showcase reverence (v. 30). One would be hard pressed to find a principle more fitting for the close of the sages' many lectures.

Paradox involving reverence and boasting (31:30, content-based). Whereas fickle charm and fading beauty warrant only temporary boasting, the reverent woman paradoxically has something to brag about (31:30; see 'Notes'). This puzzle resolves when one considers that reverence focuses honour (and therefore boasting) on the LORD. None is a more worthy object of boasting than the divine, and none better able to do so than the reverent.

Comment

Section I (31:10–12). A rhetorical question tinged with despair launches this lecture, evidently arising from the youth: 'A resourceful wife, who can find – since her purchase price exceeds corals?' (31:10). In the light of the stern maternal rebuke concerning his female associations to this point (v. 3), her son may feel dismayed by the daunting task of locating a bride who could satisfy his mother's expectations. Even if he could find such a woman, he fears her bride price would defy even his royal purse.

Although the youth's question rings as rhetorical, the poetess takes the question seriously. The sort of fellow 'who can find' such a resourceful wife will be one exhibiting trust (31:11a). Acquisitive, possessive or domineering suitors need not apply.

From this point the sage turns from answering, 'Who can find?', explaining instead, 'For what sort of woman should a suitor be searching?' She withholds until Section IV further comment about the prospective husband's qualities.

As implied earlier, the youth should seek a woman fundamentally characterized by trustworthiness (implied by the fact that her husband can trust her, 31:11a). As a first evidence of trustworthiness, she does not hoard her assets. She is not preoccupied with advancing her private empire. Rather, she invests in her household. That is why, though her bride price may be steep, she will be more than worth it. For with her 'no loot will [her husband] lack' (v. 11b).

Genuine care for her family comprises her second evidence of trustworthiness. She neither harbours offences nor pursues spiteful vendettas with biting revenge. Instead she 'reward[s her husband] with good and not evil' (31:12a). She is bent towards benevolence.

Durability marks her third dimension of trustworthiness. As years pass, onlookers will review her life and bear witness that (a) she invested in her household, (b) she behaved with caring and (c) she did so not sporadically but durably 'all the days of her life' (31:12b). The remainder of the lecture expands on these three signs of trustworthiness, corresponding to Sections II, III and IV, respectively.

LXX locates the Hezekiah material (Prov. 25 – 29) between vv. 9 and 10 of Prov. 31 (see 'Comment' on 30:14–15).

31:10. To interpret this question not as a cry of desperation, but as an exclamation of awe (inspired by the woman's great capabilities), runs contrary to the fact that it is rhetorical, assuming an answer of 'No one!' (*pace* Fox 2009: 890–891; see 'Notes' for 31:10).

Despair similarly tinged both the sage's earlier longing to find a trustworthy person ('But a person characterized by faithfulness, who can find?', Prov. 20:6b) and the Joban search for wisdom (cf. Job 28:12, 20). Job's search, like this, resolves climactically in reverence (Job 28:28; Prov. 31:30), reinforcing the likelihood that, on a metaphoric level, the Resourceful Wife represents Lady Wisdom.

Section II (31:13–24). Section II (31:13–24) illustrates two ways the Resourceful Wife invests in her household: through fabric industry and food preparation (introduced in vv. 13 and 14, respectively). Taking initiative, she leaves nothing to chance – even from the earliest of those two processes. For fabric, she procures raw wool and flax (v. 13). For food, she gathers exotic ingredients 'from afar' (v. 14).

Next the sage examines more closely her industry in food preparation (31:15–18). Supplied with ingredients earlier secured, before sunrise she will rise to have a meal ready for her family, including her employees (maidservants, v. 15). Beyond short-range meal preparation, she secures a long-term supply (vv. 16–17). Only after others have been served and sunlight fades does she turn to satisfy her own needs (v. 18).

Then the sage turns to explore further this woman's efforts in the fabric industry (31:19–22). With wool and flax earlier obtained (v. 13), she now spins yarn (v. 19). Completed garments benefit both the needy who are outside her family (v. 20) and her entire household (v. 21; note summation by 'entire', and escalation of quality by 'scarlet'). Only when their needs are met does she provide for her own apparel needs, clothing herself regally in purple and linen (v. 22).

As if feeding and clothing her family (and others) were not benefit enough, the poet observes still wider ripples of reward that flow from the Resourceful Wife's determination to invest in her household (31:23–24). Her husband enjoys substantial community esteem (v. 23). Based on context, this owes at least in part to the fame of her labours.

In addition, she turns a profit from her garment industry (31:24a). Not only does she engage in direct sales; she even markets more widely with the help of merchants (v. 24b).

31:13. Linen would serve principally for undergarments, with wool for outer garments (Waltke 2005: 529). Records from Elephantine along the Nile indicate that a quality woollen garment would cost more than two months' wages, with simpler linen garments going for a quarter the price. In antiquity, women accomplished in spinning and weaving commanded respect (524).

31:15. This woman manages a wealthy estate, given that maidservants look to her for food (Fox 2009: 894).

31:19. By engaging in spinning yarn, this prosperous woman demonstrates that she did not regard herself above performing manual labour required to achieve her goals (Fox 2009: 895).

31:20–27. A three-step palistrophe may be seen in 31:21–25. The central step focuses on honour enjoyed by the husband (v. 23). The second step refers to garment manufacture (vv. 22, 24), while the outer step describes the Resourceful Wife's confident attitude (vv. 21, 25).

Waltke also notes this, and proposes a fourth step involving body parts (31:20, 26–27; 2005: 528). However, the single saying in v. 20 does not balance evenly the pair in vv. 26–27. More significantly, this fourth step would disrupt the thematic recap of fabric and food in vv. 25 and 27, respectively, and the manner in which those two sayings frame an intervening saying with this poem's sole mention of 'wisdom' (v. 26). Consequently, despite the appeal of a palistrophe spanning 31:21–25 (or vv. 20–27), it appears incidental, secondary to the structures described earlier for these verses (see 'Form and structure', above).

31:20. This woman's kindness to the oppressed is reminiscent of the care for the others his mother urged on Lemuel in his role as monarch (31:9; Fox 2009: 897).

31:22. The woman's attention to personal attractiveness, while not overlooked, ranks last among her many priorities in Block II.A (vv. 13–22).

Section III (31:25–27). After illustrating in Section II how the Resourceful Wife may invest in her household through food preparation and fabric industry, at the palistrophic focal point of Section III the sage expands on the trait of caring – that second facet of trustworthiness (31:26, introduced in v. 12a). So renowned is her skill in 'faithful love' that it draws others to hear her 'instruction' on the topic. Cleverly the poet incorporates fabric (the first illustration of investment in her household) into the accolades describing her confidence concerning the future: 'Strength and splendour are her clothing' (v. 25a). Similarly figurative language about food (the second investment illustration) follows the focal point: 'the bread of sluggishness she will not eat' (v. 27b). She clearly exhibits caring as she 'keeps watch over the journeys of her household', v. 27a).

31:26. With good reason the trait of 'instruct[ing] concerning faithful love' rests at the pinnacle of the brief palistrophe spanning 31:25–27. Within this lecture, only 'instruction concerning faithful love' parallels 'wisdom' itself. Among the many instructions a parent may impart, none ranks higher than instruction about receiving and giving durable love.

Based on the influence of wise women in Tekoa (2 Sam. 14:2) and in Abel of Beth-maacah (2 Sam. 20:16), 'a significant, political role [was] available to women in the years preceding the establishment of the kingship in Israel' (Camp 1981: 14).

Section IV (31:28–31). A period of years would intervene between the description of the Resourceful Wife's caring nature (Section III) and the acclaim of Section IV (31:28–31) – time enough to persuade observers that her trustworthiness and benevolence were not sporadic, but durable (anticipated by the expression 'all the days of her life', 31:12b). Staging from lesser to greater, her sons begin the litany of praise, followed by her husband (v. 28). A transcript of his panegyric fills the last three sayings (vv. 29–31). Given how many 'resourceful' women he has observed, her superlative performance gleams all the more brilliantly (v. 29).

Having established her praiseworthiness (31:29), her husband discloses the secret of her success: she determined to cultivate reverence, discounting superficial charm that cannot but deteriorate. In contrast, humble reverence paradoxically gives this woman something to brag about (v. 30).

Aware that his wife has garnered the admiration not only of her family, but of the wider community as well (recall the husband's consequent prestige among the elders, 31:23), the husband beckons to the assembled crowd, urging them to join in publicly honouring her (v. 31). This lecture – and with it the entire book – ends with retribution at its lavish best: 'Give her some of the fruit of her hands, and may what she has produced praise her in the gates.'

In this manner the queen mother answers the youth's opening protest, 'A resourceful wife, who can find?' The sort of suitor 'who can find' a resourceful wife will be a suitor who can manifest an open-handed trusting outlook (31:11a). He will feel threatened neither by her creative initiative nor by her economic successes (vv. 16, 18). Instead he will bask in the honour her achievements bring him (v. 23). So secure is he in his own identity, that, without a second thought, he eagerly brags about her (vv. 28–31). Equipped with such traits, the youth can be confident of finding a resourceful woman to wed.

31:29–31. An Egyptian inscription on the tomb of Petosiris records his praise for Renpet-nefret, his 'excellent wife'. Her skill in giving counsel and her reputation for 'stretch[ing] forth her hand to everyone' parallel elements of the Resourceful Wife poem (Fox 2009: 903).

Explanation

The Resourceful Wife lecture offers enduring advice for six audiences: young men, young women, husbands, parents, children and all who pursue wisdom. Consider first what a young man may gain from this teaching.

Counsel for young men

This poem primarily counsels young men so they may navigate adolescent infatuation, cultivating discernment of character when seeking a spouse. Of greater value than superficial, fading glamour (31:3, 30) is trustworthiness (v. 11a), individual initiative that seeks to build a relationship rather than a personal empire (v. 11b) and resilient generosity that will not give way to reflexive spite or biting revenge (v. 12a). These desirable traits must be durable – not fleeting exceptions (v. 12b).

Such a spouse will possess stamina and foresight (31:25). She will diligently watch over her family's welfare (v. 27). Proven character will render her words credible (v. 26a). Her words specifically will cultivate faithful love (v. 26b). By implication, a young man should not expect a prospective spouse to exhibit traits he himself is unwilling to embody.

Counsel for young women
Indirectly, the poetess's advice benefits young women. By overhearing what sort of woman the queen mother counsels her son to watch for, they will be emboldened to defy contemporary culture's inordinate emphasis on native charm (31:30). Instead they would become women marked by trustworthiness, women displaying initiative that advances a team (not self alone), and women renowned for generosity of spirit, consistently so.

Counsel for husbands
The wise husband within this poem models in three respects how other husbands should conduct themselves. First, he will not regard his wife as a mere commodity, even a highly valued commodity (much less an accessory; 31:10).

Second, a wise husband will not micromanage his wife's initiative. He will demonstrate trust instead (31:11), encouraging her initiative in family-strengthening ventures (vv. 13, 16–18).

Third, a wise husband is not threatened by his wife's achievements. His world must not revolve around himself. At its human centre rests the corporate family unit that he and his wife together are building. He recognizes that as her achievements strengthen the family, he wins. In evidence of his personal security he praises her openly, boasting about her to others, and encouraging them to admire her, not him (31:28–31; cf. Eph. 5:28b). These traits the suitor must pursue as well, in order to become one who can 'find a resourceful wife'.

Counsel for parents
The mother and father in this poem model counsel for parents. Regarding the mother, consider three principles modelled by the Resourceful Wife. First, it is in order to care for her household that she undertakes farming, food-preparation and fabric enterprises. Her extrafamilial career is not primary.

Second, she maintains loving vigilance over each family member, long after finishing the basic responsibilities of feeding and clothing them. 'She keeps watch over the journeys of her household,' suggesting observant concern as they venture into the world (31:27a).

Third, beyond supplying tangible support of food and clothing, she invests in her family with wise insights (31:26a). Most especially she teaches them to love others faithfully, as by example, so also by word (v. 26b). The malaise of too many families today proves our need of mothers (and fathers) who masterfully teach durable love (see v. 26 under 'Comment').

As father, the husband in this poem models for his children (31:28) the high respect he has for their mother (vv. 29–31). That respect forms the foundation of his love for her. The resilient web of security woven through his respect for his wife fosters in their children the crucial capacity to trust others. Deprived of trust, we create and consign ourselves to a culture of loners, individualists assessing 'other' as nothing but threat. Given trust, we grant others the chance to reciprocate, to contribute, to create rich and supportive community.

Counsel for children

The children in this lecture model honour for their parents – in particular, how to honour one's mother (31:28a). Maturity emerges in a child when he or she begins to realize how much one's mother has contributed, whether tangibly or intangibly. Failure to arrive at this discovery does not so much detract from her achievements, as it reveals the child's narcissistic immaturity. Robust filial honour offers the cure.

Counsel for all, concerning wisdom

A sixth counsel applies to all, urging lifelong pursuit of wisdom. In one of Proverbs's first lectures, the sage urged youth to enrol with Lady Wisdom as tutor (1:20–33). Her list of accomplishments subsequently dominated an entire poem (Prov. 8). Directly the sage urged the pupil to prefer Lady Wisdom's invitation to a banquet, rejecting Dame Folly's counter-invitation (Prov. 9). Thus Lady Wisdom progressed from wisdom tutor, then appeared as credentialled counsellor and subsequently extended an invitation as a generous, wise host.

A pupil may outgrow a passing relationship with his or her tutor, with an occasional counsellor or with a banquet host. However, if Lady Wisdom were to be secured permanently as the youth's figurative spouse, that pupil would enjoy a perpetual supply of counsel.

Towards the close of the Resourceful Wife poem, the remarkable woman increasingly exhibits traits reminiscent of Lady Wisdom (esp. as wisdom instructor in Section III [31:25–27]; for an exploration of Lady Wisdom as Resourceful Wife, see McCreesh 1985). While a metaphoric interpretation such as this must not obscure the queen mother's literal counsel concerning who can find a suitable wife (v. 10), the degree to which the Resourceful Wife resembles Lady Wisdom counsels all to respond to wisdom with enduring respect – manifested most clearly in how we respond to reproof, wisdom's greatest gift (cf. Prov. 3:11–12; 15:33).

BIBLIOGRAPHY

COMMENTARIES ON PROVERBS

Clifford, R. J. (1999), *Proverbs*, OTL, Louisville: Westminster John Knox.

Fox, M. V. (2000), *Proverbs 1–9*, AB 18A, and *Proverbs 10–31*, AB 18B (2009), New York: Doubleday.

Garrett, D. A. (1993), *Proverbs, Ecclesiastes, Song of Songs*, NAC 14, Nashville: Broadman.

Longman III, T. (2006), *Proverbs*, Baker Commentary on the Old Testament: Wisdom and Psalms, Grand Rapids: Baker Academic.

McKane, W. (1970), *Proverbs: A New Approach*, OTL, London: SCM.

Meinhold, A. (1991), *Die Sprüche*, 2 vols., ZBK, Zurich: Theologischer Verlag.

Murphy, R. E. (1998), *Proverbs*, WBC 22, Nashville: Thomas Nelson.

Murphy, R. E., and E. Huwiler (1999), *Proverbs, Ecclesiastes, Song of Songs*, NIBCOT, Peabody: Hendrickson.

Perdue, L. G. (2000), *Proverbs*, Interpretation, Louisville: John Knox.

Plöger, O. (1984), *Sprüche Salomos: Proverbia*, BKAT 17, Neukirchen-Vluyn: Neukirchener Verlag.

Scott, R. B. Y. (1965), *Proverbs and Ecclesiastes*, AB 18, Garden City: Doubleday.

Toy, C. H. (1902), *A Critical and Exegetical Commentary on the Book of Proverbs*, ICC, New York: Charles Scribner's Sons.

Waltke, B. K. (2004), *The Book of Proverbs: Chapters 1–15* and *The Book of Proverbs: Chapters 16–31* (2005), NICOT, Grand Rapids: Eerdmans.

Whybray, R. N. (1994b), *Proverbs*, NCBC, Grand Rapids: Eerdmans.

OTHER WORKS

Alster, B. (2005), *Wisdom of Ancient Sumer*, Bethesda: CDL.

Alter, R. (1985), *The Art of Biblical Poetry*, New York: Basic.

Boraas, R. S. (1985), 'Purple', in P. J. Achtemeier (ed.), *Harper's Bible Dictionary*, San Francisco: Harper & Row, 844.

Bossidy, L., and R. Charan (2002), *Execution: The Discipline of Getting Things Done*, New York: Crown Business.

Brueggemann, W. (1997), *Theology of the Old Testament: Testimony, Dispute, Advocacy*, Minneapolis: Fortress.

Bryce, G. (1972), 'Another Wisdom-"Book" in Proverbs', *JBL* 91:145–157.

Byargeon, R. W. (1998), 'Echoes of Wisdom in the Lord's Prayer', *JETS* 41:353–365.

Camp, C. V. (1981), 'The Wise Women of 2 Samuel: A Role Model for Women in Early Israel?', *CBQ* 43:14–29.

——— (1985), *Wisdom and the Feminine in the Book of Proverbs*, BLS 11, Sheffield: Almond.

Cohen, Y. (2013), *Wisdom from the Bronze Age*, WAW 19, Atlanta: Society of Biblical Literature.

Crenshaw, J. L. (1982), 'Wisdom and Authority: Sapiential Rhetoric and Its Warrants', VTSup 32, *Congress Volume, Vienna, 1980*, Leiden: E. J. Brill, 10–29; repr. in *Urgent Advice and Probing Questions: Collected Writings on Old Testament Wisdom*, Macon: Mercer University Press, 1995: 326–343.

——— (1990), 'The Sage in Proverbs', in J. G. Gammie and L. G. Perdue (eds.), *The Sage in Israel and the Ancient Near East*, Winona Lake: Eisenbrauns, 205–216.

Day, J., R. P. Gordon and H. G. M. Williamson (eds.) (1995), *Wisdom in Ancient Israel: Essays in Honour of J. A. Emerton*, Cambridge: University Press.

Dell, K. J., and M. Barker (eds.) (2005), *Wisdom: The Collected Articles of Norman Whybray*, SOTSMS, Aldershot: Ashgate.

Duvdevani, S. (1970), 'בְּדַעְתּוֹ תְּהוֹמוֹת נִבְקָעוּ וּשְׁחָקִים יִרְעֲפוּ־טָל *bĕda'tô tĕhômôt nibqā'û ûšĕḥāqîm yir'ăpû-ṭāl* [Prov. 3:20]', *Sepher Yoseph Braslavi*, Society for Biblical Research in Israel, Jerusalem, 21:339–341.

Exum, J. C. (1996), 'Nurse', in P. J. Achtemeier (ed.), *HarperCollins Bible Dictionary*, San Francisco: Harper & Row, 766.

Faulkner, R. O. (tr.) (1973), 'Maxims of Ptahhotpe', in W. K. Simpson (ed.), *The Literature of Ancient Egypt*, New Haven: Yale University Press, 159–176.

Fichtner, J. (1966–7), *Proverbia* (critical notes on Proverbs), in K. Elliger and W. Rudolph (eds.), *Biblia Hebraica Stuttgartensia*, Stuttgart: Deutsche Bibelgesellschaft.

Fontaine, C. (2002), *Smooth Words: Women, Proverbs and Performance in Biblical Wisdom*, JSOTSup 356, London: Sheffield Academic Press.

Fox, M. V. (2015), 'Three Theses on Wisdom', in M. R. Sneed (ed.), *Was There a Wisdom Tradition? New Prospects in Israelite Wisdom Studies*, AIL 23, Atlanta: Society of Biblical Literature, 69–86.

Greenberg, M. (1983), *Ezekiel 1–20*, AB 22, Garden City: Doubleday.

Grewell, G. (2013), 'Rhetoric of Ridicule', PhD diss., The University of Arizona <http://hdl.handle.net/10150/312568>, accessed 29 March 2021.

Hallo, W. W. (1990), 'Proverbs Quoted in Epic', in T. Abusch, J. Huehnergard and P. Steinkeller (eds.), *Lingering Over Words*, HSS 37, Atlanta: Scholars Press, 203–217.

Heim, K. M. (2001), *Like Grapes of Gold Set in Silver: An Interpretation of Proverbial Clusters in Proverbs 10:1–33:16*, Berlin: Walter de Gruyter.

——— (2012), *Poetic Imagination in Proverbs: Variant Repetitions and the Nature of Poetry*, BBRSup 4, Winona Lake: Eisenbrauns.

Herodotus, and A. de Sélincourt (tr.) (1954), *Herodotus: The Histories*, Baltimore: Penguin.

Isocrates, tr. G. Norlin (1966), LCL, 3 vols., Cambridge, Mass.: Harvard University Press.

Jenni, E., and C. Westermann (eds.) (1971–6), *Theologisches Handwörterbuch zum Alten Testament*, 2 vols., Munich: C. Kaiser; Zurich: Theologischer, *Theological Lexicon of the Old Testament*, 1997, M. E. Biddle (tr.), Peabody: Hendrickson.

Jones, J. W. (2019), *She Opens Her Hand to the Poor: Gestures and Social Values in Proverbs*, PHSC 30, Piscataway: Gorgias.

Joüon, P., and T. Muraoka (2006), *A Grammar of Biblical Hebrew*, Rome: Pontificio Istituto Biblico.

Kinnaman, D., and M. Matlock with A. Hawkins (2019), *Faith for Exiles: 5 Ways for a New Generation to Follow Jesus in Digital Babylon*, Grand Rapids: Baker.

Koch, K. (1955), '*Gibt es ein Vergeltungsdogma im Alten Testament?*', *ZTK* 52:1–42; repr. 'Is There a Doctrine of Retribution in the Old Testament?', T. H. Trapp (tr.), in J. L. Crenshaw (ed.) (1983), *Theodicy in the Old Testament*, Philadelphia: Fortress, 57–87.

Kugel, J. L. (1981), *The Idea of Biblical Poetry: Parallelism and Its History*, New Haven: Yale University Press.

——— (2017), 'Ancient Israelite Pedagogy and Its Survival in Second Temple Interpretations of Scripture', in K. M. Hogan, M. Goff and E. Wasserman (eds.), *Pedagogy in Ancient Judaism and Early Christianity*, Atlanta: SBL Press, 15–58.

Laisney, V. P.-M. (2018), 'L'ostracon du Caire d'Aménémopé retrouvé (JE 96555)', *Orientalia* 87: 137–146.

Lambert, W. G. (1960), *Babylonian Wisdom Literature*, Oxford: Clarendon.

LaSor, W. S., D. A. Hubbard and F. W. Bush (1996), *Old Testament Survey*, 2nd edn, Grand Rapids: Eerdmans.

Lausberg, H. (1998), *Handbook of Literary Rhetoric: A Foundation for Literary Study*, Leiden: Brill.

Lichtheim, M. (1973–80), *Ancient Egyptian Literature: A Book of Readings*, 3 vols., Berkeley: University of California Press.

Liver, J., and S. D. Sperling (2007), 'Kings, Kingship', in Fred Skolnik (ed.), *Encyclopaedia Judaica*, Farmington Hills: MacMillan Reference; Jerusalem: Keter, 163–169.

Longman III, T. (2006), *Proverbs*, Baker Commentary, Grand Rapids: Baker Academic.

——— (2017), *The Fear of the Lord Is Wisdom: A Theological Introduction to Wisdom in Israel*, Grand Rapids: Baker Academic.

McCreesh, T. P. (1985), 'Wisdom as Wife: Proverbs 31:10–31', *RB* 92:25–46.

——— (1991), *Biblical Sound and Sense: Poetic Sound Patterns in Proverbs 10–29*, JSOTSup 128, Sheffield: Sheffield Academic Press.

Malchow, B. V. (1985), 'A Manual for Future Monarchs', *CBQ* 47:238–245.

Marcus, R. (1943), 'The Tree of Life in Proverbs', *JBL* 62:117–120.

Millar, S. R. (2020), *Genre and Openness in Proverbs 10:1–22:16*, Atlanta: SBL Press.

Muilenburg, J. (1953), 'A Study in Hebrew Rhetoric: Repetition and Style', *Congress Volume: Leiden, 1953*, VTSup I, Leiden: Brill, 97–111.

Muraoka, T. (1999), 'The Tripartite Nominal Clause Revisited', in C. Miller (ed.), *The Verbless Clause in Biblical Hebrew: Linguistic Approaches*, Winona Lake: Eisenbrauns, 187–213.

Murphy, R. E. (1986), 'Wisdom's Song: Proverbs 1:20–33', *CBQ* 48:456–460.

Niccacci, A. (1999), 'Types and Functions of the Nominal Sentence', in C. Miller (ed.), *The Verbless Clause in Biblical Hebrew: Linguistic Approaches*, Winona Lake: Eisenbrauns, 215–248.

Overland, P. (1988), 'Literary Structure in Proverbs 1–9', PhD diss., Brandeis University.

——— (1996), 'Structure in *The Wisdom of Amenemope* and Proverbs', in J. Coleson and V. Matthews (eds.), *'Go to the Land I Will Show You': Studies in Honor of Dwight W. Young*, Winona Lake: Eisenbrauns, 279–295.

——— (2000), 'Did the Sage Draw from the Shema? A Study of Proverbs 3:1–12', *CBQ* 62:424–440.

——— (2005), 'Wisdom', in B. T. Arnold and H. G. M. Williamson (eds.), *Dictionary of the Old Testament: Historical Books*, Downers Grove: InterVarsity Press, 984–989.

——— (2008a), 'Chiasm', in T. Longman III and P. Enns (eds.), *Dictionary of the Old Testament: Wisdom, Poetry & Writings*, Downers Grove: InterVarsity Press, 54–57.

——— (2008b), 'Rhetorical Criticism', in T. Longman III and P. Enns (eds.), *Dictionary of the Old Testament: Wisdom, Poetry & Writings*, Downers Grove: InterVarsity Press, 655–663.

——— (2016), *Learning Biblical Hebrew Interactively*, 2 vols., Sheffield: Sheffield Phoenix.

——— (2018), 'Wisdom Traditions of Ancient Israel', in J. S. Greer, J. W. Hilber and J. H. Walton (eds.), *Behind the Scenes of the Old Testament: Cultural, Social, and Historical Contexts of Ancient Israel*, Grand Rapids: Baker Academic, 499–505.

Paul, S. (1979), 'Unrecognized Biblical Legal Idioms in the Light of Comparative Akkadian Expressions', *RB* 86:231–239.

Perdue, L. G. (1994), *Wisdom and Creation: The Theology of Wisdom Literature*, Nashville: Abingdon.

Perry, T. A. (1993), *Wisdom Literature and the Structure of Proverbs*, University Park: Pennsylvania State University Press.

Posener, G. (1975), 'La piété personnelle avant l'âge amarnien (Planches 18-21)', *REg* 27:195–210.

Pritchard, J. B. (ed.) (1969), *Ancient Near Eastern Texts Relating to the Old Testament*, 3rd edn, Princeton: Princeton University Press.

Ray, J. D. (1995), 'Egyptian Wisdom Literature', in J. Day, R. P. Gordon and H. G. M. Williamson (eds.), *Wisdom in Ancient Israel: Essays in Honour of J. A. Emerton*, Cambridge: Cambridge University Press, 17–29.

Schniedewind, W. E. (2019), *The Finger of the Scribe: How Scribes Learned to Write the Bible*, Oxford: Oxford University Press.

Shafer-Elliott, C. (2018), '"He Shall Eat Curds and Honey" (Isa 7:15): Food and Feasting in Late Eighth-Century Judah', in Z. I. Faber and J. L. Wright (eds.), *Archaeology and History of Eighth Century Judah: Festschrift for Oded Borowski*, Atlanta: SBL Press, 279–298.

Shupak, N. (2015), 'The Contribution of Egyptian Wisdom to the Study of the Biblical Wisdom Literature', in M. R. Sneed (ed.), *Was There a Wisdom Tradition? New Prospects in Israelite Wisdom Studies*, AIL 23, Atlanta: Society of Biblical Literature, 265–304.

Simpson, W. K. (tr.) (1973), 'The Instruction of Amenemope', in W. K. Simpson (ed.), *The Literature of Ancient Egypt*, New Haven: Yale University Press, 241–265.

Skehan, P. W. (1947), 'The Seven Columns of Wisdom's House in Proverbs 1–9', *CBQ* 9:190–198.

——— (1976), 'A Single Editor for the Whole Book of Proverbs', in J. L. Crenshaw (ed.), *Studies in Ancient Israelite Wisdom*, New York: Ktav, 329–340.

Smith, B. H. (1968), *Poetic Closure: A Study of How Poems End*, Chicago: University of Chicago Press.

Sneed, M. (2011), 'Is the "Wisdom Tradition" a Tradition?', *CBQ* 73:50–71.

Spencer, H. (1869), *Social Statics, or, The Conditions Essential to Human Happiness Specified, and the First of Them Developed*, New York: D. Appleton.

Thomas, D. W. (1962), '*'ēw* in Proverbs XXXI 4', *VT* 12:499–500.

——— (1965), 'Notes on Some Passages in the Book of Proverbs', *VT* 15: 271–279.

Tozer, A.W. (1982), *The Pursuit of God: Tozer Legacy Edition*, Camp Hill, Pa.: Christian Publications.

Trible, P. (1975), 'Wisdom Builds a Poem: The Architecture of Prov. 1:20–33', *JBL* 94:509–518.

Tutu, D. (2000), *No Future Without Forgiveness*, New York: Doubleday.

Van Leeuwen, R. (1988), *Context and Meaning in Proverbs 25–27*, SBLDS 96, Atlanta: Scholars Press.

Veijola, T. (1992), 'Höre Israel! Der Sinn und Hintergrund von Deuteronomium vi 4–9', *VT* 42:528–541.

Waltke, B. K., and M. O'Connor (1990), *An Introduction to Biblical Hebrew Syntax*, Winona Lake: Eisenbrauns.

Watson, W. G. E. (1984), *Classical Hebrew Poetry: A Guide to Its Techniques*, JSOTSup 26, Sheffield: JSOT Press.

Weeks, S. (1994), *Early Israelite Wisdom*, Oxford: Clarendon.

West, M. (1992), 'Looking for the Poem: Reflections on the Current and Future Status of Biblical Hebrew Poetry', in P. R. House (ed.), *Beyond Form Criticism: Essays in Old Testament Literary Criticism*, Sources for Biblical and Theological Study, Winona Lake: Eisenbrauns, 2:423–431.

Whybray, R. N. (1966), 'Some Literary Problems in Proverbs I–IX', *VT* 16:482–496; repr. K. J. Dell and M. Barker (eds.), *Wisdom: The Collected Articles of Norman Whybray*, SOTSMS, Aldershot: Ashgate, 2005, 30–44.

——— (1979), 'Yahweh-Sayings and Their Context in Proverbs 10:1–22:16', BETL 51:153–165; repr. in K. J. Dell and M. Barker (eds.), *Wisdom: The Collected Articles of Norman Whybray*, SOTSMS, Aldershot: Ashgate, 2005, 45–57.

——— (1992), 'Thoughts on the Composition of Proverbs 10–29', in E. Ulrich et al. (eds.), *Priests, Prophets and Scribes: Essays on the Formation and Heritage of Second Temple Judaism in Honour of Joseph Blenkinsopp*, JSOTSup 149, Sheffield: JSOT Press, 102–114; repr. in K. J. Dell and M. Barker (eds.), *Wisdom: The Collected Articles of Norman Whybray*, SOTSMS, Aldershot: Ashgate, 2005, 63–75.

——— (1994a), *The Composition of the Book of Proverbs*, JSOTSup 168, Sheffield: Sheffield Academic Press.

——— (1994c), 'The Structure and Composition of Proverbs 22:17–24:22', in S. E. Porter, P. Joyce and D. E. Orton (eds.), *Crossing the Boundaries: Essays in Biblical Interpretation in Honour of Michael D. Goulder*, Leiden: Brill, 83–96; repr. in K. J. Dell and M. Barker (eds.), *Wisdom: The Collected Articles of Norman Whybray*, SOTSMS, Aldershot: Ashgate, 2005, 76–89.

Williams, J. G. (1980), 'The Power of Form: A Study of Biblical Proverbs', *Semeia* 17:33–58.

Wilson, J. A. (1969, tr.), 'The Instruction of the Vizier Ptah-hotep', in J. Pritchard (ed.), *ANET*, Princeton: Princeton University Press, 412–414.

Wolters, A. (1985), '*Ṣôpiyyâ* as Hymnic Participle and Play on *Sophia*', *JBL* 104:577–587.

Zimmerli, W. (1933), 'Zur Struktur der alttestamentlichen Weisheit', *ZAW* 51:177–204; repr. as 'Concerning the Structure of Old Testament Wisdom', B. Kovocs (tr.), in J. L. Crenshaw (ed.), *Studies in Ancient Israelite Wisdom*, New York: Ktav, 1976, 175–199.

INDEX OF SCRIPTURE REFERENCES

Note: Page numbers in **boldface** indicate focused attention devoted to a specific portion of Scripture.

INDEX OF AUTHORS

INDEX OF SUBJECTS

Note: Since this is a selective index, some subjects that recur frequently are omitted, such as 'section', 'unit' or 'wisdom'.